EXPLORATIONS IN THEOLOGY

SPOUSE OF THE WORD

HANS URS VON BALTHASAR

SPOUSE OF THE WORD

Explorations in Theology

II

IGNATIUS PRESS   SAN FRANCISCO

Title of the German original:
Sponsa Verbi (Skizzen zur Theologie II)
© 1961 Johannes Verlag, Einsiedeln

Parts previously published in English:
"The Contemporary Experience of the Church",
"Office in the Church", "Who Is the Church?", and
"The Church and Israel" published in
Church and World, translated by A. V. Littledale
with Alexander Dru, © 1967, Palm Publishers, Montreal

Cover by Roxanne Mei Lum

With ecclesiastical approval
© 1991 Ignatius Press, San Francisco
ISBN 0-89870-266-6
Library of Congress catalogue number 89–84206
Printed in the United States of America

CONTENTS

INTRODUCTION

The Church, insofar as she is the bride of Christ, remains enshrouded in mystery. Certainly, she is the "people of God", and, as such, in great measure accessible—resembling here the synagogue. The real distinction begins with Mary, in whom the Word was made flesh; with the Eucharist, which is the flesh, by which we are united with God's substance; and with the Holy Spirit, breathed by the risen Son of Man into earthen vessels.

The Church is a mystery of love, to be approached only with reverence. Many windows have been opened for us to see into the center, but in the most secret chamber the Church remains hidden. In faith we know this, and it is from this standpoint that we are directed to interpret what can be seen of the Church. And if that is so, then the image of the Church that results is likely to be quite different from the current fashionable ones.

Part I circles about the mystery of the center. The accent lies here. Part II treats ways of Christian living—all expressly interpreted from this center, radiating from it and pointing toward it. Very little will be said here about the vaunted adult laity open to the world. Rather, an attempt will be made to restore a balance in danger of being lost. Part III, which touches the sacramental bond between bride and bridegroom, only points the way.

This is certainly not, therefore, a systematic ecclesiology, but perhaps a few building stones for a future one.

PART ONE

THE CONTEMPORARY EXPERIENCE
OF THE CHURCH

There is a danger, when one is confronted with the many different "spiritualities" in the Church, in comparing the features of one with the features of another in an effort to determine which is "best" and which is "worst". These spiritualities include all those that have come and gone in the history of the Church, and also those that remain even today; and from among these spiritualities, of course, one is free to choose according to personal inclination or inner calling. Certainly, freedom as such, and therefore also the freedom of the Christian, has as one of its fundamental characteristics a detachment from circumscribed motives and forms that are merely ephemeral. But this is not the heart of freedom, for freedom consists also in the possibility of deciding for the best, for what appears essential. It consists in identifying oneself, in other words, with the very thing that is chosen in its living and pulsating origin and, in the strength of this unconditioned reality, in acting on the unformed and confused events of the time, clarifying them and imparting to them a consistent structure. Thus, great movements in the history of the Church have always begun by brushing aside all "spiritual" boundaries—for these tend to separatism and are of themselves insufficiently grounded in reality—and by returning to the original impulse of the gospel.

To distinguish, therefore, between the extant kinds of spirituality—which nowadays is generally the spirituality of either the various religious orders and congregations or the secular clergy or the laity or groups of laymen—is practically a useless exercise, perhaps well intentioned but more often than not (and not always unconsciously) tainted with a spirit of animosity. It is as though any one of the saints could have been thus preoccupied with his own special spirituality! This departmentalizing of spirituality, furthermore, is quite out of harmony with the ways of the Holy Spirit, whose only true purpose is to infuse into men's hearts the fullness of Christ, and this fullness

Translated by A. V. Littledale with Alexander Dru.

permits no restriction. Therefore, there can be no question of pro-
pounding, alongside all the other forms of piety alive in the Church,
one special spirituality for the Church of today. To support this idea
we must keep in mind that the Church herself is "the fullness of him
who fills all in all" (Eph 1:23). Indeed, it is the Church who imparts
offices and charismata, precisely because Jesus Christ "ascended far
above all the heavens, that he might fill all things" (Eph 4:10), as a
means to "building up the body of Christ, until we all attain . . . the
fullness of Christ; so that we may no longer be children, tossed to and
fro and carried about with every wind of doctrine . . . but speaking
the truth in love, we are to grow up in every way into him who is the
head, into Christ" (Eph 4:12–15).

In other words, what is needed is an understanding of every particular mission in the Church as proceeding from the whole Church and
destined for the growth and deepening of the life of the whole
Church. This understanding can come about in the individual only
from a love for the whole Church imparted by the Spirit of unity.

To propound, therefore, a special "modern spirituality" demands
an a priori theological assumption, or rather—since we do not want
to mince matters—a theological prejudice. The ground of this is not a
clearly worked-out, personal view but the Spirit of the wholeness of
Christ, who alone can teach us to choose out, from among the
bewildering mass of spiritualities now current, what is of real
significance, what really matters, since it represents not what man
produces in his own interest but the Spirit of the Church's fullness.
What points the way and conditions our choice are not the "high
things" of human ingenuity or originality but the "humble", with
which the Spirit enjoins us to concur (Rom 12:16) and which bear the
sign of fruitfulness. It is true that the Church's fruitfulness is not an
object of direct observation. The source whence it springs lies in the
inward, invisible sphere. When it flows outward and produces a
visible change, the connection is such that it can only be felt and
glimpsed in faith; it can never be established by the methods of
ordinary experience. Nonetheless, the Holy Spirit does not leave the
Church without some visible, convincing signs, such as the miracles
of the saints, especially those of the moral order.

Though we may not make any judgment in respect to good or evil without prejudicing God's judgment, yet we are told to recognize the tree of good and evil by its fruits, spiritual and secular. In practice, this means that while we attend to the signs of our time (to read them is part of our Christian duty), we must look for the signals that sanctity in the Church, canonized or not, has set up for us. It is there that we always find true fruitfulness and therewith the proof that the Holy Spirit intends *this* and not something else, on which, perhaps, much ink and organization are lavished. Unless the Lord build the house, the architects of modern spirituality labor in vain. But the Lord gives sleep to his own, the sleep of peaceful, "abiding" love and contemplation. Therefore, we must listen to the heart's resonance: when our heart is deeply stirred when the Church is spoken of, taking note of the direction toward which it spontaneously turns in inmost hope, where it feels directly touched, not because it has finally been talked into something but because it knows itself to be understood prior to any human utterance. It matters little to the heart whether or not the expression that captivates it has already received its final form and precision, if it is even open to misconstruction, a word of various meanings to the many; the Christian heart has itself understood.

If we take this criterion seriously—not in any fanatical or illuministic fashion but wholly in the framework of the Catholic Church, in obedience to her, attentive to her heartbeat—there results as if spontaneously, and right at the outset, a great cleavage that allows us at once to throw off half of the material that we supposed we had to carry with us. If we listen to the way the Spirit blows and to *his* signs of the time, listen therefore in a pure attitude of faith and prayer to his directing, then we can say with certainty beforehand: the Spirit of Jesus will, today as always, not give his Church anything other than the Spirit of Jesus himself. Now this means that the spirituality of the Church can, at every time and also in the present, be only spiritual, and not worldly in the sense of desiring earthly power, the power to assert herself with new and promising methods of political, diplomatic, economic, sociological organization, which would assure to the visible Church greater independence and greater influence in the world. This holds good even if these promising methods are applied primarily internally in order to tighten discipline, to cleanse and lubricate the joints, centralize the direction, ensure greater uniformity of utterance and directives, and raise the standards, moral and intellectual, of the clergy and, as far as possible, of the laity. All these are watchwords of integralism, which, as we here understand it, is at the opposite pole to the Spirit, which blows when it wills. To this extent, there exist *within* the empirical Church two opposing spirits, such as Augustine describes, following the Bible of the Old and the New Covenants, as the battle between two *civitates*; and the *Spiritual Exercises* of Ignatius (more spiritually) as the opposition of two casts of mind: on the one hand, the Luciferian, the will to power; on the other, the Christian, the will to poverty, abasement, humility. The worst feature of integralism is that, out of this mentality, which obviously should be most consciously fought against in the Christian (otherwise, why the exercise of the "two standards" in regard to the most inward, secret decision for Christ?), it makes a combined front of the visible Church and the visible non-Church and for that very reason (since the battle is fought out in the world) claims for the Church the means used by those who do not belong to it.

The program of integralism, however, may claim its appropriate place even within a spiritualized idea of the Church. It is no infallible sign of the Spirit to renounce all hold on worldly positions, all means of propaganda, organization, and centralization, all technical methods of communication and dissemination; and from, it may be, the collapse of all these positions—or, to speak plainly, from communism—to await a spiritual and eschatological salvation and start seriously thinking on Christian lines only, as it were, on the far side of the Communist era. Meanwhile, the things mentioned are at best only means and are governed by a "so far as" determined by the Spirit—the Spirit of Jesus Christ. For it is the Holy Spirit's aim to lead the Church "into all truth", the truth he "shall receive from mine", from the treasure of Jesus Christ. "*Hoc sentite in vobis.*" To hold that this *sentire* somehow follows of itself on the achievement of the integralist ideal is as illusory as the idea of a Communist regime changing dialectically into one of freedom.

The sword with which the Lord demands we should fight and

with which St. Paul fought with all his life is the sword of the Spirit. And it will be shining and sharp if the life we live is swordlike, clear-cut, so that in it the truth is reflected. It is against this manifestation of the truth alone that the real enemies of the Church are opposed, whereas the enemies of integralism may well be friends of Christ, whose severed ear he puts back and heals. Our ideals in regard to the life of the Church do not constitute spiritualities. When we pray for the Church, we ought to ask ourselves if our prayer fits in with that of Christ for the Church. We bear the superabundant treasure of Christ's glory in earthen vessels that the superabundance of strength may be ascribed to God, not to us. The life of Christ will be visible in us only if, at all times, his Passion unto death is made visible in our life (2 Cor 4:7, 10). Like St. Paul, we must be "always delivered unto death" if the true "integrality" of Christ is to be preserved in us. Thus every kind of integralism, open or disguised, is contrary *in principle* to true catholicity, which can win to itself and comprise all things only if it delivers itself up (the real Tradition principle) and dies like the seed to rise again. The principle of integralism is the wholeness, the freedom from wounds and scars of the beast in Revelation (13:12, 14). Man today, more than ever before, needs to be on his guard, remembering that all that he can achieve by his own power (and what can he not?) has no part with what "the Spirit speaks to the Churches".

I

The Church is, of her very nature, a mystery of faith, and this fact has always been present to the consciousness of every epoch of her history. The patristic age lived naïvely in this consciousness, without feeling the need to construct a distinct, self-contained ecclesiology. Man *was* the Church; he stood in the sphere of light and holiness; but reflection on the Church became necessary when the question of her structure arose. Men first became conscious of this question as they looked at those outside, as they considered the nature of heresy or

Judaism; here was a mirror in which they saw, as in a negative, the contours of the Church. It is this unreflective consciousness that alone explains, after a fashion, what is most difficult to grasp of all the various decisions in the Church's history (though they were, in fact, not conscious decisions): that of infant baptism, more pregnant for the future even than the paradoxical "*In hoc signe vinces*" of the Constantinian era, in which the Cross, the sign of the divine helplessness, was made the standard behind which the Church marched onto the field of earthly battle. It is easy to understand how, later on—by appealing to Tradition as a source of revelation—theologians sought for a primitive justification to legitimize a Christianity that one did not enter by personal decision but was unconsciously "born into", as one was incorporated by circumcision into the "carnal" people of the promise; it was going to be infinitely difficult not to take this practice as the model for the *opus operatum*.

Closely connected to the practice of infant baptism was the idea that the Church was, primarily, the "manifestation" of the risen Christ and, therefore, also of his "glory" in the world. It is an idea that for the Alexandrians (later also for the Carolingian Church) suited the militant character of the Church, whether in the spiritual field (in martyrdom) or even in the secular. Constantine's cross was in reality a sign of victory, and it was only gradually that, behind the Church of glory, men came to glimpse the inner mystery of suffering that it hid, becoming increasingly conscious of the contrast between form and content in the Church.

In the High Middle Ages, despite far-reaching sociological changes, the situation was really no different. Even the embittered controversy between the protagonists of Pope and Emperor remained on the threshold, as regards the theology of the Church, and was restricted to legal rights; it did not touch on the essence of the matter, for thought was still in the prereflective stage. The core of truth was safeguarded by prayers and meditations of contemplative love; the commentaries on the Song of Songs and on Paul and John, whose content was transmitted uninterruptedly from the patristic era to the scholastic, preserved the heart of the mystery. Great art could reproduce the mystery in its imagery, on the basis of an as yet *undisputed aesthetic and religious correspondence between the inward and the outward, mystery and form.* This relationship persisted as long as the question was not consciously raised as to what, in fact, as expressed in ideas, was the content of the mystery and what was the outward form. At most, one could say that the content was the Kingdom of God that had come with Christ, and its manifestation was Christendom, as a visible corporate body set apart from paganism, Judaism, and Islam — *Christendom,* not the "organized Church" of post-Lutheran times. Such a relationship, undefined but strongly impressed on the mind, could be justified from the standpoint of the gospel, but it is not identical with that suggested by the latter. It includes a cultural component, which nowadays we mistakenly try to elucidate with the catchword *mythical worldview.* There is a definite order of theological ideas, held unreflectively, that stands in a fruitful and mutual relationship with a definite order of cultural and philosophical ideas, also held unreflectively. The first makes use of the second in order to represent a definite mode of relationship between consciousness and unconsciousness, which seems to it just and incontrovertible. Between the theological mystery of the relationship of Christ and the Church and the aesthetic mystery of, say, a cathedral, there existed only an analogy, not an identity, and no one at that time was deceived by it. The analogy, however, held; it spoke and said enough to prevent any attempt to press beyond into the domain of the rational, after the fashion of the Enlightenment. But what it said were things that have validity only within an aesthetic symbolism in which the Kingdom of heaven "expresses" itself in the holy kingdom of earth, and which to us today, who lack this sense of symbolism, seems a terrible misconception. Within such a world system, there is a justification for the Crusades — which, however looked at from a Biblical standpoint, signify a reversion to the ideas of the Old Testament (itself the theological place of symbolism). After all, from the Christian standpoint, all the world seems alike. Wolfram von den Steinen, with his thorough working out of the "Christian myth", has rendered to Christians of today an important service by helping them toward a clearer discernment of spirits. Yet to project our modern Christian consciousness back into the Middle Ages, however illuminating they may be, is quite unjust. For it is only of ourselves that we ought to be thinking when we contemplate with astonishment, and often with horror, the too hastily drawn conclusions of aesthetic symbolism.

The situation becomes quite different at the time of the Reformation, when (despite all the courageous attempts of the "third force") the consciousness of a breach in the heart of Christendom compelled men to form judgments based on reason. These, like all judgments of the kind, however indispensable, involved tragic losses. For now the spotlight of reflection was turned on what survived of the Christianity of former times, on the undivided visible Church. And this happened in an age when, through the Reformation itself, but equally through the budding natural sciences, the old view of the world was collapsing and a myth was losing its force—and which could only be regained, if ever, through a long and devious process.

In Catholicism, the result was a breach in the Church's teaching. From now on, the central point became the "form" of the Church in the narrow sense: the three functions of the hierarchy, among which could be counted the sacraments and the forms of worship, the disciplinary laws, and theology as the teaching of defined dogma. *But the question whether this form could or should still be seen as the simple expression of the content of the inner ecclesial mystery of the Church was basically no longer asked.* In fact, it could not be considered profitably in a transition period like the Baroque, where, at one and the same time, the old aesthetic ideas, for instance, in art and in traditional thinking, were continued but were menaced or even already abandoned in natural science and the philosophies colored by it (Descartes, Leibniz, the empiricists, Kant). The medieval, nonreflective aesthetic system of the correspondence between the inner nature of the Kingdom of God and its outward appearance had to give way to a stronger sense of tension—in part the outcome of reflection—between the organized hierarchical Church as form and the inscrutable central mystery as content. The two had to be bridged, and this was done explicitly by Ignatius Loyola (in his "Rules for Thinking with the Church"), tragically in the death of Thomas More, heroically in the last *Pensées* of Pascal. Against the idea of functionalism, the epoch of Goethe, of idealism and romanticism, with its concept of the organism, harked back to the old world image, along with Schleiermacher, Sailer, and Möhler right up to Pilgrim's *Physiology of the Church* and their last offshoots in "organic asceticism" and the ecclesiology of the *corpus mysticum.* But the latter conception, as soon as it was used as the key to the entire doctrine on the Church, was seen to be defective of its very nature. *"Corpus"* and "organism" are images whose exaggerated use in connection with the relationship between the inner nature and outward form of the "organized" Church must not be overlooked. Just as we cannot defend the view[1] that the relationship between the external organization of the Church and her internal mystery is adequately expressed by the comparison of that between the body and soul, so we cannot on Biblical grounds maintain a disconnection between the two poles (even if only in the Protestant sense). Such a relationship between content and form as was introduced at the Counter-Reformation cannot be vindicated as the intention of the founder of the Church, nor can it be derived from St. Paul's image of the body (Rom 12; I Cor 12; Eph 4), in which the differentiation of the "members" cuts right across the distinction of official and unofficial, impersonal and personal, hierarchical and charismatic. The Pauline imagery is needed only to guard against hasty interpretations. If the Church is the "body of Christ," its Head, then individual Christians, considered as parts, are *his* members and not actually members of the Church, which, if taken by herself, would not be a body but an acephalous torso. It is the "Head", expressly as "raised up", who determines and distributes offices and charismata (Eph 4:11, 16), and therefore it is the Trinity (*idem Spiritus, idem Dominus, idem Deus* [I Cor 12:4–6]) and not the Church organizing herself. Likewise, the mutual ordering and subordination (which result from the imparted powers and hierarchical offices) in that light are to be understood "organically"; looked at immanently, everything is "ministerial". The free Christian obeys Pope and bishop for the sake of Christ and through his direct relation to Christ. In other words, it is through the *entire* Spirit of Christ, who is also the Spirit of the *entire* Church, that

[1] Which retains the medieval system of nonreflective "mythical" symbolism, restricted to the hierarchy.

the individual Christian is inserted as a member in the whole, "for it is not by measure that [God] gives the Spirit" (Jn 3:34). Otherwise, the New Testament would not be a covenant of freedom.

Precisely where an undialectical relationship between form and content has become unacceptable, we find, for the first time, an unequivocally spiritual movement within contemporary ecclesiology. Reflection on the nature of the Church is as alert as ever. On all sides we hear the call for a satisfactory ecclesiology. At the same time, however, we must be on our guard against facile solutions, and keep before our minds the double question: What is, in fact, the inmost essence of the Church, and—if this cannot be expressed in words— what is the form of its manifestation?

The spiritual (esoteric, we may say) medieval doctrine on the Church was that the Church is the bride of Christ, and this was a continuation of the patristic doctrine. The mystery is love, is marriage, in a depth and height of meaning that goes beyond the flesh, without denying it; for the mystery of the flesh is itself a great mystery, particularly in relation to Christ and the Church. This enables us the better to understand the splendor and exuberance characteristic of the language used at that time about the Church. But in the late Middle Ages, the ravaged form of the Church on earth was no longer transparent enough to convey her inner radiance. This was, consequently, assigned to the secret marriage of suffering of the individual mystic with the bridegroom; finally, to Luther, the countenance of the external office of the Church appeared distorted into a Babylonian mask and caricature.

Something of the personal conception characteristic of the late Middle Ages persisted in the Baroque age (mainly seen in the great figures of John of the Cross, Francis de Sales, Fénelon, and Ignatius), so that the external pomp and hierarchical order could no longer be taken directly as the "manifestation" of the hidden splendor of holiness. A hidden cleavage ran through the spirituality of the *grand siècle,* between the personal inwardness of the individual, and the Church theology formed according to Bellarmine, symptomatically illustrated in the opposition between Bossuet and Fénelon.

Now the problem has forced itself into the open, and the differences demand to be fully explored. So we inquire once again into the inner nature of the Church and come up, more consciously than did the thinkers of patristic times and the Middle Ages, against the problem of the mystery of the Church as she was at her origin. For that is what we have to embody and express in our Christian life.

But is it, indeed, possible to represent the original and inmost being of the Church or express it conceptually? Scripture speaks of the bride: this is an image that presupposes an actual subject, contrasted with the bridegroom, though united with him in the mystery of the one flesh. But is the Church such a subject? Or is it not rather the sum of the individual believers who as such are subjects by nature and not simply through the grace of Christ? Does the splendid imagery of the Song of Songs, which communicated its profound meaning in a nonreflective mode of thought, still hold good for us moderns? Or perhaps we should, with Karl Barth, demythologize what eludes clear comprehension both in the object and in our consciousness and revert to a simple encounter between person and person, to the concept of the people of God as found in the Old Testament, the Qumran scrolls, and Protestantism—as, to be sure, many among us are now proposing. This means following the *City of God* rather than the *Commentaries on the Psalms*. And it has quite a modern touch about it: the Church with her clear lines like a building designed with all the most up-to-date techniques, all that savors of myth swept away, and the mystery concentrated more or less on the Person of Christ, God and man.

We can see at once that this approach is unacceptable, since it means abandoning the core, inapprehensible but essential, of the mystery, to which the words *bride, body,* and *people* can serve only as pointers. The "bride" who, issuing from the wounded side of the new Adam, is at the same time his "body" (and only for that reason his "people") is both the one (with Christ) and the other (over against him), in a relation at once of independence and freedom for which there is no analogy in the created sphere but only in the Trinity. The Church is the grace and fullness of Christ poured out into the "other" (created) subject and is not only act but also result, yet result never separable from act. For this reason, the "bride" can never desire to think of herself as definitively "over against" her Lord but only as pressing on to closer union with him, the Source of her being. There can be no ecclesiology that is not, at its core, Christology; and if it is to proceed on the right lines, it must begin by renouncing itself. Its unity is not a second unity next to the unity of Christ: this is true of its totality of body and spirit. For this reason, the nuptial mystery of the "one flesh" can only be a simile for it, just as Eve's coming forth from Adam's side is no more than a simile, even though we take it that her soul, too, came from him. This, however, would stretch the Biblical image into a Christological one and still remain imperfect in its new application. But if Christ is the Incarnation of the God who rightly bears the name of *"Non-aliud"* (see Nicholas of Cusa)—precisely because he is the Wholly Other!—then he cannot be the "One" to whom the Church could be contrasted as the "other". The Church so understood will ultimately be unable to be an object to herself but will see herself only as the outflowing love of the Lord (and, through him, of the Trinity) and, therefore, as the love flowing out over the world for her redemption. And however conscious she may be of being a continuous expression of gratitude, of responding and confessing in faith, she will understand this not as her own independent action but as joining in with the Son's *eucharistia* and *confessio* to the Father in their common Spirit. What she can do of herself is as ordinary and insignificant as the portion of bread and wine that disappears by being transubstantiated into her Lord.

Many consequences follow from this fact, one of them being a new ecclesiological conception of marriage,[2] which only now attains its full theological significance. Another is a new conception of virginity, which is at last being freed from any suspicion of a Gnostic depreciation of the body and is seen as a heightening, rather than a diminishing, of the individual sacrament of marriage—being a direct participation in the general sacrament that is the mystery of the nuptial fruitfulness between Christ and the Church. For the exaltation of Christian marriage is always accompanied by that of Christian

---

[2] The Biblical exaltation of marriage, in point of fact, rests on (1) the "acephalous" character of woman in contrast to man (not, then, on the two-person relationship) and (2) the mystery of woman's origin from man, which can hardly be considered "retracted" by 1 Cor 11:11–12 (Eph 5 was written later).

virginity. Another consequence is a new consciousness of the Church as servant, for the mystery of her own bridal relationship is not her own appurtenance but is wholly in the Lord, in the depths of his being; and the Church, in whatever aspect she comes to view herself, can only see herself as the handmaid of the Lord. In this we have, undoubtedly, the key to the present interest in Mariology. It is as if the Church, in striving after self-knowledge, were more and more insistently confronted by God with this particular mirror, the bride without spot or wrinkle, ignorant of self-reflection, knowing herself solely as handmaid, however much she be the woman crowned with the sun, moon, and stars, the queen of heaven. In Mary the Church can look upon herself without risk of confusion, not only because she can never identify herself with Mary (for, in concrete, it is always sinners who contemplate her) but also because what she sees in Mary is always the opposite of identification. Only at the end of time can she hope to reach the level of her most exalted member, when the stain of original sin shall have been washed away, virginal integrity restored, bodily assumption into heaven completed. Till then, the Church, in honoring Mary, cannot be honoring herself, and the more she (as the Church triumphant being gathered into heaven) comes to resemble her archetype, the less liable will she be to the temptation. Anyone who clearly understands this dialectic can easily combine a tender and ardent devotion to Mary with all the contemporary warnings against Mariological exaggerations, since these are the fruit of a radical misunderstanding of the Marian principle. Mary herself had neither the vocation nor the inclination to concern herself with Mariology, and neither has the Church to construct an ecclesiology that goes beyond an outline or even beyond guarding against error or explaining her own transcendence. And just as no Christian should indulge in the contemplation of his own (infused or acquired) virtues, still less may his holy mother, the hierarchical Church, do so, for it is from her Spirit that he acquires his own spirit of humility and modesty. But if the Church, as the handmaid of the Lord, may not glorify herself, yet it does not become her sons to besmirch her earthly crowns that she does not know what to make of in this period of history. It is not without significance that, as has often been remarked, the Marian definitions and those of the First Vatican Council on the place of Peter occurred at the same period; they each support the other and elucidate their real purpose. They do so, however, only when they are considered in the Spirit of Christ and as the expression of his Spirit and are not used as a vehicle for the self-glorification of the Church, internal and external, in an earthly integralistic sense. The Marian spirit of unity with the Lord, in her virginal body and in obedience, is also the Petrine spirit of an unreflective ecclesial obedience for the sake of the Lord and his nuptial mystery, obedience even to the Cross. It is a spirit of surrender without thought of self, which, in both cases— the *Mater Dolorosa* and the crucified Peter—reaches the point of complete acceptance.

At this same point there appear, moreover, all those spiritual impulses, apparently extraneous to all the traditional social forms of the Church and desirous of drawing their sustenance directly from the Lord, that are expressly concerned with bringing not the "Church" to the world but solely the Lord and *his* love. Typical of many cases is that of Charles de Foucauld, who cut himself off externally, spatially, more and more from any visible connection with the Church so as to be alone in the desert among savage tribes, like an embodied essence of the Church, standing before the Eucharistic Lord, and letting his outpourings of grace stream through him. Then, posthumously in his sons and daughters, he sought out the most hopeless and unpromising places, with the express intention of bringing nothing to the world, neither school nor medical help nor anything to do with culture, but only the humble love of the Lord. "Ceaselessly", he makes the Lord say, "must you descend, ceaselessly humble yourselves; ceaselessly must the first take the lowest place, in the spirit of humility, in the desire to serve." "Work for the sanctification of the world, work at it like my mother, without speaking, in silence. Build your dwellings among those who do not know me, bring me into their midst by erecting there an altar, a tabernacle, and bring there the gospel, not by word of mouth but by example, not by preaching but by living it." "Example is the sole external work by which one can influence souls whose attitude to Christ is one of complete rejection." "Our hearts must be quite poor, emptied, void, free, detached from all that is not

God and Christ, in order to be rich and overflowing with his love, filled with his love, captured by his love, depending on him alone."

For Charles de Foucauld, the Church is no longer an object for contemplation but is wholly gathered up in her act of worship, in which she becomes the channel for the all-uniting love of Christ. Something analogous might be said of the standpoint and action of other groups and movements, which do not so much lead to the Church and illuminate the way as they try, simply, to be the illuminating spirit of the Church: "Blameless and innocent, children of God without blemish in the midst of a crooked and perverse generation, among whom you shine as lights in the world" (Phil 2:15). In these cases, *sentire cum Ecclesia* is raised to a higher plane, that of *sentire Ecclesiae*. This is possible only in complete self-abnegation and obedience to the hierarchy, as we have seen already in connection with the spiritual unity of the Marian and Petrine aspects. This will always be the guarantee of their purity and genuineness.

From this it may be seen that it is not due to the influence of contemporary "realism" but to a sense of what is real in the sacred sphere that we are more and more losing all taste for the pomp and circumstance designed to impress man with the majesty of the Church. There is, simultaneously, an increasing trend toward simplicity ("associate with the lowly" [Rom 12:16]), toward awareness of the lowliness of all the elements of the Church that emphasize her function as servant. "Prestige" is no longer to be sought by outward display—and the idea that the Church could acquire prestige by such means has been finally quashed by Georges Bernanos. It is now clear to everyone that—if we must speak still of prestige—the Church will gain more in the eyes of men the less she concerns herself with it and the more obedient she is to the Lord's injunctions to his disciples. In this connection it may be affirmed, not as a daring conjecture but as a simple fact, that even the numerous canonizations make comparatively little impression on the faithful, as does everything, in fact, that can be effected by organizational machinery. The faithful are impressed not by canonization but by sanctity, and mostly by those who, without human striving and human means, are pointed to directly by the Holy Spirit and by him brought into prominence. We are not here objecting to the canonization process as such. But it is today the tacit desire of men that canonization be, above all, a manifestation of sanctity, the mother calling attention to the conduct of this or that fellow saint—an act, then, of the Church obedient and serving rather than self-glorifying. Nowhere so much as here is quantity the enemy of quality.

In our day, of course, there is discernible in all quarters a certain bit of animosity toward papal centralism, an animosity that often misses the point and is pardonable at most on human grounds but not on Christian ones. Examined closely, however, this unrest is not always basically a refusal *sentire cum Ecclesia* but more often the expression of a deep conviction that the hierarchy has indeed a sacral function for the Church, but that this function is wholly one of service. This hierarchy is the crystalization of the love of the Lord, who established it as necessary for this sinful world (most necessary, in fact, when it accepts the humble task of instructing and exacting obedience in the name of the Lord). As soon as this attitude is recognized, many a fault finder is prepared for joyful cooperation. The spirituality of the hierarchy remains to this day indirectly formed and burdened by a forceful theology of the late primitive Church, the "ecclesiastical hierarchy" of Denis the Areopagite, which, unconcerned with the actuality of sin, was content to portray an ideal Church, a Church as she ought to be. This theology identified office with sanctity, the higher office with the higher sanctity, the transparency of the official function with the transparency of contemplation rapt in its sacred object. This ideal surely must be an inspiration to the members of the hierarchy, but precisely for that reason it may not encourage substitution or compensation for deficient personal holiness by the objective holiness of office (as the Areopagite was sometimes consciously or unconsciously interpreted during the Middle Ages and later). The office is no less sacred to the faithful of today than it was to former generations, but it is now soberly regarded as the means to actual sanctity and as the holier and more venerable the more clearly it represents the kenosis of Christ.

A final consequence follows. The hierarchy is no longer seen as merely the "manifesting corpus", the embodiment of the Church's intrinsic, mysterious, holy status of bride, but rather as a serving office that is to transform this original hidden holiness into an external holiness of life and love—and there has been a corresponding change in apologetics. The *notae Ecclesiae*—closely connected with the hierarchy—of fundamental theology now lose some of their forcefulness in favor of the pivotal *nota* of holiness. "By this shall all men know that you are my disciples, that you love one another"—this, surely, is *the* apologetic of Christ and the apostles. The unity of Christians, so strongly emphasized in the high-priestly prayer, is surely not of human making but a Trinitarian gift, and it can be nothing other than the expression and manifestation of this supernatural love. "*Ubi peccata sunt, ibi est multitudo, ibi schismata, ibi haereses, ibi dissensiones; ubi autem virtus, ibi singularitas, ibi unio, ex quo omnium credentium erat cor unum et anima una*" (Origen). It is *this* unity—and not one allegedly exacted by the power of the keys—it is *this* catholicity and apostolicity that can bring about apostolic effects. It might, for instance, lead a Newman from the Anglican *via media* into the Catholic Church.

All these aspects are interrelated. They follow easily once the principle from which they rise has been grasped. The fact that their multiplicity can be brought to unity may well indicate that we have accurately touched on the principle of which they are the expression.

2

A further conclusion can be drawn from the above. If the Church and the individual Christian are worthy of belief and impress by the fact that they do not point to themselves but are suffused by and show forth Christ's love, if the Church and the Christian alone can capture the world's attention by proclaiming something other than themselves, then this self-abnegation in the service of Christ is clearly the only possible way of revealing to the world the self-abnegation of Christ. This kenosis of Christ, consummated in the death on the Cross, is the very point of origin of the Church and Christian as such. It is the point of the incomprehensible generative power of Christ, who bears the entire Church within himself. She exists nowhere else but within him (and, ultimately, the entire hope, the entire faith of the Old Covenant spring from thence). As Christ has received from the Father the power to surrender his life, as he breathes forth his spirit on the Cross in an extremity of weakness, so he can also, at Easter, breathe his Spirit into the Church. His weakness unto death is his divine and his human power, his omnipotence, willing to assume the form of utter powerlessness.

The Church and the Christian are, undoubtedly, products of this unique generative power on the Cross. This does not mean, however, that, as products, they are ever separable from the act by which they originated. " 'As the Father has sent me, even so I send you.' And when he had said this, he breathed on them, and said to them, 'Receive the Holy Spirit' " (Jn 20:21–22). It is the Spirit who wills to be continually breathed forth and who, for that reason, must be ever anew breathed forth from a principle that is both Trinitarian and Christological. Ecclesial piety today is more closely bound up than ever before with this mystery. The Church community is the true product of the solitude of Christ, his solitude on the Cross, his solitude as the incomparable God-Man, which is, in turn, the manifestation of his Trinitarian solitude and ultimately of the primordial solitude of the Father in the generation of the Son. The Christological solitude is the active source of all Christian Church community. The Christian must be not only Church generated but also the Church cogenerating, regenerating: he must be the Church in origin, the Church in solitude. This is solitude that evokes community, apostolic solitude that does not go out from the Church but in which the Church herself goes out into the world. It is not private, existentialist solitude, for it is most profound community in and with Christ, just as Christ's solitude is always—even in his dereliction on the Cross—community in and with the Father. But such solitude in origin can become so abysmal as to occlude the experience of community. The Church is the pure outpouring of the Lord, the Christian the pure outpouring of Christ and Church. The Christian proceeds from community with Christ, from community with Church. Bearing this duplex community he advances toward a community to be regenerated, but he goes his way in solitude. It is ultimately the solitude of the generating Father, the Father who is such only in relation to the Son.

It does not really matter whether this solitude is realized mainly by way of contemplation or by way of the active apostolate. The Carmel is solitude in God, solitude whose meaning is generation of the Church through the Church. In accord with the tradition of her order, Thérèse of Lisieux used to describe the function of the Carmelite nuns as "mothers of souls". The lifework of John of the Cross was solitary in this most profound sense, in the midst of the Church, *as* the Church. The celebrated prayer of the Carmelite Elizabeth of the Trinity (*"O mon Dieu, Trinité que j'adore"*), on which the Benedictine Dom Vandeur has written so profound a commentary, is a pure prayer of solitude that never mentions the Church at all, for it is a prayer from the very heart of the Church. For example, Edith Stein's commentary on John of the Cross, *The Science of the Cross,* leads to the same conclusion. This agreement among the great orders (to which may be added, as representative of all the rest, Francis of Assisi and Antony of the Desert) is significant in that they all take as their starting point the sending of disciples into the world. If the movement of the synagogue and of Israel is always centripetal (*"habitare fratres in unum"*), that of the Church—from the unity of the Church—is centrifugal (*"ite in universum mundum"*). Even the autarchic abbey does not escape this law, which makes it a city set on a mountain, radiating a light that directs others to their end. The "community life" of the orders is an instrument for the self-abnegation and apostolic solitude of the individual, exercising them in renunciation of self and Christian love. *"Vita communis maxima poenitentia"*, as John Berchmans said.

This explains the missionary spirituality of the "secular institute", whose members as a rule have to go singly through the world, endowed with the strength of the Church community and carrying it into realms alien to the Church. Certainly, they have to be sowers and planters of a new Christian community, not to dwell there in comfort but to continue their journeying from there as apostles in a new solitude. It is obvious that this spirituality as a form of life is not for everyone, but it belongs, in however attenuated a degree, to the ecclesial maturity and responsibility of those who have been confirmed. One cannot be simply—today less than ever—the Church as a product; one must always be the Church producing. The Church community can never be definitively rounded off and self-contained; once it has reached this stage it must open out in the "*Ite, missa est*" to the world and to solitude.

This raises the problem of the liturgy, which today more than ever agitates the Church as a whole. The problem consists, in the first place, in recovering what is genuine and real from the accumulations of the centuries. In reaction against the untenable liberalism of making liturgy a personal matter, we must make every effort to arouse the sense of community within the liturgy, to restore liturgy to the ecclesial plane, where individuals can take their proper place in it. On this plane they must learn to be the holy people set apart instead of individuals. Liturgical piety involves a total turning from concern with one's inner state and self-abnegation to the attitude and feeling of the Church. It means enlarging the scope of prayer, so often narrow and selfish, to embrace the concerns of the whole Church and, indeed—as in the Our Father—of God himself. In fact, this violent, this often "crucifying" sacrifice of the pious subject to the ecclesial object (this is what Schleiermacher and Hegel call "community consciousness") is, ultimately, one of the conditions for the presence of the Eucharistic Lord: "Where two or three are gathered together" —that is, where individuals, in profound faith and obedience, desire to be and to realize the Church—"there I am in the midst of you."

Nonetheless, despite what enthusiasts for the liturgical movement often seem to think, liturgical piety does not replace personal prayer, the encounter of the soul with God in the intimacy of the Sermon on the Mount. Community prayer calls, in fact, for personal contemplative prayer, which becomes by that fact ecclesial prayer. When the liturgy seems not to tolerate contemplation within itself and alongside itself—especially through a busy activism, for example, when the sacred action of the altar is accompanied by the roar of loudspeakers and other machinations that make private prayer impossible—then it degenerates into a worldly thing. The Christian ought to come away from the liturgical sacrifice not with the satisfied sense of having accomplished something but inwardly strengthened, and with the ardent desire, in the words of so many post-Communions, to realize in his life what has just been sacramentally enacted. This integration of community and individual prayer has certainly begun in our time, but it is not yet well enough understood, nor approached from both directions. We yet lack adequate directives. To supply these, the older orders, whose merit it is to have abetted the liturgical revival in various regions, need only recall their own ancient Tradition (as has been done for the Middle Ages by Dom Jean Leclerq in his excellent book *The Love of Learning and the Desire for God*). In this way they can recall to life the synthesis already present in the Church, avoid the dangers and by-products of a too exterior liturgism, without forego-ing anything of value already acquired. In the absence of real, per-sonal contemplation concurrent with the liturgy, and if the cultivation of community consciousness is not accompanied by the building up of the Christian person, then his sense of himself as externally representing the Church is illusion. The unity into which he merges himself would then be simply that of a pious group consciousness after the Protestant manner and not ecclesial community conscious-ness aglow with fervor, whose direct source is the Bridegroom, Christ.

The axis of this ecclesial community consciousness is the redemp-tive love of Christ, which he imparts without diminution or compro-mise to his bride. To know the real spirit of this consciousness, we have only to recall the evangelical counsels by which Christ prepares—for those who desire it—the way to the mystery of the Cross: the counsel of virginity—for the Church is virginal in the core of her sentiments (2 Cor 11:2); the counsel of poverty in spirit and reality—for the Church is poor in all that is her own in order to be a receptacle for the fullness of Christ; the counsel of utter docility—for the Church, as body and bride, must necessarily be at the disposal of the Bridegroom. Thus it is that our generation begins to perceive that the evangelical counsels concern each believer who desires to attune his own heart to the pulse of the Church, not only in an objective performance of the cult mystery but in the *leiturgia,* the service of his whole life. And since the counsels of Christ are the key to his own

crucified love (and there is no other than his), then, according to 1
Corinthians 7:29–31, they pertain to every state in the Church and
must be observed by each. *Sentire cum consiliis* (if these are properly
understood in Christ's sense) is identical with *sentire cum Ecclesia.* We
have to rid ourselves of the superficial idea of an opposition between
the two forms of the Christian life, an idea that comes from considering only how the different states of life diverge instead of going back
further to their underlying unity. For, unless this is done, how is it
possible to understand what is meant by "the mind of the Church"?
For example, if anyone constructs a spirituality of the lay state and of
marriage from the standpoint of its distinction from the religious and
priestly state, he is thereby debarred from perceiving what lies at the
root of both, the spirituality of the Church as such. And it is the same,
too, if he assigns the "secular state" to the temporal sphere and the
duties pertaining to the Kingdom of God in the world and the
"religious state" to the new eschatological age. In so doing, he somehow presumes a split in the Church, whether he intends to or not. But
the Church, as a single *totality,* has on principle died to the world with
Christ and with him ascended into heaven, to be sent forth from
thence into the whole world. Thus the Church is bound as a single
totality to Christ's entire redemptive act, and the divergent ways of
marriage and virginity must be the expression of this totality.

This reference to the common root of the states of life is of great
practical importance for the secular institutes. Insofar as the secular
institutes understand to the core their own thought and can *live* it
(and this is not always the case), insofar as they are capable of bringing
their thought to the attention of the external Church (and this has
barely been indicated)—to this extent are they called, if not to clear
away the sterile dualism of the states of life in the Church, then at least
to lessen it considerably and to bestow on the apostolic essence of the
states of life a virtually primitive Christian newness. The Christian
layman or laywoman who lives a life of celibacy, poverty, and
disponibility, purely for the love of Christ, presents a far greater
challenge to the non-Christian and Christian world than does the
member of a religious order, who essentially lives a well-organized
and somewhat sheltered traditional life. The member of the secular

institute does not preach, but his very life is a positive and abiding witness to the presence of the Church in the world. He is in privileged, if certainly not in exclusive, fashion the Church manifest, the sign of proclamation not of himself but of the Church and of Christ. More precisely, he is a member of Christ manifest, and membership necessarily refers to the body. This is manifestation, and it is not for the common multitude but for those individuals who can withstand the perils of witness by virtue of their mission and their fidelity to this mission. This is manifestation, and it implies being prepared for frustration, being prepared to see an entire effort (such as that of the priest workers) fail the first time and to revoke that effort without, for all that, considering it completed, settled. In the case of the priest workers it was clearly a question of overcoming a bourgeois prejudice against the priesthood as such, whose civil status was called into question. Objectively, there is no reason why the witness of the ordained Christian should be more important, more meritorious, more conspicuous, more precious than that of the layman; *a priori,* the reverse ought to be expected. On account of anticlerical prejudice, the experiment with priests appears more productive of both gain and loss, and yet both the gains and the losses may have helped to dispel some of the prejudice. Those laymen who will remain in the forefront of controversy will be less in the limelight, but their witness as Church in the most worldly world will be no less effective. If they have chosen, in addition, to heed the evangelical counsels, they can the more forcefully embody the radical unity of the Church, overcoming the world, without fleeing it, by the power of self-denying love.

The example of such a life must react and already does react upon the married state and on the priesthood and on the old orders and congregations: on the married state by inspiring the realization of the counsels; on the priesthood by suggesting a more radical interpretation of the apostolate in the spirit of the Gospels; on the religious state by emphasizing the fact that even in its traditional form, this state interiorly no less is, no less must be the manifestation of the Church than are her exterior manifestations. In each case the central concern is the Church and not the specific ways of life, old or new. In each case it is a question of renouncing fruitless comparisons in favor of a deep personal awareness of Church. In each case it is a question of submitting personal piety to the focal point of ecclesial awareness. This awareness does not lie in political or cultural spheres but unequivocally in the origin of the Church in Christ, an origin that can altogether be perceived only in faith and love and in the spirit of resolute discipleship.

The Church, then, must be conceived of as having her center not within herself, as an external, worldly organization, but outside herself, in Christ who engenders her. From this it can be seen that the Church, while inwardly reaching out to the Lord, must for that very reason externally go out beyond herself into the world. Hence the characteristic that Friedrich Heer so strongly insists upon, that ecclesial love must, in its Christological core, be love for one's enemies, love and turning toward the non-Christian brother without—if in this perspective there can indeed still be a "without" in any real sense. If the Church is understood as dynamic in her very origin, as the irradiation of Christ into the world to be redeemed, then the world itself, into which she radiates, is her proper and natural sphere. On this account, the Church must have a worldly form, spatial and institutional: sacrament, hierarchy, and dogma. The non-Christian world may indeed judge her by what is institutional in her, and even her own sinful element may, for the sake of convenience and as a means of escape, cling to these institutional elements. But this does not mean that the Church in her true nature, the holy Church, has to interpret herself in this way. On the contrary: she will understand the unchangeable "bone structure" given in her foundation, in the light of its function in the living organism, whose life and activity are guaranteed by this very structure. We cannot say of any living thing that there is a "tension in unity" between the bone structure and the flesh: still less can we say so of the supernatural image of Christ, the Church, in whom everything, however conditioned by her situation in the world, is to be understood as the crystalization of the love of Christ. Seeing and recognizing this at all times was the art of the saints, and it is the same now as always. Love of one's enemies as the axial element—and not just as an incidental act of heroism—is Christian agape in the form appropriate for our time. It would not be itself were it viewed simply as a relation between members of the Church, an interchange between those already in a state of charity toward one another. Certainly, it is entirely in accord with the synoptic, the Pauline, and the Johannine teachings that the mutual love of Christians be a light in the world, drawing attention to itself—that is, to Christ, the Source of this light. But this simply means that love within the Church must not be closed in on herself but must have a far-reaching apostolic and redemptive significance for the world, as is seen today mainly in the much discussed idea of the whole world as a single family.

One further observation on this point. Once the Church is understood in this twofold transcendence in relation to the Lord and to the world, a new kind of love for her is enkindled, a love that is far more tender and devoted than any enthusiasm that might be enkindled by her visible structure. It is impossible to avoid an impression of fanaticism and narrow-mindedness as long as the Church strives for prestige or for preponderance and as long as the motive force is not love for the hidden central mystery of the Church and the urge to defend it in the external sphere. But the burning love of the Christian for this profound mystery is itself a mystery. If we think of the Church primarily in contradistinction to the Lord, as a corporation endowed with graces and the means to grace, the faithful, as members of the Church, will surely not refuse homage, admiration, and loyalty, love and obedience, today any more than before. For it is she who "has" the Holy Spirit of Christ, and from her the individual obtains a participation in this Spirit, who, therefore, is always the Spirit of the Church.

But is this way of looking at the Church adequate? Does it not envisage merely a partial aspect, which should never be divorced from the primordial mystery that is never fully revealed? For the mystery is not disclosed (since it is ultimately to be seen in the light of the mystery of the Trinity) as to how far the actual reality of the Church is in Christ (even where she presents herself as his fullness) and how far she is in contradiction to Christ (that is, as a reality engendered by his creative power). For this reason, it can never be finally settled whether the Christian only "believes the Church" or, at the same time, "believes in the Church". He believes her only insofar as she is the emanation of the fullness of Christ, who is God: and only God can one believe. This being so, then also is the Christian's love toward the Church not simply love directed to an entity apart in itself but, most certainly, love that only begins with the Church in order to become love for Christ and God, a transparent and transitive love, which, as such, is ultimately the love of the Church for her Lord and Bridegroom. Devotion to the Church in the present age will be, at its core, not love toward the Church but love that is that of the Church.

Identification of one's own life with the inmost center of the Church, where she is simply the bride in the presence of the Bridegroom, is the ultimate and abiding justification of the contemplative life. No doubt, this can be adjusted to the time in its varying details, not only in the mitigation of its observances but also, perhaps mainly, in a more radical, more consequential ecclesiological form of piety. Nonetheless, the paradoxical fact of its power of attraction shows how wrong they are who consider contemplation outdated or tolerate, at most, the *contemplativus in actione.* Mary of Bethany can never be dispensed with. *Personam Ecclesiae gerit:* she represents, in her special role, the Church herself. She actualizes in the world of human consciousness the inmost mystery of the nuptials between Christ and the Church, God and the world, grace and nature, a relation that is the mystery both of Mary's fecundity as mother and of that of the Church. It is a mystery that, in its absolute finality in itself, and in its "unconcernedness", is itself the focal point, just as, in Song of Songs, the love between bride and bridegroom is fulfilled in itself, is sufficient in its inner fecundity, without procreation, without any further action. That the contemplative life in the Church is also a life of penitence and mortification, a crucified life as well as a marriage festivity, is simply the final consequence as the Church has always understood it and still today is given to understand it through the inspiration of the Holy Spirit.

3

The transitive character of present-day devotion to the Church has one final characteristic, inasmuch as the "world" that confronts the Church is not merely an undifferentiated world (though, in principle, redeemed by the Lord of the Church) but, to a great extent, is a Christian world, or the "non-Catholic Church". Everyone nowadays is aware of what this involves, and so we can state it briefly. We feel the cleavage in Christendom much more deeply than men did in the centuries since the Reformation—not only in the West but also increasingly between East and West—and feel it as something whose guilt we all share, as inexcusable, and as a most evident obstacle to the Church's apostolic work. For us the schism is the outward indication, the eruption of a long-standing disease in Christendom. However helpless we feel in the presence of the suppurating sore—since, ultimately, it is only individuals who can come to an understanding, and the organized and opposed bodies only with great difficulty—yet we know one thing: that healing, if it is possible, can come only from the power within, from a renewal of love. The source of this love can be only the heart of Christ, and the form it takes will be preeminently that of fervent prayer, prayer for inner unity and outward reunion. It is a love that does not shift all responsibility for action onto the Lord but works along with him, doing all that can be done in the spirit of the Church, which, essentially, will follow along the lines we have sketched out in the first and second sections; that is to say, it will relate all that pertains to the inner sphere of the Church to its supratemporal, ever-present point of origin. If all this takes place within the two Christian communities in the course of their self-questioning and in the true spirit of faith, it cannot fail in the end to resolve the oppositions inherited from history. There cannot be two ecclesial truths. At the most, it is possible that different aspects come together and complete one another in the one truth, that a partial truth should sink into the background and be almost forgotten in the one comprehensive aspect, that the perspective of the whole should be lost or obscured in a partial view. If Christians of different confessions were, in mutual love, to posit the true act of faith (which always envisages that total Christian truth)—and this, if they believe and love, they are bound to do—then the love of Christ can certainly work in them many a miracle of rapprochement and reconciliation.

However, even this aspect of devotion to the Church has its dangers, for it is constantly liable to go to one of two opposite extremes; and so, when Christian love is ardent but insufficiently enlightened, there is need for supervision by the Church. Yet the love that embraces both the Church and other Christian confessions with special intimacy provides, to a great extent, its own safeguards. It knows that differences in doctrine are not unimportant and that they are not to be glossed over by a liberal approach that ignores or diplomatically minimizes them. They can be overcome only by great efforts on each side to see what in its own position is a cause of separation and of the other's defects and so bring the two together. Associations for work and discussion between theologians of different confessions are multiplying; they examine, in a new spirit of love and responsibility, both what they hold in common and what separates them. What is most fruitful so far as immediate results are concerned is present-day Biblical scholarship, where both sides now work together practically without friction. If this continues long enough, we may have every hope for a rapprochement even in the sphere of dogmatic theology. Certainly, the agreement reached in the last decades on matters of Biblical scholarship, even of Biblical theology, is unprecedented in the history of the Church since the Reformation. It makes it seem quite out of the question to revert to the usual methods of controversial theology, which ignore the results achieved by Biblical scholarship. It is in the joint hearing of God's word that we must let ourselves be jointly instructed on the unity of this word. The Catholic Church has nothing to fear or to lose thereby. She cannot be afraid of any genuine result, even though she may, under the guidance of the Holy Spirit, have to take account of new depths and bolder heights. The harvest to be reaped from the study of the Bible on all levels, from strict scholarship to that of vulgarization, is of immeasurable importance for an understanding of the Church. Here, too, the Christian consciousness is becoming greatly enlarged and open to the full import of revelation, and the Church is thereby attaining a new self-awareness. In addition, we are recovering dimensions that were present to the Middle Ages but lost to view in the religious controversies — that, for instance, of the Augustinian City of God, which comprises both Testaments. The value of the Old Testament in theological controversy is particularly great, since it affords scarcely any occasion for differences of opinion.

And now, for the first time in the Church's history since the days of Justin, the way is opened for communication between the Church and Judaism. The first dialogue, begun during the Enlightenment between enlightened Judaism and liberal Protestantism, was of little ecclesiastical significance. The new dialogue, however, which has gradually to forge a way through unforeseeable obstacles, is bound to produce results. It must be conducted in view of the New Testament origins made clear through Biblical studies, that is, at the point when the Church actually came into being in history and from which her being can never be disconnected. It may be that this aspect has not yet penetrated the consciousness of the Church and that paving the way for dialogue is still seen as a duty of reparation rather than something demanded by the present age of the Church. But if today we are everywhere concerned to gain a clear view of the ecclesial fundamentals and of what the divine intention was regarding the Church, surely the eternal situation described in Romans 9–11 as the primary one in Church and world history must be seen as more urgent and compelling than ever. The matter is far more than one of vague, human sympathy for the new state of Israel, the boldness of its experiment, the courage of its inhabitants. Nor is it merely one of that mutual rivalry between "Jews and Gentiles" through which, according to Paul, God prepares both for his Kingdom. It is, ultimately, what concerned the burning love of Paul, his "great sorrow and unceasing anguish", his desire to be "cut off from Christ for the sake of my brethren, my kinsmen by race. . . . To them belong the sonship, the glory, the covenants, the giving of the law, the worship, and the promises" (Rom 9:2–4). It concerns the wound that goes so deep into the heart of Paul and the apostles, Christ and the Church, the Lord's weeping over Jerusalem, and his own "anathematization" as the embodiment of (in the first place Israel's) sin. It concerns the ever-present thorn in the Church's flesh, the constant presence of the Cross, the guilt of which it is only too easy (as Christian Tradition has done) to turn over to the Jews. Admittedly, the Church is not the Lord. She has no power over world history, and her service as spouse is her unconditional agreement with the "inscrutability of his counsels". Yet this expression escapes Paul only when he speaks of the common disobedience of the "Jews and the Gentiles", of God's mercy equally accorded to both, and of the eschatological salvation of Israel. What a close community of destiny is theirs, and what thanks is due from the Church of the Gentiles to Israel thus brought low! The Church begins to form some idea of it in her reading and study of Scripture seeing how her daily office, the psalms, the prophets, the sapiential books are not only inspired from above but also spring from within the heart of the devout Israel led by the Holy Spirit: "If I forget thee, Jerusalem . . . " It is an inward, indissoluble unity of destiny such as existed between the beloved Jacob and the unloved Esau (Malachi 1:2–4 = Rom 9:13), who draw together while still in the fear of their estrangement: Jacob "went on before them, bowing himself to the ground seven times, until he came near to his brother. But Esau ran to meet him, and embraced him, and fell on his neck and kissed him, and they wept" (Gen 33:3–4).

The great, sweeping eschatological views of Romans 11 has been given us for a purpose: it implies certain ethical demands. As a result of it, and of God's victory over the cleft in the heart of Paul and of Christ and the Church, there arises in the consciousness of the Church a tremendous hope and love, so that the deepest source of love springs up from the chasm of the darkest tragedy of world history. Present-day devotion to the Church is dominated by the idea of the collapse of all that divides, the dismantling of the old fortifications. This by no means implies overrunning the eschatological boundaries that have been laid down. What it does imply is obedience to the enjoined meditation on the Biblical revelation, its prophetic and dialectical utterance, and its messianic hope of a final synthesis. It is by hope that the seriousness of the dialectic can be measured, a hope that is not without fear but in which grace superabounds (Rom 5:15–21). It is from the horizons thus opened up that the Christian today derives all his confidence and parrhesia. It is as if, in his darkness, this new light is something owed to him; as if the Church, more closely bound to the Cross, can thereby obtain a deeper view into the Kingdom of resurrected love.

"FIDES CHRISTI"

An Essay on the Consciousness of Christ

I. *Biblical faith as a whole*

Did Jesus have faith? To answer this question, let us begin—at first in a quite a priori fashion—with a few remarks on what the Bible has to say about "faith" and its relationship to Christ. If it is true that the Bible as a whole increasingly uses the term *faith* (in growing measure up to the prophets, and especially Isaiah) as the adequate expression for the way the chosen people related to God; and thus if, within this framework, this term also truly reflects how the individual members of the people of God related to their God of the Covenant; if indeed the Biblical idea of faith includes even more so *God's* faithfulness toward his people and assumes that this fidelity is a presupposition and prototype to be imitated (recall that the Hebraic term encompasses more shades of meaning than the Greek); then, speaking a priori, it cannot be otherwise in the case of Jesus. For it is concerning him that the law and the prophets have spoken (Jn 5:46; Lk 24:44), and it is with him that they converse on Mt. Tabor (Mt 17:3), and he is the one on the basis of whom every Old Testament believer has lived (Heb 11). And so we can say a priori that it cannot be otherwise with Jesus than that he has perfectly fulfilled and lived out the disposition on the human side that the God of the Covenant, the Father, has demanded of all men.

This is a very encapsulated summary of the link between the idea of faith in the two parts of the Bible. But in order to understand it correctly, we must at the same time draw a distinction between the Old Testament and the New Testament concepts of faith. In his well-known book *Two Types of Faith*,[1] Martin Buber has juxtaposed

Translated by Edward T. Oakes, S.J.

[1] Martin Buber, *Two Types of Faith*, trans. Norman Goldhawk (New York: Collier-Macmillan, 1951).

the two concepts, setting them over against one another. He holds that the two types of faith are fundamentally irreconcilable: for Buber the Old Testament faith is a complete attitude of man toward God, an attitude in which the moments of personal fidelity and complete surrender converge. Old Testament faith is one of hopeful and persevering patience: it is a daring trust beyond all earthly considerations, transcending all fears. It rests in the assurance that what God has spoken about himself, what he has done and promises to do, is to be trusted and held to be true and reliable. New Testament faith, in contrast, is an acceptance of a historical *fact* as mediated by human eyewitnesses: namely, that Jesus of Nazareth is the Christ, the Messiah, the Redeemer of the world, and the Son of God. Therefore, for Buber Christian faith is an essentially "dogmatic" faith, a faith *that* something is true. If this juxtaposition of Buber's were correct, then the New Testament faith could not in any way be the fulfillment of the Old Testament faith but only its replacement with something new.

But if, speaking from a Christian and theological perspective, the New Covenant is the fulfillment of the Old, then we must be able to show that the Covenant faith in the New Testament also *fulfills* the Covenant faith of the Old. That is, once again, an a priori postulate of Christian theology, but it can be made evident without difficulty. For the God to whom the believer of the Old Testament surrenders himself with his entire existence is the same God whose effective word has borne witness to itself in the history of the chosen people and then in the world as such: as deed of power, as wonder, as law and command, as promise. In these modalities God becomes present to his people as the God who approaches and is present to them in his faithfulness. In the Old Testament it is the same thing to say that one believes God and that one believes God's word, command, promise.

But if the Word has become flesh and—as Word of power, of command, and of promise—has clothed himself in the figure of a historical human fate (and in human terms how tangibly this investiture was already at work in the history of the Jewish people!), then the extent of this new and final revelation of God's fidelity to the Covenant is not even a changed *mode* of the same faith but *is* the same faith outright.

There are two reasons why it seems that one type of faith has been pushed aside for another: first, because in the New Testament the knowledge of the Incarnation of the Word of God in Jesus is first encountered as a kerygma preached by men, that is, by eyewitnesses to the Resurrection of Christ. This is a kerygma that is addressed to those who are unaware of the news it proclaims and who must therefore "believe" the ones who already know of this event. In this way the first hearers of this news move to the second moment (which of course must already be implied in the first if it is to be realized at all): they take hold of a "faith in God" by adopting the "faith of the Church", so that, as Paul says, "You accepted the Word of God which you heard from us not as the word of men but as it is in truth, the Word of God" (1 Th 2:13).

Now this kind of mediation is indeed nothing new, since of course even Moses and the prophets, and Aaron and his priest-hood, as eyewitnesses and earwitnesses, authoritatively mediated to the people the word of God, even where that word was also active in a way that was immediately historical and generally visible to others. And God unconditionally demanded along with obedience to his word a simultaneous obedient hearkening to what the mediators of this word were saying. Christ, who demands faith for himself, stands within this Old Testament Tradition of this word of God, which includes as part of its requirement the fidelity and obedience of faith.

But the proclaiming disciples also speak within the Tradition of the Old Testament prophets or of those who were otherwise commis-sioned: they are all men who have been strictly enjoined by God not only to announce something intact and undivided but also to pro-claim their message with a divine authority that requires an obedience to the messenger as well as to the message. But this means, of course, that they too must submit *their* own existence to this proclamation, all the way to martyrdom.

But the more important reason for making this distinction here between Old Testament and New Testament notions of faith lies not so much in Buber's distinction between faith *in* and faith *that* but in a second reason, to which Bultmann has drawn our attention:

In the Old Testament the pious person faithfully and obediently believes in God on the basis of his deeds. The deeds themselves, however, do not have to be "believed", since they already are visible in the history of the people. In the New Testament, however, God's deed must *itself* be "believed"; for what is made known in this deed is the life of Jesus ending on the *stauros* [Cross], who lived on earth in the form of a servant. That the "folly" of the Cross is divine "wisdom", that the crucified One is the exalted risen One, the Lord: this is not an event accessible in the light of day but only becomes evident in the word of proclamation.[2]

Now the difference that Bultmann sees is there; but looked at more deeply, it lies not in the emphasis on the mediating, kerygmatic authority of an eyewitness to a past event in contrast to the immediate encounter with the visible deeds of God in the Old Covenant, which were known to all who were affected by them. Rather, the difference lies much more in the tension within the dialectic of the very word of God itself between revelation and hiddenness, a tension that now takes on a *Trinitarian* pattern: while Jesus as Word and Son assumes the soteriological role of veiling the word (all the way to death, even death on a Cross), the Holy Spirit, who has been poured out into the world since the Resurrection of the Word, assumes the role of indicating the reality behind the veil. This activity of the Spirit as pointer, as revealer of the veiled, is an activity both as the Spirit of Christ and at the same time as Spirit of the Church: that is, the Spirit's role is to make use of the Church's witnesses, whom the Spirit uses as his instruments to unveil the veiled.

Thus the Protestant antithesis in Bultmann does not work in exactly the way it would seem to: between a fact supposedly known openly to the general run of mankind (for example, the redemption of the people from Egypt) on the basis of which the individual even today and in the future is meant to believe God; and the hidden Christian fact of the Cross and Resurrection, which is placed before the individual only in faith, defined as an existential appropriation of a fact that touches the individual on only a personal level. On the

[2] Rudolf Bultmann, article on *pisteuo, TWNT,* 6, 216.

contrary, in the New Testament there is a genuine *fides ecclesiae* that is different from the historical knowledge and faith that the people had in the Old Testament. This *fides ecclesiae* for its part is based on the original knowledge of the Faith, that is, on the way that the original eyewitnesses had been present at the events. And this is how this Faith is handed down.

Of course, the individual is not born a member of the Church by virtue of the flesh but must, to become a member of this new Israel, decide for and confess the Faith from now on as an individual. This is a genuine step forward from figure to reality. But still every Jew had personally to decide for the faith of the people too. Even in the Old Testament we find the distinction already being made between an Israel merely according to the flesh and the true children of Abraham, who alone are to form the "holy remnant". And thus too the corresponding historical activity of YHWH was not alone or primarily the long-past story of the patriarchs that was evident to the eyes of history. Rather, God's activity from the outset was something more hidden. In its decisive point it was even something hidden, because it was ultimately to be realized only in the future, as we see when we read the major and minor prophets. Indeed this was the demand not only of Deuteronomy but also throughout all of Exodus: if the people respond to God's deeds with faith, then God will also demand, through his spokesman Moses, an ever-new faith, in order that he may be able to make his divine deeds ever more efficacious.

No more than the prophets demanded on their own authority the act of faith that the God of the Covenant required did the Church of the New Covenant claim for herself or her representatives the total surrender of faith that only God could vouch for and accomplish. That the evangelical kerygma requires an obedient acceptance, one that is now thoroughly characterized as "faith", is due to its *divine* content and its divine claim to authority. But the specific kind of response the kerygma demanded was also influenced by the concept of faith prevailing in intratestamental Judaism. Here YHWH's historical activity has become a *remembered* past. God's presence gives witness to itself above all as law, a law that must be timelessly obeyed. The word of the law contains a self-sufficiency so that the term *faith that* [something is objectively true]" can already be used. The tone shifts from personal fidelity to the pious performance of the individual, to his merit, or (with Paul) his works:

> Thus God's grace and his punitive judgment are separated. By grace only that forbearance is meant that overlooks individual crimes.[3]

But while the works of the believer are indeed very much in the foreground, it goes without saying that they are fused in a single moment to the obedience to the law. This lays the foundation for both the Pauline as well as the Jacobean theology of "faith and works", both of which would not find in the classical Old Testament theology any sufficient basis for synthesizing the tension. Both theologies stand before the task of integrating anew the now separated elements: James sees how they necessarily complement each other, while Paul reverts back to the total, integrated, classical concept of faith. And so he feels he must reject a Judaistic "justification from works" that would parallel faith. In fact, Paul can only be correctly and fully understood when one has recourse to the central Old Testament view of faith that lies behind the late Judaistic either-or of faith and works (where Luther and the Protestant view of faith also unfortunately seem to be stuck) and when one interprets what even for Paul was certainly colored and stamped with purely contemporary concepts as based on the fullness of the faith of Abraham, that is, a fully integrated "faith". In this integral faith (which contains more than Luther's moment of trust and naturally also more than a mere "assenting as true" to purely dogmatic truths—a caricature, by the way, of the Catholic concept of truth), Paul integrates even the *fides Christi* as the final, concluding moment.

Only slowly did the total Old Testament faith transform itself from an implicitly to an explicitly (and theologically) integrated faith. At first the various semantic elements and concepts that only hover around the central religious behavior of Israel toward its Covenant God had to converge and then slowly grow into one another.

---

[3] Weiser, art. cit. 202; cf. A. Schlatter, *Der Glaube im NT* (1927), pp. 35f., 66f.

Weiser has described this history most luminously in the article cited in note 3 above. First, there is the etymological family of words in Hebrew around the root 'mn (to which our *Amen* belongs), whose connotations in the Niphal form encompass the semantic range "firm, sure, reliable". But more extensively and exactly, it refers to the authentic, the actual, or something definite and right. Thus it comes to mean what is trustworthy and excludes every deception and mere appearance.

When referring to God, to his word, command, and law, this term recognizes a surety and trustworthiness befitting God. It is therefore something appropriate also for man and indeed is demanded of him, as a specific attitude toward God and his revelations. God's fidelity and steadfastness (Heb: *'emet, 'emunâh*) are thus no accidental properties that might happen to be lacking: they are the expression of *God's being God.* Herein belongs the verbal adjective known to us as *Amen,* which expresses the theoretical and practical recognition by man of God's dispensation to him: *Amen* recognizes the absolute validity of God's fidelity, and it affirms the absolute resolution of man to stand by it.

In the Hiphil form *he'emin,* it is the saying of amen to something; it is the believing itself, assenting to a thing and thereby trusting the statement as well as the thing itself. This is an attitude that is founded in the quality of the thing or of the addressing person. It thus implies and expresses a two-sided relationship. If God, who establishes the Covenant with Israel, is this Person, then the faith of Israel becomes a "relationship with God, which encompasses the whole person in the totality of his external behavior as well as his interior life".

In Isaiah, faith becomes the attitude that is absolutely necessary for the existence of the Israelite, and only in unconditioned clinging to God alone does man have continued existence: "If you do not stand by me, you will not stand at all" (Is 7:9). If one compares this to the doctrine of Paul (Rom 9–10) that Israel derives its whole origin from trusting in God and thus from the spirit and not from the flesh (that is, from the mere connection with the accident of birth as such), then one realizes how centrally New Testament faith is rooted in the prophetic doctrine.

Other etymological families have gradually been integrated into the one named above. Thus we can clearly see numerous relationships emerge that were already implicit in the meaning of faith. For example, the verbal family *batach* has the basic meaning of "being situated in security", "feeling secure", and thus, by extension, "being able to trust". This gradually becomes an ever more exclusively religious and interior act in the course of the history of the suffering of the people. Then there is the etymological family of the word *chasah,* meaning "to take refuge", "to hide out", which generally characterizes the basic attitude of the psalms. And finally there are those verbal branches that express hope and steadfastness: *chakah, yichel,* and so on.

These all refer to moments that are certainly especially characteristic of Old Testament faith, but they do not in any way recede in the New Testament, since Christ too with equal emphasis stresses the necessity for perseverance; for staying awake; for remaining firm; for having a constant readiness for God, his grace, his future, his desire to make use of us. At most we may say that this meaning of perseverance in the New Testament is so strong that it is placed as its own motif "next to" faith, but it belongs so absolutely to the essence of faith that it is practically inseparable from it, so that "your faith is at the same time hope in God" (1 Pet 1:2; cf. 1 Th 1:3; 1 Cor 13:13).

The integration of these individual meanings (*Momente*) of faith into a total and unified attitude of faith is clearly a sign of a step forward in the Old Testament. Continued reflection now understands the Faith more interiorly and seriously. The New Testament neither wants nor is able to get behind this totality. Of course it analyzes the individual aspects more profoundly in the service of the same effort to deepen understanding, to make faith all the more concrete. The warning to be true to the Faith, patient in it, watchful in it, hopeful in it, means precisely one and the same religious attitude of man that had also been called for previously by God's one single, unified act in the salvation history of the Old Testament.

This single attitude should not be allowed to dissolve into congeries of isolated moral or theological "works" or "virtues" in the manner of the Judaizers (*jüdaistisch*) or of the Greek pedagogues.

Indeed, every serious philosophical ethic has always striven for this integration of man in his attitude before the divine, whether that ethic be tinged with the Platonic, Aristotelian, Stoic, Cynic or Neoplatonic palette. We should note here that the Greek family of words *pisteuein, pistos, pistis,* although originally used only as an ethical and not as a religious concept referring to God, also contains most of the meanings of the Hebrew concept of faith: above all, reliability, trustworthiness, fidelity, conviction, warranty, trust, both in the active sense (having trust) as well as in the passive (enjoying the trust of another).

Although the Greek word lacks the religious power that flowed into the Jewish word from this history of revelation, it was still the best available for the Septuagint translators for reproducing the Jewish reality. We cannot lay the blame on "Hellenization" as such for the watering down of the Old Testament concept of faith. Even the Latin *fides* possesses the same breadth of content. This is especially true of the idea of the ability to turn to God as well as to one's fellowman—and here the Latin is more closely related to the Hebrew than is the Greek term. God's *fides* and *fidelitas,* his standing by his Covenant because he stands by himself, justifies the specifically human form of *fides:* the fidelity that is founded on the recognition of *God as God,* which entails a perfect act of self-surrender. (The recent German translation of the psalms has most felicitously captured this embracive double meaning of *fides* in both God and man.)

Now if we look back, at this juncture, on our original a priori starting point, it will now seem to us to have been strengthened. The man who is perfect before God, Jesus Christ, cannot possibly relate with indifference to this integration of the true attitude of man to God as it took shape in the course of the Old Testament. It is only if we look at the distinctive New Testament meaning in the Greek term *pistis* (which means holding the announced kerygma to be true as well as the individual statements either contained in it or implied by it) that we will of course have to admit that Christ, who is the essential content of this kerygma, has nothing to do with this kind of faith. In this sense he stands over faith:

He himself does not "believe". For his own existence, the Word is objectless. He does not stand where one believes but where faith is *directed.* Or more exactly: he makes faith possible.[4]

But that does not say everything, not even the most important part. What goes unmentioned and undemonstrated is how Jesus makes our faith possible in the first place. For this is a faith that does not supersede, as it were, the whole Old Testament attitude toward God but is meant to complete it from within (Mt 5:17). But that can only happen if Jesus not only causally brings about that perfection but also, more importantly, lives it out for us as model and exemplar, receiving from God the power to be Redeemer, the power to shape and stamp within us this living model.

2. *The faith of Jesus*

Why do we then shy away from, why does the New Testament also clearly shy away from, speaking simply of the faith of Jesus? Indeed, probably because this archetypal attitude has become so perfect and thus so inexpressible in its innermost regions that the same characterization of it with the copy in us would wipe away the distance between the two. The New Testament has inserted no comprehensive, definitive term for the central attitude of the Son of Man toward God. It is such a bright light that we could not tolerate it, and so we could apply names to it only by dismantling it into its individual aspects and confining our gaze to its reflection in us.

In this dismantling process, by breaking up the pure light into a spectrum of aspects, however, we discover that his light has indeed been assembled from the same elements as the light of the Old Testament faith, only in the highest, divine-human perfection. We find everything again: the fidelity of the Son of Man toward the Father, a trust that is placed in God once and for all and yet is realized anew in each moment in time. In the Son of Man we find the unconditional preference for the Father, for his essence, his love, his

---

[4] Romano Guardini, *Die menschliche Wicklichkeit des Herrn* (1958).

will and command in relation to all of his own wishes and inclinations. We see the unflinching perseverance in this will, come what may. And above all there are the handing over and making available to the Father everything, not wanting to know ahead of time, not anticipating the hour: "No one knows that day or the hour, neither angel in heaven, nor the Son, but alone the Father" (Mk 13:32).

It is entirely a matter of indifference how one might explain in detail this "economic" ignorance (*ökonomische Unwissen*) of the Son; it is a reality, and for us that is enough. It belongs to his kenosis, which renounces all kinds of privileges and possibilities that by right belong to the *forma Dei* and thus also to the Son of Man. It is also unimportant in what way in John's Gospel the approaching but not yet arrived hour of his suffering is known ahead of time or suspected by the Son: it certainly stands on the horizon of his consciousness, as his reference to the hour shows. But its precise outcome is always given over to the Father and left to his discretion as something that does not now concern the Son, requiring neither his attention nor his concentration. He lets it be, resting in the will of the Father, in order to have the chance of nestling himself trustingly in the arms of the Father, receiving even the great hour, when it comes, purely and without anticipation, simply as being from the Father's goodness. That is the perfect attitude that Isaiah tried to induce in the Jews: "Be still; do not fear! . . . Do not trust yourselves, or you will not survive!" (7:4, 9); "In turning toward God and in peace is your salvation; in keeping still and in trust is your strength" (30:15).

The way the Son refers everything that he is, does, and says to the Father, his express will not to consider himself "good" but to refer everything to the goodness of God alone, the absolute trust in the Father (Mt 19:17; Lk 18:19), all this is the source of his power. This is the power that moves out from him in miracles and that he seeks to inculcate in his disciples as their own power to believe and, by his example, to impart. So this faith that he demands of his own followers does not pertain to him (that comes only in the reflection of John)[5]

---

[5] The only place in the synoptics that refers to faith in Jesus himself (Mt 18:6, "If anyone causes one of those who believe in me to sin") is limited in its range by Mk 9:42.

but refers to God. But he is the only one who possesses this attitude in all its fullness and who can impart it to those who have entrusted themselves to him. He trains the Jews in this faith, which they indeed know theoretically but which suddenly contains a total and immediate urgency, since the reign of God is an immediate part of it.

He explains the quintessence of the Law: right judgment (*Recht*) (*krisis, mišhpat;* cf. Amos 5:24), mercy (*eleos, chesed;* cf. Micah 6:8), and faith (*pistis, emeth,* in the sense of "faithful"; cf. Mt 23:23). He leads people to this and guarantees it with his example and with the help of God's power working in him. He calls them to take his hand and to dare to leap into God. This leap presupposes the whole being of the person: whoever hands the whole region of his self over to God without hesitation can also rest assured in the same totality of God: he can have everything from God, ask anything from him. Jesus is personally the guarantor of such totality ("Speak but the Word!"), because he openly possesses it himself (his words and works prove it), and indeed he possesses it archetypally.

One will thus concur with and endorse Martin Buber and other exegetes when they interpret Mark 9:14–29 on the basis of a total Old Testament faith.[6] "If you can, have pity on us and help us", says the father of the possessed boy. And Jesus: "If possible? All is possible to the one who believes." Then the father: "I do believe; help my unbelief." Mark "lets the father say what the disciples of Jesus actually would have said, who with this assertion had attributed their inability to cure his boy to their unbelief". This verse on the capacity of the believer is probably an authentic statement from Jesus himself, but it cannot be interpreted (as Buber notices) as "to me, Jesus, is everything possible; because I believe, I can heal the boy." For Jesus wants to point not to himself, to his own subjective power, but rather to God, to whom he prays (v. 29); he does not want to point to a property befitting himself alone: "True

---

[6] Heinrich Schlier, *Mächte und Gewalten im NT* (1958), p. 40, points in the same direction in reference to Mk 9:23: through prayer and obedience, Christ lets the Spirit of God become powerful in and through himself.

faith is no privilege of Jesus alone but is, as such, accessible to others too."[7]

One must let Jesus' demands for faith in the synoptic Gospels take effect within oneself in their entirety. This is especially true of those paradoxical passages that require the exclusion of all doubt and that insist, if one is suddenly to see, on the certainty of being heard, of being able to do anything in God and through God, even to the point of throwing mountains into the sea. In all this Jesus reveals his own most inner attitude and power and bestows part of it on his disciples. He lives and works and suffers from the certainty of being heard at all times (Jn 11:41-42). From this power and surrender—which are not the power and surrender of his subjectivity, of his "steadfastness in believing", but rather are the power and surrender of God in him—he establishes faith in his disciples. But he does not give this faith to them as some pale and atrophied vestige that resembles his faith only from afar. What he gives them is a genuine participation in what he genuinely possesses.

Only when we see this as a positive development does Christian faith become truly *Christian* faith. For it is not at all sufficient that Christ be faith's object and, at best, its cause for merit; he must also be the overflowing subject, on whom others believe as their way of participating in grace: "Help thou my unbelief!"

Jesus' offer to mediate to us the power of God in his surrender and readiness to be of service to all were understood by John as love, love in two senses. First of all, it was the love of this man who made himself available to all in a selflessness even to death, but it was also the love of God himself flowing through him: to believe in Jesus means to love him, Jesus, as love. Even this is (presupposing that God's Word has become flesh) only the final declaration of the Old Testament's loving and faithful belief in God and his saving word, as the Deuteronomic and Jeremian literature shows us.[8] The double use of *pisteuein* in John 2:23-24 is understood in the same way: "Many believed [*episteusan*] in his name, but he would not entrust himself to them [*ouk*

---

[7] Buber, *Zwei Glaubensweisen* (1950), pp. 15-19; English translation: see n. 1 above.

[8] See A. Deissler, "Psalm 119 and Its Theology" (1955) [no further reference to this article given—TRANS.].

episteusen heauton autois]": the mutuality of self-surrender is not possible under such circumstances.

Only in this way does the full light fall on the extraordinary statement in the Letter to the Hebrews, that Christ is the author and perfecter of our Faith.[9] What is meant by *pistis* is doubtlessly faith in the integral Old Testament sense, for the passage includes the long procession of Old Testament witnesses to the Faith who have all withstood and prevailed in the struggle for the Faith, persevering and hoping, on the basis of Christ. This procession gives the author the opportunity to unfold all the individual aspects of the total Faith in order to integrate them again in the end into Christ's faith. He is "the author and perfecter of the faith" because he "endured death on the Cross for the joy set before him, scorning its shame. . . . Consider him who endured such opposition from sinful men so that you will not grow weary and lose heart" (Heb 12:2–3).

Jesus not only pioneered the *agôn* of faith as a model but also did so as our archetype, thus making it possible in the first place, establishing and perfecting not only the New Testament but also the whole faith of the Old Covenant. We must concur, therefore, with Delling[10] when he interprets Hebrews 12:2 as follows:

> First of all according to the context especially of the moral consequences that result from this faith. Furthermore, however, Jesus is *archegos* also insofar as he believed in the Christian God in an archetypal way as the first human being, "perfecting" this faith in God's unconditional love (overcoming even the threshold of sin) through his death on a Cross, giving this love its concrete, unique realization in salvation history.

Thus Bauer obscures the whole issue when he does not refer to the richer semantic range that is also present in *archegos*. For it means not just "founder, establisher" but even more an "initiator, who begins the first of a series and so gives the push to what follows".[11] Spicq does the opposite, even though he refuses, in contrast to some Catholics

---

[9] *Archegos kai teleiotes tes pisteos* (Heb 12:2).

[10] In his entry for *arche, archegos,* in *TWNT* I, 486.

[11] *Theol. Wb.* (5th ed.), at *archegos.*

and many Protestants, to concede formal "faith" to Jesus because Scripture has not done that elsewhere.[12]

Archegos has basically no other meaning here than that of Acts 3:15 and 6:31, where Christ is called the "Author of life" and "Leader and Savior", or in the Second Letter of Clement 20, where he is called *archegos tes aphtharsias* (the pioneer of our immortality), or in *Epist. Vienn.* 17, where he is hailed as *archegos tes zoes tou Theou* (the Founder of our life in God).[13] In fact it is much less a matter of naturalizing and adopting this linguistic usage at any price[14] than it is a matter of becoming sensitive to the fact that the Christian and Biblical Faith as a whole is a following of Christ. For faith this is not peripheral but unconditional and absolutely basic.

From here we must once more plumb the depths of the meaning of the frequently used formula in Paul "faith of Christ Jesus"[15] or "faith in Christ Jesus".[16] In any case we cannot simply interpret the genitive as an objective genitive (especially in view of the dative of the second formula): it is not simply faith whose "object" is Christ. Nor can we simply hold the view that it is a subjective genitive either, seeing it as the act of faith of Christ himself.[17] Rather it is a third term towering over both. A. Deissmann points out the formulas parallel to "the faith of Christ": for example, "the power of Christ" (2 Cor 2:9; 1 Cor 5:4), "the wealth of Christ" (Eph 3:8; 2:7), "the blessing of Christ" (Rom 5:29), "the fullness of Christ" (Eph 4:3), and in many other places

[12] *Ep. aus Hebreux* II, 386: "It faut prendre *archegos* dans le même sense que Hb 2:10 'initiateur' ou 'chef de file' comme synonyme de *prodromos* ou *promachos,* le premier à faire ou à accomplir quelque chose."

[13] Euseb. *Hist. Eccl.* 5, 1.

[14] This is inappropriate in the light of Christian Tradition, which is founded on the basis of the specifically *New Testament* concept of faith.

[15] The expression *pistis Christou Iesou* is found in the following passages: Gal 2:16, 20; 3:22; Eph 3:12; Phil 3:9; Rom 3:22, 26.

[16] *Pistis en Christoi Iesou:* Gal 3:25; 5:6; Col 1:15; 1 Tim 1:14; 3:13; 2 Tim 1:13; 3:15).

[17] Thus J. Haussleitner, *Der Glaube Jesu Christi* (1891); *Was versteht Paulus unter christlichem Glauben?* (1895); Gottfried Kittel, *Theol. Stud. und Krit.,* vol. 79 (1906), pp. 419ff.

and suggests that we speak here of a mystical genitive (*genitivus mysticus*).[18]

Christian faith means, then, faith *within* the reality of Christ, faith that as such shares in the fullness of the truth, the love, the action, the suffering, and the Resurrection of Christ and in all the other aspects of his reality and indeed is made possible by them. According to Deissmann, "It is a faith that lives in communion with the pneumatic Christ and indeed is a faith 'on' God, in content identical with the faith that Abraham had in primordial times. And so it is unconditionally a trust in the living God."[19]

Now one cannot accept such a pure parallel between the faith of Abraham and that of Christ—as if Christ had done nothing further than restore what had originally been lost. Nonetheless, the direction of Deissmann's thought is important, for the Faith of Christ is also that. But Abraham's faith is directed in its whole sense, structure, and movement toward the Faith of Christ (Jn 8:52ff.; Gal 3:8, 4; Heb 11:9–10), which has opened access to the Father for all time.

The "mystical genitive" can be unfolded from two sides: on one side, in the manner of Albert Schweitzer in his book *The Mysticism of Paul the Apostle* (1930), in which the emphasis is put on the mystical experience of Paul, who found the truth of his existence in Christ, who died and rose with Christ, who hurried forward to meet him in the eschatological reencounter, while still encountering him mystically in the Sacrament. In short, Paul has been taken out of his former corrupt existence and placed in a new and more real existence in the reality of Christ, in which faith gives a share. On the other side is the possible interpretation of Ernst Lohmeyer,[20] for whom Paul does not think in psychological-mystical terms but in objective-theological ones. Already the fact, he says, that the substantive noun *faith* in Paul is much more often used than the nominative verbal form *believing* shows that "the word characterizes the fullness of experience much less" than "an objective content on which the believing I is directed and on which it is grounded".[21]

---

[18] A. Deissmann, *Paulus* (1911), p. 94.
[19] Ibid., p. 95.
[20] "Grundlagen paulinischer Theologie" (1929).
[21] Ibid., p. 116.

Faith *justifies* man. It is source, origin, spring, and fountain of true life, life that God considers to be life. In order to point out the whole extent of the reality of faith, Lohmeyer makes use of the Aristotelian concept of *causa formalis,* indeed of the

> *forma substantialis* that shapes matter. Just as matter is different from form and yet its own reality, so too the believer is always something other than faith itself, and yet faith determines his whole reality. One could even say, not I believe but faith in me. Paul depicted this distance with a sharp and refined pen: where he means the metaphysical principle of faith, he calls it "Christ faith", but the human act of faith is called by him "believing in Christ" or, more exactly, believing "on him".[22]

But from the figure and work of Christ the metaphysical quality of making just flows to faith. In no way is this a matter of a mere subjective application to the historical Jesus. If faith is to be a metaphysical principle, "then Christ himself is the undistorted presentation of the ultimate religious principle as such, not to be confused with any other being or work in the world." But this is only possible if Christ himself is God—the God who became man historically in Christ. Only if this tension is borne can we understand Pauline faith as a principle:

> Christ must be understood as the sole bestower of all divine things in the life of the individual as well as in the course of history and at the same time its historical carrier. . . . Only in this way can the strange term *Christ faith* be explained. It is not only the faith that Christ *has,* nor is it even the faith he gives, but above all it is the faith he *is.* For since this faith is the ground of all believing life in history, it can point to no other prototype or copy.[23]

Everything depends on the unity of Christ: only as God can he become for all the principle that he himself has lived and, as death and Resurrection, has experienced. But only as man could he live and experience what then became the principle, which in others will be

---

[22] Ibid., pp. 117–18.
[23] Ibid., p. 121.

called Christian faith. In its continuity with Abraham faith has once more shown its true historicity.[24] So faith for Lohmeyer is simultaneously the revelation of God from all eternity and the revelation in history, with all its provisionality: it is the structure of the religious attitude "between the times", which on one side is definitively over but on the other is yet to be reached in the Parousia. This means that faith determines human existence from the place where Christ himself gained access to the Father in history through his obedient and suffering existence: in other words, where God the Father turns toward the world in the obedience of the Son, in the form of a slave: as "grace", "gospel", "faith". And so Christian faith is just as inseparably determined by the stance of the Son toward the Father (where Abraham's faith is perfected) as it is by the attitude of the Father toward the Son, which as grace for the world shapes the attitude of the Son to the metaphysical principle of the world's stance toward God.

From this standpoint we must now somehow make contact with what was once known as liberal theology but which today has run into a kind of twilight because of Bultmann and his school. For Lohmeyer Pauline faith necessarily includes both poles: the historical Jesus and the Christ of the community of faith. But it is part of the foundational presuppositions of liberal theology that Jesus was a believing Jew like any other, endowed with special prophetic power, to be sure. But even Bultmann speaks uninhibitedly of Jesus' faith in miracles and prayer.[25] Indeed, of his faith as such:[26]

> On the contrary, the word *faith* does not yet mean for him what it will later for Paul and John: the obedience of man under God's revelation of salvation. . . . Faith is for him the power in certain moments of life to commit himself entirely [*Ernst zu machen*], convinced of God's omnipotence; it is the certainty that one is truly experiencing in certain moments the action of God; it is the conviction that the distant God is near if man will but abandon his

[24] Ibid., p. 124.
[25] Rudolf Bultmann, "Jesus" (1951), 13–14th ed.), pp. 145, 151f., 157.
[26] Ibid., p. 156.

habitual attitude and truly be ready to look upon the God who is near. And so one can only believe in the way Jesus means it when one is obedient. This automatically precludes every frivolous abuse of the faith of God.[27]

But one can expect God's grace and forgiveness as his free act in one's own life only when one is ready, in that grace, to forgive others too: the I and Thou between God and man is present in the I and Thou between men (pp. 167f.). In such an event of personal encounter man receives an adumbration of what kind of event it is for God, for God to be interpersonal precisely as God. And so the finite man also understands: precisely because he himself was forgiven, he must likewise show grace to his neighbor.

The question is: "How did the transition from the faith *of* Jesus to faith *in* him come about?"[28] Historical-critical research has uncovered a terminological distinction that cannot be simply brushed away: there really is a difference between Jesus' proclamation and early Christian theology, especially as it concerns the Faith. According to Fuchs, it would be a hasty conclusion if one wanted to argue purely a priori that the risen One is identical with the historical Jesus, so that we already knew beforehand that everything announced by the historical Jesus ipso facto belongs to the content of the Faith in the risen Christ. This explains, on the one hand, why Jesus did not purport to be the content of the future Christ faith and, on the other hand, why (because only faith mediates an appropriate understanding for Jesus) so much of his proclamation had to remain misunderstood at the outset.

But Paul's faith is entirely different from a serene assent to something as true. It is a struggle (2 Tim 4:7), a decision, in which there is no going back, only a going forward and further on along the path. Faith is still a wrestling and a commitment of one's whole visible life from the power of invisible life. It is a wrestling with the powers of evil, but these powers are located in man himself; it wrestles for a

[27] Ibid., p. 160.
[28] Ernst Fuchs, "Jesus und der Glaube", in *Zur Frage nach dem historischen Jesus* (1960), pp. 238–57.

share in Christ's victory, caught between weakness and strength. It is a struggle "from faith into faith" (Rom 1:17). And precisely in this dimension of faith as a struggle one is linked with what faith must have been for Jesus himself.

Both Jesus' interpretation of the law as well as his prophetic-eschatological proclamation of the Kingdom in the synoptics place him above all in the Jewish Tradition. To God everything is possible, even what is impossible to man, and "the relationship of Jesus to God's sovereignty belongs to what contradicts and is impossible to the normal outlook." And this is also true of the words of Parousia, foretelling the coming of the Son of God. Jesus' proclamation

> demands *unavoidable* decision. And it is precisely here that it becomes clear that under such circumstances we cannot easily speak of a faith in Jesus that might in individual cases dispense with Jesus' words. Thus Jesus' own faith is all the more important, although even the synoptic Gospels studiously avoid this formulation. They never say, "My faith has saved you." Jesus' faith never refers to his own faith alone in God. For that would mean that he could not be distinguished in any way from a pious Jew. But Jesus' faith also does not specially refer to his own view of God's coming.

The decisive fact lies in this: that Jesus defines those who wait on God "as those who cannot help themselves". They are the ones who are later called, and whom he himself already calls, "the poor". It is also crucial that he *risks:* not only to announce and to threaten God's coming but also to call out from the crowd those people whom God wants to visit. And he does this by including himself among them. His own faith in God was unconditional, and he dares to include his followers in this, praying, bearing with them, and thus challenging them. This is his absolute "faith", and it stands behind all of his parables. This prayerful endurance, all the way to the struggle at Gethsemane, is the place from which he goes to the Cross: this cup is drunk to the dregs:

> Jesus is distinguished . . . from his disciples because he suffers the struggle of faith for them. In this most personal incorporation he still remains distinct from them. But even so it is clear that he has

dared to believe in God's coming for them. The words of institution at the Last Supper, subsequently formulated by the Church, as well as the likewise later formulated predictions of suffering also express this way that Jesus understood himself.

God has vouched (*recht gegeben*) for this faith of Jesus by raising him from the dead and thereby has given to the believing community this faith as "a faith redounding to its benefit [*ihr zugute kommenden*]". The Christian's nearness to and distance from Christ are thus characteristic. To come to faith thus means being "placed before God together *with* the historical Jesus"; it means "*like* Jesus believing that God hear*s*". "But our faith is different from Jesus' faith because in Jesus' name it has been said to us since Easter that God *has* heard."

No doubt a bridge is being built here so as to bring closer together what seems to be incompatible. Most important is the insight that Christian faith cannot be understood except as enfolding oneself into Jesus' most interior attitude. Here is where the ineluctable truth of liberal exegesis must be seen and maintained. But this should not be taken only in the sense that one man took a chance on God (indeed, not only for himself but also for his fellowmen). Rather, God *answers* this venture with the Resurrection, whereby the One who risked everything on God is shown to be something other than a mere man. For Jesus would never have been able, without arrogance, to accomplish the totality of faith demanded of him without this more than human help.

The pastoral Letters point once more to the parallel of Christ's own confession and that of the Christian:

> Strive for justification, piety, faith, love, patience, and mildness. Fight the good fight of faith, take up the eternal life to which you have been called and for which you have made glorious confession before many witnesses. Before God who gives life to all and before Christ Jesus, who made his glorious confession under Pontius Pilate, I pray you: Keep the commandments without fail (1 Tim 6:11–13).

Between the *homologia* (confession) of the one struggling for the faith and that of the suffering and struggling Christ there exists, as in the *agon* of the Letter to the Hebrews, the closest bond, which is always an integral, integrating bond. In this struggle everything is at stake, and the only way it can be gained is by committing one's whole existence.

We might briefly pursue this train of thought as it was developed by the apostolic Fathers, in their own discussions about the integral faith that has been lived exemplarily by Christ and stamped into his followers. For Polycarp *fidelitas* is the graced perseverance in imitating the suffering Christ, "for in this he has given us an example through himself, and we have believed in this" (8, 1). For Ignatius faith is the "nail" that nails our flesh and spirit to the Cross of Christ. It is the way we are drawn into his Cross (*Smyr.* 1:1). Indeed he equates faith with Jesus' own flesh, and love with his blood (*Trall.* 8:1). Clement, imitating the Letter to the Hebrews, equates faith and obedience with the faith and obedience of the just ones of the Old Testament (*Cor.* 9–10). He sees in this the conquest of our spiritual ambivalence (*dipsuchia*) (11:23). Faith is the "clinging" "to the Father and Creator of the universe and to his glorious and abundant gift of peace" (19). Faith in Christ (*"he en Christoi pistis"*) confirms the fullness of all good and ordered life (22). All faith, then, is but the answer to God's own being, *pistis* (Ignatius, *Trall.* 3:3; 2 Clem 1).

3. Theology

It is well known how sharply later theology sought to deny that Christ had faith, although it was fully aware of counterarguments: (1) that faith is a more noble virtue than moral virtue and thus belonged a fortiori to Christ; (2) "that Christ taught none of the virtues that he himself did not possess, according to the opening of the book of Revelation: 'Jesus began to do and to teach' (Rev 1:1); but now this means concerning Christ that he is the *auctor et consummator fidei* (Heb 12:2), and thus he had to have faith in a preeminent manner"; (3) that "even the saints in heaven must still possess faith, because the glosses on Rom 1:17 (*"Justitia Dei revelatur in eo ex fide in fidem"*) say: from the faith of words and hope into the faith of things and sight". These three objections are raised by Thomas (the last two are direct quotes). And he refutes them from one simple principle: that the object of faith is the divine itself, which *we* do as yet not see. But Christ "*has seen God according to his essence from the very first moment of his conception*" (*S Th* III, q 7, a 3), and thus he cannot really have faith in the exact sense of that term. Not only do the scholastic theologians speak this way, but we find even Augustine already saying this.

Now if we proceed only from the concept of faith based on the specific differences between the meaning of faith in the New Testament in its relation to the Old, then this conclusion is unavoidable. But if we keep in mind that the New Testament concept *completes* and *perfects* the Old Testament concept, fully displaying its crucial priority, then we will not automatically emphasize the moment of negativity (the nonseeing) and thus the provisionality of the attitude of faith. To do so would obscure the perfection already lurking in the very core of faith itself: faith's definitive nature, which expresses the complete correspondence between God's fidelity and man's fidelity, would be overshadowed.

Possibly scholasticism was thinking at this point too much in the categories of the Greek doctrine of the virtues, which was primarily concerned with the qualities and circumstances of the individual soul ("my" faith, "my" stance toward God, and so on) and too little within the dialogic categories that were decisive for Israel's covenantal theology, which saw human existence as the response to God's call. And indeed these covenantal categories are the very foundation laid by God himself for his Trinitarian revelation in the New Covenant, which places the eternal life of love and blessedness in the relationality of the Divine Persons. For Greek thought, it was very difficult not to equate a "full vision" with an "exhaustive vision"—with an "overview", we might say—which too easily implies a finitude and closure in the object being seen.

Only the Neoplatonic thinking on infinity broke this pattern and opened wider doors. If one simply juxtaposes the Platonic-Aristotelian concept of intuitive or conceptual vision with the New Testament concept of faith, then of course Thomas is absolutely right: one cannot at the same time see *and* believe something. Faith by definition is an assent to something as true, based on what authority says rather than what the evidence of one's own senses attests. However, this answer to the limitations of Greek thought does not mean that the fullness of the act and attitude of faith of the Old Testament have thereby been exhaustively described, particularly in its central dynamism.

Of course there is a weighty objection to this reservation: the faith of the Old Testament is the perfect attitude of man within mortal life—the prospect onto another eschatological condition of seeing God is not presented to him in the Old Testament period, or at least not clearly. But as soon as this perspective arrives at the New Testament, then the inner provisionality of the whole attitude of Old Testament faith becomes immediately obvious. The Pauline contrast of "faith versus sight", of *in spe* versus *in re,* would now come into play (2 Cor 5:7; Rom 8:24). But this should not be treated simply according to the schema imperfect/perfect, negative/positive.[29]

For against this view speaks the principle of the resurrection of the flesh (including the "marks of the nails"), which implies the inner transfiguration and eternalization of *all* the moments that *are* the essential temporal expressive forms of God's relationship.[30] The counterpart to this reflection is the Johannine insight that God's *doxa* already radiates Christ's mortality from within; indeed, it shines at its brightest in the consummation of his suffering and death.

---

[29] This holds true even more when in Rom 8:24 Paul is discussing hope and not faith and when in 2 Cor 5:7 he is referring not to the contrast between faith and sight but to the contrast between two spheres: the one in which the pattern of Christ is formed in us only first in faith, and the other sphere in which this faith will be perfected (Kittel, *ThW* II, 372). Also, we must consider that in 1 Cor 13:12 Paul does not mean by "seeing as in a glass darkly, enigmatically" (*ainigma:* that is, mediated through the sayings of the prophets in reference to Nb 12:8 and late Jewish texts) that we are seeing unclearly or indistinctly. What Paul means is that the *prophetic* form of sight, which is the context of this passage (see 12:8), will pass away. But this does not mean (as we have yet to show) that Paul is not referring to faith (Kittel, *ThW* I, 177, *ad loc: ainigma*).

[30] We say "are" and not "have been" because this past is a mode of the intratemporal, which perhaps was not sufficiently considered by Augustine (*De Trin* XIV, c 1-2, n 3-4; *PL* 42, 1038; *De agon Chr* c 13, n 15; *PL* 40, 299).

Seen in this way, the attempt to delimit those "virtues" that Christ had and must have had from those that he "cannot have had" is difficult and elusive. We can say this even of the hope that, as a "virtue", Thomas Aquinas denies to Christ, although he possessed individual moments of their acts: "For although he knew everything perfectly, whereby faith was entirely excluded from him, he yet possessed no less perfectly what belongs to this perfection, as for example, immortality and bodily transfiguration, which he could hope for" [quote uncited—Trans.].

The whole way this question has been posed, whether Christ could have hope (and faith), had been blocked by a peculiarly narrow Augustinian definition that maintained that each person can only hope for future goods for himself.[31] The first, and for centuries the only, theologian who objected to this ban (and there in only one place) was Thomas, who established the principle that if someone was united to someone else in love, he could also hope for good things for the other person—as it were, for one's other self.[32] On the basis of this principle (even if he apparently did not know of the passage), Thomas Muniessa, S.J., held the view that Christ fully hoped while on earth and even continues to hope in heaven with all the saints for the redemption of his whole Mystical Body.[33] Pierre Charles, S.J., has pursued this development in two articles,[34] reasoning out the problem in this way: Christ's foreknowledge has not hindered his hope. Hope does not need to be uncertain. On the contrary: uncertainty is the worm in the fruit of hope and stands in contrast to its formal object. Thus infallible hope is the most perfect hope. The saints in heaven, however, hope in the sense of their earthly mission: Peter hopes for the visible Church; Christ, however, hopes for the salvation of the whole world.

This hope of heaven seems to Père Charles to be the deepest justification for the call of the saints, and both are infallible and

[31] *Enchiridion* 8, 3.

[32] *S Th* 2, 2, q 17, a 3.

[33] Thomas Muniessa, *Disputationes scholasticae de mysteriis Incarnationis* (1689), pp. 14, 28, nn. 73, 77.

[34] "Spes Christi", *Nouvelle Revue Théologique* (1934): 1009–21; (1937): 1051–75.

unchangeable.[35] Christ's hope, however, who draws all things unto himself, fulfills the hope of God himself. But Christ's hope lasts until his world mission is completed.

Certainly the decision of Benedict XII (1336) against his predecessor John XXII seems to preclude this view. Benedict XII insisted that the souls of the dead did not have to await the general resurrection (as John XXII assumed when he radicalized the opinion of many of the Fathers and medieval theologians, for example, St. Bernard) in order to enter into the direct vision of God. Rather, for Benedict XII they view God immediately after death (provided they do not need to be cleansed in Purgatory), and "such a direct vision of the divine essence and its enjoyment overtakes [*evacuant*] the act of faith and hope in them *insofar as faith and hope are theological virtues*" (*Denz* 530).

Regarding this, Charles correctly remarks that the scope of this statement extends precisely as far as the range of the doctrine being condemned, according to which the dead souls persevere in faith and hope before their judgment *because* they cannot enter into the beatific vision of God. Many theologians assume that the *habitus* of the three virtues continues on in heaven even if their acts are no longer performed. Charles cites the assertion of a late scholastic, Thomas of Argentina,[36] who holds this view and adds that he assumes that saints even perform the act of hope (with the proviso that the Pope not decide otherwise).

In the Middle Ages the situation for faith was quite different from the issue of hope, because the central definition of faith (likewise for the time subsequent to Augustine) was the *cognitio obscura,* which for that very reason left room for the freedom to make a decision for God and thus for service to others. Two distinct paths open up at this point: if one emphasizes the *cognitio,* then earthly faith, as the first preliminary radiance of the eternal knowledge of God by direct sight, becomes the *fides inchoatio gloriae.* It was then possible to permit the act of faith to ascend to the level of sight through an increasing series of qualitative jumps, just as the light of dawn emerges and "disappears" into the full light of day. Thus, only in this way is

[35] Ibid. (1934): 1019.
[36] *In Sent.* (Genua, 1585), p. 42.

faith outdone (*evacuatur*): when it is fulfilled beyond itself. This was the view of William of Auxerre,[37] Hugo of St. Cher,[38] and Albertus Magnus.[39]

But if the emphasis is put on the darkness and enigmatic obscurity in the knowledge that faith provides, which seems to be an essential feature of it (because only this darkness can guarantee the freedom and usefulness of the act of faith), then the opposite consequence follows: the sight of the countenance of God makes the act of faith interiorly impossible. This was the way Augustine had unambiguously decided, as did Bonaventure[40] and Thomas Aquinas.[41] Matthew of Aquasparta extensively discusses the question and likewise came down firmly for the second camp, on the logical ground of a wholly intellectual definition of faith. But still he entered this proviso (which is true in any case): even in heaven there is no comprehensive vision of God, for the Divine Infinity cannot be surveyed by the creature even in the light of glory. Therefore, there must be not only faith (*fides*) but also something that keeps calling for faith that can never be grasped in knowledge (*credulitas*):

> Because the blessed do not grasp God exhaustively, although they see him, they therefore come to appreciate God ever more as the One who is ever greater than what they see, so that they cannot exhaust him. And in this sense it would not be inappropriate to say that the blessed believe something because they do not *know* everything.[42]

Indeed, the same holds true even among the inhabitants of heaven among themselves, of whom each one, because he is a spiritual subject, also has his mysterious inner space into which others cannot see without further ado but which each individual must *reveal* to the other in an act of free witness. "So it happens that if an angel reveals

---

[37] *Summa aurea* 3, tr. 20, qq. 1–2.

[38] *In 1 Cor* 13:10; *Opuscula* 7, f. 110 d.

[39] 3 Sent. d 31; Borgnet 28, 586.

[40] 3 Sent. d 31, a. 2, q. 1; *Quar.* 3, 680f.

[41] 3 Sent. d 31, q. 1, a. 1, glae 1, 3; *S Th* 1, 2, q 67, a 3 and 5.

[42] *Quaset. disp. de fide,* q. 6 ad 3; *Quar* (1957, 2d ed.), pp. 156–57.

his mystery to another, this latter angel *believes* him, because he knows that the first angel cannot lie."[43]

The narrow boundaries of the scholastics' definition of faith made for difficulties on all sides. If, for example, Thomas denies that the Lord on earth had faith but attributes obedience to him on the basis of clear texts from Scripture, then we are certainly justified in asking what form and what gradation of not knowing (or refusing to make use of his knowledge of the Father) are required to make possible this indubitable obedience of the incarnate Son. And then we can ask further what basic constitutional features of temporal-finite existence — to which hope and obedience, trust and patience certainly belong — are also necessary, so that we can genuinely say of the Son that he has become like us in *all* things but sin. We will then once more encounter that exemplary core meaning (which the New Testament refuses to oversimplify) that must primarily be characterized (*angezielt*) with the word *faith,* with all its rich connotations from earlier stages in the Old Testament and which has been enriched further from its completion in the Christian order of grace.

Based on the Biblical positivity of the dialogic "covenantal faith" in Scripture, theology has again and again tried, as we saw, to insert the positive moment of faith as well as of hope into the vision and possession of eternal life. Many theologians such as Durandus and Gerson sought to have the *habitus fidei* continue on in the *visio* even without the act of faith. Thomas, in contrast, felt that this held true only for certain features of faith: its certainty and steadfastness.[44] To clarify this issue, they went back once more to 1 Corinthians 13:13 and sifted the oldest interpretations of this passage all the way to Tertullian and Irenaeus (finally displaced by the Itala): whereas speaking in tongues, gnosis, and prophecy come to an end, the love that believes all and hopes all (1 Cor 13:7) will never die out, "and so there remain (*nuni de menei*) these three: faith, hope and love". Paul Henry, S.J., has spoken for this older interpretation,[45] to which

[43] Ibid., ad 12, p. 161.

[44] Concerning all of this, see Suarez, vol. 12, p. 218.

[45] In his doctoral dissertation on 1 Cor 13:13, awarded with the highest honors at the papal university. Otto Kuss (in his *Römerbrief,* vol. I [1957], p. 151) sees 1 Cor

Irenaeus has given so unforgettable an expression[46] with Origen agreeing.[47]

Père Henry's preference was taken up once more by Dom Marc-François Lacan,[48] this time in a philosophical context. With Chrysostom he interprets verse 8a of the "Ode to Love" as belonging to the previous verse, "Love bears all things, believes all, hopes in all things, perseveres in all things. Love never fails" (*oudepote piptei*)! *Piptein* should not be understood as a literal contrast with *menein* (v. 13). That would be the case only if one had already previously decided for the *temporal* interpretation of the *"nuni de"* in verse 13, whereas the *logical,* consequential meaning is required by both the linguistic context[49] and the intentional context.[50] Moreover, *piptei* in verse 8a stands in the present tense, corresponding to the previous statements. Thus it must not be drawn to the later future statements. The expression *nuni de* never has for Paul, especially in I Corinthians, a temporal sense (5:11; 7:14; 12:18, 20; 14:6; 15:20); the meaning can be adversative only in 13:13, pointing to a contrast to the unperfected, provisional gifts in 8b–12, and so we should translate it as "while/whereas".

Thus three levels should be distinguished: (1) ephemeral charisms, (2) the three that remain (with the first adversative *dé* in 13a), and (3) love, which towers over the other two and animates them (with the second adversative *dé* in 13b). Therefore, corresponding to the whole

---

13:13 as being enigmatic: "If we interpret the phrase 'but now' [*nuni de*] temporally ('as of now') . . . then the contrast with those gifts of the Spirit that for the apostle obviously do not last is destroyed. But if looking back to verse 8 we mean by 'remain' an eternal remaining, then there arises a difficulty if we explain the eternal remaining of faith and hope that Paul himself, in a concession, has elsewhere characterized as a faith in and a hope of completion (2 Cor 5:7; Rom 8:24)." For my own way of removing this difficulty, see my remarks above (pp. 66f.) and above all the text of Irenaeus.

[46] *Cont. Haer.* II, 28, 3.

[47] *In John* X, 43; Peuschen ed., p. 222.

[48] *Recherches des Sciences Réligieuses* 46 (1958): 321–43.

[49] Verse 12 implies this: *arti* and *tote:* Why give up this clear expression for an unclear one?

[50] Of course, faith, hope, and love "now" remain. That is obvious but is also true of the ephemeral charisms!

intention of the hymn, love holds the crown. But *together* with faith and hope, it is eternal, for it forms with these two the lasting structure of Christian life: being sons and daughters of God. It is not surprising that Paul speaks in this passage both of "seeing God face to face" (v. 12) and of "these three remaining" (v. 13), for of course he is speaking in his letters above all of the theme of the earthly life of the Christian.

In his systematic reflections Dom Lacan first of all calls our attention to the fact that faith and hope in Paul have a richer resonance throughout the whole Biblical and human experience than in later theology, where they are described and defined as "theological virtues" (faith as an act of understanding, hope as an act of the will). Lacan also reminds us that Benedict XII's definition expressly is directed to both, insofar as they are theological virtues (see above, p. 68). As he does with so much else, Paul also describes faith and hope as well with an "indeterminacy of overabundant richness" (Cerfaux), as the "foundational attitudes of the Christian life". If the formulation of the inseparable triad faith-hope-love seems to stem from Paul himself, then it is still, as Lacan shows, only an unfolding of the *one* basic Old Testament stance in which the three aspects intermingle undifferentiatedly and thus are all the more inseparable. Hope lies in faith's surrender to God, and this is the perfection of the covenantal love between God and Israel: "I will betroth you in faith and then will you know YHWH" (Hos 2:20), where once more faith and knowledge (as in Paul, Irenaeus, Origen) mutually imply one another.

Love in the New Testament (*agape*) is a superabundant completion of this mutual surrender and knowledge; indeed, we should love *because* and *as* God has loved us, as both Paul (Rom 5 and 8) and John (13 and 15) agree in teaching: it is precisely love, which includes faith and hope, that is given by God and required by him as our response to that gift. The concept of the covenantal fidelity can knead this indissoluble unity back once more into its inseparability. And this covenantal faithfulness culminates in the encounter with the partner "from face to face". Certainly Paul also knows the earthly provisional modality of faith, insofar as it must stem from listening and include a doctrine assented to in obedience, whose insight must for now remain imperfect. He also knows the earthly modality of hope (*elpis* as *hypomoné*), holding fast to what is crucial; this is clear from his discussion in Romans 8:24bc–25. The *hypomoné* does not belong to the "three things that remain", for these constitute our eternal life.

Even though later theology abandoned the purely Biblical version of the foundational stance of the Christian life, yet we find again and again with the mystics that a dynamic concept of eternal life continues to break through, whereby even the creature gazing on God in the beatific vision does not cease to discover how God really is always new and unexpected and to anticipate him in ever-new surrender, trusting in him at all times.

4. *The eschatological prospect*

If faith in the Old Covenant is a stance that can never be superseded and that comports very well with a direct seeing of God (which sees his already enacted great deeds in history and creation but also an eschatological seeing of his Day of Glory when his hidden justice will finally be revealed to all), then obviously this not-to-be-superseded Old Testament stance cannot be superseded in the completion of the New Covenant. For even New Testament eschatology is the inner *fulfillment* of the Old and in no way *replaces* it with something entirely different. The resurrection of the flesh, which ever since the Resurrection of Christ has become *the* eschatological fact, is no sensible concession to a Platonic immortality of the soul in an ideal heaven divided from the temporal-spatial world here below. Rather, it intensifies the perspectival line of Jewish messianism to which even the reanimation of the skeleton in Ezekiel 37 belongs (which, by the way, is a very Jewish incident and was interpreted that way, too).

And to that Jewish messianism also belongs already as a perfecting moment within Judaism an attitude of faith that essentially transcends everything pertaining to works and what can be grasped and that exists in the paradoxical scandal of God's future for the world. Indeed, it does so out of this paradox. It lives on as a witness of what for the world is simply folly, as later Jewish messianism thereafter all the way to Sabbatism and Hassidism has lived out. Jacob Taubes has drawn our attention to these things and suspects that the Pauline *pistis* is not to be seen, as Martin Buber does, as a deformation of the old Jewish concept of faith emerging out of Hellenism but on the contrary points to the Christian shaping of an intra-Jewish messianic eschatological possibility.

Faith as "God's folly" lived out in witness by us, faith as "dying and rising with Christ" and thereby the expression of an eschatological-messianic existence, thus not only is an attitude of expectation that could then be overtaken by the Messiah's coming but also is *the definitive messianic attitude itself.* It is the coperfecting of the Messiah's form of existence, which in the New Testament is the crucified Logos—the one, therefore, who has in the name of God put to shame all of the "logical" ways of man against every future expectation of Greek "wisdom" and Jewish "works-righteousness" belief in miracles. He is the one who has done this not only for us, not only for his disciples, but rather even more in himself, in his own essence.

From here we can easily move to the final conceptual step, which in the Jewish definition is quite simple but less so for the Christian: behind this messianic existence there is no further possibility in Judaism. This possibility is the eschaton, which as such is the future of God in its ineradicable double-sidedness: for the "world" and its "peoples", judgment; for the pious believers who hope, a vision of the justice of God now revealed. Christian theology has the tendency to bring into the eschatological paradox a logical, Greek matrix by dissolving the double-sided encounter with God in a surveyable juxtaposition of steps and phases. This is justified insofar as the transfiguring side ("a new heaven and a new earth") is positioned "after" and "behind" the judging side by Scripture itself, so that it does not seem that God's gestures of judgment are the final visage that he turns toward the world. But the dissociation of the two moments can and must not go further.

In this connection we can phrase things more clearly still, as Paul can place *pistis* among the eschatological realities, even if elsewhere he tries to distinguish the "grades" of the Christian paradoxes, characterizing the death and judgment side as a change in *pistis,* the resurrection and transfiguration side as a change in *eidos.* For precisely in the same context he speaks of a "not wanting to be found naked" and of a transformation of the earthly "tent" into a heavenly one (2 Cor 5:1–7). The "tent" remains, and with it—even in the beatific vision of God's *kabôd* (glory)—there remains that mediation that the creature needs in eternity in order to withstand the inconceivable God, *precisely* in his appearing! Feuillet has tried to show[51] that the *oikia acheiropoietos* (garment not made with human hands) that we "put on" in heaven as our new and eternal clothing so as "not to be found naked" can only be the participation in the humanity of the already transfigured Christ. As Karl Rahner has shown, Christ is the lasting presupposition for our intuition of this *kabôd,* because he is God's *kabôd* in creation.[52]

But if Christ is this *kabôd* of God in creation by virtue of being a man, standing as man in all eternity before God, before the God who is for the creature in eternity ever greater and ever more inconceivable,[53] then, as Karl Rahner says,

> the human soul of Jesus, thought of in terms of quite normal scholastic categories, also stands before the incomprehensibility of God precisely in the *visio beata.* His soul does not "grasp" God; it does not "see through" God. And one can quite serenely call this Catholic dogma. But how should we label this stance of Jesus' soul before the lasting incomprehensibility of God if this is not to be, for example, only a peripheral phenomenon at the frontiers of Christ's "knowledge", the mere negative indication of the finitude of this knowledge but rather precisely in Jesus' soul the unique object, his soul's most appropriate nourishment—precisely *what* is seen. This surrender to God's inconceivability, this *excessus* that never ceases to continue, would indeed be poorly expressed if it never were to emerge into view, so long as we speak exclusively of Christ's knowledge and vision.

[51] "La Demeure céleste et la Destinée des Chrétiens", *Recherches des Sciences Religieuses* (1956): 161–92, 360–402.

[52] Karl Rahner, "Die ewige Bedeutung der Menschheit Jesu für unser Gottes-verhältnis", *Geist und Leben* (1953): 279–88; reprinted in *Schriften zur Theologie,* vol. 3, pp. 47–61.

[53] That is, *akataleptos* (ungraspable): as the Cappadocian theologians have definitively laid down for all subsequent time in their struggle against the rationalistic Arians.

But if this is true, in spite and because of the highest *lumen gloriae* in Christ, how much more is it true of his humanity, which "sees" and clings to God through his continual mediating activity? Finally, *really* to stand before God, before the inconceivability of the divine miracle making all things clear: that cannot be described, circumscribed, or constructed with the categories of the stoic *katalepsis* (seizing) but rather already demands the categories of a loving surrender that entrusts oneself to the infinite and to the knowledge that one has been accepted and loved.

We can confirm all of this from an important theme in the history of theology. All authentic religious philosophy outside of the Bible had always been saturated by the incomprehensibility of God and placed the *via negativa* over all affirming paths to the knowledge of God—not out of resignation but to express the most positive feature of the human experience of God. In his hermeneutical studies against Norden's *Agnostos Theos,* Festugière has shown how very much the thought of God's unrecognizability has emerged from within the very center of classical Greek philosophy and that it requires no "Oriental influences" to explain the negative mysticism of late antiquity.[54]

To an ever increasing extent in the philosophy of late antiquity, the *excessus* beyond all gnosis, which is the true organ for the encounter with God, bears the name *pistis*. But this *pistis* and the apophatic approach of a "philosophical" theology keep their connection with Christian theology because of the work of Dionysius the Areopagite[55] and Maximus the Confessor.[56] They accomplished this so thoroughly that it was put in the very center of theology and—as high scholasticism shows—Christian thought can no longer ignore their legacy.

In spite of his reaction against an overhasty incorporation of Neoplatonism in Christian theology, Thomas Aquinas gave more and

---

[54] *La Révélation d'Hermes Tismégiste,* esp. vol. 4 (Paris: Gabalda, 1954).

[55] *Div. Nom.* VII, 4.

[56] See Wolfson, *The Philosophy of the Church Fathers* (Cambridge, Mass.: Harvard University Press, 1956), as well as my *Gnostische Centurien* (Herder, 1941), pp. 113–14, for indices to this concept of faith in Philo, Gregory of Nyssa, Proclus, Evagrius, etc. *To gar noesai esti to pisteusai:* Tismegistus IX, 10.

more room to the apophatic tendency in his late commentary on
Boethius' *De Trinitate*. If one suspects the whole stream of philosophizing and seeks to accuse it of being an irruption from the outside into
the purity of Biblical thought, then the termination of this river of
thought in John of the Cross might seem even more dubious (*nachden-
klicher*). No doubt this Doctor of the Church owes a lot to the
mysticism of the Areopagite and medieval tradition, and he makes no
secret of it.[57] But for him the way to God is a way of Christian
experience, which he paradoxically describes as the way from an
"experiential knowledge" in the case of the beginner (experience of
sensible and spiritual consolation) into an ever deeper evacuation of
every sensible and spiritual "experience" and into an ever more naked
faith.

We would completely misunderstand him if we were to look on
this way as simply a provisional and episodic one. The dark night has
only a provisional character insofar as it is a passion, and it is a passion
only so long as the soul is not yet adapted to her exceeding object of
superabundance (*Überschwang*). But once she is so adapted, then the
night does not make way for a new light but reveals to the soul night's
own inner and superabundant light. John constantly equates the night
itself with the *contemplatio infusa,* and this is "the great burning thirst
that desiccates all bones", and this precisely because the soul is a
"living thirst for life that brings death".[58]

The soul demands the experimental transformation from every
evidence in finite spirit to the purely formal object of faith, the
evidence of God alone that has its seat in God and not in man. Thus it
is true: "I have trusted myself blindly to the pure Spirit who is a dark
night for all my natural powers."[59] And he equates "this dark night"
with that of the mystical theology of the Areopagite.[60] We see here
the counterpoint to the Alexandrian and Augustinian terminology,
which otherwise dominates Christian theology, where *pistis* primarily

[57] See *Mediaeval Mystical Tradition and St. John of the Cross* by a Benedctine of
Stanbrook (1954), as well as the *Studies in the Spanish Mystics* by Allison Peers.

[58] *Dark Night of the Senses,* chap. II.

[59] *Dark Night of the Soul,* chap. 4.

[60] Ibid., chap. 5.

is seen as the first step to *gnosis*. But even this stream of thought knows that authentic gnosis of God includes an extremely mature and fully developed form of *not* knowing, of self-surrender, in other words, of *pistis*.[61] What John of the Cross describes as "faith" in the context of the theological Tradition is already the darkly experienced participation in the *excessus* of eternal life (see *Subida* II, 24).

If we look back at the opening of this investigation, the *fides Christi* stands at the living crossroads of the Covenant between God and man. When God's Word became man, the *fides Dei* was incorporated into Christ, and God's Covenant of fidelity became one with humanity. This man who is, as the expression of God's essence and deliberate love, his Son, is the incarnate "faithfulness of God" (*pistos ho Theos*) in whom "all of the promises of God have found their Yes" (2 Cor 1:18, 20). He is, as Dionysius says, the ecstacy of the divine eros flowing out of itself, in which God hands himself over and entrusts himself to the world.[62]

Because, and insofar as, he is this, he can answer God as perfect man with a faith that gathers and establishes the faith of all mankind in order also to be the incarnate Covenant of humanity with God. But he does not go back and forth along these two ways but rather is such simultaneously. Indeed, he is the hypostatic identity of these two ways, and thus he is the substantial Covenant, the ontic bond between God and world. He is this Covenant, this bond essentially as "faith" in its wider sense and as "metaphysical principle" (Lohmeyer), so that he has become the final reality of the relation between God and world that grounds everything and that cannot be superseded.

Of course, the Church is already involved in this commitment. For the mediator, God and man, is no private person but rather the incarnate personality of God himself, who eternally transcends all individual limitations from all eternity, gaining a general human

---

[61] See the passages cited above from Origen, where he discusses a *dia eidous pistis*. Baruze emphasizes the difference of this highly mystical faith from the beginning faith of the simple. See also Maréchal, *Psychologie des Mystiques*, vol. 2 (1937), pp. 193f.

[62] *Div. Nom.* IV, 13.

relevance in the Incarnation not only "morally" but much more "ontically". This can already be discerned in the Old Testament foretype, which is primarily a covenant between God and a people, merely mediated through the person of Moses. Christ indeed occupies the place of Moses in order to perfect this role. But with him God himself joins the fray and, as Galatians says (Gal 3:19–22), makes all intermediate authorities superfluous. Thus neither Christ nor the Church, nor her hierarchy, are intermediate instances between man and God. But in faith the believer seizes the faith of the Church and the *fides Christi* immediately, for it is hypostatically one with the *fides Dei* in Christ.

The Chalcedonian "boundary" that says the two natures remain unmixed in Christ (*asynchytos*) is thus basically no boundary. Rather it is what enables us to become immediately one. It makes possible the marriage between God and creature, of which Christ, Church, and Holy Spirit are the substantive consummation.

OFFICE IN THE CHURCH

I. *The question at issue*

The chief stumbling block against which non-Catholics come up in the Church is authority, the impersonal institution. The paradox implied in the duty to follow Christ, the imitation of the inimitable, may—indeed must—be accepted: this dialectic of the impossible that is yet imposed as an obligation, of a gift that goes beyond all human capacity, in fact accords with the specifically Protestant sentiment. But what, we might well ask, can the most personal of all relationships and experiences, those of vocation and discipleship, have to do with an authority that can still function substantially despite personal sinfulness? Surely the whole logic of the gospel teaching must make us regard it as a mere means of preserving social order within the Christian community? Above all, the whole course of development from the Old to the New Covenant seems to lead in quite a different direction. Even in the Old Covenant there was little about authority, and great stress was laid on personal discipleship in faith and the people's obedience in faith as its history proceeded. In addition, such wide scope was allowed to free prophecy that it constantly checked and censured both the priesthood, hardened in its official ways, and the institutional kingship and spared no one in recalling religion to its point of departure, namely, God's great decision for the people, comprising as it did the people's decision for God, their side of the nuptial relation.

And now that the old order ought to be infinitely surpassed through God's coming in the flesh, through the wholly unexpected way in which discipleship in faith has been made a concrete reality as given by one man to another, it is inconceivable that we should revert to a stage of religion outside of and prior to the Biblical. Yet this is just what the Catholic Church does when she gives, as it were, an independent status to institutional organs and their functioning.

Translated by A. V. Littledale with Alexander Dru.

For the most part, the arguments in defense of the institution fail to meet the real objection or to allay disquiet. On the one hand, they merely refer the "structures" to Christ's positive ordinance, corroborated by an interpretation of relevant texts and linked up with proofs drawn from history. On the other hand, they point to the logical necessity of the institutions from the religious aspect, their object being to safeguard the functioning of the sacramental system and ecclesiastical jurisdiction from dependence on the "worthiness" of the person exercising it. This is easily done by adducing the disastrous consequences brought in by the sects and heresies. But this second argument does no more than commend the acceptance of *minus malum,* or perhaps a *medium sine qua non,* which should be used with great care and delicacy as the pure means to an end, which is the personal following of Christ on the part of the believer. The first argument, based on the positive ordinance of the Founder of the Church, from which there can be no appeal, cannot easily satisfy human or even theological reason or lead the *fides quaerens intellectum* to a tranquil contemplation of the doctrine. Must we, then, continue to endure a residue of unease about the institutional Church, as long as we are the *civitas Dei peregrinans,* and only afterward, when the institutional part is no more, be able to look back and see its necessity and justification? Surely, this is one of the mysteries of the Faith, all of which are linked to the Cross of Christ. It is one of the mysteries of the Church, which not only in her inmost being as the community of saints and the spotless bride of Christ but also in her visibility to the world and her conspicuous imperfection remains a pressing enigma. The answer to the difficulty, which concerns Catholics and non-Catholics alike, can be found only if personal discipleship and authority are seen as intimately connected from the very first and inseparable in both fact and idea. And this connection must mean not only that the personal practice of the believer is protected and guaranteed externally by an impersonal authority (this may well be true, but it does not dispel all doubts) but also that the very concept of discipleship, which can only be apprehended dialectically, only *per excessum,* implies that of authority and is inseparable from it.

The following study proposes to get back to that origin. It will, therefore, not be concerned with bringing out what is called a "unity of tension", such as is said to exist, for instance, between personal charisma and impersonal authority, in St. Paul's theology of the Church. There, the two are very closely linked so that, on a cursory view, authority could be seen simply as one charisma among others and subsumed under this superior concept, though the subsequent independence of the authoritative office is seen as already in prospect, or even realized. The drawback here is that this view paves the way for the argument that the institutional side, from the human and sociological standpoint, is merely the inevitable residue left over when the tide of the first enthusiasm had ebbed, when the tremendous founder personalities such as Christ and Paul had left the scene to lesser men, and the charismatic succession—as in the Old Testament judges and prophets and (according to Max Weber) in many non-Christian religions—had ceased. Is this cessation, then, to be ascribed to a law of sociology and history governing the decay of enthusiasm? If so, the whole outcome is a betrayal of the Founder's intention and a vindication of Protestant criticism of Catholicism. Or did it come about because the institutional factor is, of its nature, inseparable from the New Testament idea of discipleship? If so, and only then, the Catholic case is proved convincingly. But if it can be definitely established, important consequences follow for the common understanding of the Catholic Church. For if the two are really found to have been bound together in unity from the beginning, the Catholic Church and the Catholic way of life can only be made credible and lived in view of this origin. Here, and here alone, is the real crux of all apologetics, and all the separate proofs derive their ultimate force from this unity forged by Christ and indissoluble.

This bond of unity between discipleship and authority once proven, it is capable of being understood in various—even contradictory—senses, and it is consequently here, at the very outset, that decisions that condition all that follows must be taken.

The first decision is whether the apostles' following of Christ as recorded in the Gospel was, of its very nature, directed to the office they were to be given—whether, that is, it was expressly a training for their authoritative position, or, alternatively, whether it was a training for the Christian life in general and would only later, as if accidentally, issue in their consecration and official mission.

The second alternative is the one that any Christian free of preconceptions would spontaneously accept, seeing in Christ's relationship with his apostles a model for his own relationship with the Lord and desirous of applying to himself piecemeal the Lord's instructions to his disciples. But that would make the institution of the office something more like a mere appendage to the general initiation into the Church and so pave the way to a positivism that reduces the spiritual office to a decision of Christ to be accepted without further explanation.

The first alternative is the one that commends itself naturally to the *fides quaerens intellectum,* which spontaneously assumes an intimate connection between office and Christian living, but its acceptance would entail even more unacceptable consequences. For in this view the life of God among men, as described in the Gospel, would at its profoundest level be directed to the establishment of the clerical body—would, in fact, be a *grand séminaire* for the clergy on whom, after the ascension of the Founder, would devolve the task of handing on to the people the instruction imparted to them in virtue of the powers committed to them alone. Thus the spirituality of the Gospels would be preeminently a clerical one, and from this two opposing conclusions could be drawn. Either the spirituality of the laity must be derived from that of the clergy (somehow adapted and watered down in the process), or else lay spirituality cannot be formally contained in the clerical and must therefore be newly formed as something on its own according to the special state of life of the laity who occupy, in the order of the world, a position quite different from those who "have left all".

Both conclusions must be rejected as complete distortions and harmful in the extreme. Can there be a third way? Is it possible from one and the same history to extract both the universal and the particular, both what applies to all Christians and what applies solely to those in authority, without unwittingly falling into one extreme or the other?

The second option is closely bound up with the first; and the fact that it approximates it without being identical with it throws light on the profound mystery of the Church that is already present in the first option and rules out any hasty solution. The apostles had to leave behind all things in order to place their all in Christ, and it was into this void that the grace of their office was poured. But not everyone who leaves all things receives the exercise of authority, and not every layman literally leaves all. The distinction between the religious state and the secular cuts across that between the priestly state and the lay. All the theologians of patristic times and the Middle Ages saw, in the practice of the apostles, the foundation of the New Testament priesthood and of the discipleship of the individual Christian; and now we can either derive from it the obligations of the clergy, assimilating them to the rule of life of the apostles and the primitive Church (the regular clergy), or, alternatively (for instance, with Cardinal Mercier), direct the orders to conform to the original order of Christ (the apostolic clergy) as their ideal and model. In both cases the laity are once again excluded, and we have the same dialectic as before. Either it is true, as an unbroken Tradition from the Fathers to post-Reformation theology teaches, that the religious state in the Church today is what the whole Church was in the time of the apostles (in Jerusalem, with its community of possessions); and then the state of the ordinary laity is a concession, something outside of the original perfection of the gospel. Or else clergy and religious alike are restricted to representing a mere function within the total organism of the Church; but then it is difficult to see why the gospel confines itself to explaining this special function, and the temptation arises to supplement this—historically conditioned?—onesidedness of the New Testament writings by an approach more suited to our time.

Here, too, it is enormously difficult to synthesize the various standpoints, even when we view the question from a distance, particularly when we remember that, as a matter of history, every genuine renewal of the ecclesiastical spirit has necessarily been effected by a return to the radical position of the first age, which was undoubtedly that of the "special" way of leaving all things. But the question now begins to take on a more acute form, for the issue concerns not only the lay state but also the relationship, within the apostolic state, between spiritual office and spiritual life. If the spiritual office demands a spiritual mode of life as exemplified in the religious state, does it not follow that we must consider the ordinary form of life of the secular clergy as itself a concession and a compromise, compared with the strictness of the apostolic way of life?

There is yet a third option to be considered. It is true that the Twelve chosen by the Lord form the new, spiritual Israel. They are to judge the twelve tribes; they constitute the twelve gates of the heavenly Jerusalem. But the significant factor is that they are not themselves tribes but individuals and that the new people of God is built on the "foundation" of individuals who follow the unique individual Christ. It is only the individual who is called to follow Christ. Although the Twelve form a *collegium,* they are individuals still and not a collective, and their mission from the very beginning envisages each of them as being distinct from the others, each a missionary, on his own, to a particular country or district. At least this is the idea that follows from St. Matthew's account of the final sending forth of the apostles. It is true that in reality things turned out a little differently (for most of the apostles, it was a matter of a little missionary work in the environs of Jerusalem), but was not this collective dwelling together already a departure from the original idea? And was it not actually the beginning, the foundation for the "impersonal" character of the office? It might be rejoined that a visible community on earth, such as Christ willed the Church to be, necessitates a properly constituted body as legislature and judicature, in which the individual plays a part only insofar as he holds any office. All this is true, but we must not be too hasty to equate the visibility of the community that is the Church with that of the natural community and univocally subsume both under the same general concept. Granted that the Church is a visible community, and further, that there is within the Church a purely official element and not only a personal charisma: Can its character as community and as official body be determined and defined according to the laws of the natural community? Is it not rather the case that everything rests on the primary cell of personal discipleship, which is something quite different from the primary cell of the family; on *rebirth,* which is essentially personal, as opposed to *birth,* which is merely natural? In these days the question is posed in terms of an antithesis between a Church of the people and a missionary Church of individual missionaries; and although the manner of its resolution has far-reaching consequences, it may perhaps be reduced to a question of style in the conception of the Christian way of life. And even then, it very much affects all aspects of the Church's life.

2. *The paradox of the following*

The whole course of relationships between Jesus and men starts from his command "Follow me" (Mk 2:14; Mt 9:9; Lk 5:27; Jn 1:43). This laconic injunction demands, moreover, immediate response, and it envisages the whole of life, and even more: existence in time and in eternity. It has the unconditional sense of the nearly literal equivalent "going along behind", and only then has it the more profound meaning of a spiritual alignment behind him whose call is a command.

The response to his call is described as an equally immediate leaving all things and following him (Mt 4:20, 22; Mk 1:18; 10:28; Lk 5:11; Jn 1:39). It is essentially a leap into the void, where there is nothing but Jesus—as we see in Peter's simple statement in Mark: "Behold, we have left all things and followed you." Here the question is not yet formulated that Matthew appends: "What, then, shall we have?" Here is a human question caught up within the answer inspired by the Lord, a question that cannot be suppressed or totally overshadowed by the fact of discipleship.

This step, or leap, is, for Jesus, the condition of their becoming disciples. We see this in the episode of the rich young man, where, once again, the interpreting gloss in Matthew is originally lacking ("If you would be perfect . . . "), and it only says, "You lack one thing; go, sell what you have and give to the poor, and you will have treasure in heaven; and come, follow me" (Mk 10:21).

These three factors in conjunction constitute the gate to life with Christ. In the call, everything relates solely to the person calling. There is no set program about the way, or instruction to be followed, no ideal proposed, no law given to mark out the territory. There is no connection with anything known beforehand, no commendation of goodwill; no vows are taken. The follower is not praised for his courage or achievement, nor is he trained to make the leap, heartened by any inducement, warned about the gravity of the situation. The Lord does not first present himself, show his credentials in the manner of the head of a school, the master of an esoteric band of disciples. Everything consists in his mere call, which is his direct personal intervention, a claim on the one called. The call is absolute and, therefore, final; it is precisely the intervention of God's absolute sovereignty. Even when a miracle precedes (the draught of fish), or an appeal to an earthly teacher (John the Baptist), or to a prophecy of Scripture (as with Nathanael: see Jn 1:46 and 7:41-42), all this fades into the background—or else it is so far surpassed as to become the direct contrary (the fishers become the fished; out of Nazareth, something good comes). Even the love that follows at a distance, when it encounters the one who turns toward it, can only ask, "Where do you live?" and, from the moment of the "turning" (Jn 1:38), everything becomes a matter of the call and of going along with him.

The three disciples who recoiled from the starkness of "following" were dealt with uncompromisingly. The first, with his "I will follow you", assumed the initiative, the masculine role, and awaited the assent of the Lord. But no one can call himself or let his enthusiasm be a substitute for the call. Jesus, far from unreservedly accepting him, showed him the void, which was his own inasmuch as he had nowhere to lay his head, but it appears as a void precisely because it is not filled by the call and so made tolerable. In fact, the void is all the deeper in that the man in question is a scribe, for whom the law and wisdom have always presented a content, *lucerna pedibus meis.* The second was a disciple, according to Matthew; Luke says that on the call "Follow me", he was at once accepted as a disciple. He asked first for permission to bury his father. The natural law, reinforced by the positive, obliged him. He felt himself not only in the right but also in duty bound to frame a synthesis of the Old and New Covenants: first the Old must be fulfilled; then he is free to go over to the New. But as Jesus himself is the synthesis, it is for him, not the disciple, to frame it: "Let the dead bury their dead!" Everything apart from the God of the living (Mt 22:32) is dead, everything apart from Jesus, who is himself

the life (Jn 14:6). He alone controls the law of nature and that of
Scripture: "Of me Moses wrote", and therefore "if you believed
Moses, you would believe me" (Jn 5:46). There can be no thought of
violating a law through the following of Christ. The third said, "I
will follow thee, Lord, but first let me take leave of those who are in
my house." He was drawing up a program, dividing up the subject
matter, mapping out stages of his development. If I can get so far, then
I can take the risk. It reminds us of the scene in which Elijah casts the
cloak of the prophet's calling on Elisha, who was plowing with
twelve yoke of oxen. "And he left the oxen, and ran after Elijah, and
said, 'Let me kiss my father and my mother, and then I will follow
you.' And he said to him, 'Go back again; for what have I done to
you?' And he returned from following him, and took the yoke of
oxen, and slew them" (1 Kings 19:20–21), then followed Elijah and
became his disciple. The Lord said, "Whoso putteth his hand to the
plow and looketh back is not fit for the Kingdom of God." That is
equivalent to "[he] cannot be my disciple" (Lk 14:27) and, more
trenchantly, "[he] is not worthy of me" (Mt 10:37–38).

The literal sense of "going along with" and (corresponding to the
Jewish custom between rabbi and pupil) "coming after" (Mt 16:24) is
so strong that it constitutes the indispensable basis for our understanding of the process, and this in three respects. In the first place, in that
the pure, naked "going with" means of itself, no more than local
movement, it does not include forward progress, instruction, consecration. The whole emphasis is on being with. This is more than a mere
"coming to him", which, according to God's form of expression, is
distinct from "discipleship" (Lk 14:26–27). It is, besides, more than a
temporary "walking with", the characteristic of discipleship. In the
New Testament, "following after" is so much of a real, active process
that it is impossible to form from its verb form a general concept
describing what is incumbent on all Christians, such as is the case with
the noun "discipleship".

In the second place, the literal "walking with" and "being with"
are the exclusive privilege of the twelve apostles, so much so that
Paul, who was not then present, had the greatest difficulty in accrediting
himself as an "appendage" of the apostolic college. For him there

could not be a "following after" in the literal sense, since this was not possible at all in the time after the Resurrection. In fact, there was not a "being with" as between one man and another, only a "being in"; and this, from now on, with the corresponding and complementary ideas of "turning to the Lord", "calling by the Lord", "faith", expresses the new reality of Christian existence, until it takes on a new form, with the death of the body, though with a different meaning, that of "being with the Lord" (Phil 1:23). Here below, in the meantime, our "being with" Christ is changed into his being with us (see Mt 28:20).

Finally, in the third place, it was reserved to John, the last hagiographer of the New Covenant, to undertake the synthesis of the synoptic literalness and the Pauline interpretation into something of universal and spiritual import. John was present with Jesus from the beginning. He was the first literally to accomplish the walking to Jesus and then with him (Jn 1:35–39 is undoubtedly autobiographical and describes, prior to the calling of Peter, the characteristic quality of the beloved disciple). But this literal fact itself leads, in John's contemplation of it, to the ultimate spiritual step. Already, in the scene by the Jordan, each word has a spiritual overtone: the "hearing" of the Baptist's words, the "following" of Jesus, his "turning around", the mutual interrogation, the first appearance of the significant word *stay* ("Rabbi, where are you staying?"), especially the answer of Jesus, "Come and see", whose meaning is underlined by "They came and saw where he was staying; and they stayed with him"—here we have a summing up of the whole Johannine theology. Thus John is the first to raise the idea of "following" from the literal and earthly plane to a spiritual one. He does so in connection with the twice-repeated injunction of the risen Christ to Peter, "Follow me" (Jn 21:19, 22), meaning, as the context shows, to death and Resurrection (not simply in "feeding the sheep" or to martyrdom or into the invisible world). Where Paul sees only a community of destiny between Christ and the Christian, John sees always the older, apostolic reality of the literal "following after and behind". This is something eternal and final, so that it is even the heavenly occupation of the elect: "It is these who follow the Lamb wherever he goes" (Rev 14:4). While preserving the apostolic prerogative, John has here opened up, for all who come afterward, a breach through which they too (at a distance from the Twelve) can enter on the "following". Already this had been done by the seventy-two, whose literal following of Christ is assured but whose number itself (six times twelve) is symbolic and therewith keeps the circle opened indefinitely.

Now the expression "going along with Christ" must have a very precise meaning and imply a very pressing necessity, not only for the person called but also for the One calling. To bring this out, let us first go beyond the bare literal aspect and face the real paradox of discipleship (or following). Its significance is, primarily, salvation and its attainment. God is salvation, which has now appeared in the form of man: to be in salvation means to be with this man. The identification of Jesus with salvation comes out in the great utterances he makes about himself in St. John and also in those of the "Son of Man" in the synoptics (Mk 12:6; 12:37; 13:26; 14:21, 62). Whoever follows Christ unconditionally is "fit for the Kingdom of God" (Lk 9:62). The rich young man seeks "eternal life", and Jesus responds to his searching with counsel to leave all and follow him (Mk 10:18, 21). In John, "following" is taken more spiritually as "not walking in darkness" and "finding the light of life", Christ himself being this light (Jn 8:12). It also means to gain participation in the messianic salvation, in the goods of salvation promised by the prophets, foreseen by Abraham, which "many prophets and righteous men longed to see . . . and did not see" (Mt 13:17), but are now imparted not to anyone at all but to those who go with him and follow after him. Here we begin to glimpse the paradox: Why should salvation, which by its very nature, by the terms of its prophetic announcement, should be of universal application, be so incomprehensibly reserved to these elect? For it is that salvation "which thou hast prepared in the presence of all peoples, a light for the revelation to the Gentiles" (Lk 2:31–32). It is the visitation of the rising sun "to give light to those who sit in darkness and in the shadow of death" (Lk 1:79), the preaching of salvation to all the poor, the blind, the bruised, and the captives (Lk 4:18). What is the explanation of this exclusiveness so insisted upon?

Certainly, we can understand that so great a good, a salvation so final and complete, is worth any sacrifice. It is perfectly in accord with reason, indeed with a commercial outlook, that one who has found the treasure in the field or the pearl of great price should sell all in order to buy it (Mt 13:44–46). We can understand, in this light, that Jesus demands from those who desire to find him the leaving of all the rest, hatred of all the rest, including the seeker himself (Lk 14:26)—as indeed is demanded by a right scale of values and a clear-cut decision—and, finally, the staking of one's own life, which is what the Church after the Resurrection retrospectively included in the idea of "carrying the cross" (Mt 10:38; 16:24; Mk 8:34; Lk 9:23; 14:27). Before his own crucifixion, Jesus (who, in all his prophecies of the Passion, had never once spoken of his Cross) could not have demanded of his disciples a carrying of the cross as part of their following him. But he could demand that they stake their lives in their absolute decision to embrace the salvation offered by the Messiah. In the same way, the Lord addresses the demand to "hate" everything else and to "carry the cross" expressly to the "great multitude" (Lk 14:25–27), urging them to weigh up the entire consequences of his analogy of the "calculation of the cost" and the "king about to go to war" (Lk 14:28–33). All this he makes of general application. It concerns the arrangement incumbent on anyone if he is to participate in the goods of salvation at the end of time. In Christ this salvation is "at hand"; whoever draws near to him, who turns to him, attains it. If the Twelve were no more than a visible representation, an example to make clear the meaning of this participation offered to all, there would be nothing paradoxical in their being called and requisitioned.

But this is not so, and it is just when we pursue the matter beyond this point of general application that the role of the Twelve seems so obscure and incomprehensible. For, since they were chosen out especially, they were obviously more closely united to the person, existence, and teaching of Christ with a view to participating therein in a manner different from any others. The question then arises: In what do they participate? In Christ's teaching, through being more thoroughly instructed? That is possible, but it cannot be the decisive point, since Christ is not primarily a doctrine but a life. In his life, then? That too is possible but cannot be the whole solution; for Jesus, and he alone, was sent by the Father to "give his life as a ransom for many" (Mk 10:45); he alone is their "Master", while they are all brothers (Mt 23:8); finally, Jesus did not intend for them to become themselves "teachers" later on: "Neither be called masters, for you have one Master, the Christ" (Mt 23:10). However marvelous their progress and sublime their functions, the original cleavage, the contrast that makes possible all the rest, the fact that they are all "from below", and one only is "from above", he who is "above all" (Jn 3:31–32; 8:23), can *never* be bridged. Jesus is unique; he is the only begotten of the Father; he is what he does and does what he is.

Undoubtedly, the Lord's public life had to do with the work of teaching, and in what could he instruct the people and the disciples if not in himself? He laid open to them his heart and his feelings for them to learn to understand him. He himself is his doctrine. And since he is what he does, his disciples also must do what he does and is and, in so doing, gain some intimation of who he is (Jn 7:17; 8:31–32); in so doing they actuate not themselves but Christ in them. If this primary law is forgotten through some kind of mysticism, however well intentioned or perfervid, Christianity is reduced to the level of a merely human world religion based on one variety or other of pantheism. It is against this that the Old Testament waged war as against the age-old enemy, and the New Covenant can only mean the final victory of this conflict.

This unique relationship of master and disciple in the Incarnation of God can, of course, be subsumed under human categories, either sociological or ethical. Moreover, it is of the essence of the Incarnation that this should be so and that these categories apply not only to the Old Covenant but also to the whole of human history in the natural order. In Greek religious philosophy there was a "following of God", a placing of oneself behind God, his leading, his Providence, his will, as is so excellently expressed in the hymn of Cleanthus. What is small and peripheral orders itself to what is great and central. There is also the religious following of the wise man and teacher, through whom, in a covenant of discipleship, it was alone possible to attain, preserve, and transmit wisdom—consider Pythagoras or Epicurus. Admittedly, the Old Testament idea of a covenant had its sociological basis in the covenants of the great nations and the nomadic tribes with their own special god to whom they pledged themselves and swore fidelity and whom they "followed", literally in the case of the nomads, spiritually in the case of the higher cultures. And in the journey through the desert, Yahweh became, in reality, a God "going before" (Ex 13:21; 33:16; Nb 14:14; Dt 1:30, 33; 20:4; 31:6; etc.), who jealously watched that they should "go after" him and not after strange gods (Dt 6:14f.), not "to the right hand, or to the left", but straight "in all the way" (Dt 5:32–33). Yet, though this was an instance of the recognized fact of divine leadership, it went beyond the generality of such cases, being of a wholly unique character. Any parallels to it in religious history are far remote; they serve rather to obscure than to clarify its nature. That is why the Old Covenant speaks preferably of God "going before" rather than of the people "following". The latter term was chiefly employed negatively, not "going after strange gods", and, when positively, with an erotic overtone: Israel followed God in the desert as the Oriental bride followed her bridegroom (Jer 2:2). Generally, the injunction was simply to "walk in the way" of the Lord (Dt 5:33). Yahweh is no "wandering God", and the walking behind the ark of the Covenant has itself no magical significance. It is always a matter of following the law of the Covenant, spiritual self-commitment to God's disposition, to his wisdom. And the sapiential books know that man's relationship to wisdom is simply one of prayer for being constantly kept in his following and his status of sonship. At the same time, there was, indeed, a danger that the "wise man" of Israel should approximate too closely the wise men of Greece and Egypt, insofar as he was one who, through his dealings with wisdom, had received the intrinsic quality of "being wise". In the same period, too, the rabbis gathered round them their own groups of pupils, who followed them in the street a few paces away as a sign of reverence. But then Jesus came at the right moment to restore and bring out fully the proper and original idea of following at a distance, the idea of the Covenant of Sinai and of the prophetic teachings.

For in the Old Covenant the pillar of fire and the clouds were only figurative; and, after Israel had entered the promised land, the main thing was a spiritual walking in the ways of God. But now the following of the incarnate Son was not just figurative but rather the expression, becoming ever more exact, of a relationship with God that made quite impossible any equating of the divine wisdom that commands with man's own wisdom that obeys. And while the rabbis, as the prophets before them and now John the Baptist, had their groups of pupils, and the disciples of Jesus seemed, to all appearances, just one such group (Jn 4:2), yet the instructions they received from their master left them always in a state of surprise and disarray, since he did not impart "wisdom"; in fact, everything about him, words and conduct, indicated that he himself was wisdom. Outward and inward following, whose unity was only adumbrated in the Old Covenant, were in Jesus put on the same level. A paradox, then: the more one desires to be a "master", the more one must remain a pupil. The significance of this paradox is far more profound than in the Old Covenant or than in the case of the natural relationship of a pupil (say, to his guru). It is not just a matter of remaining in an attitude of prayer, of preserving contact with the master, but of the literal "apart from me you can do nothing fruitful" (Jn 15:5).

3. The more intense paradox of imitation

The universal religious relationship as subpersonal could favor the conception that the center of the finite person can and must be taken and absorbed into the center of the Godhead. In the Old Covenant it would have been inconceivable that "walking in the ways of God", the realization of his commands in the individual life, could have led to Yahweh's becoming immanent in the believer or the latter's absorption into Yahweh. All was at the personal level, just as modern personalism derives from the idea of the actualization of the Old Covenant in the Jews (so Stern, Scheler, Buber, Gabriel Marcel). Christianity has gone beyond personalism as it has gone beyond the Old Covenant to reach a higher plane proper to itself alone, one that, from the standpoint of natural religion as well as Biblical personalism, is bound to seem wholly paradoxical—bound, therefore, to be misunderstood. The paradox is so sharp that it is constantly liable, even in Christian theology, to take the direction either of a religious and mystical impersonalism or of a Jewish personalism. A Catholic theology that relies too much on an abstract metaphysics of being and grace, and also liberal Protestant theology, tends to impersonalism; orthodox Protestantism tends to personalism.

The crisis of the Biblical idea of "following" is reached with the intrusion of the idea of "imitation" into the New Testament. It is more or less understandable that one should be able to follow some unique personality at a distance prescribed by respect and love. But that one can and must imitate what, in virtue of his uniqueness, is inimitable, this seems, from the Christian standpoint—for there is no other, historically—a flat contradiction, if one knows what one is talking about. Granted that we make a priori an absolute distinction between an external sphere of qualities and actions that are, in some way, imitable (these of necessity would be principally the human ones) and a sphere that is absolutely inimitable, because divine and divine-human. But even a cursory view of the New Testament is enough to show that such a distinction is never made and that, on the contrary, Christ is inimitable to the same degree in which he is proposed to his followers for imitation. Terminologically, following and imitation are poles apart, and the difference is one that Protestant theology is prone to emphasize to the fullest extent; and even where the Biblical text makes unavoidable a minimum of "imitation", it gets around this with the dialectic of *peccator* and *justus*. In fact, this theology makes a point of never allowing us to overlook the element of "following" in "imitation", even in the Christian and paradoxical sense of "following". One may well ask, therefore, whether a scrupulous care not to say a word too much in this regard is not preferable to speaking blatantly and unguardedly of the Christian as *alter Christus* and of "iso-Christism" (as the ideal of the Greco-Christian mystics). Obedience to the specific Christian grace is the safeguard against both extremes, not by balancing the two but by retaining the paradox that is not to be solved in the conceptual sphere, and elucidated only in the mystery of the Trinity, which enters, through Christ, even into the life and consciousness of man and makes derisory his most daring flights of thought. What we may call "imitation" in the Christian sense is no other than the disciples' following as conceived and ordained by Christ himself, whose "leaving all things" and "going with" him were changed from a material to a spiritual act and carried out in all seriousness. This took place in four stages.

1. The doctrine of Christ is Christ himself, and so for the Christian the content of Christian existence is nothing other than its form, namely, following. This is not merely the act of entering on a course of instruction (matriculation) but is identical with it. Leaving all things means a spiritual renunciation of one's own views, mode of life, and purposes and, on a deeper level, of one's own freedom and reason, offering them all to the Master, and, according to his disposition, either receiving them back or not, or having them replaced by his own purposes and freedom and reason. In this, leaving all things is the same thing as *faith*. The Old Covenant prepared the way by raising the impersonal basic act of natural religion to the plane of the personal. This act is the abdication of finite subjectivity in view of the infinite ground of all things. In Zen Buddhism there is a similar mysterious exchange: the total renunciation of finite consciousness, knowledge, and power leads to investiture with the infinite consciousness, knowledge, and power. What is here a kind of technique, and so concealed magic, is purified in the personal encounter between Yahweh and the people and assumes the form of self-commitment into the hands of God to dispose of as he pleases. The religious man does this, not in order to be immersed in the universal reason but that the personal design of God in his freedom may be glorified in him. Hence the simile of nuptial and bridal fidelity applied to Yahweh and Israel, which, despite the Oriental subordination of the woman to the man, is the product of a genuine relationship between two persons.

Christian faith surpasses both forms. If we consider it in its first, most primitive form, there is an unmistakable likeness to the forms of the natural religions. In Mark, faith is the medium (of surrender) by which man *is able* (through surrender). Whoever can so give himself as Christ intended, indeed, as Christ himself did: in him can the supernatural take place. Unbelief prevents miracles of healing (Mk 6:5). The belief, however, of the hemorrhaging woman causes a power to go out from Jesus to heal her; her faith made her whole (5:28, 34; see 10:52). Faith demands an act of spiritual courage to leave all things and take the leap—hence the exhortation, "Do not fear, only believe" (5:36)—courage to bring the soul into unity (James 1:5; Mt 6:22; Lk 11:34) and to discard double-mindedness (James 1:8; 4:8). Paucity of faith essentially leads to godlessness, but from "Take heart . . . have no fear" (Mk 6:50; 10:50) to "Have faith in God" (11:22) is but a step. The essential point is the reference to God, which means, for Christ, to the Father who sent him (Mk 9:37); the act of faith, mediated by Christ, has the Father for object. But what Christ taught he performed in superlative fashion. While those of little faith trembled in the storm, he slept in the boat; and, though his attitude may not be described as "faith", yet it is the model and prototype of faith. Afterward, when he reproaches them and asks, "Have you no faith?" he means "faith in God", his own attitude, in which he is educating the disciples. There is also, in this connection, the case of the father of the possessed child, who said to Jesus, "If you can do anything, have pity on us and help us." Jesus, taking up the man's own words, replied, "If you can!" And he continued, "All things are possible to him who believes." The man replied, "I believe; help my unbelief!" Can the "believer" (who "can" do all) be referred to Christ? Certainly not apart from Christ, who must assist the transition from double- to single-mindedness. Can the "believer" (who "can" do all) be referred to Christ? Certainly not apart from the man, for whom he is the prototype of oneness of faith and the power of faith. Only with the power of Christ, in it and through it, "can" the man elicit the faith necessary for the miracle to happen. It is the power of Christ that takes over in him, just as the Spirit of Christ will later take over in the disciples, so that they need take no thought beforehand of what they are to say (Mk 13:11).

Here we have a contrast with the Zen teacher, who prepares and trains the wise as to how one can let the infinite spirit work powerfully in the individual; a contrast, too, with the prophet, to whom it can be given, with his office, to impart to others God's Spirit (which he is not and which does not belong to him)—see Numbers 11:25f.; 2 Kings 2:9–10, 15. St. John indicates what makes possible this higher condition in the Trinitarian formula, "For as the Father has life in himself, so he has granted the Son also to have life in himself" (Jn. 5: 26), so that he is neither indigent in his dependence nor unrelated to another in his power to dispose of his own being. His autonomy, as real as the Father's, has yet, as its inner form and prerequisite, his eternal sonship and love for the Father. This divine and divine-human form is the prototype of the Christian; he is exercised in it; moreover, as unique and inimitable, it is preëstablished both ontologically and ethically. For this reason, the relationship between the Christian and Christ is not simply a transposition, made possible by the Incarnation, of the personal relationship between the people and Yahweh onto a human plane. For Christ exercises men in faith in the Father; faith in him, of its very nature, goes further ("He who believes in me, believes not in me"—Jn 12:44), and can never remain interpersonal; it is only possible as relating to the Trinity. And for the same reason the Christian act of faith is not totally comprehensible as a personal act, but, though it is that, the crucial element is that it is supra-personal and Trinitarian, which is what makes it possible.

The general structure is thus elucidated. The leap involved by "following", leaving all things (spiritually as a completely interior act), is, in its single-mindedness and courage, sustained from the very outset by the grace of Christ. This makes the double-minded participate in his divine and hypostatic oneness, and thus—again, purely in his grace—makes possible the following of him, and empowers the Christian not only to make the leap away, but to "come to him"; not only to follow, but to "imitate". This will be clearer in what follows.

2. There corresponds to the demand for total faith and the power imparted to make the leap, Christ's revelation of his own being in its fullness. Every one of his words, every act, points to the full meaning of his existence. It is impossible, therefore, to distinguish what is to be imitated, from the inimitable. In fact, it is precisely the inimitable things about him, the messianic miracle working, such as casting out devils and raising the dead, that are enjoined upon the disciples. What is inimitable becomes imitable, for it is not so much the material act which is put forward as the model, but rather the inmost unity of the

person performing it, his unity of sentiment, that is revealed. It is never anything material that is offered for imitation, not even in the case of the washing of the feet, whose copying is expressly demanded, but always the spiritual core shown forth in the particular expression. One must always look to the heart. For this reason, the acts of Jesus can be not only unlikely but astonishing, and both together, for it is precisely the lowliness of the Lord in becoming a servant that is the astonishing thing, the more one comes to understand it. The opening of his heart in Matthew 11:25–30 (Lk 10:21–22) begins with his praise of the Father, who has hidden it from the wise, meaning both the pagan wise, who aimed at finding the infinite only through their own finitude, and the Jewish wise, who had falsely usurped the divine wisdom, without possessing the simplicity of faith. The "simple", the "little ones", however, gain a participation through grace, not actually in the Son nor the Father, but in the sphere of the mutual relationship of Father and Son, in which the Spirit moves. This is a sphere completely unapproachable by those who stand outside, but made accessible by the gracious good pleasure of the Son. It is the sphere to which the simplicity of the child is alone commensurable, and which is envisaged by the passages concerning children (Mk 9: 36–37; 10:13–16; see 24). The heart that is now revealed and that reveals him is gentle and humble, so that it is the expression of the Spirit and gives it place for its dwelling. It is not "following" that the Lord demands, but "coming to him," to be lightened from the "yoke" of the law, "which neither we nor our fathers were able to bear" (Acts 15:10), and by him will be changed and become "sweet and light," in that the heart itself (which makes known the heart of God) becomes the "law" of the "little ones". This heart will itself take up the "yoke" of the cross, of the scorn and mockery of all men, and the extreme of hatred. Here, however, it demands not the following of the Cross as an ascetic practice but only "coming to him", submission to God's own law of the heart. But, as we have seen, the demand for this submission makes submission impossible.

On that account, the words of Jesus to men are shrouded in a strange obscurity. Insofar as they convey a demand to those in grace, the elect, they give access to him and understanding; otherwise, they bring about nonunderstanding and scandal, exclusion. The parables are theological forms of speech, since they reveal enough to make faith possible and conceal enough to make unbelief possible. And it is just this "hearing and understanding" or "hearing and not understanding" that forms the content of the first great parable, that of the sower, who is the Son of Man himself (Mt 13:37). Christ, when he expounds the Kingdom of God in parables, necessarily expounds himself, not, however, as a "doctrine", but as the reality to which man can only say Yes or no.

In this consists its difference from the invitation of wisdom in the words that sum up the Old Covenant: "Draw near to me, ye unlearned: and gather yourselves together into the house of discipline. . . . And submit your neck to the yoke: and let your neck receive discipline. For she is near at hand to be found. Behold with your eyes how I have labored a little and have found much rest to myself" (Sir 51:23, 26–27). This wisdom at rest in itself after a little labor is in contrast with the open heart of God, which receives all the humbled in its own humiliation that they may find rest and can only do so by giving them to share this yoke of humiliation. In consequence, the yoke of the new law leads directly on to the yoke of the Cross, which the Christian, in his following, has to take on himself. If we want to set out all the implications of "carrying the Cross" according to the words of Jesus, we notice that the expression could not have been used before Peter's confession (Mt 16:16; Mk 8:29; Lk 9:20; Jn 6:68–69)—in Matthew 10:38, therefore, it is used in anticipation. In it we have the inmost depths of Christ's heart revealed to the fullness of faith of the Twelve (Mt 16:21) and in the heart of Christ the exposition of the Trinitarian decree from eternity (Jn 1:18; 3:16). Once again, it is not the exterior act but the interior sentiment that, as God's attitude and settled disposition, is transfused unreservedly into the faith of the Church. The follower and imitator of Christ is initiated into this attitude of God, and not into his unique and inimitable act of redemption, in such a way that he is primarily given the charge not to perform something but to let the disposition and the consequent act of God come to pass in himself; or rather, to see himself as admitted to this attitude and act of God as his true sphere, from which follows, in the absolute logic of revelation, the "go thou and do in like manner". And since God's unique resolve to redeem in forgiveness was taken in eternity, the attitude of the Christian also has an element of eternity, reaching beyond all temporal standards ("seventy times seven" [Mt 18:22]) and immune to all objections based on personal reciprocity (Mt 5:20f.). It is therefore something outside all human probability, impressive, striking, and demonstrative (Jn 13:35).

This is the context in which to view the few texts in the Gospel that speak of "imitation" rather than of "following". In Matthew 11:29, we have "learn from me", learn, that is, the meekness and humility that reflect, for men, the heart of God and that should be reflected in the disposition and actions of man, as the parable of the unmerciful servant shows. The two other passages also directly envisage the interior disposition. The first (Mt 20:26–28) is Christ's instruction occasioned by the petition of the mother of the sons of Zebedee: "Whoever would be great among you must be your servant, and whoever would be the first among you must be your slave; even as the Son of Man came not to be served but to serve and to give his life as a ransom for many." Here we have the first teaching; the example follows as a kind of appendage, an illustration, a confirmation by the most extreme instance. This doctrine, so opposite to all exercise of power in the world (v. 25), is, in order to be shown as practicable, hidden in the special sphere of the Lord. For the act of the Son of Man that is adduced in elucidation—his act, which sums up in itself all that is peculiarly his—is precisely what is inimitable and unique. Here we are not taken so far as we are later by St. John, when he demands that because "he laid down his life for us . . . we ought to lay down our lives for the brethren" (1 Jn 3:16). Only by way of parenthesis had the Gospel previously said the same: "This is my commandment, that you love one another as I have loved you. Greater love has no man than this, that a man lay down his life for his friends" (Jn 15:12–13). Matthew emphasizes the disparity: only the Lord can give his life as a redemption; it is for the disciples to make theirs the disposition to be servants and to strive for the lowest place (see Lk 14:7–11). Following the Lord to his own Cross can be promised by the Lord only after his

Resurrection as the most excellent of graces (Jn 21:18), and as such its full implications were worked out by St. Paul.

The doctrine, also, on the occasion of the washing of the feet (Jn 13:13-17), which contains the word *example,* is still a doctrine of love humbling and abasing itself; though the element of imitation, in fact the strict command of imitation, only comes in the second place, whereas the first explanation, made in the course of the action, gives it a sacramental character and therefore one inimitable by the disciples. What Jesus alone can do—to give, through the washing, community with himself, that is, to take man's sins on himself—that Peter cannot. But the disposition in which the Lord does what cannot be imitated Peter can and must imitate through the outward example and inward grace of the Lord. This distinction seems the solution, but is it really? Is it possible, in the case of the Lord himself, to distinguish disposition and action? Is not the disposition—in the very act of washing the feet—the love that goes "to the end" (Jn 13:1) and so to the Cross? And how should a sinner "imitate" this disposition of the utmost purity, indeed proper to the Godhead, unless the miracle of sacramental washing precedes, carrying over all the feeble and fragile work of the sinner into the very sphere of Christ with all its efficacy at once human and divine?

3. The point at which following can become imitation, that of "having the same mind as Christ Jesus" (Phil 2:5), is the heart and the total of all Christian ethics as summarized by Matthew in the Sermon on the Mount. It runs through all the individual commandments, not to develop them in a material sense but to bring them under the permanent Christian form, which is nothing less than Christ's own personal way of thinking. It is always pointing the way from promise to fulfillment, while emphasizing how close the promise is to its fulfillment (the Beatitudes) and yet how clearly fulfillment goes far beyond promise. The ethics of Christ is an exposition of his personal way of thinking, only to be understood in the light of his own personality. It is not framed in view of man and his possibilities but in view of Christ and what is possible to God. Thus it extends to the renunciation of one's rights, and of power, and even of one's honor, which the natural

law enjoins every man to preserve. It even goes so far as to eliminate the distinction between friend and enemy, and by way of not merely counsel but of command; not as a remote ideal but as a condition for entering the Kingdom of heaven (Mt 5:20), for obtaining the Father's forgiveness of sin (6:14–15), and for avoiding God's judgment (7:1). Human laws expressing the relationship between reality and appearances are subjected to a remorseless criticism, not because social religion is to be changed into something individual but because both the social and the individual aspects are assessed according to the attitude of the incarnate God. Thus "good works" done in public, prayer in public, fasting in the public view, give way to what the Father sees in secret. The command not to be solicitous means that the criterion is not the nature of the external work but God's judgment, showing that the whole ethic is constructed in view of God and the perfection of the "Father in heaven". It is the ethic of "but I say to you", justifying such a displacement of values, since he vindicates the most ignominious of humiliations and sufferings on the part of his followers: "Blessed are you when men revile you and persecute you and utter all kinds of evil against you falsely on my account. Rejoice and be glad" (5:11–12). From now on, what is to be made visible is the glory of the Cross. That is the city set on a mountain, the light in the candlestick, the good work that must shine before men, so that they may see it and praise the Father.

The problem raised by this ethic seems insoluble, for it is undoubtedly an ethic for men. Each commandment taken by itself seems a possibility, something within human fulfillment, so much so that the Sermon on the Mount has been seen as a summing up of the humanistic attitude. Yet, taken as a whole, it is certainly beyond human capability, utopian or eschatological. It is something that takes no account of real human relationships in all their complexity, something wholly out of this world and above it and therefore undermining the foundations of human society. If anyone does not feel this, he has never experienced a single breath of the scorching, piercing air of the gospel. Protestant attempts at a solution have this much in their favor, that they bear witness to an experience of the shock of these words. Such an attempt is the idealistic Kantian solution of the liberals, who see Christ's demands as a kind of ideal scale of values, an eternal standard by which reality is to be measured. Another is the eschato- logical solution of the radical followers of Schweitzer, for whom the Sermon on the Mount can only be seen as a (utopian) interim ethic valid till the judgment shortly to come to pass. Then there is the dialectical solution of the Barthians and the later Lutherans, for whom the whole program is actually carried out only by Christ; in him alone *peccatores* are *justi,* and Christians bear witness by their attempt to bring this program into the light. All three realize the vast, humanly unbridgeable gulf between man's real condition and the reality here demonstrated. There can never be any question of transition, approximation, advance from one to the other, in the sense of from below to above. In consequence, it can only be a matter of a lofty guiding ideal or of an eschatological miracle, with which the sinner, as such, has nothing to do.

None of these approaches to a theological ethic is adequate to compass the whole situation as given, but they do all face the diffi- culty that arises from the disparity between the human and divine standpoints. The same cannot be said of the pure religious and social ethic, which presents the Sermon on the Mount as simply a program to be realized in the sphere of the inner sentiments as Christian and human; and yet this ethic, in contrast with the other three, takes account of one side of the matter as given, namely, the sober duty of man to fulfill the program. It must, indeed, be fulfilled, but this is not humanly possible. It is possible, though, in Christ, quite apart from assuming any dialectical or idealistic gulf between the realities of earth and heaven. It is, in fact, possible in the contact between the faith that "follows" and the divine heart opening itself through grace, in the contact made by the believer in leaving all things, so as, without reflection on himself (for he must abandon and "hate" himself), to approach the Lord and, with the Lord, his Father and his human brethren. His part is to make an act of obedience in faith, and his attitude must be one of surrender to the Lord, which allows himself to be informed by him. In this respect, the Christian life is, in the strictest sense, above and beyond all psychology.

The point we have now reached is the source of the Christian mission, which, however, in its theological structure, has already reached the stage at which authority in the Church, in the strict sense, comes into being. Where the paradox of "following" results for Protestantism in a dialectic is just where, for Catholics, it results in mission and office. For the Catholic these are not factors that make it possible for man, of himself, to conjure away the disparity involved in the idea of "following"; they are what God himself takes into his own hands to end the disparity. "With men this is impossible, but with God all things are possible" (Mt 19:26). For God as Creator is a God of form and of the beautiful; for his greatest works he makes use even of sin and its consequences, and of the Cross, too, which will not "be emptied of its power" (1 Cor 1:17). The act of surrender in faith under the impulse of grace is therefore answered by God with investiture with "the form of Christ", which will be formed in the Christian (Gal 4:19) so that he, in turn, may become a "form" for others (1 Th 1:7). This form, as common to all Christians, is the soil from which springs authority in the Church, the "pattern for the flock" (1 Pet 5:3) which is a form specially established by Christ. It is not to be conceived democratically as derived from the first, but presupposes it, and thereby is understandable as a universal Christian element. The words *form* and *pattern* are makeshifts that cannot do justice to all the chief elements, notably the vitality and personality of the new life in Christ established by God, which Paul compares with "putting on" a garment, Christ himself (Rom 13:14; Gal 3:27), or dynamically, putting on "the new nature, which is being renewed in knowledge, after the image of its Creator" (Col 3:10). Yet this image (which, to be properly understood, demands a full treatment of the ancient usage of clothing and assimilating, of walking along with and transforming, to mean the same thing, is, for us, something external, whereas "form" supposes an inner principle imposing a pattern, and this Paul is equally fond of using.

This form of Christ has its source in the, so to speak, material, feminine principle of the surrender of faith, "leaving all things", and in the formal, male principle of grace giving itself and imprinting itself on the believer, in whom it is a participation, in Jesus Christ, in the life of the Trinity. This life of grace, therefore, even insofar as it is "form", is by no means "impersonal". We must not misunderstand the statement, theologically unimpeachable, that God's natural works and supernatural graces *ad extra* are *communia*. It is, rather, "suprapersonal", in the sense of a participation in the vitality of the interchange of life between the three Persons. The Christian life, lived as it should be, is evidence and confirmation, though in a mysterious fashion and inexpressible in words, of this suprapersonal quality of life, for true holiness is always a psychological enigma.

The condition for its attainment is the right relationship between man and grace. The more pliable, abandoned, and free from his self-form the believer is, the better can the divine image and the form of Christ be impressed on him. *Ecce ancilla Domini.* Consequently, the less a man himself reaches out to a form, clings to one, and the more freely in "leaving all things" he holds himself ready for the reception of the form of God and the less he reflects on his own creaturely being and fancies that he knows in advance who he is, the better the process of his being "put on" succeeds (2 Cor 5:2), and the more unhindered does Christ live in him as in one of his members, the Spirit live in him as in his temple (Gal 2:20; 1 Cor 6:15, 19). The faith that "leaves all" is, however, not one's own achievement. It is preceded by redemption through the blood of Christ, God's taking possession of man, the fact that "you are not your own" (1 Cor 6:19) and that, therefore, "those who live might live no longer for themselves but for him who for their sake died and was raised" (2 Cor 5:15). The believer is thus humbled by his faith (and through seeing what has been done for him), and his humiliation is the condition for his elevation by God (Mt 23:12; Lk 14:11; 18:14). And the more the form freely given is imprinted on and consciously present to the individual and to the community, the greater must be the bearer's sense of humility, the more profound his abasement. This applies, above all, to the ministry in the Church; and equally to the mission demanding a special holiness. The form of the Christian as it develops never has the effect of eliminating the double paradox of "following" and "imitation"; in fact, it brings it out more sharply. The more the servant, sent out and commissioned, represents the Lord—not only externally by a function to be discharged but also internally by his life and person — the more profoundly does he see himself in contradistinction to the Lord. As long as he is really the Lord's servant, nothing can be further from his mind than to equate himself, in any point whatever, with the Lord. Just because he sets this distance between himself and the Lord, the form of Christ and of God is infused into him. We may even say that inasmuch as the servant more deeply feels himself to be, on a quite other plane, different from the Lord, the more like him he becomes, like him who took on the *forma servi* and was found "in habit like to a man", obedient even unto the Cross, so that he might come to know the extreme disparity between the sinner and the Father, and, as God's Son, to surmount it.

4. Now we must look closely at the investiture with the form of Christ as shown in the gospel, not as an isolated act but in its connection with the manifestation of Jesus himself. Once again, it is Mark who takes us closest to the source. The beginning and end of his Gospel are governed by the idea of the *exousia,* the fullness of power. Its manifestation is the main point of the various callings recorded in the beginning.

There is first the *exousia* over the world of spirits. This is preceded by the temptation by the devil and the ministration of the angels in the desert and followed by the calling of the first four disciples, who leave all things. Then follow the first showing of the *exousia* in the synagogue at Capernaum, the first outbreak of astonishment, the first encounters with unclean spirits (1:23, 26, 27, 32, 34, 39). In 2:10f., the casting out of the devil is both forgiveness of sins and a manifestation of the *exousia.* Then there are the calling of the tax collectors and the feast with publicans and sinners, and the "I came not to call the righteous, but sinners" (2:17).

There is, secondly, the exousia over the law: that of fasting, which he declares inappropriate while the bridegroom is present; that of the Sabbath, of which the Son of Man is the Lord, as is evidenced both by the disciples plucking the ears of corn and by the healing of the man with the withered hand. The Pharisees are beside themselves with indignation and already resolve upon his death.

And there is, in the third place, the imparting of his own unprecedented *exousia* to the disciples, recorded in the same sentence, practically, as their calling: "And he . . . called to him those whom he desired; and they came to him. And he appointed twelve, to be with him, and to be sent out to preach and have authority [*exousia*] to cast out demons" (3:13–15). This he repeats at the actual sending: "And he called to him the Twelve, and began to send them out two by two, and gave them authority over the unclean spirits. . . . So they went out and preached that men should repent. And they cast out many demons and anointed with oil many that were sick and healed them" (6:7, 12–13). It was because of this that he was alleged to be possessed and so gave his instruction about the unclean spirit and the Holy Spirit. The theme of his encounter with spirits is continued (5:1–18; 6:7, 12; 7:25–29).

Finally, the question of *exousia* is again the central one: "By what authority [*exousia*] are you doing these things?" (11:28), but the question is countered with another and remains unanswered. The solution is given in the growing revelation of his sonship, manifested more and more as something sublime and unique (12:6, 37; 13:26, 32; 14:62; 15:2, 39). The final scene establishes once again and forever the *exousia* of those he sends forth (16:17–18).

We see, then, a unique personality who arouses consternation and bafflement wherever he goes, working miracles while remaining in his state of solitude, somewhat like a meteor impinging on the world, proclaiming his power from above over the world of spirits and asking from men no more than the courage to believe. And the most striking thing about it all is the suddenness with which his *exousia* is imparted to twelve men without education or preparation, with no period of transition; and then, so endowed, they are sent forth.

In the account in St. Matthew, the investiture with this power is no less sudden. There is, indeed, a distinction made between the passages where Christ speaks of the Kingdom of God (the Sermon on the Mount, vv. 5–7) and that in which he sends out the Twelve (v. 10). In the former, he speaks of the way of life in general; in the latter, of the conduct to be observed in the discharge of the ministry; on the one hand, of life in the world as a Christian among other men; on the other, of opposition to the world to which the apostle comes with his commission, from which he must guard himself, at whose hatred he is not to be surprised. The discourse on the Kingdom is indeed delivered in the presence of a great multitude, but it is the disciples who come to him and whom he instructs (5:2). The final Beatitude of those who are persecuted "for my sake" and have evil spoken of them is reinforced by allusion to "the prophets who were before you", obviously before the disciples. They are the salt of the earth, the city on a hill, the light on the candlestick; and, since the subject is not changed, it is to be assumed that all that follows is addressed to them, in the presence of the listening crowd. The Head of the Church is teaching the entire Church, consisting of clergy and people. There is no secret doctrine for the disciples; every word that concerns them in particular also applies to the whole Church in general, and whatever applies to the people applies in a special manner to the disciples.

Even the parables, which he afterward explains to his disciples apart, he first utters to the "great multitudes" (13:1–2, 36). And so Peter, on the occasion of the parable of the watchful servant (Lk 12:35–40), can express the doubt: "Lord, are you telling this parable for us or for all?" The Lord answers by bringing out the nature of the Church's ministry, that of the faithful and prudent steward set over the household to give it food in season and to whom the Lord has entrusted the administration of all his goods. Since he knows his Lord's will, he will be held to a much stricter account than one who does not know it (12:42–48). Likewise, the disciples are constantly admonished not to be, like the people, "without understanding" (Mt 15:16; 16:9; Mk 7:18), for to them "it has been given to know the secrets of the Kingdom of heaven", but not to the rest (Mt 13:11). It is, then, of slight importance that, in Luke, some of the Sermon on the Mount is preached to the "multitudes" (Lk 11:29f.), some to his disciples in the presence of so great multitudes "that they trod upon one another" (Lk 12:1), and some only to his disciples as the "little flock" (Lk 12:22, 32). More significant is the fact that the doctrine of carrying the cross in the following of Christ and of the necessity of hating everything occurs, in Matthew, in the discourse to the Twelve as they were sent on their mission (10:37–38) but in Luke is addressed to the "great multitudes" (14:25–27), and carrying the cross is designated as a "daily" necessity. Even the statement "whoever of you does not renounce all that he has cannot be my disciple" (14:33) is addressed to the whole people. This cannot be explained by a subsequent "ethicalization" of Christ's original and literal demand. Luke's is by no means a watered-down Gospel. The words of his Gospel, in fact, have a twofold meaning, just as they do in Matthew. In a narrower sense they are for a more restricted circle, and in a more general sense (though in no less a grave and literal way) they are for a wider circle. The distinction between the two circles is a somewhat fluid one, inasmuch as the mission discourse, taking up as it does apostleship, in Mark and Matthew is addressed to the Twelve, but in Luke to the seventy-two (10:1), who are expressly commissioned. But can we therefore say that the seventy-two are necessarily also invested with the ministry? Their being sent out "as lambs among wolves", without purse, scrip, or shoes, to announce the Kingdom, heal the sick, and thus to be worthy of the reward, can also be applied in an unforced way to the laity—say, to those Roman soldiers who, as they moved with the army from place to place, spread the Kingdom of God everywhere. Why should not the closing words be applicable even to the seventy-two: "He who hears you hears me" (10:16), since, according to the account they gave to the Lord of their mission, the spirits also were subject to them?

We may, indeed, try to establish a sharp distinction between those who follow in the literal sense—that is, all men or women who accompany the Lord in his journeys (Lk 9:1–3)—and those who do not or who are, in fact, prevented by the Lord, like the possessed Gerasene (Mk 5:18–20; Lk 8:38–39), who is subsequently given an "apostolate" in the midst of the world. But such a distinction is not altogether clear. The prohibition is made, in this case, more in view of the man's previous life than in order to establish an actual "lay apostolate". In any case, such a slender thread cannot be made to support a theological proposition. And then it is reasonable to consider the friends of Jesus in Bethany, who, though outwardly "lay people in the world", certainly belong inwardly to those who have "left all things" and, in their own fashion (Mt 26:10–13), fulfill a universal function in the Church. The same may be said of Mary

Magdalen, with her function in the Church as representative of sinners redeemed, an office performed in the public life of Jesus, both beneath the Cross and at Easter.

This is the general setting in which we should consider the various utterances of the Lord gathered together in Matthew 10 as his discourse to those he was sending out. There is no part of it that does not concern every Christian, but none also that does not receive special force and character from the circumstance of the sending of the Twelve. Some parts were spoken to them in particular and may, *per extensionem* or in special circumstances, be of application to all. Others primarily concern every Christian, and those in authority must simply pay special attention to them. These are such passages as "A disciple is not above his teacher, nor a servant above his master; it is enough for the disciple to be like his teacher, and the servant like his master. If they have called the master of the house Beelzebul, how much more will they malign those of his household?" (Mt 10:24–25). In the end, the Christian who is sent is not given any privileged reception on the part of the world, whether he is one of those formally "sent" or one of the "prophets" or one of the "just", or simply "one of these little ones" (10:40–42). The structure of existence, the "Christian form", is the same for all four.

Yet it would be a grave error to conclude from this that, in the New Covenant, there is no more than a "universal priesthood" or that authority here is nothing but a universal charismatic quality in the Church more strongly imprinted on certain individuals. The Twelve, chosen out by name from the very beginning and designated apostles in a specific sense, are they who were present from the outset and remained when most of the others left (Jn 6:66), who "continued with me in my trials" (Lk 22:28), who pronounced the decisive words of the confession and received the keys (Mt 16:18; 18:18), were given the function and authority to celebrate the Eucharist and to bind and loose sins (Lk 22:19; Jn 20:23). It was to them as a college that the risen Christ appeared; to them he finally opened the meaning of the Scriptures (Lk 24:45); to them he imparted the final commission and the great apostolic promise (Mt 28:16–20). Office and power hold fast together and are never impugned in the period covered by the Acts of the Apostles; St. Paul's whole theology of the apostolate presupposes their recognition. But this does not mean that the form of life of those in authority is essentially different from that of the others. It is, in fact, the same, and the Gospels confirm this in making no hard and fast distinction between them, without thereby prejudicing the universal transposition from the "flesh" to the "spirit", from an earthly and literal understanding to a spiritual and free interpretation. For the Son, in his mortal life, must speak and act within the world of time and space as one subject to death, but his words are "spirit and life" (Jn 6:63) and "shall not pass away" (Mt 13:31), because the Spirit hears and explains them (Jn 16:13) and makes them coextensive with all time. In the same way, Jesus expressed in geographical terms his sending the disciples out into the world (Mt 10:5-6; Lk 24:47; Acts 1:8), and the Spirit raises it to a higher potentiality in which Jerusalem, the geographical center and point of departure, is superseded, and the mission goes out everywhere from every place. Now everywhere is a "holy land", and everywhere is "strange" (I Pet 2:11), and from the mortal word comes forth the immortal meaning.

4. Form and imitation

The words *âme* and *ôme* mean "measure". To "amen" a vessel means to take its measure, its dimensions. And *ahmen, nachahmen* (to imitate) means to take the measure of a thing or person, so as to know it and in certain circumstances use it in the formation of new structures.

Christ had of necessity put himself forward as an example to his "pupils" and followers, even if this word is used only in John, and then only once (13:15). The word and the idea remain in the background, because imitation involves the interplay of two meanings: imitation of what is absolutely inimitable, of one who is unique of his kind; and imitation of those who fail even in the presence of Christ, because in him on the Cross sin is brought to the light of day. Never in the Gospel is the following, the imitation, of the Lord described as something to be achieved by degrees. The disciples are, to a great extent, stage figures, activated by the words of the Lord, by whose failures the Master demonstrates his own wisdom and infallibility and over whom, quite unexpectedly, almost like a costume, the "armor" (Eph 6:11) of an apostle and messenger of Christ is suddenly thrown along with all the powers appertaining to it: they are given a role with which they have to identify themselves. One may perhaps speak, on the plane of psychology, of a certain gradual "growing into" this role, but the decisive factors in their training are the Cross and the absolute failure of Judas, Peter, and the rest who fled (even John slept and left the Lord alone). For what happened here was no fiction, no mere exercise in humiliation, but a real, fruitful humiliation, which alone brought to successful conclusion the attempts to "leave all" and so made them capable of receiving authority.

The threefold denial is given an almost liturgical form in the Gospels, so that it is an essential part not only of the passion but also of the ceremony by which the ministry is instituted. The threefold denial recalls the threefold, Trinitarian question, "Do you love me?" (Jn 21:17) and has the same liturgical and symbolic overtones as the upside-down crucifixion of Peter foretold immediately afterward (21:18–19). This fits in with the concluding passage, which disposes, with divine irony, of Peter's question in his official capacity about John's remaining (that of the Johannine Church within or without the Petrine): "What is that to you?" (21:22–23). This brings out clearly the limits within which the holder of office in the Church is representative of Christ and also, for the last time, the appropriate treatment of the ministry by the Head, one of honor combined with an ever renewed and intensified humbling. All of Peter's qualities as they become manifest—his well-meaning impulsiveness, his evasiveness at the prospect of the Cross, his striking out from secret fear, the bravura of his faith, which makes him lose his head when he comes to reflect—all these are used for humiliation, because "the greatest among you" must become as "the youngest, and the leader as the one who serves" (Lk 22:26). Peter is, with those like him, firmly grounded in the paradox of the ceremony of institution and never forgets it. It is only thus, as stamped therewith, branded, that he can become an example to his flock (1 Pet 5:3). His denial is no chance occurrence, for nothing in the Passion happens by chance. It is necessary as an essential element in the instilling of the "form" as foreordained for the way of life of those in the ministry. Once again: the "form" is not the ministry itself. It is the unity made up of the man as he is ("a failure") and the commission given by divine grace from above. This unity gives its determinate structure to the Christian life in general and to that of the ministry in particular, its authenticity for those endowed with supernatural perception, its wholeness unimpaired by all the criticisms of the world.

This form is always represented when the disciples, in the Acts, give testimony before Jews and Gentiles, before the Sanhedrin and the Roman officials. It is especially what St. Paul means when it appears in his writings as a distinct reality that has to be recognized and can be proposed to the community for imitation: "Brethren, join in imitating me, and mark those who so live as you have an example in us" (Phil 3:17). *Typos* is actually something hammered out, stamped out, an outline to guide, which withstands every kind of verification and on which psychology, Christian or otherwise, breaks its teeth in vain. But here everything is enigmatic and becomes more so the more it is analyzed and its individual characteristics and motivational forces distinguished. What St. Paul calls form is, however, indivisible, and the only motivational force in human events, even though it is rightly perceptible only with the eyes of faith.

This image impressed has no independent status, aesthetically or ethically. In other words, however perfectly it is realized in the person of the apostle, the person himself is quite secondary, in fact nugatory, for he does not make his own imprint or present himself but is purely the material for the form and the power of God to make itself present. The *typos* can be, in a way, static, full, and perfect—and so really be put forward as an exemplar for imitation—while the person bearing it is still long engaged in struggle and imperfection. Hence the paradox of the Letter to the Philippians, which enjoins imitation of the supreme Exemplar, Christ, with his sentiments of love and suffering (2:5–11), and this "without grumbling or questioning" so as to become "blameless and innocent, children of God". And yet, this salvation is to be worked out "with fear and trembling", conscious, therefore, of one's own failings and fearful of losing it. It is a question of realizing a perfect form in the extreme imperfection of personal effort, the two opposing extremes being united by the pure grace of God, "at work in you, both to will [personal, imperfect] and to work [achievement]" (2:12–13). What is demanded of the faithful is once more demonstrated beforehand in the apostle, the one who has "left all" (3:8), who, for that reason, is free and suitable for the office of being *typos*. For the image he offers and proposes has a real power of imprinting itself (3:17), so much so that he enjoins them to look not only on this imprint but also on those already stamped with it, to walk according to them; nor does he hesitate to call them "perfect" (3:15). Yet this static image only comes to be in that Paul is convinced that he has not yet "attained" the goal, is not "already perfect", but "I press on to make it [perfection] my own, because Christ Jesus has made me his own. Brethren, I do not consider that I have made it my own; but one thing I do, forgetting what lies behind and straining forward to what lies ahead, I press on toward the goal for the prize of the upward call of God in Christ Jesus" (3:12–14).

We must observe that the "static" form, which Paul puts forward as model, is by no means the "office", nor is the "dynamic" factor the person who strives to realize the ideal embodied in the office. In fact, the *typos* is precisely the man Paul striving with such intensity (in contrast to the other persons in the ministry who "all look after their own interests, not those of Jesus Christ" [2:21]), who in the directness of his course presents an image that is adequate and compelling. The office pure and simple with its authority Paul sees only as a last resort, a threat: I have the right, the power, in virtue of my office to demand this of you, but since I have to represent Christ to you, I do not use it (Philemon 8; 2 Cor 13:2, 10). It is easy to threaten with the rod of office, but those reprimanded must be induced to prefer charity to the rod: this is the art of Paul (1 Cor 4:21). It is, indeed, no human, personal, psychological art, but a divine one: "I was with you in weakness and fear and much trembling. And my speech and my preaching were not in the persuasive words of human wisdom but in the showing of the Spirit and power; that your faith might not stand on the wisdom of men but on the power of God" (1 Cor 2:3–5). And yet, there is no absolute cleavage between the preaching and the weakness of the man. The Spirit of God is active in both and brings both into a unity established by him, for "we have received . . . the Spirit that is from God, that we might understand the gifts bestowed on us by God. And we impart this in words not taught by human wisdom but taught by the Spirit. . . . Yet among the mature do we impart wisdom . . . a secret and hidden wisdom of God" (2 Cor 2:12–13, 6, 7), It is only the combination of the two that results in the "image" to be imitated, for, were it not for his weaknesses, the foolishness, nakedness, homelessness, persecution, and calumny, the image of the crucified would not be stamped on the life of the person sent. Those holding the first place must be as "apostles, as last of all, like men sentenced to death" (1 Cor 4:9); otherwise, they are not images expressing Christ. For this reason, the gloss is correct that to the exhortation "be imitators of me" adds the words "as I also am of Christ" (1 Cor 4:16), though Paul never puts the two images on the same level. For if his own life is one marked with the form of the Cross (Gal 2:19; Col 1:24), yet the voluntary, innocent suffering of Christ is beyond all comparison with the sufferings of the "first of sinners" (1 Tim 1:15). This contrast is always presupposed when the one is held as a reproduction and expression of the other (2 Tim 3:10–12), or a just parallel drawn between Christ's crucifixion "in weakness" but living "in the power of God" and Paul's being "weak in him" and living "by the power of God" (2 Cor 13:4).

Once again we see how Paul, so far from presuming on his official position to admonish the community for its manner of life, does just the opposite. He refers to his manner of life in order to shake them out of their certainties, of being "already filled, already become rich", already reigning (1 Cor 4:8). It is not by his office that the apostle represents Christ for the community but as one humiliated in Christ, made "a spectacle to the world, to angels, and to men" (v. 20). To be a person sent, one must have died and have been crucified to the world, and this must be apparent in the office. Consequently, he owes it to the office to show forth subsequently in his person this essential condition that it presupposes. If he does this, then, and only then, is the office discharged in a Christian way and has the same theological and apologetic force for both Christians and non-Christians as the

Christian's witness with his life, which, indeed, is a witness only as a dying with Christ into the new God-given form.

This makes clear the meaning of 2 Corinthians 5:11–21, where Paul attributes the source of the official mission to the fact of dying with Christ and to the "new creature" that results. This dying with Christ is not simply to be understood sacramentally (Rom 6:3f.; Col 3:3) as a fact but is the outcome of the "charity that presses us", from the thought that "if one died for all, then all were dead . . . and may not now live to themselves." This radical self-renunciation, in order "to live in Christ", means becoming "a new creature". This "new creature" is, moreover, not only a passive transference into Christ, but—since the form of Christ is imparted to us—an active sharing in him, an active reception into us of Christ's mission: "All this is from God, who through Christ reconciled us to himself and gave us the ministry of reconciliation; that is, God was in Christ reconciling the world to himself, not counting their trespasses against them, and entrusting to us the message of reconciliation. So we are ambassadors for Christ, God making his appeal through us. We beseech you on behalf of Christ, be reconciled to God. For our sake he made him to be sin who knew no sin, so that in him we might become the righteousness of God" (2 Cor 5:18–21).

Christ's being made sin is something over and above his person and office; it is the outcome of his perfect love and obedience to the Father, these two being identical. The Christian, the apostle, is steeped in this form of Christ and made a new creature; and in him, therefore, only one form can come into being, one that is the product of love and the ministerial office indissolubly conjoined. The "ministry of reconciliation" between God and the world can only mean the "beseeching word of reconciliation", though "the Kingdom of God does not consist in speech but in power" (1 Cor 4:20), and, consequently, for the discharge of this embassy of Christ and collaboration with God (2 Cor 6:1), nothing short of total commitment of life is sufficient (6:4–10), putting "no obstacle in any one's way, so that no fault may be found with our ministry" (6:3). Paul lays abundant stress on the special commission given him by God, the ministerial charisma, which is passed on by the imposition of hands (2 Tim 1:6); and it stamps the person called to be a *typos* for the Church in that he puts his whole life at its disposal. Likewise, the First Letter of Peter makes those in the ministry a *forma gregis* in that, far from exercising it under compulsion or by compelling others, they are, like Peter himself, "witnesses of the sufferings of Christ", which means two things: presence, as betrayer and bitterly repentant, at Christ's Passion, and witness thereto by his own passion (1 Pet 5:1–4).

This life of bearing witness is as unique in Christianity and beyond rational analysis as is the mystery of Christ himself. In this aspect, the form of life of Paul and of every Christian is just as much an article of faith (part of the *credo Ecclesiam*) as are those concerning Christ. But the official character of the apostle and his disciple is no harder to accept than the possibility of the Christian form of life in general. As Paul is *typos* for the communities, so are the communities of Judaea *typos* for those of Thessalonica (1 Th 1:7). Nor does either consciously aim at "exemplarity", for "it is required of stewards [only] that they be found trustworthy", neither judging themselves nor caring how others judge them (1 Cor 4:3). The Christian does not belong to himself but to God and the Church, and only so is he *typos* and "fellow workers of God" (1 Cor 3:9). In himself he is nothing, merely a "servant" (1 Cor 3:5; 4:1; 2 Cor 4:5). And precisely in the extent to which Christians are servants can they be fruitful and become "fathers" of the communities (1 Cor 4:15; 1 Th 2:7, 11). What is not capable of analysis is the relationship between surrendering what is one's own and imparting to others what is divine, wherein what is also imparted is what was surrendered and is now become new. The lover, who desires to possess nothing and gives up all he has, in fact possesses all things, and the most needy can enrich all men (2 Cor 6:10).

This, however, is the mystery of God in Christ himself; and, therefore, the Christian *typos* reaches out in an uninterrupted ascent from Paul to Christ and to God. He thus carries on the gospel idea of following and imitation, supplementing, it may be, the more Jewish terminology by the more Greek one of "imitation" but preserving its content. If the Sermon on the Mount demands that Christians "be perfect, as your heavenly Father is perfect" (Mt 5:48), namely, in *caritas,* which makes no distinction between friend and enemy, Paul says the same, in effect, when he urges Christians to "be kind to one another, tenderhearted, forgiving one another, as God in Christ forgave you", and to "walk in love, as Christ loved us and gave himself up for us, a fragrant offering and sacrifice to God" (Eph 4:32 to 5:2). Once again, following and imitation refer to the central disposition, to humility and gentleness, love, forgiveness, mutual reconciliation, patience in bearing with weaknesses and scandals. In such a way does Paul present the great exemplar of the Son coming down in the form of a servant, in obedience and the ignominy of the Cross (Phil 2:1–11); so too does Romans 15:2–7 point to Christ as a model for the "strong", who are to bear the infirmities of the weak and not to please themselves: "Welcome one another, therefore, as Christ has welcomed you, for the glory of God" (15:7). Yet again, Paul this time adducing his own example intermediately, in 1 Corinthians (10:32 to 11:1): "Give no offense to Jews or to Greeks or to the Church of God, just as I try to please all men in everything I do, not seeking my own advantage but that of many, that they may be saved. Be imitators of me, as I am of Christ."

Paul and Christ can even be conjoined with the community as a single exemplar (1 Th 1:6–7). The unity consists in having "left all things" and having taken up obediently the divine commission. In this way, the Thessalonians can, through receiving the word in much tribulation, be themselves imitators.

Orthodox Protestantism, in contradistinction to pietism, has always, as it does today, rejected the idea of an *imitatio* of Christ as ignoring the distance between him and us, and tantamount to a sacrilege. It is, however, not without interest to observe that, in view of the mimesis texts of St. Paul, this attitude can only be sustained, so it seems, by emphasizing the authority of the apostolic office. For Michaelis, the *typos* is not so much the pattern to be copied as the exemplar to be followed. In Philippians 3:17, though Paul associates himself with other "models" in the community, he has, indisputably, a place apart, grounded in his apostolic office. And although he puts forward his conduct as a model, yet in the demand "be imitators of me" he claims, above all, obedience. It is the same, especially, in 1 Corinthians 4:16; likewise, in reference to this passage, also 1 Corinthians 11:1, and the same in I Thessalonians 1:6, and Ephesians 5:1. Even the other passages where his quality as a pattern is given special prominence, as 2 Thessalonians 5:7 and Philippians 3:17, the factor of his authority is not to be ignored.

We do not contest this factor of authority; in fact, we are glad that it is so frankly recognized. And it is equally clear that Paul, when he puts himself forward as a model, intends only, by his relationship with Christ, to lead men to the unique Lord (2 Cor 4:5). He alone is the image, to which we are "conformed", according to which we are "reformed" through God's grace and the actions of his sacraments but also through our cooperation in action and contemplation (Rom 8:29; 2 Cor 3:18). Paul is a "model" precisely in that he directs himself according to the model of Christ, or rather has been directed according to this model by God's grace, which has given him the ministry. But we are associated with him in virtue of the indissoluble unity of the Christian form of life, which is put forward by Paul as our model only because it is to be understood, not in an ethical or psychological way but in a representative way. With the apostle in particular, and those in the ministry in general, this form has the character that belongs to the office, a character that, as a special "revelation" of the power and authority of Christ "in" the person revealed (Gal 1:16), appears, in actual life, as a heightened, publicly manifested, image of Christ (2 Cor 4:8f.), and this precisely "for your sakes" (v. 15). This instrumental character of the apostolic life, whose humiliations are designed for the exaltation of the community, and suffering for its consolation (1 Cor 4:8–10; 2 Cor 1:6–7), is not a mere functioning of a law of the ministry, in virtual independence; it is simply the "law" of Jesus Christ himself applied to those sent. It is a wholly personal manner of representing Christ, his being poor that we may become rich (2 Cor 8:9), that balance in the Mystical Body that is what manifests, in the social sphere, the heart of the Redeemer. Here too the law holds good according to which the ministry, far from being in contrast with personal following, in fact derives from it, is embedded in it, and that its apparent impersonality is no more than the manifestation of the Trinitarian superpersonality as a constitutive element in the Church by the will of its Founder, the sphere that personal following, by the grace of God, ultimately reaches. If this were not true for the laity also, it would be impossible to understand why and how they should imitate those in the ministry and take them as their model. But as for those in the ministry, their office is so rooted in the very heart of their following that any division between ministry and life, any reliance on the functions of the ministry without personal involvement and sacrifice, can only be an affliction to Paul (Phil 1:15–17; 2:20–21; 3:18–19; 2 Tim 4:1–6), and therefore to Christ whom he represents (Phil 3:10).

All this is confirmed in the other epistles of the New Testament. That to the Hebrews makes Christians followers of all those who believed before them and, if we take together all the examples adduced, calls faith a spiritual "leaving all things" in order to stake everything on the promise of God, "going out, not knowing where" (11:8), "sojourning in the land of promise as in a foreign land, living in tents . . . he looked forward to the city that has foundations, whose builder and maker is God" (11:9–10). No possessions, therefore, even in the holy land, only a prospect of a heavenly country. Considering "abuse suffered for the Christ greater wealth than the treasures of Egypt" (11:26). "Mocking and scourging, and even chains and imprisonment (11:36) but also overpowering of earthly contrivances: conquest of kingdoms, exercise of justice, valor in battle (11:33–44). Thus faith is, indeed, a protective form into which man enters by leaving himself, which exposes him naked to God's loving chastisement (12:4–11), while at the same time assuring him an impregnable fortress, armor that cannot be pierced. And always "looking to Jesus, the pioneer and perfecter of our faith, who for the joy that was set before him endured the Cross, despising the shame. . . . Consider him who endured from sinners such hostility against himself, so that you may not grow weary or fainthearted" (12:2–3). Undoubtedly, here Christ himself (as in the beginning of Mark) is seen in the form of life that, with us, is called faith, even though it may be disputed whether faith is ascribed to him formally or *eminenter*. What is certain is that, by his form, he is the author and finisher of the form of faith. In chapter 13, which is certainly by Paul and perhaps comes from a lost epistle, the leaders of the community are mentioned: "Remember your leaders, those who spoke to you the word of God; consider the outcome of their life, and imitate their faith" (13:7). Looking to the end (*respice finem*) is what brings out the full meaning of their life as a form of faith. This is what is put forward for imitation and now expressly bound up with obedience to those in charge of souls (13:17).

Peter's first letter places the believer straightway in the supernatural form of faith. He is "born anew to a living hope", "to an inheritance ...in heaven", through his existence in this form directed to the eschatological manifestation of salvation. Here also the prophetic existence of the Old Covenant is adduced as serving and ordained to this form of faith of the New (1:1–12). This form requires, as in the Old Covenant, the reproduction in man of the holiness of God (Lev 11:44), walking as "obedient children" in the form of God himself and therefore walking "in fear", all the more so as they are children redeemed by the "Lamb without blemish or spot" (1:14–19). Instead of being "fashioned" according to their former desires (1:14), there is now "obedience for love" (1:22); they must be "built up" into the edifice of Christ, the "chief cornerstone", and in it, through him, offer themselves as a spiritual sacrifice. This sublime form is "honor" for the obedient in faith but a scandal to "them that believe not"; once again and finally, by this form, Hosea separates those who are the "people" from those who are "not my people". Again this form is, for the Christian, "conversation", a reality of grace, undeniable and lived, to be shown to the world, that wrongdoers "may see your good deeds and glorify God" (2:1–12).

Obedience to secular authority must be, therefore, to calumniators (of the Christian form as an eschatological revolution), a proof of their belonging to a higher order; the Christian status of "servants of God" must be shown by their good conduct in the secular sphere (2:13–17). In fact, submission to an inconsiderate and hard master becomes an opportunity for the servant to imitate the *forma Christi*. "For to this you have been called, because Christ also suffered for you, leaving you an example, that you should follow in his steps. He committed no sin; no guile was found on his lips. When he was reviled, he did not revile in return; when he suffered, he did not threaten; but he trusted to him who judges justly. He himself bore our sins in his body on the tree, that we might die to sin and live to righteousness. By his wounds you have been healed. For you were straying like sheep, but have now returned to the Shepherd and Guardian of your souls" (2:21, 25).

This is perhaps the strongest passage in the New Testament for the *imitatio Christi* and, like those in the Gospel, brings out the paradox in all its sharpness. Since the form of the Christian in its entirety has been brought about by the sufferings of Christ, and he, in suffering unjustly, bore our sins and carried them to the Cross, we ourselves were originally represented in his sufferings as those wrongdoers whom we now have to bear with in imitation of him. *In tanta similitudine major dissimilitudo.* The contrast cuts across the similarity in such a way that the more the similarity comes to the fore, the more profoundly does the contrast stamp itself on the follower of Christ. Therefore, any danger of confusion with the Redeemer is made more and more remote. Everything in our form is his, even when some merit seems to accrue to us. This is something that Peter constantly repeats in various forms. The Christian form of life for wives preaches more eloquently than the word. It is above all the "being subject", the adaptation to the form, which is for them the married state in the concrete. But the husband must also adapt himself to this ordering, since he and the woman are "joint heirs of the grace of life" (3:1-7). All are obliged to Christian love that does not render "reviling for reviling" (3:9), that "suffers for righteousness' sake" and thus "reverences Christ the Lord" (3:15), him who "died for sins" (3:18) that we, having died, might live with him through resurrection and baptism (3:19-22). Our being exposed before the world, which fails to understand our new way of life, speaking evil and persecuting us (4:3-4), is incapable of harming us (3:13). We are "armed", because we live in the "will of God" (4:2; 3:17; 4:19; 5:6), under whom we humble ourselves and on whom we cast all our care (5:6-7). We are not to trouble ourselves about the form of the Christian but to be content to know that it springs from "the same thought" as the form of Christ suffering (4:1). Consequently, each must, in serving, "administer" his particular form as Christian, his "grace", whether it be mutual charity or hospitality or the gift of speaking the word of God or a "ministry" that may be given in the

power of God (4:7–11). The "elders" should be "examples to the
flock", the "young men subject" to them, both commanding and
obeying in the same spirit of humility (5:1–5). All should know that
"participation in the sufferings of Christ" is a matter of "joy", in fact
of "glory", the reverse of shame and the proof of the rightness of the
way, for "the time has come for judgment to begin with the household of God" (4:12–19).

James refers not so much to the pattern of Christ as to that of the
prophets and Job in their patience (James 5:10–11), but even so, from
his insistence on the command of love, with its self-abasement (1:9–10;
4:10) and its stooping to the humbled (2:2–8; 15–17), the image of
Christ clearly emerges (2:1). If he commends action (1:25; 2:14–26),
he mainly stresses meekness and patience (1:3, 20–21; 3:13, 17; 4:1;
5:7–11), which includes restraining the tongue (1:26; 3:1–12); and this
is simply to adapt oneself to the form freely engendered by God,
coming down from him as a good and perfect thing (1:17–18). Like
the Old Testament wisdom, it can only be prayed for (1:5–7) in a
spirit of detachment from possessions, since these are the greatest
hindrance to entrance into the form of God (4:13–5:6).

For John, this form is simply the eternal love between the Divine
Persons and therefore hardly comprehensible as "form". Yet the dialectic of the transition from one's own existence (in sin and the confession of sin [1 Jn 1:8–9]) to the forgiveness of sins (1:9; 2:12; 3:5) and
rebirth out of God to sinlessness (3:9) enables us to see the actual
becoming of the form. The act of love is the essential thing, as in
James 3:17; but only when it proceeds from "abiding" and therein
persists, does it have its source in the form of God (3:6). Whoever
loves has knowledge, and whoever keeps the word is in charity
(2:3–5; 3:6). All this is the echo of the being and conduct of Christ.
For God first loved us (4:19) and sent his Son into the world as a
propitiation for our sins, that we might live through him (4:9–10).
We are, therefore, already inserted into love, and so it is only obedience to the reality and not our own achievement if we let what God
has done in us through Christ be verified by acting accordingly.
"Beloved, if God so loved us, we also ought to love one another"
(4:11). "By this we know love, that he has laid down his life for us; and

we ought to lay down our lives for the brethren" (3:16). "He who says he abides in him ought to walk in the same way in which he walked" (2:6). All this is, indeed, a "commandment" (3:22-24; 5:2-3; 2 Jn 6), but it is more, since it is Christ's dwelling in us. The Spirit given to us (2:20-28; 3:9; 3:24-4:2; 4:13; 5:6-8) makes us God's children, who must also love his eternal Son (5:1-2).

All these variations on the single theme of following Christ reproduce the same motive, which continues always in the clear-cut form it had in the beginning, and whose mysterious riches will never be exhausted. The first leap of faith that leaves all things is never over and done with; it remains a constant determinant of the form and enters into it, and the humility of Christ can only be our form by our being continuously humbled on account of our having caused the humiliation of Christ. Only in this way can Paul go almost to the point of assimilating himself to Christ and ascribe to the individual Christian in his sufferings (as distinct from the Church as a whole) a share in the expiatory power of the Passion (Col 1:24). Only thus can Christian love, which destroys the self in order to build up the whole body, be thought of as participating in the fruitfulness of Christ and in his self-renunciation (Eph 4:16). Without this working of the Spirit of Christ in the members, *purely* through the objective, sacramental, and official mode of action, nothing in the body of Christ is built up and established. The whole objective and official element is simply the substructure and means to bring forth the subjective form of Christ in each Christian.

5. Historical sketch

The history of Christian ideas consists in the perpetually renewed attempt to follow Christ's commands and example, to understand his design and his commission, to explain them and make them fruitful for each succeeding age. The gospel always remains, and so does man, the sinner and the hearer of its message. Its exposition, however, may vary in two ways. It may proceed from within, from the Holy Spirit who explains Christ to the Church and shows ever new aspects of his

Person and doctrine. Or it may proceed from the historical situation, which also throws new light on these, and may involve new demands on the Church and the Christian. It is thus possible that interpretations varying according to the time and the particular emphasis may yet meet at the center, just as different transverse sections of an object may all pass through the center. They will be consistent with one another only insofar as they actually make contact with the center and radiate forth from it, and insofar as, despite their external differences, they are ultimately in affinity. It is hard to make the temporal developments fit into a rational scheme (such as Hegel did for world history). Even should the sequence of external events be brought within a scheme that elucidates them, the designs of the Spirit, who breathes where he will, cannot be wholly perceived and ordered this side of eternity. The temporal significance and direction that are undoubtedly present and must be assumed can only be divined here and there.

1. The first period of the idea of the following of Christ is characterized by the fact of martyrdom. This was brought to bear by the persecution of Christians, together with the expectation of the imminent end of all things, as also by the tenor of the apostolic writings, many of which (Thessalonians, Philippians, Hebrews, 1 Peter, the letters in Revelation, among others) were written to fortify men under persecution, and others composed under the threat of martyrdom (the prison letters; 2 Peter; those to Timothy, Titus, and Philemon; 3 John). It is but a step from these to Ignatius of Loyola. The apostles had, in fact, not produced any detailed commentary on the words of Christ but only explained, with astonishing freedom and independence, the meaning and import of Christ, of his death and Resurrection. Certainly, his words and miracles were also recorded, but the main point of the kerygma consisted in his death and Resurrection. And this was the focal point for the Christian; here was the sphere in which he had to follow Christ. The response of the Church in martyrdom was the best and most literal that could be conceived. But although the liberal interpretation may have been the *typos* and the compelling example for all Christians, the right response of the time, it was not applicable to all times and conditions.

2. Even before the persecutions ceased, the need was felt, in the third century, to adopt a position vis-à-vis the religious culture of the time. The incarnate *Logos* became the true *sophia* or *gnosis,* and following him in love by overcoming the passions (*apatheia*) became the true philosophy. The Greek and Gnostic idea of negation of the world through spiritual ascent and turning away from the finite through imitation of the divine life was confronted by Christian virginity as a positive response. Philo had already fashioned the synthesis between the Greek "following of God" (Pythagoras, Plato, Epictetus) and the Biblical "walking in the ways of God", as also with the late-Judaistic imitation of the attributes of God. It is extremely difficult, if not impossible, to say where, in the theology and spirituality of the Alexandrians and Cappadocians, the ancient Platonism and stoicism are simply used as a means of expression and where Christian thought (though it involved some limitation upon its life-giving paradox) is made subservient to the ideas of the time. Both trends can be present in one and the same thinker; beneath the far-reaching adaptations and concessions, there may often enough lie concealed a genuine Christian integrity. It is much the same with the great heresies of the time, Gnosticism and Arianism, which on the one hand brought out the true nature of Catholicism and on the other not seldom compelled the emergence within it of an antithesis more or less dependent on them. Does the mystery of the Cross really find a central place in Origen's system? Is his wholehearted idea of the following of Christ perhaps of a too ascetical nature, a necessary training for the perfect mastery of the gnosis; and is this not also the case with the struggle against the devils on behalf of the Churches taught by the *Didascalia?* We may ask, also, if with him, and Methodius, Gregory of Nyssa, even Ambrose and Augustine, the idea of virginity is wholly free from the spiritualism of late antiquity and whether the "following of God" with its bold paradoxes in the "life of Moses" of Gregory of Nyssa is really the continuation of the gospel following of Christ and of the Old Testament walking in the way of God. Even with the great St. Antony, who started such a genuine Christian movement when he took so literally the command to "leave all things", we may wonder if going into the desert, with such exclusive emphasis on the inner life, was not

a restriction of the Christian ethic to a single aspect of it. At all events, the desert spirituality, bound up with that of neighboring Alexandria, could easily shift the idea of the following of Christ onto a sidetrack, with the consequent risk not so much of forthright errors, but— though fought against by a prudent discernment of spirits—of being misled by the contact of Christianity with the Asiatic world religions. Evagrius—from whom the way leads directly to Mount Athos and Palamitism, and indirectly, through Palladius and Cassian to Western monasticism—aimed, through the renunciation of all images and concepts, to attain to the inner light of the soul, and through it to the divine light of grace, in which, ultimately, the uncreated Trinitarian light of the Father might itself shine forth. Even Augustine was deeply involved in the Asiatic approach of the Neoplatonists and only by degrees found the way from a religious philosophy with Christian affinities to a genuine theology of following the Cross. On the whole, the idea of following was alien to Hellenism. The personal master-and-disciple relationship of classical philosophy had long since become obsolete, and there remained the "imitation" of God, the theory of prototype and copy with the ascent by contemplation from faith to vision.

Nevertheless, the passing of antiquity saw the emergence of a Christian form embodying all the Greek and Roman thought forms, one that continued as the definitive, almost the sole form actuating the medieval Church. The Benedictine rule, whose mysterious author, so hard to depict historically, is revealed in his unparalleled influence down the ages as a formative Christian force of the highest potency, unites charisma and ministry, authority and love, zeal and discretion, the Roman and Christian character, in such a way as to be practically a model for all Christian discipleship. It is a model that did not set itself up as a rival to the gospel, one that remained so open in its readiness to serve that it could be developed in all directions, in the holiness of the hierarchical ministry and of personal asceticism, in missionary activity and in the stability of contemplation, in the life devoted to the liturgical *opus Dei* and in a Christian humanism in the Tradition of antiquity. It is the moderate and mature superpersonality of the Benedictine form that enabled it not only to produce out of itself almost all subsequent forms of monasticism but also to set its mark, directly or indirectly, on Catholic culture at all levels right up to modern times.

3. With the onset of the Germanic era the tendency was reversed. Young nations, divided up into small tribes, were naturally familiar with the idea of following and trusting the leader, and a connection was easily established between the march of the Jews through the desert and the wandering of the nations. The ethos of the "Heliand" was at great pains to distinguish this secular loyalty from the loyalty of faith of the apostles to their leader, Christ. The transposition, which in some respects was almost too easily achieved, came up against extraordinary difficulties in others, as in the providential betrayal by Peter and the flight of the disciples. Nonetheless, it was achieved, and the great preacher-poet was able to persuade his hearers that Peter had to undergo the shame of felony for the sake of his subsequent office and the knowledge of human weakness. All through the Middle Ages the ethos of personal following prevailed, and the more it was impregnated with the Christian spirit the more marvelous were its fruits. But the two ideas were so close that they were not always sufficiently distinguished, and noble actions inspired by the secular idea were often too hastily taken as Christian in essence. In the tragedy of the Crusades, in the subtle tension between St. Louis and his follower de Joinville, in the story of Parsifal and the Arthurian tales in general, we can see both the similarities and the differences in all their varieties. From the consecration of the sword and the initiation of the knight to the ceremony of anointing the King, we can see how the secular relationships of leader and follower were sacramentalized; even at so late a date, the Pope sent a consecrated sword to Charles of Lorraine and Prince Eugene. St. Ignatius raised this idea to a wholly spiritual plane in his contemplation "De Regno Christi", which set its distinctive stamp on the spirituality of his society. Apart from the secularized Teutonic order, this is practically the only place where the idea has persisted up to the present.

4. The movement toward poverty that broke out among the Christian people was contemporary with the feudal world and (in a hidden

fashion) a part of it; it began long before Francis and, in its origin, was a reaction against the rich and princely Church: it lay on the fringe of orthodoxy. What the "poor men of Christ" longed for, from Robert of Arbrissel, Joachim, Norbert, Arnold of Brescia, and the Waldensians onward, was direct contact with the Christ of apostolic times, the literal acceptance of the idea of "leaving all things", which had almost disappeared under the pomp of the Church's representatives. Francis brought the movement from the fringe right into the center of the gospel. His second rule brought together all the texts on the following of Christ under the idea of poverty, in which the stress was laid on this following, poverty being the sign of the will's firm resolve. But for him poverty was not only a means and an expression but also a real end, since Christ willed and had to be poor to redeem us, poor in order to show us to the Father as utterly destitute. If the spirituals departed again from the center to the fringe of orthodoxy, it was still the spiritual school of the *Poverello,* the spiritualization of his idea of poverty, that became the spring of modern spirituality. Franciscan poverty was conjoined, in Bonaventure, with the "becoming nought" of the Areopagite. He was followed in this by Eckhart or Tauler, of whom the latter was a decisive influence on Spanish mysticism and also on that of France in the *grande siècle.* Poverty of life and of the spirit as the following of Christ was the constant ideal of the Brethren of the Common Life, of the *devotio moderna,* which produced Erasmus. He attempted, by the methods of philology, to bring about a rebirth of the pure gospel and the primitive Christian Tradition. In so doing, by skillfully bypassing both the Reformation and the Counter-Reformation, he founded what Friedrich Heer has christened the Third Force.

5. The idea of "following" never managed to establish itself in Luther's mind; it was cramped by his too narrow idea of faith. Yet he better than anyone else could have finally Christianized the Germanic idea of discipleship and freed it from all accretions. He might also have liberated the Franciscan heritage, present in German mysticism, from all Neoplatonic coloring and handed it on to the new age. Neither of these things happened. His *fiducia,* an essential element in both the

Old and New Testament faith, remained isolated (and so was contro-
verted, instead of being absorbed through a right understanding, by
the Counter-Reformation idea of faith). The Christian paradox of
Tauler's mysticism could not, in fact, be preserved in the Lutheran
dialectic. In the late Middle Ages there was a growing rift between
the institutional Church and the Church of the personal interior
life with its practice of mysticism and poverty, but now the two
broke completely apart, and it became quite impossible to envisage
any origin for the Church's ministry in the personal following of
Christ. Consequently, after all sorts of compromises had been tried
within Protestantism in the course of its history, the final victory
was bound to lie with the upholders of the personal inner life. These
were the most powerful figures. In this connection, we may mention
Pascal and his image of Christ, since he was so strongly affected by the
Jansenist doctrine of predestination; and Kierkegaard, whose assault
on the liberal pastorate was the fulfillment of his life and work.

Even the Counter-Reformation was divided, more deeply than
appears at first, by two contrasting trends. Its apologetics upheld the
Church as a hierarchical structure, and the great saints of the Baroque
era were certainly a proof of its truth; a triumphant architectural style
was used to glorify both at the same time. But, as in the late Middle
Ages, the true spirituality followed other, more hidden ways; it was
concerned with the individual who, in his following of Christ, sought
and realized the "Kingdom of God within" (Lk 17:21) by "interior
prayer". Since, however, this was pursued with a kind of mystical
directness—we have only to think of Berulle's teaching on the reproduction of the "interior states" of Jesus—it did not, in fact, any longer
convey the Christian "inner form". Form became exterior representation, in opposition to inwardness (the two are, more or less, embodied
in the opposition between Bossuet and Fénelon). For that reason,
psychology gained the upper hand, the description and scrutinizing
of the mystical and other states, and the Christian commission was
seen as a step, not without danger, in the direction of exteriority
(Lallemant). The Catholic romantic movement, also, was dominated
by the idea of inwardness. Hence it is that a little book, the *Imitation of*

Christ, was so important at that time and during the subsequent period. Hence, too, the rescue from oblivion of German mysticism, and the emphasis, where the Church was concerned, laid on community of love in the Holy Spirit. Twentieth-century personalism continues along these lines, though it is primarily the product of Protestantism (Kierkegaard) and of Old Testament Judaism (Scheler, Buber). "Form" as impersonal is here seen as pertaining to the "office" or to the religious life in its ordered claustral form, and over against it stands the life of the laity as "personal"—an opposition that, carried to its conclusion, can only destroy Church unity, as it has already done once.

This rough and ready account brings out clearly how the different epochs emphasized different things, which all meet in the center of the gospel, but since none of them actually constitutes this center, especially when the first impulse weakens, the outcome is a lack of balance. Christian antiquity obviously put the accent on virginity. With Tertullian there was a clear basis in eschatology for this, but from the Alexandrians on, there was a Platonic motive: a spiritual way of life seen as a condition for contemplation. It would be wrong to exaggerate this one-sidedness. The patristic treatises on virginity are thoroughly imbued with the spirit of the gospel, profound and stirring. Nor is it the literal following of the counsels that brought a one-sided attitude but the adoption of motives of flight from the world and of a too negative asceticism. These were already perceived by St. Augustine as bishop: If the Kingdom of God is not of this world, is then, perhaps, the desert also not of this world?

The medieval cult of poverty is admirable and astonishing for its thoroughness, but here too we may say that its weakness lay precisely in its strength, in its liberal fashion of following Christ. Francis was fully conscious that what mattered were the heart and the spirit prompting it. For him, freedom from all earthly goods and ties was what characterized the bride who leaves all, who is betrothed not to poverty but to the Divine Bridegroom in the common possession of poverty. Yet it was the literal acceptance of poverty, combined with the "literal" sharing of the stigmata, that was responsible for the distortions of the Franciscan theology of discipleship and imitation, increasing in volume from the *Tractatus* of Salimbene to that of Bartholomew of Pisa—designated by Luther as the monks Eulenspiegel and Alkoran—who discovered, one by one, all the qualities of Christ perfectly mirrored in Francis, set up by the spirituals as the new spiritual man and founder of the third age of the Church. The transference of the idea of poverty on the spiritual plane, effected by the Dominican mystics, freed it from this one-sidedness and restored it to the center. Rightly understood, they could say a great deal to us today.

For Ignatius, following Christ is essentially obedience, but the obedience of the feudal relationship as continued in the Spanish ideas of kingship and knighthood, as he knew it in his youth bound up with the late medieval love service. With him, this idea of discipleship became interiorized, personal, corresponding to the new age just beginning: the vow of fidelity is the response befitting the noble heart when it contemplates the life of our Lord. The *Spiritual Exercises* proceed by way of encounter between Christ and the individual, leading up to the crucial point where his allegiance to Christ is placed at the service of the Church's hierarchy. When the Pope, as the supreme head of the Society, commands any mission, this is seen and accepted as the direct command of Christ. This is personal obedience subordinated to the Church's ministry, self-renunciation carried to the utmost: magnificent indeed but always liable to shift from the attitude of loyalty and discipleship into an impersonal striving. This is, in fact, what occurred in the collapse of the German knighthood idea into the Prussia of the Hohenzollerns and of the Kantian imperative.

For Ignatius, then, obedience as the central attitude of the Church as bride of Christ is the true core, the most sublime concept of discipleship: *ecce ancilla.* But obedience, once detached from this inner disposition (perhaps more through the one who gives than the one who receives the commands) and seen simply as a tool for the use of the hierarchy as such can and must lead to abuses. These are utterly remote from the conception of the Founder, who, with all his realism, always held firmly to the ideal aspect of the Church; but it is a danger still to be reckoned with on account of the hidden cleavage, already described, in the post-Reformation Church. Nonetheless, Ignatius, more than anyone else, succeeded in passing on to the present age the gospel idea of discipleship as a living reality. He has done so in that he neither takes for a criterion the person of the follower nor lets it be wholly merged in the function. Instead, he has always in view the higher center of the living Christian form, which takes hold of the person (according to the "journey to the hell of self-knowledge" of the First Week) for the service of the Lord and thereby secures for him true freedom.

6. Difficulties resolved

We can now consider the three difficulties enunciated at the beginning and see how they can be resolved. The solution, it is true, is accessible only to those who are ready to go so deeply into the root of the matter that the unity of all its factors emerges of itself. This unity lies in God rather than in the Church, since the unity of the latter lies not in itself but in the Head. The Church is a manifold of members, which both differentiates it from the Head and slackens the bond between the two. "Now there are varieties of gifts, but the same Spirit; and there are varieties of service, but the same Lord; and there are varieties of working, but it is the same God who inspires them all in every one" (1 Cor 12:4–6).

The gifts, service, and working of each individual are not these individuals themselves; they are the "form" or "function" in the living organism of the Church imparted to each one. "All these are inspired by one and the same Spirit, who apportions to each one individually as he wills" (ibid., v. 11). There is no member of the Church who, precisely *qua* member, does not have his "member form", and this is something common to all "gifts, service, and workings". In fact, the qualities of member and member form are strictly identical. The eye, ear, and foot, which Paul adduces in comparison, are not some sort of neutral entities that accidentally take on the functions of seeing, hearing, and walking. They *are* these functions, which, in order to be themselves, are materialized in a definite corporeal structure. In Christ, whose body we constitute, is materialized a distinct function of man, proclaimed by him in the Holy Spirit. This function, viewed apart from the body of Christ, may indeed be specified as part of the order of creation, but as this particular function it is related as matter to the form given by Christ in the Holy Spirit. "For by one Spirit we were all baptized into one body—Jews or Greeks, slaves or free—and were all made to drink of one Spirit" (ibid., v. 13), the Spirit that has made us functions of the unity. We can see at once that this idea of function has nothing in common with modern functionalism, which presupposes the depersonalizing of the individual harnessed to his task. The totality whose functions the baptized become is not an industrial or administrative collective but the Person Jesus Christ, divine and human, in his function of revealing and imparting the triune personal life of God. Consequently, functionalizing the person baptized into Christ can only mean elevating his isolated created personality into the state and wholly new setting of the divine life so revealed and communicated. This mysterious operation becomes at once evident when we look at the actual "functioning" of the Church, for where is the human person more "holy", more redeemed, than in the place where he attains to holiness? Consider Paul, Augustine, Bernard, Teresa: all the power and energy of their personalities we see developed far beyond their natural potential. At the same time, this happened in the complete renunciation of self, in leaving all things, and in "hatred of self" (Lk 14:26). Everything about them became the expression and active functioning of God in the Church, and only in this higher setting is it comprehensible and explicable.

Once again, it is to our shame that Protestant theology had to recall us Catholics to this Biblical functionalism and so restore to us the ultimate foundation of the Church ministry. Oscar Cullmann's *Christology of the New Testament,* based on Karl Barth's idea of revelation in his *Church Dogmatics* (vol. I, part I), shows how the chief titles of Christ—Prophet, Servant of Yahweh, High Priest, Messiah, Son of Man, Kyrios, Redeemer, even Logos and Son of God—express what God wills to be in his work of saving the world. In opposing an exaggerated actualism that would merge God's Trinitarian being into his act of revelation (seeing him solely as revealer)—*esse sequitur agere* — both Barth and Cullmann emphasize the fact that we attain to God's being-in-itself only by means of his action-for-us, and that the Bible offers no possibility of framing a doctrine of God's being-in-itself in abstraction from his working in the order of revelation, even though, in the function, the person as such is always manifest as its prerequisite. One can only agree with those who are still wary of interpreting the Biblical data in the Greek terminology of Nicea, Ephesus, and Chalcedon, provided that it is always realized that the conciliar formulas were intended to preserve the full import of these. Protestants undoubtedly exaggerate the contrast between the Biblical-Hebraic and Greek modes of thought with its generalized philosophical approach; they view philosophy only in its most arid scholastic form. The fact is, however, that one can only frame a constructive philosophy of being in the categories of actuality, and natures cannot be understood otherwise than as sources of acts (*natura est principium actum*), form only explained in relation to its finality (though this is not to be taken in the narrow, technical sense of the Enlightenment), and to the being of the thing itself (*esse sequitur formam*).

Christ, as the Father's Word sent and incarnate, passes over from the *forma Dei* in which he abides into the *forma Servi*. Paul throws further light on the idea by the two additional terms *image* (which means not "similarity" but "sameness of form") and *shape* (which likewise refers to form, in fact to the living form of expression, character, conduct). Thereby he indicated the inward character and the depth of the form assumed. It is no mere external way of acting, a sort of disguise, while inwardly, in character and being, one remains something quite different. On the contrary, the principle itself from which the acts issue has the form of a slave, is actually man, and the humiliation is precisely the passing over from being in the one actual form to being in the other; and so the mystery of Christology consists precisely in this "passing over", which means more than a simple addition of a second nature to a first. It would be no humiliation if, in passing over to the being of a slave, he ceased to be God; but the entrance on the form of a slave must nonetheless be seen as a real movement, an event for him too, a becoming and an "emptying" (Phil 2:5–8).

It is by analogy to what Christ did in descending that the Christian ascent, wrought by this descent from the "shape of man" into the form of a member of the Church, must be understood, even if there is no question of any structural identity with the hypostatic union. But what Christ is by nature we must be, through him, by grace; and, as he is wholly the "man-for-others" (Karl Barth), his Person as Redeemer being wholly given over to the function of redeeming, so the redeemed human person must become, through its being made a member in Christ, a function in the Mystical Body. Here we must distinguish between a temporal aspect of the Church's existence, which lasts to the final judgment and the fulfillment—the only thing of which we have exact knowledge—and the eternal aspect of the Church's being, of which we are only given an intimation. In the temporal aspect, not only the individual in the Church is to be understood functionally; the Church as a whole retains, as regards the entire world to be redeemed, a functional aspect. The Church is, at one and the same time, the redeemed world in course of becoming and Christ's instrument for the full redemption of the world. Consequently, the individual member of the Church in time is not, actually, functional as regards the Church, as if it were the executive bearer of this function. He is, rather, functional in and with the Church as a whole. His being as function is the expression of his being as part of the Church, and the bearer and executor of the function is plainly Christ, indeed the Trinity: "You are the body of Christ, and individually members of it" (1 Cor 12:27)—not then members of the Church but members of Christ. The function-being of the Church (and of the individual members), far from excluding the personal life as an end in itself, actually includes it, so much so that it remains the indispensable center of activity, as is shown in the chapter on charity (1 Cor 13) that follows the one about functions (1 Cor 12); for charity fills all functions, not as if they were something disparate to it, but as its own living organs, distinct one from the other.

We are now in a position to answer the questions broached in the beginning. The most important insight, which conditions all the others, is that of the functional and representative character of the Christian form of existence, in which the human opposition between person and function is no longer applicable. For this reason, any ecclesiology that is based on this opposition and, for instance, assigns what is personal to the laity and what is functional to the clergy starts from a false premise. Though the cleric has a function that the layman has not, yet functionality on the Christian plane applies no less to the layman than to the cleric. At the most, it could be said that the functional character of the Church as a whole (and so of all its members) is more clearly shown in the cleric than in the layman and that in the cleric it has its own functional character more visibly presented. The recollection of this fact is one of the sources of anticlericalism, just as Paul's stress on himself as *typos* earned him little sympathy in the Christian communities.

Our first conclusion offers no difficulty. The question raised was whether the training of the apostles, in the gospel, was a training for the clerical state (in which case it has no direct concern with laity) or for the Christian life in general (and then the inner connection of orders and jurisdiction with this training is no longer clear). But the question, in view of all that has been said, is wrongly posed, since it is not a matter of alternatives but of an inner and necessary unity. Christ trains the disciples (as also the people) in the Christian form, which as such is beyond the distinction of clergy and laity. But this common possession is not to be confused with the Protestant idea that the priesthood of all believers is the foundation of the special state of the clergy, in that the powers inherent, collectively and democratically, in the Church are imparted by it to individuals. The hierarchy, as is clear in the texts, was directly established by Christ and the origin of its special commission is not to be traced casually to the Church as a whole. This does not rule out that the functional side of this special commission may be a particular expression of the general functional form of the Church. Consequently, what is special is not something added, externally and positivistically, to what is universal. It is, rather, a special imprinting by Christ on the universal form, whereby it can and should be, in a more special way, *typos,* model, and pattern of this universal.

The second conclusion follows equally naturally. It is quite true that faith, in the Scriptural sense, presupposes as basic principles leaving all and hating all, for anyone to be a disciple of Christ at all. It is also true that this faith, demanded of everyone, represents the human contribution to the God-given form that is sanctity. And so it follows that the so-called ordained state, or better, the religious state, which achieves in fact this leaving all according to the counsel of Christ, can, once again, be nothing else than the special manifestation of what is implied in the general state of the believer, whether this be exemplified by a layman in the world or by a cleric. Granted that the literal leaving of all things (external goods, bodily fruitfulness, and spiritual disposition over oneself) results, in the Christian setting, from a special call of Christ, yet this "special" call itself, like the response to it, is analogously present in the general Christian form of life. It is no more a question of identifying the function of Christian holiness simply with this specialized call (as if only those in the clerical or religious state were canonizable) than of denying outright the inner connection between specialized holiness and the specialized call. It is indeed obvious that this external leaving all things is the prerequisite willed by God for a man to devote his life undividedly to the service of God's Kingdom (inside and outside the Church). But holiness, both general and special (and the distinction is, obviously, not a hard and fast one), exists only as a form bestowed. The religious state, therefore, is not to be valued according to the degree of subjective striving (which may be just as great, or greater, in the secular state) but primarily in respect of the meaning and scope of the mission imparted, to which, admittedly, one's personal endeavor ought to correspond. The final proof of all this is St. Paul's membership theory, according to which higher qualifications (and personal distinctions) directly signify higher types of function (which means service for the whole body, especially the "weaker members")—1 Corinthians 12:21–26. Laymen who object to the greater honor shown by the Church to religious and clerics might well reflect on these verses.

The third point at issue was that between the idea of a "personal Church" and a "people's Church." Indeed, the more personal and distinctive calling, with the more personal and distinctive response of the one called to his vocation (whatever form it takes), brings about a correspondingly greater isolation, makes him more independent in his missionary role, placed, as he is, in the front line of the Kingdom of God. The graces of confirmation have brought a man to his full stature as a Christian when he is able to represent the Faith uncompromisingly before the world, not merely before his fellow Christians. For this reason, the Church is always, in her *potior pars,* her special quality as Church, a missionary Church, a Church of witness and of martyrdom. With all that, she does not cease to be a community, but one of a very special sort: basically a centrifugal community (going apart, as it were, precisely in that which unites her, in Christ's missionary call), in contrast with the synagogue, which always as today (in Israel) has been a centripetal community and is only missionary *per accidens.* Accordingly, the question is where we are to place the center of the Church: whether in her spiritual locus, which, however, is necessarily embodied in a minority, or where by far the greatest number is to be found, though they certainly do not embody her pure idea in the clearest fashion.

At the present time, we are able to look back on the history of the following of Christ almost from an eschatological plane and formulate a doctrine accordingly. It is a doctrine that, so far from preventing, actually stimulates us to seek and find a form of Christian discipleship relevant to the time and its spirit, which, in the light of the various attempts in the course of history, will avoid, as far as is humanly possible, any one-sided and materialistic conception. The forms developed in history may correspond, afterward as before, to special vocations, which—for instance, the purely contemplative life—are theologically as appropriate now as in times when they were more consonant with the existing culture. But, in addition, there is something like a form in the *kairos* of the present time, a form that seems given when the Christian tries to live in the world and in a secular calling a specialized Christian vocation along the lines of the Christian counsels. In this he will be, for all states of the Christian life, a specialized witness to the general form of sanctity that is the basis of all Christian living.

WHO IS THE CHURCH?

I. *Figure and myth*

To frame the question in this way is to presuppose that the Church is "someone", in other words a person. A person, however, seems definable only as a spiritual center of consciousness of free and rational acts. How, then, can the Church be a person in this sense? We are, of course, wont to attribute to the Church all kinds of acts: the Church wills this and that, rejoices, suffers, permits one thing or another, commands, forbids; above all she prays, thanks, intercedes, hopes, sacrifices, and, as regards men, she instructs, admonishes, feeds them. In a number of these cases, the average Christian has in mind the ecclesiastical hierarchy, which in its activities represents, at least in his eyes, the Church, if it does not exactly coincide with her. In other cases, he sees expressions of the general life of the Church, or perhaps rather expressions of her life that, while elucidated and transmitted by the hierarchy, must ultimately be ascribed not to the latter but to the Church in general as their subject. And so the question emerges anew: How is this general subject to be understood?

The most obvious course is to explain it as a collective subject, in the same sense as the natural groups, family, race, people, state, mankind are said to be subjects, and so we predicate of them certain acts and relationships. There is good reason to designate, as is often done, collective subjects as real and not merely figurative persons, since a family, say, or a people is essentially more than the sum of its members. Yet, since a people possesses no center of consciousness of its own but at most one that is made up of the centers of the individual persons, one may well hold that there is merely an analogy between the individual and collective persons. We can, therefore, clarify the issue by asking whether the subject Church can be subsumed under the category of collective person, and whether we are to understand statements about it in the same way as statements such as

Translated by A. V. Littledale with Alexander Dru.

"The people wills", or "The state declares". Even in these cases the collective act is posited, or at any rate made public, by a group, large or small, of responsible individuals, such that the relationship of these to the whole body is susceptible of many gradations, from democracy to absolutism. A government may consider itself more as the expression of the collective will and feeling (though it can never be absolutely this), or else the people may agree to accept the dispositions of the government as the expression of its own attitude and so to follow them out and comply with them.

However the relationship between the principle and the consequences may vary, some such relationship must always be present. But, as regards the Catholic Church, when we look more closely, no secular form of constitution can be predicated of it. It is true that, externally, it seems to have a pronounced monarchic and aristocratic constitution that attributes all initiative to the Pope and the bishops holding office *jure divino* and is by no means representative of the "will of the people". At the same time, however, these rulers are "believers" equally and in the same sense as all the rest. They do not follow their own will, not even representing anything like a spiritual *"raison d'état"*, but discharge their office in absolute dependence on the real supreme Head of the Church. This Head is the glorified Christ, his Person transcendent over the whole Church, sovereign and unaccountable. For him it is no sort of hubris but a simple statement of fact to make the equation: *L'Eglise, c'est moi.*

If we take this literally, we already have the answer to the question "Who is the Church?" The subject of the Church is, then, simply Christ; he posits and is responsible for her acts in the sense of St. Augustine's reiteration against the Donatists: it is not Peter who baptizes, nor Paul, nor Judas, but Christ alone. We can see, then, why we feel the inappropriateness of making the Church one of a number of "collective persons". No collective, in the secular order, can be in this way referred to an individual subject, so as to take its origin therefrom and be so utterly dependent on it. The Church, however, is "Christ living on"; she is, to use Paul's great analogy, *Christ's body.* This means, if we allow its full range of meaning, that the Church, in regard to her Head, is not a person on her own, a new and second one. The "body", in the sense of the simile, forms, together with the "Head", one being; that is, she is a person only "by grace" of the "Head".

It is not part of the nature of the Head, in Paul's simile, to need a body in order to be a person. Christ, being God, has no need of a Church. But it is absolutely of the essence of this body that it should need this Head in order to participate in his personality and, in that way, to be a body at all. The entire "organism" that the Church forms, and as which Christ willed her to be and founded her, together with her hierarchical structure and monarchical apex, is, taken by herself, headless, acephalous. The consciousness or self-awareness ascribable to her as to a secular corporation is far from being that intended for her in reality and that she ought to and, in fact, does possess, because it is poured into her by Christ. The verse of the psalm,

> It is like the precious oil upon the head,
> running down upon the beard,
> upon the beard of Aaron [133:2],

was, for the Fathers, an eloquent image of the grace flowing down in abundance from the Head onto the body, which owes this grace, preeminently, its participation in the personality of Christ.

The simile of a body answers the question "Who is the Church?" only in a negative sense; she is, and cannot be other than, an extension, a communication, a partaking of the personality of Christ. This is comprehensible in some degree only if Christ is seen as both God and man. He became so as to be of the same nature as we are and so to be our Head, and this in order to impart to us, through his humanity, the Trinitarian life he shares as God. We cannot, then, stop, at Christ's self-consciousness, for this, as human, cannot be set apart and understood in isolation from his divine consciousness, which includes the whole Trinitarian consciousness. Thence grace, as participation in the divine life, flows into the Church, through the mediation of Christ, grace that has its own "consciousness" in the divine virtues of faith, hope, and charity. These three are personal spiritual dispositions that impart an essential "life" of God, but one that is conscious, though for the time being still veiled, and disclosed in its full "consciousness" only in the world beyond. "Life", when predicated of God, in St. John and Scripture generally, means nothing "biological". It is used to express the whole intimacy and intensity of the divine thinking, feeling, and willing.

This applies also to the analogy of the vine, in which the "biological" element is obviously an expression of both the ontological and the personal inwardness of Christ's dwelling in the Church. The clarity of his thinking, the strength of his willing, the consistency of his love, all make up the life that flows into us from him, without which we can do nothing but that when present enables us to bring forth the awaited fruit. Here the unique principle of life dwelling in Christ is more strongly emphasized than in the simile of the body. Even when the comparison is drawn between the stock that is not seen and the fruit that is so evident, the whole achievement of the branches yet belongs to it, more clearly than in the other simile, in which the body is understood as the product and prolongation of the Head. The least tendency to independence on the part of the branches as regards the stock would be the beginning of a withering process and lead to their being cast into the fire. There is nothing fruitful in the branches that does not come from the stock and, though unseen, really preexist there: *Quis in Christo est omnis Ecclesia.*

The last image of this, one frequent with the Fathers, is the origin of the Church *from the wounded side* of the crucified Lord. There is no doubt that subsequent theology owes a great deal to St. John's picture of the opening of Christ's side and the flowing out of water and blood. There can be no doubt at all that, for John, water and blood represent all the sacraments, nor that the whole event, of which the presence of Mary and the beloved disciple beneath the Cross forms a part, signifies the extreme of love, at once divine and human, in its self-manifestation. It is equally certain that, for John, Christ's giving up his spirit to the Father at the moment of this gift from within his body has a Trinitarian and ecclesiological sense and is connected with the glorified Christ's gift of the Spirit at Easter. Spirit, water, and blood, in their unity, are the "three witnesses" of this unique divine and human love, and their unity has evidently to do with the inner essence of the Church. That the Church essentially originated on the

Cross[1] and represents the creative achievement and outcome of the Passion suffered on man's behalf is theologically undeniable. The only question that remains is what the reality issuing from Christ's dying body was in fact: whether solely the attributes of the spirit and body of the God-Man being poured forth externally in the sacramental forms—and thereby the Trinitarian grace granted to mankind in Christological form—or whether in the crucified, dying representative of humanity some element of preexisting sinful man must be deemed present so as to be a kind of second agent cooperating in this founding and outpouring of the Church. If the latter is taken as the more consonant, then the transition from the image of the Church as body to that of the Church as bride is accomplished imperceptibly.

In the great text of Ephesians 5, the comparison between *husband and wife* on the one hand and Christ and the Church on the other obliges us to take the image of head and body in a nuptial and personal sense. In this setting, "head" means the ruling partner, the lord, in a marriage; "body" means completion and unification in the physical nuptial order. This transposition demands, henceforth, the maintenance together of both statements: the personal, in virtue of which the Church is a "someone" whom the Lord loved and for whom he delivered himself up, a "someone", therefore, who in a certain way already existed; and the somatic, in virtue of which the Church is what she is, namely, the glorious one without spot or wrinkle yet owing her origin wholly to this event of the Cross. The paradox, not to say contradiction, Paul could sustain only by bringing to it his prior theological understanding of the doctrine of the sexes, the origin, that is, of the first woman from the rib of man, whereby she is said to be both "his own flesh and blood" and a "person" for whose sake the man is to "leave his father and mother and cleave to his wife". And since this twofold statement of Genesis, to which Paul refers, is inapplicable to Adam and Eve, since Adam had no parents to leave, it must have to do with the future. And so Paul, who elevates the sex relationship from type to antetype, is yet undoubt-

---

[1] Certainly, as we will show, on the Cross as inseparable from the Easter event, especially as it is understood by St. John.

edly thinking of the simultaneous realization of both aspects in the relationship between Christ and the Church. Those Fathers who speak, in connection with Ephesians 5 and Philippians 2, of Christ leaving and coming down from the Father (and, with Origen, also from the "mother", the "heavenly Jerusalem", after Galatians 4:26), in order to cleave to his bride in her fallen state on earth and estranged from God, simply make fully comprehensible Paul's statement that Christ loved the Church and gave himself on the Cross for her; and the second explanation adopted by them is equally in accord with Paul's train of thought—the Church, purified on the Cross and made glorious without spot or wrinkle, was previously lacking in such purity and splendor and was endowed with these qualities only on the Cross, in the New Covenant.

There are, then, two divergent images of the Church. On the one hand, the Church is seen as originating wholly from the dying Christ; on the other, she is considered preexisting. From these, there follow the equally divergent aspects of a Church that is no more than the outpouring and prolongation of the twofold nature of Christ and of a Church that confronts Christ as a "someone", a subject, a person. Paul, in his tremendous vision, conjoins these seeming incompatibles; and we may well ask, seeing that the passage in Genesis did not require but merely prompted it, if he could have done so apart from the background of the contemporary mythical Gnostic way of thinking. This was prone both to personalize abstractions and also to represent the world principles in sexual terms, making them emerge from the primal source as a male-female couple. There is no need to postulate this as directly influencing the theological process, but it suffices to see it as working in the background by way of suggestion, facilitating the approach, and providing the occasion; while the inner theological treatment of the themes, once provided, proceeds independently. Thus the abundant fruits yielded by the conception of the Church as bride of Christ in the patristic age, and also in the medieval exegetes following the Fathers, are quite independent of any Gnostic prompting and ascribable to the convergence of a great number of Biblical themes. But a time came when the bride image became blurred and lost its hold on men's minds, and this is true today for the general consciousness of the Church. The analogy of the body has been resuscitated and is again in vogue, but this had not happened to the analogy of the bride. The reason for this hesitation in ecclesiological thought must now be examined.

2. The problem of the Scriptural basis

It is today generally recognized, of course, that the Genesis image, which St. Paul applied, of Eve coming forth from Adam's rib must itself be taken as a piece of religious symbolism ("myth"). But this image, so striking and rich in theological content, ought to be the origin of the spontaneous act of hypostasizing the Church, making her the bride, a person contrasting with the Divine and human Bridegroom; for the image of bride, in its content, goes beyond that of the "Mystical" Body, though of course without contravening it. This had to be made explicit, since one might well think of a "bride" who was not, at the same time, "body", as was the case with the Old Testament Israel of Zion, God's betrothed or spouse (no essential difference for Jewish law, since the man's marriage rights were already conveyed in the betrothal, though to be exercised only after marriage). "For your Maker is your husband ... and the Holy One of Israel is your Redeemer, the God of the whole earth he is called. For the Lord has called you like a wife forsaken and grieved in spirit, like a wife of youth when she is cast off, says your God" (Is 54:5–6). "Go and proclaim in the hearing of Jerusalem, thus says the Lord, I remember the devotion of your youth, your love as a bride, how you followed me in the wilderness, in a land not sown" (Jer 2:2). Further, all these texts that speak of judgment, denouncing Jerusalem's adultery, enormously strengthen the realism of the image, making it operate so forcefully that one can hardly speak any longer of a mere image. In addition, these texts establish a singular continuity, little noticed in theology, between the disfigured bride of God in the Old Covenant and the bride of Christ in the new, expressly said to have been bathed and washed and therefore glorious and unspotted. Later, we will go further into these correlations. For the moment, it is just a matter of seeing that Israel, as Yahweh's spouse, is indeed a kind of subject, but nothing in the nature of a "body" of God.

The physical correlation is reserved to the New Covenant. Israel is, above all, God's people, and as such a collective subject, even if of peculiar constitution and value. It never saw itself in any other light—except, perhaps, in that later period when Gnosticism had already started. In fact, even at the beginning and at the zenith of its course, it saw its relation to Yahweh as analogous to that of other peoples to their God leaders, nor did it deny the existence of their religious covenants but only their lawfulness. Furthermore, we may take the whole manner of thinking of this early period to have been "mythological", for it regarded, unreflectingly, both the peoples and their gods and the hierarchies of divinities as real unities. It was a very human, realistic mode of conception, saturated with imagery, which ceded only to philosophy with its power of abstract thought, and which may well have left its mark on the simile of the marriage of Yahweh with his people. The nuptial simile, indeed, was not exclusive to Israel but was used and misused over and over again by other peoples. Its use by Israel was distinguished from that by the neighboring cultures only in its absolute purity and severity, indeed in its predominantly sharp and juridical form—though the distinction is an essential one. The exceptional case is that of the Song of Songs, though it still follows the general line in that there is never even a hint of reference to the relations between Yahweh and Israel: this is an amazing piece of discretion observed even by the latest compilers of the corpus of writings, who no doubt included it in view of its allegorical meaning. It must, then, be the case that the sensuous portrayal of the two lovers was meant to become, in the history of Christian theology, the predestined *typos* for the development of the New Testament nuptial relationship between Christ and the Church, although here again the problem of the Church as a subject on her own is presupposed and alluded to instead of being faced squarely and thought out.

It is difficult to assess, in this context, the import of the few *synoptic texts* that bridge the gap between the nuptial theology of the prophets and that of Paul. What stands out, here also, is their discretion, which goes so far that it is always doubtful whether Jesus was describing himself as the Bridegroom of the new redeemed community or was merely adopting the nuptial simile as the traditional image of the messianic era. In the parable of the ten virgins, there is probably no allusion to any bride;[2] the whole significance of the parable is the necessity of being always on the alert. The parable of the royal marriage feast (Mt 22:1-14) is about the judgment and is obviously cognate with that of the wicked husbandmen (21:33-46). Matthew puts them in close proximity. The passage about the "marriage guests" (Hebraistically called "sons of the bridegroom"), unable to mourn so long as the bridegroom is with them (Mt 9:15), cannot well be taken as a public declaration by Jesus of his messianic character. It is more like an application of a simile of Jesus by the community for its own acknowledgment of his being the Messiah. There remains only the word of the Baptist in St. John's Gospel (3:29) that he who has the bride is the bridegroom, and the Baptist, the friend of the bridegroom, hears his voice and rejoices. This too can be reduced to a figure of speech, if we see in the Baptist the one who brings in the bride, he who, in the prevailing custom, had to bear witness to the bridegroom of the bride's virginity. Accordingly, the purport of the statement would be the friend's unselfish love. Such a minimizing of the text, however, is not obligatory; and it is far more probable that the Lord, of set purpose, took the marriage image for the messianic era and applied it to himself. This means no more than that he took it in the received Old Testament sense, according to which the bride is none other than the people as a collective entity, the community elected by the Lord.

We are still, in fact, a long way from the Pauline parallel of the physical relationship between man and wife, since the Lord himself, in his various utterances, does not anticipate what the creative "word of the Cross" (1 Cor 1:18) would later express. And though, in the synoptics, the bridegroom is spoken of in quite clear fashion, it is remarkable that there is no mention of the bride, even in the parable

---

[2] The reading "to meet the bridegroom" seems the original one; "and the bride", a later addition (Mt 25:1).

of the royal marriage feast. It is left completely open who the bride is: whether the bridegroom, in fact, has an individual bride, of whom the invited guests are friends or relations, or whether the nature of the bride is to be looked for as present, in a hidden manner, in the guests, the "children of the bridegroom", the ten virgins, and so in those very persons to whom the Lord is speaking. Again, the words of the Baptist, in St. John, taken by themselves, do not point to anything beyond the messianic connection; they do so only if taken as part of the general content and significance of the Gospel, along with the Word being made flesh (1:14), the marriage feast at Cana (2:1–11), the "temple of his body" (2:21), the return to the womb in order to be reborn (3:4), the giving of his flesh and blood for the life of the world (6:33f.), the fountain of living water flowing from him (7:37–38), his freely giving his life for the sheep (10:17), the royal entry of the "daughter of Zion" (12:15), the vine and its branches (15:1–8), his giving his mother to the disciple (19:27), the opening of his side (19:34), the breathing of the Holy Spirit (20:22), the hand in the wound (20:27)—and, the outcome of all this, the designation of the Church as "the elect lady and her children" (2 Jn 1) and the eschatological vision of the spouse of the Lamb (Rev 21:22).

If we consider all these together, there is no doubt that, for St. John in particular, the relation between Christ and the Church goes far beyond that between Yahweh and Israel. A far more intimate relationship has been created and communicated through Christ's bodily nature, one transcending even that conveyed in the nuptial image of the Letter to the Ephesians, though including it. It is an intimacy more implied than expressed, and yet, in spite of it, St. John is as silent as the other evangelists on the personal character of the bride Church. Even in the final eschatological vision of Revelation, he shows it only as in an image. He describes her appearance, adornment, splendor radiating outward, just as does the Deutero-Isaiah, but never goes so far as to personify her. He ascribes to her no personal act, never exhorts her to rejoice, to marvel at the multitude of her children. In fact, he lets her personality merge with her social aspect, describing her as a city with a high wall around her and twelve towers, dwelling on their position and names and describing in detail the interior arrangements, lighting, occupants, water supply, and structure. Only at the end of the book and of the whole of Scripture do we hear a word from the bride, her only word, uttered in unison with the Spirit: a cry of longing to the Bridegroom: "Come!" (22:17).

Throughout, John is always more reserved than the prophets, who ascribe a much more varied personal activity to the faithful virgin and faithless prostitute Zion. Though he presupposes a far closer union as an existing fact, he restricts the personal confrontation of Bridegroom and bride to a minimum, and even the bride's cry at the end can very well be interpreted in the context of the collective idea. With this accords the fact that John, who has nothing about the simile of Head and body, carries on the two other great Old Covenant symbols of the Church, that of the "vineyard" (Is 5:1f.; Jer 2:21f.) and that of the "shepherd and the flock" (Jer 23:3f.; Ezek 34). The first he uses as an image of the community of being between Jesus and the faithful, the second as an image of the Church's collective unity reinstated by the shepherd.

If we go on to examine the theology of the Fathers, we find it difficult not to speak of an extension and amplification of the bride motive that is not certainly authorized by Scripture: the Church (even though come forth from Christ, or purified and exalted by him) is made a subject on her own, with a womanly beauty, whose form and adornment, feelings and sentiments, destinies, humiliations, and exaltations can be described. A powerful contribution to endowing the Church with a personality and life of her own was made from the earliest times (of Justin and Irenaeus) by the parallel drawn between Mary and the Church, which, in the twelfth century, came to pervade the commentaries on the Song: the Church as bride, difficult to grasp in herself as a person, appears as it were polarized in the person of Mary, and Mary herself as crystalizing around herself the whole community of the faithful. This idea may well have been, up to the present, the most suggestive for a personal conception of the Church. It is certainly the only one that, theologically, retains its force and is taken seriously. But, as with the older ecclesiological motives, the question must be asked: What is the theological justification for this extension? Has it any Scriptural basis? Is it viable for us today? These questions cannot be evaded.

The contemporary doctrine of the Church goes further than an ecclesiology of the hierarchic and sacramental structure that communicates the grace of Christ; it is focused primarily on the simile of the body. Two phases may be distinguished of what is, in fact, a reaction against the official Counter-Reformation theology: the first is that of the organic conception of Catholic romanticism, and the second, in the present century, that of a renewed attention to the ideas of St. Paul, culminating in the encyclical *Mystici Corporis* and the theologies preceding and following it. The basic fact to be realized is that the Church is something more than a "structure" set up by Christ, an institution designed to shelter and sustain a multitude of believers in Christ, as a formal element enclosing a material one. It is something that, in a mysterious way, is connected with the corporeal nature, the humanity, of Christ, preluded by his Incarnation, prepared by his preaching, and finally established by his death on the Cross and, above all, by the Eucharist as the fruit of the Passion: a mystical participation in his hypostatic union, his Person subsisting in two natures. What this change has above all restored to prominence is that the body of Christ in its three forms (*corpus triforme*), the real, the ecclesial (mystical), and the Eucharistic Body, can be one and the same, inasmuch as the Eucharistic Body is truly and actually the real body but in a way that permits it to incorporate those who receive it as a Mystical Body.

This mysterious relationship, which can never be fully elucidated, goes far beyond the plane of the visible structure of the Church or rather shows its true significance and its whole scope. The mystery, however, as a Eucharistic one, is involved in this structure and given over to its charge; it is accessible to the individual believer only in the framework of the hierarchical structure. In this way, the doctrine of the *corpus mysticum* reacts powerfully on the conception of the hierarchical Church, giving it an added strength, and depth of meaning: the Sacrament is confected by the priest, and through the power of his orders the laity participate in it. And what is true of the Eucharist is basically true of the other sacraments (with certain exceptions, to which we shall return).

It is equally true of the Church's external and internal jurisdiction, which imprints the real ecclesiological form on the life of the Christian even in his inmost acts.

To such an image of the Church, in which the institutional and the Eucharistic-sacramental elements are so bonded, the matrimonial simile is almost an embarrassment. For if the two elements together illuminate the reality set up by Christ, signifying his spiritual achievement as well as his manhood, Passion, and Resurrection, nevertheless it only *formally* illuminates *that* reality that awaits the faithful, the "structure" that fulfills and completes them materially. The sacramental structure and the grace it contains are the aspects of the Church that proceed directly from Christ and pertain only to those who are able to constitute a complementary reality. But it is difficult to see how this formal element, taken by itself, can be the basis, even figuratively, for a mutual personal relationship. Certainly, no one would want to say that this formal aspect, this form-giving (and *esse sequitur formam*) structure, taken by itself, is the Church; for the latter requires its material complement, the faithful themselves, who only become the people of God when "informed" by the Church structure and only represent the full reality of the bride of Christ within this structure. At the same time, it remains true that the faithful, both individually and as members of the community, can pertain to the Church as bride only insofar as they come within this form. They belong by grace of this form; they belong insofar as their lives are in harmony with this form and allow it to exist in them and work in them; for this form contains and imparts to them the grace of Christ and the Trinity, which makes them living members of the Mystical Body. But if the Church, as institution and sacrament, cannot be designated in the proper sense as bride of Christ, then the Church fully constituted (of form and matter) can rightly bear the personal name of bride only insofar as the people of the Church, coming under this form, receives it into itself and lets it work there—as a community, in other words.

This, much abbreviated, is roughly the line adopted by Charles Journet in his work *The Church of the Word Incarnate,* the fullest treatise in ecclesiology in our time. He is fond of citing the dictum of

St. Thomas that Christ, Head and Body, *computatur quasi una persona*[3], for everything that formally constitutes the Church and whereby she draws men to Christ is physically and morally an outflowing of Christ, who represents the *personalité mystique efficiente instrumentale* of the Church. Moreover, Journet says, "since Christ as man is King, Priest, and Savior, it is in the likeness of his Kingdom, his priesthood, and his charity that he sets his stamp on the Church, making henceforth with her but a single living being, a single mystical Person inundated with grace from on high. Of this mystical Person he constitutes himself, by his sacred humanity, the mystical personality effecting it but only instrumentally", since the ultimate agent is the Trinity itself, or, *per appropriationem,* the Holy Spirit. As the Source from which the prayer of intercession ascends, Christ and the Church in conjunction form a single mystical Person. Likewise, such a Person is formed by the Holy Spirit and the Church together as the source from which grace descends and works its effects. "The Church's life is, indeed, inseparable from its Source, from the Word of God in the order of intercessory prayer, from the Holy Spirit in the order of action. Yet the Church can be contemplated also for herself, in abstraction from her source from which she is distinguished. . . . Here is the place for the bridal comparison. The Church then appears as a created collective person, distinct from Christ as bride from Bridegroom and from the Spirit as creature from Creator." But it is clear from the whole context that such an abstraction is wholly artificial, since the underlying distinction between "uncreated" grace (as the *direct* effect of this presence) in the preceding case does not essentially elucidate anything, since the created grace itself cannot for a moment be thought of apart from the uncreated. One cannot even say that the formal element here under consideration is already described in the Bible as "body of Christ", since this necessarily includes in its definition the concrete members as the material element. Still less is the formal element to be designated the "bride".

Consequently, we are obliged to affirm that, if there is to be a nuptial (and so some kind of personal) contradistinction between Christ

---

[3] *S Th* III, 49, 1.

and the Church—however this may subsequently be determined—
the basis of it lies, indeed, in God's life imparted but no less essentially
in the subjectivity and personality of the real subjects who form the
Church.

3. Peter and Mary

Let us accept this view, without prematurely drawing the conclusion
that, in so doing, we fall back on a purely collectivistic conception.
What it excludes is simply the naïve, unreflecting hypostasizing of the
"bride", although ultimately such a hypostasizing, once fully clarified
by reflection, will be perfectly acceptable as an adequate expression of
the mystery. It excludes, in addition, the view prevailing in the late
Middle Ages and the Counter-Reformation as a consequence of a
weakening of the earlier insight; the view, that is, that the hierarchical
and sacramental structure of the Church is the Church in the strict or
formal sense, while the "sheep" ruled by the hierarchy and merely
receptive of the sacraments belong only to the "material" element of
the Church. On the contrary, the whole structural aspect of the
Church is also mediating and instrumental, and even the various
modes of divine communication in the Christological graces of the
Church are not an end in themselves but are for the sake of those who
receive them. The whole purpose of the formal structure and sacramental grace is to reach out to the man as he actually is, to penetrate
his being and raise him to the status of member of the mystical Head:
only thus is "the Church" constituted.

The encounter that, at its maximum intensity, merits the name of
marriage is personal and takes place between God as person and man
as person, though all that gives this encounter an ecclesiological stamp
is its prerequisite only and is not the encounter itself. Admittedly, the
whole complex of those things instituted by God for salvation is the
most sublime, the richest in mystery, the most inaccessible to the
human mind, of all that is. Nonetheless, it is there for the sake of the
individual creature and fulfills its purpose only when he is reached
and brought home to God. Much in these institutions is, in the

deepest sense, conditioned by time and disappears when fulfillment is reached in the next world. That is the case with the official, hierarchic structure of the Church and her individual sacraments and also with certain provisional forms of the life of grace they impart: faith and love in their veiled condition, the cardinal virtues as conditioned by time and the necessity of struggle. What never falls away is the nuptial encounter between God and the creature, for whose sake the framework of the structures is now set up and will later be dismantled. This encounter, therefore, must be the real core of the Church. The structure and the graces they impart are what raise the created subjects up to what they should be in God's design: a humanity formed as a bride to the Son, become the Church.

The bride is essentially woman, that is, receptive: one who, through acceptance of the seed but also through all her own female organs and powers is made competent to bring forth and bear fruit. In bringing forth at birth (which, in a broad sense, includes her care of the child and his feeding and upbringing to full independence), woman gives to man the complete, superabundant response. It is to such a Christian womanly role that the creature is educated by the structural, sacramental Church: the office and the Sacrament are forms of communicating the seed; they belong to the male aspect, but their end is to lead the bride to her womanly function and fortify her in it. Part of this, indeed, is her ability to receive a supernatural seed, an ability that itself is capable of development from a low to a high potential; and it includes, besides, the power to preserve the seed, to make it bring forth much fruit in the "good ground", a hundred-, sixty-, and thirtyfold (Mt 15:8–9). In the supernatural sphere of the Church one cannot assume an encounter, on equal terms, between two partners for the imparting of the seed, as one can in the natural order. Here, on the contrary, the preparation of the female partner is, fundamentally, conjoined with the nuptial act of union, and both together are meant by St. Paul with the active verb "to present" (Eph 5:27). Considered in the terms of Church law, it is true that the representative of the "office" has the masculine function of the one who gives, and the "laity" the feminine one of receiving; but it does not follow that the clergy are "more", the laity "less", the Church. The reverse is, in fact, the case, since the active communication is instrumental, the passive reception is the end, essentially ordered, to indeed basically one with, the female activity of seed bearing, giving birth, and educating.

Admittedly, this distinction between means and end is not of itself sufficient to make clear the genesis of the Church as a subject in her own right, since the structures by which grace is mediated do not exist apart in a sort of space between Christ and the Church; they belong to the latter. In this connection, it is pertinent to take note of the fact that Christ also did not establish them in a void but in the growing faith of his disciples, a faith already come to maturity in Peter's confession: "Lord, to whom shall we go? You have the words of eternal life; and we have believed, and have come to know, that you are the Holy One of God" (Jn 6:68–69). This is a faith that knows and is able to express what it knows, a knowledge it owes not to "flesh and blood", but to "the Father who draws", the Father to whom faith makes men tractable and docile (Jn 6:44–45). The Church's faith is the womb that can bring to birth, to assist which the Church's functions were framed. This makes the foundation, in the gifts it brings, strictly parallel to the demand of following Christ even to the death of the Cross, likewise a gift of grace given and assured (Jn 21:18–19). The functions belong to the Church bearing and giving birth; her womb is where they are preserved; there they were received and from there are imparted.

This alone explains why, for the Fathers, it was precisely in her sacramental action that the Church appeared as a mother's womb giving birth, and as a mother bringing up those born to her. "The Church lies in anguish", St. Methodius says, "and bears the *psychike* anew as *pneumatike*; for this reason, she is also a mother. For as the woman receives the man's yet unformed seed, and, in the course of time, brings a complete man to the world, so, we may say, the Church continually receives those who betake themselves to the *Logos,* shapes them into the image and form of Christ, and makes them, in the course of time, citizens of those blessed eternities.... Those whom she gives birth to are the neophytes, ... and these receive the characteristics, the human mode of Christ, because the image and form of the *Logos* is impressed on them and born in them through perfect *gnosis* and *pistis,* so that in them Christ is born in a spiritual manner. And, therefore, the Church is pregnant and in travail, till Christ is formed and born in us, in order that each one of the saints may be born as Christ through his participation in Christ." Here the antithesis between office as directed to an end and reception as the end envisaged is resolved in a higher identity, in that the womb of the Church effects prototypically in the individual what the individual himself will have to bring about through his being patterned in this womb. This again supposes that the Church as prototype, if she is to be able to perform the sacramental function, herself possesses not only the "objective holiness" of the structures but also the subjective, personal holiness of faith, love, and hope realized in act. Therein she is already, in the fullest sense, the bride who can make to the Bridegroom and his "word of the Cross" (1 Cor 1:18) the creaturely, bridal response expected of her—creaturely, because her love is believing and hoping, not seeing and possessing; bridal, because her loving faith and hope are formed supernaturally by Christ's "word of the Cross".

All of this can be expressed in a different way: if the content of the ecclesiastical structure is, for the Church herself, "objective spirit", whose scope and range can only be measured and grasped by the divine subjectivity (for God alone completely "understands" his own Word, which the disciples proclaim; God alone fully perceives the greatness of the grace that they mediate sacramentally; and God alone knows the divine severity inherent from its foundation in the Church's jurisdiction, when it is applied according to the mind of God), then this "objective spirit" necessarily presupposes a "subjective spirit" to receive it. This is Peter's faith. It is obvious, however, that it does not inhere absolutely and exclusively in the subject, Peter. Its existence is only witnessed and represented by Peter at the promise of the office (Mt 16) and its bestowal (Jn 21), as is abundantly clear by the Lord's threefold question before the investiture. What this act brings out above all is that Peter's subjective spirit is not equal to the objective spirit of office and Sacrament, not only because Peter is a sinner and his sinfulness was never more terribly revealed than when he was confronted with the demands inherent in the spirit of the office but even more so because Christ alone can bring unison into the two sides in the uniqueness and singularity of his mission as Redeemer and Sacrifice, one only who can bring together in unison the divine demands of worship and expiation inherent in the priestly office. The identity to which the office points cannot, by any means, exist in the Church, but solely in the Lord, as the Church's Head and Bridegroom.

Yet, and just because of this, this identity must be reproduced in the Church; for the Lord wills to see his Church standing before him, not as a singular, palpable failure but as a glorious bride worthy of him. Here the Marian principle in the Church necessarily comes into play. Mary is the subjectivity that, in its womanly and receptive manner, is enabled fully to correspond to the masculine subjectivity of Christ, through God's grace and the overshadowing of his Spirit. The Church flowing forth from Christ finds her personal center in Mary as well as the full realization of her idea as Church. Her faith, with its love and hope, in its womanly openness to the divine, the Divine-human Bridegroom, is coextensive with the masculine principle, embedded in the Church, of office and Sacrament, even though it is not part of its womanly character to comprehend totally, in the manner of the Bridegroom, the objective spirit therein contained. She is not the Word but the adequate response awaited by God from the created sphere and produced in it by his grace through the Word.

For this, undoubtedly, a special grace is needed, qualitatively different from that of the rest of the faithful, which elevates the Marian response of faith to the status of principle and exemplar of the response of the entire Church. Mary's faith, as the fruitful womb of the Word, is privileged on two counts. In respect of its origin, it is a faith proceeded from her "immaculate conception"; in respect of its end, it is a faith destined to bear the fruit that is not only Christ's body but also himself as Head. This fruitfulness, therefore, which was previously predicated of the Church as prototype of the fruitfulness of the members, when, from being born, passively, in baptism, they actively bring forth the life of Christ, in themselves and in the Church—this paradigmatic fruitfulness is, in Mary, so far surpassed, raised to such potency, that she not only does what the Church does—bring forth Christ—but also does it archetypally, in that she lets the Head of the Church take flesh in her, him whom the Church will, in turn, deliver from out of herself. The process on the ecclesial level, whereby the soul born of Christ in turn conceives and bears him, in the order of the body, this process is elevated to become an archetypal process in which Mary, preserved from original sin by the grace of Christ's Cross, conceives and bears him in the order of the Head. In the former process, the objective stainlessness of the Church (the "infallibility of Peter") always effects and supposes a constant purification of the Church by water and the Word, and, therefore, the Church becomes a "glorious bride" only as she is actually made pure. But in the process on the Marian level there can be no question of a subjective, personal purification as an actual event. Mary, preserved from the outset, has undergone no such purification. In Mary, therefore, the Church is not only infallible in the official Sacramental sphere (though always fallible subjectively and existentially, always defective and hopelessly falling short of the ideal inherent and proclaimed). In her the Church is also personally immaculate and beyond the tension between reality and ideal.

It is on this very account that Mary also stands above and beyond the purely mundane encounter of bridegroom and bride and opens it out into the infinity of the divine Eros insofar as God himself accepts her word of faith and fidelity, and as she is overshadowed not by the *Logos* as such but by the Holy Spirit, who carries the Father's seed into her spiritual and bodily womb, the fruit of this marriage being the Incarnation of the Son, who, in his entire being, is Head and Body, Bridegroom and Bride. There is certainly no question of making a personal distinction, in the union of husband and wife, between the man giving and the seed given, and from this standpoint Mary, as prototype of the Church, is rightly called the bride of the incarnate Word. Nonetheless, what is brought about here is not a repetition of the sex relationship but its prototypal realization between God and man; and God, known and received in this intimate fashion, can only be the God in three Persons. On this account, Mary receives the Son as seed of the Father through the realizing act of the Holy Spirit of Father and Son. And it is for the same reason that, in the sphere of the Church, the actualizing of the sacraments is the work of the Holy Spirit, who places the Father's Word in the womb of the soul for it to generate and give birth. This again does not prevent the Church being the Son's bride, since this entire participation of the created world in the Trinitarian Divinity is the working and prolongation of the incarnate Word. Mary is given to us as prototype so that the Church may never forget the Trinitarian dimension of her nuptial mystery; just as Christ, too, as he went about on earth, always situated it in relation to an openness to the Trinitarian life.

There is another thing that this reveals, namely, the reason why, according to St. Thomas, the Fiat of the mother of God was spoken *loco totius generis humani* and not, for instance, *loco totius Ecclesiae.* (It could equally be said that, in her, the Church speaks her Fiat to God for the whole human race.) The Word was, in fact, carried into her life of faith in a womb, in order to become flesh. It is part of her mystery and being that the Word became flesh, not only in but also from her, that her self-giving response to God was understood and required as something involving the whole person, something both spiritual and of the body. One cannot divide this response into two parts: one spiritual, her active acceptance of faith; the other bodily, her passive utilization as womb for God becoming man. It is for this very reason that she participated in the formation of the hypostatic union in her own manner, a purely womanly one of surrender. And when the Fathers see the actual *connubium* between God and man realized in Christ himself, in the indissoluble union of the two natures, this is also no purely physical occurrence, with its matrimonial character exclusively derived from the side of God and his intention. It is a real two-sided mystery of love through the bridal consent of Mary acting for all the rest of created flesh. In Mary's flesh is meant "all" created "flesh" (Jn 17:2) to which God wills to espouse himself; and since Mary is *caro ex qua,* she is also *fides ex qua.* But the hypostatic union is the carrying out and thus the final indissoluble sealing of the covenant of fidelity, which marks with its sign all future vows of fidelity in the Church: those of baptism, of marriage, and of virginity.

Mary's abiding physical virginity is the bodily aspect of the abiding inner virginity, which means the exclusiveness, of her spiritual faith. The glorification of virginity by the Fathers, which they apply both to the Church's virginity and to that of those vowed to it and of each individual member of the Church, even the married, is directed, fundamentally, to a Marian virginity, itself primarily the expression of a personal attitude to the God coming to meet them nuptially. Once again, we can follow out two themes in this glorification: the Church, from her very origin, is virginal (as distinct from the synagogue, so often reproached by God as an adulteress). Also, the Church, as the one "purified" by Christ, has become "virginal", and as she is constantly protected by this grace, she must keep herself in the virginity received and not fall away from it again. But both Mary and the Church are fruitful precisely because they are virginal. The exclusive character of love, which virginity involves, is in each the condition for bearing the fruit of God. The themes interlace in the happiest way when the two acts—the "purification" of the Church and her divine marriage—are seen as one, as in the celebrated Benedictus antiphon of the Epiphany.

Dom Odo Casel has brought out the idea (originally Syrian and subsequently adopted in the West) that the Epiphany is the feast of the marriage between Christ and the Church in that the baptismal water of the Jordan was also understood as the fructifying water of the marriage: "In the river Jordan has the Church become espoused", sings the Syrian Church during matins of the vigil. The bath of the bridegroom is, at the same time, the marriage bath of the bride, since the bride herself is present prototypically in the flesh of the bridegroom. For this reason, the Epiphany can be, in the East, both the baptismal day of all believers and the day of the consecration of virgins; for the sacramental bath is itself the enactment of the nuptial mystery, and the consecration of virgins is done to exemplify the marriage between Christ and the Church, being the explication of what had been begun in the baptismal vows and fulfilled in the conferring of the Sacrament. What essentially demonstrates this for us is that the sacramental baptism received by the individual Christian was originally received by the Church herself, and indeed in the flesh of Christ, which, nuptially united to his Godhead, is the source of the "Mystical Body".

The outcome of our study so far is that the first step to answering, in a positive way, the question as to the subject of the Church is to relate it to Mary's faith, fruitful because virginal. Alois Müller has rightly shown that the patristic parallel between Mary and the Church, though it contains all the elements for the solution, failed of final elucidation because it was never made sufficiently clear that Mary's faith was what made possible her bodily conception of Christ, and so there was no advance beyond a mere parallel between her bodily bringing forth and the Church's spiritual bringing forth. But once all doubt on the point was overcome, the act of Mary was seen, absolutely, as the basic subjective act of the Church. For Mary's personal act, by reason of its uniqueness and eminence, can be two things at once: the subjective and absolutely complete ground for the subjective act of the Church as such (always qualitatively superior to every act, defective as it is, of the individual); and, since Mary is also an individual believer within the Church community, the subjective and absolutely complete ground of each personal act of faith within the *communio sanctorum.* At the same time, it must always be borne in mind that, as we said before, the subjective act of the Church, even in its perfect fullness in that of Mary, is always one of womanly surrender—an act not of dominance and comprehension (which pertains to the Head) but of humble, handmaidenly following and service. Its character is not one of masculine gnosis, desire for knowledge at all costs; for Mary on earth did not seek after knowledge but was content to keep and contemplate the word in her heart. Even the theological and pastoral knowledge and understanding that the risen Christ laid up in the memory of his Church in opening, for forty days, the Scripture to his apostles was placed deep within this spiritual womb of womanly contemplation. And so, in this respect also, the prophecy was fortified: *femina circumdabit virum.*

Mary, in giving birth spiritually and physically to the Son, becomes the universal Mother of all believers, for the Church as body is born of Christ and is herself Christ. Mary is the prototype of the Church, not only because of her virginal faith but also equally because of her fruitfulness. This is, indeed, not autonomous (as that of the goddesses of fertility) but wholly ancillary, since it is Christ, not Mary, who brought the Church into being by his Passion. All the same, she took part, as an intermediary, in this creation by the universality and unrestrictedness of her Fiat, which the Son is able to use as an infinitely plastic medium to bring forth from it new believers, those born again. Her presence with him at the Cross, her agreement to his abandonment of her to the Church in the midst of his dereliction on the Cross, her eternal role as the woman in labor (Rev 12), show how fully her self-surrender is universalized to become the common source, the productive womb, of all Christian grace.

4. *"Anima ecclesiastica"*

Mary's special role as regards the new people of God in the history of salvation gives part of the answer to the question "Who is the Church?" It cannot give the whole answer, but what it can do is usher in the complete answer, since it is the infinite disponibility of her attitude of faith ("Be it done unto me according to thy word") that makes her the ideal (moral) and real (physical) womb of the Church. Her own person, in its faith, love, and hope, has become so supple in the hand of the Creator that he can extend her beyond the limits of a private consciousness to a Church consciousness, to what the older theology since Origen and Ambrose is accustomed to call *anima ecclesiastica.*

This *"ecclesiasticizing" of the individual consciousness* is, however, available on a different level to every man regenerated from the private existence of the natural state and the still more cramped bounds of sin consciousness estranged from God, regenerated, that is, to the Church through the death of the old man and endowed with the consciousness of the new man. The truths propounded here are such as the "old man" cannot grasp, eluding the subtlest philosophical dialectic of alternation with its progressive broadening out of consciousness into the Absolute. The fact is that the dying and burial of the old man have already taken place *en Christô,* and so likewise the resurrection of the new, who lives *en Christô,* ontologically, and so, of necessity, also consciously. "Therefore if any one is in Christ, he is a new creation; the old has passed away; behold, the new has come" (2 Cor 5:17).

The newness in question consists not in a diminution, still less in an extinction of personal consciousness, but in its being taken along in faith into the consciousness of Christ: "It is no longer I who live, but Christ who lives in me; and the life I now live in the flesh I live by faith in the Son of God, who loved me and gave himself for me" (Gal 2:20). "And he died for all, that those who live might live no longer for themselves but for him who for their sake died and was raised" (2 Cor 5:15). "If we live, we live to the Lord, and if we die, we die to the Lord; so then, whether we live or whether we die, we are the Lord's" (Rom 14:8). This constantly renewed and variously expressed expropriation of man, in which he dies to himself, is, in its positive aspect, his appropriation by God, to "obtain salvation" (1 Th 5:9). The expression is never used in a singular sense, however: it always refers to God's own people (1 Pet 2:9), and only as such are they called to "obtain the glory of our Lord Jesus Christ" (2 Th 2:13). This taking up of the "I" and the "we" through God into Christ is often described by Paul as a changeover from consciousness of one's own action to consciousness of God's action taking place within us: "Not that I have already obtained this or am already perfect; but I press on to make it my own, because Christ Jesus has made me his own" (Phil 3:12). "But if one loves God, one is known by him" (1 Cor 8:3). "What we are is known to God" (2 Cor 5:11). "You have come to know God, or rather to be known by God" (Gal 4:9). And, eschatologically: "Now I know in part; then I shall understand fully, even as I have [now already] been fully understood" (1 Cor 13:12).

What kind of consciousness this is of the new man, according to Paul (and also, of course, John, Peter, and James), comes out most clearly from his use of the personal pronouns. Paul makes copious use of the first person singular. His "I" has astonishing vitality, diversity, agility: in fact, with regard to the community, it has a kind of omnipresence beyond space and time—*absens corpore, praesens spiritu* (absent in body . . . present in spirit [1 Cor 5:3]). He uses "I" in speaking of such a commonplace thing as the plan of a journey that he propounds, but also in speaking of the vertiginous height of his solitary calling in God's plan of salvation: "You have heard of the stewardship of God's grace that was given to me for you, how the mystery was made known to me by revelation, as I have written briefly. When you read this you can perceive my insight into the mystery of Christ" (Eph 3:2–4). His "I" is of such unique character, is so patterned on Christ and imitative of him as to be recommended, in its turn, for imitation. It had its beginning at Damascus. It is the "I" of Christ's mission, the "I" transformed into the servant of Christ, from flesh become spirit. It is ecclesiastical, and manifests itself—brings out its own anatomy before the eyes of all—only because it is a paradigm of the mission, the functional side of the Church, of membership in the body of Christ. It knows itself as utterly divested of ownership of itself; belonging wholly to Christ and the communion of saints, it would prefer to die so as to be with Christ, that being by far the best—but it no longer knows any personal preference: what is best for Paul is what serves the Church best, and for her sake he continues to live (Phil 1:23–25).

We can see from this that to attempt to write a psychology of Paul is no less absurd, in principle, than to do the same of Christ. The personal reality that drives forward with such impetus cannot, by its very nature, be contained in these categories, although it does not destroy them (which is what tantalizes the onlooker so much) but makes sovereign use of them. It is because the "I" of Christ harbors the Father and the Spirit in circumincession that he can release out of himself the Mystical Body with all his personal members, their missions of sanctification and functions of love. And because the Trinitarian "I" of Christ wills to dwell in those who love him (Jn 14:23), the "I" of Paul is not only entirely dominated by this divine life but also harbors, for its part, the communities entrusted to him, which he brings forth in travail out of himself (Gal 4:19), and to which he is father, mother, and nurse. His "anxiety for all the churches" (2 Cor 11:28) is a womanly weakness, accepted in order to produce manly strength, a weakness that, together with Christ, is the ignominy of the Cross and a spectacle to men and angels. Yet even on this plane the law holds good: "Children ought not to lay up for the parents, but parents for their children. I will most gladly spend and be spent for your souls" (2 Cor 12:14–15). He justifies even his severity as an educator by this love and lets his tenderness shine through all his harsh measures. And he so utterly experiences the glory of Christ pervading him that he has no call whatever to glorify himself but is wholly and entirely the glory of the churches.

This "I"—explicable in terms of the mission and not of psychology—
which the Church bears in herself and has expanded to become the
anima ecclesiastica, is now able to think and to say things about the
Church, quite beyond the reach of a personal "I". This occurs when,
in the course of its official function, it has to contrast itself with the
"you" of those in its charge and can, therefore, include with its own
content the content of the churches and communities—and so, also,
the content of the "you". In such cases, it can use the ecclesiastical
"we" in statements bearing on salvation, which none of the individuals addressed could presume to do. Take the beginning of the Letter
to the Ephesians, where the Father's eternal plan of salvation is described
from predestination onward, and where the "we" designates the
Church of the predestined. In this "we", Paul himself is, of course,
included. His assurance of salvation is as absolute as that of the
Church herself (which prevents neither him nor the actual Church
from supporting this assurance by fervent prayer and penance—"lest,
while I preach to others, I myself become a castaway"). But he
absolutely includes within it the community of which he has actual
charge, not in a vague, rhetorical "we" but in the "we" of the father,
of the responsible apostle, who gathers his children around him as a
hen gathers her brood under her wings (Mt 23:38); yet the parrhesia
for doing so he derives from his mission and office. It is only when
admonishing and censuring in his function as educator that he opposes
himself to the community or, at any rate, excludes himself from it *ad
tempus;* while in his preaching office he includes himself, and his
consciousness of the Church can compensate for any lack of parrhesia
in the utterance of others. "Become as I am, for I also have become as
you are" (Gal 4:12). That is, you too must allow yourselves to be
formed by the Church: "And we exhort you, brethren, admonish the
idle, encourage the faint-hearted, help the weak, be patient with them
all. See that none of you repays evil for evil, but always seek to do
good to one another and to all" (1 Th 5:14-15). It is clear from this
that the "Church of the saints" not only "represents" the Church of
sinners, of the imperfect, the struggling, but also carries them and is
responsible for them before God. With Christ it empties itself, so as, in
weakness and shame, to bring in the least member and to be able to

represent each such, not only in word, in reprimanding, but in deed and in truth.

Thus the opposition between "I" and "you" ("Thou") is always reconciled by the "we" that joins them together, and the transition from one to the other is smooth and imperceptible.

"We" can mean (1) the person of Paul in his office. The plural, then, expresses the neutralization of the person by his office but, at the same time, emphasizes the function, which, as such, is always represented by a plurality of subjects. The transition from this "official" to the "theological" (carrying and including) plural remains imperceptible (see 1 Th 3:1, 3–4, 6f., where, in verse 5, the "I" suddenly emerges from the "we"); (2) the hierarchs, for instance Paul with Timothy and Silvanus as joint authors of the letter, where Paul either purposely includes the others or, forgetting them for the moment and speaking from the fullness of his own heart, includes them only implicitly. The "party of the hierarchs" can also pass over, without a break, into the "party of the Church", since the teachers have confidence in it manifesting what is taught in its mode of life; (3) on this account, "we" can simply mean the Christians in the Church, Paul and the community together.

"You" is either (1) the individual community spoken to or (2) a considerable section of the Church, for instance, the Gentile Christians, to whom Paul speaks as a Jew from the other side, or alternatively, the Jewish Christians, to whom Paul appeals as the apostle of the Gentiles. But it can also be (3) simply "you Christians", you baptized, dead and risen in Christ; and then its scope is coincident with the "we" in the last signification. In this case, it is indifferent whether Paul uses "you" or "we": he is carrying on the inner colloquy of the Church with herself; he gives utterance to her self-consciousness, either as he is authorized to do so or (which comes to the same thing) as the voice of the whole. This applies equally to questions of fact and of obligation. Consequently, it does not matter if the instruction proceeds from the "we" to the "you" (1 Th 4:1f.) and then again comprises both in a common "we" (4:14), continuing in the "you" only again to include the "you" in the "we", and to establish a rigid exclusion from those not belonging to the Church and from their conduct (5:5–10). In

Galatians 6:1–10, "I" alternates with "you", "thou", and "we"; all facets of the Church consciousness that never impairs the person but protects and elevates it to a superior order.

This analysis shows that the birth of the new man, belonging specifically to the Church in the grace of baptism, in the outpouring of faith, hope, and love through the Holy Spirit (Rom 5:1–5), means the extension of the narrow limits of the individual sinful subject as compared with the subject of the Church. This does not imply that the believer becomes Christ substantially, nor does it mean a direct participation in the hypostatic union; nor, indeed, a progressive pantheism according to Eckhart, or as Hegel teaches in such an extreme sense. On the other hand, the mysteries of the *communio sanctorum*, the degree of the mutual circumincession of the members, their mutual power of representation before God, their community of goods even of the most inward, the monadic power to love to draw everything on itself and into itself (as described in particular by Tauler) and, as a result, to extend itself over everything and, while remaining a single heart, to become one *cor mundi*: these mysteries cannot be adequately mastered by means of purely philosophical distinctions ("*entitative* singular, *intentionaliter* universal"). The theological paradoxes are sharper, and it is simply a question of preserving their sharpness and not reducing one side to the other. They are paradoxes that thrust themselves on our attention from the indwelling of the Trinity in the Church: for the Church is uniquely the sphere that binds God and creature together. Therefore, where the most improbable event must necessarily occur—where, that is, the individual person, penetrated by God's dwelling in him—is both elevated and sublimated in his personality and opened to and made the portion of the community. Here too the mysteries of the Trinitarian relations and of their opposition in identity cannot fail to impinge; and the mystery of Christ himself, who in the Church is at once himself (his Body) and another (his Bride), works out in the Christian's life of grace in the Church. But with all this, the fundamental law of the creaturely status is not to be held superseded and overborne by the divine paradoxes to which man is raised. On the contrary, his elevation is what brings out clearly, confirms and fulfills the ultimate end of the created being as such (*gratia perficit naturam*). Looked at in this way, the laws of the *corpus mysticum* are commendable to reason, and that is why Paul could borrow his image of the body from the Romans. It is reasonable that the member should sacrifice itself for the *bonum commune*, as Cicero says, and after him Caiaphas (Jn 11:50), unconsciously prophesying, that is, not suspecting how truly he spoke. And it is equally in accord with any rational social order that the strong should care for the weak and so bring about a balance (Rom 15:1f.; 1 Cor 8). But just how far this law can go is made manifest only in the Church.

5. Unity in analogy

It follows that the Church is most fully present where faith, hope, and love, selflessness, and tolerance of others are found in the highest degree. Thus the concepts of "more" and "less" come into the Church, and the categories of proper and improper enter at the borderline where a living, loving, hoping faith passes, through mortal sin, into a "dead faith". These categories altogether dominate the ecclesiology of the Fathers. Later, when heretics definitely misapplied them, they were relegated to the background, making way for a univocal idea of the Church, but one tending of necessity to a certain minimalism. Still, in the long run, they remain indispensable for ecclesiology. They are dangerous only when they are warped and so lead to inadmissible conclusions: for example, that the sinner, who possesses no more than a dead faith, can no longer be a member of the Church, or that the Church of the saints and the official, institutional Church are magnitudes of different orders, of their nature disparate. We must keep two aspects simultaneously in mind and hold them firmly: first, the Church is a unity—Trinitarian, Christological, and plainly characterized as such in her own structure; and, secondly, this unity is imprinted analogously on the members. Here it is not a question of the *analogia fidei*—the allocation of faith by God according to the quality of the mission of the members—but of the categories of proper and improper and, within the former, of the degrees of intensity within the participation.

The Fathers saw these two aspects expressed in the unity of the bride, the one single dove, and the plurality of her companions, those who follow in her train. "*Sponsa enim ipsa perfecta ecclesia est, sponsus Dominus, adulescentulae vero cum sponsa sunt inchoantes animae et per novum studium pubescentes*" (St. Gregory the Great). Origen had already given this interpretation, Origen, who was so fond of emphasizing the (fluid) analogy, in the Church, of the "simple" (or "progressive") and the "knowers" (or "perfect"). The "perfect" are those who have the *anima ecclesiastica,* having allowed their consciousness to merge with that of the Church, and so represent in themselves the essence of the one bride. One would have to blind oneself to the facts if one refused to admit that, for the Fathers and even for the High Middle Ages, the "proper" Church was that of those with living faith, those who love, and that, despite all the misapplications of this view by the Montanists, Novatians, Donatists, Messalianers, the extreme Origenists, and, later, the Bogomils and Catharists, despite all the Church's theological defenses against these, the original, early Christian idea of an irrefragable partnership of Church and love, Church unity and love unity, lived on vigorously. Augustine himself, who had carried on in this field a bitter war against the "pure Church" of the Donatists and the sinlessness of the Pelagians, preferred to abandon the "unspottedness" of the present Church and to make the "stainless bride" an eschatological reality rather than to retreat from the idea of this partnership. Certainly, the Church is full of sinners, but *inasmuch* as they are sinners, they cannot be counted in with the Church. They can only be in her as "improper", "so-called", "seeming", "reckoned", "pretended" members but cannot, *qua* sinners, express membership in the one body of love. It must be clearly noted that Augustine, in this, had no thought of splitting the Church into two (apparently irreconcilable) magnitudes: a Church of saints, the true one, and a Church of the external institution. He had no more idea of doing so than any of the other Fathers or the scholastics.

Admittedly, Augustine's idea of the Church has within it a line of demarcation, derived from elsewhere, which has, indirectly, an ecclesiological consequence and is not without a causal connection with the final cleavage in the Protestant idea of the Church. Let us look first at the relationship between the proper and the improper Church before Augustine. From the Gospel onward, there is a "bearing" of the sinners in the Church; it is not without significance that, in John, Christ's answer to Peter's acknowledgment of the Messiah contains a reference to the presence of Judas among the Twelve: "Did I not choose you, the Twelve, and one of you is a devil?" (Jn 6:70). The line constantly taken by Paul in his ethical teaching is that Christians should bear with one another, that the more perfect (the "strong"), in particular, should endure the less perfect (the "weak"). The only kind of excommunication he uses is medicinal, leaving to God judgment on the question of definite membership. John, however (in the name of the Church), puts himself already in the situation of the final judgment, when he distinguishes between sins that are not unto (eternal) death, for which one can intercede, and those unto (eternal) death. "I do not say that one is to pray for that" (1 Jn 5:16). But can the line of demarcation between these two sins (not to be confused with our distinction between mortal and venial sins) ever be established in the temporal sphere? And as long as there remains a glimmer of hope for an apostate's conversion, surely the Church is obliged by the command to bear with and pray for him?

This command was taken absolutely by the pre-Augustinian Fathers as the rule of the Church. Origen describes the "perfect" or "gnostic" as the one who intercedes with God for the "imperfect", in fact, as the strong in Christ fighting the Pauline fight against the powers of darkness, on behalf of the weak. The "gnostic" or "knower" is, for Origen, precisely the "teacher", whether through theological instruction, if he is capable, or through the example of his life, preeminently through martyrdom. And so, out of Paul's teaching and his idea of the fruitfulness and convincing witness of holiness, we have the image of the Church wonderfully described, for example, by Methodius:

From the "rib" of the Son made Man and lying dead on the Cross (the rib being his spirit), God took the matter from which to form for him his "life partner". "I mean, of course, the souls betrothed and espoused to him; for it is the frequent usage of Scripture to call such the whole multitude of believers, and so the Church; and in this way the more perfect and advanced are brought together into the one person and the one body of the Church. The higher souls, who have a more inward grasp of the truth, cast away, in their perfect purity and perfect faith, the follies of the flesh, and thus become the life partners of Christ; to him they are, according to the words of the apostle, betrothed and espoused as a virgin, in order that they may receive within them the pure and fecund seed of doctrine and cooperate as helpers in teaching for the redemption of others. But those who are still imperfect and only beginners in doctrine will be drawn by the more perfect into the pregnant womb of the redemption, and formed as in a mother's body, till they are born and brought to existence unto the greatness and beauty of virtue; for these, in turn, thanks, to their progress, have become the Church and cooperate in the birth and training of other children, in that they accomplish the immaculate will of the Logos in the womb of their souls as in a mother's body."

This image of the Church constantly recurs throughout patristic theology. It is a dynamic image of love, a love striving upward to the perfect and, at the same time, descending with Christ to sustain and protect what is weak. This love, then, is not only a general well-wishing of children for one another but one explicitly Christlike in form, and only thus a Christian and ecclesial love, not stopping at the things "the heathens also do" but going on to what Christ has done and what each member after and along with the Head ought to do in the commission and power of Christ. Paul first demonstrated in himself this law of bearing the Church in its full application and had, as it were, to experience in himself what is necessarily implied in the specific holiness of the Church. Therefore, the Fathers did not stretch the idea unduly in applying this active "bearing force" of Christian love to all who earnestly love Christ and the Church more than themselves and become martyrs to her, whether or not by the shedding of their blood. This is what shows whether, in the consciousness of the individual, the Church outweighs the personal "I", and whether a "fellow runner" in the Church is a "bearer of the Church", a "pillar" (Rev 3:12). It is here that the consciousness of belonging to the

Church objectively becomes the more profound consciousness of participating in the Spirit of the Church.

The "ecclesiastical hierarchy" of Denis the Areopagite rounds off aesthetically this ancient image of the Church and is also responsible for its currency in the Middle Ages. In it, the official hierarchy is incorporated into this comprehensive scheme and interpreted accordingly. The sharp antithesis between the perfect and those on the way to perfection is toned down and reconciled by means of a third, intermediate stage of those who, themselves the object of mediation, begin already to act as mediators. The main import of the word *hierarchy* is drawn from the primitive Christian interpretation of the Church in terms of love; its Neoplatonic guise is purely external. Primarily, it signifies the inner hierarchy of sanctity, to which the official hierarchy is subjoined in a secondary sense. Nonetheless, the love inherent in the Church is itself present impersonally in the office, in accordance with the essential character of Christian love (as a participation in the heavenly hierarchy of the divine love itself).

This image of the Church, in the Middle Ages, came to be centered on Mary, and in this way its inmost truth was brought out. Previously, the "stainlessness" of the holy Church, viewed empirically, could be considered only as an ideal to which she approximated. The apostles were held to be preeminently the core of the actual Church "without spot or wrinkle"; "*Ipsi [apostoli] enim sunt non habentes maculam vel rugam aut aliquid hujusmodi, vera ecclesia*" (Origen). To them were added their successors, the martyrs, and, after the time of Origen, the holy Doctors, as evidenced by Bede: "Through the word and example of the holy Doctors, the whole structure of the Church, according to Bede, is held together. To them is entrusted the care of the Church, and there is no doubt at all that their firmness is not to be shaken. . . . In the heart of the saints, therefore, the one, true doctrine of the Church is constantly assured; in the works of the saints, the virtue of the Church is ever resplendent and beautiful." Bede was aware of the weaknesses of the empirical Church, those even of its holiest members, and spoke, therefore, as though the Church's stainlessness were a matter of approximation: the Church is realized insofar as sanctity and love are realized: complete sanctity and love, which constitute the "form" of the Church, are, then, to be found in the Head alone.

This opens up three different ways of approach. The Church's sanctity can be held (in the context, for instance, of the Song of Songs or of the Letter to the Ephesians) as an "idea" laid up in heaven above the present reality and informing it. Or else it is seen (and this is closely connected with the first) in the indestructible character of the hierarchical and sacramental structure set up by Christ, thus, in practice, settling the question of a subject of the Church. Or finally, it is centered on Mary's immaculate conception as its personal fixed point. According to this view, Mary stands, as the universal womb bearing progeny, behind the sanctity of the apostles, and great significance is given to her presence with the apostles at Pentecost and receiving the Spirit, so that she is, in a very real sense, able to communicate her Christian wisdom to the apostolic Church. Thus, as Bede tells us, "Philip of Harveng never tires of extolling the maternal activity of Mary in the first ages of the Church, bringing forth the apostles, as if bearing them, out of the darkness of ignorance, bringing them up and forming them, and, as the Mother of all, presiding over them, and, through her constancy in faith, calling the vacillating disciples to order." This somewhat external, imaginative presentation gives place to a more interior one in German mysticism, which brings out the idea of the essential fecundity and apostolic character of love (even— and especially—of silent, contemplative love), and so attains to a far deeper comprehension of Mary's role as Mediatrix of grace. She is seen as spreading her protective cloak over the whole of Christendom, and making some part of her stainlessness flow out over the bride, the Church. Philip's "education of the apostles" by Mary, which, it is true, has been taken as referring to the sphere of love and fidelity rather than to that of their office, now makes way for the idea of a sheltering of the whole official side of the Church in Mary's maternal womb, which bears, brings forth, and silently represents it. It is significant, however, that even at the beginning of the thirteenth century, John of Pecham saw the Church's unity wholly in terms of love and holiness, into which even the unity of obedience to the hierarchy was integrated. For him, Church unity is (1) unity of love, by which all are one heart and one soul; (2) unity of divinization (that is, of grace), which makes all members of the one Christ; (3) unity of ecclesiastical communion in faith and the sacraments; (4) unity of the hierarchical connection, to which belong the common obedience and also the unity of the apostolic succession from Christ; and (5) unity of common sentiments (unanimity).

This whole system of ecclesiology, centered on the strongly dynamic idea of love in the Church, ascending and descending, bearing and being borne, and with its organic completion in Mary's immaculate conception, suffered a contraction as a result of the predestination taught by Augustine in his later years. According to Augustine, the final separation spoken of in St. John's letter is something close at hand, definite and tangible: the proper Church (of those who really love) is now explained as or hardened into the "Church of the predestined", and the improper Church (of those in mortal sin within the Church) similarly as the mass of the damned. It is not that Augustine had any thought of empirically determining this final separation; but the line separating, once and for all, the "two kingdoms" ran hidden beneath the earthly frontier between Church and non-Church, though not simply coincident with it. According to John, one did not pray for the reprobate; even Christ on the Cross, according to Thomas, could not pray for them. Bearing others in love has certain bounds, even though, for the time being, not verifiable. The fruitfulness of love is not simply infinite. The Church of the elect shuts herself up within herself, and as a result the dark shadows cast a gloom over Christendom from Augustine to Gottschalk and Calvin, disturb men over the question of their own personal salvation. And, with all this, Augustine in his anti-Pelagianism sees sin present everywhere. The Church's stainlessness is eschatological and, for the present, is wholly withdrawn into its divine Head. In him, through him, the body is freed from sin. For Augustine, the central image is that of the Head and the body—that of the bride and Bridegroom is merely explanatory of this. Just as we speak of a distinct closed period of Church history ending with Constantine, so we may also speak of a closed Augustinian period in ecclesiology (which, though quite different, is nevertheless connected with it below the surface); both of these are now beginning to open up.

The image of the Church, that of dynamic love bearing and being borne (which in its totality is borne by Christ, by God), an image that sees in the Church all gradations of holiness from the highest, most unsullied sanctity of Mary to the very brink of damnation, in fact even beyond it, in the case of the gravely sinful who are yet, in some way, members of the Church—this image is the justification of these two statements: that the Church, the more "properly" she is the Church, the more stainless, the more conformed to Christ she is, the more Marial, and that she still remains the Church even in the sinner, since he has some velleity and is being borne by the suffering members of the Church, deficient and estranged though it be, and as struggling and in course of conversion. The Church, at her core, remains unspotted and a pure bride. In this, she is distinguished from the synagogue, which, according to the prophets, can become a brazen harlot. There is a certain continuity between the Old and the New Covenants in that the Church, in her ("improper" but "true" members) sins and falls, and the words of the prophets never cease to apply to us as members of the Church.

This is, in fact, the image of the Church already adopted once one takes seriously the question "Who is the Church?" For the only satisfactory answer is that she consists of real subjects. She is not a *mere* collectivity that, in comparison with the real interconnection between one generation and another of mankind as a whole, always has something fictitious and accidental about it. Real subjects, then, but only such as participate through divine grace in a normative subject and its consciousness. And if this participation is possible only through infused grace, then that in which they participate is divine: the supreme subject demanded by the question posed can only be the Divine itself. Mankind gains participation in it through Christ and the sphere that is his (*en Christô*) and that he has prepared as Redeemer, namely, the Church. Insofar as this sphere is his own, he is her consciousness; and insofar as she makes to him the response of a woman and a bride, she has her supreme, normative subjectivity in Mary. Finally, insofar as the one grace streams through her, this grace makes all spirits, in all their personal varieties of missions and spiritual ways, converge in a single consciousness, opening in Mary to Christ, and through Christ to the Holy Spirit of the three-personal God, who in the beginning overshadowed Mary and, since Easter and Pentecost, dwells in the Church.

This image of the Church also gives a convincing sense to the "myth" of the Church fallen from heaven for whose sake Christ leaves the Father and the heavenly Jerusalem, the mother, in order to go in search of her on earth and to form with her one flesh. For, in fact, the subject estranged from God, namely, the man Adam and, in him, mankind, is really fallen from paradise and gone into an alien place far from God. Adamic humanity, and none other, was what the Redeemer went to seek. It alone was the subject out of which he willed to form his pure Church. This humanity was, in God's predetermination ideally, and in the first parents, really holy and unstained. Its turning away from God, which could not be put right by man, its banishment to a bodily state subject to the passions and death, likened by Ignatius to an existence in prison among wild beasts, are quite enough justification, on Biblical grounds, for the core of the apparent myth. But the return home is achieved not by a gnostic form of spiritualization but by the transformation of the flesh estranged from God through the sacrificial fire of the Cross, in the mystery of the "one" sacrificed flesh of Man and woman, Christ and Church.

6. *A unity of unities*

This brings us to one last element in the solution of the problem that still remains to be clarified. We found ourselves unable to accede to the view that the Church formally consists only in sacramental grace imparting the form of Christ and that the human persons taken up into her constitute only the material aspect. That would be to overlook the essential aim: to make the person a member of the Church. Admittedly, that theory appears to be borne out by the fact that the *Ecclesia* of Christ (in contrast with the holy people of old, which was also a people in the natural order) is an assemblage made up entirely of individuals called out of the world, individuals who must expressly renounce their natural connections so as to be incorporated into a new, heavenly people, whose foundation and unity come wholly from above. The Fathers saw Psalm 45 as prophetic of this: "Hear, O daughter, consider, and incline your ear; forget your people and your father's house; and the king will desire your beauty."

Here the people who must be forgotten are a pagan people; there can be no question of an allusion to the racial community of all men in Adam. Nor does the theologoumenon of the first Adam, who comes from the earth, and the second, whose origin is in heaven (1 Cor 15:45f.), speak of a substitution, but of a redemption in time, in which the second Adam presupposes the first, in order (as the context shows, which deals with the Resurrection) not to discard him but to perfect him by his transformation. "Just as we have borne the image of the man of dust [Adam], we shall also bear [by our resurrection] the image of the man of heaven" (ibid., 49). "We sigh with anxiety; not that we would be unclothed, but that we would be further clothed" (2 Cor 5:4). For that reason, the Son took flesh from the generation of Adam, and for the same reason the Fathers, in particular Ambrose, saw the formation of the hypostatic union as the real and primordial marriage union, that of God with the whole of mankind: "*At vero postquam Dominus in corpus hoc veniens contubernium divinitatis et corporis... sociavit, tunc toto orbe diffusus corporibus humanis vitae celestis usus inolevit.*" This passage, representative of many, especially from the Greek Fathers, shows that the marriage of Christ and the Church is to be interpreted only against the background of an, as it were, fundamental marriage with mankind as a whole. This being so, the encounter of the "unity from above" with the "unity from below" cannot be without significance for the formation of the Church's unity as well. The unity from below is characterized for the Redeemer as the unity of the *massa damnata* tainted with original sin, and the unity from above—God in Christ in the Church—envisages as the ultimate subject of the gift not individuals taken up out of the *massa damnata* but nothing less than mankind. It is for this that Christ made satisfaction on the Cross; to say otherwise would be Jansenism.

If this is fundamentally correct, then the next question still remains difficult: that of the significance to be attributed to the unity of mankind in relation to that of the Church. Athwart this question lies the freedom of the divine choice and the divine judgment, and it is impossible to work out a systematization on the lines of Origen and Gregory of Nyssa. Nevertheless, the old allegory—older than the Alexandrians—of the one lost sheep sought out by the shepherd and brought home can rightly be applied to mankind. And, basically, the Fathers meant nothing else when they spoke of Christ coming down to earth to bring home his fallen bride. One can only say, then, that the Church represents mankind, stands to it in a necessary, dynamic relationship, even if this cannot be clearly elucidated. We come to our closest understanding of it when we see the Church as the body of Christ, the body he joins to himself to carry out his work of redemption in the world and in mankind, when we consider the Church's "coredemptive" function—on its own plant—and, in it, her role of mediatrix to the world. Then the whole range of the Church between those who bear and those who are borne, or between the perfect, the advancing, and the beginners, would be no cosmos closed in on itself but in its totality something instrumental. To be in the Church would be tantamount to an assignment, however inchoate or rudimentary, in the work of the redemption of the world.

Unless one sees the whole matter in this light, the *gratia perficit naturam* is not allowed full scope, and *natura* means merely the individual persons representative of human nature, and not the latter's real totality. Nor would it be metaphysically possible—unless one were to follow a Platonist conception of man—to make a complete disjunction between person and race, so that, if one section of mankind were redeemed and brought into the new unity of the Church, and the other failed to be so transplanted, the original unity that God created and whose reestablishment he had in mind (Eph 1:10) would still be unimpaired. But as it is, we see the supernatural unity framed on the lines of the natural, the latter being taken up into the former, admittedly in such a way that, in this aeon, the unity of the two unities retains a historical, discriminatory, and representative character as the "struggling Church" of Jesus Christ, as a positive institution equipped to bear witness inwardly and outwardly to the reconciliation of the world achieved in principle, to its redemption still awaited at the end of time. Then the Church's consciousness has really something to do with mankind's consciousness: knowing that mankind is envisaged in God's plan, she can know herself (in the humble awareness of her election) as representative of mankind before God, in faith, prayer, and sacrifice, in hope for all, and still more in love for all. For Christ died for all, and the Father loved all so much as to give his only begotten Son for them; and Christian love must see in all men those redeemed by Christ, potentially and perhaps actually members of his body.

It is through the Church that God and man encounter one another, and the Church's consciousness cannot be in any way closed in and bounded; it is open on both sides, to God and to man. Yet it cannot simply be restricted to being this open center, for we must take account of the nuptial simile, which, in its full sense, is a simile of movement (man going to woman in procreation, woman turning to man in giving him back the perfected offspring). There is no such thing as a Church consciousness simply contrasted with Christ, for the Church, bride as she is, is also his body, informed by the consciousness of the Head; and inasmuch as she has her own existence, she stands open to him, to serve as handmaid. In fact, even this mystery, this movement, cannot be ultimate, since Christ cannot be divorced from the Trinity, and that which passes over from him to the Church, in the depths of their intimacy, is the entire Trinitarian life in course of communication.

The Letter to the Ephesians gives us the stages of this unity: "Eager to maintain the unity of the Spirit in the bond of peace. There is one body and one Spirit, just as you were called to the one hope that belongs to your call, one Lord, one faith, one baptism, one God and Father of us all, who is above all and through all and in all" (4:3–6). The unity founded, and therefore to be lived, in faith and love is, in the first place, the unity of the "Lord", in whom Christians are "one body", indeed precisely as the Epistle to the Galatians says, "one" (3:28). But, since "the Lord is the Spirit" (2 Cor 3:17) and his words are "spirit and life" and "the flesh is of no avail" (Jn 6:63), consequently "one body" implies "one Spirit", and this body-Spirit is the sacramental form of the Church, to which belong the "one faith" (as certified formula and infinite content) and the "one baptism" (as rite and infinite efficacy). But this infiniteness of the Spirit is the presence of the Trinitarian God in the Church-body and therefore the ultimate and highest orientation to the Father of the work effected by the Son and the Spirit. To him is directed the "one hope that belongs to your call", so that the Church may be not only the fullness of Christ but also the fullness of the triune God pouring himself out into creation, as Tertullian so boldly says: *"Ubi tres, id est Pater et Filius et Spiritus Sanctus, ibi Ecclesia, quae trium corpus est."*

This should prepare the way for a final word on the Church as bride. If the Church is to be unalterably a unity (with the Bridegroom Christ) in contradistinction to him, and if she is thus representative of the opposition of mankind as a whole (as creature) to God (as Creator), then the opposition of God and creature in her will be sublimated, overcome, and fulfilled by being merged in the opposition within the Trinity that accompanies the identity.

7. Trinity, Incarnation, Church

We return now to the question of the nuptial union between Christ and the Church, in which she becomes not only "one body", but also, as has been said above, "one Spirit". For Christ, who made over his body to the Church before the Passion, breathed his Spirit into her at Easter. If one considers the image, which Paul calls a "great mystery" (Eph 5:32), in the light of this very fulfillment, then we find it elucidated from above, while it, in turn, illuminates the mystery of the Church.

The marriage union presupposes three things: (1) two persons, who, even in the union, remain "unmixedly" (*asugchutōs*) persons, and only so are in a condition to experience physical union as a rapturous encounter of their spirits or persons; (2) a physical union of such a kind as to make them both truly "one flesh", as is shown externally by the result, the child, in whom the share of both is not only physically but also metaphysically indistinguishable; (3) a physical opposition of the sexes that represents the opposition of the spiritual persons in the bodily sphere and at the same time makes possible their union in one flesh, this irreducible opposition being the basis of the irrefragable union.

By uniting these three, man gives the real proof of his being the center and crown of creation. Here nature (the material, subhuman, vital creation) and spirit (superhuman, angelic essence) come together and complete one another in a creative act. For procreation and birth, in the subhuman sphere, presuppose imperfect individuation, the immersion of the individuals in a common ocean of biological life, and it is only as representing this that they fulfill the act of reproduction, which is of necessity sealed by their incomplete individuation in death.

The angelic spirit, in contrast, has a monadic structure and does not reproduce itself. However profound and fruitful the mutual encounter of angels may be held to be, they certainly have no part in the animal experience of rapt submission to the invasion of the life force, whether specific or generic.

But how man is able to conjoin the two must be the most profound mystery of the natural order: the encounter of spirit with spirit under the sign of bodily coalescence on the one hand, and, on the other, a bodily union whose rapture and fruitfulness is, as it were, a natural sacramental sign and indication of spiritual union—for the fruit is, beyond anything that might be expected, not only a new individuation of universal life but also incomprehensibly a new person. Undoubtedly, the theory of creationism, taken by itself or superficially, fails to do justice to the power of human coition, since it must certainly exceed that of the animals and is conjoined with the divine primary cause, without which the coming into being of a person would be inexplicable. The Thomist theory of a succession of forms, each higher than the preceding, during the development of the embryo, though very ingenious, possibly minimizes the human share too much and unduly splits up the spiritual, animal, vegetative soul in *fieri* (not in *esse*). However this may be, it is certain that the child is a product not only of husband and wife but also of earth and heaven. And it is man's incomprehensible, irrefragable glory that in marriage (which biologically bears, even for him, the germ of death) he can make a mutual and personal asseveration of immortality, of a love, that is, that precisely because it can reproduce and die knows itself immortal. Truly, for him the infinite emerges from the finite, like foam on a troubled sea.

Paul, however, calls this a great mystery in relation to Christ and the Church. The lines leading up from the natural to the supernatural mystery, which is a mystery of faith, can still be drawn only tentatively and by way of suggestions. The most difficult line is the first: marriage requires two persons. We have attempted to give some intimation of the personality of the Church. We could not hypostasize the Church, nor did we wish to see her as a mere collectivity. Neither is there a collective person resulting from the merging of the individual persons. There is absolutely no analogy for the reality that revelation calls the bride of Christ; and since God's Trinitarian consciousness in Christ is embedded in her to make her a bride, an individual subject, this subject being is itself a mystery of faith. We attempted to clarify it through the encounter of God's unity with mankind's, an encounter that raises the latter unity (which consists of innumerable persons) to a participation in the three-personal Spirit-unity of God; an encounter, however, that is fulfilled in history and in the event involving the incarnate God and the persons of the elect, who have already received, and mirror forth, the Spirit of Christ and the Trinity. It is only when God sees himself in the mirror of the creature that there have been response to him and an encounter with him. But he can only see himself in a living mirror, in which the character of man as created in the divine image is stamped with the seal of grace and so becomes a part of the total and adequate response. This sublime elevation of man as an ever-personal being, yet with a sexual role, is the place of the unity of the bride.

The second element, that the bride is here the very body of the man Christ, is less difficult to understand. It is true that we are again confronted with a mystery that cannot be educidated: that of the Eucharist, which must be presupposed in order to understand the real bodily character of the bride as something supernatural, imparted by Christ. But Christ is a real man, and, as such, he also touches the biological plane and that of subpersonal individuation; and were it not for his union with the Church on this level also, the marriage

simile could not be sustained. Nonetheless, the emphasis in the union
is not on the first Adam, the man of dust—on the *bios*—but on the
second Adam, the man of heaven—on the Logos and the *pneuma*. Of
man it was said: " 'The two shall become one.' But he who is united to
the Lord becomes one spirit with him" (I Cor 6:16–17). Here, the
flesh alone is of no avail; here the bare sacrament also is of no avail: it
is only the Spirit, placed by the Lord in flesh and sacrament and
received by faith, that makes the fleshly sacramental bridge capable of
bearing its load. Yet even the marriage symbol pointed in this direction and was therefore a "great mystery". The fleshly element was
already seen as a "sacrament" of personal encounter, but only fully so
when marriage between Christians became a true sacrament and was
understood in light of the mystery of the union consummated by
Christ and his Church. Nevertheless, in the following chapter (I Cor
7), Paul sets virginity above marriage, since that is the way in which
the believer, going beyond the earthly simile, gives himself directly
(from without the center of the Church, as person) to the Lord,
nuptially, and is fused nuptially with him. This is certainly true in the
pneuma, but also in the mystery of the "one flesh" that Christ and the
Church form together. Virginity outside the Church can only be a
negative and ascetic concept, but within the Church it is the pure way
of participating in the mystery of flesh and spirit of the God-Man that
is fulfilled in the Eucharist, Cross, and Resurrection.

The third element, the mystery of the opposition, has already been
presented in its Christological setting. The Church is not, purely and
simply, Christ. She is not hypostatically united to God who dwells in
her. In this opposition, therefore, she is receptive to her Head and so
has a feminine role. She is Marial, in the sense already explained. In
this consists the fulfillment of the creaturely opposition that underlies
the mystery of love and fecundity in the bodily sphere, a fulfillment
that is only to be derived from the highest sphere, that of the Trinitarian opposition of Persons in identity of nature. It is comprehensible
that the seal of identity should be imprinted from above on the
oppositions that arise in salvation history: thus, too, the opposition
between Christ as Bridegroom and the Church as bride is subsumed
in the identity of the one Christ, Head and Body, who, as *Christus*

totus, is for Augustine "one person", and for Paul the "one" (see Gal 3:28). This seal of identity imprints itself right through the unity Christ-Church until it reaches that most fundamental opposition that rejects identity, because in it the dissimilarity is ever greater than the similarity — the opposition, that is, of God and creature. In the hypostatic union (and its imperfect participation in the Church), even this irreducible abyss, without being eliminated, is bridged and tunneled by the power of God's love.

In these three points, then, marriage is a symbol of the redemption. If the first, the irreducibility of the subjects, were lacking to redemption, then instead of redemption by grace, we should have a pantheism that eliminates the creature. If the second, the one flesh as sacrament of the one spirit, were lacking, then the unity would not be truly brought about, and we should remain with that juridical conception that is generally (whether rightly or not) laid to the charge of Protestantism. If the third, the relative opposition of the sexes, were lacking, we should lapse into a kind of religious homosexuality, in which the creature would relate himself to God in a masculine fashion, a sin of which non-Christian mysticism is guilty in a subtle way, as is, in a less subtle way, religious magic, whose perverse encroachment on God himself (appearing in angelic form) is depicted in the story of Sodom and its destruction. Consequently, a typical pagan utterance like that cited by Paul in Athens ("We are indeed his offspring" [Acts 17:28]) can really be adduced only in a marginal sense and for purposes of illustration. With God there can be no union of the same sex but only a feminine dependence on God, as taught by Paul and Augustine: no taking but only a being taken. As the individual believer lets himself be taken by God, becoming a handmaid of the Lord, so the Church awakens in him and, in feminine fashion, reflects the Spirit of the Lord. It is both the lowliness and glory of woman to be obliged and to be able to receive in this way. But since we are sinners, this humility must be instilled into us by humiliation: "But we have this treasure in earthen vessels, to show that the transcendent power belongs to God and not to us" (2 Cor 4:7).

If we consider the marriage act not so much from the angle of the partners as from that of the offspring, it can be seen to involve three elements, in ascending gradation, all of which are necessary for the production of offspring: a material element—seed; a biological element—life; and a personal element—immortal spirit. Though these elements are easily distinguishable in the abstract, the distinction is very difficult when it comes to the actual sources of the operation. With animals, and even with plants, the material element, the seed, itself contains the life that is to be built up, but, at the same time, this life is an offshoot of the total life of the species, in fact of cosmic life in general. With man, in contrast, since a spiritual person is produced, the "world soul" is not the only active agent—God, personal and creative, is himself active.

The Church likewise originates from a "seed", which is the body and blood of Christ delivering himself to death for the life of the world. But the "life" by which he is a living being is his "Spirit", which, as was shown, must be both divine and human spirit: the spirit that was breathed forth on the Cross with water and blood and sent back to the Father, and that is, therefore, inseparable from the Holy Spirit whom the risen Christ breathed on his Church (Jn 20) and sent down upon the Church after the ascension, when he forms once more a joint principle of spiration with the Father, as a Spirit at once Trinitarian and Christological in union with the Father. In this community of spiration, which involves the participation of the Father in the whole work of building up the Church, we see the third element in the process, the cooperation of God the Creator.

For the Church to come into being, a productive act is required, and this extends from the Man dying on the Cross (who lets body and spirit and person flow out of himself so fully that he is himself all outpouring and seed, that the Creator dissolves in the creation the priest in the sacrifice)—extends through the communication of his own both human and divine spirit into the very mysteries of the generation and spiration within the Trinity. Here indeed the person is not distinguished from the life flow in which the Father is active generation, the Son passive generation, where being Son and being Word of the Father are not distinguishable, and breathing forth and being breathed forth are identical as one event, though they involve the eternal relative opposition of the Spirit to Father and Son, whose identical love is the Spirit.

Thus it is evident that the self-outpouring in death and Resurrection of God's incarnate Word into the Church is truly the pouring forth of the Trinitarian life externally. The virginal man Christ is wholly (as Hamann most profoundly divined) the generative organ (*instrumentum conjunctum*) of the eternally generating Godhead and the central organ in that it belongs to him alone to make himself (in the Eucharist) a seed and, at the same time—beyond any analogy with the way in which man and the Creator cooperate—to pour out his Spirit into what is produced, through his joint spiration with God the Father.

At this point, we must mark precisely the distinction between creation in nature and supernature on the one hand and between generation in nature and supernature on the other. Natural generation presupposes the sexual partnership, but the female partner, the Church, that is to originate from Christ, is not yet in existence. It must first of all come into being by generation through the Cross, Resurrection, and Ascension. There is eros when the love that generates can *pre*suppose the natural *pre*presence of the one loved (in its difference as in its similarity of nature); *agapē,* on the other hand, creates out of complete *self*lessness that which is to be loved. But the Son's creation of the Church is not the same thing as the Father's creation of the world, for it presupposes the latter and fulfills it in grace. It is, therefore, on the level of "nature" analogous to eros between the sexes, but on the level of "supernature" analogous to the Father's act of creation, since grace can never develop out of nature. On the level of nature, the subject humanity is presupposed, as the individual humanity of the separate persons no less than as the collective reality and unity of all the individuals descended from Adam and Eve. Into this natural unity is poured the seed of the dead and risen Word of God. But the analogy with nature seems preserved through Christ's relationship to Mary, in which the purely natural unity raised to a real feminine partnership in Mary's Fiat, comprising all the inchoate acts of assent and faith of the old Zion as well as of Peter representing the Church and of the other apostles and disciples, represents the true matrix of the Church to be brought forth. If we bear this in mind, it becomes almost palpably evident how Mary (and, conjoined with her, the entire supernatural reality of faith in the world around Christ) is both the prerequisite and womb of the coming Church as well as being herself the Church generated, since Mary's preredemption and the faith of the Old Covenant also refer back to the generative redemptive act of Christ. The Church as the female partner is both produced and presupposed in the generative act of Christ. Otherwise, this would not be both divine and human.

This being so, the feminine character of the Church as a subject is, moreover, posited and presupposed; and it is not only presupposed in the sense that nature (created humanity collective and personal) is presupposed as the subject of attribution, to which the grace of rebirth can be given, but also, as implied by the Old Covenant, Mary and the Church of those who believe and love—which involve a believing subject informed by grace. But this inchoate subject, the Church, is fulfilled only in the mystery of the Holy Spirit, who is embedded in her as her inmost ground, and who can therefore constitute it in its perfected state because he is a Divine Person precisely *as* testifying to the eternal opposition of the Persons. In virtue of this divine *coincidentia oppositorum,* he is the Founder and Foundation of the "other", the bride—who, yet, is as such the "one", the body—and out of the oneness of the "Spirit of Christ" creates in all believers the "opposition of being" resulting from the same Spirit of Christ. Simultaneously, then, he makes the One out of the Other (that is, he brings back the creation, which as regards God is the Other, into the divine law of life, and subordinates to it this otherness), and at the same time makes the Other out of the One (that is, from the hypostatic union of Christ he brings forth the double subject Christ-Church). Thus the return of the creature into God becomes simultaneously the outgoing of the divine life, which, entering into the creature, draws it into the eternal opposition of the persons in love and through love.

"CASTA MERETRIX"

I. *The theme*

When Luther dares to equate the Roman Church with the whore of Babylon, it strikes us as the height of blasphemy. But he was not the first to coin the phrase. Similar things can be found in Wycliffe and Hus, and their language was not a complete innovation but the violent simplification and coarsening of a very old *theologoumenon.* This in turn has its origins in the Old Testament, in the words of judgment spoken by God, the betrayed Husband, against the archwhore Jerusalem, and in the New Testament's application of these texts, which are so fundamental to the Old. Now it is true that the Church regards herself as profoundly different from the unfaithful synagogue; in her there is at least one identifiable place where she is perfectly pure and unchangeably faithful. No believer, no Christian theologian (including Luther), would ever doubt these truths. But is that the only thing she has to be? Could the real *Ekklesia,* made up of *these* particular believers, be something different? Christians of other times have unhesitatingly acknowledged that it would be rash to deny these possibilities a priori.

Two examples from the Middle Ages, as "High" gives way to "late". On the summit of Mount Purgatory, after all kinds of testing and purging, *Dante* sees the Church approaching in an allegorical procession. A carriage, the Church, is being drawn by a griffin, the eagle-lion symbolizing Christ in his two natures, surrounded by the theological and cardinal virtues. Enthroned in the carriage, as a symbol of the pure bride, is Beatrice, whom the poet glorifies as the *anima ecclesiastica.* But to meet Beatrice, he has to go through a final, terrible, and remorseless confession. Beatrice's reproaches, harshly and mercilessly hammering down, smash the lover to the ground. His shame, his infidelity, is there for Church and world to see. She had warned him from heaven, but the warning was·fruitless, and so she

Translated by John Saward.

sent him into hell. And now she demands full repentance, total confession, of a kind that is possible only when a man meets the spotless love of God. Only when the shattering experience of confession has taken place is the poet allowed to go through Lethe, the waters of oblivion; only when he has done penance does he leave behind him the essentially earthly experience of estrangement from love, the constant inability to do enough, the fall from the height of "first love" (Rev 2:4–5); only then, when he has been duly prepared, can he receive the paradisal vision. When he awakes, he no longer sees the heavenly glorification of the Church. All that is left is the carriage with Beatrice and the seven virtues and seven gifts of the Spirit: the earthly equipment of the Church. Now, newly purified, he has to experience the transformation of this form of the Church (Canto 32). The Church carriage is tethered by its shaft to a tree. Shaft and tree are of the same wood: the shaft is the Roman See; the tree is the earthly kingdom. An eagle swoops down on the carriage: the persecution of the early Church by the Roman state. Then a bony fox comes out of the carriage: the heresies. But Beatrice drives the fox away. Next the eagle covers the whole carriage with his plumage: Constantine takes the Church under the secular wing of the state. A dragon tears off a piece of the carriage: this may symbolize the Great Schism or Islam. The rest of it is entirely covered by the feathers: secular power and wealth spread out over the Church, and her true nature almost entirely disappears beneath. Finally, emerging from the carriage, come the seven heads and ten horns of the Beast of the Apocalypse: the Church appears as a monster. In fact, the whore of Babylon herself replaces Beatrice in the carriage and flirts with a giant (the King of France), who out of jealousy abuses her and finally abducts her: Avignon becomes the Babylonian captivity of the Church. The poet see this not as an external accident but as an appropriate internal symbolic punishment. The next canto begins with the lamentation over the fallen Jerusalem—*Deus, venerunt gentes . . .* —intoned by the seven virtues. Beatrice, when she consoles them, almost has the appearance of Mary at the foot of the Cross. "A little while," she says, "and you will not see me", because of the obscuring of the present form of the Church. "And again a little while": Beatrice, here expressing

Dante's hope, promises an avenger and deliverer. The appalling defilement of the Church is compared to the first sin: violence is here done to God himself (33, 58).[1]

The great Bishop of Paris, *William of Auvergne,* was one of the most serious-minded theologians of his time. Even as a *magister,* he combined immense erudition and knowledge of the theological and philosophical Tradition with keen insight into the state of the Church. "In his lectures and writings he reacted with a vitality all of his own and in language of a bluntness and graphicness without parallel in the works of other scholars of the thirteenth century."[2] This is illustrated in the following passage in his commentary on the Song of Songs. The verse where the Bride is compared to one of Pharaoh's chariots provides an opportunity for praising the flaming chariot of the Church militant, within which glows the fire of the Holy Spirit. But then the image is turned round.

> It is obvious that everything nowadays is topsy-turvy. The Church is more like Pharaoh's chariot than God's! It hurtles down into the abyss of wealth and sensuality, even into sin. The wheels of the Church's teachers have come off the track and are far removed, in their unlikeness, from Christ. . . . Today the chariot of the Church is no longer moving ahead but falling behind, because its horses are running backward and dragging it after them. It is no longer strong steeds that are chosen for ecclesiastical office, but young foals of little relatives, with neither chest nor withers for pulling.

---

[1] *Savonarola,* in his poem on the corruption of the Church (1475), may have been directly inspired by Dante. He too mourns "the chaste maid" and "noble mother", who, through the pressure of imperial power, wealth, and secularization in Rome, has gradually been transformed into the whore of Babylon:

> Then I spoke up: "Lady, tell me, I pray,
> Who wounded thee so deeply in this way?"
> "The whore of Babylon", said she, "by shameless lies
> Has trapped me, made me her chosen prize."
> "But can't we", I asked, "fight the hag by war?"
> "In vain", came the answer, "is the battle's roar.
> Silence is the wisest course of all.
> Weep without words and keep thy counsel."

[2] H. Riedlinger, *Hoheliedkommentare des MA* (1958), p. 241, We give the text in Riedlinger's transcription.

> On the other hand, there are stallions: in heat, degenerate in their unbearable lust . . . wild in impatience and wrath, ripping their reins, snapping their harness.

If one thinks of the Church as the bridled war-horse of Christ himself, then it must be said that the modern leaders of the Church have bridled it "not as a horse but as a donkey". They force the Lord himself to "sit at its rear end". Then William denounces the avarice of the clergy, who are far more concerned with their income than with the salvation of souls. In fact, they prostitute Holy Church, because for squalid gain they invite all and sundry to shame her. And so her nipples are cracked and her breasts torn out, in a word.

> "The sons of Memphis and Tahpanhes have deflowered you, even to the crown of the head", as Jeremiah says (2:16).
> "Thou art all fair, O my love, and there is not a spot in thee." . . . Yes, all fair is she. Her individual members have a befitting beauty of their own and are coordinated to each other. This applies to the members of the Church: to the head, the company of the prophets; the neck, the Doctors; the shoulders, the martyrs; the breast, the confessors; the arms, the defenders of the Faith; the hands, the subtle preachers and those who do the works of wisdom. "All fair", too, is the human soul. . . . The opposite is true of Babylon: she is the mother of all harlotry and idolatry on earth, as we read in the seventeenth and eighteenth chapters of the Apocalypse. She is of extreme ugliness.

Then follows a description of sinners in the Church, the licentious, the teachers of lies and false wisdom, those who are as brazen in their sin as the men of Sodom:

> Whether they be clerics or laymen . . . they teach and suggest carnal things under the pretense of humanity.
> And now it appears that Isaiah's threat (4:17) to her [the bride] is fulfilled: "God has made bald the crown of the head of the daughters of Zion." By depriving her of the contemplation of doctrine and heavenly wisdom, he took away her forehead, and we see the words of Jeremiah fulfilled: "You had a harlot's forehead; you would not blush" (3:3). He took away her eyes, for, according to

Isaiah (56:10), all her watchmen have become blind. The eyes of her prophets and princes, who for her saw visions, he has closed (ibid., 29:10). Her cheeks are ashen; her lips are bloodless, the sure sign that her soul is ossified.... As we read in the book of Lamentations, "From the daughter of Zion all her beauty has departed" (1:6), so that in truth it can be said of her, as Isaiah says (21:4), "Babylon, my beloved, has become an abomination to me." God's beloved is the Church, so long as she walks in the footsteps of the Fathers. But now she has become Babylon through her heinousness and infestation by unclean spirits. For God himself she has become an abomination. Is there anyone who would not be beside himself with horror at the sight of the Church with a donkey's head, the believer's soul with the teeth of a wolf, the snout of a pig, furrowed ashen cheeks, the neck of a bull, and in every other respect so bestial, so monstrous, that a person seeing it would freeze with terror? Is there anyone who would not regard and describe this dreadful perversion as Babylon rather than the Church of Christ? Is there anyone who would not call it a wasteland rather than the city of God? ... Heretics call the Church "whore" and "Babylon" because of the appalling scandal of the Church being overrun by the degenerate and carnal, a mob so large, riffraff so noisy, that the other members of the Church are hidden and cannot be seen. Although the heretics may have rightly felt and spoken in this way about the degenerate and those who are Christians only in name, they did not extend these terms of abuse to all Christians. We are no longer dealing with a bride but with a monster of terrible deformity and ferocity.... It is clear that it cannot be said of her in such a state: "Thou art all fair, and there is not a spot in thee."

William is not alone in using this fierce language. Odo of Cheriton speaks in a similar way, while the great Dominican exegete, later Cardinal, Hugh of St. Cher, takes over much of William's commentary word for word.[3] Although such texts should not be regarded as dispassionate theology, they nonetheless powerfully raise a theological question. Do the Old Testament's words about the archwhore Jerusalem have any kind of application in the New? Can any theological idea concerning the old people of God, especially one as impor-

---

[3] Riedlinger, pp. 255f.

tant and central as this, be written off as totally redundant and irrelevant to the New, of historical interest only? Convinced that it was impossible to deal with the matter in this way, Erich Przywara developed his passionate "Theology of the Hour", which he called "Covenant Old and New". In what follows we want to do something much more modest. We shall assemble some of the material (by no means all of it!) from the theological Tradition that shows how strongly the great theologians felt that this idea was still relevant to the New Testament. Ours is a purely historical undertaking. We intend, without prejudgment, by critical examination and in temperate language, to set out the most important themes. It will then be for the theologians to draw their conclusions. They should do this calmly, and yet not so anxiously that, by maneuvering and making subtle distinctions, they empty the whole thing of content and render it harmless. Without endangering the immaculateness, holiness, and infallibility of the Church, one must look the other reality in the eye and not exclude it from consideration. Much would be gained if Christians learned more and more to realize at what price the holiness of the Church has been purchased.

2. The theme in the Old Testament

The theme of the Covenant as a marriage between God and his people was alive in Israel long before Hosea. It is a way of teaching the people about God's justice and love. His love is jealous and exclusive, lordly and yet totally committed and devoted to his wife, a love that expects from her an exclusive love in return. Without lengthy explanations, the other theme is placed directly alongside: deserting Yahweh, Israel's God and Covenant Lord, is like adultery. Israel must expect from God the same treatment reserved for the adulteress and wife turned whore not only in the law but also in the logic of love and fidelity.

"You shall worship no other God, for the Lord, whose name is Jealous, is a jealous God, lest you make a covenant with the inhabitants of the land, and when they play the harlot after their gods and sacrifice to their gods and one invites you, you eat of his sacrifice, and you take of their daughters for your sons, and their daughters play the harlot after their gods and make your sons play the harlot after their gods" (Ex 34:14-16, the Yahwist). The sacrificial regulations in the "law of holiness" forbid the Jews to "slay their sacrifices for satyrs, after whom they play the harlot" (Lev 17:7; cf. 20:5). However, retrospectively, in Deuteronomy Yahweh says to Moses: "Behold, you are about to sleep with your fathers; then this people will rise and play the harlot after the strange gods of the land, where they go to be among them, and they will forsake me and break my Covenant that I have made with them" (Dt 31:16). The book of Judges describes the beginning of this constantly repeated adultery (2:17; 8:27, 33; cf. 1 Chron 5:25; 2 Chron 21:11, 13), and the psalms declare the punishment that by law it deserves (72:27; 105:39).

A new dimension opens up with the prophets, especially Hosea, who is commanded by God to go to a harlot, to marry her, and to have children of harlotry, upon whom the shame of their mother will fall. This shows that God wants to give his relationship with his people an incredibly vivid reality. It is no longer the legal relationship of the earthly wife with her heavenly Lord. It is the relationship of love of a God humiliated by the woman's adultery, a God who in his wrath discloses more his own "shame", a God who, by taking back the harlot, by betrothing her in justice and changing the names of he sons, shows the "weakness" of his love. Clearly, the harlot should have been rejected, but God's love humbles itself to woo her back. There is nothing even remotely suggestive about this love, nothing of the unsavoriness of the heathen gods' relations with their peoples. Yahweh is the God who is strong and gentle and yet, from the very beginning, betrayed. It is he who led the people through the wilderness (11:1-5; 12:10; 13:4-5), he who relentlessly threatens and yet promises the victory of his tender love.

Isaiah takes up the theme fleetingly: "How the faithful city has become a harlot, she that was full of justice. Righteousness lodged in her, but now murderers" (1:21). But Jeremiah, following Hosea, develops it at length. Yahweh reminds Jerusalem of "the devotion of [her] youth, [her] love as a bride, how [she] followed [him] in the wilderness"

(2:2). But seeing that she has "played the harlot with many lovers" and would now like just to return to Yahweh, he raises the bitter question, which will become more and more pointed in the course of the book: "If a man divorces his wife and she goes from him and becomes another man's wife, does she still have the right to return to him?" (3:1–2). No, God must abandon his former beloved to her enemies and to wild animals (12:7–9). He forbids the prophet to intercede for her (11:14). "I will not pity or spare or have compassion, that I should not destroy them" (13:14). And yet everything is still bound up with the mystery of God's love. Even the rejection is to be seen as a kind of guidance, a way to a new election, though that, of course, given such hardening of the people's hearts, can be accomplished only through God's "everlasting love" (31:3).

In Second Isaiah the rejected wife is so abandoned and humiliated that God can console her only in the misery of exile. The shame will be taken from her. God cares for her with a love like a mother's (49:15). But the profundity of Hosea has gone. There is no longer any talk of taking back harlots, runaway wives; a bill of divorce has never been issued (50:1). "The mystery of divine love is . . . weakened in that it now approximates more closely to the kind of conduct required of man in his communal relationships."[4]

In contrast, Ezekiel, with his vivid depiction of Israel's shameless adultery, exploits the image to an almost unbearable degree. In a first chapter (16), he tells the whole story from Israel's first election. In a second chapter, he describes the infidelity of the two separated halves of the kingdom: Samaria under the name of Oholah ("her own tent") and Jerusalem under the name Oholibah ("my tent in her").

In both descriptions the imagery has been so intensified that the characteristics of the archwhore Jerusalem merge with those of the archwhore Babylon. Jerusalem's adultery is, in fact, portrayed as being far worse than that of her "sisters" Samaria (the northern kingdom, infected by heathenism) and Sodom (the manifest depravity of the heathen world).

Jerusalem was originally a "foundling", of heathen descent. Her

---

[4] W. Eichrodt, *Theology of the Old Testament,* vol. 1, ET (London, 1961), p. 255.

father was an Amorite, her mother a Hittite. On the day of her birth she was cast out on the open field, naked, unwashed, her umbilical cord uncut, and there, on the ground, writhing in her own blood, she was found by God. He brought her up, she became sexually mature, and yet she is still naked. "You were at the age for love, and I spread my skirt over you and covered your nakedness; yes, I plighted my troth to you and entered into a covenant with you, says the Lord God, and you became mine. Then I bathed you with water and washed off your blood from you, and anointed you with oil. . . . You grew exceedingly beautiful and came to regal estate. And your renown went forth among the nations because of your beauty, for it was perfect through the splendor that I had bestowed upon you" (16:3–14). We should note here motifs that will be taken up in the New Testament: the *Ecclesia ex gentibus* washed clean in water, the clothing with the mantle of grace, the perfect glory of God bestowed upon the bride, the plighting of troth, the nuptials.

But the bride, foolishly trusting in her beauty, uses her renown "to play the harlot" and "lavishes [her] harlotries on any passer-by". Out of her gracious adornments she makes "gaily decked shrines": the old heathen shrines in Israel, which were places quite literally of cultic sexual depravity in the service of the goddesses of fertility. The literal accuracy of his description gives the prophet's words their extreme astringency without lessening their permanent relevance to times and places where they do not apply literally. Religious sensualism is inevitably accompanied by religious sadism: Jerusalem slaughters her children, whom she had borne to and for Yahweh, and sacrifices them to Moloch: "You slaughtered my children and delivered them up as an offering by fire to them." And in all this she never remembers what God has done for her (15–22). Not content with increasing her harlotry to exorbitant proportions by offering herself at every street corner, Jerusalem reverses the usual practice: instead of receiving payment for her harlotry, she pays her lovers to use her as a harlot: "None solicited you to play the harlot; you gave hire, while no hire was given to you" (30–34).

God takes revenge.

I will gather all your lovers, with whom you took pleasure, all those you loved and all those you loathed. I will gather them against you from every side and will uncover your nakedness to them that they may see all your nakedness. And I will judge you as women who break wedlock and shed blood are judged and bring upon you the blood of wrath and jealousy. And I will give you into the hand of your lovers, and they shall thrown down your vaulted chamber and break down your lofty places. They shall strip you of your clothes and take your fair jewels and leave you naked and bare. They shall bring up a host against you, and they shall stone you and cut you to pieces with their swords, and they shall burn your houses [35–41].

In Jeremiah (4:29–31) the fall of Jerusalem is portrayed precisely as a sexual murder: the prostitute is killed by her paramours. Again we should observe the continuation of the motif in the New Testament. This time the archwhore is Babylon. By the judgment of God, all her fornication rebounds upon her. She too has committed fornication with all the kings of earth and quaffed the cup of intoxication that was her reward. She too has made rich the merchants of the earth. She too drips with the blood of the saints (Rev 17:2, 6; 18:3f.). And she too is given up to the hatred of her lovers, who make her desolate, rob her, devour her flesh, and burn her up with fire (17:16; 18:8).

Ezekiel has one final crescendo: "Like mother, like daughter". All the demonism of her heathen origins has reasserted itself in the daughter, in the one who was endowed with more grace than her sisters Samaria and Sodom. At first she seemed to lag behind them, but soon her bad behavior had outstripped theirs; they did not commit "half the sins" of Jerusalem. Previously God exposed her bodily shame; now he does it to her spiritually. Her shame will make the other two appear righteous (44–52). But then the unthinkable happens. God has mercy on the archwhore who broke every covenant. Mindful of his covenant in the days of her youth, he enters into a new covenant with her, this time an "everlasting" one. And yet the word *shame* runs like a refrain through the celebratory conclusion: "Then you will remember your ways and be ashamed when I take your sisters, both your elder and your younger, and give them to you as daughters, but not on account of the covenant with you. I will establish my covenant with you, and you shall know that I am the Lord, that you may remember and be confounded, and never open your mouth again because of your shame, when I forgive you all that you have done, says the Lord God" (53–63). It is precisely the new and everlasting forgiveness, justification, and marriage that bring about Jerusalem's most extreme exposure. Her situation is just like that of mankind at the beginning of St. Paul's Letter to the Romans. First of all, God abandons it to the logic of its religious perversions (including sodomitical homosexuality). But then humanity divides into two groups. Israel, endowed with more grace, fell more grievously than the Gentiles: "As it is written, 'The name of God is blasphemed among the Gentiles because of you'" (Rom 2:23). And so it is not Israel's covenant fidelity and merit that count, when God, out of pure grace and fidelity, remembers his covenant promises, and "every mouth is mute, and the whole world must be held accountable to God" (3:19). And is it not essential that Christ's Church too was finally founded in the sight of Peter, mute in his shame and tears, thrice humbled for his threefold betrayal?

Ezekiel plays through all the motifs again in Chapter 23, this time with a modulation into the political key. After the Egyptians Oholah (Samaria) takes the Assyrians as her lovers, yet without giving up the Egyptians. And so the Assyrians uncover her nakedness, rob her of her children, and slay her with the sword. Oholibah (Jerusalem) behaves even more wickedly. After the Egyptians and Assyrians she makes love with the sons of Babel, sends messengers to them, and commits fornication with them, whose sexual power is like that of rutting asses and horses. But God rouses her lovers against her. They cut off her nose and ears, rob her of her children, tear off her clothes, rip off her jewels, chop her up, and throw her into the fire. Her sister's cup of frenzy passes to her. She must drain it to the dregs and chew its shattered fragments, which gash her breast from the inside. For she has desecrated God's oil and incense by using them for her lovers, and in God's own house, too. She has sacrificed to alien idols the children she had borne to God. This time the parable ends with the extermination of lewdness through the extermination of the lewd.

After the exile the theme fades away. The past is transfigured. The picture of the eschatological future is unclouded. The individual comes to the fore in his struggle with God (Job), in his confession of sin and his trust in salvation (the psalms). And then suddenly, unrelated to the imagery of the prophets, connected only conceptually with the rest of Scripture, there emerges the Song of Songs: from its main theme the New Testament will develop the theology of the Church. In the apocalyptic literature the two images, which the prophets had linked in a tremendous drama (this interconnection was the core of the whole of the old revelation), appear unrelated and apart, as pure white and pure black. The Qumran texts bear witness to this eschatological dualism; its final form is in the images of the two women in the Apocalypse of St. John. For the abyss that yawned in Ezekiel, when confronted with New Testament grace, opens up even deeper recesses: not only Hades, into which the prince of Tyre descends (Ezek 27, 28), in which Pharaoh is buried (31, 32), but hell in the full sense, which really blazes only when it comes face to face with the new heaven of the grace of Christ. This fulfills and surpasses the great either/or of the law, which is in its most intense form in Deuteronomy.

3. *The theme in the New Testament*

Compared with the explicitness verging on crudity found in the prophets (and in another form also in the books of law and wisdom), the New Testament seems at first restrained. In contrast to the *fortissimo* of the judgments of the Lord, here speaks one who is "meek and lowly of heart": "He will not wrangle or cry aloud, nor will anyone hear his voice in the streets" (Mt 11:29; 12:19). But this soft speech is heightened power, the quietest blazing of the hottest flame. In any case, the Son is not sent to say again what the prophets said. He fulfills what they said, and not a jot of it is without significance. He presupposes the prophets; the New Testament cannot be interpreted without the Old. He takes the prophets up in such a way that the great political events and the great rhetorical diatribes "become human" on the stage of his own life.

At this level of one human being meeting another, the scenes in the gospel involving sinful women always fascinated the Fathers of the Church. Ultimate forces and decisions stand in the background; after all, here human beings meet God himself in human form. Mary, the Lord's Mother, looks after the beginnings and the Child himself, but then her figure almost entirely disappears to emerge just once more (and then only in John) at the foot of the Cross (alongside Mary Magdalen the sinner). Between these two points, it is the sinful women who are to the fore: the harlot in Luke 7; the dubious Samaritan woman with her five or six husbands; the adulteress of John 8; the Mary of John 12 who, at least in her action of washing the Lord's feet, resembles the sinner of Luke 7; and the Magdalen, from whom seven demons were driven out, the woman splashed by the blood of the Cross, the first person to proclaim the Resurrection to the Church. This graphic evidence, together with the repeated assertion that Jesus eats by preference "with tax collectors and sinners" (Mk 2:15–16; Mt 9:11), that he is "a glutton and a drunkard, a friend of tax collectors and sinners" (Mt 11:19), justifies the words of judgment: "Truly, I say to you, the tax collectors and the harlots go into the Kingdom of God before you. For John came to you in the way of righteousness, and you did not believe him, but the tax collectors and the harlots believed him" (Mt 21:31–32). And so the son who squandered all his property on prostitutes will celebrate the banquet with the one who stayed at home with the father (Lk 15:11f.).

The Bridegroom comes in the sign of the wedding banquet (Mt 11:19) and is "seen and justified" by the "bride" herself as a "friend of tax collectors and sinners" (ibid.). His personal presence provokes explicit memories, with contemporary relevance, of the "great whore Jerusalem" of Ezekiel 16. Again and again, in the person of her official representatives, she is called "an adulterous generation" (Mt 12:39; 16:4; Mk 8:38). Moreover, as *St. Paschasius Radbertus* rightly emphasizes (*In Mt* 1, 6, 11; PL 120, 447C), it is Jerusalem that Jesus is thinking of when he upbraids Chorazin and Bethsaida, unrepentant, yet the scene of many of his miracles (cf. Mt 11:20–21). These cities, to which so much was given, represent Jerusalem. This is the implication of the recurring comparison with the sinful cities, for whom it will be more tolerable on the Day of Judgment than for the "beloved city". On two occasions, as in Ezekiel, the city "justified" in this way by Jerusalem is "Sodom", or "Sodom and Gomorrah" (Mt 10:15; 11:23–24; cf. Jude 7). Linked with this are the words addressed to the Pharisees: "The tax collectors and the harlots go into the Kingdom of God before you" (Mt 21:31). But increasingly the city with which Jerusalem is compared can also be "Tyre and Sidon". In the Old Testament, Tyre (and Sidon with it; Ezek 28:20–33) is the archetype of arrogance and self-glorification, for which it is thrust into the pit. It is virtually the archetype of Antichrist. And yet on the Day of Judgment it will be more tolerable for Tyre and Sidon than for the whore Jerusalem. It was, after all, these cities that the Lord met in the person of the Canaanite woman, with her "great faith", when he "withdrew into the district of Tyre and Sidon" (Mt 15:21–28). The city can also be "Nineveh", the Assyrian Babel, and "the Queen of Sheba", who will arise at the judgment against the great whore Jerusalem. The new and greater thing demands it: "Something greater than Jonah is here! Something greater than Solomon is here!" (Mt 12:41–42). This condemnation of Jerusalem by Gentiles, tax collectors, and harlots is a "self-condemnation" (12:27, 37). Taking up the other great images of the prophets, the Lord says that it is the destruction of the "vineyard" (Mt 15:13; 21:33f.), the leaving of the "flock" (Lk 15:4), of the "righteous persons who need no repentance", who shift the guilt of "extortion" and "adultery" from themselves to the tax collector (Lk 18:11) and in so doing make the temple of God a "den of robbers" (Mt 21:13).

St. James (4:4–5) takes up the old prophetic image when he challenges those Christian souls that find space for earthly desires: "Adulteresses! Do you not know that friendship with the world is enmity with God? . . . Or do you suppose it is in vain that the Scripture says, 'God yearns jealously for the spirit that he has made to dwell in us' [or, 'The spirit that he has put into us yearns jealously for God']?" Whatever the exact words of this lost text may have been, there is a clear reminiscence of the jealous relationship of God the loving Bridegroom and Zion the unfaithful bride.

As for the repentant prostitutes in the Gospel, in these episodes all the light falls on the Lord, on the liberation from sin that he brings about. There is no stress at all on the prostitute herself; she serves as just a demonstration. In fact, in the case of the woman taken in adultery, the Lord first of all points out the Jews' solidarity with her and then absolves her almost incidentally, as a matter of course. The light falls on the assertion that "Christ loved the Church and gave himself up for her, that he might sanctify her [consecrate her, *hagiazein*], having *cleansed* her by the washing of water with the word, that he might present the Church to *himself* in splendor, without spot or wrinkle or any such thing" (Eph 5:25–27). That is the important thing. The question of what he purified her from and what she was like before is left entirely in the dark. The prostitutes, too, come into the light only at the moment when they have already been attracted by his grace, when they kneel at his feet in sorrow for their sins. All the light falls on the act of putting them back on their feet, on the absolution. But what becomes of the woman who has been absolved? Can we say that she has been confirmed in grace?

"Go and sin no more!" (Jn 8:11). It is up to her not to sin again. The house may be empty, swept, and garnished, but the devil may return with seven others worse than himself, "and the last state of that man becomes worse than the first" (Mt 12:45). The same is true of individual sinners. It is true of stumbling Peter and his fellow apostles: "Simon, Simon, behold, Satan demanded to have you, that he might sift you like wheat, but I have prayed for you that your faith may not fail; and when you have turned again, strengthen your brethren." Peter's promise to go with the Lord to prison and to death shows he misunderstands what the Lord is promising and immediately earns him this other assurance: "The cock will not crow this day until you three times deny that you know me" (Lk 22:31–34). Peter is sustained by a prayer that protects him from Satan, but not so protected that he cannot fall, deny, come so very close to Judas. The same thing is said to him when he confesses the messiahship of Christ: "Did I not choose you, the Twelve, and one of you is a devil?" (Jn 6:70). It would be incredible if such words and events referred only to the actions that founded the Church and had no relevance to her continued existence.

The New Testament speaks of the safeguards granted Christ's Church, but at the same time, in harsh juxtaposition, there is the threat of abuse, the possibility of defection. Nowhere is the immaculateness of the bride an established fact for the bride just to accept and not to worry about any further. The relevant text from St. Paul shows this clearly: "I feel a divine jealousy for you, for I betrothed you to Christ to present you as a pure bride to her one husband. But I am afraid that as the serpent deceived Eve by his cunning, your thoughts will be led astray from a sincere and pure devotion to Christ. For if someone comes and preaches another Jesus than the one we preached, or if you receive a different spirit from the one you received, or if you accept a different gospel from the one you accepted, you submit to it readily enough" (2 Cor 11:2–4). Where on earth does this susceptibility of the Church-bride come from, this curiosity and lustfulness? What makes her turn her head? Why does she heed every passer-by? Why does she not let herself be led by the apostle to her one and only Lover? Every epistle of the apostle shakes with this fear. Apostasy and relapse are always possible. No sacrament, no receiving of the word and Spirit, gives definitive assurance of salvation (Heb 6:4f.). The frightening thing is not so much that they themselves go astray but that they "despise authority" (2 Pet 2:10; Jude 8), the *kyriotês* embodied by the God-Man on the Cross. "They crucify the Son of God on their own account and hold him up to contempt" (Heb 6:6). "If we sin deliberately after receiving the knowledge of the truth", in other words, if we consciously and deliberately spurn the Cross, "there no longer remains a sacrifice for sins" (Heb 10:26). Since with the Cross we stand at the end of all the ways of God, there is not, as there is for the whore Jerusalem, a final promise overcoming all shame. That promise has already been fulfilled in the Cross. In fact, in a mysterious way, the Cross of Christ stands in an unimaginable position beyond all sin, even the ever-greater sin of the old and new bride. The person who tries to get beyond this absolute terminus, who is content with it, the one who has "spurned the Son of God and profaned the blood of the Covenant by which he was sanctified, and outraged the Spirit of grace", falls into a fiery abyss very different from the one experienced by Persephone's crowd: "the hands of the living God" (Heb 10:29–30).

In this sense the Old Testament mystery of the prostitute is surpassed in the final mystery of all, the mystery of the Cross. In fact, already in the Old Testament, especially in Hosea, the shame of the daughter of Zion is reflected on the shamed God-consort (as it were, *Dieu cocu*). And when, in Ezekiel, Zion is asked to experience shame at the very moment of her final engracing, it is as if she were bearing God's shame with him. On the Cross the shame is definitively taken on and endured, in a way beyond all imagining, for the redeemed Church and humanity. Consequently, the Church feels her shame nowhere more deeply than in her crucified Lord and in what, as an unfathomable grace, he allows her to feel with him. At its innermost and purest core, the harlotry of the new daughter of Zion merges with the supreme "folly of the Cross" (1 Cor 1:18), with "what for the world is foolish", "what for the world is shameful", "what for the world is without nobility", "of no repute", "even things that are not" (1 Cor 1:27–28), which God has claimed for himself. Now this idea of a humiliation and dishonoring that goes as far as nonbeing (*mê on*) comes from the Old Testament. It can be seen in the names of Hosea's "children of harlotry". Paul cites the passage expressly (Rom 9:25–26; cf. Hos 2:23), as does Peter (1 Pet 2:10). It is this that God took upon himself to shame the wisdom of the Greeks and the Jews' demand for signs, a humiliation surpassing all possible derision, every kind of contempt, and it is this that, as a seal, as a pure grace of the Cross, he has impressed upon the Church. The Jerusalem ensnared by the rulers of this world, stripped by them of her garments and all her finery, her shame held up to ridicule, finally hacked down and hurled into the fire: that Jerusalem's final place is none other than the Cross. That is why Christians are also called to take the shame of Jesus upon themselves by leaving the old Jerusalem (cf. Heb 13:13).

So can the Christian settle down and put the Cross behind him once and for all? He could only do that if he allowed himself to think he had the "perfect love" that "casts out fear" (cf. 1 Jn 4:18), that total eschatological "confidence on the Day of Judgment". But he is a liar if he maintains he has no sin (cf. 1 Jn 1:9), if he thus fails to move, time and time again, from the Old Testament to the promise and hope of the Cross, if he fails to approach Jesus, time and time again, in the company of all the sinful women and men who encounter him, if he fails to acknowledge him, all the time as if for the first time, as his Savior. People like to accuse the apostolic Church of a somewhat naïve assurance of salvation, and yet with what insistence do the apostles remind the Church of her origins. She must never forget from where she comes. She must keep her former shame before her eyes in the attitude of Mary Magdalen, in a gratitude, like hers, of confession and adoration: "Formerly, you were . . . !" (Gal 1:13; 4:8; Phil 3:4f.; Eph 2:11–12; 4:17–24; Titus 3:3; 1 Pet 1:14, 18; 4:3–4, etc.). The real Church is as real, as physical and full-blooded, as the old Jerusalem. How could anyone consign her to a pure eschatological grandeur beyond the reach of all peril, safe from all shipwreck? (The Fathers interpreted St. Paul's shipwreck in Acts 27 as a symbol of the historical Church.) How could anyone restrict her to the bare structures she is given and guaranteed from above? That would be to cut her off from historical reality, from all faith, hope, and charity (which can be "heroic" only in the face of peril). Neither "in the Church" nor "as Church" is there a "subject" that can be identified with an existence that is guaranteed and trouble-free. For "Church" can find salvation and security only in the Cross of her Lord (and not in herself). And if she knows that she is the fruit of the Cross (and every Christian knows that is what he is), then the only way for her to live is to follow the way of the Cross in penance and conversion. That is how the Church sees herself before God in the liturgy, which is her surest *lex credendi:* "Keep, we beseech thee, O Lord, thy Church in thine unfailing mercy, and since without thee human frailty cannot but fall, keep her ever by thy help from all harm and lead her to salvation" (Collect, 14th Sunday after Pentecost). "O Lord, we beseech thee, let thy continual pity cleanse and defend thy Church, and since without thee she cannot continue in safety, preserve her evermore by thy grace" (Collect, 15th Sunday after Pentecost; cf. Collect, 1st Sunday in Lent). Here and everywhere the Church prays for herself, not just for her children, with whom she might be identifying in a mother's attitude of "as if". All these people praying together are the Church of Christ, these people who beg for the grace that purifies, sanctifies, protects.

The central issue in what follows is the way in which patristic theology handled and interpreted the recovery and translation into the New Testament of the Old Testament's "revelations" about Jerusalem. Was too much or too little taken over? And what is the final shape that emerges for Biblical-speculative theology of Biblical revelation taken as a whole?

4. *The Rahab theme: the salvation and purification of the prostitute*

Exegetical theology has never failed to notice the clear and deliberate way in which St. Matthew selected the female figures in Christ's genealogy. According to *Anselm of Laon,* these are named "to show that Christ was to be born not only of the Jews, but of the Gentiles; not only of the righteous, but also of sinners" (*In Mt* 1; PL 162, 1239C; cf. *St. Paschasius Radbertus, In Mt* 1, 1; PL 120, 67C). *Rabanus Maurus* underlines this idea:

> Legitimate spouses are passed over, while four foreign women are taken up in Christ's genealogy: Tamar, sitting at the road side in the garb of a whore; Rahab the harlot, joining herself to Salmon, prince of the tribe of Judah from Jericho; Ruth, coming from Moab after her husband's death and joining herself to Boaz; Bathsheba, who conceived through the adultery of King David. In the literal sense, this took place so that we might admire the supreme mercy of God, because, to destroy the sin of man, he deigned to be born not simply of human beings but of sinners and prostitutes. In its spiritual sense, however, these women symbolize the Church that was to come from the error of the Gentiles to the Lord [*Hom. in Evang.* 163; PL 110, 458].

One of the three Old Testament harlots is mentioned three times in the corpus of the New: Rahab. It was she who let Joshua's two spies into the city of Jericho, hid them, and then by her cunning protected them from being hunted down by the King's men. While their pursuers look for them on the Jordan plain, Rahab tells them to make their way through the hills. She makes a profession of faith in Yahweh and receives an assurance from the spies that, if she keeps the agreement, she, her family, and everyone staying in her house will be spared when the city is taken. The spies give her a sign by which her house can be recognized: a scarlet cord, hanging out of her window over the city wall, will indicate to the attackers that this is the house to be spared. And that is what happened. The rest of Jericho is utterly destroyed, but Joshua spares the house of Rahab, "and she dwelt in the midst of Israel to this day" (Jos 2:1–21; 6:17, 22–25).

In Jewish speculation at the time of Christ,[5] Rahab is already a symbolic figure. On the one hand, she is an example of the saving power of good works (Strack-Billerbeck I, 21); on the other hand, she is endowed with the spirit of prophecy (Josephus, *Ant. Jud.* V, 1, 13), because she acknowledges the true God and the election of Israel and foresees the fall of Jericho. All on her own, she admits the people into what will later be the Holy Land and opens up for them the way to conquest. Her spiritual role is central. She really does invite symbolic interpretation. For the Jews, she is already a type of the Gentiles who are incorporated into the people of God, the *ekklesia* (Strack-Billbeck I, 22). What the New Testament has to say about her must be seen against this background.

For theology inspired by St. Paul, Rahab is the witness to justification by faith. "By faith Rahab the harlot did not perish with those who were disobedient, because she had given friendly welcome to the spies" (Heb 11:31). For theology inspired by St. James, she is justified by works. "And in the same way was not also Rahab the harlot justified by works when she received the messengers and sent them out another way?" (James 2:25). The special place given Rahab alongside the most important figures in salvation history indicates the distinction she already enjoyed in the thinking of this period. Now while these two texts, like the original story in Joshua, do not give any particular emphasis to her earlier profession, Matthew must have made mention of Rahab in the Lord's genealogy (Tamar, Ruth, Bathsheba, and Rahab are the only women mentioned) with this

---

[5] For the whole chapter, cf. Jean Daniélou, "Rahab, Figure de l'Église", *Irénikon* 22 (1949): 26–45, reprinted in *Sacramentum Futuri* (1950), pp. 217–32. I have used and partly expanded the texts cited by Daniélou.

aspect in mind. The Christian Tradition will develop both aspects
further. Rahab the convert, the prophetess, the woman incorporated
into the Church, in fact the Church of the Gentiles itself—and Rahab
the harlot. For the Fathers, the first aspect predominates. Origen,
though, says that Rahab and Tamar became types precisely because of
the role they play in Christ's genealogy (cf. *Hom.* 28 *in Luc.;* Rauer
IX, 173).

Development, based on Jewish and New Testament Tradition,
begins already with the *Epistle of St. Clement.* Combining Paul and
James, the Pope says, "For her faith and hospitality Rahab the harlot
was saved" (12:1). Moreover, the scarlet cord has a significance for
him: "It showed beforehand that through the blood of the Lord there
would be redemption for all who believe and hope in God. You see,
dearly beloved, not only faith but prophecy is found in this woman"
(12:7–8). This "sign" can be compared to the streak of blood from the
slaughtered Passover lamb, which the Jews had to paint on their doors
to protect them from the angel of death who struck down the
firstborn of Egypt. For Clement, this is also the "sign" of the Blood
that redeems both Jews and Gentiles: "The sign of the scarlet cord . . . for
its part reveals the Blood of Christ, through which the unrighteous
and former prostitutes out of all the nations are saved, if, having
received the forgiveness of sins, they do not sin any more" (11:3).

St. Justin Martyr (*Dial.* III, 4) extends this theology of redemption
by placing the flood and the ark alongside Rahab and the rite of the
Passover lamb. Here too there is salvation from general destruction.
Rahab's house and those present in it become the saving ark and thus
a symbol of the Church, the Church that, since Rahab came from
Jericho, is precisely the Church of the Gentiles.

In the work of *St. Irenaeus* the theme gains in intensity:

> Thus Rahab the harlot condemned herself, because she was a
> Gentile and guilty of all sins. Nevertheless, she received the three
> spies [*speculatores:* in Greek philosophy *kataskopeusai,* "to spy out",
> also means "to examine" and is used of Providence and its gover-
> nance of the world], who were spying out the whole land—in
> other words, Father, Son, and Holy Spirit—and gave them a place
> of hiding. And when the whole city in which she lived, at the

sounding of the seven trumpets, fell into ruins, Rahab with all her household was saved through faith in the scarlet cord. This explains what the Lord said to those who did not accept his coming, the Pharisees, who despised the scarlet cord, in other words, the Passover, the redemption, and the Exodus of the people from Egypt: "The tax collectors and harlots enter the Kingdom of heaven before you" (Mt 21:31) [*Adv. Haer.* 4, 20, 12].

The three saving events—the ark, the Passover lamb, Rahab's cord—are definitively linked and, through the Matthew text, more strongly related to the Old Testament theology of the harlot. And that is not all. Irenaeus invokes Hosea's treatment of the theme and brings Rahab into connection with the idea of redemption through marriage: she becomes the "Church to be sanctified through communion with the Son". That is also the significance of Moses' relationship with the Ethiopian woman: the wild olive branch (of which St. Paul speaks) is grafted into the holy trunk.

In the first of the Easter homilies in the tradition of *St. Hippolytus* the thinking progresses from the Passover lamb to Rahab as the Church: "The fact that the entire victim had to be eaten in the individual houses and none of the meat was allowed to be taken out means that only one house contains salvation in Christ—the Church universal. Once she was distant from God, but now she alone belongs truly to God, because she received those sent by the Lord Jesus, just as the household of Rahab, the former harlot, had received the spies of Jesus [Joshua] and were the only people to be saved when Jericho was destroyed" (PG 59, 724; cf. Hippolytus' commentary on Daniel 2:19; Bonwetsch I, 1, 79). One of the fragments of Hippolytus' works has something similar: "These twelve spies (cf. Nb 13:1) are the type of the holy apostles, and Moses is the type of Christ. Just as he sent twelve men to spy out the land of Canaan, so Christ sent out his apostles in order to scan the world in his name and for the sake of the gospel" (*Frag. in Num.* 13; Bonwetsch I, 2, 104). Here we have strong endorsement of the Tradition of seeing Joshua, because of his name's similarity to "Jesus" (his first name was Hosea!), as a special type of the Lord. In light of all this, Rahab really does become the Church of humanity, as the next stage in the theme's development, Origen, shows so clearly.

Origen is the classical exponent of the theology of Rahab. No one after him will add anything really new. As he meditates on it, every detail of the story becomes significant:

> Rahab means breadth [*latitudo*]. What is this breadth if not the Church of Christ assembled out of sinners as well as harlots? . . . It is this "breadth" that received the spies of Christ. In the book of Hosea there is another harlot, whom the prophet is instructed to accept, as a symbol, of course, of the Church assembled out of the Gentiles. . . . From a prostitute she [Rahab] becomes a prophetess, for she says: "I know that the Lord your God has handed over this land to you." So you see how the woman who was once a whore, godless and impure, is now filled with the Holy Spirit. To things past she bears witness, in the present she has faith, and the future she prophesies. So Rahab, the "breadth", extends and grows until she reaches the four corners of the earth. . . . But let us see how this wise harlot behaved with the spies. The advice she gave them was mysterious, heavenly, with nothing earthly about it: "Make your way through the hills", in other words, do not go through the valleys, avoid what is base, proclaim what is sublime. She herself places a scarlet sign on her house, by which she escaped the destruction of her city. She chose none other than a scarlet sign, as a symbol of the Blood, for she knew that no one could be saved except in the Blood of Christ.

And now we come to the theology of the one house. "The former harlot receives this instruction: 'All those to be found in your house will be saved.' If anyone wants to be saved, let him come to the house of the former harlot. Even if it is someone of the [Jewish] people who wants to be saved, let him come to this house to find salvation. Let him come to the house in which Christ's Blood, as the sign of redemption, is to be found. . . . And let no one deceive himself, no one delude himself: outside of this house, that is, outside the Church, there is no salvation. If anyone leaves it, he is guilty of his own death." The sign at the window represents the sacraments: the water of baptism and the Blood of our Lord. With the ark and the Passover lamb, the house of the harlot forms the third great symbol of redemption and the Church. "The people in the house escape the coming

Judgment of God, when, at the sound of the trumpet, Jesus our Lord conquers and overthrows Jericho [this world], and only the harlot and all her household are saved." But Rahab remains in the holy people to the present day. This cannot be interpreted literally. "If you want to see more clearly how Rahab was incorporated into Israel, consider how the wild olive branch is inserted into the trunk of the cultivated olive tree, and you will understand how those inserted into the faith of Abraham, Isaac, and Jacob are rightly regarded as incorporated into Israel until the last day. For we wild olive branches, taken from the Gentiles, who once were prostitutes, worshipping stone and wood instead of the true God, have been inserted into the cultivated tree to this day" (*Hom. 3 in Jos.* 4; Baehr VII, 304–6; *Hom.* 6, 4; ibid., 326).

What is remarkable, indeed unique, about this statement is that Origen takes the phrase *to this day* to mean that the Rahab episode has an abiding relevance (he will give us several other testimonies to the same effect). In this passage what is abidingly relevant is not so much the transformation of Rahab from whore to holy Church as the engrafting of the Gentile Church into the Jewish Church. No other Father has felt so strongly as this spiritual master that the Old Testament cannot be superseded, and not only the Old Testament but also the economy and people of the Old Testament. This is the reality in which the Gentile Church is rooted, into which she is engrafted even now and will be time and time again, in the sense that she owes her salvation and sanctification to her admission to the people God originally chose for himself. Origen insists that the process and event of the Gentile Church's incorporation is a living reality. This position is in marked contrast to ecclesiologies that either forget and pass over "the Church of the Jews" (experiencing and describing the Church of the New Covenant as simply "the Church of the Gentiles") or regard the synagogue as the "unfaithful bride" left behind by God, thus allowing Christians through the centuries to do the same (cf., for example, the pseudo-Augustinian *Altercatio Ecclesiae et Synagogae,* PL 42, 1131–40, where the synagogue is simply dismissed as *adultera et moecha,* 1131A, 1135D). In contrast, *St. Augustine* says in the most emphatic way that the New Testament inteprets Hosea's harlot to mean the Church, not

Israel according to the flesh, but the Church of Jews and Gentiles according to the promise (*C. Faust. Man.* 22, 89; PL 42, 459–461). The implanting of the Gentiles into the Jewish Church is an act of purification. *Origen* shows this has abiding relevance when he comes to the "moral sense" of the passage, that is to say, when he applies it to the individual soul, albeit in connection with what is affirmed about the whole Church: "The harlot who received the spies sent by Jesus did it so that in future she would be a harlot no more. Now the soul of each of us was this harlot while it lived in vice and lust. But it has received the messengers of Jesus, the angels, whom he sent before his face to prepare his way" (*Hom.* I *in Jos.* I, 4; ibid., 292).

The phrase coined by Origen—"outside Rahab's house, the Church, no salvation"—inevitably became an axiom for *St. Cyprian.* It provided him with a graphic image to express his basic idea about the Church's unity. "It was said to Rahab, who prefigured the Church, 'Gather into your house your father and your mother.' . . . Do you think you can live when you leave the Church and build new dwellings and different homes? After all, it was said to Rahab, in whom the Church was prefigured, . . . 'Whoever leaves the doors of your house shall be guilty' " (*De cath. eccl. unit.* 8; CSEL 3, I, 217; cf. *Ep.* 69, 4; 3, II, 752–53). The harlot theme is inactive in Cyprian.

St. Jerome, in the Origen Tradition, speaks more pointedly, "Rahab, the justified whore, contains us" (*Ep.* 22, 38; PL 22, 422). "Rahab the harlot, as a type of the Church, hung from the window a cord containing the mystery of the Blood, so that her house, when Jericho was destroyed, would be saved" (*Ep.* 52, 3; PL 22, 530; cf. *Adv. Jovin.* I, 23; PL 23, 243A). Similar things are said in the *Altercatio Simonis et Theophili* (TU I, 3 [1883] 33), which also refers (34) to Hosea's harlot.

The Song of Songs mentions that the bride has a "coral necklace" (1:10). *Theodoret,* in his commentary on the passage, is reminded of Rahab's scarlet cord. This gives him the opportunity of interrelating, in the reality of the Church, the harlot of the Old Testament with the bride of the New. "By referring to the coral necklace, he reminds us of the harlot Rahab, who was her type and prefiguration in the Old Testament. For by receiving the spies sent by Joshua the son of Nun, she was deemed worthy by them of eternal salvation" (*In Cant.* 2, 4; PG 81, 129C). However, in his commentary on Joshua, Theodoret stresses the fact that the Church, who once was a harlot, must not forget her past: "Let no one regard the image of Rahab as unworthy of the Church. Listen rather to the apostle: 'We ourselves were once foolish, disobedient, led astray, slaves to various passions and pleasures, passing our days in malice and envy, hated by men and hating one another' (Titus 3:3), and again: 'Once you were darkness, but now you are light in the Lord' (Gal 4:8). And yet again: 'Do not be deceived; neither the immoral, nor idolaters, nor adulterers, nor homosexuals . . . will inherit the Kingdom of God" (1 Cor 6:9–10), and he adds immediately, " 'And such were some of you, but you have been justified . . . ' Just like Rahab the harlot" (*Qu. in Jos. int.* 2; PG 80, 462).

St. Cyril of Jerusalem identifies himself more with St. Matthew's version of the Rahab Tradition: "The type of Jesus saved Rahab the harlot when she believed. But the true Jesus said: 'Behold, the tax collectors and prostitutes go before you into the Kingdom of God' " (*Cat.* 10, 11; PG 33, 676C; cf. *Pseudo-Chrysostom, In Meretricem;* PG 59, 533).

For *St. Hilary* the Rahab episode, together with the reality and symbol of Hosea, moves to the very center of typological theology: "We have called the [Hosea] text to mind chiefly so that now, as we consider Rahab, we can show her to be a type of the Church. Church and harlot can with certainty be compared, because we can show that the harlot united to the prophet has been wedded by God in eternal expectation of faith, justice, and wisdom" (*Tract. Mysteriorum* II, 5; *Sources Chrétiennes* 148). In the spirit of Origen, Joshua is interpreted as a foreshadowing of Jesus; he is the type of the New Covenant, just as Moses, who led the people through the wilderness but not into the promised land, was a type of the Old.

The story [of Rahab] is one long chain of important images of salvation and of the spiritual goods that were to come. The harlot receives the two men sent by Jesus to spy out the land. In other words, the sinful Church receives the law and the prophets sent to spy out the faith of men, and she confesses that "God is in heaven above and on earth beneath". From the same spies she receives the sign of salvation in the scarlet cord, clearly a symbolic color, signifying in dignity kingship and in the bodily sphere blood. Both are proper to the Passion, for thus was the Lord's robe procured. The houses daubed with this blood in Egypt were spared, with this blood the book of the Covenant was sprinkled, with it the people were sanctified. Every member of the family found outside of the house made himself guilty. That means whoever is found outside the Church will be guilty of his own death.

Like Origen, Hilary gives the image an eschatological slant: "For six days Jericho, the type of the world, was encircled. On the seventh, at the sound of the trumpets, it collapsed, and Jesus spared the whole house of Rahab . . . because she confessed the Incarnation of God, and because Jesus gave her the sign of scarlet" (II, 9–10; 154–57).

In his twelfth treatise (Ed. Batiffol, *Tr. Origenis* [Paris, 1900], pp. 128–39), *St. Gregory of Elvira* has arranged the Rahab theme, together with the other harlot motifs from Scripture, in a kind of fugue. In so doing, he makes vividly clear the interwoven unity of the theme in the Bible. We shall return to some of these motifs later. Gregory wants to draw our attention to the *oikonomia* of the *mysterion*: "Why Rahab? I do not think she was mentioned by chance but with prophetic good reason. For this harlot meets me in many passages in Scripture, not only as the hostess of the saints but also as spouse. After all, Hosea, the holy prophet, is commanded by the Lord to take a harlot as a wife . . . and the same Lord, who is our Redeemer, when he was sitting by a well in Samaria, spoke first of all with a harlot. . . . And finally a harlot washed the Redeemer's feet with her tears" (129). "This Rahab, though called a harlot, bears prophetically within herself the sacraments of the Virgin Church and the shadow of the things to take place at the end of time." The traditional themes are unfolded: idolatry is adultery, so the Church from the Gentiles is called a harlot; she receives the messengers sent by the Lord. And when at the end of the world, at the blast of the trumpet, Jericho collapses, only the people in the harlot's house will be saved. But the Church is Christ's bride, washed clean through baptism: "From being the harlot she once was, she becomes virgin, in accordance with the Lord's words to the Jews: 'The prostitutes will go before you into the Kingdom of heaven.'" So by "prostitute" Jesus meant the Church of the Gentiles. Gregory portrays both Rahab and Mary Magdalen as an image of the bride of Christ. He compares the scarlet sign to the red of the bride's lips in the Song of Songs and links the sparing of Rahab's house with the deliverance of those who ate the Passover lamb in Egypt. Having presented all these themes, he then gathers them together. He sees them circling round a central point—the contrast between "once" and "now". "Once, while we dwelt among the Gentiles, we were not his people, but through faith in Christ we were destined to be transformed into his people and be called sons of God. And the Church too, before being taken to himself by Christ, was once unbeloved, but then was destined to become his beloved" (133). The flood and the ark are drawn into the analogy, and the Jericho/Rahab episode now becomes the vivid illustration within history of the two great destructions—at the beginning of human history and at its end. "The flood, the Passover, and the Rahab story are the three great *sacramenta* that contain the Biblical theology of redemption."[6]

A few more testimonies can be cited, though they change the general picture very little. First, *St. Augustine:* "Rahab represents the Church of the Gentiles. That is why the Lord says to the arrogant Pharisees: 'Truly, I say to you, tax collectors and harlots will go before you into the Kingdom of heaven' (Mt 21:31).... 'I will be mindful of Rahab and of Babylon' (Ps 86:4)... not only of Rahab, but also of Babylon. But for whom will he be mindful? For those 'who remember me' (ibid.)" (*En. in Ps.* 86; PL 37, 1106). *Cassiodorus* (*Exp. in Ps.* 86, 4; PL 70, 619) repeats the statement. What is important here is that Rahab (who really refers here to Egypt but is taken by the patristic exegetes to mean the historical person) is mentioned in the same breath as Babylon, *the* great harlot. Theologians coming after Augustine dwell on the wonder of the transformation of harlot into virgin. Augustine himself had emphasized that Christ "redeemed his Church from harlotry with demons and made her a virgin" (*Serm.*

---

[6] Daniélou, op. cit., p. 43.

188, 4; PL 38, 1005). *St. Caesarius of Arles* makes the same point: "That harlot, dearly beloved brethren, symbolized the Church, who, before the coming of the Lord, used to play the harlot with many idols. But Christ, on his coming into the world, not only set her free from fornication but also changed her, by a great and mighty miracle, into a virgin" (*Serm.* 116, Morin I, 483). *St. Fulgentius:* "Rahab symbolizes the Church of the Gentiles.... By receiving the spies of Jesus, she, who hitherto had played the harlot with idols and was a godless whore, became a woman of faith, fidelity, and chastity" (*De rem. pecc.* 20–21; PL 65, 543–45). Similarly, *St. Paschasius Radbertus* (*Expos. in Mt.* I, 1; PL 120, 61CD) and *Pseudo-Ambrose* (*Serm.* 46, 15; PL 17, 698–99). *Rupert of Deutz* goes into more detail and adds a new idea, which we shall have to consider more closely later on (in part 7): the parallel between the whore who "gives herself to every passer-by" (Ezek 16:25) and the womb of the Catholic Church, which is open to receive all who come to her: "This whore, of noted faith and illustrious memory, ... symbolizes the Church that is gathered, and gathers, from the Gentiles.... The spies rested in her house, and she refreshed the depths of her soul by opening her door to them and receiving the word of salvation.... Before they entered her house ... she was a whore, a bed of demons, a brothel of idols. But when they had entered, and she had received them, she became pure, the chaste virgin of one husband, his one friend, one dove, one immaculate, one perfect woman" (*De op. Trin.; in Jos.* 10; PL 167, 1008–9; cf. *In Cant.* I, 3; PL 168, 887BC). *Durandus* too links the two themes: the Church "is presented in the image of a harlot, because she was assembled originally from the heathens, and because she closes her womb to no one who returns to her" (*Rationale div. off.* I, 14 [1859] 12). The idea of this comparison was first developed by *St. Ambrose,* who excelled in the discovery of such bold ideas, as will be seen. The man on the roof, says the Gospel, must not come down—in other words, must not return to the world. "But I know a roof on which Rahab concealed the spies sent by Jesus. Rahab as type was a whore, but as mystery the Church, which is linked to the Gentile peoples by consort with the sacraments" (*In Luc.* 8, 40; PL 15, 1776).

The idea of the Gentile Church as a converted harlot is so common that it can also be developed independently of the Rahab story, especially when the Church is seen in universal perspective and is identified with the human race that is to be redeemed. This is true of *Aponius,* for whom "the Church consists of all those who have faith in Christ, the Church who, before the coming of the Bridegroom, lay in her own blood" (cf. Ezek 16)" (*In Cant.* I, I, p. 6; ed. Bottino-Martini [Rome, 1843]). Thus in speculation connected with Ephesians 5:26–27, the Church's bath of purification may be taken to mean in general terms redemption or more specifically the sacrament of baptism, or more narrowly still the baptism in the Jordan in which Christ both purified his bride "his flesh" and married her. The famous Epiphany antiphon expresses this idea: "Today the Church is joined to her heavenly Bridegroom, since Christ in the Jordan has washed away her offenses" (*Hodie coelesti Sponso juncta est Ecclesia, quoniam in Jordane lavit Christus ejus crimina*).[7] From the fact of the one true bride's purification, *St. Cyprian* concludes that she has exclusive legitimacy: "Only the Church that has been joined and united to Christ spiritually bears sons, as the apostle says: 'Christ loved his Church and gave himself up for her, that he might sanctify her, having cleansed her by the washing in water.' If Christ's bride and beloved is she who by Christ alone has been purified and cleansed in the bath, it is clear that heresy, which is not Christ's bride and cannot be cleansed and sanctified in his bath, can also not bear sons for God" (*Ep.* 74, 6f.; CSEL III, 2, 804). The numerous Syriac liturgical and theological texts[8] all vigorously insist on the act of cleansing, but they say very little about what the "poor bride" (Jacob of Sarug) was before her cleansing. *Cassiodorus* speaks of the cleansing bath when commenting on Psalm 50: "That the Gentile Church, which was covered with the filth of its sin, may be cleansed through union with God" (PL 70, 358; cf. *St. Augustine, In Joh. tr.* 57, 5; PL 35, 1789).

[7] On this whole theme, see Casel, "Die Taufe als Brautbad der Kirche" *JLW* 5 (1925); Hieron Frank, "Hodie etc. Ein Beitrag zur Geschichte des Epiphaniefestes", in *Vom christlichen Mysterium* (Patmos, 1951), pp. 192–226.

[8] In Frank, pp. 202–7.

The Fathers kept returning to the idea that the former whore has been miraculously transformed into a virgin. They were not afraid of applying to the Church the graphic proverb (Prov 30:20): "This is the way of the harlot: she eats, and wipes her mouth, and says, 'I have done no wrong.'" "This harlot is a type of the Church. Once she dwelt among the Gentiles, depraved by idolatry, disgraced by the fornication of idle superstition. The crowd of false gods had made her an adulteress. . . . But once our Lord Jesus Christ had poured the pure water of baptism over her, she received the washing away of both her crimes and her earlier name through the grace of faith. By God's grace the former harlot becomes a virgin" (*Pseudo-Ambrose, Sermo de Salomone* 46, 15; PL 17, 698). And again on the same proverb: "What it says about the adulteress applies to the woman that is the Church. Formerly she followed idols and whored after foreign gods, but once . . . washed in baptism, she is convinced she has never sinned. She becomes pure, dies to the devil, is reborn for God" (*Pseudo-Ambrose, Sermo in Prov.* 30, 19–20; 47, 5; PL 17, 702A; cf. *St. Isidore of Seville, Alleg.* 73; PL 83, 111A). Finally, *St. Anastasius of Sinai*: "This is the way of the adulteress: she eats, and wipes her mouth and says, and says, 'I have done no wrong.'" This is the way of the conversion of the Church that has faith in Christ: she whores after idols, but then she renounces them, and the devil is washed clean from her sins, receives forgiveness, and says, 'I have done no wrong'" (*Quaest. et Resp.*, PG 9, 593AC, with use of a text from Hipploytus, though Bonwetsch does not accept the attribution: Hipp I, 2, 176–78; PG 10, 624). *Origen,* without reference to the proverb, asserts the same truth: "It can happen that someone who has sinned and has now ceased to sin is called 'sinless'. Thus our Lord Jesus Christ prepared for himself "a glorious Church without spot", not because any individuals within the Church have ever been without "spot" but because they no longer defile themselves, a Church "without wrinkle" not because the "wrinkle" of the "old man" has never adhered to them but because they no longer have it" (*Hom. 2 in Luc.,* Rauer 9, 14).

What Rahab is for the theology of the Old Testament, Mary

Magdalen[9] is for the New: the former harlot converted into the Christ-loving soul. In fact, at the foot of the Cross, she quite explicitly becomes the symbol of the purified Church, entrusted on Easter Sunday with bearing the message of salvation to the apostles and the world. This is particularly clear when Mary Magdalen is identified, on the one hand, with the sinful woman who anoints the feet of Jesus in Luke chapter 7, and, on the other hand, with Mary of Bethany, who also anoints him. The former sinner meets the future virgin, the pure contemplative and friend of the Lord, and the two converge to the point of identity. "The harlot was transformed. She was no longer a harlot but became more honorable than a virgin" (*Pseudo-Chrysostom, In Meretricem et Pharisaeum,* PG 59, 531). "The harlot who washes the Savior's feet and dries them with her hair is the type of the Church, gathered from the Gentiles. To her these words apply: 'Your sins are forgiven you'" (*St. Jerome, Ep.* 122, 3; CSEL 56, 66). *St. Augustine* likewise identifies the woman bearing the jar of ointment with the Church (*En. in Ps.* 21, 2; PL 36, 171).

According to *Origen,* when Mary Magdalen anoints the feet of Jesus, she is the penitent Church, the Church at the beginning of her conversion, in contrast to Mary of Bethany when she performs the same action: "When she begins to serve God and to know Christ, the Church on earth is his 'footstool', just as that penitent woman, that sinner, lay at Jesus' feet at the beginning of her conversion, having not yet been permitted to empty the fragrant ointment of her good works over the head of Christ. For her desire was this: to be at Jesus' feet and to anoint him" (*Serm. in Mt.* 8; Klost.-Benz. II, 13). Similarly, *St. Ambrose* says that the two distinct anointings were carried out by the same woman: the first is carried out by the Church inasmuch as she is a sinner, the second by the Church inasmuch as she is making progress toward sanctity. More will be said later about the fact that the Church of the saints adopts the gesture of the Church of sinners (*St. Ambrose,*

---

[9] On the subject of Mary Magdalen, we can cite here only a few illustrative texts. A comprehensive collection of texts, which shows the different roles played by the many women mentioned in the Gospels, can be found in Urban Holzmeister, "Die Magdalenenfrage in der kirchlichen Überlieferung", *ZfkTH* 46 (1922): 402f. 556f.

In Luc. I, 6, 12–35; PL 15, 1671–78). *St. Paulinus of Nola* follows this interpretation and adds the lovely detail that the Church of sinners washes herself by pouring oil over Christ, cleanses herself of her sins by drying his feet, loves herself by embracing him in love (*Ep.* 23, 32–33; PL 61, 277–79). According to *St. Gregory the Great,* who liked to distribute the figures in the gospel between the synagogue and the Church, the Pharisee in Luke chapter 7 is simply the Old Testament, whereas "the sinful woman, following the footsteps of the Lord, covering his feet with her tears, symbolizes the Church converted from heathendom. And this woman can symbolize us too, when, having sinned, we turn back wholeheartedly to the Lord" (*Homiliae in Evangelium* 2, 33, 5; PL 76, 1242). Similarly, speaking in general terms, *St. Peter Chrystologus:* "See, a woman who once was a sinner, known all over town. Who is this woman? Without doubt, the Church. In which town? In the town of which the prophet says, 'How faithful Zion has become harlot' (Is 1:21; Jer 11:16–17)" (*Serm.* 95; PL 52, 467–68).

Most of the texts referring to Rahab and Mary Magdalen stress the transition in time: once she was a whore; now she is a saint. Secondly, they place special emphasis on the Gentile Church: once she played the harlot with idols; now she is chaste and faithful to Christ. Only the greatest of the theologians of the patristic age go beyond these two categories: *Origen,* who regards the whole unabridged Old Testament as a model, a visual aid, for the Church; for him, what was relevant in the past has to be still relevant today. And *St. Augustine,* starting from somewhat different premises, holds a similar view. For the Church's great Doctor of sin and grace, the difference between the engracing of Israel and that of the Gentile Church is not so great. Thus, in the famous sermon about the two harlots who argue over the dead child in the presence of Solomon:

The two women are the synagogue and the Church. . . . Both were harlots, for the Apostle says that Jews and Greeks are all equally in a state of sin, for any soul that turns away from eternal truth to indulge in earthly filth goes whoring away from God. . . . But one mother woke up and realized, not by her own merits, for she was a harlot, but by God's grace, that a son had been given her — the work of evangelical faith. . . . Yet both were harlots, because all had been converted from worldly lust to the grace of God. The only things she could really confess to be her own were her sins. The gift of fruitfulness comes from God [*Serm.* 10; PL 38, 92–95].

It is worth placing *Rabanus Maurus'* interpretation alongside St. Augustine's:

There can be no doubt that the Scriptures call both the synagogue and the Church adulteresses and prostitutes. At first sight, this seems blasphemous, but then we turn to the prophets. Hosea takes a harlot to be his wife, has children of harlotry, and later marries an adulteress.[10] Ezekiel calls Jerusalem a whore, because she chases after her lovers, opens her legs to every passer-by, sets up a brothel in a public place. Christ, therefore, came to lead prostitutes to marriage. . . . Similarly, the prostitute in the Gospel (Lk 7), who washed the feet of Jesus with her tears and dried them with her hair, the woman whose every sin was forgiven, clearly represents the Church gathered from the Gentiles. I have spoken openly about this, so that it does not seem incongruous to call both women prostitutes, to one of whom, by the judgment of Solomon, was given the custody of the son. The attentive listener will ask how a prostitute can represent the Church, who has neither spot nor wrinkle. But we are not saying that the Church remained a prostitute, but simply that she used to be.

Rabanus Maurus then goes on to show that the Church lives in the same house as the synagogue, that she gave birth in the chamber of the synagogue (in other words, in the sphere of revelation), that the synagogue crushed her own child to death, and then tries as fast as she can to make the Church's children her own ("Read the whole of Galatians!"). The dispute of the two women before the King is thus the great conflict in the early Church between St. Paul and the Judaizing party. The fact that the Church would rather give her living child to the synagogue than see it cut in two

[10] Following one version of the Latin text, a good many of the Fathers find both a harlot and an adulteress in Hosea.

represents St. Paul's concessions to St. James' party (*In 3 Reg.*, 3; PL 109, 127–29).

For *St. Augustine* and the exegetes who follow him, as we shall see, the really pure Church is an eschatological concept. It is only these theologians who are able to some degree to overcome the deficiency in the Rahab theology of the Fathers: the overhasty replacement of the spurned synagogue by the chosen Gentile Church (the theology of history to be found in Romans was surely warning enough about the dangers of that idea). Patristic theology (and almost all theology following it) has given insufficient consideration to the truth that "salvation comes from the Jews", that the Gentiles have been engrafted onto the "holy trunk", that the *theologoumena* of God's ancient people are transformed and taken up into those of the new people of God, for whose sake (1 Cor 10) they once were abandoned. This deficiency also weakens the idea of *metanoia* as something relevant to the Church as a whole: the turning from old to new as something with an absolute and permanent relevance, an unending process of coming from the old and moving into the new, the dynamic of all existence and reality in the Church. In the words of *St. Gregory the Great*: "Let the Church cry out, 'I am black but beautiful', black by your judgment, but beautiful through the radiance of grace . . . black by merit, beautiful by grace . . . black by myself, beautiful by gift, black from the past, beautiful through what I am made to be in the future" (*Cant.* 1, 5; Heine, 183; PL 79, 486–88). As a concrete community of believers, the Church always exists in this tension, and so concretely she looks in two directions, as *St. Dionysius the Carthusian* shows. She is always both "spotless Church" and "disfigured Church", always both "virgin" and "harlot", for "the whole, through the diversity of its parts, can get conflicting names". "Thus the Church is called disfigured, estranged, bloodless, or whorish with regard to believers without charity or good works, yes, those who have been befouled by vice, whose souls are not brides of Christ but adulteresses of the devil" (*In Cant.* art. 12; *Opera Omnia* VII, 368B; art. 18, 406B; Riedlinger, op. cit., pp. 396f.).

4a. Hosea: redemption through union with the harlot

In the Rahab story the chief character is the woman; through her faith, or through her works, she is cleansed and saved. It is she who opens the gates to Joshua/Jesus the Redeemer. It is likewise Mary Magdalen who goes in person to the Lord. In the Hosea story the light falls on the man and his humiliating action. Hosea is the image of the mercy of God and of the extreme self-abasement of his love. Only through this love is Israel the harlot, type of humanity in the Church, saved and her descendants are renamed. Here at last the theme reaches its unfathomable depths of meaning.

Hosea does what he does in fulfillment of the mission given him by God. He is, in that respect, the type of Christ. But what he does is not only degrading for him; it is also ambiguous and easily misunderstood by other people. That is why it was possible and logical for the Fathers to see other carnal unions in the Old Testament as pointing to Christ and the Church—for example, Samson's relationship with the Philistine girl ("His father and mother did not know that it was from the Lord, for he was seeking an occasion against the Philistines" [Jg 14:4]), and especially with Delilah, who robs him of his strength; Moses' marriage to the Ethiopian woman; even David's adulterous affair with Bathsheba.

In these texts the stress falls on the action and intention of the man, an intention that is unrestrictedly redemptive. If we look at the other partner in the relationship, it is clear that the role of bride cannot primarily and properly be played by a delineated, delimited Church, because that would mean that God's saving plan in Christ applied to only a section of humanity. No, "the bride" here means simply "the flesh": first, the flesh of Christ himself as, so to speak, the primal and archetypal Church, and then, by means of this assumed flesh, "all flesh", the whole of humanity, which is meant to be in the Church and is being progressively incorporated into her. This universalist motif is thus not primarily ecclesiological; it functions as a counterweight to the Rahab motif, which is all too limiting in its implications.

St. Irenaeus introduces the theme with his customary realism:

It pleased God to take his Church from the mass of sinners. She was to be saved through union with his Son, just as this harlot was sanctified through union with the prophet. And for this reason St. Paul says that the unfaithful [*infidelis,* unbelieving] wife is sanctified by the faithful [believing] husband (cf. 1 Cor 7:14). What the prophet did by a symbolic act, Christ, as the apostle shows (cf. Eph 5), did for the Church. In similar fashion, Moses took an Ethiopian woman to be his wife.... The marriage of Moses was a pointer to the marriage of God's Word [*Adv. Haer.* 4, 34, 12, Harvey; cited in Pseudo-Ambrose, *Serm.* 46, 15; PL 17, 699].

Earlier (4, 22, 1f.), in connecting with the foot washing, Irenaeus had already spoken of "the Word washing away, by himself, the impurities of the daughter of Zion", so that the whole body of Christ should, to its very feet, be sanctified and led to purity.

St. John Chrysostom explains the appearance of prostitutes in the genealogy of Christ by the brisk assertion that "God espoused to himself a prostituted nature, which the prophets from the beginning declared to have taken place with respect to the synagogue" (*Hom. in Mt.* 3, 4; PG 57, 35).

St. Jerome gives a rich orchestration to the theme in the prologue to his commentary on Hosea (which refers to the now unavailable commentaries of his predecessors, *Origen's* above all, but also those of Origen's disciple *Didymus* and of *Apollinaris):* "Who, at the very beginning of the book, would not be scandalized when Hosea, first of all the prophets, is told to take a harlot as his wife and does not refuse? ... No frown creases his brow.... He just goes straight to the brothel and takes a harlot to his bed. And he does not introduce her to the ways of marital chastity but shows himself to be a real debauchee and wastrel. After all, he who joins himself to a prostitute becomes one body with her (cf. 1 Cor 6:16)." The answer to this question is to be found in the New Testament:

Then we understand who Judah is, the patriarch chosen as king, and we are not surprised that the holy man went in to Tamar as if she were a harlot; nor that Samson (whose name means "sun") loved Delilah (whose name means "poor") and, having been on her account mocked and condemned to death, slaughtered thousands of his enemies; nor that Salmon, by Rahab the harlot, begat Boaz the just, who covered Ruth the Moabitess with the corner of his cloak, and, as she lay at his feet, transferred her to the head of the gospel; nor do we wonder why King David had so many wives and appointed as his successor on the throne none other than the son he begat by Bathsheba, or why it seems that not only harlots but even adulteresses are pleasing to God. And so we read in this same prophet [Hosea] that he had carnal union first with a whore and then with an adulteress.... This is the woman, the harlot and adulteress, who washed the feet of Jesus with her tears, dried them with her hair, and honored them with the ointment of her confession.... And lest we think that what she did was a small thing and refer the *nardos pistikos,* the faithful ointment, to something other than the Church, the Lord helps us grasp its meaning ... when he says: "Truly, I say to you, wherever the gospel is preached in the whole world, what she has done will be told in memory of her." This is the harlot of whom the Lord says to the Jews: "Truly, I say to you harlots and tax collectors will enter the Kingdom of heaven before you." For you refused to receive the Son sent to you ... whereas this harlot with kindness received my spies, two sturdy lads, one of whom I sent to the circumcision, the other to the Gentiles.... In the Song of Songs she says of herself: "I am black but beautiful."

Having assembled these various Biblical motifs, Jerome considers Hosea's relationship with the harlot in more detail. He shows, when expounding the text *quia fornicans fornicabitur terra Domino* (1:2), that the important thing is "not so much the prophet's liaison with a harlot as the whole human race's defection from fellowship with God". Now Jerome adds that here are three distinct ways in which the harlot and the adulteress can be interpreted. First, they can be taken to represent, respectively, the ten tribes of Israel and the two tribes of Judah. But these, in the books of the prophets, usually symbolize the Gentiles on the one hand and the Church that comes from David on the other. But since Israel (Samaria) was not really Gentile but a degenerate form of the Jewish people, the third line of interpretation sees the two figures as expressing the relationship of heresy and Mother Church (*In Oseam,* prol. and cap. 1; PL 25, 855–64).

There is no doubt that this whole exegesis derives substantially from the lost commentary on Hosea of *Origen*. He had already observed that the genealogy of Christ that descends from God mentions the sinful women, while the ascending one does not. St. Matthew mentions Tamar, Rahab, Ruth, Bathsheba: "Since Christ came to take upon himself the sins of men, he took over, in descending into the world, the person of sinners and depraved humankind' (*Hom. in Luc.* 28, Rauer 9, 173). Two commentaries dependent on Jerome's are those by *Haymo* (PL 117, 11f.), who incorporates quite extensively the Ezekiel theme of Jerusalem the archwhore, and *Rupert of Deutz* (PL 168, 15f.), for whom the whore is none other than the human race, to which God goes in order to extract from it the children of promise, the people of Israel. But they keep on playing the harlot (Rupert refers to Ezek 16), and finally they split into the double harlot of Ezekiel 23. To one of the two, Oholibah, God goes one last time, "when the Son of God was born of her flesh in the virgin's womb' (22A). So Hosea's action is a sign for yesterday, today, and tomorrow, "for this race, unfaithful to God, has played the harlot, still plays the harlot today, and will go on playing the harlot" (22B).

Also in the Jerome Tradition is *Pseudo-Rufinus'* commentary on Hosea (PL 21, 962f.), though it limits itself to the historical interpretation: the whore is Israel (964CD). This is true, in the main, of the great Hosea commentary of *St. Cyril of Alexandria* (PG 71, 12–328), which inspired *Theophylact* (PG 126, 563f.). However, Cyril does strongly emphasize how much Hosea's humiliation clarifies the word of God and refers to St. Paul's desire to be anathema for the sake of his brethren. The prophet's action sheds light on "all our pneumatic communion" with the Lord (33A).

For *St. Hilary,* the mystery of Hosea is one of the primary components of Old Testament typology:

> We should have no hesitation in seeing here a prefiguring of the Church. The Apostle himself thought that what was said to Hosea about the sons of this harlot applies to the people of the faithful, because he says to the Corinthians . . . [then follows not 1 or 2 Cor but Rom 9:24–26]. What took place physically in the prophet,

namely, conjugal union and procreation (for the harlot bore him three children, the first of whom, at God's behest, was called Israel,[11] the second Not-Loved, and the third Not-My-People), is confirmed and accomplished by God to teach us a spiritual lesson. For "in justice and faith" the Lord took to be his bride the harlot married to the prophet. He did this when he made "a covenant with the beasts of the field", that is, with the humans rendered inhuman by the law of this world, and with "the birds of the air", that is, with those who live in the vanity and vacuity of this world, and with "the serpents of the ground", that is, with those who carry within their bodies a poisonous, lying soul. And he broke the "bow" (in the serpents), the "arrow" (in the birds), and "warfare" (in the beasts of the field) (cf. Hos 2:18ff.).

Israel is begotten as firstborn son, chosen out of all the nations of humanity, but he loses the promise:

> In the first place the harlot is chosen as bride for the God of faith and justice, and then Not-Loved and Not-My-People, born of the harlot, are called "sons of the living God". Now we must call to mind the words of God, by which the prophet was instructed to take an adulterous woman as his wife, because we are taught that everything has been prefigured by the events of the Old Testament and will be fulfilled in and by the Lord. Thus the union of the prophet with the harlot is meant to show us that Gentile ignorance has been united to the teaching of the prophets, and that the children of the two are to be given new names: "Not-Loved" becomes "Loved", "Not-My-People" becomes "My People"; off-spring of a harlot mother become sons of God [*Lib. myster.* II, 1–4; CSEL 65, 30–32].

St. Hilary sees Hosea's sexual intercourse with a harlot as a type of the union of divine revelation with sinful humanity, the fruit of which is the people of God, the sons of God. *Pseudo-Ambrose* goes one step further and describes Christ himself as fruit; in other words, he sees the hypostatic union as a marriage between Divine Word and human flesh. "The Lord demands marriage with the woman who had committed fornication, and the fruit of this marriage is Christ. The

[11] The name in fact is Jezreel, where Jehu slaughtered the descendants of Omri.

name 'Jezrahel', meaning 'divine birth', is bestowed by the Lord on the son born of the harlot (that is to say, of Hosea's wife, who had been a harlot). . . . A pious union of dissimilar spouses took place when the Word was made flesh, for the consorting of divinity and flesh is irregular. . . . God took flesh to himself and assumed a soul. Through the unwonted irregularity of the Incarnation, God has regularized the union, so he may be all in all" (*Apol. David* 2, 10; PL 14, 908). Pseudo-Ambrose is also familiar with the other interpretation of Hosea's harlot, which applies it to the Church; this, however, leads back to the Rahab theology (*De Salom.* 15; PL 17, 698f.). The interpretation that sees it as referring to the flesh of Christ is decisive, because in this personification of the *caro* we can see the destined unity of all flesh, indeed of all "sinful flesh" (Rom 8:3), whose guilt the flesh of Christ will take up into itself (2 Cor 5:21). "The flesh wanted to adhere to Christ. It hurried to the marriage so as to be "one spirit" and to become the flesh of Christ, the very same that before had been the flesh of the harlot. It remembered that beforehand it had fallen in Eve, when it had preferred bodily lust to the commandment of heaven" (*Exp. in Ps.* 118, 1, 5; CSEL 62, 8).

What concerns us here is not the general idea of the hypostatic union as a marital union—that is common enough in the Fathers[12]—nor the widespread view that Christ's flesh is itself the primordial Church, from which derive, through the assimilation of all other flesh, the Church and the *Christus totus* (St. Augustine, *In Ep. 1 Joh. tr.* 1, 2; PL 35, 1979). No, our concern is with the view that it is precisely through the Incarnation that adulterous humanity is restored. Citing Jeremiah 3:1 ("If a man divorces his wife and she goes from him and becomes another man's wife, will he return to her? . . . You have played the harlot with many lovers, and would you return to me? says

---

[12] Texts in M. J. Scheeben, *The Mysteries of Christianity*, ET (St. Louis, 1946), pp. 372ff. *Dogmatik* III, p. 141; J. Schaid, "Heilige Brautschaft", *RAC* I, 557 ("The marriage of the Logos with human nature"). Cf. St. Ephrem, *The Hymns on Faith* (ed. Beck), Hymn XIV: Christ weds his flesh and, through the flesh, the Church, while his once beloved synagogue "woos the calf" (p. 47). However, in several hymns Ephrem celebrates the holy harlots who are images of the Church (*Hymni de Ecclesia et Virginitate*, nn. 17, 18, 22, 27, etc.; Lamy IV, 546f. 558, 584).

the Lord"), *St. Gregory the Great* gives us this reminder: "Ponder well, brethren, the weight of such kindness. Behold, he calls, and the very ones he brands as befouled he takes in his arms and kisses, the very ones he complained had deserted him" (*Hom. in Ev.* 2, 33, 8; PL 76, 1245).

In a famous sermon of *St. Augustine,* which Hugo Rahner regards as genuine but Dom Morin ascribes to *St. Caesarius,* the Hosea mystery becomes the mystery of Samson and Delilah:

What was the meaning of Samson? If I say he signified Christ, it seems to me that I speak the truth. However, the thought immediately occurs to anyone who reflects: Was Christ overcome by the flattery of a woman? How is Christ understood to have gone in to a harlot? Then again, when did Christ have his head uncovered or his hair shaved, himself robbed of courage, bound, blinded, and mocked? Watch, faithful soul. Notice why it is Christ, not only what Christ did but also what he suffered. What did he do? He worked as a strong man and suffered as a weak one. In the one person I understand both qualities; I see the strength of the Son of God and the weakness of the Son of Man. Moreover, when the Scriptures extol him, Christ is entire, both Head and Body. Just as Christ is the Head of the Church, so the Church is his body; and in order that it might not be alone, it is the whole Christ with the Head. Now the Church contains within itself both strong and weak members. . . . There is a further fact that must be admitted: in association at the sacraments, the imparting of baptism or participation at the altar, the Church has both just and unjust men. . . . The harlot whom Samson married is the Church, who committed fornication with idols before knowing one God but whom Christ afterward united to himself. . . . When Samson went in to the harlot, he was impure if he did so without reason, but if he did so as a prophet, it is a mystery. . . . He took away the city gates through which he had gone in to the harlot and carried them to a mountain. What does this mean? Hell and love for a woman Scripture joins together; the house of the harlot was an image of hell. It is rightly considered as hell, for it rejects no one but draws to itself all who enter. At this point we recognize the actions of our Redeemer. After the synagogue to which he had come was separated from him through the devil, they shaved his head; that is, they crucified him on the site of Calvary, and he descended into hell. . . . All saw the fact that he went in, but the fact that he arose just a few knew, remembered, felt. Moreover, he removed the city gates; that is, he took away the gates of hell [St. Caesarius, *Sermon* 118, ed. Morin I, 491–99; ET, *The Fathers of the Church,* vol. 47 [Washington, D.C.: 1964] , pp. 184ff.].

When it passes from the harlot Church to the harlot hell, the sermon appears to be digressing. In fact, at a deeper level, the connection is preserved: in both cases what is involved is the overcoming of the sin of the world.

But it is the image of David's adultery with Bathsheba that gives the idea its most vigorous expression. Once again it is the Ambrosian Tradition that takes it furthest. Ambrose himself introduces the image. He describes David's arrogance and presumption in claiming that he would never be moved (cf. Ps 29:7), followed by his fall and humiliation. But then he asks whether there might not be a deeper mystery in the fact that it is precisely the offspring of his adultery who was to be David's successor on the throne. Perhaps the death of Bathsheba's first husband and her affair with David point in some way to the Church. "Christ is called David. . . . To him is wedded the Church, and she, by the seed of the Word, filled with the Spirit of God, gives birth to the body of Christ, that is to say, the Christian people. She is the woman who is 'bound by law to her husband as long as he lives' (Rom 7:2). That is why her husband died—so that she would not be an adulteress by being with another man. Here, then, we have a mystery in the figure, a sin in history; guilt through man, mysteries through the word" (*In Luc.* III, 38; PL 15, 1605).

The second (spurious) *Apology of David* takes up Ezekiel's image:

[Adam] became naked to himself after becoming guilty of sin. In him the whole human race was denuded through the succession of nature. . . . Christ saw his family naked and loved it, for Christ loves the holy soul. Thus Jesus loved Lazarus and Mary, and Christ loved his Church, though naked, though not yet clad in the beauty of the virtues. . . . He saw her, he before whom all things are laid bare (cf. Heb 4:13), from whom the inner secrets of the heart cannot be hidden, for he is the searcher of the heart and reins (cf. Jer 17:10). . . . He saw his Church naked. He saw, and he loved her. He saw his beloved naked, and as the "Son of Charity", he fell in love with her. . . . Here we have not the scandals of adultery but the mysteries of charity. . . . Where you have faith, you need not fear adultery.

But the mystery of love can be foreshadowed, by way of type, in adultery.

Adultery took place as a type of salvation, for not all adultery deserves condemnation. Indeed, the prophet was told, "Go, take to yourself a harlot for a wife" (Hos 1:2). It is the Lord who commands there to be a marriage with a woman who was a harlot. Now, as we have said, the fruit of this marriage is Christ. . . . If, then, union with a harlot can be pious, so too can association and union with an adulteress. This applies to the Jews. However, as regards divine things, I do not dare to speak of adultery, even of a pious kind, so as not to offend anyone with the sound of my words, even if their reverent meaning is manifest. What can be said more cautiously, even if less clearly, is that a pious union of dissimilar partners took place when the Word was made flesh. For the nuptials of divinity and the flesh are not lawful, nor is it the case that, as flesh is united to soul, soul to flesh, in a natural covenant, so divinity and flesh, as it were, keep the law of the marriage bed. . . . By taking [Bathsheba] to himself, God the Word made the union lawful. The nuptials in the Song of Songs point to this mystery, the nuptials whereby the Church is married to Christ, and flesh to spirit. And so the bride runs around looking for God's Word, for the wretched flesh, wounded and naked, adulterous in all things yet immaculate in Christ, looks for her Redeemer. This flesh Christ united to himself to make it immaculate. He joined it to himself to remove the adultery. And since it was under the law, it had to die, in order to be free of the law, so that, through that death, what one might call the marriage between law and flesh could be dissolved. Thus the flesh died in Christ, so that we, having died to the law through the body of Christ, as the apostle says (cf. Rom 7:4), might belong to another, to him who rose again from the dead . . . so that we might rise again . . . as Christ's new marriage [*Apol. David* II, 10; PL 14, 903–9].

Cassiodorus makes the general point that "it was appropriate to those [prophetic] times that the future mysteries of the Lord should be announced by an act of this kind, that what among men seemed blameworthy should be shown to have a spiritual meaning, a reference to the great mystery". He refers to Hosea and Tamar and, on the subject of David and Bathsheba, follows Jerome and Augustine. Bathsheba signifies the Church or human flesh in general. David is Christ. "Just as [Bathsheba], while washing, unclothed, in the Kedron brook, delighted David and was compelled to accept the King's embraces while her husband was slaughtered at royal command, so the Church, that is, the congregation of the faithful, as we know, is cleansed of sin's defilement in the bath of baptism and united to Christ our Lord" (*In Ps.* 50; PL 70, 358).

For *St. Paschasius Radbertus,* too, David is Christ, who, from his "solarium", looks out on the earthly Church: she washes herself in baptism and yearns for heaven. "As foreseeing, he saw the predestined. As Bridegroom, he loved the one he had called, so that as lawful husband, he might in spiritual marriage unite her, the justified, to himself. But for Bathsheba to be married to David, her husband Uriah had to be murdered"—in other words, Jewry (*In Mt.* 1, 1; PL 120, 66–67).

The *Opus imperfectum in Matthaeum* is odd: "In his very worst sin, David was a symbol of Christ and the Church. Just as he, happy on his terrace, saw and desired lovely Bathsheba and made her his own, even though she was still married to another man, a Hittite, so Christ, happy in his highest heaven, saw the Church of the Gentiles, lovely in her heart, displeasing in the filthiness of her errors . . . for she was still the mistress of the devil: he desired her and made her first his own. . . . And that is what Christ does with every upright soul" (*Hom.* 1; PG 56, 620).

Later the Bathsheba image is played down. *Gerhoh of Reichersberg* will serve as an example.

David is the image of Christ, Bathsheba of the Church, Uriah of the devil. Just as Bathsheba, as she washed unclad in the Kedron brook, pleased David and was found worthy of the King's embraces, while her husband, at royal command, was slaughtered, so the Church, that is, the congregation of the faithful, through the washing of sacred baptism, is cleansed from the defilement of sins . . . and the devil, against whom the apostles waged war, was destroyed. . . . Bathsheba did not sleep with her first husband after being joined to David; neither does the Church. . . . Do not be surprised that an adulterer symbolizes Christ, an adulteress fore-shadows the Church, and a chaste man represents the devil, for it is no good for vice to be written in letters of gold, just as it is no disgrace for virtue to be noted down in ink [*In Ps.* 50, 1–2; PL 193, 1602–3].

Despite the blatancy of the imagery, this allegorizing of the David story is in danger of detracting from the seriousness of the reality to which the image points: the Incarnation of God, his extreme self-humiliation. It is only this extreme humiliation (going down into "harlot flesh") that is the instrument and precondition for the transformation of "harlot" into "saint", of fallen humanity into immaculate Church. Some of the Fathers used Solomon's proverb about the washed harlot saying she has done nothing wrong to describe the wonder of a Christian good conscience. However, there are no less insistent voices that, at the same time and in sharp dialectical contrast, warn the purified never to forget their past, the condition from which they were delivered.

5. *The Eve motif: heresy as harlotry*

The bride, the Church, is preserved in her chastity by the Bridegroom. She knows this is pure grace. But she can know it only if she has consciousness, and she has consciousness only in the human beings who form her. Now these human beings are nature, not grace. As human beings, they have been brought into unity and elevated above and beyond themselves in order to form the Church. Left to themselves, they can fall back again on themselves and become sinners. The dialectic of existence in the Church lies within the undeniable reality of these two poles: "There is an infallibly pure Church! It is made up of fallible human beings!" St. Paul is forever recalling this dialectic, even when he speaks of the nuptial mystery: "I feel a divine jealousy for you, for I betrothed you to Christ to present you as a pure bride to her one husband. But I am afraid that, as the serpent deceived Eve by his cunning, your minds will be corrupted and led astray from simplicity toward Christ" (2 Cor 11:2–3). The verses that follow show that the "deceiving" of which Paul is thinking here is the corruption of Christian doctrine. He speaks of the preacher of "another Christ", "another Spirit", "another gospel". The unity of the Church is the "simplicity [*haplotês*] of your spirit" toward the Bridegroom. Alien doctrine under the cloak of Christ, of the Spirit, of the gospel, means the ruination of this bridal simplicity and thus the disintegration of the ecclesial mind, the pursuit of an alien spirit, infidelity, adultery— this time in the image of the primal infidelity, the infidelity of Eve.

The Fathers saw the unity of the Church as two inseparable things: something given, an institutional grace, but also something to be achieved ethically through love and faith. It is not surprising, then, that they had the elemental feeling that heresy, the ruining of the ecclesial mind, is an intensely dangerous spiritual fornication. *Origen* has most to say on the subject. On the one hand, he describes and experiences the mystery of this ruining as the continuation in the Church of the Passion of God's Word (*Hom.* 18 *in Jer.* 12; Klostermann 3, 168; ibid., *Hom.* 10, 2; Klostermann 3, 72; *Comm. in Jo.* 20, 6; Preuschen 4, 334). On the other hand, he is particularly sensitive to infidelity hidden within the heart, the infidelity that comes from listening to alien spirits. "The human soul is very lovely. She has a wonderful beauty. . . . Certain adulterous and sordid lovers, attracted by her beauty, want to corrupt her and 'commit fornication with her'. Wise Paul, therefore, says, 'I am afraid that, as the serpent deceived Eve by his cunning, your soul will be corrupted' (2 Cor 11:3). In carnal fornication our bodies are corrupted, but in spiritual unchastity our 'spiritual senses' are corrupted, and the soul herself is wounded" (*Hom.* 7 *in Ezek.* 6; Baehr 8, 396).

Fornication of the body is execrable. For what is more execrable than to violate the temple of God, to take the members of Christ and make them the members of a prostitute (cf. 1 Cor 6:15)? Far more execrable, though, is that general fornication that contains every kind of sin. It is called general fornication when the soul, the soul that has been admitted into fellowship with the Word of God and united to him, so to speak, in marriage, is corrupted and violated by some stranger.... As long as the soul clings to her Spouse and heeds his word and embraces it, she receives from him, without doubt, the seed of the Word. As he himself says, "By your fear, O Lord, we have conceived in the womb" (cf. Is 26:18).... If the soul, then, has conceived by Christ, she bears sons, for whose sake it is said to her: "She will be saved through childbearing, if she continues in faith and love and holiness with modesty" (1 Tim 2:15).... But if the unhappy soul deserts her holy marriage with the Divine Word and gives herself up to the adulterous embraces of the devil and the other demons, deceived by their allurements, she will also, without doubt, bear them sons, of whom it is written: "The children of adulterers shall not come to perfection, and the seed of the unlawful bed shall be rooted out" (Wis 3:16).... The soul can never exist without bearing children. She is always giving birth, always bearing sons [*Hom. 20 in Num.* 2; Baehr 7, 187–89].[13]

Finally, Origen refers to Romans 7 and distinguishes three situations: (1) the husband is alive, and the wife lives with him, that is, under the law; (2) the husband is alive, and the wife is unfaithful to him, acting in accordance with "the other law in her members", which seduces

---

[13] *Methodius* argues on exactly the same lines. Because the soul bears within her the glorious image of God, "evil spirits lust after her, plotting and striving to defile her godlike and lovely image, as the prophet Jeremiah shows, reproaching Jerusalem, 'You have a harlot's brow" (3:3) . . . they desire to commit adultery with every soul betrothed to the Lord." And *Pseudo-Macarius* (*Hom.* 15, 28; PG 34, 593D): "It is like when a young woman finds herself in a house with a young man. Flattered by him, she gives in to him, commits adultery, and is thrown out. That is how the terrible serpent of sin treats the soul. He entices and urges. And if she consents, the bodiless soul partakes of the bodiless evil of the spirit; spirit partakes of spirit. Yes, the person who gives in to and accepts the thinking of the evil one commits adultery in his heart." For *St. Gregory of Nyssa* (*De virg.* 15; PG 46, 384B), every sin involves fornication.

her into adultery, "for every opposing power that wins a victory in the human soul and mixes with her commits adultery with her"; (3) the husband dies, and the woman is free to marry again—the husband who can never die, the Word of God. This is why, says Origen, Jesus addresses the synagogue not just as "evil" but as an "adulterous generation" (Mt 11:39). And so "the Word of God abandons the synagogue of the Jews and goes off to take a 'wife of harlotry', the people, that is to say, of the Gentiles, who were harlots when Zion was still a faithful city" (*Comm. in Matt* 12, 4; Klostermann 10, 75).[14]

This last text broadens the motif ecclesiologically, but usually it is applied to the individual soul as she hovers between being faithful to God and being unfaithful to him by going off to the devil. The idea emerges already in *St. Hegesippus,* who says of the Church in Jerusalem that she is still a pure virgin because she has not been infected by any heresy (Eusebius, *Hist. Eccl.* III, 32, 7).[15] *Clement of Alexandria* uses strong words: "Any person who lives like a heathen in the Church, by deed or word or even just by thought, introduces fornication into the Church, [Christ's] body" (*Strom.* VII 14, 87–88, 1; GCS III, 62, 24f.). *Origen* applies the great Ezekiel text about unfaithful Jerusalem to those who leave the Church to join the heretics. The devious methods of the myriad Gnostic sects of his time must have almost forced the image upon him. "Opening a brothel on every street": that is what the heretics do when they take the words of Scripture and make themselves shacks in which to commit fornication. "She goes to Moses, to Isaiah, to Jeremiah, and collects honey from their writings." In those who remain within the Church, the adultery is secret; in those who leave the Church, it is open. Using images from the Song of Songs, Origen shows the difference between true virgin Church and false harlot heresy. "The breasts of the chaste are unbroken, but the harlots' breasts are slack and wrinkled. The breasts of the chaste are erect and swell with maiden vigor. They accept the word of the

---

[14] Cf. Lieske, *Theologie der Logosmystik bei Origenes* (1938), 149, Methodius, *Symp.* 6, 1.

[15] Further texts: *Clement of Alexandria, Strom.* III, 12, 80, 2; *Origen, Comm. in Jo.,* ad 3: 20 (Pr. 520); *Theodoret* and *Ambrosiaster* on 2 Cor 11: 2 etc. (J. Schmid, "Heilige Brautschaft", *RAC* II, 556).

Bridegroom and say, "Between my breasts he shall rest'" (*Hom. in Cant.* 2, 3; GCS 46). *St. Cyprian* adapts the theme to mean that the Church as bride really cannot be now led astray: "The bride of Christ cannot be defiled; she is inviolate and chaste.... Whoever breaks with the Church and enters on an adulterous union cuts himself from the promises made to the Church" (*De unit. Eccl.* 6; PL 4, 502–3; ET, M. Bévenot, S.J., *Ancient Christian Writers* 25, pp. 48f.). *St. Gregory of Nyssa,* too, calls the heresies harlots (*Or. in suam ordinationem;* PG 46, 548C). For *St. Ephrem,* the heretics are "deceitful suitors, trusty when sent out but now changed into tricksters", promoting themselves instead of Christ.' They tried to imitate the beauty of the Bridegroom in order to snare the bride. They "shamed the bride of the Son", and she, "her love now dissipated, clothed herself with the name of a slave" (*Hymn.* 24 *Against the Heretics* BKV² vol. 61, 91–92). *St. Augustine* calls the heretics harlots' sons who do not attain their inheritance. They may be children of Abraham but not of the lawful mother (*Civ. Dei* 16, 34; PL 41, 513). Once again, in the sermon on Samson already quoted:

> "Samson was angry because a friend married his wife" (cf. Jg 14:19, 20). This friend prefigured all heretics.... By departing from the Church and the gospels, they attempt through adulterous wickedness to seize the Church, that is, the body of Christ, as their portion. For this reason that faithful sevant and friend of the Lord's bride says: "I betrothed you to one spouse, that I might present you as a chaste virgin to Christ" (2 Cor 11:2). Moreover, through the zeal of faith and a rebuke, he touches the person of his wicked companion: "And I fear lest, as the serpent seduced Eve, so your minds may be corrupted from the truth that is in Christ Jesus" (cf. 2 Cor 11:3) [*Serm.* 364, 3; PL 39, 11641; ET, *The Fathers of the Church,* vol. 47, pp. 185f.].

In the sermon on Solomon, also mentioned above (*St. Caesarius,* ed. Morin I, 489f.), the two harlots disputing before the King are the Church and Arianism. The Church struggles for the unity of the Child, whereas guilty heresy is content to see it divided.

The context in which the idea is presented by St. Paul, who is the thread that links every stage of its development, prevents any kind of

Pharisaism. It is not a question of people in the Church complacently leaning back on the bride and looking down on the adulterous heresies outside: it is the possible apostasy of those entrusted to the Lord as his bride that Paul fears so much. *Origen* supports him in that view. He sees the origins of the open adultery of Church division as lying hidden within the Church, in her secret or open sinfulness. The frontier between holiness and heresy runs through every member of the Church. *St. Augustine* will complete this Origenist and general patristic view of the Church with his doctrine of the two cities, of *caritas* and *cupiditas,* which, like Origen's Church, have existed since the beginning of the world, indeed from before the world's foundation (*Comm. in Cant.* 2; Baehr 8, 157–58). For Augustine, the division between them cuts through the heart of the individual. According to both, the Church as pure bride is as much a "spiritual" as a historical reality. For the individual she is never so much a "historical reality" that she is not also something "spiritual" constantly to be strived and prayed for. True, the Church has her grounding in Mary, but in her members she constantly tends to lapse back into being Eve, or at best to strive upward from Eve to Mary.

Rupert of Deutz describes how Eve-Church, sunk in the depths of Hades, cries out, as redemption draws nigh: "I will greatly rejoice in the Lord. . . . For he has clothed me with the garment of salvation" (Is 61:10). "I had been stripped bare in Adam. With fig leaves I hid my nakedness. In a pitiful coat of animal skins, I was thrown out of paradise. But now, in place of leaves, my Lord and God gives me the garment of salvation. In place of the itchy fabric of desire, he clothes me with the first stole of baptism and the remission of sins. In place of the skins of mortality, he girded me with the second stole of resurrection and immortality" (*In Is.* 2, 36; PL 167, 1352D).

In this context we must point out a further, very strange kinship between ideas. *Luther* was no more the inventor of the "harlot reason" slogan than he was of the jibe that the Roman Church is the whore of Babylon. Behind lay an allegorical interpretation of the commandment in Deuteronomy: "When you go forth to war against your enemies . . . and you see among them a beautiful woman, and you have desire for her . . . then you shall take her . . . and she shall shave her head and pare her nails, and she shall put off her captive's garb, and shall remain in your house and bewail her father and her mother, and after thirty days . . . you may marry her" (Dt 21:10–14). Origen did not fail to see this fair captive as worldly wisdom, who can only be wedded after due paring and penance (*Hom. in Lev.* 7, 6; Baehr. 6, 390–91). St. Jerome (*Ep. ad Pamm.*; PL 22, 44) takes up the idea, and, by so doing, he gives it a long and memorable history in the Middle Ages. Henri de Lubac has written about the motif, with equal measure of learning and humor, in his history of spiritual exegesis ("La belle captive", in *Exégèse médiévale* I [1959], pp. 290–304). The fair captive's fate varies from theologian to theologian.[16] Many are terrified of her and would be glad to get rid of her. Others fawn on her. St. Thomas confines himself to the Biblical rule (*Boeth. Trin.* 2, 3). Only St. Bonaventure[17] actually utters the word that is never far from the others' lips: "whore". "The Jews refused to listen to wisdom from the mouth of wisdom; and we who possess Christ within ourselves refuse to listen to his wisdom. This is the supreme abomination: that the most beautiful daughter of the King is offered to us as a bride, and we choose to be coupled with the filthiest servant and to deal with harlots; and we want to go back to Egypt, to the lowliest food, since we reject the food from heaven. . . . Do not love the harlot and dismiss your wife" (*Collations on the Six Days* 2, 7; 19, 18; ET, José de Vinck [Patterson, 1970], pp. 268, 293). The whole problem of faith's relationship to knowledge, of theology as divine wisdom and human thought, comes to the surface here in the imagery of the holy nuptials.

6. The Jerusalem theme: sin in the Church as harlotry

The seriousness of the issue dawns on us when we stop seeing the bride's infidelity as something largely outside her, in heresy, and realize that it exists inside her. At this point the Church cannot avoid

---

[16] On this see G. Söhngen, "Die Theologie im 'Streit der Fakultäten'", in *Einheit der Theologie* (1952), p. 14.

[17] Cf. J. Ratzinger, *The Theology of History in St. Bonaventure,* ET (Chicago, 1971), pp. 154f.

confronting the Jerusalem texts of the Old Testament. All Christians are sinners, and if the Church does not sin as Church, she does sin in all her members, and through the mouths of all her members she must confess her guilt. *Cassiodorus* formulates it explicitly in that way: it is the Church who, in her members, confesses the copiousness of her sins (*In Ps.* 25, 10; PL 70, 180). And *St. Bernard* says; "Were the bride to say that she had nothing black in her, she would be deceiving herself, and the truth would not be in her" (*Serm. in Cant.* 25, 3; PL 183, 900B). "Once the Church has attained salvation", says *Eusebius,* "she remains in constant need of that same salvation" (*In Ps.* 39, 10; PG 14, 850). Even Charles Journet, who scrupulously protects the Church as such from having any blemish, cannot avoid ascribing to her confession of sins and acts of penance, supported by grace. Similarly, *Origen* depicts the Church, symbolized by the Queen of Sheba, approaching Christ-Solomon: "'She opened her heart to him', in other words, by confession and penance for her earlier sins, and she told him all that was in her heart" (*Comm. in Cant.* 2; Baehr 8, 119). Now this act is one that the Church never ceases to perform, and surely all the other acts that accompany it—pleading for the grace of fidelity, anxious yet trustful clinging to the God who is man's only strength and stay, "standing over self" (as St. Augustine says)—are likewise acts of ecclesial feeling and praying:

> We are the Holy Church. . . . Let us honor her, for she is the spouse of such a great Lord. What else can I say? Great and singular is the condescension of the Bridegroom. When he found her, she was a harlot. He made her a virgin. That she was a harlot we must not deny, lest we forget the mercy of him who set her free. How can we fail to call her a harlot, when we think how she lusted after idols and demons? There was fornication of the heart in all: in some, of the flesh; in all, of the heart. And he came and made her a virgin. He made the Church a virgin. In faith she is a virgin. In the flesh she has a few consecrated virgins. In faith all her members must be virgins, men as well as women.

Then follows the citation of 2 Corinthians 11:2–3: "Thus the Church is a virgin. She is a virgin, and a virgin may she be. May she be on her guard against the seducer, lest he prove to be a corrupter" (*Serm.* 213, 7; PL 38, 1063–64). This *caveat* rings out even more loudly in *St. Ambrose:* "Not in herself, daughters, not in herself, but in us is the Church wounded. Let us, then, be on our guard, lest our fall be the Church's wound (*Caveamus igitur, ne lapsus noster vulnus Ecclesiae fiat*)" (*De Virginitate* 10, 48; PL 16, 278D).

The trembling of the penitent Church, the Church that "stands over herself", achieved very early and memorable expression in the writings of *St. Hippolytus.* Again it is Mary Magdalen who represents the Church kneeling at the feet of Christ. "I clasp the feet of Christ. Let me not fall back to the ground, lest I succumb to temptation. The serpent is after me. He is again trying to use me to set a trap. He is again out to conquer Adam. Lead me into heaven!" "Accept Eve! Accept the woman who is no longer naked, no longer wearing fig leaves but clad with the Holy Spirit!" (Hl. ed. Bonwetsch TU 23 [NF 8], 65–66). This text is all the more remarkable because Hippolytus rejects the idea of a Church made up at the same time of both righteous and sinners. The Church-bride can be "beautiful" only when she does penance (ibid., 40) and hears the words: "Be consoled, daughter; your sins are forgiven" (ibid., 47). In the commentary on Daniel the Church appears as Susanna, while the two old men are the devil, who threatens and tries to ruin her (1, 18; Bonw., p. 30). "In truth what befell Susanna is to be understood as something happening here and now to the Church." The two old men are the Jews and the heathen, both bearing the Church false witness (1, 20, p. 32). They are joined (1, 21, p. 33) by "those who call themselves Christians but are not in reality". In 1, 22, with a reference to St. Paul's words about the serpent's seduction of Eve, the earnest entreaty is made that she should not be seduced (p. 34).

St. Ambrose, in his own works, took over many of these words of Hippolytus about the Song of Songs (references in Riedlinger, pp. 20–23). To understand them correctly, we need to remember that in Hippolytus there is what one might call a "presentialism", the conviction that these texts have a present relevance. For example: "The Church does not cease to give birth, in her heart, to the word, who is persecuted by unbelievers" (*De Chr. et Antichr.* 61; PG 10, 780). And again: "Understand, O Man, the text, 'The mouth of the Father has brought forth a good word' (Ps 44:2). And now a second word appears, brought forth in the holy. The word constantly gives birth to the saints, just as the word is constantly brought forth by the saints" (*In Da.* I, 9; GCS I, 17). Thus, for Hippolytus, the transition from synagogue to Church is a permanent present reality. The synagogue is the Church of the past, the past of the Church. "I am black but beautiful, daughters of Jerusalem. I am sinful, but still more am I lovely, for Christ has set his heart on me" (Hl. TU p. 35). Through the liturgy and its *Hodie,* the Christian is enabled to stand within this "transition". Just occasionally, he looks beyond the present tense of Christ's saving mystery to another equally important present tense, to an event that is also Christ's work—the transition from Old to New Covenant. *Pascha* means transition, passover, "for at this time the Church, through baptism, passes from unbelief and infidelity to faith and fidelity" (*Beleth, Rationale* 113; PL 202, 118).

The same "presentialism" enables *Origen* to apply the prophetic texts to the Church. For example:

> Blessed is he who is ever born of God. For the righteous man is not born of God just once, but constantly, in every good work, God gives birth to him. This can be explained by reference to the Savior. The Savior was not begotten by the Father at some specific moment; no, the Father is forever begetting him. The same is true of the righteous. The Savior is the Radiance of [the Father's] glory, but radiance is not emitted at a certain moment. It radiates as long as the light shines. Thus the Radiance of God's glory is begotten eternally. . . . And the same is true of you, inasmuch as you possess the Spirit of sonship [*Hom.* 9 *in Jer.* 4; PG 13, 356–57].

Origen's commentary on Ezekiel, in twenty-five books, has been lost, but Homilies 6–10, translated by St. Jerome, give us a reasonable picture of the master's thinking. In what follows we shall present a few important passages:

> What is it I admire about Ezekiel? The fact that when he was told to bear witness and to make known the iniquities of Jerusalem, he thought not of the danger in which his preaching might place him

but only of obeying the instructions God had given him and saying what he had been commanded to say. It may be a mystery, a revelation of hallowed insight into Jerusalem and the things said about her, but the fact remains: he prophetically accuses her of "harlotry", of "playing the harlot with every passer-by". He bears witness with a voice of condemnation. He rebukes the city for her crimes. But because he had the confidence to do God's will, because he was ready both to die and to live, he spoke without trembling. . . . "Thus says the Lord: your root and your birth are of the land of the Canaanites; your father was an Amorite, and your mother a Hittite" (Ezek 16:3). What city was so lofty and held her head so high in the world as the "city of God"? And yet, reassuring herself of these great things, that she was so close to God, his very own city, she sinned, and because she sinned, the Holy Spirit declared her to be a degenerate foreigner. Her father was an Amorite, not God. So long as she did not sin, her Father was God. When she did sin, an Amorite became her father. So long as she did not sin, the Holy Spirit was her Father;[18] when she did sin, a Hittite became her mother. . . . If such things are said of Jerusalem, to whom in Scripture so many exalted and wonderful promises are made, what will become of wretched me if I sin? Who will be my father, my mother? . . . If I sin, who believe in Christ Jesus and have given myself to such a great Master, who will be my father? Not the Amorite, a far worse father. Who? "He who commits sin is born of the devil" (1 Jn 3:8). And again: "You are of your father, the devil" (Jn 8:44). . . . So if I become a sinner, the devil begets me in my sins, and makes his own the words spoken by God the Father to the Savior, "You are my son; today I have begotten you" (Ps 2:7).

"On the day you were born, your umbilical cord was not cut" (Ezek 16:4). . . . He presents Jerusalem allegorically as a newborn baby girl. However, we should realize that everything said about Jerusalem applies to all the human beings in the Church. So our first state is as here described. God forbid that our third should be like Jerusalem's! All we who once were sinners are called "Jerusalem" by God, and our beginning is as here described. The second stage applies to us when, after God has visited and made himself known, we persist in our sins. Of the third evil, which we totally detest, we

---

[18] Origen clearly wrote "mother" here, but Jerome has altered it.

shall speak when the time comes. . . . Just as in the male the foreskin is circumcised, so in the female the umbilical cord is cut off . . . but she sins, and so her umbilical cord is not cut off. . . . "You were not washed with water for salvation" (Ezek 16:4). Let us look at the things that happen to Jerusalem, so that they are not reproduced in us. . . . We who have received the grace of baptism in the name of Christ have been washed, but I do not know who has been washed "for salvation". Simon [Magus] was washed, and, having received baptism, he remained in the company of Philip. But he was not "washed for salvation"; he was condemned by the person who said to him in the Holy Spirit, "May your money perish with you!" (Acts 8:20). It is very hard for the one who has been washed to be washed "for salvation". Pay heed, catechumens; listen to what has been said here and prepare yourselves . . . so that you are not like those who are washed, but not "for salvation", who receive water, but not the Holy Spirit. . . . The very things said here to Jerusalem will be said to every sinful soul who appears to have faith. So I will not climb up to greater matters and probe what surpasses my powers and talents. "You were not rubbed with salt" (Ezek 16:4). Jerusalem is at fault. She was not worthy of the salt of God. If I believe my Lord Jesus Christ, he himself will make me salt and say to me, "You are the salt of the earth" (Mt 5:13). When I believe the Spirit who spoke in the Apostle, I am seasoned with salt and can keep the commandment, "Let your speech always be gracious, seasoned with salt" (Col 4:6).

"And you were cast out on the open field." Why? "Because of the depravity of your soul on the day of your birth" (Ezek 16:5). Can anyone have a depraved soul on the day of his birth? He is describing our passions, human vices, and habitual depravities. . . . If we sin again after the regeneration of baptism and the receiving of God's word, then "on the day of our birth" we are "cast out". All too often we find people who have been washed in the "bath of second birth" but who do not bring forth "worthy fruits of penance" and enliven the mystery of baptism with no greater fear of God than they had as catechumens, with no greater charity than they exercised as hearers of the word, no holier works than before. The fate of such people is described here. . . . But see the mercy of God, behold his singular clemency. Although Jerusalem is "cast out on the open field", he does not so despise her that she remains cast out forever; he does not so abandon her to her depravity that he completely forgets her and never raises up her from where she lies. Notice what follows: "And as I passed by you . . ." (Ezek 16:6). You were cast out, but I came to you; you had fallen, but I did not fail to visit you. "I saw you weltering in your own blood" (ibid.), as if to say, I saw you guilty of murder, guilty of blood, guilty of mortal sins. . . . "I caused you to multiply like the grass of the field, and you grew up" (Ezek 16:7). . . . I came to you, visited you in your abjection, and caused you to multiply. . . . "Your breasts were formed, and your hair grew, but you were naked and dishonored" (ibid.). Whoever does not "put on Jesus Christ" (cf. Gal 3:27) is naked. Whoever does not put on "compassion, kindness, lowliness, meekness, patience, forbearance" (cf. Col 3:12) is dishonored. . . . "And I passed by you" (Ezek 16:8). A second time he comes to her, he sees her sinning, and, because of her sins, he departs. And yet he comes back again. Again the kind and merciful God visits her. "And I came to you and saw you, and behold, it was your time and the time of your corrupters" (ibid.). What does "your time" mean? The time of maturity, when fornication becomes possible. . . . And who are the "corrupters"? While we are small, those who want to come and corrupt us—bad Christians, unclean spirits, demons—have no chance of corrupting us. But once we have grown up and are able to sin, they look for an opportunity of corrupting us. . . . And because this time had come, our Lord Jesus Christ came again to visit wretched Jerusalem, that is, our sinful soul. "And I covered you with my wings" (ibid.). . . . Blessed is the one whose shame is covered by the wings of God; blessed is the one who wants to persevere in the blessedness in which Jerusalem did not want to persevere. . . . After so much that made him return, he turns back once more. After so many visits, for the first time he enters into a covenant with her.

"You became mine, and I washed you in water. After all these things, I took you and washed you myself for salvation, and I cleaned away your blood from you, and anointed you with oil, and clothed you in bright raiment . . . and you ate fine flour, honey, and oil" (Ezek 16:8–13). But after [all this] wretched Jerusalem is again upbraided for her harlotry. . . . Let us take care that, after the pure words of "fine flour", after the sweet words of the prophets, after the "oil" that "gladdens the face" (cf. Ps 103:14), the oil with which we "anoint our heads" to make our fasting acceptable (cf. Mt 6:16f.), we do not lapse again. And we do not just anoint ourselves with oil; we enjoy it. "You became exceedingly beautiful!" (Ezek 16:13). He praises her beauty, praises her fine appearance, her lovely form. "You came to regal estate" (ibid.). What progress, regal estate! "Your name went forth among the nations" (Ezek 16:14). All this befits one who has begun to be free of the world, who is progressing toward the blessed life; yes, it is right that such a person should have renown in the world. But God forbid what follows next! It is written to instill fear in the hearers' hearts. After the beauty, after the renown, wretched Jerusalem begins to commit fornication. So "do not boast about tomorrow, because you do not know what the day to come has in store" (Prov 27:1) . . . and again: "Look to yourself, lest you too be tempted" (Gal 6:1).

"Your renown went forth among the nations because of your beauty, for it was perfect through the loveliness that I had bestowed on you, says the Lord God, but you trusted in your beauty" (Ezek 16:14–15). Beautiful Jerusalem became proud and puffed herself up in the awareness of her beauty. And because she became proud, and did not humble herself, and did not give God the glory, listen to what is said to her: "You committed fornication because of your renown, and you lavished your fornication on every passer-by. And you took your clothes and stitched them into idols for yourself" (ibid., vv. 15–16). The things I used to adorn you, the things that made you lovely, you have used to make idols. . . . The "clothes" are the divine Scriptures and the meaning in them. Heretics tore these clothes and stitched text to text, linked word with word, but not with the right and proper links. By stitching together their impieties, they made "idols" for themselves, by which they tempted many into believing and agreeing with their cult, and into accepting a bogus [Church] discipline.

Let us, therefore, beware of the heretics, whose manner of life is blameless, although it is perhaps the devil rather than God who teaches them how to behave. Just as bird catchers put out certain foods as bait to trap the birds more easily through the delightfulness of the taste, so, if I may dare to say so, there is a chastity of the devil that is a snare for the human soul. Through this chastity, meekness, and justice, he can the more easily catch and trap us in the net of false doctrine. The devil uses various tricks to attack and capture wretched man. He gives the evil a good manner of life to deceive the onlooker and brands a bad conscience on the good. He lays traps for me, a preacher in the Church, so that by my conduct he can bring down the whole Church. People in high places are particularly prone to attack from the devil. The idea is that, through the conspicuous downfall of one person, all may be caused to stumble, and faith be upset by the corrupt morals of the clergy. . . . The prudent person is not tricked by the heretics' meekness into accepting their teaching, and my sins do not cause him to stumble. He considers the dogma, concerns himself with the faith of the Church. He recoils from me in horror, but he accepts the teaching, as the Lord says: "The scribes and Pharisees sit on Moses' seat, so practice and observe whatever they tell you but not what they do, for they preach, but they do not practice" (Mt 23:2–3). This text applies to me. I teach good things but do the opposite. Like the scribe and Pharisee, I sit on Moses' seat. . . . Let us not imitate anyone. If we want someone to imitate, then the model given us is Jesus Christ. In sacred Scripture we have a record of the acts of the apostles and the deeds of the prophets: this gives us a sure example to follow. . . . But if we choose to emulate the wicked and in the same breath say that they teach one thing and do the opposite, then we are acting against the commandment of the Lord. . . . Yes, wretched Jerusalem sinned greatly. Time and again, through the prophets, God tried to lead her back to better ways, but she would not heed his counsel or accept his commandments. And so God has doubts. He says that he does not know what to do. " 'How', says the Lord, 'shall I restore your heart?' " (Ezek 16:30). . . . You are held fast by the bonds of many sins. Your trespasses prevent your life being restored by my words. I tried to restore you often enough, speaking through my saints, but you did not listen. And now I do not know what to do, and so I say to you, "How shall I restore your heart, seeing you did all these things, the deeds of a brazen harlot?" (ibid.). . . . Those who do not give up their religion altogether but are conquered by sin and try to hide their sin are like a blushing harlot. But those who completely abandon their religion to the point where they do not care about the bishop, the

priests, the deacons, the brethren, and sin with total effrontery—
these people are like a "brazen harlot". . . . We were not at first told
that Jerusalem had sisters, but now he adds, "You are the sister of
your sisters, who cast off their husbands and their children. . . . Your
elder sister is Samaria, she and her daughters who dwell at your left
hand, and your younger sister, who dwells at your right hand, is
Sodom with her daughters" (Ezek 16:45–46). . . . Virtue makes Christ
my brother, and when I am good and consistently virtuous, he says
to his Father, "I will declare your name to my brethren; in the midst
of the Church I will praise you" (Ps 21:23). . . . Now just as virtue
makes the Lord Jesus my brother, so iniquity gains me many
brothers; yes, as it grows, iniquity bears brothers for me. At the
beginning Samaria was not sinful Jerusalem's sister, nor was Sodom.
But when she had advanced in wickedness—as we have just shown—
she found herself in the middle between two sisters. . . . Who are
these two? . . . Schism and separation made Samaria what she
is. . . . So when we Church people sin, we are not far from the
heretics and their depraved doctrines. Whoever sins has bad faith. If
our conduct is evil, Sodom is our sister, for the Gentiles are Sodom.
And so when we sin, we are the brethren of heretics and heathens. . . .
"Behold, these were the iniquities of your sister: pride, fullness of
bread, and abundance" (Ezek 16:49). . . . Which is the greatest sin of
all? . . . Self-importance, pride, arrogance is the sin of the devil. . . .
Now pride's raw material is wealth, rank, worldly glory. Very
often, for those who hold ecclesiastical office, the order of priest
and rank of deacon can be the cause of pride. How often priests
forget about humility! As if the purpose of ordination was to put
an end to humility! As if they did not have to pursue humility
because they had received a dignity! As Scripture says, "The greater
you are, the more you must humble yourself" (Sir 3:18). . . . Think
how often the gospel condemns the pride and boasting of the
Pharisees. The Pharisee stood and prayed like this: "God, I thank
you that I am not like other men, extortioners, unjust, adulterers,
or even like this tax collector. I fast twice a week" (Lk 18:11). But
the publican, humbly and meekly standing far off, did not even
dare to lift up his eyes, and said, "God, be merciful to me a sinner"
(ibid., v. 13). And the publican "went down to his house justified"
(ibid., v. 14), not justified absolutely but justified in comparison
with the Pharisee. . . . For it is one thing to be justified, another to

be justified by another person. Just as the tax collector was justified by the Pharisee, so Sodom and Samaria were justified by comparison with sinful Jerusalem. We ought to realize that, on the Day of Judgment, each one of us will be justified by another person and condemned by another person. Even when we are justified by another person, that justice is more an occasion of shame than of praise. If, for example, I am found to be guilty of sodomitical sins, and then someone else is brought forward who has committed two kinds of sins, I am justified but not justified in the sense of being just. I am justified in comparison with the person who has committed several sins. I am judged as just, although I am far from justice.... I do not want to be justified by the wicked, because such justice is shameful. I am anticipating, because the prophet now goes on to say, "Your sister Sodom and her daughters have not done as you and your daughters have done.... Samaria has not committed half your sins; you have committed more iniquities than they and have justified all your sisters by all the iniquities you have committed" (Ezek 16:48, 51). Sodom sinned. Samaria also sinned. Jerusalem is covered in sin.... There is only one who is justified by all and justifies no one. Therefore "in your sight no man living shall be justified" (Ps 142:2). Abraham may have been just. Moses may have been just. Every illustrious man of the past may have been just. But compared with Christ, they are not just. Compared with his light, their light is like darkness. Just as the light of a lamp is darkened by the rays of the sun and fades like any other lightless stuff, so it is with the light of the just. The light of all the just may "shine before men" (cf. Mt 5:16), but before Christ it does not shine.... Before sunrise, the bright moon and the sparkling stars of the firmament shine in their stations, but when the sun rises, they are hidden. The same is true of the light of the Church. Like the moonlight, before the rising of that true light, the "sun of justice", the Church's light shines and is bright before men. But when Christ comes, it fades away before him. It says somewhere else, "The light shines in the darkness" (Jn 1:5).... Anyone who gives this matter long and diligent consideration cannot be proud when he sees his light reckoned as darkness in comparison with the greater light.... "The iniquity of your sister Sodom is pride" (cf. Ezek 16:49). When we read what is written about the destruction of the Sodomites, we should not say, "Poor old Sodomites, no more does the earth bring forth its fruits for you! Unhappy people, so greatly to be pitied; you have had to endure such dreadful things, such gloomy things!" No, instead we should apply this text to our own hearts. We should examine our "reins and thoughts", and then we shall find that those whom we pity exist within us, and that the sins of Sodom, Egypt, and Assyria, indeed all the sins listed and condemned by Scripture, can be found within ourselves. ... It is not hard to see that nothing so leads a man to arrogance as wealth and abundance and the consumption of great riches and rank and power. At a higher level it is easy to see that I feed my pride when I have understanding of the word of God, when I am wiser than others. "Knowledge puffs up" (1 Cor 8:1). Those are the Apostle's words, not mine.... Such a great man as the Apostle Paul needed a blow from "an angel of Satan" to strike him, to keep him from being "too puffed up" (cf. 2 Cor 12:7).... Before Uriah came along, no fault was found in David. He was a blessed man, blameless in the sight of the Lord. But because he became conscous of his spotless life, he said what he should not have said: "Hear, O Lord, my justice.... You have tried my heart and visited it by night. You have tested me by fire, and no iniquity was found in me" (Ps 16:1, 3).... And so he was tested, stripped of help, so that he might see what human infirmity can do.... He found himself in the very sin of which he boasted he was free.... The first thing is to commit no shameful deed, but to do only those that can gaze upon God with untroubled brow. But since as human beings we often sin, we should remember that the second plank of salvation, after shameful deeds, is blushing and lowering one's eyes out of shame for one's crimes rather than going around with a bold face as if one were guilty of nothing. After shameful deeds it is good to be shamed.... So a great blessing is reserved for Jerusalem, if only she will believe the Lord who says to her, "Be ashamed, and bear your shame, for you have justified your sisters" (Ezek 16:52). Let me give you an example from Church life. It is shameful to be separated from the people of God and the Church. It is a disgrace in the Church to leave the order of priesthood, to be thrown out of the diaconate. Of those expelled, some stir up trouble, while others accept, in all humility, the judgment made on them. The rebellious ones, smarting with the hurt of their dismissal, gather people round them and make a schism.... They do not accept their disgrace.... But the ones who, in all humility, leave the judgment in God's hands, whether or not they were justly dismissed, the ones who patiently endure the sentence passed on them, these receive mercy from God, and from men the summons to return to their former grade and forfeited glory. If someone complies with the instruction, "Be ashamed", if he carries out the divine command that follows, "Bear your shame, for you have justified your sisters", he will see the grace that repays him mercy for shame.... What is promised? "I will reverse the aversion of Sodom and her daughters, for you have justified your sisters Sodom and Samaria" (Ezek 16:53). ... First, I will reverse the aversion of Sodom, secondly of Samaria, thirdly of Jerusalem, and if I reverse the aversion of Sodom and Samaria and Jerusalem, they will be restored to their ancient state, first, Sodom ... secondly, Samaria ... thirdly, Jerusalem.... Those loved more by God will receive salvation last. Sodom, justified by Jerusalem, is the first to receive mercy: Sodom represents the Gentiles. Samaria—that is, the heretics—receives salvation in second place. Thirdly, as if they were unworthy of a more rapid remedy, the people of Jerusalem are restored to their former state. The Gentiles receive grace before us; so do the heretics, when we offend God, when sin weighs us down. The closer we are to God and the nearer we are to blessedness, so, when we sin, the further we are from him and it, the nearer we are to the most terrible and extreme punishments. For the judgment of God is just, and "the mighty shall be mightily tormented" (Wis 6:7), whereas the smallest deserve the swiftest mercy. Smallest of all is Sodom, and after her, in comparison with Jerusalem, not Sodom, Samaria is very small. ... And if I find that I am Jerusalem, a sinner in the middle between my sisters, when will he "reverse my aversion"? When I hear the words "bear your shame" (Ezek 16:54).... And this is the end of the promise: "I will remember my Covenant with you in the days of your youth, and I will establish with you an everlasting Covenant. Then you will remember your ways and be ashamed ... that you may never open your mouth again because of your shame, when I forgive you all that you have done" (Ezek 16:60–63). Even when my many sins are expiated, I cannot open my mouth. Even when he forgives my misdeeds, I am no stranger to shame [*Hom. in Ezech.* 6–10; Baehr 8, 378–423].

Origen chooses his words with great care and moderation. He is speaking of the human members of the Church, not of the Church as such. And yet he is speaking of these human beings as forming and representing the Church. The more "ecclesiastical" they are, the more he has them in mind. Above all, he is thinking of those who are the Church's official leaders and preachers. He spares them as little as the prophet spares the whore Jerusalem. But at the same time he speaks existentially. He must be speaking, especially in this sermon, of himself. The Church would be pure if he were not so impure. Here as elsewhere (for example, in the magnificent seventh homily on Leviticus), he presents himself as the unworthiest of all and takes all the guilt on himself. The force and sincerity of this gesture help him convince other believers that the gravest, the most momentous guilt is to be found in Jerusalem, in the members of the Church. And the more pharisaically proud they are of their ecclesiastical purity and *gnosis,* the guiltier they are.

St. Jerome, in complete dependence on his Alexandrian master, writes a commentary of his own on Ezekiel chapter 16. "Jerusalem" can be understood in four ways. It is either the city burnt by the Babylonians and Romans, or the heavenly city of the "firstborn" (cf. Heb. 12:23), or the Church in the sense of the "vision of peace", or the individual souls that know God by faith. Some think they can apply the text to the heavenly Jerusalem, but the Church does not accept that interpretation, lest we be compelled to refer all the details of this present prophecy to the heavenly powers—their downfall, torment, and restoration to their original state." After this elimination of an extreme Origenism (the Gnostic myth of the fall and *apokatastasis* of the heavenly Church), Jerome keeps the three other interpretations—the Old Covenant, the Church, the soul—and gets them to shed light on each other. " 'Your father was an Amorite, and your mother a Hittite' (Ezek 16:3). If *she* had to listen to such things, what will become of us, called from Gentile filth and cleansed of all stain in the Savior's bath, if we defile the garment of Christ and lack a wedding robe at the feast?" (*In Ez.* 16; PL 25. 130CD, 131C). And when God passes by naked Jerusalem: "What mercy! It was not enough to see her once, weltering in her blood, and to call her to repentance, but once more he visits her." The washing is baptism. The anointing is confirmation, through which Jerusalem receives the name of Christ (135B–37A). The shoes she is given are the preaching of the good news (138A). The new garment is Christ (137BC). She becomes the "fragrance of Christ" and finally Queen (140B, 143B). "Let us apply everything we say about Jerusalem . . . to the Church. If, according to the Apostle, Jerusalem is our mother (cf. Gal 4:26), and our mother is the Church, it follows that Jerusalem is the Church, the mother of the firstborn enrolled in heaven (cf. Heb 12:23)" (143CD). "[God says to her:] It is by my kindness and incredible generosity that you are allowed the title of Queen. . . . But what kind of discernment is this? Trusting not in God's mercy but in her own beauty! The higher a person is, the more he has to fear falling and, by fornication, abusing his title" (144B). In what follows this fornication of the Church is interpreted first of all to mean heresy, then immorality in the broadest sense. Jerusalem gives herself up to every passer-by, spreads her legs at every street corner. "A double curse is directed at our Jerusalem, whether she be the Church or the souls of believers when they are negligent and give way to every kind of vice: 'Woe, woe to you' (Ezek 16:23)" (149B). "She imitates the whore of the book of Proverbs [5:2ff.; 7:10ff.]. Openly in public places and on street corners, as foolish youths pass by, she invites them to her embraces. She pollutes the beauty of her soul, which she received as a grace from God the Creator. All her senses are full of indecency. All her thoughts encourage vice. She opens her heart, spreads out her legs, and fornicates with her Egyptian neighbors. She follows their example, the example of the heathen, people who boast of their indecency. She is so wicked she even surpasses them in indecency" (149CD). So she is given up to the punishment of the heathen. "Our Jerusalem" too will be punished in that way "if we neglect the holy ordinances of God". "And so great will be wretched Jerusalem's censure and ignominy that even the powers hostile to us will blush at the magnitude of our sins" (151CD). "She did not imitate the cunning prostitutes who like to raise the price of lust by holding back, thereby driving their lovers to distraction. . . . 'You fornicated three times in your daughters.' This can be attributed literally to Jerusalem . . . or to the Church and to believers who have been led astray ... who have committed fornication of every kind in body, soul, and spirit. ... The daughters of the fornicating Church are, first, the souls of believers, secondly, the souls of those led astray by heresy, whose guilt reflects back on the mother [*quarum culpa refertur ad matrem*]" (153A–54A).

> "And after you there will be no fornication." In other words, compared with yours, all later fornication will seem less heinous. Whatever we said about Jerusalem refers to the Church and to the souls of believers. They give away their wedding gifts—gold in thought, silver in speech, the clothes that cover our ugliness and shame. They give them to their lovers, either the hostile powers or the teachers of perverted doctrines, people who maintain that unchastity is not harmful, that the lust that overcomes the sexual organs demands copulation by a law of nature, that we can eat everything indiscriminately, because food is there to be consumed, that prudence is necessary if it is to our advantage ... and other things of that kind. In accepting such opinions, wretched Jerusalem, in whom there should have been the "vision of peace", turns keenness of thought and charm of speech into turpitude. And to spite her spouse, she goes off to her lovers in the very finery with which her husband, in the superabundance of his goodness, had adorned her [155AC].

In comparison with the sins of Samaria and Sodom, Jerusalem's sin is the greatest of all.

> Samaria and Sodom [in other words, the heretics and the heathen] often commit less grave sins than those who are thought of as Jerusalem [in other words, Churchmen, *ecclesiastici*]. Thus it is said to the Corinthians, who believed in Christ, but were encumbered with deeds of wickedness, "It is reported that there is immorality among you, and of a kind that is not found even among pagans" (1 Cor 5:1) (159D). ... Sodom and Samaria may be bad, but they have not sinned half as much as Jerusalem. "The servant who knows his master's will and does not do it shall receive a severe beating" (cf. Lk 12:47) (162BC). ... We corrupt our brothers and sisters by our sins, when our sins incite them to greater wickedness. Let me explain myself more clearly. Someone in the high office of priest-

hood does not behave well, and so by his conduct he defiles its dignity. Will not the imitation of his vices corrupt the layman, his brother? For "whoever causes one of these little ones to stumble ought to have a millstone fastened on his neck and be drowned in the depth of the sea" (cf. Mt 18:6). . . . Who can doubt that of three sinners, three impious men (the Gentile, the heretic, the Churchman), the one with the greatest dignity deserves the greatest punishment? . . . On the other hand, the least of the three deserves mercy. . . . As St. Peter says, "The time has come for judgment to begin on the house of God" (1 Pet 4:17). And in our prophet Ezekiel the men wielding axes are told, "Begin with my holy ones" (cf. Ezek 9:6). Jerusalem's sisters repent before she does and are restored to their former state, but she continues to bear her disgrace. . . . We read the same thing in the gospel: it will be more tolerable for Sodom on the Day of Judgment than for the city that did not accept the apostles (cf. Mt 10:15) [162C–64B].

If at last Jerusalem is welcomed back to grace, "It will be through my mercy, not [her] merits, and then she will be ashamed and say with the Apostle, "I am not worthy to be called an apostle, because I persecuted the Church of God" (1 Cor 15:9). "And you will never open your mouth any more because of your shame" (Ezek 16:63). . . . From this we learn that, even when by God's mercy we have got back our former glory, or rather when we have received the eternal Covenant of the gospel, having pleased God in all that we do, we still have the memory of our past sin, and our mouths remain closed for ever, because we have been saved not by our own works but by the grace of God" (167AC).

This patristic way of speaking was not likely to please a more sensitive age, as we can see from Savonarola's thirtieth sermon on Ezekiel:[19] *Sono alcuni che dicono che li propheti non si expongono della Chiesa presente: Va, legi un poco santo Hieronymo et sancto Gregorio e li altri doctori che toccono questa expositione!* See also Savonarola's thirty-second sermon on Ezekiel:[20] "Despicable Church! 'I lavished lovely garments on you,' says the Lord, 'but you committed idolatry with

[19] *Prediche de Fra Hieronymo sopra Ezechiel* ven. 1520 fol verso.
[20] Ibid., fol 92 verso.

them.' The vessels were abused for pride, the sacraments for simony. In your lust you have become a shameless whore" (he describes this very vividly: *Selected Writings and Sermons* [1928], pp. 165f.).

Through *Rabanus Maurus* (*Commentaria in Ezechielem;* PL 110, 665–94), most of Jerome's commentary is passed on to the Middle Ages.

The great admonitory sermons of Origen and Jerome shed light on the deep inner connection between the destiny of the Church as a whole and that of her holy or sinful members. Church, abstracted from all her members, is no longer Church. Her destiny is in her members, theirs in her. The sins of the sons and daughters reflect back on the mother, which is why she has to pray in her members and beg for her own salvation. *St. Hilary* gave this strong expression: "The Church is made up of tax collectors and sinners and heathen. Only her second and heavenly Adam has not sinned. She herself is a sinner and is saved through bearing children who persevere in the faith. 'Adam did not sin, but the woman was led astray and fell. But she will be saved through childbearing, if they persevere in the faith' (1 Tim 2:14–15). Now, of course, this does not mean that the woman is not saved from her sins by the Lord and is baptized in vain and had to be redeemed through the merit of childbearing. On the contrary, not even childbearing guarantees her salvation. She is only saved if the children she has borne persevere in the faith' " (*Lib. myster. De Adam,* CSEL 65, 5–6). Similarly, *Rupert of Deutz* applies the Old Testament names to the mother because of what the sons have done: "The woman clothed with the sun is Holy Church. Scripture in many places describes her as the woman united to her spouse, God, and loved by him. However, occasionally, because of the vices of the wicked and the sins of those who have fallen into idolatry, she is rebuked as a whore" (*In Apoc.* 7; PL 169, 1041).

It is true that the Church "has" the Holy Spirit, but that does not mean that the Church as a whole—and each of her members—does not have to pray constantly for the presence of the Spirit. It is true that the Church is immaculate (in the sense that she is the place where God sanctifies human beings with his grace), but that does not exclude but rather includes the Church's unceasing confession of sin.

"The Church stands in prayer, so that she may be cleansed in confession. And that is how she stands as long as she lives here [*stat Ecclesia in oratione, ut mundetur in confessione; et quamdiu hic vivitur, sic stat*]" (*St. Augustine, Serm.* 181, 5, 7; PL 38, 982). Being near or far from the light of grace is a reality for the Church too: "Thus speaks the Church: 'I am "black', I am a sinner, because 'the sun has discolored me, because at times, when my Creator removed himself from me, I fell into error'" (*St. Gregory the Great, In Cant.* 1, 5; Heine, 183).

The Church, who is able to see and condemn herself in this way, has this strange duality within her: standing where she is, thinking of how she ought to be, she can reject within herself what ought not to be. *St. Peter Damian* links this duality once again with the symbol of Rahab. It struck him that the house of Rahab was besieged by the ark of the Covenant—in other words, that the Church was to be found inside as well as outside Jericho. "Church conquers Church! It does not seem unreasonable to me that the ark of the Covenant and the house of the harlot, which is being besieged, should both symbolize one and the same Church, since there are different kinds of members in one and the same Church. Some do the besieging, walking round the city with sacred preaching. Others, in the bulwark of their infidelity or corruption, have to be captured by weapons of saving doctrine. Some already belong to the house; others by the aversion of misdeeds are still alienated from it" (*Serm.* 57; PL 144, 825C–26D). *St. Bede the Venerable* had already spoken in similar fashion (*Exp. sup. Jes. Nave.* 7; PL 93, 419). He in turn must have borrowed his ideas from *St. Ambrose:* "Outside the city walls the name of Jesus gave the attackers victory. Inside the sign of the Lord's Passion gave the attacked salvation. And so because Rahab understood the heavenly mystery, the Lord says in the Psalm: 'I will be mindful of Rahab and Babylon'" (*De fide ad Grat.* 5, 10, 128; PL 16, 674–75).

The same idea of two sides to the concrete reality of the Church can be expressed in a different, harsher way. The abuse, by the sinners within her, of the Church as a pure and bridal mystery can be presented in the imagery of fornication, except in this case the Church herself is not a "harlot" but a woman abused passively and against her will. Take, for example, a fragment of *St. Hippolytus*, which is prob-

ably part of the *Benedictiones Jacob*. The text "You went up to your
father's bed" (cf. Gen 49:4) is applied to the "people" (i.e., the Jews),
who go up to the "bed of the Father" (i.e., the Church) to ruin her by
persecution and calumny (Bonw. 1/2, 55–56). Mention has already
been made of *Clement of Alexandria*'s assertion that anyone who lives
in a heathen way in the Church, by thought, word or deed, commits
fornication with her (*Strom.* 7, 14, 87–88, 1). This coarse image was
bound to appeal to the Middle Ages, during which the original
patristic imagery faded away. Thus *St. Bernard* would never call the
Church a whore, but he does say that the bad shepherds who devas-
tate the Church "prostitute" her rather than "institute" her (*Serm. in
Cant.* 77, 1; PL 183, 1156A). In a vision *Hildegard of Bingen* sees the
Church covered in dirt, with ragged clothes and filthy shoes. She
looks like a child who has been rolled around a pigsty. She bewails the
devastation that has come upon her. Once, in the blood of the Son of
Man, she was chosen as his immaculate bride, but now she has been
soiled and plunged in filth by "fornicating and thieving" priests. In
her the wounds of the Bridegroom open and bleed afresh. They open
as long as the wounds of sin open in the lives of men. But these
wounds, too, have been soiled by priests. The visionary sees a drawn
sword hanging over the clergy. They are corrupt in what they are and
what they do. "And I saw how this sword was poised to strike at not a
few of the places inhabited by religious people, just as Jerusalem was
struck after the Passion" (Letter 52; PL 197, 269f.; H. Rahner, *Mater
Ecclesia* [1944], 104–6).

To conclude, a rather bombastic text:

> The state and face of the Church are in these days so wretched that
> it is hard to think of a text one can decently apply to her. One,
> though, that comes to mind is the story of the Israelite's wife in the
> time of the judges who for a whole night was raped to death by the
> men of Gibeah. Her husband found her dead early the next morning,
> her hands stretched over the threshold. He placed her on his
> donkey and took her home, where he cut her body into twelve
> pieces, which he sent to the twelve tribes of Israel, stirring every-
> one to compassion and zeal for revenge.... Who is this woman,
> who left her father to be the wife of an Israelite, if not holy

Church, who left her father (the devil or the world) to be joined in marriage to Christ? Just as the woman in the story often left her husband and returned to her father, so the Church, growing cold in her love for Christ, goes off to socialize with the world, or its prince, the devil, in the house of infidelity and immorality. But whenever that happens, Christ, her husband, calls her back, and through the mouths of pastors and doctors, by the infusion of his Spirit of love, he revives ardor within her, saying to her, as it were coaxingly, "Hearken, O daughter, and see, and incline your ear; forget your own people and your father's house. So shall the King desire your beauty" (Ps 44:12). While the Church here below walks among proud and depraved men, she is violated by their proud and depraved . . . doctrines and morals. And though the Church has many times suffered from wicked and depraved men, she has never been more shamefully subjected, so it seems to me, to corruption than she is today with an unbridled gang of Simoniacs assaulting her chastity to satisfy their lusts. It is like the boats in the gospel: "Both were filled, so that they began to sink" (cf. Lk 5:7). They did not sink, but they were in danger of sinking. In the same way, we can say of the Church that her corruptors are abusing her all night (the hour of darkness!) so much that she is dead, i.e., close to death. Yes, in many parishes, the vital fire of the sacraments, from which they could have drawn life, has been totally extinguished, just like the fire of the altar of the Lord, which was kept alight through so many years of the Babylonian captivity, is said to have been extinguished at the time when Jason and Menelaus were buying the priesthood [*Gerhoh of Reichersberg, Syntagma de statu Ecclesiae* 12; PL 194, 1458–59].

7. *The Tamar motif: the Church in the form of a harlot*

When they spoke of the Church as the fulfillment of Rahab, the Fathers made contradictory demands. On the one hand, the Church must forget what she used to be, a harlot, and in the future think of herself only as the virgin bride, indeed, as mother of Christ: "I have something wonderful to tell you, something wonderful but something true. If she so desires, this harlot can in no time at all become a virgin. She is 'virginified' and conceives and bears the Son of God. 'Out of your fear, Lord, have we conceived and given birth. We placed the Spirit of your salvation on earth' (Is 26:18, LXX). So you see. . . . Rahab the harlot can conceive and give birth to the Redeemer" (*St. Jerome, Tr. in Ps.* 86; *Anal. Mared.* 3, 2; 104–5). "What is inimical to Christian faith about a harlot abandoning her fornication and being changed into a chaste spouse?" (*St. Augustine, C. Faust.* 22, 80; PL 42, 453). On the other hand, the very same Fathers insist that she should never forget her origins; in fact, her very salvation depends upon her remembering.

The tension is heightened in the Hosea story. There the harlot, who bears the self-humiliating and humiliated prophet's children, not only cannot forget her background but also constantly has to confront it in her children's names of shame until the day the Lord changes them into their opposite. And unfaithful Jerusalem (in Ezek 16 and 23), the last to be taken back, can really only accept the fact of being taken back in the deepest silence and shame. Thus, in some incomprehensible way, the two things must be true at the same time: the past has been graciously crossed out and totally overcome, and yet something from the past lives on and clings to the present, something formal and somehow constitutive.

Here a new Old Testament motif becomes important, the very subtly told story of Judah and Tamar. Let us briefly recall the details. Judah, the son of Jacob, lives away from his brothers among the Canaanites. He takes Shua's daughter as his wife and receives from her three sons, Er, Onan, and Shelah. He gives Tamar to Er as his wife, but Er dies, so he asks Onan to raise up progeny for his brother from Tamar. However, Onan does not want children that will not be his own, and so each time he spills his seed on the ground. He likewise dies. Shelah is still a minor, so Judah sends his daughter-in-law home. He puts her off, but he does not give her to Shelah when he comes of age, because he does not want a third son to die. Tamar hears that Judah is coming to Timnah for the sheep shearing, so she changes out of her widow's weeds and sits down, her head veiled, by the side of the road. She wants a child of the blood of her husband, Er. Judah sees her and takes her for a cultic prostitute. Tamar makes Judah give him three pledges until she receives from him the promised kid from the flock. She becomes pregnant. Judah's friend comes with the kid, but nothing is known in the district of any cultic prostitute. Three months later it is reported to Judah that his daughter-in-law has played the harlot and is pregnant. Judah orders her to be burnt. She is led off, but Judah recognizes her by the three pledges and calls out: "She is more in the right than I am, because I did not give her to my son, Shelah" (whose wife she should have become by leviration). The twins brought into the world by Tamar are the ancestors of David.

The striking thing about this story is that, though in different ways the subject of prostitution is touched on or alluded to, there is no actual prostitution. In the literal sense, according to the law and custom of the time, what we have here is a lawful choice of mate under the appearance of harlotry. The Fathers understood this perfectly well, even though they were probably ignorant of the details of the legal convention, and applied it to the Church.

To begin with, we have three fragments from *St. Hippolytus'* commentary on Genesis (in Bonwetsch's literal translation):

> Tamar is the type of the holy community, and Judah is the type of Christ. The name "Judah" means "the tearing down of the enclosures", so Judah represents the King. And when it says, "They reported to Tamar and said, 'Behold, your father-in-law is going to Timnah for the sheep shearing' ", the people who do the reporting are a type of the prophets and apostles, who inform the community of the coming of the Messiah. And just as Tamar adorned herself and went off to meet Judah and changed out of her widow's weeds, so the holy community changes out of her old ways, puts on the garments of piety and faith, of lovely hope and trust, sets off to meet Christ, who came from the stock of Judah, and adorns herself with the garments of the New Covenant to make glad the heart of the King, who came to redeem the world [*Fragm. in Gen.* 38, 14; Bonw. 1/2, 95].

> Judah did not desire Tamar with animal lust, but all took place by Divine Providence, to ensure the propagation and survival of the line. Likewise, Tamar, Judah's daughter-in-law, did not sit down by the busy thoroughfare to earn a harlot's fee. She cherished the hope

of getting progeny for the line and race of Abraham, for she, as a descendant of Esau, was of the race of Abraham, and Judah thought she had caused the death of his sons, Er and Onan, and was cursed with infertility. After sleeping with her, Judah gave three pledges—a seal, a cord, and the stick he held in his hand. These were the pledge that he had slept with her. Likewise Christ has given his Church three things: his Body, his Blood, and baptism. And if Tamar was saved by three things—the ring, the cord, and the stick—Holy Church was delivered from idolatry by three things— the confession of faith, the Body and the Blood, and for her children she chose deliverance from worldliness through Christ. And we receive his Body and his Blood, because he is the pledge of eternal life for all who approach Him in humility [ibid., pp. 95f.].

The third fragment describes Tamar's pregnancy and how, on the way to being burnt, she shows Judah the three pledges: "Tamar is now the type of the holy community, and Judah the type of Christ. And just as Tamar, to be free of shame, hoped for progeny for the race of Abraham, so the holy community hoped to keep the commandments of Christ and obey the words of his holy apostles in order to be freed from the shame of the old life and the stench of idolatrous sacrifice" (ibid., pp. 96f.).

Hippolytus is well aware of the sinful appearance of the episode, but he places no emphasis on it in his exposition. The motif comes out more strongly in *St. Augustine,* probably not without the influence of St. Ambrose. We shall postpone our consideration of the vitally important texts of the latter, because he develops his ideas in terms of Mary Magdalen's example rather than Tamar's. Augustine is concerned to show against the Manichees that the dubious appearance of many episodes in the Old Testament is either just a matter of appearances or can be justified by its prophetic significance.

In Tamar we must see the people of the kingdom of the Jews, to whom, from the tribe of Judah, the kings came, as it were, as spouses. Her name is rightly translated as "bitterness", for it was she who gave the Lord gall to drink. . . . Tamar changes her clothes, so her name is also translated as "changing". The name "bitterness" can still be kept, but it is now not the bitterness of giving the Lord gall but the bitterness of Peter's tears. For Judah is translated into Latin as *confessio,* "confession". Bitterness can be mixed with confession to indicate true repentance. Through this repentance the Church, seated amidst all the Gentiles, becomes fruitful. . . . And the whorish habit [*habitus meretricius*] of Tamar is the confession of sins. For Tamar is already the type of the Church called from out of the Gentiles [*C. Faust. Man.* 22, 83–86; PL 42, 454–258].

Augustine adds the further detail that the harlot Israel is transformed by her *confessio* into the Church. The transformation and marriage first take place in the hidden depths of the heart; the pledges for it are produced openly only later.

St. Jerome's interpretation of the "prophetic whore" (*scortum propheticum*) is directed at the Jews. For him, Tamar is the symbol of either the Church of the Gentiles or, as seems more appropriate here, the synagogue. She was first rescued from idolatry by Abraham and Moses (Judah's first two sons); then, after committing adultery and disowning the Redeemer, she spent a very long time without altar, priest, and prophets (in other words, she did not marry the third son); finally, she longs once more for contact with her original husband. Thus, when the fullness of the Gentiles has come in, all Israel will be saved (*Ep.* 123, 13; PL 22, 1055AB).

St. Zeno of Verona constructs a subtle allegory out of the Tamar story (*Lib* II, Tr. 15; PL 11, 434–39). The essential features of his interpretation are as follows. Judah is ancient prophecy. Er is the Gentiles. Onan is the Jews, who spill the seed of God's word. Shelah is Christ, still a minor and not yet ready for marriage. Judah's dead wife is the faith of the synagogue. Judah's union with the veiled Tamar ("rightly taken for a whore") is the union of revelation with the still unrecognizable Gentile Church (who "had greater faith in prophecy than the Jews did"). She receives the pledges and is then no more to be found, because she has meanwhile been washed clean in baptism. When she becomes pregnant, the Jews accuse her of adultery: she has violated the Sabbath and broken the traditions. But she can produce the pledges of revelation and prove she is the lawful heiress.

St. Bede the Venerable simply reproduces the ideas he receives from the Tradition (*In Gen.;* PL 91, 266–67). In his commentary on St.

Matthew's Gospel, *St. Paschasius Radbertus* takes over, word for word, the main ideas of St. Augustine. However, in his opinion, Judah and Tamar—symbols of Christ and the Gentile Church—cannot be entirely excused (*In Mt.* I, I; PL 120, 55A–58). He emphasizes strongly that all the women named in Christ's genealogy are harlots.

For *Rupert*, as for Augustine, Tamar represents bitter penance, which takes place publicly on the crossroads (between the law and grace) and is unafraid of the appearance of harlotry (817B). But Judah is Christ, who unites himself to the penitent Church and, through the one conjugal union of the Cross, begets two peoples. The salvation of both Jews and Gentiles is assured (*De Trin. in Gen.* 8, 29–30; PL 167, 515–18). *Pseudo-Hugh of St. Victor* (*Alleg. in Vet. Test.*) also follows Augustine (PL 175, 652), as does *St. Peter Damian* (*Opusc.* 60; PL 145, 858A).

Anselm of Laon sees in Tamar "the ancient people, to whom two husbands had already been given", but they were bad shepherds and spilled the seed of God's word on the ground. Shelah, who is not given to the people, represents (as in the earlier interpretations) the interruption of the postexilic succession of the kings of Judah. So at last comes Christ/Judah, announced by John the Baptist/Hirah. "Tamar, the Church, wanted to marry him but in a changed form, no longer as the Jewish Church but as the Church of the Gentiles and in appearance a whore, for in former times she had often played the harlot with false gods, and for Judah she had been a woman, as it were, unknown." But Hirah does not find her, "because the Church has meanwhile accepted the faith and ceased to be a harlot" (*In Mt.* I; PL 162, 1239).

St. Isidore of Seville takes over Augustine's interpretation almost word for word. "Tamar changed her clothes. She also changes her name. From synagogue, she becomes Church. But she really does have to keep the name 'bitterness'. . . . Through penance the Church dwelling among all the Gentiles will be made fruitful. . . . The behavior of the harlot is the confession of sins. For Tamar is the type of the Church that comes from the Gentiles" (*Quaest. in V. T., in Gen. c.* 39; PL 83, 270). *Rabanus Maurus* takes his exposition from Isidore (*Comm. in Ruth* 14; PL 108, 1220; *In Paralip.* I, 2; PL 109, 289–90). *Rupert of*

Deutz explains the "harlot" motif by relating Tamar to the other harlots in the genealogy of Christ. The appearance of public prostitution that Tamar gives is the Church's public penance, through which she confesses she has been a sinner (*In Gen.* 8, 28–30; PL 167, 516–17). "Tamar veils her face, and the Church blushes at the errors of her former ways, and sits by the roadside, where Christ meets her in baptism" (*De div. offic.* 1, 9, 2; PL 170, 241).

St. Ambrose emphasizes the *habitus meretricius* of the Church in truly memorable words. The "house of Simon", which Christ entered as a guest, is the world. "This woman heard that Christ had come, and so she went off to Simon's house. Now the woman could never have been healed, if Christ had not come down to earth. We might say of her that she entered the house of Simon because she had within her something of a higher soul [one that had come down from above], or something of the Church, who came down to earth to gather up one people in her fragrance." We have already seen that Ambrose believed the sinful woman to be Mary Magdalen and contrasted her with Mary of Bethany: both symbolize the Church, both anoint the Lord, but the former anoints the feet, the latter the head. "The first is the one closest to us, as a person but also as representing a certain stage of progress. For we too have not yet renounced our sins. But where are our tears? ... Perhaps Christ did not wash his own feet, so that we could wash them with our tears. . . . And perhaps that ointment could be provided by no one but the Church, who possesses countless blooms of the most varied fragrance; yes, no one but the Church, who rightly took on the appearance of a sinner, because Christ too took upon himself the form of the sinner [*Ecclesia . . . quae merito speciem peccatricis, quia Christus quoque formam peccatoris accepit*]" (*In Luc.* 6, 21; PL 15, 1672–74A).

St. Paulinus of Nola follows Ambrose so closely that he reproduces the crucial sentence word for word.

> Since Mary Magdalen is the symbol of the Church to be called out of the Gentiles, she was given the privilege of handling all the signs of the mystery of salvation. With the ointment she poured out, she herself was anointed. Her penitent tears became for her a cleansing

bath, her heartfelt love the sacrifice. Yes, her hands and mouth were allowed a foretaste of the living and life-giving Bread, and her sucking kisses a first draught of the Blood of the Chalice before it became Blood in the Chalice! Blessed are they who were able to taste the Lord in the flesh and with their own bodies to welcome the Body of Christ. . . . Blessed is she who was given the privilege of being the type of the Church! At the Pharisee's house and meal it was not he but the sinful woman who was justified and absolved. . . . The Church was to correspond to her head, even in type, and so she appropriately assumed the form of a sinful woman, because Christ himself assumed the form of the sinner [*Ep.* 23, 32–33; CSEL 29, 1, 188–89].

From now on, we see a deep transformation and relativization of the earlier themes. There is something about the essential form of the Church (and this is not her most inconspicuous feature) that is reminiscent of sin, conditioned by sin, something that in the present context always means infidelity and fornication. And yet it is not guilt but assimilation to the form of the sinner assumed by her Head. A profound explanation of this from the patristic age can be found in the texts assembled and interpreted by Hugo Rahner under the title *Mysterium Lunae*. [21] The relationship of sun and moon is seen as an unceasing marriage and is applied to Christ and the Church. The central mystery is this: at the very moment of her greatest proximity to the sun, in the *synodus* of the wedding, the moon becomes the new moon, in other words, dark and black; she seems to have disappeared, to have been, as it were, annihilated. But in this Selene is only imitating the setting sun, which symbolizes Christ's kenosis and Cross. She is closest to Christ when she assumes the same kenotic form. The sun has to go down before the moon can shine brightly, and so the moon's brightness, lent her by the sun, bears witness in earthly night to the night of the Cross, the return to the "superbright darkness" of the Father. But it can also be interpreted to mean that "while Christ shone in the flesh on earth, Christ's Church could not yet gleam, for she still lay in the west, that

[21] *Zeitschrift für katholische Theologie* (1939): 311–49, 428–42; (1940), 61–80, 121–31.

is, in sin" (*St. Anastasius of Sinai, In Hexaem.* 4; PG 89, 902A).
However, for *St. Ambrose,* the changes of the moon are clear evidence for St. Paul's doctrine of the subjection of the cosmic elements to vanity for the sake of sin: "It is for you that Luna suffers.
By the will of God she has been subjugated. It is not by her free will
that Luna changes. She sighs; she is in labor on account of her
changeability. She never ceases to yearn for your redemption" (*Exaem.*
4, 8, 31; CSEL 32, 1; 137). These observations are then transferred
to the Church. She is subjected to change, yet in her essence she
does not wax or wane: *obumbrari potest, deficere non potest* (4, 2, 7;
p. 115). The Cross overshadows her, and the coming light of the
Resurrection falls upon her (4, 5, 22; p. 129f.). For *St. Augustine,*
too, the changeableness of the moon/Church is connected with
Adam's fall from divine constancy (Rahner, 436f.). Especially in
Letter 55 to Januarius and in the *Enarrationes,* Augustine loves to
use the moon symbol to describe the changes and chances of the
Church's destiny in this world. It is the destiny of being in transition
(*transitus*), something completely provisional, a fate conditioned both
by the fall and by the form of the redemption. As Luna, constantly
having to change, the Church is ordered toward a double end, as
Origen so magnificently explains (*Hom. in Num.* 23): she makes herself
superfluous and disappears into the unique light of the sun that is
Christ, and yet in the very act of disappearing she becomes a partaker
of eternal light.

To return to our theme, we must say that the *forma meretricis*
adheres so closely to the Church that, having been, so to speak, in its
final aspect transfigured and rendered harmless, it becomes one of the
marks of the Church of the New Covenant in all the beauty of her
salvific mystery. The synagogue's departure from the Holy Land to
go to the Gentiles was the infidelity of Jerusalem, "the opening of her
legs at every street corner in the world". And yet it is that very
movement outward to all the nations that is the mission of the
Church. She must mix and unite herself with all nations and not shy
away from this new apostolic form of intercourse. Once again it is *St.
Ambrose,* the boldest adventurer in this theology, who gives us the
most striking formulation:

This Rahab—in type a harlot, in mystery the Church . . . did not refuse intercourse to the many men who came her way. The more lovers she has, the chaster she is: a spotless virgin without wrinkle, untouched by feelings of shame, public [*plebeia*] in love, a chaste prostitute [*casta meretrix*], an unfruitful widow, a fruitful virgin. Harlot, because thronged by many lovers, with all the enticements of love, but without the stain of transgression, for "he who is joined to a harlot is one body with her" (1 Cor 6:16). Unfruitful widow, because, if the husband is absent, she cannot bear children, but if the husband is there, she gives birth to this people, this great crowd. Fruitful virgin, who bore this multitude with the blessing of love and without the use of lust [*In Luc* 3, 23; PL 15, 1598].

And again, when speaking of the roof under which Rahab sheltered the spies: "I know a roof where Rahab hid the spies sent her by Jesus. In type Rahab was a harlot, but in mystery the Church, coupled with the Gentiles by the consort of the sacraments" (*In Luc* 8, 40; PL 15, 1776). Clearly, when seen in the context of this passage, the Samaritan woman's apostolic preaching and Mary Magdalen's bearing of the Easter message to the apostles come to have special symbolic force. One text out of many must suffice, in this case about the Samaritan woman: "O apostolic harlot! The harlot proves to be mightier than the apostles. She preaches Christ even before the Passion and the mystery of his suffering and Resurrection: 'Come and see the man who told me all the things I have done!' (Jn 4:29). I spread my sins abroad to guide you on the way. 'Is he perhaps the Messiah?' See the woman's intelligence. See the sincerity of the harlot!" (*Pseudo-Chrysostom, In Samaritanam*; PG 59, 541).

8. The Babylon motif: the spirit of confusion

All the motifs and symbols discussed so far, even that of the archwhore Jerusalem, could be applied to the Church, because it was always possible to see her at the same time, in her essential core, as the immaculate bride. For the prophets, even Jerusalem's rejection was one episode between her first and final eschatological election. But the picture is very different when we pass from the "archwhore Jerusalem" to the "archwhore Babylon", an image that makes its first appearance in the Old Testament (Jer 50–51) and is then broadly unfolded in the New (Rev 17–19). Now, of course, the features of the two archwhores merge with one another in order to describe the character, crimes, and downfall of the terrible powers opposed to the Church. These not only play the whore, like Jerusalem, with all the mighty ones of this world but also intoxicate themselves with the blood of the martyrs, the children of the Church. In the Apocalypse, confusion between Babylon and the "beloved city" is not even thinkable.

This ultimate irreconcilability of the spirit of Christ's true Church with the spirit of Babylon constantly led the heretics of the Middle Ages to identify the Roman Church with the great Babylon. The contrast expressed in this appelation, with its implication of an absolute reform of the Church that would alter her very essence, reduces all the different sects to their common denominator. "One basic piece of evidence can be adduced ... to support the view that medieval heresy originated in the widespread movement for Church reform and not primarily in a late resurgence of Gnosticism: the central importance that all the sects attribute to the question of the Church, and the arrogant, unbending opposition of all the heretics, from the eleventh century onward, to the Roman Church. All agree in recognizing her in the image of the great whore in the Apocalypse, in the Babylon of 1 Peter, in the *Ecclesia malignantium* or *diaboli,* who has falsified the pure evangelical Tradition. She is contrasted with the *Ecclesia Dei,* the only legitimate continuation of the apostolic Tradition through all persecution, all poverty, and all suffering" (Rafael Morghen).[22] According to Stefano di Borbone, the Waldensians say, "The Roman Church is the whore of Babylon, and those who obey her are damned" (*Romanam Ecclesiam esse meretricem Babylon, et omnes ei oboedientes damnari*).[23] The apostolic brethren confess that "there is a double Church, the spiritual and the carnal, the spiritual composed

---

[22] *Osservazioni critiche su alcune questioni fondamentali riguardanti le origini e i caratteri delle eresie medioevali* (*Archivio* 67 [1944], 98–151, p. 146).

[23] *Tract. de haeresi* (in *Bibl. max. vet. patr.* or *Thesaurus* of Martène), col. 1779.

of those people who live in total poverty, the carnal of those who live in wealth and privilege. . . . It is this Church of which St. John speaks in the Apocalypse and which he calls Babylon.[24] Peter Dominicus, a Beghard, adds that "in the sixth phase of the Church, in which we now live, the Roman Church, under the name of 'Babylon', has been cursed by Christ, rejected and destroyed, just as the old synagogue of the Jews was rejected by Christ."[25] There is abundant proof of the Cathars and Albigensians describing the Church in this way.[26] And there is no need here to list all the examples from the late Middle Ages, from Hus, Wycliffe, and Luther, from the whole world of the sects right up to the present day.

We are concerned only with Catholic theology, with the question of whether the application of this Biblical symbol to the Catholic Church is in any way defensible or at least understandable. We gave two examples at the beginning: William of Auvergne and Dante. We could also cite *Savonarola,* but he can be regarded even less than these two as a witness *sine ira et studio.* The same is true of the spiritual Franciscans, for whom, as earlier for Joachim, the clash between the *Ecclesia spiritualis* and the *Ecclesia carnalis* within Catholicism becomes the crucial question in Christendom.[27] But over these too lies the half shadow of condemnation.

What we need to know is the theological way in which an orthodox use of the Babylon symbol became a possibility to be considered. The question can be answered quickly and unequivocally by looking at *St. Augustine*'s *City of God* and at his general doctrine of the Church, which is characterized by two fundamental tendencies. First, there is a vigorous, spiritual, and dynamic concept of the two opposed kingdoms: where the spirit of *caritas* reigns, there is the Kingdom of God, Jerusalem; where the spirit of *cupiditas* reigns, there is Satan's kingdom,

[24] Limborch, *Hist. inquisitionis* (Amsterdam, 1692), pp. 99f. (R. A. Knox, *Enthusiasm,* p. 111).

[25] Ibid.

[26] More examples in Arno Borst, *Die Katharer.* Schriften der Monum. Germ. 12 (1953).

[27] Ernst Benz, *Ecclesia Spiritualis* (Stuttgart, 1934). Grundmann: Religiöse Bewegungen des MA Hist. Stud., vol. 267 (Berlin, 1935).

Babylon. Secondly, dependent on the first point, there is a sharp division between the Church's sacramental form and her spiritual, grace-given content. The form can validly exist outside the Catholic Church (so, against the Donatists, there is no rebaptizing of converted heretics) but without the grace-given content, which opens up only on entry to the Church. These two elements together produce the typically Augustinian Church ethic, the idea that much of the spirit of Babylon can hold sway within the Church-Jerusalem, that it is only on the Last Day that corn and chaff in the Church are separated, that meanwhile wheat and weed have to grow together entwined. A third point, concerning the theology of history, emerges in the *City of God*. In the Old Testament, Babylon/Assyria (alongside Egypt) was the embodiment of the great power opposed to God. However, by the time of the New Testament, its historical power was at an end, so, for the Mediterranean world, Rome took over the role of the new, second Babylon. Augustine argued that in the spirit of Rome we find the spirit of that worldly mentality that is hostile to God. It is well known that the Roman Emperor's "conversion" to Christianity aroused little enthusiasm in him. In contrast to Eusebius and his own disciple Orosius, he continued, and gave a new spiritual application to, the old Christian theology of opposition to the world.[28]

St. Augustine's *City of God* had a most powerful influence on the Middle Ages' theology of history; indeed, one might say it was almost the only influence—though admittedly the medievals underestimated its anti-Roman and antiimperial tendency. No wonder, then, that where it was studied and understood in depth, it set off on the track that we are now following. An example will explain what we are saying and provide the "missing link" in our chain of proof. It comes from the writings of *Gerhoh of Reichersberg*, who was, if not the greatest, then certainly the most powerful and—in terms of his knowledge and mastery of the theological Tradition—the most accomplished of the German theologians. Ardently involved in the struggle for reform within the Church, passionately devoted to the purifica-

---

[28] W. Kamlah, *Christentum und Geschichtlichkeit,* Untersuchungen zur Entstehung des Christentums und zu Augustins "Bürgerschaft Gottes", 2d ed. (1951).

tion of the Church in theory and theology as well as in practice, he was predestined to develop ecclesiology in this direction.

Outside the Church there is no salvation, and so sacraments outside the Church are valid in form but contain no life (*sacramenta mortua, Tr. adv. Sim.* 19; PL 194, 1353, with reference to Augustine). The Church is formed by the love of Christ and Christians. She is above all a spirit, the spirit of the city of God from Abel onward as opposed to the spirit of the world from Cain onward (194, 14–15): the spirit of Babylon, of "confusion", of "muddle", which is at its most dangerous for the Church when it is a spirit of deviously inconspicuous confusion between the sacred and the secular (194, 27, 40). This is the spirit of Babylon, and it can break out in the Church at any time. For Rome is "the second Babylon, and we rejoice to see it transformed into the city of Zion" (194, 16). Gerhoh loves and admires this Christian Rome. He even admires "the Church structures daily growing on the ruins of Jericho, gleaming with golden images . . . clearly showing how the house of Rahab has been saved, that is to say, Holy Church built on the faith and name of Peter" (41C). But the "second Babel" (66C), in its very splendor, has the tendency to accommodate the spirit of the old Babel, and "it is a tragic spectacle to see an almost entirely Babylonian people dwelling in your midst, Jerusalem" (40A), a people dedicated to "the rebuilding of Jericho" (41B). The Babylonian takeover, the new Babylonian captivity of God's people, has four stages, according to Gerhoh, which more or less coincide with the stages outlined by Dante by which the abuse of the *religiosa judiciaria potestas* goes deeper and deeper. First, the Jews abused it, by condemning Christ; then the pagan emperors, by persecuting Christians from without; then, after Constantine, the heretical emperors by threatening the true Faith from within; finally, false Christians, the fornicators in body and spirit, the corrupt clergy above all, but also the Christian emperors who lead the Church into simony (193, 689–90). Things have gone so far that nowadays the best people in the Church are like Elijah, having to flee from the modern Jezebel into the wilderness, where they hardly have the wherewithal to live (781f.). Elsewhere the stages are identified with the horses of the Apocalypse. Red represents the emperors from Nero to Diocletian, black the Arian emperors, gray (a mixture of black and white) the false Christians, whose lives no longer correspond in any way to the Faith they profess. "Elijah is persecuted by Jezebel, the rich and godless woman, yes, by the great mass of the godless. Like a real prostitute, she goes whoring with the devil, and in the Apocalypse she is called the 'mother of all harlotry'" (*Comm. in Ps.* 17, 5; 19, 3). The *cathedra Moysis* has imperceptibly become the *cathedra pestilentiae* (789; 946–48). The radiant moon/ Church has become the *luna obscura:* "Mere dignity of office without dignity of merit" (*sola dignitas officiorum sine dignitate meritorum*) (795–96). The Antichrist has not yet arrived, but "he is coming with all power to sit in my temple, the Church, boasting that he is God ... so that, were it possible, even the elect would be led astray, those who are the apple of my eye, chosen not only so that they themselves should not go astray but also to protect the whole body of the Church from the darkness of error" (850CD). This is the very same spirit against which the prophets railed

> when the Jewish priests in the glorious and sumptuous temple were boasting and saying, "This is the temple of the Lord, the temple of the Lord, the temple of the Lord!" (Jer 7:4). But "the voice of the Lord shatters the cedars"; that is to say, he humbles the false boasters, giving the lie to their lies. They commit robbery in the temple, which should no longer be called the temple but a den of thieves. And by the righteous judgment of God, the King of Babylon will come down and lay waste all the temple's treasures.... Thus it came to pass, first through the first Babylon, then through the second Babylon, Rome. The Jews were taken prisoner and all their treasures plundered [194, 113AB].

In the Old Testament, the spirit of Babel was first a living reality in Jerusalem herself: her captivity in Babel was just the consequence and punishment of that. The same thing happens again to the Church in the New Testament, because she has "abandoned her first love". Gerhoh stays close to the ancient prophets (he is totally silent about the gospel). At the same time he takes the wind out of the sails of contemporary heresy by constantly praising poverty, humility, and self-abnegation as the spirit of Christ and thus the true spirit of the Church and by making this lament: "The words of the rich, the mighty, the proud, the perverse overpowered us who are poor, weak, lowly, who have been converted to you, O God, and are ready to return to Jerusalem from the midst of Babylon" (194, 57D). In a subtle allegory he proves that the Euphrates, on whose banks the Jews sat and wept, is really one of the rivers of paradise, which flows through the middle of Babylon, but has meanwhile been poisoned by many foreign waters, so that it "is fit for drinking not so much by the captive citizens of Jerusalem as by those of Babylon" (194, 93AB). For Gerhoh, the warrant for this image of the poisoning of the pure gospel is not just heresy but also the worldly additives of philosophy and poetry and the new dialectical spirit made fashionable by Abelard.

His love and enthusiasm for the Church are genuine. He has no difficulty at all in singing her praises as the pure and immaculate bride. But like Hippolytus, Origen, and Augustine, he sees that she is only true to the spirit of her Head and Bridegroom when she clings to him in unceasing prayer. "The soul of the whole Church . . . becomes a partaker of the divine nature when she clings to what is above her and thus receives the power to govern what is beneath her, namely, the whole body of the Church" (PL 193, 1135). His idea of the Church is as concrete as that of the Fathers: he does not distinguish between the Church's form and the people who make her up. That is why he can go further than Augustine does in his *Enarrationes* and makes the psalms (when it is not expressly Christ who is praying) the prayers of a humiliated, contrite, weeping, penitent Church. "The whole Church training herself in penance" (*Tota Ecclesia semetipsam exercens in poenitentia,* 712A); "I the penitent Church, or I any penitent in the Church" (*ego poenitens Ecclesia vel ego quilibet poenitens in Ecclesia,* 1102B); "I the penitent Church, or I any penitent in the Church, long to be like the penitent Peter" (*huic Petro poenitenti ego poenitens Ecclesia vel ego quilibet poenitens in Ecclesia cupio assimilari,* 1104A); "I the penitent Church, or I the penitent ecclesial person" (*ego poenitens Ecclesia vel ego poenitens ecclesiastica persona,* 1114B; 194, 169); "All the tears of the whole totality of the Church" (*totius universitatis Ecclesiae universales lacrimae,* 1019A); "I, the Church, do not consider myself to be pure, as the Novatianists and Cathars do. I know how many sinners I have within me, and I do not refuse to do penance but say, 'Forgive us our trespasses' " (1135AD).

Gerhoh prays with the Church and her great Tradition of prayer. For him, the Church prays together with all sinners, and all sinners pray in her. In his prayers all the arrogant negations and refusals of the sects are deflated. Gerhoh's spirit lives on in William of Auvergne and Dante, in those in the Church who inherit the Franciscan spirit, in German mysticism and the *Devotio moderna,* in Savonarola,[29] in John Fisher, Erasmus, and Thomas More. It also lives on in *Luther* as the heir not just of sectarian ranting about the Church as the "great Babylon" but also of the old Biblical and patristic theology of the "bride" as a "little whore" (*meretricula*), who in Christ is redeemed from her harlotry through the *admirabile conubium et commercium* — the wonderful nuptial exchange, which Hosea foreshadowed:

> This is how the "nuptials of Christ" are seen as the final resolution of the mystery of the "nuptials of Israel". Ezekiel provides the theological prophecy. . . . Augustine completes the nuptial theology of Origen: "Great and unique is the Bridegroom's condescension: when he found her, she was a whore; he made her a virgin. She must not deny she was a whore, lest she forget the mercy of him who set her free. . . . Yes, he came and made her a virgin" (*Serm.* 213, 7, 7). So it is not just a question, as it is in the Old Testament, of an "eternal marriage" with the murderous, adulterous archwhore, who lies slain in her own blood. No, that "shadow", that "type", is elevated into the "physical reality" of a whore who lusts after false gods and then becomes a "virgin" again. For the nuptials of Christ in the New Testament, this transformation is a unique, constitutive experience, and yet it is ever new, something that is always "here and now" and "today" in the sense of the *memoria* and the *hodie* of the liturgy. Each Good Friday, in the Reproaches, the bride-Church, speaking as the converted Jerusalem, confesses to the murder of the Lord. Then, having gone through the mortal silence of Holy

---

[29] "A few weeks before he died, he gave a lecture to priests and religious on the corruption of the Church. . . . 'Rome', he exclaimed, 'is a second Babel, the seat and center of all vice. . . . Rome is more godless than all other cities and nations, more godless even than the Turks and the heathen; it is polluting the whole Church' " (J. Schnitzer, *Savonarola* II [1924], pp. 708f.).

Saturday, she receives from Christ the Bridegroom the *Exsultet,* the "exultation" of the ever new Easter nuptials. He only fully celebrates his "Resurrection in death", for his bride/Church, because of the mortal nothingness of her guilt, is constantly being resurrected [*E. Przywara, Alter und Neuer Bund* (1956), pp. 281f.].

9. *The Shulamite motif: "I am black but beautiful"*

The self-portrait of the bride in the Song of Songs, with its blithely confessed dialectic, will form our conclusion. Her blackness indicates either her lowly rural origins (she is "sunburnt"; Cant 1:6), which the King humbly accepts, or perhaps it is the sign of some great trial (cf. Job 30:30; Lam 4:8). But her blackness takes nothing from her beauty, which the Bridegroom in his rapture constantly praises. For the Fathers, all the "spots and wrinkles" observed and bewailed in the Church do not for one moment compromise her immaculateness. This is true even of such a severe critic of the concrete condition of the Church as Origen. What makes this position all the more remarkable is that the Fathers never dream of dissecting the Church, à la Journet, into her "formal" and "material" elements, with the formal element (in the sense of the indwelling of God's Spirit through Christ in the sacramental/institutional dimensions of the Church) being essentially invulnerable, while the material element, the people of the Church, belongs to the Church in the sense of being contained and informed by her. For the Fathers, the two elements are absolutely intertwined; the aspects of "grace" and "merit" are not separable even in thought. Unity and holiness are both given and preserved and exercised in faith. The unity of Christians is essentially love, that is to say, responsive bridal fidelity and consent to and under the Bridegroom. And so—here patristic ecclesiology does agree with Journet—the question of membership of the Church really does involve analogy. At the lower limit the man in a state of mortal sin is a member supported, through God's grace, by those who have faith and love, and the ones who really love are, of course, all members in fellowship with one another, supported by Christ but also supporting one another, actively living out the Church's unity of love. For the Fathers, the foundational rock of Peter's faith, secured by Christ's Passion and prayer (cf. Lk 22:32), is inseparable from the eternally assured truth (of doctrine) and love (of life). To the patristic mind, an "infallibility" bestowed only from above without a simultaneous responsive love from below, from the heart of the bride, is quite unthinkable.

At this stage the Church has not yet fully realized that the great symbol and embodiment of this responsive bridal love is the all-sustaining love of Mary. And so other groups of Christians representing sanctity stand alongside her. First and foremost, there are the apostles, whose subjective holiness, for the reason we have just given, is greatly exalted by the Fathers (for example, Origen). Then there are the martyrs, who, through their conformity to the Son of God, who "gave his life for his brethren", participate directly in his holiness. Finally, we have the Doctors, who in their own way are martyrs and confessors: as successors of the prophets, they bear witness to and expound, in the Holy Spirit, the infallible truth. All these form the radiant heart of the "immaculate bride", the Church. Here every *anima ecclesiastica* must abide and adhere.

But the "bride" is always in motion, distant from Christ in sinners, close to Christ in those who have charity, and so, as *Origen* explicitly says (*Hom. 2 in Cant.* 4; Baehr 8, 47), she is always both black and beautiful. The speculations about Rahab and Tamar are relevant to this. The Gentile Church (which, for the Fathers, is the *whole* Church, because they regard the synagogue as totally rejected) is always moving from blackness to beauty in baptism. She, one and the same subject, is (in her temporal origins) black, but (henceforth) beautiful. And however much for this reason she has to "forget" (cf. Ps 45:11) her former cast of mind, she must remain "mindful" of the fact that she has been redeemed by pure grace and raised up from being a whore to being a bride. One cannot imagine patristic ecclesiology without this double tension between "black" and "beautiful" in time as in space.

Both the blackness and the beauty, as both dogmatic and existential notes of the Church, are stressed in some well-known words of *St.*

Ambrose. Here is the light that makes the mystery clear: "How can the Church, made up of defiled people, be undefiled? First, by God's grace, insofar as she has been cleansed of her trespasses; secondly, by ceasing to commit misdeeds, through the quality of not sinning. She is not immaculate from the very beginning, because that is impossible for human nature. It is by God's grace and her own quality, by henceforth sinning no more, that she appears to be immaculate [or rather seems to be one who has always been immaculate, *ut immaculata videatur*]" (*In Luc.* I, 17; CSEL 32, 21). Confirmation in grace is chiefly an attribute of the Church as a whole, as "the company of all the saints" (*coetus omnium sanctorum*), "as if all were one person" (*quasi omnium una persona, Origen, Comm. in Cant.* I; Baehr 8, 90), whereas the constant struggle out of sin's remoteness from God to love's closeness to God is chiefly an attribute of the individual, of us who are still always "stinking in sins and vices" (*in peccatis vitiisque foetemus, Origen, Hom.* I *in Cant.* 3; ibid., 34): we have to be educated by *Ecclesia,* taken by her into herself (ibid., 35, 55). So the Fathers have no difficulty in calling the Church "defiled" with reference to the sinners who belong to her. For *Origen,* the Church, in her members, is respectively either *speciosa* or *turpis* (*Cant.* I, 6; ibid., 36). *St. John Chrysostom* can speak of a "leprous Church" (*Hom.* 44 *in* I *Cor.* 4; PG 33, 379), *St. Augustine* of a "limping Church" (*Serm.* 5, 8; PL 38, 59A). Sinners are glad to be called the dirty feet in the body of Christ (*St. Jerome, Adv. Jov.* 2, 29; PL 23, 326; *St. Caesarius, Serm.* 83, 3; PL 39, 1907; *St. Ambrose, Ep.* 41, 26; PL 16, 1120).

St. Augustine is the only one to introduce a new aspect into this doctrine of the Church. As his reactions to Pelagius grow in strength, the immaculate sanctity of a human person of earth becomes increasingly dubious to him, or rather it becomes an eschatological ideal. With this shift—from an early Christian idealism to a disillusioned realism—two new possibilities come into play. First, one can reduce the Church's immaculateness to that part of her institutional life that is outside the human sphere (in particular, the sacraments); the absolute purity of the bride, composed as she is of human beings, is then explained as an eschatological grandeur, toward which the Church strives. Alternatively, one can preserve the old ideal with subtractions and concessions and treat the immaculateness of the bride as a relative grandeur.

St. Augustine's last word on the subject is this: "The saints themselves are not free of daily sins. The Church as a whole says, 'Forgive us our trespasses!' She thus possesses spots and wrinkles. But through confession the wrinkles are smoothed out, the spots washed away. The Church stands in prayer in order, through confession, to be purified, and as long as men live on earth, that is how she stands" (*Serm.* 181, 5, 7; PL 38, 982). Again in the *Rectractions:*

> Just as the "washing of regeneration" (cf. Titus 3:5) cleanses from the guilt of all sins that human birth has inherited and wickedness has incurred, this perfection cleanses us from the stain of all vices without which human weakness cannot exist in this world. It is in this way, too, that we must understand the words of the Apostle: "Christ loved the Church and gave himself up for her, that he might sanctify her, having cleansed her by the washing of water with the word, that he might present the Church to himself in splendor, not having spot or wrinkle or any such thing" (Eph 5:25–27). For here there is "the washing of water with the word", by which the Church is cleansed. But since the whole Church, as long as she is here, says, "Forgive us our debts", she is certainly not "without spot or wrinkle or any such thing" here. However, it is from what she receives here that she is led to the glory which is not here, and to perfection [*Retr.* I, 7; PL 32, 593].

He reinforces the point again at 1, 19; col. 617; 2, 17, 637–38). Similar words can be found in *St. Jerome* (cf. *In Eph.* 5, 27 [PL 26, 564D–65A] with *In Jer.* 6, 29 [Reiter, p. 413]).

In this Augustinian perspective, toward the end of the patristic age, *St. Peter Chrysologus* once more sees Magdalen/Church resting at the feet of the Lord, just as *St. Hippolytus,* at the beginning, immortalized her in a perpetual gesture of supplication. The latter's great fear is lest the purified Church should fall again from her sinlessness, while the former is motivated by an acute contrition that strives toward the final eschatological purification:

> "And behold", it says, "a woman in the town who was a sinner". . . . It was in this town [of perfidy, *perfidia*] that this woman, that is, the

Church, was bearing up under the depressing guilt that sprang from the heavy silt of so many past sins. . . . Therefore, with welling love she sheds her tears upon the feet of the Lord. . . . She . . . kisses them with praising lips and pours out the whole ointment of mercy . . . until [*donec*] he will come back to her and say, . . . "Your sins, many as they are, are forgiven you, because you have loved much." For the remission of sins will take place then [*tunc*], when all occasion of sin will be taken away, when all the matters conducive to sin will be gone . . . when the "flesh of sin" will become flesh altogether holy, earthly slavery will be exchanged for heavenly domination, and the human army will be raised aloft into the Divine Kingdom [*Serm. 95, de Magd.;* PL 52, 468–69; ET, George E. Ganss, S.J., *The Fathers of the Church,* vol. 17 (New York, 1953), pp. 149–51].

Then there is *St. Isidore of Seville:* "At the end of time, death, the last enemy, will be destroyed, and the one and only house of Rahab, the one and only Church, will be delivered from the destruction of the ungodly, at last pure and free of the shame of fornication through the window of confession in the blood of the remission of sins. Until this happens, as long as the world lasts, she remains as a whore in Jericho" (*Qu. in Vet. Test.;* PL 83, 371B).

Finally, *St. Thomas Aquinas:* "To be a 'glorious Church not having spot or wrinkle' is the ultimate end to which we are brought by the Passion of Christ. Hence this will be in heaven and not on earth, in which, 'if we say we have no sin, we deceive ourselves', as is written [1 Jn 1:8]" (*S Th* 3a, q 8, a 3, ad 2; ET, Fathers of the English Dominican Province, vol. 15 [London, 1924], pp. 141f.).

The other solution (for which Riedlinger supplies numerous texts), which contents itself with a relative immaculateness of the Church, is really just a temporary solution, a meager compromise between the old idealistic ecclesiology and St. Augustine's realistic ecclesiology. The etymology of *pulchra* is given as *gravi ca-rens pul-vere* (*Honorius of Autun, Cant. tr.* 1, 1; PL 172, 372D). The absence of grave sin in the better members of the Church is sufficient justification for the statement. This opinion is superseded, absolutely and dogmatically, from the moment that *St. Bernard* brings Mariology into the foreground and when the bride emerges, in the commentaries on the canticle, as the link and central point between the *Ecclesia* and the *persona ecclesiastica.* A place has now been found where a relative immaculateness depends upon an absolute immaculateness and beauty; this is particularly true when, through late medieval Franciscan theology, the Immaculate Conception becomes widespread. From this point on, the early Christian, pre-Augustinian ecclesiology can be reconciled with Augustine's without compromise. We have three motifs: a bride who is even now absolutely holy (existentially and not just institutionally); a Church that is blemished both now and to the end of time; a bride who is eschatologically pure. These three can exist simultaneously and interdependently. Indeed, they are mutually and fruitfully complementary. It is even possible for Rahab to meet Mary (*Gottfried of Admont, Hom. festiv. 77;* PL 174, 1025):

> Our redemption in Christ was not accomplished until he had died. The same is true of the continuation of the redemption that takes place in the Mystical Body: it will not be finished for the whole body until that body has ceased to live here below, that is, at the end of time; it will not be completed for each member except at the death of each member. Sin will not be suppressed until that comes to pass. As long as this world endures, there is time for sin, since we are in a time of trial. All this goes together.... Sin caused the redeeming death of the Savior; sin will also cause the passion and death of the Mystical Body, in which redemption is at work. In the Savior's death, however, the sin belonged exclusively to others; in the death of the Mystical Body, in the death whereby mankind redeems itself, the sin belongs not to others but to men themselves. Accordingly the two passions must differ. The Passion of the Head was spotless.... The passion of the human race lacks this purity; it conquers.... The law of sin rages malingnantly in all men. And the "body" of Christ is designed for men, for all of them such as they are, to make them better than they are. This objective it accomplishes, in great part, by the quarrels and sorrows men cause one another and themselves, whether unconsciously or voluntarily or, as often happens, in a mixture of unawareness, malice, and good intentions.... Mankind is sinful. It bears the burden of its former crimes and adds to it by its present crimes.... Consequently an

intense desire for justice and love, a longing for a better mankind in a better world, is formed and quickened in it, not without the aid of grace. But the longing is so vague in the obscure and incommunicable depths of conscience, and its manifestations are so incoherent ... [that] we have the tragedy of a blind and raging giant, who turns his own weapons against himself and rends himself to pieces in the night. Such is the humanity that makes up the Church. We are dealing here with a delicate subject that is a source of dismay and scandal. We can readily understand that the Church should have its martyrs and that the innocent may be persecuted or succumb to illness. But that Christ's spouse, whom he has taken to make her holy and spotless, without defilement or blemish of any sort, that Christ's body, which God has chosen from eternity to adorn with the grace of adoption in purity and sanctity, should be a body of sin, that it should be demeaned by pettiness and malice and that its moral miseries should figure so largely, even in its most characteristic activity, seems impossible to concede. But it is so. The holy Mystical Body is a body in which redemption is accomplished and yet not accomplished; in which sin is ever present and active; in which each generation as it rises imparts renewed vigor to sin; in which, finally, sin has its necessary place, a place from which it has to be dislodged, a place in which occur most of the trials that will cast it out, a place in which redemption is at work.

Undoubtedly baptism, which applies the redemption to each individual, completely eliminates from the soul all the sin that was actually in it. But baptism does not dry up the source of sin, as the Council of Trent clearly teaches (D 802–6). The baptized person will have to struggle against the forces enticing him to sin and also against himself, for he will often be his own chief tempter. He simply cannot avoid all sin (D 833), and a terrible possibility will always hover over his life: the possibility of losing his eternity. Similarly, the source of sin remains in the Church militant in general, for what baptism does in the individual, the death of Christ has done for the whole Mystical Body. The Church is made up of sinners; hence her great prayers are the prayers of sinners, "Forgive us our trespasses"; "Holy Mary, Mother of God, pray for us sinners." Sin is in the Church, contagious and ineradicable, like the weeds in the field that are forever obstinately encroaching, and it will not be exterminated until the Church militant herself is no more, on the Last Day, the day of the harvest.

The holiness of the Church is not less real for all that, but it is realistic holiness, the sanctity of the Church militant. The Church is holy by reason of what God has placed and wrought in it, but it is not holy because of what men contribute of their own resources or because of the activity they perform in it so far as that activity proceeds from them alone. Woe to those men who proclaim that they are just and better than their fellows! . . . A profound similarity links the members of the Mystical Body to the most depraved of nonmembers, and those who try to be sincere are quite aware of this fact. But then, if the members of the Mystical Body are sinners, they will have to act as sinners, and, even when they wish to rid themselves of their sins, they will give many an indication, by the very way they rid themselves of their sins, that they are still laden with them. Exception must evidently be made for the actions of the Church that are the actions of Christ, for example, in the administration of the sacraments and the solemn proclamation of dogmas; there we find nothing but holiness. But everywhere else, wherever man acts as man, in all the deeds of even the best of Christians and the most exalted heads of the Church, human frailty and human malice and human traces of human sins frequently and inevitably betray themselves. The very saints do not wholly escape these miseries except at the instant of their full spiritual maturity, when they come to die. We have to believe that grace tends to safeguard the pastors of the Church in proportion to the importance of their acts; but it does not suppress them; that would be to suppress man [Émile Mersch, S.J., *The Theology of the Mystical Body*, ET, Cyril Vollert, S.J. (St. Louis and London, 1951), pp. 305ff.].

THE CHURCH AND ISRAEL

The dissensions that accompany the foundation of anything new are so destructive that the harm they have done seems irreparable. Catholics and Protestants at first used harsh and violent language about one another, until, growing tired, they gave it up. Now they are slowly beginning to look upon the cleavage as unnecessary and tentatively to resume communication—but the harm caused by that strife within Christianity is trifling compared with the dissensions and division brought about by the sword that Christ set up in the midst of his earthly Kingdom, the sword spoken of in the Bible, which pierced his own and his Mother's heart and also the heart of the Jew called to be the apostle of the Gentiles, who confessed to having "such great sadness and continual sorrow in his heart" that he could wish to be anathema to Christ if that would but take away the reproach from his people.

Now, if the dialogue between Jews and Christians, almost though not entirely in abeyance for a thousand years, is to be resumed, one thing is clear: it must be resumed at the very core, the pulsating heart, of the Bible. Furthermore, those who, in fact, completed the cleavage of going further (although, in their own view, guiltless) should suffer more on its account than those who have remained as they were. There is an element of harshness and abruptness in the New Testament situation that no dialogue can mitigate, unless it is to become quite unreal. The passage of two thousand years has not altered this situation by bringing a synthesis nearer, nor can one ever hope to reach agreement beyond the Cross and the Resurrection, as it were, on a purely human level. Nothing can alter the fact that Jesus left the Jews to themselves, that the apostles, after their initial attempt at a dialogue, systematically did likewise. Is his failure with the people of Israel a deficit impossible to repair, a congenital defect, so to speak, of his religion? And a still more searching question: Has not, perhaps, the anti-Jewish front of all the Gospels and the apostolic writings

Translated by A. V. Littledale with Alexander Dru.

been responsible for the frightful anti-Semitism running through the Church's history, which certainly remains a blot on the Church viewed empirically, and also provided Christians in their instinctive hatred with the plausible excuse of theological justification and obedience to the Bible?

We have no qualification, as Christians, to answer these questions; our obligation is to hear God's word and to try to think in obedience to it. All well-intentioned fraternizing between Jews and Christians, all roundtable discussions must, if any result is to accrue, be conducted in the presence of God's word. But this at once tears us apart, since what for us is God's word, the New Testament, and especially Romans 9–11, is not such for the Jews. Let us, however, attempt the only course possible for us Christians. Let us speak to our Jewish brothers through the word of God, through Romans 9–11. We shall find that three fundamental theses emerge.

First: *Israel's obduracy enters incontestably into God's plan of salvation in its historical working characterized by election and reprobation.* Now, this implies three things.

1. Paul's statements belong to the theology of history. They are made from the standpoint of the divine way of acting and so utterly transcend human perspectives of salvation history as well as the plane of human works. God is the author of the problem, and to him alone belongs its resolution. The uncompromising harshness with which they are stated, deliberately intended to wound and scandalize, serves solely to bring home to man his incompetence in the whole matter. Has not God the right to choose and to reject, to have mercy and to harden? You object: Why then does he punish? Paul does not answer the objection but brushes it aside: O man, who art thou that repliest against God? Cannot the potter break up the vessel? Is not the whole Bible, from Moses to Hosea and Isaiah, full of instances of this kind, of the injustice of God? Later, Paul elucidates all that can be elucidated but only to end in praise of the "unsearchable counsels and unfathomable ways" of God. Everything up to the very end remains his plan, his execution, his mystery. Whoever intervenes with good

advice, like Peter, dissuading the Lord from his Passion, is the adversary, Satan, and comes under God's displeasure.

2. The whole point at issue is clearly the obduracy that is the sign of God's rejection. The expressions are heaped up: "blindness", "hardness", "obduracy", "deafness", "snare", "trap", "stumbling", and finally, "rejection". The problem is not whether Israel is to blame for this fate, which St. Paul affirms expressly and incontrovertibly and demonstrates at length: the guilt lies on those who put works in the place of faith, the tangible results of what is fleshly and earthly in the place of being led by the promise and the Spirit. But this is only a sort of parenthesis in St. Paul's train of thought. He shows only incidentally that God's rejection was just, which really did not need to be proved. The one important thing here is that Israel's condition is due to a sovereign act of God, infinitely surpassing anything man might have done to bring it about. Human guilt is certainly present within the all-embracing act of God, but it does not determine this act, and this is shown by the fact that it is embraced by the act of election and reconciliation as by that of reprobation and condemnation. God rejects, *because* man is guilty; he also has mercy, *because* man is guilty. The final, decisive *because* rests with God.

3. This twofold action of God's is clearly concerned with history, secular and salvation history. It is the greatest tragedy in the history of Christian theology that this truth should have been so completely ignored. From the time of Augustine, Paul's statements have been taken out of their context in the history of theology, have been applied to individuals and referred to their eternal salvation or damnation, to heaven and hell. But they are not concerned with this at all. It is true that Paul elucidates the twofold action of God with reference to various personalities representative of the people, to Isaac and Ishmael, Jacob and Esau, Moses and Pharaoh; but are we to conclude that Ishmael, Esau, and Pharaoh are eternally damned? More especially since the idea of eternal hell can be only a New Testament one, which presupposes the elimination of that of the common Hades or Sheol. The theology of predestination that prevailed from St. Augustine throughout the Middle Ages and on to Luther

and Calvin—whether well founded or not—can most certainly not appeal to the great Pauline passage on God's twofold action in salvation history. So far is this from it that, as Karl Barth so convincingly shows in his *Church Dogmatics,* even the New Testament statements on individual reprobation and election should be read in the light of these social statements on world history and salvation history and not vice versa. But we are not for the moment concerned with this, only with the fact that God's total and indivisible, if two-sided, action upon mankind is concerned with its salvation, expressing in both aspects the divine economy of salvation.

Second: *The reprobation of Israel serves to the election of the Gentiles, who, as the elect, are the spiritual Israel and have their lasting roots fixed in the old Israel.* Using this theodicy of history, Paul illuminates the mystery of the dual nature of God's action without thereby depriving it of its character, its mystery, or making it comprehensible, after the manner of Hegel, in terms of a philosophy of history. Once more, three things are implied:

1. Israel's reprobation serves to the election of the Gentiles: this statement is made with the utmost clarity. Certainly, Israel is not to blame for not having believed in God. It is not this, however, that affects the Gentiles but solely the interim state of blindness to which God has destined Israel in her guilt, a state that allows those formerly blind to see, those formerly deaf to hear the word proclaimed. Never are the elect granted any sort of right over those blinded, no spiritual right either to lord it over them in their humiliation, no right to mockery, revenge, persecution, anti-Semitism. The shadow cast over Israel by God comes from God. It is the shadow of God himself, given solely as a mirror for those entered into the light, to make them realize the darkness from which they themselves came and into which they fall back if they "puff themselves up"; to show them that they must ascribe their election solely to grace; and, finally, to illustrate the indissoluble union and destiny binding those in darkness and those in the light. Indeed, St. Paul goes so far as to say that the Gentiles owe their "engrafting" to the fact of the Jews being

"cut off", and so to God's action on them, not to their own sinful action, their self-blinding, which is, indeed, included in the former. This brings those rejected and cut off into a unique relationship to the Messiah, who for the world's redemption was "made sin" by God: as we Christians cannot look on him without seeing the wounds caused by our sins— since, innocent, he bore them for us—so guilty Israel, according to Paul, suffers for the world's redemption, and in the burden laid on Israel that assumed by us is clearly incorporated. And so anyone who strikes Israel strikes the Messiah, who, as God's suffering Servant, gathers up in himself all the afflictions of God's servant Israel.

2. The election, however, that for a time is taken away from Israel in order that the Gentiles may be incorporated is the same as the old, unique election of mankind in Abraham, Isaac, and Jacob, into which the universality of peoples is now incorporated. Here the Jews and Gentiles can be seen as inextricably intertwined, in so subtle a way as to suggest God's direct leading. Where Israel is concerned, this means that it was, from the outset, a function of the final election of the Gentiles—so much so, in fact, that it was not the fleshly Israel that came first in God's plan, in order to be the promise of a subsequent spiritual Israel, but, as Paul shows in detail, the fleshly Israel, which was, from the first, based upon the spiritual. Fleshly generation is the work of man, but Isaac's generation was itself a function of the spiritual promise of God to a sterile couple and of Abraham's spiritual faith in that promise. This recurring doctrine of Paul occurs here significantly. The same is true, later, of the birth of the twin brothers, where the natural order is reversed—and equally throughout the whole destiny of the people, of which only a remnant attains the promise, while the greater part comes to grief in the desert, in exile and diaspora. Their collapse is the collapse of the fleshly Israel: the remnant is the distillation and quintessence of the spiritual Israel, which was intended from the very beginning. From this it follows that the dialectic of election and reprobation did not take place only between synagogue and Church but was present already within Judaism and the law: the Church of the Gentiles only participates

therein as fulfilling it and, henceforth, as the spiritual Israel, forming a single figure together.

This must, therefore, also be considered in relation to the Church, for if the universal Church is the fulfillment of the promise made to Abraham, she is, in fact, to use Paul's image, grafted onto the olive tree, whose own branches lie beside it, cut off in order that the wild branches may be inserted. "If some of the branches be broken, and you, being a wild olive, are engrafted in them and made partaker of the root and sap of the olive tree, boast not against the branches. But if you boast, consider: you do not bear the root, but the root bears you." What is striking about this crucial passage is that it makes no mention of Christ, who is on every other occasion described as the foundation, the vine from which the branches flourish and are fruitful. Where is Christ to be found in this image, which only illustrates the relation between promise and fulfillment, Israel and the Church? On both sides, certainly. He is the true fulfillment, the rod from the root of Jesse; and although he was before Abraham came to be, and Abraham for his sake obtained the promise, he is still the true seed of Abraham, the prophet foretold by Moses, the true son of David, the true servant of God described by Isaiah, the true flesh and blood of his Jewish Mother Mary. According to the flesh, he is an Israelite, which means that he is also the flower and fruit of the entire Israelite faith, hope, love, prayer, and suffering. Jesus is at once a Jew and Son of the Father: he has his enduring roots both in Abraham and in heaven. And the Church that issues from Jesus' life and death, being rooted in him, must likewise have its roots in both.

3. Paul adds two further qualifications: he says that what is still visible of Israel, side by side with the Church, consists of severed branches. And yet the Church is grafted onto not a dead but a living root, from which she draws the sap that he describes as "holy". "If the root is holy, so also are the branches." Consequently, there is something present in the Church of the Gentiles—and this is the crux of the matter—something that is older than herself, in virtue of which she is what she is. This is the ancient, *irrevocable* promise of God to his people. From this, it necessarily follows that if the Jewish promise,

transcended so as to refer to the salvation of the whole world and giving the people a representative character in the process of redemption, if this promise, fulfilled in Christ's sacrifice made in his representative capacity, is present as a living and holy root in and under the Church, then it is evident that the Church, too, participates in the sap of the root, that is to say, in the redemptive destiny of holy Israel in its representative character, the destiny fulfilled in Jesus Christ. The Church, in other words, in spite of her character as light and fulfillment, still shares in the Judaic and messianic destiny of suffering in her role of representative and bears a promise that carries her beyond herself, which can only be fulfilled at the end of time. It must be realized that this does not mean that Israel's promise lives on elsewhere than in the Church of Christ. Nor is it said that Israel has, theologically speaking, a historical mission to fulfill in mankind, different from that of the Church, as is constantly alleged. Hypotheses of this sort, whether proposed by Jewish thinkers, by Judeo-Christian historical theologians, or by Christians like Soloviev (in his celebrated essay *Das Judentum und die christliche Frage*) or Léon Bloy (in *Le Salut par les Juifs*), have a millennialist character: they transfer what belongs to eschatology into the historical future, thus making it a matter of historical progress. This distortion is indeed the one remaining chance open to Jewish ideology, with whose Communist or liberal stamp we are familiar. The idea of progress can perhaps be buttressed by a theology of creation, but there is no room for it in a history of grace and salvation understood in a Christian sense. Yet, in spite of all, Israel's promise is not dead. It lives on to the very end, to the moment when the holy root bursts forth, blossoms and bears fruit, in the spiritual Israel of the greatest of the sons of Abraham. The two destinies, then, lie not alongside but within one another, corresponding to the one, sole promise and fulfillment.

Third: *Israel's rejection, as a factor of salvation history, points to an eschatological salvation common to it and the Church, in which rejection and election are brought into equilibrium.* The intertwining of the two destinies is carried through by Paul to its ultimate consequence.

1. Insofar as Israel's hope has been realized in Jesus Christ, present though hidden in the Church, it has been objectively fulfilled, and for Israel too. But insofar as Israel, for the time being, has been deprived of the perception of this fulfillment (Mt 23:38–39; 2 Cor 3:15; Rom 11:10) and yet cannot cease to hope in the promise without ceasing to exist, its hope must be the same as that of the Church. Because the Church hopes for the return of Christ, who will make the reconciliation of the world by the Cross, hitherto hidden, into its manifest redemption in glory, Israel's expectation of salvation is justified both objectively and subjectively, and the sufferings she endures for her own and the world's redemption are to be seen in the same light as this hope, insofar as it is present. Peter, in his sermon in the temple, expressly acknowledged the rightfulness of this hope of the Jews, excusing them on the ground of ignorance for the death of the Messiah, a death that served for the world's redemption. "Repent therefore, and turn again, that your sins may be blotted out, that times of refreshing may come from the presence of the Lord, and that he may send the Christ appointed for you, Jesus, whom heaven must receive until the time for establishing all that God spoke by the mouth of his holy prophets from of old" (Acts 3:19–21). Paul speaks to the same effect, and with the same unrestricted generality, in regard to the salvation of the chosen people: "And so all Israel should be saved, as it is written: there shall come out of Zion he that shall deliver and shall turn away ungodliness from Jacob. And this is to them my Covenant, when I shall take away their sins."

It is no concern of Christians to distinguish in Israel's attitude what is deliberate persistence in defiance and what is a survival and continuance of genuine hope. Their task is, rather, to draw Israel's hope in the darkness into the Christian hope in the light, aware of their responsibility to bear the light on behalf of those in the dark but also, remembering Paul's warning, in fear of the light, which knows itself to be borne by the darkness (for roots are always in darkness).

2. The destiny of each grows alike in their long waiting for the full and final redemption and produces a sort of harsh symmetry: "As you also in times past did not believe God but now have obtained mercy

through their unbelief, so these also now have not believed for your mercy, that they also may obtain mercy." For the Jews, first light, then darkness; for the Christians, first darkness, then light; their roles unchangeable in the economy of salvation in time and yet, seen from the pinnacle of God's eternity, symmetrical and balanced and transcending whatever "jealousy" is occasioned, indeed intended, by the one-sidedness of election: "God has included all in unbelief, that he may have mercy on all." Their mutual jealousy over election evaporates in the prison common to all, and finally even the legitimate antinomies are dissolved — antinomies independent of any human antipathy or hatred — and rooted in the true functions pertaining to their respective missions, which allow of no reconciliation of differences on the purely human level, such as the liberal Jews would like. Honor is thus accorded to what is merely human and, still more, to the religious and theological zeal of Jews and Christian alike. But over and above all, sole honor to the one Redeemer of both: "Who is it that has first given unto him, that he must be repaid? For of him, and through him, and unto him are all things: to him be the glory for ever. Amen."

3. The sap of the living root of Jesse ascends through Jesus Christ out of the Old Covenant unto the New. God allowed the sap of grace and wisdom to mature and condense in the Old Covenant for a thousand years, manifesting the process for all times in the sacred Jewish books. If Christ is the transcendent synthesis of the whole, we still need to gaze, again and again, on the parts, if we are not to misunderstand the power of the whole. Whenever the Church forgets the power, the drive, the *kabôd*, the tremendous prophetic insistence of the Old Covenant, if only for an instant, she falls at once from the height she occupies, her salt becomes tasteless, her image of Christ begins to resemble the Christ of the pre-Raphaelites. Even when she pays exclusive attention to Paul and neglects James, the Jew, with his philosophically stringent demands for the practice of love in the secular sphere and for changes in the social structure, his tirades against the rich, his religion of actions and works, the Jewish element that, in fact, pervades all the Gospels, the Church is no longer universal and catholic. No doubt, there is a permanent Jewish demand

on Christendom, which is no other than the enduring demand of the Old Covenant on the New.

As a result of Biblical research, we Christians of today know better than past generations that the Bible is not a book fallen from heaven, mechanically inspired, but that its inspiration developed and came to completion in the heart of the Israel that fought, prayed, and suffered untold pain. We can no longer subscribe to the view of the Fathers, who so strongly felt the transition to the Church as a change in the legitimate ownership of the sacred books. When she received Israel's noblest legacy, the Church obtained not just vegetative sap from the root but also human sap, the lifeblood of Israel, mingled with her high consciousness of mission and the dark depths of sufferings that this mission entailed. Ultimately, they are two chambers of the one heart that beats, which indeed beats on the cross of the world, where the dividing wall was broken down and all hate was overcome in the flesh of the suffering Christ, so that in his person, the two are made one, in the single new man who is our peace (Eph 2:14–15).

Year by year, the Church prays on Holy Saturday:

O God, we see your wondrous works of old enlighten even our own day. For the salvation that you bestowed by the power of your right hand upon one nation, as you rescued them from the Egyptian persecution, is not conferred upon all nations by means of the water of regeneration. Grant that the peoples of the whole world may become the descendants of Abraham and share the prerogative of Israel. Through Jesus Christ.

PART TWO

CHARIS AND CHARISMA

The promise of Jesus and its fulfillment in the Acts of the Apostles show us the Church, which has become alive at Pentecost, as being the work and the dwelling place of the Third Divine Person, the Holy Spirit. The Church is his temple as a whole (1 Cor 3:16) and also in each individual member who is expropriated of himself in favor of the Spirit (1 Cor 6:19; Eph 2:22). But in the new, grace-filled *analogia personalitatis,* the infinite and the finite subjects do not simply remain alongside each other; they live in a "fluidity" flowing into one another, something for which there is no further example on earth; the Christian is "drenched" with the Holy Spirit (1 Cor 12:13), a text that points to the relationship of the Spirit both to the water of baptism and [at the relationship of the Spirit] to the flowing Blood of the Eucharist. Note, for instance, the image of the love that is poured out in souls through the Holy Spirit (Rom 5:5), or the image of the flowing mutual union in the act of marriage as the explanation of what it is to "become one spirit" when one adheres to the Lord (1 Cor 6:17), or "being dipped into" the Spirit as into water (Jn 3:5): here the water, together with fire and air, clearly forms the closest metaphor for the qualities of the Spirit, "subtle, mobile, penetrating ... all spirits and streaming through them, more in motion than any motion" (Wis 7:22–24). In this analogy, the Christian is completely indwelt by the Holy Spirit, whose praying and sighing completely fill him and pass through him (Rom 8:26f.); he is driven by the Spirit (Rom 8:14); he is instructed by the Spirit; indeed, he receives the direct testimony from him (Rom 8:16; 1 Jn 5:9f.). For this reason, the Christian is quite fundamentally "a man of the Spirit", a "pneumatic [person]" (Gal 6:1), "one conforming to the Spirit" (*ho kata pneuma;* Rom 8:5)—provided that he gives place to the Spirit in himself and permits him to have the upper hand over what is fleshly and egotistic, provided that he thus is a *teleios,* a fully grown Christian person who has matured to the "experience of the Spirit" and bears the fruits of the

Translated by Fr. Brian McNeil, C.R.V.

Spirit (Gal 5:22f.), having attained to the gnosis of what "God has revealed to us through his Spirit" (I Cor 2:10; cf. Eph 1:17–18). Seen from the perspective of the Spirit, this revelation is universal: "You have the anointing from the Holy One, and you know everything . . . and you need no further instruction" (I Jn 2:20, 27), for "the Spirit will lead you into all the truth" (Jn 16:13).

The Church of Christ, together with the existence of the believer in her, is decisively marked by this fact, that nothing can surpass the presence of the Spirit, which is absolute "fullness", "fulfillment", and in this sense is the presence of eternity or (what amounts to the same thing) the eschaton. While this certainly possesses on the one side qualities that are analogous to an earthly and historical process of spiritualization—a certain "removal" of the barriers and narrownesses of the factual reality of time and space into the medium of a universal act of understanding, which makes for interiorization—at the same time, it has quite other qualities, apparently the opposite of these, which come from the fact that the Holy Spirit of God is the *concretissimum* and not in the least an "abstract" medium, the *personalissimum* and not in the least a mere "objective" spirit, the one who is most free even in the manner of choice and decision and not in the least the mere place where one is freed from the narrowness of the historical dimension. Yet, once again, this second range of qualities does not remove the first, as one can see in the orientation of the entire dispensation of salvation from promise to fulfillment, from type and anticipatory image to truth, a process that has already its prefiguring within the Old Covenant (in the way in which the latest period can carry out the illuminating reflection on the past generation of the historical facts by means of a particular presence of the Spirit as inspiration, no longer to carry out the tasks of judges and prophets but to understand, interpret, and write down) but that can truly take place and come to completion only when Jesus, after his death and Resurrection, distributes the fullness of the messianic Spirit.

The incomparable quality whereby the Holy Spirit is at once both that which is most universal and that which is most concrete gives grace in the New Testament the quality of being at once the "universal" grace of the Mystical Body of Christ—grace that takes the individual out of his limitation and incorporates him in the circulation of life of the highest divine-human life—and "particular", extremely personal grace as the elevating and perfecting through the Holy Spirit precisely of that concrete uniqueness and quality of being in the image of God that belongs to the created spiritual subject. Otherwise, the believer would enter not the eschatological fullness but at best a spiritual communism that would represent without fail a danger to his personal gifts. If only the former were grace, it could be described as a general ontic determination of the finite subject, perhaps in such a general way that it would not in the least be necessary for him personally to be aware of this *elevatio* and *participatio naturae divinae,* this elevation to the divine nature and participation in it; the Church herself and incorporation in this would then be simply "objective Spirit". But since this possibility is excluded, thanks to the personal nature of the Holy Spirit, a personal *experience* of faith (as the New Testament bears witness from start to finish) corresponds absolutely to the "faith of the Church" when this is lived genuinely, just as there corresponds to the universal grace a particular determination that has precisely this human person in view and marks him out in a unique manner: as election before time began, as the vocation and the justification of precisely this sinner, as a particular sanctification in the context of the Church for the task and mission that belong to him and to no one else.

The (universal) *charis* is also necessarily at the same time a (particular) *charisma.* "Each one has his own *charisma,* one of one kind and another of another kind" (1 Cor 7:7). "To each one of us is grace bestowed according to the measure [*metron*] with which Christ has distributed it" (Eph 4:7; cf. 4:16: *en metrô(i) henos hekastou*). "Each one according to the measure [*metron*] of the faith that God has allotted to him" (Rom 12:3). The universal, catholic *pistis* appears in this last text precisely as given always an individual form in the essences of the particular missions and commissions, but immediately after this, Paul has the *charisma* pass over again into the universal *charis,* by adding, "But each is equipped with different *charismata,* each according to the *charis* that has been given to us: if it is prophecy, then we are to make use of it according to the analogy of *pistis*" (12:6). However this "analogy" is to be interpreted—whether it refers to the universal faith of the Church or (better, in this context) to the personal faith of the individual as having a share in this[1]—here one can and must speak of a *distinctio realis* between *charis* and *charisma* within the one total reality of the redeemed existence, and this distinction is, at its core, an analogy; indeed, it is the innermost point of the *analogia entis,* the innermost point of created being when it has attained its determination and shares in the eternal being within the Godhead. The *charisma* declares that the age of the Holy Spirit is not universal in such a manner that it would not encompass also the fulfillment of everything that belonged to the events of history: precisely the age of the Holy Spirit brings the fulfillment of the historical commission (such as was possessed by Moses and the judges and kings), the prophetic commission (as this came directly from the Holy Spirit to the individual personalities who were called), and the commission of inspiration (which communicated likewise a direct insight and understanding of the depths of God and of his historical revelation). Indeed, it comes to be seen that what was "historical" in an earthly sense in the people of old—an isolated, occasional fact that occurred seldom—has become a thoroughgoing vocation of the believer in the new people because of the universal presence of the Spirit, since it is no longer individuals who are priests and kings in the new people but everyone (1 Pet 2:9; Rev 1:6), and this is precisely because these two terms are no longer a merely "general" vocation of the people as such (as in the Old Covenant: Ex 19:6) but the gift of a participation in the one and unique and eternal Priest and King, Christ.

The more deeply one attempts to grasp the unity of the universal and the particular, as this has been sketched briefly here, the more sublime does the mystery become. This has initial analogies in the natural realm, for example, in the way in which a great personality who sets his mark on history—e.g., Shakespeare—can determine the universal spirit of his people by stamping it with his own utterly personal and already somehow suprapersonal spirit, but these initial analogies converge on a constantly receding point that is unattainable

---

[1] Cf. Kittel, art. *analogia, Theologisches Wörterbuch zum NT,* 1, 350f.

for men and is attained only in the Holy Spirit and in his work of fulfillment.

One must first consider to the end the line of the "removal of what divided" in Christ, the bearer of the Spirit: "removal" of the dividing walls of sin but then immediately, on a deeper level, also the removal of the barriers of vocation set by God between Jews and Gentiles in the period of the history of salvation that stood under sin (Eph 2:13–18) and the removal of the barriers within the Jewish people between chosen priests and those who were not chosen. But there is also the removal of the barriers set up in nature itself that oppose the different beings one to another: barriers of culture (educated and uneducated), of social position (slaves and free), and of the sexes (man and woman) (Col 3:11). This removal is due to the unique work of Jesus Christ carried out vicariously for all: in love, he has gathered together all the differences and changed what was negative—service, receptivity, suffering, loss, poverty, abandonment by God—into the expression of what is most sublimely positive and so has relativized all the differences "in himself" (Eph 2:15). This is indicated by the interpretation given of the Church by going back into the origins *before* all differentiation: to Abraham, the father of all believing Jews and Gentiles (before the edict concerning circumcision and the law: Rom 4); to Noah, in whom God made an eternal Covenant, not only with one single people but with every created being (Gen 9:16–17, where the prefiguration is surpassed in Christ, who brings redemption even to those who refused to believe at the time of Noah: 1 Pet 3:18f.); and ultimately to Adam and to his universal position as the source and midpoint of the entire human race (Rom 5; 1 Cor 15). But when the origin is recovered, it is not reestablished in the sense of a mere *restitutio in integrum* of paradise; rather, it is absolutely superseded, because the second Adam comes from heaven, and the Church that he founds looks ahead to the Jerusalem that descends to earth.

The midpoint of this whole event remains the integration of all individual values in the person and the life work of Jesus Christ, in whom initially all differentiation is leveled out—until only he, the only image of the Father (2 Cor 4:4), is left—so that it can then unfold anew from him and in accordance with *his* Spirit. The only continuity that exists from the Old Covenant to the New is the one that passes through this "bottleneck" of the unity of Christ. That which is old, the work of the Father, is affirmed anew by Christ and by the meaning that he gives: man and woman affirmed by the mystery of Christ and the Church, Christ and Mary (Eph 5), slave and free (1 Cor 7:21) from Christ's humiliation and acceptance of the status of a slave (Phil 2:7; 2 Cor 8:9). There is thus also no direct communication between the "hierarchical" priesthood of the Old Testament and the New other than in Christ, in whom, as we have seen, it is initially the general kingly priesthood of the new people that is instituted. But since this is in him, there is no room for any "democratic" interpretation of this universal priesthood; just as it has the character of what is universal at its root, so it has also the character of the gift bestowed in each individual case by Christ, i.e., of the *charisma* (in the all-embracing sense of 2 Tim 1:6; cf. 1 Cor 12:28), and this guarantees both the direct relationship to Christ of the new "hierarchical" offices and an ultimate harmony of all the charisms—both the hierarchical charisms of office and the others that are given to the laity—in the one, inscrutably free power that the Head has to distribute them to the members (1 Cor 12:5; Eph 4:11f.), the power that the Holy Spirit has to distribute them to all the "charismatics" (1 Cor 12:11). In this sense—and in this sense alone—all graces, including the hierarchical graces, derive from the single womb of the one kingly and prophetic priesthood of Jesus Christ, where no more differentiation is possible; from this source proceed all the charisms, in all their differentiations, as the univocal "sanctifying" ecclesial grace of the universal kingly and prophetic priesthood of the believers.

So true is this, that it is also the final confirmation of a mystery of the creation, to which G. Siewerth has pointed in a decisive manner: on the one hand, it is not possible to interpret the created beings as "limitations" or unfoldings of the one act of being that could somehow be arrived at by means of speculation: they arise from the abyss of the divine freedom in a direct manner, and it is in this way and not otherwise that this freedom wishes to be imitated; it maintains a unique relationship, proper to the divine uniqueness, to each individual form. But on the other hand, it is not possible to pour and subdivide the act of being into the created beings: rather, it retains its transcendence over against these, and this is also the basis of the real ontological difference. The fact that *charis* and *charisma* can be differentiated from one another yet not separated from one another ultimately points us to this dimension.[2] No matter how uncomfortable it is to make this point for the organizing systematics of philosophy and of the Church, it cannot be avoided. The relationship between God, as the absolute Origin of all bestowal of grace and all vocation, and the particular individual in each case who receives grace and calling can never be revealed in its entirety in the Church, and even what the Church is permitted to learn of this is revealed to her only thanks to that act of humble but utterly free spontaneity in which the believer, imitating the Christ who was brought low, allows himself to become transparent before the representative of Christ. The same thing is made clear once again in the dialectic of the personal conscience, which remains in all circumstances (even in the case of an error) the *norma proxima* of conduct and must at the same time submit and accommodate itself to the *norma remota* of the truth that is proclaimed by the Church. This is the dialectic—which emerges much less clearly in the case of the average sinner (who always has something about the Church to criticize) than in the case of the saint—between ecclesial obedience and personal mission, which can lead to the most dramatic, apparently insoluble inner conflict that is the total dilemma of Catholic existence, from which there is no way out and yet which ultimately— by passing through the Cross—*can* become, and demonstrably often enough has become, the resurrection both of the ecclesial disposition and of the personal mission. Naturally, these situations involve exposure to risk and (seen from an earthly point of view) even despair, because this is an extremely subtle equilibrium that can of course also become delicate and tragically distorted when it is seen in the context of the standpoint of the visible Church; the accompanying Provi-

[2] From this point, it is possible to show the obviousness of the statement of theologians (naturally, within its limited validity) that one who commits mortal sin does not necessarily lose his charism. If *charisma* cries and shouts out inherently for *charis,* then the Christian *commission* has such power even over one who resists and denies that its persistence not seldom brings him back to grace.

dence and the especial protection of the divine grace do not contain any ready-made guarantee here of a "happy end" in the ecclesiological sense but rather require (as always) a genuine personal obedience not only on the part of the individual who receives the mission (this is more than obvious) but also on the part of the representatives of the Church, who have the duty to see to what is right here. And yet these situations, time and again, are the situations that are decisive for the whole of the Church's life. The fundamental condition for such an obedience also on the part of the member of the hierarchy is the acknowledgment that the *charisma* is present, not only in exceptional cases but also normally in the living, believing Christian, and all the more certainly and effectively the more love he puts into living his faith. It is only on the basis of these individual commissions, which are received directly from the Head (Eph 4:11), that the Church's life is built up as the *ramification* of the fullness of Christ in his Mystical Body; but this is necessary, because the Church is a true image of the flowing eternal life of God only when this ramification takes place, not exclusively out from unity by means of the gifts bestowed by the hierarchy but "*toward* unity", "*toward* the full-grown man", "*toward* the mature measure of the fullness" (Eph 4:13) through the "work of service" of all the members, the "performing of the truth in love" by the whole of the holy *laos* and thus of all the laity, "growing in all things *toward* Christ who is the Head" (Eph 4:14–15).

After all that has been said up to this point, and especially after the last text that has been quoted from Ephesians, it will be understood that it is not possible to separate exactly office and charism, although it is fully necessary to make a distinction up to a certain point. For the offices listed at Ephesians 4:11, "apostles, prophets, evangelists, pastors, and teachers", belong to the ramification of the unity (out of the freedom of Christ, who is the one who sends), but with the precisely indicated aim of "building up the saints for the exercise of their *diakonia,* so that the body of Christ may be built up". It follows that the works of service or "charisms" of the laity belong to the subsequent reintegration of the fullness into the unity that now is also possessed subjectively; the "offices" go forth, while the charisms return.

But one should note that among these offices there stands, built firmly into the whole (by means of the parallel texts Eph 2:20; 3:5; 4:11), prophecy on the part of the layman too, which is an essential part of the proclamation of the gospel and may not be excluded under any circumstances from the service of worship (I Cor 14; cf. I Th 5:20), because it is an aspect of the "dwelling of the fullness of the word of Christ" among the believers (Col 3:16). But then there is nothing to be surprised at when I Corinthians 12:28f. links the "charisms" without any observable break in continuity to the offices, although this of course is done more from the point of view of the official quality, of the commission, of the mission for the sake of the body as a whole, in keeping with Paul's intention in this part of the letter, whereas in Romans 12 the whole list slips over onto the side of the charisms, of the return to unity through "praxis" (12:4). Here the differentiation of the charism (12:6–8) can pass over, without any observable boundary, into the general principles of the Church's ethics (12:9–21), something that once again shows clearly that the especial element of the individual charism in each case is always formed from the matter that is common to the whole Church; one can call this *the especial form of what is general*,[3] although this (as has been established already) does not mean that it would be possible to deduce the especial from the general. The Church herself cannot produce the charisms in keeping with her genuine or supposed needs. She cannot herself produce or "order" from God the necessary commissions and the saints that she needs. She must open up her prayer and allow God to give her all this.

The spectrum of the charisms can go from the sublimest "miracles" and utterly extraordinary things, as Paul emphasizes in I Corinthians 12 and 14, to the least noticeable, apparently quite "natural" fulfillments of one's task and services. But "whatever has been bestowed for service (calling) in the Church always bears in itself the nature of a gift of grace, even if this is true to many various degrees, even when an apparently natural talent and a natural inclinate is given the

---

[3] Cf. "Toward a Theology of the Secular Institute", below, pp. 421–57.

occasion to employ its power for the sake of the Lord and of the Church".[4]

One can say that a living *sensus Ecclesiae* is always an understanding of the mysterious analogy between *charis* and *charisma,* for the fact that the especial cannot be deduced from the general and for the portrayal of the traits of the existence of the general in each individual. Naturally, if one is to hold on to this analogy of grace and contemplate it, one needs a free and fearless spirit that does not tremble for the Church's unity, and still less for the prerogatives of the hierarchical offices, with every wind that blows. One needs a broad spirit that is able to throw a bridge in itself over the tension that is at issue here between the particularity of the ("charismatic") privilege and the universality of the grace that is displayed by the one who receives the privilege—coming from the unity and making for the unity—for the sake of the generality. This is the only way to justify Mariology and the doctrine about Peter within Catholicism. No matter how exceptional the privileges of Mary and Peter (and in a broader sense, of all who have received privileges) may appear, privileges that are not to be traced back to any human source, they are nevertheless only portrayals of general characteristics of the Church, since the Church is the one bride of Christ, virgin and mother, conceived immaculate, called in grace to share in the work of redemption, and taken up bodily in grace to share in the transfiguration of heaven. In their broadest sense, the "charisms" of Mary set forth the essence of what the Church is. Peter's (negative) infallibility and (positive) gift of teaching and being shepherd make visible the indefectibility of faith in Christ and of the deeply "knowing" "instinct" of following him (Jn 10:4–5, 8, 14–15), which belongs to the Church as a whole and has its home in the *sensus fidelium.* The same is naturally true of the sacraments too, since their particularities cannot be anything other than creative concretizations, instituted by God and bestowed out of his freedom, of the universal grace that, precisely for this reason, must possess their "spiritual truth" in each individual Christian's "behavior

---

[4] V. Loch and W. Reischl, *Die heiligen Schriften des Alten und Neuen Testamentes,* vol. 5 (1885), pp. 61f., on Rom 12:6.

in love". The Fathers of the Church had an especially keen awareness of this, precisely in their intrepid thinking. They were able to speak so boldly of the *sensus spiritualis* of the Eucharist precisely because, for them, this "spiritual sense" in no way threatened the "sacramental sense" or even merely competed with this (as, for example, in the periods of the Reformation and Counter-Reformation); rather, each presupposed the other; each supported and shed light on the other. We have true communion with the Head only when we love our fellowmen, i.e., when we have communion with each other as members; this, however, is not to be understood in a flat "moral" sense but is to be understood in a "mystic", "real", quasisacramental sense, thanks to the gift of self made by the Head and to the re-presentation of this in the Eucharist. There exist an analogy and a circumincession between the sacramental sense and the spiritual sense, permitting us to gauge the force and extent of the general priesthood of the laity. The same holds true for confession and absolution. What one must see, and what insightful theology too has always seen, is that texts such as Matthew 18:18 and John 20:22f. have a double sense, such that both elements emerge at the same time and inseparably: both the particular hierarchical and sacramental sense *and* the general, lay sense—which is, however, not thereby diminished, rendered colorless, or weakened. So true is this that the context of Matthew 18 demonstrates almost the converse: here the spontaneous act of forgiving in love and of remitting guilt has the absolute priority over the ecclesiastical tribunal of confession, which here stands almost as the instance that one should have recourse to only in the most extreme emergency. If this is not necessary, if everything is absolved in the forgiving love between the members of Christ, this is clearly much better. The particular character of this sacrament is thus marked also by a negativity that lies in sin; this is not true of the Church's forgiving love, and it cannot be true in the same sense of the sacrament of the Body and Blood of the Lord.

In the sacraments of ordination (and in other consecrations of life such as monastic profession and the consecration of virgins), the personal element is linked in a new way to the ecclesiastical-sacramental grace. This is expressed when a candidate is admitted to the seminary or to the novitiate of an order, and in a certain manner also when a bridal pair is admitted to a church marriage in the presence of the representative of the Church: this does not constitute a denial of the element of the personal vocation of the candidate through God's free grace or the freedom of the marriage partners in their choice of one another and the force of law inherent in the assent that they give to one another. The oscillating relationship between *charis* and *charisma* emerges obviously here. If one wishes to construct a theory of the priestly vocation, it will not be possible to agree either on a purely subjective-charismatic hypothesis or on a purely ecclesial-objective hypothesis: rather, it is necessary to take into account the *distinctio realis* that wholly governs the undivided act of God's grace. The bishop can choose his candidates, but he cannot do this without himself obeying the unfathomable law of the calls that come from God. In the same way, the candidate must obey his superior, but this is because his own, inalienable inner "holy call" (2 Tim 1:9) directs him to the Church and to obedience to the Church—directs him indeed with such force that it is precisely through the "laying on of my hands" that the "*charisma* of God" dwells in the one who is ordained and is awakened to a new glow even as *charisma* (*anazôpurein to charisma;* 2 Tim 1:6) through renewed reflection on the sacramental grace.

The same is true, to a stronger degree, of the totally charismatic process of a vocation and a decision to imitate Christ by "leaving all" and "laying hold of" virginity. Once again, and to a greater extent, this decision, which is the gift of God's grace, permits the deepest, mysterious foundations of the Church herself to appear as in a flash of lightning: *she* is poor, the virgin, obedient, and the individual wishes to be this too out of love for her; just as the Church (in Mary and in all the saints) is this vicariously for all, the individual in his turn who is called wishes to be this vicariously for her and for all who are in her. The Church Fathers have always emphasized that the life of the evangelical counsels, which emerges as a particular charismatic class of persons, was the general form of life at the beginning of the Church (Acts 4:32f.).[5]

In conclusion, it is clear from the entire structure that has been

[5] E. von Severus, "Das Monasterium als Kirche", *Enkainia* (1956): 230f.

sketched here that even if everything that is "charismatic" is linked to the character of the individual as a member of the body and thus underlines the individual's service in the community, the particular grace that has been communicated to him may not for this reason be "reduced to a service" and in this way "turned into a thing", since it must also be seen as something that exists for its own sake, to such an extent is it—as the expression of the universal being of the Church— the unique favor bestowed on him by the God of grace. It is true that the organ of the body serves the body as a whole; but at the same time it is an unfolding of the fullness of the body, a unique form and beauty, which does not disappear even when it is referred back to the unity in the return to the totality but is absolutely preserved in the "full-grown form of the mature man". From this point of view, indeed, the "office" appears in the Letter to the Ephesians as something much more at the service of something else than is the *"charisma"*, since it is the whole essence of the office that it should aim at awakening and building up the services rendered by the individual members of the body, since it is not a passivity on the part of the laity that corresponds to the activity of the clergy but a new activity that is only now genuinely an activity with its purpose in itself: no longer an external office but "the inner man through the Holy Spirit . . . rooted and grounded in love", in order to have the power "together with all the saints" of seeing the incomprehensible four dimensions of the divine love and "to be filled to the measure of the entire fullness of God" (Eph 3:16–19). And now we see once again, more clearly, how the office by itself—which we would always so much like to separate conceptually from the realm of what is charismatic—nevertheless cannot be thought of, even in conceptual terms, without this realm, and how the office, in the praxis of life, can even less act as if the charismatic realm did not exist. For if the offices flow from the one fullness of Christ, of the High Priest and Lamb of God who died on the Cross, then they themselves are crystalized love (and not "administration", "organization"), a form in which the fullness presents itself as it unfolds itself; but this fullness, precisely by doing this, is already returning to itself by drawing into itself even what is not yet held within its grasp, by means of the organs that have been put forth into life. This means that there is no going forth that is not simultaneously an act of return, no individualization of service that does not transcend itself into the universal dimension of the ecclesial and divine love.

A living analogy governs the relationship between office and charism. The layman, who does not belong to the hierarchy, is not in the least without his office in the Church, when he has his *charisma,* and those who belong to the hierarchy are under obligation to perceive, acknowledge, and develop with all their power these "offices" too, which lie in the commissions given by God. Indeed, so much is it true that they have to orient their own privileged office toward the services rendered by the laity that they ought to understand and carry out this office of theirs much more as a charism than as an office: as a particular grace of God given for the sake of the others, but a grace that requires "unfolding anew" every day—in the furnace of humility and of the gift of self—in order to correspond (however imperfectly) to the character of their office and to show that the Spirit who animates the hierarchical office is the embodied Holy Spirit.

THE LAYMAN AND THE CHURCH

According to Paul, the Church is the "fullness of Christ", his *plérôma*. This fullness is a richness that mocks every intellectual attempt to master it—not because it is irrational but because it continually poses new tasks to the understanding, tasks that can never be completed. The understanding moves about in this fullness like one who swims in the sea. One who wishes to tackle a central problem in the Church, such as that of the lay state in her, may not hope to master the fullness with a few sparse lines: he must dive down with living faith into the living mystery and seek to fashion a statement out of the fullness, to the extent that this is given him in faith.

The Church has three levels. The first and innermost level is her eternal and historical locus of origin, where she becomes herself and where she becomes the womb for all that is in her. This is the place of the Incarnation of God, of his descent into the flesh of the Virgin and into his own flesh; both are one flesh, and thus Christology cannot be separated from ecclesiology: the formation of the hypostatic union does not take place in Mary without her consent and cooperation; as such, this formation is itself already a nuptial, ecclesial mystery. This first level is supraministerial (or suprasacramental); in accordance with an ancient ecclesiastical Tradition, one can also call it pansacramental, since all the individual sacraments and all ministeriality have their root in the universal sacramentality of the flesh of Jesus Christ (as a historical, Eucharistic, and Mystical Body). The second level is that of the ministerial (sacramental) and hierarchical, which represents the structure of the Church, established by Christ himself, which is not to be superseded or relativized by anything else in the interim period between the Incarnation and the perfecting of the Kingdom at the end of the ages. It is on this level that there obtains the relative antithesis between priest and layman. The third level is the "subministerial" (subsacramental) level of the Christian life of the members, which is the goal both of the first and of the second levels; yet this

Translated by Fr. Brian McNeil, C.R.V.

Christian life is nothing else than the unfolding of the essential basis of the Church, by means of the sacraments, in the members, who are the branches of the vine. In this goal, there is no longer any fundamental difference between the priest and the layman, although his position in the world of creation brings special functions and tasks for the layman. For the goal of the entire ecclesial reality is the salvation and rescuing of the world, and the Church—as the supernatural society of those who have received grace and who have been made members of the body of the Redeemer—does not stand as an end in herself but presupposes the world of creation for her meaning and purpose: her being and her work are open to this world and pour forth upon it. Since the world is the Kingdom of God in the process of becoming, and the Church is the yeast at work in the world, it is not possible to make a precise separation of the two. It is only in a superficial perspective that the Church can be called a *societas perfecta* "alongside" the secular (civil) society. For one thing, the material on which the Church works is present in the Church herself—nature, the world, with their ordered structures and regular patterns such as the family but also the social structures of society. For another, the material of secular society is not merely secular but also Christian (and thereby ecclesial), in that the members of the state are Christians and, more generally, are persons who stand within the realm of grace and redemption. The layperson moves in this border region as one truly at home in it, and this boundary is so fluid that it is impossible to make a sharp distinction between the situation in which the lay Christian is active as a member of the Church in the Church, and the situation in which he is active as a member and representative of the Church in the non-Christian world. This existence on the margin (between Church and world) is not a distance from the center but is a central ecclesial existence, because the Church herself is the place of the continued embodiment of God in the world, a reality that radiates forth and wells up beyond her own self.

1. *The supraministerial basis of the Church.* We shall first consider this basis in itself, then as the basis of the ministry, and ultimately as the basis of the (subministerial) vitality. The root from which the Church

unfolds is the Incarnation of the Son of God, the Word of the Father, in whom already everything was created and given an orientation toward his coming in the fullness of time. The incarnate One could not be the Omega of all creation unless he was already its Alpha, the firstborn in whom everything has its existence, even the ordered structures of creation with their laws, which he one day—in a progressive fashion in his Incarnation, in the Church, and in the perfected Kingdom—will absorb into the order of his redemption. The fundamental law of the order of redemption is vicarious representation. If the Son, who takes the place of all before the Father, seeks the consent of humanity in order to become man, then this is the consent of a single woman (*consensus virginis loco totius humanae naturae; S Th* III, q 30, a 1, c: "The consent of the Virgin in the place of the whole of human nature"); and when this Virgin shall have become the bride-Church, then her Fiat will be vicariously representative of the whole human race. This is so because the order of redemption is an order of sacrifice, and the lance that pierces the Son is at the same time the sevenfold sword that transfixes the Mother Church. Vicarious representation means election on behalf of those who are not elect; this was already Israel's destiny and mission, and Israel's tragedy was already that it failed to recognize this meaning of its election, which it referred back to the elect people itself. But the mystery of the election of Maria-Church to share in the bodily and spiritual fertility under the Cross remains the deepest and most impenetrable of all the Catholic mysteries: the one who was redeemed (proleptically) on the basis of the Cross becomes a contributory cause of the redemption, drawn—on the basis of grace alone!—into the whole dispensation of grace. It is fundamentally the same mystery that is meant when Mary is called the Mediatrix of all graces and it is said that there is no salvation outside the Church, for in each case one is saying that all the grace that is mediated to the world through Christ alone (and therefore possesses a Christological, incarnational form) has also a Marian-ecclesiological aspect because this is how the Lord has freely disposed things in his grace. The Father did not throw his Son out into a world that was sheerly opposed to God: rather, he had constructed a path of grace in Israel that led to him, a path that narrowed down and opened into the purity of the Virgin. The fullness of the grace that descends from heaven is wedded to the grace that has been prepared on earth: the Yes of Mary (and with it, the Yes of all of us) enters, and is absorbed in, the total Yes of Christ to the Father (2 Cor 1:19–20). The Yes of the handmaid submits itself to the royal Yes, which itself takes on the form of a servant and, when it is glorified, takes up the handmaid's Yes too into the glorification of its Kingdom. Out of this nuptial mystery, as a participation in it, light is shed both on the foundation of what is ministerial and sacramental as the structure of the Church and on the Christian life as its fullness and its goal. The ministry in the Church has the purpose of bringing the fontal mystery of the Church to the individual believers intact and undamaged by human limitation and sin. The *contents* of what the ministry mediates in its threefold form as priestly, prophetic, and pastoral ministry is only this mystery: divine, triune life in the incarnate form of the love between Christ and his Church. But the particular *form* of the ministeriality too, the vessel in which the Lord distributes the treasure of grace to the Church, is not constructed of any other material: the ministry is no contradiction of love and life; it is no foreign element that has been added on *ab extra*. It is crystalized love, like water that has taken on the form of ice for a period: the time of the winter that lasts until the Last Day, the time when "we are on pilgrimage far from the Lord" and need discipline and impersonal severity because we are not yet separated from the sinful world. It is of course true that in Mary, in her who is the womb mystery of the Church and who already possesses the eschatological immaculateness, this form, which is the continuation of the Old Testament hierarchy, is already superseded a priori. But we are not Mary or the bride Church; we are sinners who are in continual need of purification and sanctification; for us, the threefold ministry of the Church cannot be superseded until the end. But let us never forget that the ministry itself is wholly and completely God's incarnate love for us. The ministry has the purpose of awakening the third, the Christian life in the Church. This is the unfolded fullness of the fontal mystery. Faith, love, hope, and all the virtues are this unfolding of the innermost bridal fertility, and the virtues are fruit only by being themselves fruitful: new seeds and kernels of the original life that they scatter abroad into the world. There exist in the Christian life—mediated by the sacraments and the ministry but not identical with these—particularly close and central forms of participation in the supraministerial and pansacramental mystery, viz., those forms of life that explicitly make the Marian-ecclesiological law of life their own law, when the whole existence enters the obedience, poverty, and virginity of the Cross and redemption. This is why the vows that give entrance to this form of life that belongs to the entire Church are not an eighth sacrament alongside the others.

2. *The ministerial structure of the Church.* The ministerial structure of the Church is the highest wisdom of the Church's Founder but also his free creation. There is no possibility of deducing it a priori from what has been said about the basis of the Church, and still less by analogy with other religions and with structures that are similar to the Church. It is a positive institution, which is not to be relativized in a liberal manner or by means of a theology of history (Tertullian, Joachim of Fiore, the Protestant Reformers), and in this connection is just as original as is the supraministerial foundational mystery of the Church herself. To such an extent does it belong to the visibility of the Church in this world that even Mary, as a visible member of the Christian people, stands under Peter.

This ministeriality, however, has several aspects that share equal importance. In a first aspect—which is true but external—the priest and the layman stand over against one another as the man with the ministry and the man without the ministry. For although there exist in the membership of the Church manifold functions, charisms, and missions that pertain to the laity, these can never be set in comparison and rivalry to the hierarchical ministry, nor can one relativize the hierarchical ministry in favor of these; nor can one derive the hierarchical ministry (even in a merely historical perspective) from the charisms of the primitive Church, or derive both the ministry and the charisms as equal functions of the members coming forth from the common matrix of the supraministerial Church. But at the same time one will note that this first aspect, where ministry and nonministry seem to stand over against one another like "plus" and "minus", is a relationship and a comparison in the supernatural order, in the communion of the saints, where there is no spiritual "private property". The "plus" of the ministry belongs not to the minister but to the Church and thus to all the believers; the ministry is not an end in itself but a service, and the minister, together with the Lord, is the servant of the parable who goes around to serve those who sit at table (the laity). It is not in mere appearance or out of humility but in reality that the apostles stand "in the last place of all" (1 Cor 4:9). The one who takes on a ministry is exalted only by abasing himself together with Christ. This is the only reason why the layman looks up to the man of the ministry, just as Peter looks up to Christ who kneels before him. "The greatest among you shall be like the least, and the one who is at the head shall be like the servant. For who is greater, the one who sits at table or the one who serves?" (Lk 22:6–7). In the Church, there exist no other dignity and "reverend state" than the love that bends down and gives itself.

In the second aspect, priest and layman appear as transmitting and receiving the graces of the redemption that are mediated through the ministry in the vessel of sacrament, word, and government. But the capacity to receive graces is no *passio* but a particular form of *actio,* of which the layman becomes fundamentally capable through the sacrament of baptism, with a capacity that is ever increased by means of other graces and sacraments. One may compare this relationship of transmission and reception (as the fundamental categories in the second stratum of the Church) with the relationship between the Father and the Son, for in the act of redemption the love of God the Father too takes on ministerial traits (in the highest form of all, at the Cross), and the sovereign freedom of the Son takes on the traits of receptive obedience (Jn 5:19); it is only as the servant of the Father that he becomes the Lord of the handmaid-Church. However, one should not forget the Holy Spirit of love, in whom the unity of Father-ministry and Son-service continually reveals itself anew as love. Consequently, one can also compare the same relationship with that between man and woman; the "passivity" of the latter is not in the least inactivity or lack of interest; her character as vessel and womb is naturally and spiritually the exact correspondence to the potency of the man, which has a meaning only when it is oriented to her; in keeping with nature, when she receives the man into herself, this takes place in a total act of love in which she, while receiving, is no less active than the man, though only in a different, a feminine manner; her bearing of the male seed and her giving birth are the goal of the coming together in one and show fully how active her receptive role was. (One could pose the question whether the eras that have held the role and position of woman in low esteem are not the same periods that have viewed the laity with belittlement.) One should not deduce an ecclesiastical "equality" between priest and layman on the basis of this comparison, but one must say that priest and layman, each in his particular state, together form the one "royal and prophetic priesthood" of the Church, in such a way that the ministry and all its functions find their meaning and the basis for their existence only in this totality. This means that the *opus operatum* of the sacraments, and of the Mass in particular, is possible on internal grounds only in the simultaneous positing of the receiving community, which is present, joins in the celebration and the sacrifice, gives its consent, and gives the work of salvation its fullness and rounds it off. Everything that is ministerial stands within the brackets that go from life to life—the life of Christ and the life of the members of his body—and its only function is in the transmission of the sparks to and fro. The "faith of the Church" is the spiritual milieu in which alone it is possible for what the ministry performs to occur, and the laity form this milieu on equal terms with the priests. They have a proximity here to the mystery of Mary, who is the sphere that consents to the Incarnation of God and thus makes it possible. Since the Church as bride is always present, the validity of a Mass does not depend on the presence of a layman (as server or present in the church); but each person who is present as one who consents to and joins in the celebration multiplies the fruitfulness of the action and helps the ministerial act to attain its goal better, viz., to open up the new life of grace in the Church and in humanity.

In the third aspect, one must reflect on the fact that the life of grace transmitted by means of ministry and sacrament is the bestowal of a share in the universal, kingly, and prophetic priesthood of Jesus Christ, in the manner in which Christ has perfectly fullfilled in himself the three ministries (which cannot be precisely separated from each other) both according to the order of Aaron and according to the order of Melchizedek, and as he, the only King, Prophet and Priest, gives all his members, fundamentally and equally, a share in his three ministries. All possess the kingly freedom of the children of God; all are initiated into the full truth and share in the divine instruction (Jn 6:45); all have an active part, as Church, in the spiritual sacrifice of Christ through true spiritual sacrifices. While all of this is mediated by the Head of the Church through the hierarchy, which shares in his mediation, this does not mean any share in the hierarchy itself and therefore this will be better dealt with thematically in the third section, where we shall speak of the life of the believers.

A fourth aspect, however, shows us the layman as sharing in ministeriality itself. This does not mean that he would ever receive a share in the particular powers and functions of the hierarchical priesthood (for that would imply that he would cease to be a layman) but rather that he can exercise certain rights within the sphere governed by the hierarchy and perform acts that either pertain to him by right as a Christian or else are specifically entrusted to him by the hierarchy. In the realm of the sacramental: every Christian, man or woman, can baptize, can introduce a fellowman into the Church. The exercise of this power, which even non-Christians possess, is permitted by Church order only in case of emergency. Christians can administer the sacrament of marriage to one another: this shows what a close link matrimony has to the supraministerial universal sacramentality of the Church (as an image of the relationship between Bridegroom and bride). Yet one must add that this power, which seemingly breaks through the hierarchical-sacramental order, is based primarily in the exceptional position held by matrimony as an institution of the natural order that is here raised into the supernatural order and made a sacrament. Only one analogy (though an imperfect one) to this exists in sacramental confession, because in this too the acts of the penitent, contrition and confession, belong to the inherent contents of the sacramental act, and also because the absolution contains an element of the reestablishment of reconciliation with the Church, which can be thought of as represented in a genuine (even though nonhierarchical) manner by a layman. This is why many great theologians, including St. Thomas, have attributed a quasisacramental effect to confession to a layman, which was in vogue in the West roughly from 1000 to 1500 A.D. (4 *Sent.* 17, q 3, a 3, qla 2, ad 1). One's Christian neighbor is not just any fellowman; Christ is in him; he can mediate Christ and the Church, and his presence in the life of other persons can be a true, effective presence of the mystery of redemption. The world—both the believing world and the unbelieving—can and should see how great is the power of Christianity in the miracles and (nonhierarchical) powers of the love of neighbor. Without treading too close to the genuine and full sacrament of confession, which only the priest is permitted to mediate, one might ask oneself to what extent a Christian doctor, judge, or teacher might claim that the *quodammodo sacramentalis* of St. Thomas' formulation applied to his Christian mediation to God too, when he receives the disclosure of other people's consciences. Finally, one must say that the "royal priesthood" that is bestowed on the Christian in baptism is bestowed not only in a spiritual sense (for the offering of his own life to God) but also in a sacramental (although not hierarchical) sense, since he becomes a member of that Church, which is always as a whole the subject of the Eucharistic celebration and, as such, in principle cannot dispense with the faith and the prayer of the community if the sacrificial act is to possess its fullness. The *plebs tua sancta* that is mentioned in the Canon belongs fundamentally there with its consent, indeed with its cooperation in prayer and sacrifice.[1] If one then emphasizes the kingship in the threefold ministry, which in hierarchical terms is the pastoral ministry, then here too a certain form of participation by the layman

---

[1] In the sense of the *actuosa participatio* of which Pius XI (*Divini Cultus,* 9) and Pius XII (*Mediator Dei,* no. 91, in Herder edition) speak; naturally not in the sense of a coconsecration on the part of the faithful or of the necessity of their assent for validity (*Mediator Dei,* 94).

can exist; one need only think of the role of the princes since Constantine and Charlemagne, of the rights that the laity had at certain periods in the election of the clergy, as participants in the councils, as administrators of the Church's goods, etc. The significance of this distinction is best seen in the third aspect of the threefold ministry, the function of teacher. Although there is no question of the laity's being able to assume the hierarchical function of the authoritative proclamation of the word of God to the Church, nevertheless lay preaching and lay proclamation have existed and exist today, with the tacit or explicit permission or indeed with the commission of the hierarchy. We are not yet speaking of *the* proclamation, which is an obligation for every Christian as the apostolate of the Christian life in word and example (we shall discuss this in the third section), but of the explicit sharing in the preaching of the hierarchy. There exists the *missio canonica,* which authorizes the layman to give public instruction as a catechist in the name of the Church. For long periods in Church history there exists the lay sermon: in the early Church as a charismatic sermon, approved by Paul, inserted into the order of divine worship and held before the community, something that was practiced at least until the fourth century; in the Middle Ages, the lay sermon, which was permitted with restrictions in a small ecclesiastical circle, while it has continued to be normal *ad extra,* in a missionary context, until the present day. There exists the teaching authority of Christian parents vis-à-vis their children, which derives from the sacrament and from Church order (to say nothing of the order of nature). And beyond all this, there exists a special charism of teaching, viz., prophecy, which is not simply identical with what is called mysticism today; as a charism within the Church, it gives the one on whom the Spirit has been bestowed a right to be heard by the Church, even if not in public and not by reason of an official ministry (cf. Scheeben, *Dogmatik* § 12, nos. 166–67). There exists, with the guidance and the consent of the ecclesiastical Magisterium (the Imprimatur!), a wide theological, ascetical-spiritual, and apologetic teaching activity of the laity in the form of writing; this was already the case in the period of the Fathers (who were often well known as lay theologians and were therefore given a position in the ranks of the clergy) and has increased in the modern period. The gifts of prophecy (in the wider sense: as the interpretation of divine matters, also of Sacred Scripture, as the Middle Ages understood these gifts), the "gifts of tongues" (likewise, according to medieval exegesis, the ability to find the correct words for divine matters), the charisms of wisdom and of knowledge, the discernment of spirits: none of these are bound to ministerial ordination. It is often only the constraint of the external circumstances in which they live that prevents the laity from developing fully in the Church the gifts that have been bestowed on them.

We have set all this out from the perspective of the ministerial structure of the Church. By definition, the layman does not belong to the ecclesiastical hierarchy, but he stands in the closest relationship to it. The Lord has formed both states in a mutual relationship; they have their roots in the common matrix of the Church and more precisely still in the common sacramental basis of the kingly prophetic priesthood, on the basis of which on the one hand the hierarchical ministry is built up as the dispenser and administrator of truth and grace, and on the other hand the lay spiritual priesthood is built up as the receiver (in order to hand on further!) and realizer of what has been received in the realm of the Christian life. The layman looks up with reverence to the ministry, for without its mediation he would have no access to the source of salvation. But the priest looks up with reverence to the layman, in whom he sees the purpose and the goal of his servant function: "Let each one consider in the Lord the other as higher than himself."

3. *The sphere of life.* For this period, the final time before the judgment, the ministry is the casing that protects life. Thus the sacraments are Christ's guarantee that the grace of his Incarnation is always available in its heavenly, incomprehensible fullness, without alteration or reduction or accommodation to the narrow subjectivity of men. And the Magisterium and its apostolic Tradition are the guarantee that the truth of Jesus Christ, which towers above all that can be thought, is

handed on intact, in forms and formulae that express it correctly while at the same time correctly concealing it and taking care of it, so that, when the Holy Spirit wishes it, new, unheeded, not yet evaluated treasures of the revelation can be disclosed to the later generations. A great part of this unfolding of the fullness of Christ in the Church devolves upon the holy people, the *laos hagios*. For the truth of Christ is one with his—divine!—life; its theoretical formulation, as this can be provided for by the Magisterium in preaching and instruction alone, remains always two-dimensional; but Christ as the Way, the Truth, and the Life is three-dimensional and pluridimensional. Paul speaks continuously of the superabundance of the truth of Christ, above all that can be defined and understood, and of the necessity that should understand precisely this "above and beyond". The meaning of sermon and sacrament is attained only where the truth of the life of Christ is displayed in life, in the millionfold variation of Christian existence: that which is hidden in the formula and in the sacramental vessel discloses itself, comes to its goal; the seed finds its soil; the form and the formula find their life. This has nothing to do with modernism. In the order of the letter, and in conceptual terms, there is no possibility of superseding the letter and the concept, just as in the order of the ministry there is no development that can supersede the ministry (this is said against Joachim). But since all of this aims at realization in life, it is from the very outset "superseded" by life itself; life has the strict obligation to make the transition from doctrine to realization, from the objective to the subjective. This is the sphere of the "freedom of the Christian man", which proceeds as fruit from hierarchical obedience (something that Luther did not see). This sphere of realization is absolutely the center of the Church, even if this center has the strange character of being located on the boundary between supernature and nature. "The field is the world" (Mt 13:38), the Kingdom grows only out of the soil of the world, of nature and its laws and structures, although this is undeniably through the unfolding of its laws that lie in the heavenly grain: the Cross and love. It is therefore a false perspective to consider the ministry (in its relative freedom from the world and its purer supernaturality) as the center of the Church and the position of the layman as the Church's margin, looking on the living construction of the Church in daily life, in the apostolic act of radiating out into the world, as a kind of extension of the Church from what is her own realm, where she is truly at home, into an area that is foreign to her, almost as a work of supererogation, where what is being displayed in life is the innermost and necessary essence and its original effect in keeping with its nature. We understand this better today than did early Christianity, with its one-sided eschatological orientation and the one-sidedly monastic Middle Ages, which put even the laity under the prefix of monastic life.

The duty of the layman, after his own sanctification, is the portrayal of what is holy in the realm of the profane, the realization of the Kingdom of God in the kingdom of this world. Only, he must not forget that, until the end of the world, this realization will not take the form of a straight line but can come about only through Cross, tribulation, persecution, and martyrdom. The character of Christian life and work as a struggle, the fact that all undertakings are exposed to danger and perhaps doomed to death, the collapse of everything that has been built up into the flames of the Last Day: none of these provide any reason to transpose the center of the Church's life from the sphere of life into the sphere of the structure, out of the sphere of the goal into that of the means—simply because, thanks to the divine promise, the structures and means are exempt from this exposure to danger. The structure is the armor-bearer behind the battling knight, and *he* cannot seek refuge behind his servant.

One could take the Christian artist as the archetype of the layman—not because his activity is essentially different from that of the rest of the laity but because it is possible to use it as an image of the working of the layman.[2] The one who builds a church must portray that

---

[2] We have, by the way, a special reason to emphasize this in German Switzerland. The group of living Catholic artists who build and furnish German churches today is unique in the whole Catholic world; one can say that this group is the only point at which Swiss Catholicism today has international, indeed intercontinental, significance and impact and is the only Catholic analogy to the worldwide influence of the theology of Swiss Protestantism. Unfortunately, one cannot say anything even approximately similar about any other area of the life of the spirit.

which is holy, supernatural, and heavenly with the media of the earthly material and worldly technique; indeed, he must help the church itself to arrive at a form, for the church and for the world around that looks at it. Apart from all considerations of necessity and utility, he must make visible the dimension of beauty that belongs to the truth, a dimension that does not find sufficient expression in the conceptual formula alone and yet must play a decisive role in the mystery of the Incarnation. Beauty belongs together with freedom; the duty to protect it belongs therefore less to the ministry and its obligations than to the realm of the living act of giving a structure that is carried out by the laity. It is admittedly true that the guiding image of the artist that has been set out here is too narrow, since the art that he creates is intended first and foremost for the Church, while the layman primarily stands in the world and is to bear out the Christian spirit into the world's professions and structures. But, as has just been observed, it is impossible to draw a clean dividing line here between working with worldly material for the Church and working that brings the Church's spirit into the world. It is not possible to determine exactly the moment in which the layman changes from being a member in the Church to being a representative of the Church in the world, because this moment does not exist at all. (Nor can one say, in the case of a genuine Christian artist such as Bach or Mozart, which of his works are spiritual and which are worldly.) All Christian activity is the incarnation of the invisible grace in the visibility of the world: the activity of parents for their children; of the educators who have to give form to the noblest material; of the doctors, lawyers and judges, thinkers and planners, authors, publishers, and booksellers. The material that all of these employ is worldly and, as such, is both Christian and non-Christian. Their Christian working— the sowing of the seed, the kneading of the dough, healing and raising up, judging and evaluating, separating and uniting, clearing the ground and planting anew—is all the working of the Church in the field where she is truly at home: the world. Truth and life display themselves in this activity in a progressive incarnation: with the new answers there continually arise new questions, and the layman must encounter these in his free responsibility and power of making decisions in his maturity. In this, he will pay heed to, and follow, the directives of the Church's ministry; but the ministry and its representatives will remain in a genuine dialogue with the truth that is brought forth, developed, experienced, and very often won only at the cost of hard suffering in the sphere of life. In our age, where the differentiation of competences in the various worldly spheres is taking place with appalling speed, an ever greater importance attaches to the role of informing and advising the Church's ministry, a role that belongs to the laity and has always been exercised by them. The sociological regrouping from the Middle Ages to the modern period, which has transformed the Church from a fortress guarded by ramparts to an open city with satellite towns that wander uncertainly into the countryside, emphasizes insistently this change in the position of the layman. The Roman authorities and those among the bishops and parish priests who are open have therefore become convinced long ago of the practical indispensability of a consultation of the laity, of the need to call together specialised commissions, and of the readiness to react with confidence to what these say wherever they have the weight of professional competence behind them, and they have acted accordingly. This is a case of consulting not foreigners and outsiders but brothers in the Lord, who are inspired and illuminated by the same Holy Spirit, who are empowered by their charisms and ministries in the *Corpus Mysticum* to speak a word that is to be taken with full seriousness and who also are almost always seriously resolved to speak such a word. And the whole concern of the ministry ought to be directed to developing this spirit of responsibility on the part of the laity through instruction but also through an attitude of confidence and the desire to learn. Here, the ministry will have the experience that the concern that it brings to bear will come back to it as sixtyfold and hundredfold fruit. It is only in the body of the laity that the *plérôma* of Christ can unfold itself; the ministry has the obligation of giving to this body of the laity — which is the only place where the seed can germinate — whatever it possesses of the contents of the truth and life of Christ that has been handed down by Tradition. In the context of the changed situation, one can also speak of a certain change in the form of the *sentire cum Ecclesia* (e.g., over against the famous rules in St. Ignatius' *Spiritual Exercises*), not as far as the attitude itself is concerned but certainly as far as the manner in which it is manifested is concerned. In an epoch with an extremely high degree of publicity, which easily comes to know about things that have been covered up, in a period of unchecked democratic criticism of what is done by all those in positions of responsibility, in an age of increased average education and wide reading, it can no longer be acceptable to protect the Church and those in authority in the Church by hushing up and embellishing mistaken acts and actions (Gide has accused us Catholics of habitual lying); rather, wherever the layman has competence, he must speak of these matters more openly than was the case before; where possible, he must defend them, but where this is not possible, he must distance himself from them, whether in dialogue with the superior in the Church himself or in public. There exists an increased share in responsibility, on the part of the laity, for the acts of the Church before the world.

But perhaps the ultimate riches of the world of the laity can be unfolded from this lay world only when the understanding of the position and the responsibility of the layman in the consciousness of the Church has been linked organically to the understanding of the evangelical counsels. These are linked, in an inherent manner that can never be superseded, with the concept of the Christian fullness of life and the hundredfold harvest. It would only be necessary to enrich the monastic exegesis of the counsels, which hitherto — taken as a whole — has been the dominant interpretation, indeed virtually the only interpretation, by means of a further exegesis. The monastic life is turned away from the world; its role in the Church of the past and of today as exhortation, clarification, and help from above remains alive and is not disputed. But the gospel is not inherently monastic, and its directives have a validity that goes further than this. Mary is not a nun, but she is Mother *because* a virgin. Christ is not a monk, but he is King *because* he is poor and obedient unto death. It is not through Catholic "action" that the world will be redeemed but through poverty and obedience and an exclusive orientation toward God. And it would be in keeping with our advanced age if Catholics were to learn better to understand that responsibility for the world goes well with obedience, disposition over the world goes well with poverty, experience of the world goes well with virginity—indeed, that the ultimate fruitfulness, even in the realm that is most truly that of the laity, can be expected precisely from this source. Let the one who can grasp this, grasp it. But the one who can grasp it is not the one who psychologizes but the one who thinks Christologically in obedience to God's word. What the Middle Ages founded in a one-sided and provisional way for the warrior and the hospital brother must be extended today to the whole breadth of the professions of the laity, in a way that begins from the autonomy of the lay state and from its own problematic, not as a kind of "third order" appendage to the monastic world, and not necessarily by means of "lower orders" (diaconate of the laity), which would threaten to make the laymen who had received such a qualification into appendages of the clergy. The fullness of the subjective imitation of Christ lies in the counsels, and life in the counsels is subject to a guarantee by the Founder of the Church that is no less objective than his guarantee of the fullness of the objective powers of the hierarchy (Mt 19 and parallels). A nonclericalized state of the counsels in the Church would offer the best guarantee of a balanced, living equilibrium. But even this could be only the leaven that disappears, the grain of wheat that dissolves in death, and the fruit that would arise (to the extent that this can be visible) would have to be observed in the layman with family and possessions and the right to make dispositions, and indeed in the non-Christian world that surrounds him.

The body of Christ exists and is at the same time in a process of becoming; this is why Paul compares it with the human body, which grows up to maturity by testing its own strengths and displaying these in the matter that is brought to it *ab extra.* The basis of the Church and her structure cannot grow; but the sphere of life, which is formed predominantly by the laity, can indeed grow. The men of the ministry (who, as members, must grow like all the others) are keepers and gardeners of the growth. The duty of the laity is to be the growth and the blossoming that alone can convince the world of the truth of the teaching of Christ.

PHILOSOPHY, CHRISTIANITY, MONASTICISM

I. *Ipsa Philosophia Christus*

We moderns lack all the necessary presuppositions to grasp, from within, the way in which the ancient Church of the Fathers, and still of the Middle Ages, viewed monastic life as "the Christian philosophy" itself. For what we today understand as monasticism is a form of life that is very different from the kind of existence lived by the average, "normal" Christian, a form of life that is not in the least comprehensible on the basis of the average standard: it appears as a speciality, something that "exists as a kind of accessory" in the Church and presumably becomes more and more marginal all the time, even if it may earlier—probably for cultural reasons—have stood much more strongly in the center. It seems to us almost absurd to make a central point of reference out of a monastery, especially out of a contemplative and enclosed monastery to which ordinary people have no access.

There was a time—the time in which the West was born—when monasteries were focal points both of the Church and of culture. When all structures of order collapsed during the period of the mass migrations, the monasteries were the first to put down roots again in the endless quicksand and to permit what was formless to crystalize around them to a culture that was inseparably both secular and spiritual. These were periods in which the classical spirit, which had disappeared in external terms, still lay in the atmosphere in internal terms, since the religious ideal of a "philosophical life", i.e., of a life for the divine truth that was hidden in the world, was still something graspable and attractive, and the synthesis for which the Fathers had striven between the philosophical and the Christian *theôria* or *speculatio* was something self-evident and illuminating.

It is well known that the Fathers gave the name of "philosophy" to

Translated by Fr. Brian McNeil, C.R.V.

a Christian life lived in consistent praxis in the world.[1] The presuppositions for this reside, to begin with, in Hellenism, where the philosopher became more and more identical with the theologian, the one
who speculated about the Divinity; he was expected to devote his life
to this occupation and to find therein, as Plato and Aristotle demanded,
his highest happiness—but it was also expected that his practical
existence would reflect his wisdom. Asceticism belongs to philosophy
no less than does the contemplative habit. This is why the bridge
spanning philosophy and the revelation of the Old Testament could
be built even before Philo,[2] who then undertakes the reconciliation
of the two as the theme of his work: "The royal road to God can be
called 'philosophy' among the Greeks; in the law it is called 'the word
of God'" (*Poster. Cain.* 102); the law is the philosophy of the Jews.
Justin, who converted from pagan philosophy, is the first Christian to
make the identification: "I discovered that this is the only certain and
sufficient philosophy" (*Dial. c. Try.* 8, 1); when the apologists employ
the word in their petitions to the emperors, it is meant more *ad usum
delphini;* but Clement of Alexandria will give it a definitive home in
the Church and thereby overcome the violent opposition on the part
of a Tatian and a Tertullian. "Philosophy strives for wisdom of the
soul, correct judgment, and purity of life. It is full of inclination
toward, and love of, wisdom and undertakes everything in order to
arrive at wisdom. Among us, those who strive for the wisdom of the
Creator of the universe and Master, i.e., for the knowledge of the Son
of God, are called philosophers" (*Strom.* VI, 7, 55). Clement himself
gave his chief work the title *Stromata* ("Carpets, or concerning the
true philosophy"). "The true philosophy is the one transmitted to us
by the Son" (*Strom.* I, 18, 90). "According to Scripture, it is easier for
a camel to pass through the eye of a needle than for a rich man to be a

---

[1] G. Bardy, "'Philosophie' et 'Philosophe' dans le vocabulaire chrétien des
premiers siècles", *Rev. Asc. Myst.* (1949; Mélanges Viller): 97–108; J. Leclercq, "Pour
l'histoire de l'expression 'Philosophie chrétienne'", *Mél. de Sc. Rel.* 9 (1952): 221–26;
F. Dölger, "Zur Bedeutung von Philosophos und Philosophia in der byzantinischen
Zeit", in *Byzanz und die europäische Staatenwelt, Ausgewählte Vorträge und Aufsätze*
(Ettal, 1953), pp. 197–208.

[2] Bardy, op. cit., p. 89.

philosopher" (*Strom.* II, 5, 22). Origen too can speak on occasion of the "true philosophy of Christ" in contradistinction from pagan dialectic and rhetoric (*Gen. h.* 11, 2; Baehr. 6, 103), and for him this philosophy is just as much practical as theoretical, demanding the imitation of the Logos, poverty, celibacy, domination of the passions, strict asceticism: for Origen, all of this is meant only as the supporting structure that will permit the spirit to be free for the divine *gnôsis*,[3] for that which he calls (without mental reservations) the perfection of faith in the vision of the truth. Only a small shift is now needed before it is possible to give the designation of the genuine Christian philosophy to the anachoretic movement that will soon begin, the withdrawal into the wilderness either for the eremitical or for the cenobitic life. Eusebius of Caesarea is a witness to this shift, partly by way of appeal to the prophets of the Old Testament who dwelt in the lonely places, in the desert, in silence, and partly by way of appeal to Plato's *Theaetetus* (*Praep. Evan.* 12, 29). His *Church History* relates that already at the beginning of the second century, "a very great number of disciples, touched in their souls by the divine Logos, burned with vehement love for philosophy and, first following the Redeemer's command by distributing their goods among those in need, they then left their homeland and took on the work of evangelists" (*H. E.* 3, 37, 2). Chrysostom calls the Christian life in general "the highest and most useful philosophy" (*In Mt. h.* 31, 3; PG 57, 374), but he also speaks insistently of the "philosophy of the monks" (*In* 1 *Cor. h.* 6; PG 59, 52), which he praises as the "divine philosophy in conformity with Christ". Similar language is used by Isidore of Pelusium.[4] Monasticism understood itself as a "pneumatic philosophy" that—in a Christian manner that is parallel, for example, to the description that Porphyry's life of Plotinus gave for the Platonists—makes the soul and the spirit ready for the *theôria* through the utter engagement of the "praxis". For the philosopher among the monks, Evagrius of Pontus, Christian *theôria* will be divided into two parts: the contemplation

---

[3] Völker, *Vollkommenheitsideal des Origenes* (1931), pp. 44–62.

[4] Texts in Viktor Warnach, "Das Mönchtum als 'pneumatische Philosophie' in den Nilusbriefen", in *Vom christlichen Mysterium* (1951): 135–151.

of the world in orientation to God and in the light of God (*theôria phusikê*) and the contemplation of God in himself (*theôria theologikê*). Although this is a teaching peculiar to the philosopher monk Evagrius, he does not stand alone with the general idea that monasticism and philosophy are identical for the Christian: his opinion is shared by Mark the Hermit, Nilus, Cassian, and Maximus, chiefly because this form of life has as its essence and its program the full "practical" commitment of one's existence with a view to the highest "theoretical" goal, the vision of God. But it is precisely this that seems to them all not an innovation, and still less a copy of Greek models, but the only fully legitimate continuation of the earliest Christian Tradition. Viktor Warnach formulates the universal view when he says, with reference to Nilus, "It belongs to the essence of monasticism that it continues the 'apostolic life' that consists in the following of Christ in a gift of self without reserve. This is why the ideal of the monk is nothing else than the perfect Christian life. In the early period, every Christian was a monk, because he was ready for martyrdom for the Lord. But as the worldwide Church grew out of the small community of the apostles, and lukewarmness and an earthly attitude entered the Church along with the masses, an ascetic *taxis* [class] of its own came into being."[5] Although none of these Fathers would have called into question love's position as the highest Christian virtue, nevertheless they were equally firm in asserting that the true goal of the monastic life was to be sought in *gnôsis,* in the knowledge, experience, and vision of God.[6]

This point is taken up anew by the Middle Ages: the ancient "Christian philosophy" had

> meant the practical discernment of the true value of things and of the vanity of the world, proclaimed in the whole existence of those who renounce the world. In the monastic Middle Ages, therefore, as in the period of antiquity, "philosophy" does not denote primar-

---

[5] Ibid., p. 136.

[6] "Charity is the door to the vision of essences [*theôria phusikê*], which is followed by the knowledge of God [*theologia*] and the ultimate blessedness" (Evagrius, *Cap. Pract. ad Anatolium;* PG 40, 1221C).

ily a theory in the modern sense or a technique of knowledge, but a wisdom that is displayed in life, a way of life in keeping with reason. It is, however, possible to live in keeping with reason in two ways: the first is a life following the wisdom of this world, as the pagan philosophers had taught this, and this is the *philosophia saecularis* or *mundialis*. The other is a life following the Christian wisdom that is not of this world but already belongs to the coming world: this is the *philosophia spiritualis* or *divina. The* philosopher *tout court* and the embodiment of philosophy is Christ: *ipsa philosophia Christus.*[7] He is the incarnate Wisdom of God, and Mary, in whom the mystery of the Incarnation was accomplished, is called the "philosophy of the Christians": they must become pupils in her school: *philosophari in Maria....* [8] This integral Christianity, this existence wholly consecrated to God and *conversatio coelestis* find their realization in the monastic life. It is for this reason that the legislators and models of monasticism are regarded as the masters of philosophy. The monasteries are "schools of philosophers", "gymnasia" in which one learns "the philosophy of St. Benedict".[9] Bernard is praised because he "introduced" the monks of Clairvaux into the "disciplines of the heavenly philosophy";[10] Adam of Perseigne asserts that he has "dedicated himself to the Cistercian philosophy".[11] To live as a monk means quite simply "to philosophize"; Du Cange gives no other medieval synonym for this word in his dictionary than *monachum agere,* "to live as a monk". The concept of *philosophari* is applied both to the monks who live in community and to the hermit monks [J. Leclercq].[12]

When high scholasticism has the tendency to maintain this equation of monastic life and philosophy, this is only something that results from the most important *auctoritates* it follows. First there is

---

[7] Dom H. Rochais, "Ipsa philosophia Christus", in *Mediaeval Studies* (1951): 244–47.

[8] Leclercq, "Maria christianorum philosophia", in *Mél. de Sc. Rel.* (1956): 103–6.

[9] Bruno of Querfurt, *Vita S. Adalberti* 27 (*MGH* 55, IV, 609); Peter of Celle, *Ep.* 75; PL 202, 522.

[10] *Exord. magn. hist.;* PL 185, 437.

[11] *Ep.* 6; PL 211, 598.

[12] *L'Amour des Lettres et le Désir de Dieu* (1957), pp. 99–100.

Dionysius, for whom all of Christian life finds its summit in the contemplative act, in the spirit's existence as light and fire: it is this alone, through a process of streaming over, that makes a fruitful action in keeping with God possible. Then there is Aristotle, for whom the philosophical-contemplative act is the highest and most blessed act on earth—a teaching that Thomas Aquinas adopts and elevates in a Christian sense in his theory of eternal blessedness. If the Franciscans follow Dionysius (and Augustine, whose thought is not essentially different at this point), the Dominicans follow Aristotle and Thomas; both follow also at the point where the ideal of monasticism opens itself out to the world in their orders and draws into itself the practical work of love of neighbor. For Thomas, however, this is possible only when the monk, whose essence it is that he has consecrated himself as a holocaust to God (2a, 2ae, 186, 1c), does everything in his active love also while "looking toward God", with the consequence "that in such men, the action streams forth from the contemplation of the divine" (2a, 2ae, 188, 2 ad 1). Cajetan comments on this passage that two things are said simultaneously here: first, that an act of pure contemplative love and of the gift of self to God alone is the presupposition for a subsequent active act, and second, that even in this latter act there must be present an act of latent contemplation, if the regard to God is to hold sway over its intention and its execution. It is therefore logical that the order whose action consists in studying (i.e., predominantly in philosophizing in a human manner), in order to purify and to make fertile the divine contemplation, and at the same time in preaching, in order to irradiate in love the light of the divine philosophy, must be the most perfect order (2a, 2ae, 188, 5–6). The synthesis of Aquinas, in the clarity of its distinction and unification, remains a model. Thomas sees the face of the triune God coming into view in the formal object of philosophy through the medium of the Christian revelation, and if it is already the case that almost the whole of the worldly philosophy aims at the knowledge of God (*C. Gent.* 1, 4), how much more will this be true of the "Christian philosophy", if the one who philosophizes pursues his goal of knowledge with the appropriate passion and exclusiveness, which now is given the name of the absolute self-sacrificial gift of self!

Later on, there will exist the danger that either the formal object of philosophy is dissolved into theology and that one thus lapses into a Christian positivism to which it is no longer possible to apply the ancient term *philosophy* in any meaningful and comprehensible sense; or else that the formal object of theology is brought into such close proximity to the formal object of philosophy, or is ultimately identified with this, to such an extent that Christian contemplation is once again dissolved into the contemplation of being—a path to which much in Eckhart and in Nicholas of Cusa points ahead and a path that is later trodden to its end by the idealists.

If one excepts a flowering of patristics and of Platonism in the humanism of the Renaissance, where the notion of the Christian philosophical life too makes itself heard—although in a more vague way that is no longer related to monastic contemplation—then the meaning of this word was no longer put into practice after the Middle Ages. But it is perhaps no exaggeration to make the understanding of the justification and the necessity of the contemplative religious life in our own age dependent—not in a historical sense but in a sense that is objectively related to the matter itself—on a deeper understanding of this word. The appreciation of this is disappearing more and more, not only in the surrounding world (which cannot be expected to understand it) but even in the Christian people, for whom the contemplative life threatens to become an exceptional and marginal phenomenon that has no longer anything to do with the generality of people. While it is still true that the ideal of this form of life is often admired as a lofty and steep ideal, or is at least allowed to possess validity, it is considered in this context as an ideal that has no longer any intrinsic vital reference to the totality of Christians. The classification of believers into a fixed structure of the states of life—state in the world, religious state, priestly state, lay state—gave an initial impulse to this encapsulation of the contemplative life, along with the idea that a very special vocation was necessary also for this very special path; and since this can be the affair only of a few chosen ones, the contents of this path too will be something exclusive, almost something esoteric. Besides this, there arose along with the mendicant orders the idea that Christian contemplation and action were fundamentally compatible, and precisely the justification by Thomas Aquinas that has been mentioned above—since he presented as the most ideal order the order that knew how to unite genuine contemplation with its overflowing in action—encouraged the idea that a purely contemplative existence was after all something one-sided and that one could give what was specific to it a place in a higher synthesis. For ultimately, the Christian is not normally able to live removed from the world in the wilderness or behind monastery walls; it is enough for him to dwell in God's presence in his spirit and his heart while he is concerned with the works of love of his neighbor in accordance with the Lord's command. Thomas has set this forth in a very beautiful way:

> One can be in the world in two ways: first through bodily presence, and then in terms of one's disposition. Thus the Lord says to his disciples, "I have chosen you out of the world", and yet he also says about them in his prayer to the Father, "These are in the world, but I am coming to you." Thus, while the religious who are occupied with works of the active life are in the world in terms of bodily presence, they are not so in terms of their disposition; for when they are occupied with an external matter, they do not do so like those who ask something of the world but only for the sake of the divine service; they "make use of the world as if they were not making use of it", as it is written at 1 Corinthians 7:31 [2a, 2ae, 188, 2 ad 3].

Is there any reason, therefore, why it should be impossible to seek God in all things in the world and to find him, and to be *in contemplatione activus* on the basis of an enduring settled presence of the spirit to God that accompanies all that one does, instead of fleeing from the world (although one will not be rid of the world even in a monastery) in order to bury oneself in an inactive contemplation?

The only answer that today's theologians are accustomed to giving at this point is the differentiation of the missions and charisms; the charism of the purely contemplative life can also be one among these. And just as the charisms permit various sides of the one Church to become visible, so this charism would have the role of recalling the "eschatological" orientation of the Church to the coming new age by embodying this. It is indeed true that the contemplative life does this, but it is not true that the orientation to the eschatological dimension is the specialty of one state of life within the Church. This is why Thomas Aquinas makes a painstaking distinction between the distinctions of the ecclesial charisms (2a, 2ae, qq 171–78) and the distinction made within the Christian life in terms of action and contemplation (ibid., 179–83): the contemplative life is not in reality a charism. And although Thomas understands the two lives essentially as external forms of life, one could and should think further at this point and understand them as two aspects of the one and only Christian existence, and these aspects can also appear in a variety of emphases in a variety of external forms of life.[13] Absolutely all Christian life is "eschatological" because in baptism the Christian has been crucified to this world along with Jesus, has died to it and been buried, and has risen along with Jesus—as a citizen of the new age and from now on only as a foreigner and pilgrim here below on earth. No matter in what state of life each one lives, he must take this fundamental state of affairs to heart and must give expression to it through his existence; the one who is active must do this no less than the one who is contemplative. But what significance has a purely contemplative life in this perspective?

We shall attempt to find the path to a solution on the basis of the ancient designation of this life as Christian philosophy. But first, an objection: Is not this fusion of philosophy and monasticism something strange for us, something that can be understood only in historical terms, for one period of time in the Church's history when the classical religious philosophy—Plato, stoicism, Neoplatonism—was the living atmosphere breathed in by everyone, when the Christian still lived in the sphere (the "myth") of the classical world model, and when the path to God—in Greek and in Christian terms—seemed simply to be identical with the path out of the world and its multiplicity into the purely spiritual universal One that lay above the world? And in the Middle Ages, is it not customary to see philosophy and

---

[13] Cf. my commentary on these questions: vol. 23 of the German-Latin edition of the *Summa*, pp. 431–64.

renunciation of the world as belonging together wherever philosophy thinks predominantly in Platonic spiritual terms or in stoic monastic terms, and wherever the practical preparation of the human person and his schooling in the philosophical act coincides with radical asceticism, the mortification of all emotions and passions that would bring turbulence with them? And is it not the case that, since the Middle Ages, we—even we Christians—look with increasing scepticism at this classical path toward God (through turning away from the world and ascetical spiritualization and deepening), because it seems to us not to take with sufficient seriousness man in his form as spirit and body, in his full and good secular character, and because (something with graver consequences) it neither does nor can pay attention to the Incarnation of the Word of God and to its religious consequences?

This objection would hold good if one could truly write off Greek thinking as something that has become obsolete. Hegel and Heidegger do not share this opinion. Even if much in the classical cosmological world model must be "demythologized", and modern natural science offers new outlines for a philosophy of the material world, the Greek question about the being of what exists is as new today as it was in the age of Heraclitus and Parmenides, of Plato and Aristotle. This is no question that can be solved in order to make further advances; it challenges the spirit to encounter the mystery of reality. As long as the human spirit exists, this problem will confront it with the question of the relationship between God and the world, the absolute and the relative, the eternal and that which passes away. It is only in the presence of the mystery that the human spirit will make its distinctions and its renewed unifications; it is only in the presence of the mystery that it will be obliged to accept that the sphinx's question of who he himself is, is posed to it. The concrete forms of Platonism, of Aristotelianism, and of stoicism are time conditioned, but the question that they pose for themselves and that remains posed for all who follow them cannot fade. And if the question about being remains, then it is not simply to be solved even through the Christian revelation. It is indeed true that the Logos has taken on a wholly different vitality here, has begun to speak personally, and has spoken about the *Arché*, the Origin, about the one who is his Father and the Father of all beings. But does this mean that the question about being, the question that being poses to man, is superseded? Is it not rather the case that this question is only now revealed in its whole profundity, as all the Church Fathers and the great scholastic theologians held, from the Cappadocians' teaching about God to the teaching of Dionysius, Victorinus, and Augustine, from Maximus and Boethius to the great speculative scholastic theologians, to Eckhard and Nicholas of Cusa?

Now, it was certainly always the case that to be a philosopher was understood as an election, as the bestowal of a grace, and that a group of hand-picked initiates clustered around the great seers and thinkers. And although a philosopher may perhaps have begun in the realm accessible to all (the "exoteric"), he will end up, like Plato, in the realm of the esoteric, if he remains true to his call and the inexorable question presses upon him: not because he abandons the conceptuality of thought in favor of the irrational but because through everything the mystery fascinates him ever more forcibly. The only thing worthwhile is to hold oneself open to this mystery, and the mystery does not loosen its grip on the one who has once dedicated himself to it with all his love; he must yield up his eros to the ascent that purifies by passing through all the renunciations, for the one love for wisdom demands everything.

Protestantism does not tire of discrediting the eros of antiquity, which presses forward into the mystery of being, by setting it in contradiction to the divine agape that descends to men. This is possible for Protestantism only to the extent that the question of the being of all that exists is not urgent for it, and because being appears to Protestantism to be a mere concept. Here, however, it is only the uncomprehending negation of an equally uncomprehending position that, confronted by all the questions thrown up by scholasticism, has forgotten only the one question that decides about all the others a priori, although this is a question that no man can avoid posing, whether explicitly or implicitly. For everyone who thinks is, in a rudimentary manner, a lover of truth and wisdom, since he cannot live without truth, nor can he desire truth without affirming the reality that bears all things. But how greatly obscured the light of true being is in most people! They live half-smothered under the surface of the water, rising above it scarcely ever for a breath of air by entering reality and its unbearable splendor. They hang on with desires and anxieties, with plans and instincts that drive them, within a shell that they are afraid to break through—they know indeed that reality exists, but they want to know about it only in a subdued manner, by hearing someone else speak about it, in a recollection that makes it obscure.

Nevertheless, it is only the one who chooses and decides in the presence of the highest light of reality who is wise, and this is why Plato installs the philosopher as the king of his state: he lifts his head above the clouds, he sees the truth, and his instruction mediates the truth to all those who govern and work under the covering clouds. But the one who causes the true light to disappear from the gaze of the contemplating (pure or theoretical) reason, subordinating the latter to the acting (practical) reason, is a leader of the blind, and—as Plato has prophesied—history will demonstrate where it leads them.

For the first Christian centuries, the Christians were called by God himself to be that light of the world that the wise man who sees God ought to be. The truth was laid open before them, revealed to them; they know who God is and what he wants of men. They can bear witness, in theory and in practice, to this wisdom even to the men who still grope in the mist of paganism. In their petitions to the emperors (who included the philosopher Marcus Aurelius), the Christian apologists not only plead that the Christians be spared; they also offer the light that has newly appeared as a help in guiding the peoples. They do this not only out of a diplomatic consideration but also out of a philosophical conviction that they can still possess because the Christianity of the age of the martyrs shines in the freshness of a sunrise that has just taken place, and the martyrs give an unheard-of testimony with their blood to the power and the light of the new philosophy. As late as in the *Contra Celsum,* the elderly Origen will adduce the philosophical relevance of the Christian truth, its "evidence on the basis of spirit and power", when he attacks the loftiest and most venerable philosophical principles of the Greek world.

This lasts as long as the splendor of the sunrise persists. Where the world makes its entrance into the Church, the atmosphere becomes turbid and the true light that Christians ought to be for the world—and that they are when they look at the light—must be sought beyond the smoke-filled air of the cities: this is the meaning of the *anachôrésis,* the "withdrawal" into the wilderness. One cannot say that these men who withdraw are people weary of activity, who yearn for pure contemplation. That would be a falsification of the historical state of affairs. The earliest monasticism has an astonishingly practical orientation, but it wishes to fight the true battles of the spirit, in which the monk, through the utmost heroic endeavor, overcomes himself and the demonic powers in and around himself, so that in this way he may come into the true light of God.[14] The *pathos* that, in our materialistic world, still bears a distant resemblance to the *pathos* of those who withdrew from the world, is the *pathos* of the first scalings of mountains, of the great technical and sporting achievements, of flight in space. Even the work of Evagrius of Pontus, the most extreme "Gnostic", is filled with the tactical directives of a military commander for the battles against the demonic illusions and for the cunning with which one can outdo the most cunning of all deceivers, who again and again substitutes a form of light for the pure light, as indeed Paul has said (2 Cor 11:14). Everything depends on the synthesis of act and truth, of *praktiké* and *theôria pneumatiké.* The *theôria* is genuine only when it has been attained on the path of the *praxis,* and the *praxis* is genuine only when it leads upward into the light of the *theôria.* Accordingly, the monks had not the least desire to be "contemplatives" as opposed to the "practical Christians in the world": rather, they desired to put the primitive Christian synthesis into practice in its purity and to display it before the eyes of the Church, which was becoming more worldly.

The outcome of this is a double program for our research. The first line of investigation concerns the relationship between Christianity

---

[14] "The naked demons struggle in battle with the anchorites, and they give weapons to the more careless brethren, who fight against those who live as cenobites and practice virtue in the common life; but the second battle is much milder than the first": Evagrius, *Cap. Pract.* 5 (PG 40, 1224A).

and philosophy. This line must be pursued with due consideration, and we shall take good time here, since it is necessary here to uproot prejudices that have become deep rooted and are widespread still in the theology of our own days: above all, these are the prejudices concerning the meaning of eschatology and the position of the various Christian "states of life". It is only when a certain amount of clarity has been achieved here that it is worthwhile to go over to the second line of investigation, in which Christian life and monastic life encounter one another. At any rate, one thing is clear: such an encounter is and remains for many Christians and for most of the spectators from the outside who are not directly involved an offense and a constant source of annoyance. This cannot be altered in the present age of the world; it is an aspect of the Cross that the Church bears and that she herself portrays in her innermost and indissoluble structure.

But now we begin once again from the very beginning, as if nothing had been said up to this point.

2. *The Christian life as philosophy*

"The world is deep, and deeper than the day had thought. . . . Woe says, 'Pass away!' yet all pleasure desires eternity." Nietzsche's "Song of the Night" wishes to succeed in hearing the "words of midnight" in which the existence of the world and of man in the world gives expression to itself in that which is covered in silence. The one word is a transience, which does not hover over things like a cruel fate but is inscribed in their blood and their essence: since they are woe, they pass away, and the transience itself is woe and yet, in order that woe may pass away, is affirmed by their very essence. Since they are pleasure, pleasure of being itself, they affirm this being in the "great Yes and Amen", and they would not exist if they did not wish and need to be eternal.

All human reflection, every myth that interprets being, every religious and philosophical construction of any importance, knows that existence is constituted in this way and points out of transitoriness into the direction that leads to eternity. The zone and kingdom of transitoriness is not eternal being itself, and therefore one can term this transitoriness a mere coming to be, an "apparent being" (*maya*), mere "being with the character of appearance" (*phainomenon, aistheton*), going to the very border of a sheer separation, of a sheer nonidentity, to the principle that underlies both space and the time that flows past: matter as nonbeing. This purely transitory element is the periphery; the true, eternal being is the center. That which is purely transitory is the surface, while that which truly endures is the center of gravity and the midpoint. And an existence that understands the meaning is an existence that sets out upon the direction from the periphery to the center and therefore possesses a knowledge (of whatever kind) concerning this center.

All human wisdom that deserves the name indicates paths that lead to this center. This cannot be simply the distraction of everyday life with its insignificant multiplicity, and therefore it demands that one close one's eyes, that one turn aside: the significance of this turning aside is that it is a turning toward unity, a "purification" from the self-alienation of that which is related to unity in man, in order then to be open to an "illumination" that comes from the unity and to encounter it and grasp it in a "unification". From this basis, life in the multiplicity is no longer to be lived as a share in the distraction, but out of the strength of the unity that is discovered and held fast in all the multiplicity. Here, it is not important in what terminologies this instruction is set forth, whether it presents itself more as an idealism for which the external world is the mere "appearing" of a central subject, or more as a monism for which the world is the mere mode of an all-embracing subject, or (and this distinction is more significant) whether the issuing forth of the One into the Many is (more positively) a portrayal, unfolding and revelation of the One, or (more negatively) a falling away of the unity from itself, a darkening of its light, such that being begins to reel: *monados kinetheises,* "when the monad is moved". . . . But not even this antithesis is fully significant in the ultimate sense of the word, because the Many must derive from the One in the one way or the other and must display the traces of the unity even in the darkening and dispersal and thus must lead back to the unity. The negative aspect will correspond more to the "path back": all this is not the One that I need and seek; it only obstructs the access for me; I must deny it and leave it in order to find the One. The positive aspect will have to be associated more with the fact of having found the unity and with the new egress from the unity into the multiplicity so that now the One is rediscovered in all things.

This movement is absolutely present in human nature, and every anthropology (or psychology in the classical sense of the word) that engages to any extent in sensible reflection can and must uncover this movement. It is true that man understands and expresses himself in this, but it is false and a prejudice to conclude from this that he thereby understands only himself and not the absolute that is inscribed upon his nature (in whatever way), only his own existence and not being (in whatever way this can be grasped in his existence). This conclusion, which is drawn in the name of a certain kind of Christianity, cuts thought short and thereby conjures up a schizophrenia between philosophy (which is inherently denied) and theology (now dismissed to a superficiality and sheer positivity). By encountering himself as one who already exists, man discovers in himself the movement that consists in having gone forth and in having to go back. It is a further question, what depth, what gradient this movement takes on for him. On a superficial and thoughtless level, it can content itself with the idea that it has been generated and brought forth by the *Magna Mater Terra* or by the womb of the *natura naturans,* and that its fate is the necessity to return in death into this all-embracing principle of universal life. On a deeper level, it can catch sight of being itself as that which generates and which takes back, and thereby — to a greater or less conscious degree — come to see the horizon of the absolute as the interior horizon of human existence. It can bring this absolute (in whatever manner) into a positive relationship to the finite subject and lend it something like a supersubjectivity: as the sun of the good, which radiates forth its light without jealousy, reveals itself in all individual beings, and takes all back into itself. Ultimately, in the Christian sphere, this movement can free the relationship to the ground of being from all entanglement in nature and destiny, transposing it into the light of a highest personal freedom: then the idea of the creation finds space within this relationship and thereby also the idea of a personal love that is primarily God's love for the creature, and at a second stage the answering love of the creature for God.

This means that the revelation of the Bible too takes its place in the scheme of the world religions of humanity, which, in a schematic unity, are nothing other than the expression of human existence itself. When the living God addresses his creature in freedom, then he is addressing precisely his creature that he has already thought of in this manner and made ready with a view to this free address. The openness of the horizon of the "great nature", and more deeply of "being" and of the "absolute", and more deeply still of that "One" and "Good" that surpasses all the names of being and to which the finite person entrusts himself unconditionally: this openness does not infringe upon the divine freedom, since this is the only source from which it can derive. Christian thought from the very outset has therefore understood this open scheme as the "empty" space of all the positive revelation of God; here it is not very important whether it is structured more in a Platonic manner (in the Alexandrians, in Augustine and Dionysius, Boethius, Scotus Eriugena) or more in an Aristotelian manner (in high scholasticism), in a more Eastern (Asian) or Western manner. Let us make this simplifying statement about Christian intellectual history: Asia, as the matrix of the high religions, stands also behind Plato and Plotinus, and Aristotelianism, especially scholastic Aristotelianism (and including precisely that of Aquinas) is—as far as the fundamental religious scheme of egress and return goes—no less Platonic (Augustinian-Dionysian-Boethian) than the religious schematism of the Church Fathers. From the baroque period onward, stoic (immanent-monistic) motifs press more strongly into the foreground without altering the foundational religious scheme in depth.

Even the God of the Bible, whose unique light pierces ever more clearly through the initial fogs of polytheism and of the numinous feeling about the world, in keeping with the increasing ascent of revelation, is not the first to explain to men what "a god" is, since that is something that they know from the very beginning. He sets the right God in the place of the false gods, the mighty and living God in the place of the powerless (and therefore unauthenticated) gods, the

One in the place of the many. He reveals how the true depth of being really is. And since men were content to go no further than their inchoative schematism (which they interpreted and explained to themselves by means of myth), the process whereby they are led more deeply until they encounter the true God cannot consist merely in leading them further beyond what they already know but must consist in a radical relearning that starts at the very basis. For if God is eternal being as the one who is absolutely living and sovereign, and if the creature came forth from him, then the process of turning around (*epistrophē*) to him means not only turning away from the many to the One but also a conversion from human thoughts to God's own sovereign thoughts. In order to teach us these and to open up the access to them from within, God sent us his Word, his Son, who brought us his Spirit by becoming a man like us, by dying for us in our stead, and by rising up to God (which means that "all have died" and are risen: 2 Cor 5:15), in order to lead us with himself in the Holy Spirit to the Father. In this way, God takes the initiative in filling with his own contents man's empty and formal schematism.

If one separates (in Protestant fashion) the contents of the revelation from this schematism, the historical revelation becomes something purely or predominantly "positive" that man must make his own, in rather the same way in which a schoolboy must make his own an object of study that is foreign to him; this is something that he cannot even (like Meno) discover, as his reflection continues, as present, concealed and forgotten, in the depths of his own spirit. The articulations of salvation history are utterly incalculable, the deeds and words of Christ are the contradiction of every human hope and supposition, and it is only through this self-denial on reason's part, which is at the same time reason's obedience to the historical positivity, that the Christian learns what "faith" means, the gift that the finite reason makes of itself to the absolute. It is only this step that truly posits the category of the "hereafter", a category that is foreign to Christian antiquity and to the Christian Middle Ages, although their Christianity was certainly not a "Christianity of this world only" simply on that account. The basis for the fact that the "last things" — toward which human life is oriented in its straining beyond its own sphere, which belongs "to this world"—belong to the "hereafter", is a concept of God that posits the reality of God beyond the boundaries of man and of his human world, as that which is wholly Other. Karl Barth has given this boundary with originality the name "death line", because the creature can cross this boundary only—if at all—by dying in the encounter with God.

It is possible to take one further step, and this step has in fact been taken. The medium of the positive revelation of God is historical time, which—through the event of salvation—has become capable of making revelation in its orientation to its own end. Since the incarnate Word of God broke across to us from the far side of the death line and, by dying vicariously for us, crossed this line to reach God, this means "the end of the ages" in the midst of history. We live in the face of this end (1 Cor 10:11), although we have not yet reached it; "in faith", we "make haste" toward God's rest (Heb 4 and 11), although we shall share in this rest only when Christ returns and the temporal order has finished for us too. The earliest Christianity lived in a total orientation toward this end of time, and the Church as a whole lives in orientation to this, waiting impatiently and yearning ("The Spirit and the Bride say, 'Come!' And let the one who hears, say, 'Come!' ... He who bears witness to this says, 'Yes, I am coming soon.' Amen! Come, Lord Jesus!": Rev 22:17, 20); but this life is led in a special way, as it were in a specialist manner, by those who have renounced what belongs to the earth once and for all in order to lead an "eschatological existence" in the Church, above all the priests and religious.

If one sets this isolating perspective once again within the scheme of religion as a whole, this scheme makes it seem questionable, and it becomes doubly problematical when seen against the background of the total form of what is Christian. This questionable character necessarily infects also the form of a Christian kerygma that would bear decisively the stamp of such a form; it would be difficult for a religion, a philosophy, or a world-view to find in it the fulfillment of their own inchoative and unfulfilled or incorrectly fulfilled tendencies. Three questions arise:

1. Is God that which lies beyond man and the world, because he is the One who is "wholly other"? Or are not precisely Dionysius and

Nicholas of Cusa right to attribute the highest immanence to God because of his transcendence, giving him the name *Non-Aliud,* the "not-other", because of his uniqueness and unity? It is not possible for him to be the unique One without at the same time being, in each thing, the ground of its creaturely (individual) otherness and (species) unity; he cannot be Being *tout court,* without this implying that each being, when it looks into the ground of its own being, looks up to him, whether it knows this or not. There cannot exist any ontology without theology, no matter how formal the manner in which one would develop the ontology. The path to being, which is the path of reason in general, is the path to God. The lesser evil occurs when this path is initially interpreted and misinterpreted idealistically or monistically, because the keenness of the reason's capacity to see and to distinguish is not able to achieve more than this without a revelation on God's part; it is worse when the attempt is made to lead man to God on a path that bypasses the natural movement of his reason and contradicts his reason, for this kind of positivism casts suspicion of heresy upon the path that is inscribed upon nature and forces it into atheism out of opposition to a positivist Christianity.

Man's knowledge of the sphere of holiness, of the mystery of being at the origin and at the end of life—and therefore, concealed under each one of his moments, the knowledge that he is alienated from this mystery that holds sway in the inner realm of being and of life, but that there must exist a mysterious path that would lead him back to the inner dimension and into that which is essential—is a knowledge about the immanence of God, which must be understood by the Christian and must be lived out in the presence of religious humanity as something that is fulfilled in Christianity. In this knowledge, Christianity is not more "of the other world" and not more eschatological than any religion that is truly a religion and not merely a superficial ethic of life. The religious man, who sinks through the appearance of things into their ground, need not be far removed from the Christian, when the latter "goes into his inner room, shuts the door, and prays in secret to the Father" (Mt 6:6). It may be true that the former remains in a forecourt (which is full of danger, because he tends to view this too quickly as the definitive goal), while the latter penetrates into the true sanctuary; but even the latter will make his way through the forecourt, whether he consciously articulates this step or not. Augustine was accustomed to articulate the step by calling the path to God the entry into the depths of one's own heart, but then the entry out beyond the depths of the heart to the depths of God, warning that one should not linger (in a Neoplatonic manner) in the "sinking down" into the (philosophical-religious) inner dimension of the spirit but should rather pour out once again this entire inner dimension (*memini et effudi in me animam meam:* Ps 41:5) out beyond oneself into the true ground of God, who is *interior intimo meo* but is precisely genuinely *interior,* "more deeply within", and is therefore to be sought *via* "the inmost depths of myself", *intimum meum.* The fact that the first step consists in "purification" and "renunciation", by closing one's eyes to the multiplicity in order to attain the repose of the One, must not be interpreted by Christians to mean that they would be obliged to renounce the "multiplicity" of the religions and join the one, historical positivity, in order to destroy the multiplicity of the religions on the basis of this positivity. The positivity is not the One and can only be a message from the One; naturally, this is a message that comes through human living and dying, in which the One conceals itself in the act of revelation. Asia has succeeded in the highest art of being reconciled to fate, to the One that is somehow impersonal, especially when one knows that one is the emanation and articulation and protuberance of the One; Asia has perhaps succeeded here better than Israel, which was provoked to contradiction by the personality of the One, alongside whom there exists no Other (Dt 4:35; 32:39; 1 Chron 17:20; Is 45:18; Dan 3:96), for it is easier to submit oneself to a law of being that is necessity than to submit oneself to a divine will with a freedom to demand obedience in positive ordinances. It was Jesus who united personal obedience with the "meekness" (Mt 11:29) of Oriental submission to form a law of being—Jesus, who always does what pleases the Father (Jn 8:29) in a way that goes further than a moral identification to become an identity of substance (Jn 10:30).

That which is historical and positive bears witness to this unity and unification, and it has value only to this extent. It is not only an indication of this unification but is also prototypical for the whole creation. This means that the contemplation of Jesus, who always looks on the Father and sees all things in the Father, is the superabundant ideal for the religions of the world. It is not (as for many Christians) only a miraculous privilege based on the unique hypostatic unification between God and man, which cannot be attained by anyone else and in which one can only "believe"—and this act of believing in it then takes the place in man of what in Christ is the act of seeing—but is rather the archetypical highest instance of all religious yearning and endeavor on the part of mankind, of mankind's struggle to surrender itself to God and to bring all of existence into harmony with the absolute law. This is something that lies in Christ himself beyond grace and nature, and when human nature is incorporated in Christ, grace opens up the access to this for man. Grace is the indwelling of man in God and of God in man, not only ontically but also quite definitely in an existential manner, when man opens himself and permits the Holy Spirit of God to take control of his own spirit. The goal of the endeavor of the religions—man as the vessel and transparency of God, the man with a bodiliness in whose spirit the Spirit of God dwells (Abbot Joachim too conceived of this as the meaning of the revelation of the word, and he saw this ideal as something that was insufficiently the aim of contemporary Christianity) —this is the human person arrived at the point to which Jesus wished to bring him.

2. Since all the religions must necessarily be spiritualistic and monistic, they must also all be "eschatological". If finite man takes the ascending path to the absolute, the only way for him to seek this path is through the release of his finitude from its limitations, through the renunciation of the sensual dimension and the concept of reason. This is the path of negative theology, for which the Areopagite opens up a broad gateway into Christian theology. There exist religions, such as Buddhism, that believe they have said everything with the path that releases from limitations and hold that they have thereby found the liberation from finitude (which as such is suffering) and redemption.

Other religions, such as Taoism, dare to take the next step beyond this by denying even the denial and thus giving the finite a positive place within infinitude (as the identity of both identity and nonidentity). The Christian mystery of Easter is inscribed upon this empty schematism: the death and Resurrection of the God-Man. His death is truly the passing away of the man who is exiled, not merely into the limitations of finitude but into the limitations of the sin that alienates him from God, and this takes place at the "boundary of death", which thus becomes the boundary of judgment; but his death is still more (and this goes beyond the schematism to become the genuine revelation of the "inner depths of God": I Cor 2:10–11) the making known of the heart of being itself: the pouring forth of being itself: the pouring forth of the *Theios Erôs* beyond all limits until it reaches into the very depths of all that opposes God. Here death is the language of the eternal life of love, "illumination" and "anxiety" of existence (in Heidegger's language) as the place at which the eternal light shines out. This mystery cannot be captured with a merely dialectical methodology that sets forth the schematism in the form of a movement, because the miracle of the Resurrection passes through the holes in the "grid" such a methodology sets up. But this miracle already holds sway in a hidden presence, where the eternal flame of love chose for itself the sacrifice of Golgotha to be consumed: love consumes in order to transfigure, in order to preserve on a higher level. The Resurrection must transfigure finite existence and give it a secure place in the eternal being of God. Transfiguration is more than what idealism (that of Gnosticism and of India and of Hegel) understands as the sifting out of the eternal kernel from the husk of time and space: the spatial and temporal as such is made eternal, the finite and limited as such is released from its limitations, and that which is necessarily lost and made futile in the vanity and transitoriness of existence is preserved in a superabundant fashion. The *frustra* (without reason, to no purpose) of all earthly endeavor is given shelter within the *gratis* (without reason, without cost) of the eternal love. The entry into the depths of the bottomless abyss of Hades is the raising up above all things into the bottomless abyss of the Godhead. The ascension to heaven in a visible portrayal is the social, necessarily spatial, and temporal image for this, but the reality that is expressed in this image is precisely the dissolution of the external world of space and time, which for the future makes proclamation no longer as the mere unfolding of its own created essence but as the vessel of the eternal essence and light that portrays itself therein, "so that God may be all in all" (1 Cor 15:28). The idealistic-monistic pantheism of the religious schematism thinks in a straight line from the data of nature, but the resurrection of the flesh surmounts the natural problematic of God and creature through the sphere of God's free self-portrayal in the finite substance in order to arrive precisely in this way at a "deification" of its essential limitedness that does not destroy nature.

If one begins from the position between God and the creature, this eternal life appears predominantly as "seeing": the eternal light becomes visible in the eye of the created spirit. From the perspective of the mystery of the Resurrection, it appears on a yet higher level as "love", since the process whereby the finite yearning is made red hot by the infinite Trinitarian eros more than fulfills every created love of "I" and "Thou" by bringing it into the love of God, in which the personal relationship of "I" and "Thou" reposes in the identity of substance. It is only when one has grasped that the "resurrection of the flesh" can have no other basis than the Trinity that one has also grasped what answer Christianity can offer to the world religions of Asia. The negative precondition for this would be that one keeps the historical positivism, beyond which the West cannot progress, far removed from the mystery of the Resurrection. The Resurrection is not a continuation of the events within time and space and thus a "second", "other" life that is stuck onto the end of time and space. One must allow this end to keep its inner meaning, and therefore one must allow the presence of this ending to retain its genuineness in every moment of time of our existence: How else could the transitoriness of what belongs to the earth be experienced, the pouring away of the substance of our life into nothingness—an experience that is necessary in order that it may be the vessel that receives the infinite pouring away of God? Otherwise, one would rob man of his most precious possession, and one would rob God of what is most necessary to him. But of course, it is true that no one brings both ends into an existential unity: Who can, at one and the same time, *truly* die and rise up to God in hope? Only the God-Man achieves this to the full; for the rest of us, the *real* death is blotted out of sight in him by the certainty of the Resurrection; this is a pure gift of grace, which also contains a concealment of the whole outline in order to spare us. One must look to Christ in order to know all that is truly involved here and to know why it is not merely "forensically" true but also intimately and really true that "if one has died for all, then all have died" (2 Cor 5:15).

In the Resurrection, earthly existence is not prolonged but is revealed in its hidden divine depth. Nothing here below is lived out to the full, no joy and no renunciation: in all that men do, the word of the Lord holds good, "They know not what they do." This is true not only in the sense that an objective spirit of the race comes into activity at a higher level than the subjective spirit of the individual (in the "cunning of the reason") but also precisely in the sphere of what is most interior and personal, in the unique act whereby the person entrusts himself to a human "thou", and indeed (in faith) to the divine "Thou". But everything has already its divine depth; it has in Jesus Christ its "hidden" but utterly real life lived in heaven, which will not begin but will "appear in glory, when Christ our life appears" (Col 3:3–4). It is repeatedly emphasized that we have not only died with Christ but have also risen with him and are in heaven with him (Rom 6:3–11; Eph 2:6; Col 2:12), no matter how much this is for the moment only to be grasped sacramentally and in faith and hope. It is not possible to employ techniques of meditation to cross over this concealing barrier, because its fruitfulness for eternal life itself means that it must not be broken down. And when God, for reasons of the apostolate (2 Cor 12), permits mystics to have proleptic glimpses of glory, this is not because of a claim on their part—as the crowning of their own endeavor—but in order to bring everyone into a stronger faith and hope. The concealing barrier now points us clearly to a temporal future: to the end of one's own life, which however never stands as a rounded-off entity by itself and therefore has an inherent connection with the end of humanity and of time as a whole; and it is only at this end that "the resurrection of all flesh" can be awaited. And yet, alongside this clear Biblical statement, there stands in equal clarity the statement already mentioned, that everything is already full reality in the depths of the believer, where not only does he seek God but also God has found him, where it is not he who looks on God but God who looks on him (1 Cor 13:12; 2 Cor 5:11; Gal 4:9), where we have already gained access "to the *Civitas Dei Viventis,* to the heavenly Jerusalem, to the countless hosts of angels, to the community of the firstborn in their feast" (Heb 12:22–23) and truly belong to this as fellow citizens and members of the household, not as resident aliens (Eph 2:19). This means that the "virgins" who follow the Lamb in heaven need not be dead in order to be there. This means that it is not tenable, in Biblical terms, to draw a sharp demarcation line between a present resurrection that would be "merely spiritual" and the "bodily" resurrection that will one day happen (the latter being understood as the genuine resurrection, the former only as a figurative form of speech: Jn 5:24–29; 6:39–40, 51, 58; cf. 2 Cor 5:1–4). Rather, we have to do with a mystery of that which "is not yet fully disclosed": "What we shall one day be, is not yet revealed; but we know that when it is one day revealed; we shall be like him" (1 Jn 3:1–2). The eschatological barrier that is set up by Scripture prevents us from reaching out on our own ahead of time from the sphere of faith into the sphere of sight, the foolish illusion that we can bring about our own resurrection into God through our own ascents and techniques. The resurrection will be brought about by God alone, who has raised up the Son at the right time. Our cooperation in this is our "being crucified with Christ" (Gal 2:19), when "I" and the world are crucified to each other (Gal 6:14). Thus, God takes false concerns away from us, and at the same time the work of transformation, to the extent that we cooperate in this, can be a work of all who love and not only a work of a small elite, like advanced Oriental contemplation. But this does not mean that Christianity replaces contemplation by action (love by its works); the whole of Christ's self-giving love streams forth from the point where he looks on the Father and therein always does what pleases the Father. If some members of the Church dedicate their whole lives to this contemplation, that does not mean that the others are dispensed from it: in faith, all must continually make a spiritual reality of their having died and been raised up and "having been given a place in heaven" with Christ, no matter to which stand in the Church they belong. They must live their married lives in precisely the same "eschatological" manner as the virgin and the celibate must live theirs: in both lives, the *Theios Erôs* must cast its splendor over everything and hold sway over everything. If some individuals in the Church are called to "philosophize" in a Christian manner, to contemplate the mystery of real being in its authentic difference between eternal and temporal being, between heaven and earth, death and resurrection—just as there also exist a natural talent and vocation to philosophy—nevertheless, one cannot call this Christian philosophizing "eschatological", or at most only in the misleading sense in which the act of philosophizing is customarily called a training in dying; in reality, the philosophical eye, like the theological-contemplative eye, takes in both poles. This is something that belongs to the essence, and in what is essential there is no specialization; laymen who neglected this "philosophy" would be truly second-rank Christians who would deserve to be included with contempt among those whom Origen calls the *haplousteroi* (the "simpler ones"), those who give only imperfect realization to what it is to be a Christian.

3. The Christian lives in the fellowship of the saints, whose unity cuts right across the realm of the "living" and the "dead"—if one can call "dead" those who continue to live with God. Religion has aimed from the very outset at such a linking of the two realms in one: the Chinese and Egyptian cultures identified the center of gravity of human existence precisely as lying astride the boundary between life and death. Life draws wisdom and courage from the power of the dead, who form the majority, and true culture is oriented toward the judgment of the dead, which is the entry to eternal life. But Plato's world too (for example, in the *Laws*) embraces both realms; the same is true of Schelling's *Bruno* and *Clara,* and the reconciliation between both realms is the last note that sounds in Rilke. The embrace of both is not only the achievement of the solitary philosopher, while the crowd remains attached to the illusions of transitoriness; it is also

within the field of vision in social terms and is determinative of primitive and of high cultures that seek to establish for the society the correct relationship of proportion between earth and heaven. This does not mean that culture is in flight from the world; it understands the parabolic character of finite existence and seeks to raise up into the consciousness of all something that the society as such cannot attain, viz., the specialized philosophical disposition; and it does this by means of representative institutions, above all, by means of the religious cult. The cultic sacrifice is a vicarious symbolic reality that, in a genuine act of renunciation, portrays the general renunciation to which man is forced by the gods and by fate as something that is understood and accepted. In the firstfruits of the harvest, the whole harvest is sacrificed; that is to say, it is brought into relationship to the divine point of neutrality between death and life; in the libation to the gods, the whole drink is consecrated to them; and so on. The harvest of time is brought from the very outset into "the eternal granaries". Although in individual cases a great deal of anxiety and of magic may have played a contributory role here, this does not sully the objective motif itself, which belongs to the schematism of religion. Initially, Jesus' parable of the rich man and his harvest (Lk 12:16–21) does not go beyond this scheme; it recalls the philsophy of existence as a whole and clearly presupposes this; and when Luke immediately links to this parable the logia about not being preoccupied about life and about the body, he goes beyond this philosophy only in the sense that he carries it further: from God, there comes not only the blessing on human culture but also the personal loving concern of the Father, who shelters in the hands of eternity the temporal being that entrusts itself to him and allows one to sell all that one possesses in order to have one's incorruptible treasure in heaven, "For where your treasure is, there is your heart too" (Lk 12:22–34).

This measure of proportion between earth and heaven, which is the measure of proportion of all the high cultures, is thus presupposed and taken over in Christianity in order to be raised up to its highest intensity. This is doubtless the justification for the fact that Christianity likes to keep alive the memory of the classical period in a civilization that is more and more forgetful of this measure of proportion and that entrenches itself in what is purely earthly. This could be just as well the memory of China and of Japan and of ancient Egypt, to the extent that they embody in their religious culture the sense for measure. The fact that Christianity itself fulfills this measure does not mean that it embodies the contrasting pole of a "culture of that which lies beyond death" over against the one-sidedness of a "culture of that which lies on this side of death" and demands an "eschatological disposition". If this were correct, then the true Christian would be the one who lives in pure orientation to the so-called sphere beyond death, and the one who is concerned for the measure between earth and heaven would be one who makes compromises. Such an attitude would be much more to be expected in an idealistic-monistic religion than in a religion of the Incarnation of God, since in the latter the order of creation must be brought to its superabundant fulfillment. The "anxious concern" of the "Gentiles" is rebuked by Jesus and is condemned as "little faith" when Christians share it (Lk 12:30); yet Jesus does not overlook, for this reason, the fact that "all the hairs on your head are counted" (Lk 12:7). The fear of the Gentiles does not get beyond the prospect of bodily death and the attempt to ward this off, but the fear of the Christian is to be the fear of God: "Fear the one who has the power, out beyond death, to cast you down into hell; yes, I tell you, fear him" (Lk 12:5).

For this reason, the Christian's work in bringing in the harvest of the world into God's granaries is, in the truest sense, a work of culture. Culture spans the arch between heaven and earth and therefore between the spiritual soul and the body. Work on the spiritual soul is no less a work of culture than work on matter, and thus the work of the priest who carries out pastoral care, and the work of the contemplative at prayer in his monastery, who prays and sacrifices for the salvation of the world, is no less a work of culture than is the work of the Christian layman in the world. The education of souls for God with the Christian means of the word of God and the sacraments is only a little distant from the activity of a teacher who forms the subjective spirit of his pupils by immersing them in the objective truth, as this has been preserved by the educational material of mankind (in the holy word of humanity and, as it were, in natural sacraments). Both have before their eyes the love of truth, *philosophia*, with the renunciations this involves, as the ideal disposition in life. Instruction in history will not only hammer lifeless dates of battles into the heads of the children but will also train them in the idea that great intellectual personal decisions alter the course of the world for generations because they leave their mark on the genuine events of history. Christian instruction in the Bible emphasizes, among these decisions, that taken by Christ, which has left its mark upon the whole of the history between God and humanity and decided the course of this history. There exists a genuine analogy between the inspiration of the artist, of the legislator, of the religious and philosophical wise men on the one hand, and the word and the existence of the prophets and of Christ on the other hand—even if there is a qualitative leap of difference between the two.

One must be careful not to let the link between a meaningful activity willed by God and its reference point in eternity become too thin and too theoretical. The "good intention" that relates the worldly activity to God's will thereby also sets it within the context of his earthly and heavenly plan for the world, and even if the position that the individual occupies in this plan is not clearly visible, we know nevertheless that this position exists. It is, of course, true that everything in the world must pass through the fire of judgment on the Day of the Lord, and that it ought in fact to be built up by us and set free by us with a view to this fire; but this no less true of the spiritual than of the worldly realm, for it is not only the form of this world that passes away but also the form of the Church together with her ministries and sacraments and her hierarchy; all of this is "scaffolding" around the house of God, which is building itself up. Indeed, Paul speaks of this testing and destroying fire of judgment precisely with reference to the "spiritual" act of building on the part of pastoral work, to the "synergistic" act of building together with God: "The fire will demonstrate how it stands with the work of each one" (1 Cor 2:9–13). There are also some who, in this work, "destroy . . . God's field, God's building, God's temple: God will destroy such a one" (3:9–17). But if the work is built upon the right foundation, then, whether it is "worldly" or "spiritual", it will pass through the fire and be saved. Concern about the works of human culture is vain; it is as if God, who has counted every individual hair, could despise the work of his own work and fail to give it a safe place in his eternity along with man. "Their works follow them" (Rev 14:13).

Christian wisdom, as the word about the Cross, is true wisdom, even when it seems to be folly to those who are on the path to destruction (1 Cor 1:18); it is the truth of the genuine initiation, not a wisdom of this world or of the rulers of this world, who are removed from power (1 Cor 2:6–7). It is only a difference of secondary importance whether one seeks to make this Christian wisdom as far as possible plausible from below, as the fulfillment of natural wisdom (as Thomas Aquinas does), or presents the Christian wisdom in its own illuminating logic and in its contradiction of the empty sinful wisdom of men, as Augustine does in his mature years. In any case, the wisdom of the crucified and risen Christ is a wisdom that bestows the true God-given content, the true concreteness and color on the abstractions of the philosophical and mystical schematism and thereby, as the "word from God", also fulfills all the words of the creation.

3. Monasticism and philosophy

It is only from the breadth of this reflection that it is possible to make the special life that the Christian leads in a monastery understandable. It does no harm if initially the impression is given that the considerations that we have set out here would make monasticism superfluous, because the philosophical and contemplative act is not only something the Christian may properly carry out but is also something that is demanded of him in a wholly special way. If, in the natural sphere, one must be born with the appropriate gifts in order to become a philosopher, the Christian receives the endowment for this in his rebirth, which the Fathers call *phôtismos,* "illumination" of the spirit and of its inherent capacity to see. If the Christian is the true philosopher, who has received in Christ the mysterious measure of proportion between being and that which exists, what is then the point of a specialized contemplative life? At any rate, as we noted at the beginning, this could not be a "charism" in the specific sense: it could not be anything other than the portrayal in life of the Christian totality. It must be the preservation of the awareness of this totality where Christians are constantly at risk of forgetting being thanks to their absorption in what exists, of forgetting, thanks to their absorption in their apostolic and other actions, the vision of the light that makes everything possible, governs and justifies everything. Seen in this way, monastic contemplation signifies nothing less than the beating heart of the Church—not, in fact, a single organ but the central power that lets the blood of the entire life, which sustains and gives life, flow into that which takes on individual form in accordance with the charge that is given.

One should not begin by giving at once a purely supernatural interpretation to that image that St. Thérèse of Lisieux uses, as if it were the gift of self made by the souls that sacrifice themselves for Christ and die with him that, through their "merits", would achieve the necessary graces for the brothers and sisters who were fighting in life outside. This is true, and it will indeed be the crowning of all our other reflections. But one should not spring over the intermediary steps; and these emphasize, to begin with, the legitimate and absolutely necessary transposition of the natural requirement of contemplation, as this has been made by every worthwhile philosophy since Plato's *Republic,* although this is something—like many other postulates of a culture that is worthy of nature and of man—that modern technical civilization, as it has run amok, has made people forget. Where the natural guiding image has been lost, it would not help if Christians were to desire to share in this rush downward into death by emphasizing more strongly the active side of Christianity, that which is "directed toward the world" (in order to sanctify through their *présence* something that is essentially unholy), while themselves losing thereby the equilibrium proper to creatures; rather, they must restore to the world, out of their own higher light, what the world in its blindness no longer sees, even when this is pointed out to it with the biting irony of an Aldous Huxley. Christian philosophers such as Maritain, Gustav Siewerth, and Josef Pieper never tire of describing the ravaging natural consequences of the loss of contemplation and of indicating the medicine for this.

As Plato knew, however, and as all the high cultures have known with him, this medicine can lie only in a life that is lived for the divine truth. "My daily ten minutes" of contemplative prayer *ad usum laicorum* are not going to make good, for Church and world, the loss of a life lived for the truth. These ten minutes are better than nothing at all, and they will awaken in the laymen who practice them seriously the wish for deeper contemplation and the wholesome regret that they cannot find more time for this. This bad conscience, this feeling that there is a substantial lack, is certainly no small thing in the general hectic life; it is like the rumbling stomach of the undernourished Christian spirit, the outline form of a function that is unconditionally required in the domestic economy of the Church. Let us attempt to set out the distinguishing characteristics of this function, in that which makes it specifically what it is.

I. *Philosophy,* "love for wisdom" is, as the word itself says, an act of love. The true philosopher here loves, not his own act of knowing—which can transform itself into an addiction for sinful man—but the matter itself: the mystery of being, which discloses itself by concealing itself in all that exists. His heart burns with fire for this; it is for this that he has time, leisure, a vacuum (*otium, vacare*). He understands that the only way in which he himself can share in that which is above time is to have time for it. It is only in a painful sacrifice and renunciation of the multiplicity that makes its impact en masse and of the importunateness of the individual things that the stream of time bears along in its course, that the sun of reality, the "idea", rises up to meet the spirit. For the Christian, the sun of God has revealed itself in the humble heart of Jesus Christ with its renunciation, and now Christians are permitted to contemplate the light of being itself in this heart that is rendered mild (*praüs*) and leveled down (*tapeinos*) by humility and humiliation, if they have become "simple" (*nēpioi:* Mt 11:25, 29), have "hearts emptied out" and are "poor in spirit" in order "to see God" (Mt 5:3, 8), if they possess the "single" (*haplous*) eye that sees everything lit up by the rays of the One (Mt 6:22; Lk 11:34).

The formal object of theology—the mystery of God in his divine depth as this discloses itself in Jesus Christ—is configured to the Christian simple heart; these two seek to be alone together and must be alone together. This is the gospel of the one thing necessary. It is not simply "faith" that is characterized thus, not simply the "hearing of the word of God", and not simply "love" that perseveres beside Christ while the sister Martha is occupied with the many things she has to get done; rather, made possible by all of this, but going beyond all this, it is the pure mutual relationship of God and man, existing for one another, reflecting oneself in each other. This is also quite certainly more than what is usually called "prayer" in the gospel, viz., man's speaking with God when he exposes his distress, his need, his veneration of God to him. Beyond this, it is a being for the being of God. Worldly philosophy can be inclined to describe this being above all the individual acts (which is configured to that which exists) as an inactivity or a pure passivity, and even in the Christian realm many have repeatedly misunderstood contemplation in this way. But Mary of Bethany is not "empty": she hangs with every fiber of her heart on the mouth of the Word, she listens attentively and takes it in with her whole being; in faith and love, she is the fullness that receives the fullness of God as this pours itself out.

Because the God who reveals himself to her is the eternal love itself, the readiness of her heart, beyond acts of love, is likewise substantial love that she has poured out from the finitude of individual acts into her whole substance. This is why Christian contemplation is more than natural contemplation—amazement and ecstasy at the miracle of being. Christian contemplation is truly itself prayer, the primal act of prayer: all the individual acts can be nothing more than rays sent forth from this. And Evagrius is right here to equate theology and prayer in both directions: "If you have knowledge of God [*theologos*], then you truly pray, and if you truly pray, you have knowledge of God" (*De oratione,* chap. 60; PG 79, 1180B). For Evagrius, the all-important point is that the spirit no longer stops short with "what exists" (with "forms"), whether these are sensual or intellectual, but encounters the light that is presupposed in all the forms as the precondition of their having form and of being comprehensible. The true encounter is not reflection about God (since this can take place only by means of creaturely contents and concepts) but the act of seeing through all the forms to God: "The science of Christ needs not a dialectical soul but a dioratic soul" (i.e., a soul that "sees through": *Gnostic Centuries,* IV, 90).

The decisive thing is the act of seeing through, not the mystical act of rising above all forms in order to see the light of God outside all form. Whatever may be the case about the possibility of an unmediated experience of God in this life, this is neither promised nor a possible object of one's striving, not even in a contemplative monastery. For not even the philosophical act needs to be limited to that mystical intuition of pure being of which Plotinus said that he had received it only in lightning flashes and in very rare moments. But it is one thing to pay heed, in the contemplation of what exists, to the being that reveals itself; it is another thing to have the light of being only at one's back and to be absorbed in looking at and attending to what exists. Thus it is one thing in the Christian Faith too to presuppose contemplation only as something objective in order to be absorbed completely in action that has to do with the world, and it is another thing to sense continually the primal mystery of God's self-giving love through all the revelations of God in Sacred Scripture and in the Christian life and to let this be the central experience in all experiences. But whoever does this?

To be such a vessel for God would be the Church's role. She ought, at least somewhere or other, to make an existential reality of who and what she truly is, what act constitutes her, and to what *otium,* what *vacatio* she is called. And where she made this a reality, she would be totally herself; she would possess her true summit and center, which lie quite elsewhere than in the visible center of her administration. For there she would not become visible in individual acts; rather, her act would coincide with her being and would disclose this. The Christian who resolves to devote himself to the contemplative life enters the center of the Church; he renounces, so to speak, existence as an individual person, an individual member of the Church. He becomes anonymous; he makes a present of his heart to the Church and receives from the Church her heart. For the sake of the totality, he rises above being a part. But this is not a pantheistic totality (which always remains the temptation of the philosopher) but that totality that is the world's answer, bestowed and made possible by Christ, to the totality of God that pours itself forth upon the world: the unity of the Church. No one, therefore, is so totally expropriated as the contemplative. No one else has so little hope and expectation of personal satisfaction as he. He is not only this or that individual person over whom God disposes for the benefit of the totality; he is an aspect of this totality over which God disposes for the benefit of the parts.

2. At this point, the second characteristic can already be seen. Contemplation of being within the sphere of the Church is a being dedicated and taken up into the mystery of the nuptiality between God and the world, which has its glowing heart in the marital mutuality of Christ and the Church. But here, the renunciation of all beautiful bodies and souls made by the philosophical eros for the sake of the one beautiful thing becomes the divine renunciation itself: it becomes the *kenôsis* of God's *agapē,* its emptying out into human form, into obedience and Cross, and it becomes the communication of this cruciform pattern of all love to the bride-Church. Precisely this sacrifice of the bride to the Bridegroom and together with the Bridegroom is the Christian surmounting and perfecting of the philosophical act. This becomes ever clearer in the course of the history of Christian spirituality and mysticism: from the form, still largely clothed in the language of Greek philosophy, found in Clement, Gregory of Nyssa, Dionysius the Areopagite, Scotus Eriugena, *via* the Cistercians and the Victorines, where the element of the Trinitarian-Christological love becomes predominant, to Suso, Tauler, Teresa of Avila, John of the Cross, Francis de Sales, Clorivière, where the element of the Passion in this love becomes prominent. One can follow the path that has been taken best if one sees the changes in the concept of the night, which begins entirely in the realm of philosophy—night as the disappearing of every creaturely form before the "brilliantly shining darkness" of the divine formlessness and wilderness—until gradually

that side of the night that has to do with suffering emerges: night, not only as the pedagogical withdrawal of the light and the initial condition of the creature in which it is not accommodated to the superabundant light of God (as is still predominantly the case in John of the Cross) but truly as the night of the Cross and of Holy Saturday, the night of the experience of the distance of God, imposed by God in order to configure the person to Christ (as in many modern mystics). One must, however, note that the emergence of the Christological-soteriological motif cannot count as the replacement of the earlier philosophical motif but as its elevation and fulfillment in Christian theology. Then the mysteries of the contemplative life, which for modern man are concentrated above all in the Carmel, although in reality they belong to the essence of all contemplative existence in the Church, lose their apparently private character and, instead of being a special path, become a mystery of the Church that affects all and ought to be comprehensible to all; they become the existential side of what Christians celebrate every day in the Holy Mass in sacramental fashion: the bride is sacrificed together with the Bridegroom; she is placed together with him under the one knife of the Father on Moriah; the Mother of the Lord shares in the state of being abandoned ("See, there is your Son!") with the Son who is abandoned by God on the Cross.

At this point, the philosophical *otium* of contemplation becomes the *otium* that is urgently required by God for the Cross. The mysteries of the night normally require that one be free and have time for contemplation. Although even the active Christian in the world receives the gift of particles of this suffering of the Cross, the active commission that has been given to him does not normally permit God to train him in the state of abandonment by God: the one who is active for God is one who continually needs strengthening and consolation. It is not a question here of small "deprivations of consolation", which he too must go through, in order to come to know God through the "discernment of the spirits" and not to be attached to worldly illusions that try to deceive him. It is a question of the bride's great participation in Christ's suffering, and this demands the life of contemplation. Even in the case of the contemplatives, God remains sovereignly free to determine how he shares out the night of the Cross. This can happen on the authentically mystical level, as John of the Cross has described. It can happen in intermediary stages, as in Thérèse of Lisieux, or—as happened with great cruelty in the case of the little Bernadette—in the customary round of everyday faith, in being forgotten by the world, being put in a corner by a mother superior and by one's fellow sisters. When Christians in the world hear about these things, they raise their hands to heaven about "the way things are in convents". But they do not see things as they really are: they see sociological conditions where they ought to see theological conditions.

In the act of theological contemplation, the one who contemplates is not at his own disposal: he becomes a sacrifice of the light that he contemplates. And this is something that goes far beyond the manner in which philosophical contemplation transposes the contemplating subject and makes him a function of being itself: in the theological act of seeing, it is not the summit of the spirit but the living person with flesh and blood who surrenders himself and becomes an accepted sacrifice. It is a human sacrifice, just as the Cross of Christ was, *inter alia,* also the fulfillment of all the religious attempts at human sacrifice. These were only attempts, because no man is permitted, even for the sake of God, to make a sacrifice of his fellowman. But on Golgotha, God offered himself in sacrifice to God, and in the sacrifice of the Son, in love's agreement with him, the Church-bride too can permit God to dispose of herself in the same way. This is the "sacrificial cult, in keeping with the spirit, of the offering of your bodies to be a living and holy sacrifice that pleases God" (Rom 12:1). Contemplation is a genuine sacrificial act on the Church's part and is in this way too an absolutely required existential complement of the Holy Mass.

3. As an existential act, however, it possesses a concreteness in the Church; it is not only an *opus operatum* made objective; it must be possible to say where, when, and by whom this act is performed. Here, the third element of the contemplative becomes vitally important: the fact that one is chosen and called to this. Someone must do it, and

it is God who designates this "someone". In similar fashion, in the sagas and myths of the peoples, the god indicates by lot or by some other means the sacrifice that is to be slaughtered. This election is above all the means in which the elect nature of the Church-bride becomes concrete. It is more an ecclesiological than a personal election. It falls upon someone or other—just as, for example, every tenth prisoner is shot in a war—and it falls upon the chosen one not primarily because of a particular psychological inclination or aptitude ("all this will be given to you in addition") but first of all because of an act of election. The one chosen knows that he must do it. He goes not because he is striving to acquire something for himself, because he desires his own perfection, because he wishes to flee from the world, or for any other personal and egotistical reason; he goes because he must. He does not go for himself; he goes for all. And therefore his departure has an effect on all.

The charge of caring for contemplative vocations is incumbent upon the Church as strongly as if they were the apple of her eye; and this is what they indeed are, according to Origen and other Fathers: those who see God are the eyes of the Church. They require an exceptional spiritual guidance in their monasteries; the job of chaplain in contemplative convents cannot be taken by simply any elderly priest who is unfit for other work. The care for vocations to the contemplative monasteries is incumbent upon the teaching Church: the sermon of the parish Mass must again and again explain and make understandable the meaning and the urgency of this vocation for the Church and for the world. But, unfortunately, the secular clergy is often no less ignorant and unconcerned here than the laity. The Church "outside" must accompany the Church in the enclosure in thankful love and concern; she must have enough of the Christian spirit to understand the holy silence that reigns there, without thereby letting the curtain of forgetfulness fall down in front of the monasteries. There are very many material and spiritual forms of help, even if it were only a letter as a sign of life, an act of thinking of those in the monastery.

In the Church, the monastery possesses a visibility, even if it is above all the walls that people see. The enclosure and the stability that the Benedictines vow bestows on the binding of the one chosen to God an earthly and sacramental form of definitiveness. This is, as it were, something corresponding to the indissolubility of marriage. Everything in marriage and in the monastery depends on the maintenance of this situation, at this place, in this time, in the binding to this person. To change one's monastery and "leap over the walls" is not far from divorce. Even this Christian and theological-sacramental sign has a natural basis, as the history of the Benedictines proves. In the chaos of the mass emigration, stability was the salvation; here it was possible for roots to grow that brought the shifting sand dunes to a halt. Here the grain of wheat truly fell into the ground and, dying, brought forth fruit a hundredfold. Here, in the sacramental sign, the Johannine "abiding" (*menein*) were the clearly visible criterion of Christian love and thus also the origin of new culture. Here the sign raised up on the mountain was the magnet about which, in visible and invisible form, hearts and spirits oriented themselves. One should not underestimate the power of this sign even in today's spiritual dissolution and technical hectic. A city (such as Zurich or Stuttgart) that lacks a monastery is a city that lacks a heart.

Certainly, it is important how alive a monastery is. But it is not the psychological perspectives that help us further at this point, but only theological perspectives; only the renewed strengthening of those who live an exposed life, and whose isolation has often caused them perplexity about the meaning of what they do. A path like that taken by Edith Stein from the philosophical contemplation to the theological contemplation is a light that sheds its beams for a great distance; even the Christian philosopher in the world ought to be able to find orientation by means of this light. The same is true of everyone who aims to realize something of the Christian philosophy in his life in the world.

PRIESTLY EXISTENCE

I. *Christ the priest*

In the religions of the primitive peoples, there existed and there exist today magicians and medicine men; in the developed religions there existed priests. Can they still exist today? Or, putting the question in another way: in Israel of old, which flourished in the period of the developed religions, there likewise existed priests. But can they still exist after Jesus Christ? The more that civilization removes itself definitively from the realm of the classical period—and this perhaps means also, the more that Christianity, now spread over the whole globe, reflects upon what is specific to the New Testament in its difference from the Old Testament—the more questionable will what Catholicism understands under "office" and "hierarchy" be to it. Even to us Western Catholics, the form that the priesthood has retained in the Christian East appears archaic; our Western-Roman form appears much more archaic to our Protestant brethren; it is against this issue that their protest is directed, the protest that to a large degree forms the cement bonding the divergent sects and tendencies. The response of the Catholic Church cannot consist of an increasing isolationism that, knowing in secret that it is not in step with the times, trusts in a purely supernatural manner in a miracle of God's guidance and Providence and indeed, like the baroque Counter-Reformation, perhaps glorifies its own triumph on all the walls. The response must be made in the direct encounter eye to eye with the peoples and the men of today, and this is possible only if one has listened adequately to both sides: if one has listened to the Founder, to learn what his final and genuine intention was, and if one has listened to the world of today, to learn what paths can be taken to make this institution credible and meaningful to it. In the New Covenant, an institution *is* a paradox; the others are correct to sense this, and it must be borne, presented, and lived out as such. It is possible to soften the paradox *ad*

Translated by Fr. Brian McNeil, C.R.V.

intra by spiritualizing it and, like modern Protestantism, dividing it into the "universal priesthood" of the individual and the official function that someone or other can assume for a period and is thus to be justified in categories that are purely worldly and sociological. But it is also possible to soften the paradox in the other direction by institutionalizing it (this will be the tendency in the more comfortable Catholics) and letting it stand as an erratic block that can be justified only in a positivistic sense out of the words of the Founder.

If one considers priesthood historically, it seems that three conditions are required in order for it to be allowed to exist. The first is an *awareness of being a people.* Only peoples, great and small, have priests. If the institution is general in a people or in a region, then the social structure that bears a priest can be small: an extended family, a kin group, a clan. Victorious peoples can force their religion and thereby also their institution of priests on the peoples whom they have conquered and thus make this institution respected beyond the confines of their own area; both of these crossings over, however, indicate the normal centerpoint: the institution is supported by a consciousness of being a people. The institution is plausible for the individual ego precisely to the extent that it is dominated by the "ego" of the people, by the collective "we", and finds and understands itself to be embedded therein. In the strict sense of the term, there is no individual destiny; what looks like this can be explained only on the deeper level as a communion of the individuals in the destiny of the family, of the people as a whole, and on the basis of the history of the people and prophecy concerning the people. And no matter to what extent individual figures tower up in a determined and determinative manner in this destiny, still it is the common prosperity and doom that incorporate and embody themselves in these persons; therefore, the saga and the heroic epic are concerned with all, and, even when they are heard and viewed for the hundredth time, they remain exciting and relevant. And even the gods are truly living only as one's own gods: friends or foes of the people and woven by destiny into the common determination of the people.

To the extent that this natural awareness of being a people is strong, the second element is living too: the visible social expression

of the relationship to God of this awareness in a particular *institution.*
The transcendence of the representative person who is a priest to his
office and function corresponds to the transcendence of the individual
consciousness to the "we" of the people. There already exists the
representation of the people in the head of the clan, the prince, the
King. And this too, which has to consider and bring about the earthly
good and prosperity of the tribe or people as its first duty, cannot be
separated clearly from the religious function. Early peoples make no
distinction between the sacred and the profane, and thus there must
exist a great variety of relationships between kingship and priesthood,
from the attempt by one of the two sides to equate them, *via* the inter-
weaving of the functions, to a clean distinction that has been thought
out subtly but does not leave the two without any interconnection.
The fact that priesthood and kingly court stand in a very intimate
relationship is not to be evaluated in a "psychological" sense (as if it
belonged to the character of the priest to strive for power and to
flatter power), but is the analytic result of the essence of human
society, as this was understood by the primitive peoples and by the
high cultures. Above all, the priest is the one who addresses the social
prayer to the god or gods, prayer accompanied and supported by the
social sacrifice that attests the seriousness of the homage and of the
prayer for prosperity. The fact that he is also the guardian of the
knowledge of salvation, which as such is also always a knowledge
about the way to reconcile the gods and to put them in a good mood,
is the result of this, but it does not follow that he must therefore also
be the one who transmits profane knowledge. In this sense, the
"school problem" has existed from the very beginning in one form or
another.

Because in this religion of the people the living encounter with a
divinity is always portrayed and religion has always in some manner
the character of a personal exchange, every religion of the people is
also in some way a religion of revelation. But revelation means a
making known of the word and will of God, and since this is addressed
to the people as such, it must once again be a social function. Who is
endowed with the gift of experiencing the instruction of the god?
Originally, this can be determined only by experience. The one who

has truly received this gift is also given authority: initially, when what has been prophesied of good or evil comes true, and then through all the prophecies concerning the common good that are correct. Once again there are points of contact and of conflict between the official institutional priesthood and the prophet as the mouthpiece of the god: it is obvious that one would choose the latter also as the people's spokesman in the presence of the god, and it is obvious that the official priesthood should claim for itself the role of this mouthpiece of the god. Nevertheless, the god is not to be captured in institutional structures, and thus the tension always remains possible, as is seen, for example, in ancient Israel, in which from the beginning the circles of the "prophets", from which the great prophecy gradually arose, were different from the circles of the weighty priesthood.

It is not surprising that Israel had such a priestly institution, since, despite its particular position as the people of God, it possessed a strong national self-consciousness. This is an institution that is entirely built into the people, since one particular tribe exercises the priestly functions, while its particular position and its particular traditions do not call into question its genuine tribal membership of the people. It is unimportant whether this priestly service is originally exercised in a decentralized manner in individual scattered sanctuaries or is centralized later by the kingship in the city of David. Nor is it important whether it unites itself with the kingship to the point of identity after the captivity. It is above all a sacrificial priesthood that gave itself its own law in the "priestly code" and gave itself careful historical legitimation. Although it repeatedly had points of contact with the prophetic function, it never absorbed this into itself; God's word remained free and was not to be forced into any institution. In this freedom, God's word took up a critical if not hostile position over against the official priesthood and pointed to the questionable character of a merely official service of worship. Only when the major prophecy died out in Israel did the priestly circles inherit the charism of inspiration; they created the wisdom literature and edited the final form of the sacred writings. But thereby they reached an interior boundary. Apart from Ezekiel, the prophets scarcely foresaw any institution in the old sense for the messianic time, and even in Ezekiel, the new temple with its liturgical service is a symbolic-idealistic portrayal. The bloody sacrifices continued to be offered, but their interior religious justification was the object of so much doubt that many circles of the pious distanced themselves from them. The fact that Israel today does not think of building a new temple with new sacrifices, and that thus a new priesthood is superfluous, is a clear indication of the time-conditioned character of that temple service, which did not even wait for the New Covenant before it outlived itself. This makes it strangely clear that the religion of Israel, even in its interior, "supernatural" structure, belongs at a precisely determined place in world history; nothing else can be expected, if the closer *praeparatio evangelica* was genuinely to be borne by a historical people that, as such, has its precise place in space and time and thereby also its unique context in the historical setting: Egypt, Assyria, Babylon, Greece, and Rome. The dispensation of salvation makes use of the sociological categories that are contributed by this historical position in order to prepare the way for Christ through these (and not simply bypass them). Indeed, we can take a step further and say with caution that not even Jesus' criticism of the formalism of contemporary Judaism—not only from an ethical perspective, as the morality of the Pharisees displayed this formalism, but also from a liturgical perspective, as indicated by the cleansing of the temple—stands in a hermetically sealed historical space; it is made at a point in time that is ripe for this criticism, a point that can understand it correctly and not see it merely as blasphemy against God, although on the other hand it has nothing in common with the Sadducees' liberalism or with any other Hellenistic liberalism. For what Jesus intends to put in its place is precisely not what was expected at that point in time but something that was a fortiori scandalous both for Jew and for Greek: the Cross.

But the Cross of Christ is no institution. It does indeed embrace in itself the truth of all the institutional sacrifices of mankind but in a uniqueness and personality that essentially burst open every institutional framework. In the institution, the person cannot and must not be decisive: the office is hereditary or can be bestowed anew through an election. It is irrelevant who carries out the function, provided only that the person in question corresponds to the demands made by the office. But in the case of Jesus Christ, everything depends on the person; and by "giving" itself "as a ransom for the many", this person undertakes the reconciliation of the world. It is essential that he is a priest, but he is a priest through a personal installation on the part of God, not through heredity or delegation. It is essential that he is the correct spotless sacrifice, but he is this not on the basis of an immaculateness laid down by law but on the basis of unique, unrepeatable personal holiness. This coincidence of priesthood and sacrifice cannot be the product of mere chance and thus repeatable; rather, it is so essential that here the person absolutely coincides with the office: because he is *this* one, he can, may, and must accomplish the sacrifice, and he can, may, and must be himself this sacrifice. If one considers what is the ultimate purpose of the institution of the peoples—the reconciliation of God and the people, of heaven and earth—then one must admit that precisely this was what was fundamentally awaited, although it could not be constructed by man. A presentiment of it existed in the sagas and myths that speak of human sacrifice or that truly carry it out, within and outside the Bible, although here the full innocence of the sacrifice is never attained and still less the identity of the one who sacrifices with what is sacrificed. Precisely this is what was awaited, the only thing that could give satisfaction, while there is something improbable and utterly unsatisfactory about the construction of a "legal purity" valid in the impersonal sphere of the institution, which as such would achieve influence over the ethical-religious sphere of the person.

But when once the point of identity is attained—and it can be attained only once—then it is also attained once and for all (*ephapax, hapax:* Heb 9:12, 26–27; 10:2, 10) and recapitulates in itself the plurality and generality of the institutions belonging to space and time, which are only shadows, "while the body belongs to Christ" (Col 2:17). Thereby, he brings essentially the "end of the times" (Heb 9:26), and indeed his sacrifice is as essentially unique as the human death itself, which he accomplishes and uses and thereby supersedes as a whole: "As it is laid down for man to die once, and judgment follows this, thus Christ too has made sacrifice of himself once in order to take away the sins of all" (9:28). According to this text, after the action of Christ there is no continuation in the order of actions, any more than there is any continuation of historical life after death. Just as death becomes judgment for the totality of the life that has been lived, so Christ's sacrificial death becomes the judgment for all sins but also for all the sacrifices and priesthoods that are connected with these sins. Time, the Letter to the Hebrews goes on to say, and repetition in time is the result of the insufficiency in eternity of what has been done; indeed, the periodic offering of sacrifices is essentially a celebration that recalls (*anamnēsis*) this failure. The liturgical sacrifice offered "day by day" (*kath' hēmeran*) is abolished by the "definitive" sacrifice, because the external order of sacrifices of "holocausts and expiatory sacrifices" has been interiorized, the will of God himself has been accomplished, and thereby the temporal liturgy has been rendered superfluous (Heb 10:1–18). For the future, only one is the "Priest exalted over the house of God", only one is "Mediator" in whom all who follow him upon his way find an equally immediate access to the eternal sanctuary (Heb 4:16; 7:19, 25; 10:1; Rom 5:2; Eph 1:4; 2:18; 3:12; Col 1:22). Sins against the liturgical order now become immediately sins against the celebrant of the liturgy himself, who offers himself: to sin in the face of his sacrifice means, as far as lies within one's capacity, "to crucify the Son of God afresh and expose him to public contempt" (Heb 6:6), "to trample underfoot the blood of God . . . and to insult the Spirit of grace" (10:29). For now the whole liturgy is transposed inward, into what is essential. The altar of the New Covenant, from which those who minister in the tent have no right to eat (Heb 13:10–11), is the Cross, just as the corpses of those animals whose blood the high priest brought into the sanctuary were burnt "outside, before the gates of the camp". This place outside, before the place of the earthly liturgy, is the place of the Christian sacrifice, and it is here that those who follow the one who was cast out must likewise "go out", "by bearing his shame" (13:13). There remains for them the "continual sacrifice of praise" of thankfulness, energetic proof of which consists in "doing good" to the poor and in "contributing one's goods in common" (13:15–16).

There remains something else beyond this: the meal that is to be celebrated in memory of him: the liturgical "commemoration of sin" (Heb 10:3), which is replaced by the "memorial of me" (Lk 22:19; I Cor 11:25). This is no memorial that sinks down once again into the law of the periods of times, into the futility of a periodic celebration, but something that cannot be superseded, since it makes present what is definitive and makes full satisfaction. Besides this there is the forgiveness of sins, which likewise, according to the Letter to the Hebrews, has taken place in principle *ephapax,* "once for all": this does not have to be created now for the individual in time but only needs to be applied and made present for him. Thus it is with everything that recalls the ancient liturgy in the fellowship of the redeemed, in the New and eternal Covenant: the accent no longer lies anywhere on the act of the mediating priest, which in its temporal and spatial character creates the linking of a people with God, since this access is in principle open, precisely not through the human celebrant but through the act of Christ, and from now on all thanksgiving (*eucharistia*) must be carried out in orientation to this act and in this act.

This means that what is called in the New Covenant the function of the "president", of the "minister", vis-à-vis the people of God has a wholly different basis from that in the non-Biblical and even in the Old Testament religion. The function of mediator has passed unambiguously from the priests to Christ; it is not they who carry out the sacrifice, but he. If later, in order to honor these "ministers" in their function, the Old Testament title of "priests" (*hiereis*) was once again attributed to them, one cannot forget for a moment, in this transposition, the original, essential transposition of the realities; or, as far as the German word *Priester* is concerned, one would have to recall continually its derivation from the simple term *presbyter,* the "elder", "president". One must keep in view all the time the difference in structure between the Old and the New Covenants, something that cuts through everything and begins already in the sociological givenness of what is called "people" on each side of the dividing line.

In the New Covenant, "people" is not at all primarily a new variation of a reality already known from the ordered structures of nature with fundamental roots in the interconnection of the sexes and the dimension of the prepersonal and subpersonal that is conditioned by this. It is precisely this interconnection that is dissolved here and is indeed denied for the sake of the formation of the new community (Mt 10:35–37), just as the categories that make distinctions within the people and between the peoples are explicitly transcended (Gal 3:28; Rom 10:12). The foundation for membership derives not from below but from above, from predestination, vocation, and sanctification "in order to be conformed to the image of his Son" (Rom 8:29–30). Those who are called in this way are not individuals but have de jure an immediate relationship to God; i.e., they have been mediated by the Son himself to the Father. It is of course true that the "people" is not constructed only at a secondary stage out of these "predestined" persons, as if these were already sharers in the grace of Christ before they became a part of the people and members of Christ. This means that there is not a single moment in their real existence in which the sacramental service of the New Covenant would fail to make its active contribution to introducing them into the reality of the Church and indeed of constituting them as the Church herself, as the holy assembly in his name, through the commemorative celebration of the Lord who is made present. Nevertheless, this does not prevent the Church of Christ from consisting of persons who are free in the Christian sense, i.e., who have an immediate relationship to God through the Son—a fact to which the practice of infant baptism should not blind us—and that their essential community and character as people are located primarily in Christ and in God and, as this heavenly *Civitas Dei Viventis* (Heb 12:22) not only has her Head and her noblest members in eternity (ibid., 12:23) but also possesses her own true essence there as "a Kingdom that cannot be shaken" (ibid., v. 28). No matter how good and sufficient the equipment of the earthly form of this Kingdom may be, it can never come to a perfectly rounded form on earth as the form in which something eternal is manifested, nor can it compare itself in its membership, its various functions and offices, with an earthly people and corporate society (even with one that is in part religious). It is quite simply misleading to make comparisons on a purely sociological basis, with the tacit presupposition of a univocal concept, between pagan, Jewish, and Christian priesthood and its hierarchical articulations. The foundation of pagan priesthood is primarily natural and anthropological, while the foundation of the Christian priesthood is primarily Christological and can be explained only on the basis of obedience to the explicit instruction of Christ; in the case of the Old Testament priesthood, there exists a specific mixture of natural elements and elements with a supernatural positivism; certainly, the historical basis is to a large extent natural, and this basis remains, because Israel is an earthly people even when its natural structure is exploited to such an extent in a supernatural manner through the divine revelation.

The original designation for what can still count as "priestly" after Christ and in reference to him is simply "service", *diakonia, ministerium* —service of Christ's mediatory function. To the extent that this is simply service, it falls univocally under the governing concept of the entire Christian service; its specific difference is the special instruction (and thereby the commissioning and empowering) by the Lord to serve him in such a way in his community. It is, of course, possible to understand the priesthood of the ancient cultures too as a kind of "service of the people", but it was essentially more than this precisely at the point where Christ did not mediate: the essence of the civil function bestowed at the same time a natural and societal dignity on the functionary, an elevation above the people to whom he mediated, a closeness to the gods, a competence in all matters that had to do with God. One must be quite clear that all these titles and positions of preeminence pass in Christianity primarily to Christ, and that he alone, out of his full authority, gives the Church "her full structure for the work of service" (*pros ton katartismon tôn hagiôn eis ergon diakonias:* Eph 4:12). Now, since the particular "service" of priests possesses simply the form of the general service and has at most the duty of giving a particularly emphatic expression in life to this general form, there exists in the Church no separate priestly attitude, no specific priestly ethos; rather, there holds good for the ethos of these servants—only with the highest degree of urgency—what Christ transmits to the disciples as the law that characterizes the attitude of all Christians: "The kings of the Gentile peoples lord it over them, and those who have power over them call themselves 'benefactors.' But with you it shall not be so: rather, the one among you who is greatest shall behave like the least, and the one who leads like one who serves. Who is greater, the one who sits at table or the one who serves him? Is it not the one who sits at table? But I am among you as the one who serves" (Lk 22:25–27). But it could be deceptive to look to the conduct of Christ, who is after all their "Lord and Master" (Jn 13:14), for Christ *is* Lord and abases himself to take on the attitude of the slave, and honor is due him for both reasons: because he is Lord, and because his true lordship only shines forth the more gloriously when he abases himself. But the servant is a priori a "slave", and when he sets himself in the last place, the place of the one who serves, he is doing nothing special, nothing that he ought to be honored for; what he does is great only because it reflects the attitude of the Lord—and this is great and striking in the Lord, not in the servant. And the shimmer of glory that de facto radiates over from the Lord onto the servant, for example, where the world persecutes, despises, and hates the Christians for the sake of *the name of Christ* (Jn 15:20–21), must suffice for them as the reward given by the Lord's love, because even persecution and scorn and hatred are precisely what they have a right to: "The disicple must be content when he meets the same fate as his Lord. If they have called the master of the house Beelzebub, *how much more* will they give this name to those who belong to his household" (Mt 10:25). There exists, therefore, no dialectical path by means of which the Christian servant—whether he is a servant like any Christian or this special servant who is the priest—to deduce, from the position of the service below, a new claim to be above and to receive a mark of distinction. The position of the servants above is an eschatological promise (Lk 22:28–30).

It may be true for a long time that, precisely because Christ is the true Mediator and because the Church's sacramental acts are his acts that are carried out only ministerially by the official servants, the essential work cannot be dependent on the perfection and the state of grace of the minister; but it nevertheless remains just as true that the ecclesiastical service in which Christ trains his apostles and which he hands over to them is conceived, sketched out, and handed over in a wholly primary sense as a service of humble and descending love. Here too, no parallel can be drawn between the official character of a priest of the high cultures, and even of Israel (despite the ethical instructions given to the Levites), and the official character of a Christian servant. In the former case, it is appropriate to make a fundamental distinction between the official dignity and the person who carries out the office; but in the New Covenant, the ministry would not genuinely stand under the sign of Christ unless the office that was bestowed shared in the structure of his unique office, which essentially means that the whole person is used, and used up, for the office. The long line of heresies, from Montanism *via* Donatism and the antihierarchical sects of the Middle Ages to Protestantism have correctly recognized this origin of the office in the personal attitude of Christ (and in the corresponding *requirement* made of the Christian), but they have drawn false consequences from this for the validity of the acts carried out by the office. The office itself is an ecclesiastical-societal form of the presence of Christ, and precisely (as ministry) of the humiliated Christ among those who are his, a *memoria passionis Domini,* "memorial of the Passion of the Lord", while *that* which this ministry has to transmit, that for which it is permitted to serve as a ministerial vessel, is the glory of the exalted Christ who bestows grace on his body.

Is there anything surprising, then, in the fact that the whole care of the Lord, when he is equipping his apostles for their office, and especially when he is equipping Peter who is to be the Rock, should aim at humiliation? Not only does he merely recommend humility to them: he takes every opportunity to humiliate them, as a group or individually, in his own presence and in front of each other. This is so intentional that it goes far beyond the corrections that the head of a school imparts to the group of disciples who are learning from him. If it is correctly understood, the depersonalization into the office that is made in the New Testament can be comprehended only as the highest effort on the part of the person to give away into the office all that he "gives away", and the only way in which *this* self-renunciation, which is perfect love, is brought about by grace is through the imitation of the Cross, which is precisely the journey into humiliation. But again, this is the journey into the humiliation that is quite clearly deserved, in strident antithesis to the undeserved humiliation of the Lord—and yet, precisely only in imitation of him. Or, better: in the weeping antithesis to which Peter, who denies Jesus, is led, in order to receive the threefold bestowal of his office precisely in the sadness unto death caused by his threefold betrayal.

Ministeriality in the New Testament may not in the least be understood only on the basis of a minimal guarantee for which Christ is the surety: the guarantee that, despite the insufficiency of the person who holds the ministry, the functions of his ministry retain their validity for which the Lord vouches—the correct interpretation of the word of God in the teaching office of the Church, the correct dispensation of the Christian sources of grace to those who receive the sacraments, the correct guidance of the flock. All this is true and is already grace in exuberant profusion: grace above all for the Christians who reach the Lord, who never fails, even in the priest who fails; and grace also for the priest, since it is only thanks to this guarantee that he is saved from doubting the act he performs. But if this were all, then Christ would have made the Old Testament institution the instrument of his mediation of salvation. No: if in future there is only *one* priesthood, his priesthood, then this ecclesial participation must be set into *his* form, which is that of personal love and the gift of self that goes as far as death. The instrumentality of the Catholic priest derives from the instrumentality of Christ, and this leads inexorably to the Cross. Peter is trained pitilessly to bring him to this point. The promise of the keys follows a personal act of inspired faith and confidence and opens directly into the promise of the Cross, in the first betrayal by Peter ("That shall never happen to you!"), his characterization as "Satan" and "scandal", and in the command to deny himself, to take up his cross, and to lose his life (Mt 16:13–26). The bestowal of the keys takes place in the opposite order: it draws the chosen one aside and elicits from him an act of love that he obviously cannot be responsible for either as a human being or as an ordinary Christian: "Do you love me *more than these?*"—and this, all the less, since the threefold question obviously alludes to the threefold betrayal that the office bearer has already made, so that, in the total collapse of his private person, Peter can borrow for himself only the love that is required: he borrows this from the Lord and from the Church, in order to be able to offer the personal love that he is commanded to offer out of the treasure store of love that belongs to the total personality of the Church. The Founder institutes the office in this person, who is at one and the same time humiliated to the utter depths and sanctified by love's faith; but this office is at once interpreted as a following "where you do not wish to go", i.e., to the Cross: it is only as a "lamb that is led to the slaughter" that Peter can pasture the flock as the representative of the chief Shepherd, in the unity of sacrificing and being sacrificed that is the fundamental law of the priesthood of the New Testament. The sacrificing of the love that gives its life for the sheep is no personal accessory (even if a desirable one) of the office but the *conditio sine qua non* of the very bestowal of the institution on the Church, of that institution that then — *inter alia* — includes in itself the minimum guarantee that has been mentioned. This is why the Lord will hear nothing of letting Peter off lightly. No one is treated so roughly, no one humiliated so often and so publicly, thrown into the water (spiritually and literally), as Peter. Nor has the Father let the Son off lightly, when it was a question of the office. One can be Pope only in a persisting terror that never belongs to the past but befalls one again and again anew. And the first feeling that Christians ought to have for the priest in his office is compassion. So radical is the expropriation into the love of the Church that the only aspect of the "dignity" that can be felt at first sight is the burden of the *diakonia*.

The emphasis in this context lies on the unity of the form of the Christian as the foundation of every Christian life, whether or not it is entrusted with an office. Everyone who leaves the slavery of sin (in which he was "free with respect to the law") to enter the freedom of Christ, becomes free of sin in order to become a "slave of righteousness", a "slave of God", "to bear himself into obedience as a slave" (Rom 6:15–23). The word *parastesai,* which is continually repeated (to present oneself, to offer oneself, to place oneself at disposition), is the same word that is used for the "presentation", the "making ready" of the bride by the one who leads her to the bridegroom or by the Bridegroom himself (2 Cor 11:2; Eph 5:27), the "stripping of power" of the free person who disposes of her own life so that she may enter the obedience of marriage, which is the bride's way to reflect the ministerial descent of the Bridegroom. For this reason, the instruction to humble oneself by seeking the last place holds good, not only for the one with an office but also for every Christian. For entry into membership of the body of Christ means entry into the very law of Jesus' life: the form of being a member is identical with one manner of portraying this specifically Christian love. In terms of the Christological contents, there is absolutely no difference here between the official and the nonofficial charisms. Whatever may be entrusted to the individual Christian, he possesses it in order to let it bear fruit in the community, and both the contents of the gift and the manner in which it is given—and these two belong very closely together—must take place in the manner and form of Christ.

It goes without saying that the *sacraments* of the Lord, which are to be administered by the Church, cannot form any exception from this rule. For they are the vessels of the love of Christ *katexochen,* "par excellence", and this means that the act of dispensing them cannot be something by itself that is separated from this content; rather, in its manner and in the process of being carried out, it must be something demanded and shaped by this content. It is, however, impossible for the content (and consequently also for the act of dispensing, i.e., the communication and imparting of this content) to be something without a side that is universally Christian and affects every layman, because otherwise the most interior and most important mysteries of Christ would have to be innaccessible to the layman, and one would have to hypothesize a kind of quantitative distribution of the Christian mystery that would contradict its essence. Let us take a few examples of this:

"Confess your sins to one another and pray for one another, that you may be healed; for the prayer of a righteous man has great power" (James 5:16). This confession can also include the sacramental confession before the presbyter (who has just been mentioned, at 5:4), but, as the allusion to the "righteous man" shows, it does not exclude the layman. Something similar will have to be said about the words of institution of confession, which certainly express in a special way the bestowal of authority on the college of the apostles, but—precisely because these are the representatives of the Church as a whole—

intend in a genuine (though not officially ministerial) way to include every ecclesial person too (Jn 20:22–23). The forgiving love is, in a decisive manner, that which forgives sins: both the sin of others and one's own sin (Mt 5:23–24; 6:12), if this "mutual" forgiving (Mt 18:35) takes place in reflection upon and reference to the fact that one has oneself been forgiven by God (Mt 18:21–34), concretely, through his Son. The parable of the merciless servant illustrates in Matthew the instruction about the *correctio fraterna,* which absolutely must begin in the personal sphere and is to penetrate the official and legal sphere of the Church only in a case of emergency (Mt 18:15–17). It is extremely important that between this teaching, concerning every Christian, about Christian conduct in love vis-à-vis a sinful brother and the parable about the merciless servant, which just as certainly concerns every Christian, there is set the sentence: "Truly, I say to you, everything that you bind upon earth will be bound in heaven, and everything that you loose upon earth will be loosed in heaven" (18:18). The official aspect of these words was already emphasized in the case of the promise to Peter (16:18–19), and it is therefore advisable to interpret them in a more general sense in their repetition, as referring to every Christian, since each one has a share in the Church's omnipotence in love and prayer, an omnipotence that is promised and bestowed on her as a whole, especially when she makes use of it for fraternal love in keeping with the intention of the Redeemer. It follows that it is no longer something misguided, when the early Church attributed a real power of forgiving sins to the charismatics, in the power of whose prayer with God one can have especial confidence, even if this power of forgiving was not an official authority (declarative) but a power of intercession (imprecative). One should also note that the most important "sign" of the Messiah was the *exousia,* the "authority" over the contrary power of the unclean spirits, and that this sign (also as the most important sign) was at once handed on to the apostles and contained in itself the authority to cleanse man from the power that fought against God. Something similar is true of the gift of the discernment of spirits. But in Paul, we see both included in the list of the charisms (1 Cor 12:9–10: *iamata,* bodily cures, but with a spiritual meaning; *energemata dunameôn,* exorcisms of devils; *diakriseis pneumatôn,* evaluation and distinction of the spirits, something that presupposes that one brings influence to bear upon them). In all this, there is expressed a certain participation of all the faithful in the pastoral office of the Good Shepherd: Cain's surly question, "Am I my brother's keeper?" is unthinkable on the lips of a Christian, to the extent that a service of love has been bestowed upon him and perhaps also a special "charism of exhortation" or of "almsgiving", of "works of mercy" or something similar (Rom 12:6–8). This already implies that, even as a simple member of the laity, he has his share in the handing on of Christ as the Word of God; this is also due to the fact that all are directed "to let the Word of Christ in all its richness dwell among you, and instruct and urge each other on in all wisdom" (Col 3:16); apart from this, "the gift of speech enlightened by God" (prophecy) can be bestowed on every layman (Rom 12:6), a gift that must "not be despised" (1 Th 5:20) and can be accompanied on the one side by the gift of supernatural "mysterious languages" and on the other by the gift of the "exegesis" of such languages but is centrally the "speaking of spiritual prudence" (*logos sophias*) and "speaking of deep spiritual insight" (*logos gnôseôs:* 1 Cor 12:8, 10).

Since the sacrament of the Eucharist is the making present of Jesus Christ for the community, which celebrates in thanksgiving (holding Eucharist) in the form of his substance that has been offered in sacrifice and given away so that it can even be the nourishment of men, here too the participation of all the believers overflows the boundaries of the priestly authority, which, without consideration of its clear boundary lines, appears as embedded in a dimension that belongs to the Church as a whole. One the one hand, we have — according to the same chapter in Matthew and in the same context — the *exousia* of every prayer made in the fellowship of the Church to make the Lord present: "Wherever two or three are gathered in my name, there am I in the midst of them" (Mt 18:20). This is neither the universal presence of the risen One nor his personal presence in the heart of the individual who prays and loves (Jn 14:23); it is more than the "hidden manna" that is promised to the one who conquers (Rev 2:17) and the right to eat "from the tree of life" (Rev 2:7), more than the act of opening when one hears the voice of the Lord who stands at the door and knocks, "so that I may eat together with him, and he with me" (Rev 3:20): it is explicitly the act of becoming present in, for, and through community: through the "harmonizing" (*sumphônein*) even of only "two of you", something that does not even presuppose that they are physically present with each other (*epi tēs gēs,* "on earth") and that has "any" Christian "prayer whatever" as its content (Mt 18:18–19). Origen goes further and demands that Christ be made present, not only through prayer but also through the gift of one's own life in suffering, something that John absolutely demands of Christians in the imitation of Christ (1 Jn 3:16); such a capacity of the apostles, of the disciples, and of every saint who truly makes a gift of himself, to offer out of his own substance a true bread and a true wine to his brethren (*Lev. hom.* 7, 5; Baehr. 6, 386–87), can of course be conceived of meaningfully only within the Eucharistic self-giving of Christ: as a mystery of the fruitful Vine.

There is another point at which the ministerial element flows over onto the Church as a whole, and this finds expression in the capacity of the laity to perform certain sacramental acts: in principle, every layman can and, in case of emergency, must baptize and thereby imprint on a fellow Christian the indelible seal of belonging to Christ, and this is certainly nothing smaller than the bestowal of the character of confirmation by the bishop or the priest; every Christian couple in matrimony can, in the presence of the representative of the Church and in case of emergency even without him, give to one another the sacrament of marriage, the indissolubility of which penetrates deeply into the character of the Church as primal sacrament, while orders and the bestowal of jurisdiction have an internal logic that necessarily presupposes an ordained minister who dispenses the sacrament. Much (not everything) in the question of drawing the boundaries here depends on the judgment of the Church herself, which imparts to her members the salutary measure of *exousia.* On the other hand, the Church, which is built "upon the foundation of the apostles and prophets" (Eph 2:20), was familiar at the beginning, before the apostles laid hands on others, with a celebration of the Eucharist by "prophets" who possessed no ordination other than the call by God and were legitimated for this act by their charism; Judas

Barsabbas and Silas in the Acts of the Apostles are already examples of this (13:1f.; 15:22-32), and probably also those who spoke in tongues and the prophets of Corinth (1 Cor 14:16), and in any case the "prophets and teachers" of the Didache (11:3f.), who are those with the vocation to celebrate the liturgy in that book—ordained bishops and deacons are "also" to be admitted to celebrate the liturgy in addition to them. Odo Casel demonstrates that in 1 Corinthians 12:28 and Ephesians 4:11 "apostles, then prophets, then teachers" are the members of an original charismatic hierarchy that was still at this stage instituted by God and is only abrogated by the ordinations carried out by the apostles, while appearing, in the consciousness of the Fathers, as something that has not been totally abolished: thus in the Canons of Hippolytus (6, 43f.; Achelis p. 67), where martyrs need no further human ordination because they "have attained the spirit of the priesthood" through their confession, and where in the case of a confessor who had not been tortured, while the ordination was to be carried out, that part of the ordination prayer that called down upon him the Holy Spirit was to be omitted. Similar texts are found also in several letters of Cyprian (38, 39, 40).[1]

2. Form and law

Does this mean that we are drawing close to a Protestant understanding that either deduces the hierarchical priesthood from the universal priesthood of all believers (in a democratic manner) or else acknowledges no priesthood at all other than the latter? Not in the least. The clear boundary line that is drawn in the postapostolic Church between the hierarchical office and the realm of the charisms lies at the point where that which has the force of *positive law* in the natural society is drawn by her Founder into the supernatural society of the Church in order to be the vessel for his supernatural intentions. We must describe and delimit this law from various angles.

---

[1] "Prophetie und Eucharistie", *Jahrbuch für Liturgiewissenschaft* 9 (1929): 1-19.

a. *The Christological foundation and form of the hierarchical law*

Positive law, with a legislative, executive, and judicial authority, belongs by natural law and essentially to an established human society of people and state, irrespective of the legislative source from which this positive institution is thought to be derived. Just as man as a being cannot be thought of without a historical character (something that everyone accepts today), so it is impossible to think of him as a social being without the sphere of the law (something that is often too little heeded by theology). An Incarnation of God that did not lay claim to this sphere could not count as a full entry into the human world. We need not consider here the question whether or not this sphere existed in the paradisal society, whether the sphere of law as we know it belongs to the primary or to the secondary natural law, or (in other terms) whether law exists *ratione peccati*, "by reason of sin", or whether it is only its "capacity to coerce to obedience" that points to the fall, and whether it is possible to think of law in paradise as concealed, so to speak, in spontaneous love, and "suspended". The question is pointless, because Christ came into a world of sin and, both in his own existence and (a fortiori) in the Church that he founded, took account of the way in which this world was constituted. Behind this human law there stands divine authority, whether one wishes to derive the law from a direct divine institution or from a social contract, both according to philosophical reflection and according to the teaching of Paul (Rom 13:1-10) and of Peter (1 Pet 2:13-17): no matter what kind of man he is, the one who legitimately holds the power is the one who portrays the divine order and the divine judgment in the world.

Christ makes use of this sphere, in order to allow something in particular of his own essence to become visible through it, something that doubtless could not be made clear in any other way: his "obedience unto death, indeed unto the death on the Cross" vis-à-vis the authority of the Father. It is indeed true that the infinite love that becomes visible in this obedience of the Son both as the love of the Father and as the love of the Son and as the love of their common Spirit is the highest degree of personal love that we are permitted to see in faith; but in order to prove that it is Trinitarian love, it goes precisely beyond all the boundaries of what can be seen as "personal" in the created world and can be made comprehensible. Precisely the descent from "Son of the Father" to "Servant of Yahweh", from the absolute intimacy in the bosom of the Father to the alien condition of obedience to an authority: this descent "for the sake of sin" into the "form of the sinful flesh", this clothing and concealing of the contents of love in the form of judgment and of the inexorable judicial execution: precisely this is the appearing of the superhuman, divine, triune love. Thus it is not enough to follow Anselm's theory of satisfaction and deduce the necessity of the Cross in keeping with secular juridical thinking; one must go beyond this to assert that this form (imposed by sin) is precisely the correct appearing of a pure, divine content.

This means that one cannot deduce the juridical sphere in the Church as a residue produced by the collapse of the original charismatic sphere, as Buber has attempted to show in the case of ancient Israel (*"Gotteskönigtum"*) and Sohm has attempted to show in the case of the Church.[2] The authority of the Father vis-à-vis the incarnate Lord, which the Father hands over to the Son so that all may honor him as they honor the Father (Jn 5:22), is handed over in turn, just as it is, as absolute authority, to the Church. It is only in this way that an interpersonal relationship between men, independent of the quality of the individual person and possessing a universal validity (not only for a "circle" or a "confederation"), can represent the absoluteness of the authority within the Godhead of the Father to the Son and the authority of the Son over the Church within the dispensation of salvation. On the human level, it is a genuine authority that is not softened down, a genuine law that does not need to give up its own structure in order to become the bearer and the transparency of something that is divine and divine-human. But once again, this law has its ultimate legitimation only in the fact that its content is the divine-human sublimity of Christ's obedience in love, and that it is understood and lived as the expression of the revealed absolute relationship of love between the Father and the Son in the Spirit.

[2] Harnack's analysis of canon law as the combination of a purely human law and a law of pure *charis* is equally unsatisfactory.

This divine-human obedient love of the Son is of such a kind that, in order to find a vessel in what is human, into which it can pour itself, it needs both the highest personal relationship between man and man as the love that makes a gift of itself, bears all things, endures all things, and forgives all things (1 Cor 13), *and* the legal relationship that is independent of all personal vacillations and influences, something that bestows on the human act an unassailable competence for the sake of a supernatural common good. But here the law that holds sway is identical with the legislator himself; Christ is the Lord *and* the living law of his Church. This conception of an encounter, indeed of an identification, between that which is human-personal and that which is human-impersonal is theoretically so bold that it can ultimately be justified only on the basis of the Trinity itself and is therefore doomed a priori to be misunderstood by all who are unwilling to accept this mystery of God. It is also so bold in practical terms that the hazardous enterprise of adopting it as a law of one's existence seems something superhuman and can be justified and guaranteed as a possible form of life only on the basis of Christ the Founder. The gospel at once points to such an adoption of responsibility on the part of Christ, since the Lord does not in the least wait until the disciples have had an appropriate personal education, before he gives them (almost already when he calls them) the *exousia* over the enemy of God, the evil spirit, while also bestowing on them the authority of the word of God vis-à-vis men: "The one who hears you, hears me; the one who despises you, despises me" (Lk 10:16).

Human words break down when they attempt to describe this form of existence, because here it really holds true that *gratia non tollit naturam*, "grace does not remove nature", and because nature needs an *elevatio* if it is to unite on their own level, out of the power of the hypostatic dual nature, things that are contradictory without damage and without distortion. Practically and ethically speaking, this means that the priest should announce that he has genuine authority vis-à-vis the faithful and that he should receive genuine obedience from them, but he should understand and present this genuine authority as the authority of Jesus Christ by behaving only as their "servant". But the authority of Christ is based on his office, which is identical with

absolute love and therefore displays itself in the Church with equal
immediacy as fraternal love: this is why the authority of the priest
must be displayed in his life in such a way that it points to the love of
Christ and at the same time permits fraternal love to become visible in
the priest's behavior. This love requires of him that he carry out his
office in the spirit of Christ's love for men and thus in absolute
selflessness and in the gift of his life for his brethren. But it demands at
the same time—since Jesus' love for the world derives from his obedient love for the Father—that the priest's gift of himself in love give
account of itself primarily vis-à-vis the Lord and keep to the measure
laid down by the Lord, just as the Son does vis-à-vis the Father. The
Son is bound to the Father's will and to his earthly law, and he cannot
establish the New Covenant and its love in any way other than by
fulfilling the Old Covenant and its prophecy and its disposition of
righteousness—and indeed its threat of righteousness. He must put
more love into his works than into his words.

The central difficulty for the priestly man is how he can make his
personal love transparent to the obedient love of Christ and make
what is an impersonal legal attitude at the same time credible as
Christian brotherly love. He must not bind in a personal manner to
himself the fellowman whom he loves but must lead him by way of a
genuinely human relationship of brotherly love to the love of Christ.
He must let his love open out into the love of Christ, not by withdrawing it from his brother but by making himself transparent and perhaps
also by drawing attention to the legal side of the relationship. But this
transparency is not a flight into the shelter given by authority from
the situation between one man and another. Here lie the greatest
dangers for the priest, because here authority is misused in a subtle
way in order to mask a lack of the love that holds firm. The reference
to law and authority is used to break off abruptly discussions in which
he ought to hold firm. This reference can often be appropriate, but
just as often it covers up a latent anxiety at the prospect of being
exposed to the unprotected, defenseless character of an encounter
between men. The point is not that the priest should absolutely let
himself be insulted by a crowd without understanding or by embittered
individuals; the point is that he should not wriggle out from the

seriousness of the genuine confrontation with the brother whose brother (not master) he is, and that perhaps—if he has in fact wriggled out or is one who chronically wriggles out—he is willing to have his mistake pointed out to his face and admits it. Since the office can so easily be used as an impregnable fortress, since the preacher speaks from the pulpit without any dialogue (a tremendously dangerous interpersonal situation) and he all too easily looks on this situation as the situation that is normal for him in his relationship with his fellowmen, there exists for the priestly class an unmasking psychology that every office bearer must look squarely in the eye again and again, to see whether it does not perhaps apply to him. Peter sinks as soon as he reflects on himself and has thereby to fight against anxiety. The priestly form of life can be lived only in pure, naïve faith and thereby out of the power of Christ; every act of looking back upon oneself produces the anxiety that at once necessarily takes refuge behind the office and brings the "dignity" forward.

The dignity lies in the fact that Christ creates such a transparency in the priest that he, as one who is totally a servant, can let the Lord, who stands above him, become transparent. The more he serves, accordingly, the better does the transparency succeed. The more he applies titles of dignity to himself, the more opaque does he become. Most of these titles contradict an explicit prohibition by the Lord. "Father", "pater", "abbot", "papa", and "abbé" stand in opposition to Matthew 23:9; "master" and "magister" in opposition to Matthew 23:8; "doctor" (in the ecclesiastical sense) in opposition to Matthew 23:10; "lord" (*Dominus, Dom*) and "my lord" (monsignore) in opposition to Luke 22:25; "your Grace" (*euergetēs*) likewise in opposition to Luke 22:25; and "your excellency" and "your eminence" in opposition to the instruction at Matthew 20:26–27; 23:11; Mark 9:35; 10:43–44; Luke 22:25; and John 13:13–17. Apart from the titles "brother" and "servant", which are permitted, at most only the title "prelate" would come into question, since it expresses in material terms the office of presiding, but under the condition that every curate or chaplain would have a right to use it. How long—after the close of the feudal period, in which there were imperial and prince archbishops—

will these obsolete and Christianly incomprehensible titles continue
to be dragged along in the Church's baggage?

The ministerial character of the hierarchical law is shown also in
the fact that the law emerges with all the more emphasis, the more the
one who hears the word, who obeys the pastoral staff, who receives
the sacraments, is willing to acknowledge the office and submit
himself to it, i.e., the more the mutual attitude of service that Christ
commanded in love shines through the one who gives and the one
who receives. Here this law is a juridical imitation of the love of the
Lord himself, who has never showed his legal claim to men outside his
love and permitted this legal claim to emerge only when he encountered
love that he had awakened or encouraged. Indeed, more than this: the
relationship in law, which can be determined in isolation to a certain
extent, that Christ has as King and Lord over a soul comes into the
light where he can dispose in sovereignty over a soul that is totally
given over to him in the sense of the mystery of redemption, just as
the Father has disposed over him: by concealing the love and bringing the law into the foreground. But precisely this situation is exclusively the function and revelation of love and displays the opposite of
what is the aim of the legal sphere in human society, viz., the establishing
of the common good even where love is lacking in individuals. We shall
have to discuss this also immediately after the present point. Here the
decisive thing is the Lord's example, which furnishes the ultimate
legitimation of ecclesiastical law, the example in which law does not
stand in any "tension" over against love but is instead the expression of
love. Not only the expression of the Trinitarian and thus of the more
than (individually) personal love but also the expression of the dispensation of redemption with this love that is concealed because of the
Cross, but which is revealed on a higher level precisely in the Cross
for the one who believes. On the way to the Cross, and nowhere else,
is the word uttered: "Yes, I am a King"—but a King whose "Kingdom
is not of this world", i.e., does not possess the boundaries and structures
of merely earthly kingdoms but has its center of gravity in heaven.
This does not mean that "this world" (Jn 19:37) does not also belong
explicitly to his Kingdom ("All *exousia* in heaven and on earth has
been given to me": Mt 28:19)—and the inclusion of this earthly sphere

in his law also makes "canon law" possible—but for the time being (before the Last Judgment) he applies his law only in such a way that it may be "the law of redemption", which is a function of love, and at the same time a "law of revelation", which has its starting point and its domicile in heaven and, in its passage through the worldly spheres, once more is directed to heaven or (in the *exousia* over the spirits) to hell. This already implies that in the example Christ gives up to his death there is no possibility of carrying out any separation between the Lord and the Servant: he is not Lord at one time and Servant at another but shows that he is Lord precisely in the center of his abasement in service, which arouses such astonishment because it is possible to grasp by means of this both that it is something that contradicts his true being as King, *and* yet that it provides this with its most sublime and most appropriate expression. When, in his meekness that descends to us, he nevertheless "speaks as one who has power" (Mt 7:29), when he proclaims in his acts that he has the power to forgive sins (Mt 9:6), so that people exult that "God has bestowed such great power" (9:8), nevertheless this always blazes forth from his humility, which forbids the apostles to employ any purely worldly use of force (Lk 9:56; 22:49–50). The Greek, and especially the Alexandrine, theology has always pointed out that Jesus never used his heavenly power on earth to coerce and overpower but always *peithei, suasione,* meekly encouraging, persuading from within, advising, helping. This fact does not as such simply include the thesis of nonviolence as found in India, in Tolstoy, and in Reinhold Schneider or the Protestant denial of all genuine canon law instituted by God. But it does point with all seriousness to something that is not only 'hinted at' from afar in all the Church's legal acts, but truly comes into view: the Redeemer's attitude of love.

The only way for the priest to attain, in some measure, this Christological unity of authority in humility, in higher humility where higher authority is demanded, the raising up of the authority through the deepening of the humility, is in fact through a prayer that is utterly alive and through the continuous act of submitting his entire existence in love and obedience under the image and the authority of Christ. For the ability to copy such a unity is pure grace, although it certainly is a promise of grace that is included in the grace accompanying the mission of the one who willingly allows himself to be formed by the grace of Christ. It is, however, not a grace that does everything by itself but one that requires the humble obedience of the man who holds the office, so that it can imprint the character of the Christological paradox on this lived obedience. And the priest can give the truly convincing example and demand of others only what he himself has experienced existentially in this way in his obedience to Christ.

b. *Ecclesiastical law and ecclesiastical voluntariness*

The second delimitation is already hinted at in what has just been said and must now be developed. Civil law is instituted by God (Rom 13:1) in order to maintain order by means of "the sword" for the sake of the common good. This *exousia* is "God's helper and executes punishment on the one who does evil; this is why one must submit to it" (Rom 13:4–5): in interior terms, this submission is due to the fact that one is a sinner, but, to the extent that this *exousia* represents God's power as Judge, one must also submit to it in exterior terms as a free son of God (Mt 17:24–27; 22:15–22). The *exousia* that Christ bestows on his apostles and on their successors is not a law for sinners but the "law of the Kingdom of heaven", and indeed the law of the *hidden* Kingdom of heaven that is coming on earth in the *visible* Church: in its hiddenness, the Kingdom of heaven cannot have the same total organization as an earthly commonwealth. The fullness of power is not based originally—as in the case of the latter—on the body of the people as a whole (in dependence on God's power) in such a way that each member has a share in this power by natural law and therefore makes legal claims on the civil authority to protect him and promote his good; rather, the fullness of power rests only in the heavenly Head of the Mystical Body, who hands it over, precisely not originally to the Church as an entire body (in parallel to the state) but to the apostles whom he sends out and to their successors: to the Pope in undivided totality, to the college of bishops (likewise with an unmediated relationship to Christ but in harmony with the Pope and leaving his primacy intact). This means that canon law is fundamentally a genuinely clerical law, a law that is precisely determined and delimited *as* law by the explicit will of the Founder to equip his official representatives, whose duty it is to proclaim the coming of the God of the Kingdom and to make this visible and credible in the ecclesiastical institution, with the powers necessary for this task.

This particular structure of ecclesiastical law is seen most simply in the *potestas praedicationis* (also called, less characteristically, the *potestas magisterii*). The apostles (and their successors) have received from Christ the power to proclaim the word of God "not as a human word, but as that which it is in truth, the word of God" (1 Th 2:13). This power means that they have the authority and the ability to go beyond everything that men—even those with charismatic gifts—can say about their own proclamation and to state that their kerygma is the word of God. To make this "right" credible, they cannot appeal to anything (not even directly to the inherent quality of their word) other than to the command and the power to preach that they have received from Christ. It does not immediately follow that one can deduce from this "right" a corresponding obligation on the part of the hearer; it is not the immediate concern of the preachers, as such, whether men are willing to listen or not, whether they become converted or not. Accordingly, they may not employ any human means to bring about (still less to compel) such a relationship of law between themselves and their hearers; they may not even entrap the hearers with the means of an all too human rhetoric; rather, aware of their whole human impotence, they must entrust to God alone the power of persuasion (1 Cor 2:3–5). So, when they find closed doors, they should not continue to insist on a "right" and force their way in; rather, as the Lord himself did, they should go on their way and leave those who were not ready standing where they are (Mt 10:12–15; Lk 4:30; Jn 8:59; 10:39; 12:36). This is how the apostles behaved everywhere. And since Jesus did not even acknowledge that his (unbelieving) hearers had the right to learn from him what authority he had to claim God's word for himself (Mt 21:27), the disciple likewise who has received an office does not owe a reckoning to anyone: "I care little whether I am judged by you or by any human

body; indeed, I do not even judge myself . . . my Judge is the Lord"
(1 Cor 4:3-4).

Strictly speaking, therefore, the power to preach the gospel to the
peoples does not in the least establish a particular right vis-à-vis these
peoples. Christ alone has the "right" to send the apostles, because he
alone possesses authority over the peoples; he possesses the right as the
Son of God and has also won it for himself as Redeemer on the Cross.
When the apostles and their successors preach to the peoples, they can
refer them only to this right of Christ; they themselves do not possess
it. In other words, it is possible to infer a right from their commission
only where converts already exist, where there is the Church. By
definition the Church is unique, and so there is nothing that would
correspond to the "international law" as opposed to the spiritual "civil
law", i.e., to canon law; only the Redeemer, who is the Judge of the
world, possesses such an "international law". In the same way, there
cannot exist *jure divino* anything like an interecclesiastical (interconfessional) canon law, since, from the Legislator's point of view, the
division of the Church is *the* crime.

The situation of the apostle who is sent out becomes different only
where it is no longer vis-à-vis the world that he carries out the
proclamation, but within the Church vis-à-vis those who are baptized,
for here the right of the shepherd (*potestas regiminis*) is added to the
right of proclamation because of the sacramental power (*potestas
sacramentalis* or *ordinis,* in the broadest sense) that is being exercised.
But not even this new legal relationship may be simply constructed in
keeping with the schema of natural and positive secular law; it must at
once be considered and developed in its own particularity as canon
law. The fundamental difference lies in the fact that, whereas one is a
member through nature and compulsion of the human society that is
tainted by original sin and therefore both can and must be brought
back to order and kept in order through coercion by the forces of
order, one can and may be a member of the Church only voluntarily
out of thankful love for the Lord who has redeemed. The baptism of
infants does not alter this in any way in principle, for the one who has
reached the age of reason must now supply the voluntary decision
and the sacrament must be ratified; otherwise, he must leave the

Church. Above all, this is not altered by the fact that a great deal of resistance to our own will to baptism and our will to be in the Church continues to exist in us who are weak and hesitant and subject to the consequences of original sin; and the Church's teaching and pastoral authority may and must confront this resistance, not only with personal exhortation and help but also with institutional means. But if it is possible here to speak of something like legal coercion, of the power to compel obedience to the spiritual law, this is never in the sense of the secular authority as vindicative law; the function of the vengeance that achieves a legal equilibrium between crime and punishment is simply not entrusted to the representatives of the Church, who have no share in Christ's judgment of the world that he will execute upon the good and the evil in the name of the Father. In this age of the world, no one can grasp the inner relationship between this judgment of the world and the law of redemption, nor is anyone entrusted with the authority to see it as a whole and to regulate it. Rather, all that they have a share in is the "law of the redemption": their (limited) authority to exhort, and indeed to punish, not only to loose but also, under the appropriate circumstance, to bind, is exclusively a function of the redemption that is to be displayed and spread by the Church: it is not vindicative but pedagogical. It must lead to love and instruct in love, and Paul, who occasionally makes use of this authority—where he does not simply threaten this (a very important point) as a "possibility" (1 Cor 4:21: "Shall I come to you with the rod, or in love?" 2 Cor 13:2: "When I come to you the next time, there will be no indulgence!")—does so, even in the worst case like that of "handing over to Satan", always with a view to betterment (1 Cor 5:5; 1 Tim 1:20). In other words, the ecclesiastical punishment up to the point of "excommunication" and "handing over to Satan" is not at all to be equated with the act of "leaving" the unbelievers "standing where they are" if they do not accept the proclamation of the Kingdom. Neither of these is vindicative; the earlier is the conduct of the Kingdom, which is as yet only "arriving" and does not force its way through where it is not accepted; the second is the conduct within the established fellowship of the Church, in which ultimately everything is based on love and therefore gives a training, even only with the means of postponement, of penitence and of exhortation, in the love that has been accepted in principle but has not yet been understood aright in its consequences. Christ and the apostles never excommunicated those who did not wish to accept the word and to belong to the Church; they have "left them standing", and this is something quite different. The refusers have excluded themselves from Communion. There is no occasion for the Church ever to depart from this mode of conduct, which is fundamental for the whole of canon law, and to lay claim for herself to the manner of thinking of secular vindicative penal law. This holds true of the underlying sense of all the paragraphs in the code of canon law *De poenis*.[3]

Naturally, the Church's leadership has the authority to build up and carry out an internal order in positive law, consisting of many individual regulations, within the Church in order to exercise the legal pastoral authority (*potestas regiminis* or *jurisdictionis*). A *potestas coercitiva* too belongs to such a legislative and executive authority. Nevertheless, in all this legal context one must always keep precisely in view the origin and the purpose to which the legal authority is oriented: the totality is a law of redemption, the portrayal of Christ's commission to carry out reconciliation in the world, and thus even what appears as punitive authority within this context in Christ himself or in those in the Church who bear his commission must belong, in the strict sense that is visible to everyone, to this specifically *Christian* redemptive authority (and not, for example, merely to a general *bonum commune*). Thus, for example, the confessor must utter a genuinely judicial sentence about the sinful condition of the penitent, but he may not understand this sentence as something deriving from the sentence of judgment of the Last Judgment but only as something deriving from the verdict of grace that goes forth from the Cross. Paul's teaching is valid for the whole Church, including her legal dimension: "Do not avenge yourselves, beloved, but leave space for the judgment of wrath. For it is written: 'Vengeance is

---

[3] This is true also for the *poenae vindicativae* listed in canons 2291ff. of the (1917) code in distinction from the *poenae medicinales* or censures (which include excommunication, interdict, and suspension), for even the former are governed by the presupposition that one can be in the Church only on a voluntary basis.

mine; I will repay, says the Lord'" (Rom 12:19; Dt 32:35). The Middle Ages, which brought the secular and the spiritual authority into an organic unity, took great care to distinguish the spiritual and the secular sword and arm and yet could easily come to transgressions of the boundaries and to confusions that over a long period were able to establish themselves as customary. This is why it is important always to recollect the specifically spiritual character of the Church's law, although here the term *spiritual* does not in the least deny or reduce the genuinely legal character (law either is or is not) but only indicates its distinctive constitution. Thus, for example, one can ask oneself whether it is in keeping with the mind and the intention of the Church to *"punish"* by excommunication groups of Christians who are no longer willing to stand by the confession of their divinely established order (which includes obedience under the Pope), or whether the word *excommunication* does not in fact mean something different here: the simple recording of the fact that those who have left voluntarily no longer wished to belong to this community that exists in this manner, and that, if they should return, they would not really require to be absolved from a *"poena" (excommunicationis)*.

The office of pastor implies that those who "preside" in the Church have to take care for an order in the Church that is human and at the same time regulated in the Spirit of Christ. This instruction of the Lord is the point from which flows everything else that is regulated by canon law and leaves the broadest freedom to those who preside, provided only that they take heed to the Spirit and the intention of the Lord. The result is a *jus ecclesiasticum* that does indeed depend on the authority given by the Lord but in every other respect is a genuine human law. Where the Lord himself did not lay down explicitly the particular competences (and these essentially affect the clergy), the Church's office has the duty of resolving the question of authority, e.g., by entrusting to the laity this or that competence, greater or smaller competences in ecclesiastical matters and functions, enlarging some powers and withdrawing others, etc. In this field, which as such embraces *jus ecclesiasticum,* not *jus divinum* (*jus Christi*), one can speak of a greater or lesser sphere of competence of the laity, whereas there is no "lay law" corresponding to the narrower realm of the obligations and powers of the clergy; we shall discuss this more precisely below.

The task of the clergy is the ordering of the reception of the sacraments, the regulation of worship and of religious instruction, and the formation of Christian life in private, in homes, and in public. Behind the function in general (not behind the individual directive) stands the Founder's will that there should exist order, and the Christian obeys this will when he bows to the ecclesiastical house order. The distinction is easy to make and is often drawn clearly in Paul: the individual directive comes from the Apostle, but he "has also the Spirit of Christ" (1 Cor 7:40, 25). Nevertheless, the Apostle and the Church can draw on the authority of Christ to make a decision in a serious case, as Paul does in the problem of charismatic persons in Corinth: "If anyone believes that he possesses the gift of prophecy or any other charism, then he should also recognize that what I am writing to you is a commandment of the Lord. If he does not recognize this, then let him [or: he will] not be recognized either" (1 Cor 14:37–38). But the function of regulation is not the primary content of ecclesiastical life, which lies in love and in all the areas in which this can be applied by the Christian (and even the area of legal relationships is only one of these among others), areas in which the decisive note is given by the free spontaneity of love, "being driven by the Spirit" (Rom 8:14), by that inner obedience that is one with true freedom. It can be the sign and the expression of this freedom when one who conforms as closely as possible to the divine freedom renounces the manifestations of his own freedom and makes this decision expressive by binding it to the ministerial authority of the Church to issue commands. Such a Christian obedience is charismatic and presupposes a special, insistent vocation to this by the Holy Spirit, a vocation that makes it possible for the one who binds himself in this way to live his fetters as the expression of a highest freedom and of the imitation of the Cross.

c. *Ecclesiastical boundaries of canon law*

Here we have already touched on the third particularity of the "clerical law". No matter how open to misunderstanding and how back to front it is to deduce this law from an originally charismatic ordering (as something left over after the great charisms died out, something that is perhaps regrettable but perhaps also something quite natural and acceptable), it is also important that we see that God is not obliged to limit himself to the path of the Church's authoritative bodies, which he has instituted, when he is imparting his graces. Alongside the hierarchical law there exist the missions and charismatic tasks and offices, which derive from God with the same immediacy as the vocations. Do they form a legal order by themselves, something that would be independent of the hierarchical order? They are not, at any rate, so independent that the hierarchy would be dispensed from exercising its function of ordering with regard to them: obedience to the hierarchy was and is in all cases of a tension between office and charism always the criterion of the genuineness of the latter. But this does not mean that the office could ignore as something irrelevant the charisms and the divine commission that, in certain circumstances, lies in them (perhaps a commission directed to the office itself, perhaps to the universal Church, and perhaps only to a limited circle). Where the ecclesiastical testing of the charisms is necessary, it is an aspect of the ministry of those who administer the order of love that has been established by the Head, because this order stands at the pure disposition of the Head and otherwise does not need to be wholly visible. This is the meaning of the last episode of the Gospel of John (cf. 20:1-10 with 21:20-23). The "apotheosis of the office" with which the Gospel of John ends demands, as the final precise definition—after the whole love of the Church had been demanded of Peter in an official manner, and he had received the commission to be shepherd and also the promise of his own cross—the reference to the sovereignty of the true Head of the Church who does not need to give any account of himself to Peter. The boundaries of the office do not necessarily coincide with the boundaries of love, and the task of determining these boundary shifts goes beyond the tasks of the office. "What has that to do with you?" The immediacy of relationship to Christ that the charismatic order possesses (because this immediacy simply belongs to the interior personal order of grace and makes this visible in part) must be taken into account by the office, just as the charisms must take the office into account. But charisms can receive from God an equipment and an urgent commission that can be very similar to the official commission with its character of law; they present a kind of "divine law" that, however, remains only personal and neither limits the legal character of the hierarchical office nor calls it into question in any other way. The office is lasting and institutional, while the charisms are personal, even if one cannot absolutely assert that they die out with the death of the person: charisms of saints continue to work through the ages; charisms of founders of orders set their mark upon whole generations of religious and awaken a particular kind of charismatic imitation and charismatic obedience. This too must be given its place by the office in the ordering of the universal Church, and thus the chapter *De religiosis,* with all the relevant derivations and accompanying forms, has its place in canon law. Out of the fullness of its own authority, the office can bestow legal competences on this charismatic order (on the abbots and other superiors), so that there are a compenetration and a mutually complementary working in this field of a charismatic structure of command and obedience and of a structure of command and obedience that belongs to canon law. Even if the theological origin of the personal vocations to follow Christ has an immediacy of relationship to Christ and is thus charismatic, and the whole stand of the counsels, since it is an immediate institution of Christ, does not depend on the hierarchy, nevertheless it submits in terms of canon law to the hierarchy's competence, and the hierarchy must be concerned, within the limits of its possibilities, to form the stand of the counsels in the spirit of the gospel.

Charism is usually understood as a particular and personal commission given to the individual Christian in grace, with roots in his personal baptismal grace and in the mission that he receives in confirmation. But this means that the charismatic element points us back to the element of grace in Christian existence in general: all canon law stands at the service of this dimension, and, in keeping with its innermost essence, it has an immediacy of relationship to God and to Christ. Everything in the Church—and therefore the legal dimension too—must encourage as best it can this immediate exchange between God and his creature, and it never has the right to insert itself as an intermediate, mediatory stage. The appearance of a conflict can arise only because this encouragement itself is something demanded by God. For there can be no doubt that there is more for the layman in the Church, on the basis of the grace of baptism and confirmation, than merely the "right" to exist in the clerically administered Church and to receive passively the sacraments that are dispensed by the clergy, viz., something that is as radically positive as Christ's missionary command to the apostles themselves. Everyone who is baptized and confirmed is called and empowered to be Christ's witness in the world, and he may and must be a witness to the point of committing his own life, to the point of martyrdom. This is the nobility and rank of the Christian; this is both his "obligation" and his highest freedom, in which he is permitted to make known with joy his gratitude to his Redeemer; and he perceives anew, and more intensely, that the fact that he is permitted to do this is grace. No Christian has any privilege vis-à-vis another Christian at this innermost point, since even the vocation of the apostles does not stand "higher" than that of any one of the baptized; this means also that the original baptismal mission of the layman cannot be derived as a delegation from the clerical authority, since it is subordinate to this authority only at a secondary stage as the body that is competent in all matters of Church order. But this means that the original baptismal mission of the layman is not to be understood as a "right", any more than we were willing earlier to see the commission of the apostles to preach as a "right" vis-à-vis the peoples. It is something that the apostles may and must do, something rooted in the commission given by Christ's grace, accepted in love for him, experienced and affirmed in its urgency. And to whom should the apostle who proclaims Christ be able to announce a right? The establishment of a genuine right began for the apostle at the point where he was to "pasture", in the commission and out of the power of Christ, those who converted voluntarily to the Lord, "building them up" and "forming" them to be Christ's "body" and "bride". This is the specific character of the clerical commission, which marks it out over against the general commission of the laity to bear witness, which has its roots in love's immediate relationship to Christ; this commission would fail to recognize itself and would reduce itself, if it wished to interpret and understand itself in the sphere of canon law; and the laymen who claim "more rights" in the Church do not know precisely what they want. What they call their "right" (that which they are permitted to be vis-à-vis Christ) is neither strengthened nor improved by being written down in the code of canon law. Compared with this mighty "law", the small participation in the clerical function of ordering (and it cannot be more than a small share, if they wish to remain laymen and not become members of the clergy) would be virtually a microscopic speck. These claims of the laity can arise only at the point of intersection of two misunderstandings: that the clergyman with his function of service "has more" than the layman in Christian terms, and besides this, that what both have in common can be expressed on the level of "rights and obligations". But what the clergyman "has more" is essentially a burden for the sake of the laity's freedom—naturally, a burden that is itself a function of love (and thereby, of freedom): closer following that leads into the binding of the Cross. The layman should therefore ask himself seriously what it is that he is in fact demanding: Is it rights in the sense of the rights of citizens (e.g., the right to share in decision making)? Such rights do not exist in the least. Or is it the only Christian privileges that truly exist: a closer binding to the Cross? Why then does he not choose the clerical order or the religious state?

This is what must be said on the fundamental, theological level. On the practical and psychological level (which, however, is much less relevant), one can always bring forward many things; above all, much (including the formulations of canon law and "concessions" of the clergy) that would permit the layman to have a more living conviction of his original mission and would also offer him concrete opportunities to carry out this mission, although the layman (just like the clergy in its pastoral care within the Church) may never forget that, for the one who is baptized, the essential area of the mission is not so much the ecclesiastical sphere as the world that lies in darkness and the shadow of death "outside".

3. *Priestly life yesterday and today*

The threefold sharpening of the definition of the particular legal character of the hierarchy urgently draws the attentions of its bearers to the fact that everything in this law is based on a commission of Christ, i.e., on obligations to him, and that thus everything about this office is a service of the Lord and of his community, that the priest is a servant from every point of view and a lord from no point of view, because the function of being Lord and of ruling as Lord belongs alone to the heavenly Head and, at best, to the community that has arrived at "lordship" through this service (1 Cor 4:8). This lack of correspondence between achievement and reward (in the form of respect, dignity) belongs to the following of Christ in office. Paul of course knows the category of "praise" and of "self-praise", which for him belongs inseparably to the wholeness of the person. But the praise of the apostle and of the office bearer in the Church lies not in himself—even when the community may boast of him—but alone in God (1 Cor 1:31; 2 Cor 10:17) or then in the community, which is his own reward (2 Th 1:4; 1 Th 2:19–20); precisely for this reason, all that he can boast of in himself is his weakness, his kenotic existence (2 Cor 11:30; 12:5, 9), and this in turn means making his boast in the Cross of Christ (Gal 6:14) and not in his own deeds done in the service of the gospel (1 Cor 9:16), but at most in the consciousness "of having lived not in the wisdom of the flesh but in the power of God in the world" (2 Cor 1:12). Thus Paul can boast with a loud voice of his existence in mission, which has given him a place in the following of the Lord, and he himself posits this boasting as "folly" vis-à-vis a fleshly self-praise (2 Cor 11:16–18). But when he boasts, it is precisely not of his office as of an objectively valid dignity independent of his existence that as such would demand respect: he sees and describes this office exclusively in the context of his humiliated existence (2 Cor 12–13). The contradiction, the dialectic between the first place, which he is guaranteed by the office, and the "last place of the one condemned to death" (1 Cor 4:9) brings him necessarily into an ambiguous reputation that his enemies in the communities delight in exploiting. An unambiguous earthly honor and dignity are not to be separated out from this tangle: the dishonor of Christ has come into the whole complex and matted it together.

The "dishonor" that relentlessly presses to the fore again out of all ecclesiastical "dignities" is the unique and the great opportunity of the Catholic priesthood in this age. If it does not wish to be misunderstood and taken for something else in the form of the history of religions, which we sketched at the beginning—for this would mean that it belonged definitively to a past that has long been superseded and that modern Protestantism, modern Judaism, and the modern "philosophical faith" would be easily vindicated over against it—then the priesthood itself, and out of itself, must produce the evidence before the world that it—as office, as "impersonal" function—stands or falls with Christology, and that surely means with the person and the existence of Christ. If its only self-justification is in terms of general sociology, then the game is up for it, no matter how much those versed in the natural law may demonstrate that a "priesthood" too belongs to a "people" and that modern humanity has become degenerate by losing this awareness. The apostles are, precisely, the apostles of Jesus Christ and are not to be placed on the same sociological grade as the temple priests of Memphis, Delphi, and Rome. The opportunity for the Catholic priest lies in the fact that, in the manner in which he is a priest as well as in the manner in which he (and also the people, whom he represents) understands his office, he demonstrates the difference between the Church and all other religious groups in history and in the present.

Here there lie decisions that have to be taken in all seriousness by the Church's priesthood and that it cannot simply leave to the general Providence of the Holy Spirit vis-à-vis the Church. These are decisions that make urgent demands of the clerical self-understanding and of its self-definition in the face of the world of today, and which can be made credible to the world not by means of conciliar words alone but only through a consistent behavior and attitude. Without doubt, there always lies an "excessive demand" in the Church's office, as long as one looks only at the human strengths, and this lack of proportion between the human wretchedness and the immensity of the commission is assiduously revealed by the gospel in the education of the apostles and especially of Peter, the fisher of men. If one has cast even a fleeting glance at this construction, one will not fail to see this fundamental lack of proportion, even when one cannot accept that it is spanned through grace in the faith of the humbled man who is the Rock. But what this distant spectator absolutely expects to see is the awareness of this fundamental lack of proportion: in other words, the existential pointer to Christ that lies in the office and in the way in which it is carried out, the evidential character that becomes everywhere visible, that man by himself cannot do this, and that, if he does have the ability to do something, he understands this as a miracle from above and not as his own achievement; in short, a humility that is no mere decorative virtue but is the basis that makes everything possible.

The crucial test of whether the clergy understands itself as a ministerial function (or misunderstands itself as a ruling function) most probably lies, for the eyes of their fellow Christians (who, after all, are the only ones able to make an objective judgment here) in the image of Christianity that the clergy portrays for them. This is a correct criterion but also a severe criterion that has no mercy on the clergy, since it presupposes the self-understanding of the clergy that was demanded above in the framework of the total Christian reality and of its interpretation. Not only a mistaken self-understanding but also the very lack of a self-understanding will make itself known immediately in the Church's proclamation and will have its effect. This correct self-understanding must in fact always be active if it is to be an effective agent against the chief emphasis of the clerical perspective that comes into play almost automatically when the man who holds office reflects on Christ and on his Church. Only where he quite consciously keeps before his eyes in an ever renewed fashion the pure servant function of the office does he succeed in making this function transparent to the matter itself. Otherwise, the perspective slides away, unnoticed and virtually automatically, that which is without emphasis receives the emphasis, that on which no light falls is lit up, the spectacles become that which is seen, the medium becomes an end in itself.

Such transfers of emphasis not only affect the position of the clergy within the Church but also go on to have an effect through all the articles of the Faith. Faith itself becomes, in a "clerical perspective", primarily *fides ex auditu,* the acceptance of the apostolic preaching of the Faith, and the question whether faith is present is tested simply on the basis of this acceptance. But the center of the Faith does not lie in the relationship of the believer to the one who brings the message of faith, whom he hears, but to the word of God that is heard and to which he entrusts himself utterly as the living and incarnate God. The "hearing" of the Church's kerygma is (and also remains) the entrance into "listening" to God, which is the essential thing; the believer believes "the Church" only in order to obey the one word of God with and in the Church and as Church (in which there is no longer any distinction between clergy and laity).

Of its very nature, the clergy tends to picture to itself the Church under the image of a parish or a district, as a flock that can somehow be taken in at a glance, a flock on which it can carry out its functions. This mutual relationship of pastor and those who receive his pastoral care, something saturated in itself, appears as the ideal and perhaps already as the real prefiguration of the "one Shepherd and one flock", although this overlooks the fact that the "one Shepherd" is Christ, not the Pope, and that the "one flock" is humanity as a whole, not the few sheep within the realm of the Church. This reductive image can have unhealthy effects in various directions, above all by obliterating the openness of the Church to the world, the missionary character of the Church wherever she is, so that, for example, the aim in missionary countries is to transform the missionary territory (with its own forms and methods) as quickly as possible into a Church territory divided up into districts and parishes, while either postponing decisive missionary tasks consciously "till later on" (e.g., the intellectual and also practical problems of the mission to Islam) or simply forgetting them. This fantasy, which goes only as far as the parochial structure and somehow lets the diocesan priest who administers his parish always unconsciously see the missionary religious priest who works in a freer manner as a marginal phenomenon of the ordinary pastoral care, not seldom affects even missionary congregations today, although the opposite ought really to be the case. A Church that is not open to the world in her totality would have ceased to be the Church of Christ. "We all stand in the frontline."

The clergy has the duty of ordering and encouraging the reception of the sacraments, and this means that it tends to measure and to perceive the Christian quality of Christians simply by means of their reception of the sacraments. No one will deny that this is absolutely commanded by the Lord; but still less may one overlook the fact that the reception of the sacraments, like everything in the Church, is ordered to the life of Christian love; and the pastor should not be unaware that many people who go seldom to the sacraments (or perhaps do not go at all, for reasons of the milieu in which they live, or because of an insurmountable aversion to something that the pastor himself can see only as an external factor) permit Christian love to shine forth more brightly than others. A parish priest in Paris, with a parish in which only a small percentage of the Christians go to church, has laid the emphasis on first persuading the others to undertake a commitment of practical charity to those who are poorest and thus to open from within the access to the meaning of the sacraments for these poor people—and the meaning of the sacraments certainly lies elsewhere than in living on one's own spiritual resources.

The clergy has the duty of preaching the word, but the sermon is not the form of the word of God, only its mediation. The gospel does not stand at the service of the proclamation and is not a treasure trove and a commonplace book of quotations for the preacher in the pulpit: rather, the sermon's function is to lead to the gospel as it is in itself. The same is true of catechism and of all the other expedients of Christian instruction *ad usum delphini*, "for the use of the young". The same holds true on another level even for the liturgy as a whole and in its individual parts: no matter how important it is that the Christian people celebrate in a worthy manner the memorial of the suffering of Christ, it is just as essential (precisely because of the importance of this) that it should at once pass through all the ceremonies to find the meaning and the matter itself, and that it should never see the ultimate goal in the ceremonial, no matter how beautiful and dignified this may be. That which is simple and unemphasized deserves to be given precedence here over the sumptuous and theatrical, whether the people are more participants or spectators.

The clergy has the special task of meditating on Christian doctrine in order to present it to men in the appropriate manner. This meditation, this *intellectus fidei* that is theology, does not have its ultimate emphasis (like a human science) in itself, because faith too, on which it meditates, has its emphasis not in man but in God. Theology, as a science and a doctrine, has a double orientation that takes it beyond its own boundaries: to the *rationale obsequium* of the rational human being in his prayer to God and to the proclamation to the world in keeping with the meaning of the word that is proclaimed and with the age of the world to which it is proclaimed. Theology is therefore no private possession of the clergy in which the laity receive only a meager share in a weakened "lay theology" that is once again prepared *ad usum delphini;* to the extent that it is more than a mere help for proclamation by the priest, theology is the treasure of the whole Church's understanding of the Faith.

The clergy is alone in the Church in carrying out an official function with which, as we have seen, the charisms and mission of the laity can never compete on equal terms. But this does not give the clergy the authority to build up the self-understanding of the whole Church around the clerical state as its midpoint, as if it were Peter and not Jesus who was the real center of the Church, and as if the highest ecclesial act, against which everything else would have to be measured, were obedience to the hierarchy and not rather the genuine *caritas* —just as the apostles always understood this and proclaimed it. Today, we have once again learned what the age of the Fathers and the Middle Ages had never forgotten: that the Church is the Kingdom of God on pilgrimage on earth, the seed that is growing up oriented toward the Day of God, the people, the body, and the bride of Christ, standing in a mysterious partnership with the whole world that is to be redeemed, the world that the separated hierarchical sphere must never allow to be forgotten.

We could continue, and we should have to go through the list of the shifts of emphasis that often seem unimportant within the Church but take on a truly tragic breadth in the interconfessional dialogue, because they are projected in gigantic dimensions. The occasion for the division of the Church in the sixteenth century lay at any rate already present in such shifts of emphasis, and it is better that the Catholic should admit these in the ecumenical discussion than that he should obfuscate them for the sake of apologetics. It is perfectly possible that the future of Christianity depends on these seemingly small details, which, of course—seen in the light of the gospel—are not at all small details. The credibility of the Christian message in Africa, South America, in the lands of Islam, China, and Russia, and ultimately in the whole world, depends decisively on these emphases. They affect not so much the general ethical weakness of the Christians, their bad example, which has impressed itself so unforgettably above all on the colonized peoples, as the negligences and lazy indolences that demonstrate themselves in the self-understanding of the ecclesiastical structures. The conflict between human weakness and objective structure of the office is unavoidable; indeed, one must go so far as to say that the structure itself would be superfluous if there were no weaknesses of this kind. But one thing is the divine grace, which overcomes the insufficiency of men thanks to the official mission; another thing is the human presumption that seeks "behind" the office a covering for one's own failure and uses the office to strike back where the person is intended as the object of criticism.

We have already said how difficult it is, at least in theory, for the Catholic priest to live out existentially and display the tension between office and person in the personal encounter with men. In practice, of course, the grace of office has an astonishingly reconciliatory effect in the priest who is humble: that which appears impossible from a human perspective comes as it were automatically, and the power of the promises of Christ shows itself directly to be effective. The hieroglyph of a priestly existence, taken all in all, is not essentially more mysterious and hard to read than the hieroglyph of the Christian life as such, for this is "having died and risen with Christ", a "no longer do I live"; it is an existence out of gratitude and out of the commission that has been received, no matter in what state of life the individual now lives. Everywhere, the pivotal point between nature and grace eludes our grasp, the pivotal point that nevertheless pervades the whole form of the existence and gives it a structure for itself and for others. This hidden point, with which everything is concerned, lies in Christ, in the triune God, and it brings about simultaneously the deep hiddenness of the existence and its naked, seemingly unprotected exposure, its rest and its confusion, its light of faith and its darkness of faith. Who would think of finding a ready-made formula to describe this mystery—although this does not mean that the form of the Christian appears to the world as something illegible and muddled?

Thus it is also with the priest: Who would presume to make a neat analysis of the distinction in him between office and person? The office, as we have seen, is based in its very structure on the Person of Christ and on the triple Personhood of God; and precisely for this reason it demands of the office bearer a renunciation that bursts open the boundaries of his all too narrow human and sinful person—in order to permit him, in such a depersonalization, to share in the highest personal sphere. If the office in the Church keeps on awakening the appearance of impersonality both in the one who bears it and in the layman, and will continue to do so until the end of the world, it is precisely this aspect that is the transient and provisional character of the office, and both, the cleric and the layman, are required even now to do all that they can to see through this sphere into the realm of the personal, divine-human love that bears and forms all things, even the office. The careful observer can deduce that this realm exists and that it has an effect, by means of a humanism that is not merely Christian but precisely Christological, something that belongs precisely to the clerical state, a certain equilibrium and clarity that Christian laymen do not simply have as a matter of course. It is precisely the "great laymen" in the Church who are mostly mischief makers, pikes in the pool of carp, people who ask questions rather than answer them, insistent, reformers—one may think, for example, of the list of the great Catholic thinkers of modern France. They are not concerned with balance, and this is not only because they have not studied theology long enough and in a sufficiently Thomistic mold but also because their commission is different. But how important it is that the exposed layman too have behind him the authority and guidance of the priest who lives in the Christian equilibrium that is both natural and supernatural or at least know about his personality and quietly take orientation from him! Thus he can venture upon the risk *ad extra*, because he knows that it has succeeded at the decisive point "in the interior". It is perhaps only the Catholic priesthood that will still be able to show to the coming generation what "existence in representation" *truly* means (and not only historically, traditionally, or in terms of having noble blood). For this reason, the new theological reflection in the Church, even in today's Church, on one state of life should never be carried out without the simultaneous deeper study of the other state or states. One would not have thought far enough ahead, if one were to wish to speak of an "awakening of the laity" today simply because little can be hoped for from the clergy in the coming period, because it has, so to speak, played out its role for the time being and is transferred back from the "frontline" to the "interior", and perhaps also because it is hopelessly unmodern, and a reform of the clerical education and order of study seems to go beyond the self-regulating powers of the clergy. How could such a renewal program of the Church dare to look the Church of the apostles in the face! Let us awaken the laity, as much and as loudly as we wish, but let us awaken just as much—and even more—the clergy to its inalienable task, not in the hinterland but at the frontline. The concern of the worker priests was the right concern: not only the laity but also the clergy must assert themselves in the situation of exposure. Even if their solutions came before their time and were in part mistaken, their concern remains as fresh and as urgent as ever.

Audite haec, omnes Domini Sacerdotes, et attentius intelligite quae dicuntur. Caro quae ex sacrificiis sacerdotibus deputatur, Verbum Dei est, quod in Ecclesia docent. Pro hoc ergo figuris mysticis commonentur, ut, cum proferre ad populum sermonem coeperint, non hesterna proferant, non vetera, quae sunt secundum litteram, proloquantur, sed per gratiam Dei nova semper proferant et spiritualia semper inveniant. . . . Nam et Dominus panem, quem discipulis dabat, dicens iis: "accipite et manducate", non distulit nec reservari jussit in crastinum. "Hear this, all you priests of the Lord, and understand more attentively what Scripture says. The flesh that is assigned to the priests out of the sacrifices is the word of God, which they teach in the Church. For this reason, therefore, they are exhorted by mystical symbols that, when they begin to address their words to the people, they should not bring forward things that belong to yesterday, nor should they say old things that follow the letter only, but by the grace of God let them always say new things and always discover spiritual things. . . . For when the Lord gave the bread to the disciples, saying, "Take and eat", he did not break off any part or order it to be reserved for the morrow" (Origen, *Homily on Leviticus* 5, 8; Baehr. 6, 348–89).

TOWARD A THEOLOGY OF
THE SECULAR INSTITUTE

With the Apostolic Constitution *Provida Mater* of 1947, the Church gave official recognition and validity to a new form of the life of the counsels or "state of perfection". In spite of their primarily canonical form, this and other related documents convey with great conciseness the entire theological basis for the possibility of such a new form of the life of the counsels. Both the fact itself that this state already exists in the Church and its preliminary theological justification are of great importance for the theology of the Church and, through it, for Christian theology in general.

The significance of this new life form has perhaps not been adequately recognized and appraised until recently, because in our time another movement in life and thought has made almost exclusive claims on ecclesiological energies. I speak of the movement that for the first time has awakened the laity as it lives a secular life form and has urged them to participate in the Catholic Action of the hierarchy and, beyond that, to undertake a more independent development of their self-responsibility and their involvement where they find themselves in the world. The "theologies of the lay state", which nowadays are sprouting on every side, correspond to the concerns of the times. Here battles are fought and new land is conquered; here an irrepressible restructuring of Christian consciousness seems to be taking place, a restructuring based on the insight that the lay Christian possesses full responsibility as belonging to the people of God, pre-

Translated by Erasmo S. Leiva-Merikakis.

Translator's Note: A key term in this article is *Rätestand* or *Räteleben,* which I have translated, respectively, as "state of the counsels" and "life of the counsels". The standard English phrase in this case would be "religious life". In spite of the fact that a phrase such as "life of the counsels" poses stylistic problems by leading to an undue clumsiness of expression, I have judged it best to keep it in this case, since the point of von Balthasar's efforts seems precisely to be the clarification of the many ambiguities connected with a phrase such as "the religious life". The same could be said for other expressions that occur less frequently.

cisely as he stands with both feet in the world: in its work, its cultural struggle, its economy and politics. In earlier centuries, and partly for reasons of cultural history, the state of the counsels and that of hierarchical functions were considered to be the very center of the Church. From our new perspective, however, we have come to see the clerical and religious state as a superstructure designed by the Founder of the Church himself as an aid for his people and their Christian *life*. The reason for being of the clerical and religious state would then consist in a certain *exemplariness* (in the case of the state of the counsels) and in the *mediation* of the salvific goods necessary for a supernatural life (in the case of hierarchical functions). On the one hand we have the *life* itself and on the other the *"structures"* (Congar) necessary for a supernatural life. This point of view could be summarized by saying that the layman is the light of the world, while clergy and religious are the light of the laity.

While the origins of secular institutes in the nineteenth century were heavily obstructed by the opposition of the old orders,[1] this opposition has today almost totally disappeared. Present opposition, or at least the objections to the idea of a secular institute, results from the newly awakened consciousness of a laity seeking to grow secure in its own life form and tasks. It comes partly from the laity itself but even more strongly from the side of theologians who seek to help the lay state to develop its own particular "theology". We must first, therefore, listen to these objections, which come primarily from the area of central Europe, excluding the East, Italy, and Spain, areas that in this case behave in a more "catholic" manner and are able to think more impartially and in a less complicated fashion. The objections may, in part, be formulated theologically, but in part they are merely "atmospheric" in nature. Because the latter are perhaps more decisive, we will try to clarify them to the point where they can be understood and, when necessary, refuted. In a second section we will attempt to sketch very briefly a theology of the different life forms in the Church so as to situate the "new" state of the counsels theologically. A third section will give summary responses to the objections.

[1] Cf. Jean Beyer, *Les instituts séculiers* (1954), pp. 52ff.

I. *The objections*

1. In the age of the vanishing personality, of the mass man who swears by slogans and thinks according to the newspapers, it seems that the chief concern in the Church ought to be the preservation of the robust, free, strong, Christian personality. But this free personality grows and matures when an individual assumes in a Christian spirit a portion of worldly responsibility. Through his existence he will give shape to something that no one else could supply and that can hardly be continued by anyone, but from which all others, in *their* freedom, can derive strength and nourishment. Péguy, in his portrait of *Joinville* and in his *Note Conjointe,* Bernanos in his writings on the times, and Guardini (influenced in this by Scheler) in his studies on personality have raised the kind of human being we envision above others who do not sufficiently mature into their freedom and who escape from it into a protective and "relieving" obedience. Bernanos above all has pointed to the confusing of genuine obedience with a false pliancy as being the most dread danger for Christianity today, since this confusion becomes an accomplice of modern irresponsibility and introduces mass man into the Church in the name and under the mantle of "obedience to the Church".[2] Bernanos does not criticize the obedience of the orders, but in the transferral of this ideal to the lay Christian in the world he sees the worst of all pious falsifications. *"Vous avez mis les peuples au collège!"* ("You've put the people into a prep school!") he exclaims. A healthy state of affairs can come only from clearly distinguishing between the obedience of the vows (with its legitimate sacrifice of freedom) and the obedience of the laity, which, on the contrary, is only to be derived over and over again from the full power of freedom and responsibility. Writes Bernanos: "Christian obedience has, by nature, a heroic character. . . . Those people who are ready to obey blindly are the same who suddenly *dis*obey blindly. To obey without argument is not at all the same as obeying without understanding; a total docility is not as far removed as one might think from total revolt."[3] Modern man is

---

[2] Cf. my book *Bernanos* (Hegner, 1954), pp. 28f., 488f., 517f.

[3] *Chemin de la Croix des âmes* (1944), p. 465.

only too ready to obey. Even in the area of obedience within the Church today we can detect a certain strain of servility, an excessive manifestation of submissiveness. Here again we can quote Bernanos, this time from a famous letter to Amoroso Lima concerning Catholic Action: "It seems to me that in this day and age there is only one perfectly legitimate activity either for Catholic Action or for any Catholic at large, only one not involving any risk: this is the apology for ecclesiastical authority and its methods, the delirious exaltation of its smallest successes and the covering up of its failures." Here the question arises: With the new life form in the Church, is not the monastic ideal transferred to laymen living in the world? Is this ideal not transplanted from a habitat in which it is justified to one that is foreign to it and where it can only create dangerous confusion?

Would not the best way to proceed be to follow Karl Rahner's suggestion[4] of making a clean distinction between the two states, their inner life forms and their existential ethics? On the one hand, we have the "clergy" (which includes the state of the counsels and all persons among the laity who work primarily in the service of the clergy); on the other, the laity. The members of secular institutes then belong clearly to the "clergy". Ernst Michel would surely be happy with this separation, since it serves to remove from the clerical sphere the layman's proper place between Church and world while at the same time helping him attain to his own self-image.

2. We could also look in another way at the modern danger of a "flight to obedience": namely, as a particular instance of a general flight to the counsels, which, with our changed sociological circumstances today, may have lost their characteristic heroic trait and have even, perhaps, become the more secure path to follow. We are familiar

---

[4] "Über das Laienapostolat", *Schriften zur Theologie,* vol. 2 (1955), pp. 339–73. Cf. my disagreements with Rahner in "Wesen und Tragweite der Säkularinstitute" ("Monatsschrift des schweizerischen Studentenvereins", *Civitas* ll [1956]: 196–210). The present article was written before K. Rahner's article in *Orientierung* (Apr. 30, 1956) appeared and ought not to be taken as an answer to it. I postpone a definitive discussion for a later time.

with a taunt made by laymen to religious and no longer to be taken merely in jest: "You make the vow of poverty, but *we* keep it!" In a time when real estate, properties, and family fortunes were amassed, it was a meaningful gesture to renounce all things in order to be poor for Christ. But today it is different. Modern man often possesses nothing, either because he has lost it or because the capitalistic or communistic state takes it from him. A Christian who lives his Faith today usually does not cling to his possessions, since the little he earns is precisely what he needs to subsist. Could a "vow of poverty" essentially change anything in this situation? Considerations about the "meritoriousness of actions" no longer mean much to the people and the Christians of today. Does anything *really* change when one enters an order, other than the fact that the Christian who earns his living in a (secular) order will find himself financially much better off because of his celibacy and his being supported by a community than a poor devil with wife and children? In this manner, the gesture of "forsaking all things", seen in a sober light, changes into its opposite, into a leap from uncertainty into a greater earthly security. We could say similar things about virginity. Is remaining celibate today (and this "today" is important!) not making things much too easy for oneself, in the same way that one makes them easier by remaining "poor" (that is, socially secure) or by remaining "obedient" (that is, without ultimate personal responsibility)? On the one hand, first exclude all the theological prejudices against Christian marriage that still remain active among us from earlier periods and then look at the theology of marriage, still in development and still with so much to discover and clarify. On the other hand, exclude all the elements of enforced fatality about modern celibacy (for instance, the surplus of women, for whom not even special orders can be founded, or the factual impossibility of exercising certain vocations—such as that of teacher—in the context of marriage). Then consider the degeneration of modern man to the status of a worker bee and the tremendous need for self-denial and surrender in a modern marriage. After all these considerations we may at least be permitted to ask wherein exactly lies today the great privilege of celibacy.

This second objection may be summarized as follows: in spite of the fact that the greatest dignity goes *in abstracto* to the evangelical counsels and that no one would think of attacking them, the question must be raised whether, given our world situation today, the way of the counsels has not become the easier way, while the layman's stance in free self-responsibility and in the total battle for existence has not become the more difficult way, difficult not only in a worldly sense but also in the Christian sense, which would make of it the more valuable way theologically.

3. With our first objection there emerged the danger of a false docility on the part of the lay Christian. But what if the obedience of the life of the counsels should now reappear in the lay state itself? In other words, what if in the plane where free and responsible decisions are expected there should in reality seem to operate a "remote control" through obedience? Would this state of affairs not undermine every human trust? Erich Przywara, along with Bernanos, has given radical expression to this objection by assigning the life of the vows exclusively to the cloistered contemplative monastery (be it Christian, Buddhist, or Taoist) and by including in the crisis the "active orders" that come out from the cloister into the world. Writes Przywara:

> In orders whose members are active in education, the situation can go so far that the pupils are educated according to a diluted "rule for novices", resulting in a conflict with the life encountered later in the world. In orders whose members are dedicated to scholarship, there become established "schools of the order" that, as with the Dominicans, are bound by oath to a particular doctrine of thought [*iuramentum in doctrinam S. Thomae*], or that at least may not teach certain doctrines, as in the case of the Jesuits with Bañezianism. In the concept of "order", then, there is always the danger that, once a group goes beyond its original form, a living and rigorous "faithfulness to principles" (as Josef Pieper has rightly termed the spirit of Thomas Aquinas) may be replaced by sterile "regulations of obedience" that are supposed to be a sure "way of perfection" for the members of the order but that have little left in common with a supposed "faithfulness to principles". The natural consequence is a

latent distrust,[5] even on the part of truly Catholic circles, concerning the actual competence of all religious. There is in these cases a great uncertainty as to whether one is dealing with concrete persons who speak and act following real personal conviction and vision, or whether one has to do with an anonymous "center of command" behind the person. The situation goes hand in hand with the fact that in certain areas of the Church hierarchy the entire Catholic laity is referred to and considered to be "those who receive commands".[6]

We must conclude by asking how unbearable this state of affairs will become when the "remote control" blatantly assumes the appearance of self-responsibility, as seems to be the case with secular institutes, especially when their members work in intellectually responsible cultural positions.

4. Against the above it could be objected that it would take a strong personality in the first place in order to span such an arch and attempt to follow Christ so radically in the midst of the real world. But do we live in an age that fosters and produces strong personalities? And if we cannot take strong personalities for granted, will the new life of the counsels be strong enough itself to produce them on its own? Seen in a sober light, does it not all rather resemble an arena of mediocrity? All of these numerous small and half-anonymous groups and conventicles that today call themselves proudly "secular institutes" and that until recently could even have raised themselves to the status of "congregations": are they not something like "orders for the little people"? They form associations as plentiful as the secular welfare institutes and are just as faceless, limited, and philanthropic. Compared with one of the great orders of the past, do they not give you the impression of tiny lot gardens on the outskirts of a big city, set up alongside an old and noble park of the baroque period? Does not this new form of the religious life correspond all too closely to modern "lot-garden humanity", which delights in the faceless and rejoices when nuns' wimples fall only because it feels uncomfortable with

[5] Emphasis mine.
[6] *Humanitas* (1952), p. 868.

anything blatantly religious in today's cities and is shocked at the mere encounter of a priest on the street? Should we really be glad that things continue to grow and bloom on all sides in the Church today, if not exactly upward, then at least in breadth? Do we not in this way make a virtue out of a necessity when we speak of the "humility" of a Church that itself goes down into namelessness along with those who have become nameless? Is this descent a sign of vigor—or of exhaustion?

5. We should here have the courage to think our thoughts to the end. Does this apostle of Christ who intermingles with the proletariat and wanders off into the Churchless and Godless distances really "haul the world home"? Does he not remain separated from the world precisely by his "counsels" as by a glass wall? Would it not be better to renounce this real or supposed "perfection" in order at least to be a man among men, a human Christian among human Christians? Will the celibate ever really be able to share and, therefore, to understand the cares and burdens of the married person? Does not the size of the rift that separates both life forms become manifest precisely in the attempt at a mutual rapprochement? What is the point of relieving the overburdened mother for a couple of days, of caring for her children, of counseling those about to marry, if all of this occurs only "from the outside" and in no way involves interior participation? The question is so urgent precisely because for the first time in Church history the social problem has arisen with such force. (Here we have only to think of Péguy's road to socialism and of what he brought back into the Church with him, or of the discussion stimulated by Gertrud von le Fort's *Garland of Angels*.) Is not the old "state of perfection" (already the term!) something hopelessly individualistic, not to say egotistic? Is it not precisely this that has time and time again erected a wall within the Church community, dividing the better people from the ordinary folk, the spiritual "bourgeoisie" from a "Church proletariat"? Does not this "condescension to the people", as envisioned by secular institutes, retain the same slight stench of arrogance exuded by those "Ladies of Charity" at the time of Vincent de Paul?

In other words, in the face of today's society, we must seriously investigate to what extent the "structure of the life states" within the

Catholic Church is really and exclusively founded on theological principles or to what extent it is merely historically and sociologically conditioned. The tendency is unmistakable to emphasize ever more what the states have in common—i.e., the command to love (Scheler, A. Adam, Lippert)—and to understand this love as a human-Christian totality that integrates eros into charity.[7] The very concept of a "state" is here exploded and inundated by the "one thing necessary" that requires a totally human and incarnational form. And the new saint is the one who does not shrink back from this crossing of the boundaries demanded by the new consciousness of what it means to be human. This is the step forward that has been awaited by humanity and hints of which we can perceive, for instance, in the novels of Graham Greene. Does not the solution given by the secular institutes in comparison strike us by its unimaginativeness, timidity, and feebleness? Is it not a case of "both-and", a compromise that is as such already condemned to ineffectiveness?

These have been a few of the most important objections. There are many others that we cannot here enumerate. The ones we have outlined contain so many issues that a whole book would hardly suffice to resolve them. We will juxtapose to them a few suggestions[8] intended to stimulate further meditation. Even our answers will be in only outline form.

2. *Situating the states theologically*

We have attempted to listen to and seriously to consider the objections that are variously made out of a sincere concern for the form of the Church today. We tried to give expression even to unconscious and unavowed misgivings, since a spiritual state of affairs is often clarified

---

[7] Cf. Friedrich Heer's *Christian Marriage in the World* and all of Erich Przywara's later writings.

[8] We will be concerned only with an understanding of the *Duae Vitae* ("two lives"). The other field of tension between "clergy and laity", hierarchy and people, must be wholly left aside here. For this reason, we have given no consideration either to clerical secular institutes.

by those factors more than by conscious ones. We could say that in the countries of central Europe two different trends coexist. A *factual* tendency toward the life form of the secular institutes is undeniably present, as substantiated by the number and variety of foundations. But this tendency still lacks a theological basis. The chief representatives and shapers of the spirituality of the Church, however, are thinking and acting in a different direction. The spiritual soil in central Europe is still largely unprepared for the new idea to thrive there. Aside from a certain curiosity that would like always to keep up to date, we can speak of no deep interest on the part of ecclesiastical circles.

The new ecclesiology of the laity assumes two apparently diametrically opposed forms, which are in effect not finally incompatible in their basic tendency. On the one hand, one could emphasize the postulate of a clear distinction and separation of the "two lives", one eschatologically taken out of the world for the service of the Church (state of the counsels and state of the priesthood), the other rooted in the world and taking its Christian stance within the world situation (the vocation in the world as envisioned by Ernst Michel, Karl Rahner, and also Bernanos in his own way). On the other hand, following the example of Guardini, one could seek above all to win back the spiritual values of the evangelical counsels for the lay state in the world, for the development of the full Christian personality, with a consequent deemphasizing of the separation of the states. This double tendency can be an opportunity to pose the question concerning the structure of the states in the Church, something that we will here do in a purely schematic form because of the need for brevity.

The most important thing is for us to remind ourselves again from the outset that the Church is a mystery. As body and bride and fullness of Christ, the Church partakes in his human and divine being, and she therefore reaches down into depths that no ordering spirit can fathom. Now, her exterior, visible structure is the manifestation of the reality of this mystery. It is not, therefore, surprising if the structures that each "state" in the Church represents, both for itself and in the reciprocal relationship of all the states, do not ultimately become fully discernible but must remain mysteriously dialectic, unlike the corresponding secular and political structures planned by men and corresponding to finite human nature. It is not surprising if the structures of the Church in the course of the ages develop out of one another in new ways without prejudice to the pristine form of the Church, established by Christ and unshakable.

All of this must be stressed precisely with regard to the new life forms in the Church. We will see in what follows that the "theology" of secular institutes cannot simply be deduced from the already present and accustomed structure of the states. Such a "theology" demands a bold and, at first, unusual theological effort that will perhaps continue to be required for a long time. If this were not so, the Church could have simply subsumed the new form under the older "states of perfection" and not, fully conscious of what it was doing, have founded a new state of the counsels as it did in *Provida Mater* and *Primo Feliciter* by developing a subtle, analogical relationship between the new state and the existing ones.

In order to evaluate the implicit theology to some extent, we must integrate it into the context of a theological doctrine of the Church. The field of tension within which the life forms in the Church find both their common and their distinctive elements can be developed in two dimensions. It goes without saying that both of these are Christological, since life-styles and states in the Church can be nothing other than forms of the following of Christ. But, since they are also intended *for human beings,* they both exhibit *a human form,* tailored to their nature, even if, as supernatural possibilities, they are not to be developed or justified purely from their own nature.

The *first field of tension* is that between eschatology and Incarnation. According to Paul, Christians have, by the power of baptism, died to the world, been buried with Christ, risen with him, and thereby been incorporated into the heavenly, eschatological Kingdom. As citizens of the approaching Kingdom of heaven, they are foreigners on earth. They await the Kingdom from heaven and, at the same time, help it achieve its breakthrough out of the world (Eph 4:15f.). From this eschatological character of Christianity we could describe the state of the evangelical counsels interiorly as being the taking seriously of the

Christian's call out of the old eon and into the perfect discipleship of Christ, while the state of life in the world would remain a kind of "concession" to the old eon (*syngnōmē:* I Cor 7:6). In this way we could justify a view of the state of the counsels that could be traced through the whole history of the Church, which says that it does not embody a "second ethos" alongside that of ordinary Christians but is merely the radical expression of the one and only Christian ethos.[9] Against this view, we must remember that eschatological existence does not imply a vanishing of the world, a hyperspiritualization, or a turning away from history or from earthly work and culture but rather a point of departure for the Christian's mission into the world *as it is.* The Christian is sent into the world in the name of the risen Lord to whom the world belongs as a whole (Mt 28:18f.), since it was established and created through him and for him (Col 1:16–17) and since, precisely through his Resurrection, he has been enthroned as Ruler of the entire cosmos (Phil 2:9–11). Far from contradicting the Incarnation, the Resurrection rather manifests its fulfillment. In the Incarnation, the seed of the definitive Kingdom of God is implanted into the kingdom of the world. In the Resurrection, on the contrary, the Kingdom of God has become so powerful that the entire kingdom of the world appears implanted into *it.* From this perspective the "Christians in the world" appear in a much more positive light. Alongside eschatology we have the Incarnation; alongside dying and rising into another sphere we have an existence in the sinful world, a life consecrated by God himself as a witness to the ongoing process of the world's redemption. In this light, even the priestly and the religious life emerge as that "auxiliary state" (*secundario et instrumentaliter,* says Thomas) that has "left the world" only in order better to go into it with Christ, to be a leaven for the Church and the world, in action and contemplation, to bear fruit a hundredfold in the field that is the world. In this way the religious state, too, is a radical form of "Incarnation". The vows of the orders, therefore, have always been considered to be but the radical fulfillment and ratification of the

[9] Cf. my introduction to the *Rules of St. Basil* in the second edition of *Die Grossen Ordensregeln* (1961).

vows of baptism. If baptism, for Paul, is a dying and rising with Christ, with the effect that the baptized now experiences himself as a stranger in a cosmos still subjected to the "forces of the world", then this universal Christian truth becomes a total life form in the life of the counsels. But "mystical" death is at the same time "mystical" Resurrection and, therefore, an anticipation of a hidden existence in the glory of Christ, with the end of "appearing together with him" in his own time (Col 3:4).

In seeking to establish a harmony between the religious and the secular states, then, we can arrive at the following formula: insofar as the Church is a *new eon* within the old, to that extent she has been uprooted from the old eon. This aspect of the Church is manifested primarily, although not exclusively, by the life of the counsels. But insofar as the Church is a new eon *within the old* (which in any event has itself, in Christ, already struck roots in the new eon), she remains yoked to the world and its total destiny. But even this formula does not yet sufficiently describe the relationship between the Christian states of life. To achieve a satisfactory description we first need to review the second Christological field of tension. We will first summarize it in order then to enter into the inner dialectic of these two fields of tension.

The *second field of tension* is that defined by general and particular vocation. The way of a more intimate discipleship as embodied in the counsels is shown both by the Lord and by Paul to be something total and integral in its exclusiveness. In comparison to secular life, with its "dividedness" and worldly "cares", the way of intimate discipleship is to be unconditionally preferred. The Magisterium and the ecclesiologists have always kept watch over this hierarchy of preference. The Council of Trent formulated a definition (sess. 24, can. 10) to affirm this order as a reaction to the leveling tendencies of Protestantism. But this order of preference is ethically justifiable only when it is seen in conjunction with a particular vocation, taking this concept in its full breadth of meaning, which ranges from an inner "must" to a freely chosen "may". Otherwise it would be impossible not to give the impression that whoever does not choose the "better part" remains a second-rate Christian. Because the Christian acts of "call" and "choice" launch one on the way of what is "objectively better", this "objectively better" thing is not the better thing for everyone. Ecclesially speaking, however, even this distinction is acceptable only provided the "objectively better" thing is not only of a personal nature but is a better thing for the Church as well and, therefore, for society — provided, in other words, that exclusive claim to life with Christ leads to a universality in the mystery for all that is Christ's Church. Since all Christians partake in this mystery of exclusive universal love in Christ's Church, for that very reason we can say that, in a general sense, *all* are among "the called" (*klētoi*). And here again, the life of the counsels appears as but a radical form of the one life in Christ shared by all. If this were not so, Paul could not have taught an ethics for all Christians, taking the unique story of his own vocation as a point of departure, nor could John have discoursed on love in the Church, always setting his own special love as an example.

We must now penetrate somewhat more deeply into the meaning of this network of relationships. Let us begin with the *first field*. There we saw that the "dying and rising" in the life of the counsels is a radicalizing — in the total interior and exterior form of existence — of the basic stance of a person in the Church. We can, therefore, say that the first state of life simply places the Christian moment in high relief as a "form", while in the second state this moment is always intermixed with the world as with a "matter". In the form-ality of the first state, the Christian moment possesses a purity and also a universality that it no longer has in the second state, where it finds itself intermixed with the world as with a matter. There is here involved an *individuatio ratione materiae* (a "specificity derived from matter") and, therefore, also a division into parts (1 Cor 7:34) and a "specialization" that, theologically speaking, are foreign to the first state. This first state is *forma informans vitam ecclesiasticam* (a "form that shapes the life of the Church after itself"), in the image of the Lord — a leaven in the dough of the Church, and the dough must absorb *all* of the leaven into itself, must take *all* of the radical spirit of death and Resurrection into itself, and not merely a part of it. The life of the counsels is, thus, the spirit of the whole and not a thing for specialists. Whatever there is about it that may be considered special exists only to serve its availability to the whole. It becomes salt only in order to season the whole. The life of the counsels is, then, the moment of totality in the Church, the moment that by its presence keeps the particular from losing the spirit of a catholicity understood as wholeness. To say it in the shortest possible formula, the life of the counsels is *the particular instance of the general.*[10]

But this presupposes that this "general" is itself a "particular" over against something even more "general". Over against that part of mankind existing outside the Church, the general character of the Christian state as such is that of a community of faith that, through Christ's word and sacraments, partakes in a very particular way in the total mystery of his suffering and rising for the redemption of the world. This faith community, constituting the totality of the Church, but with the life of the counsels at its heart, is thus the light and the salt and the leaven for the whole world.

As long as this first aspect dominates the field of vision—Christian radicalism both as "form" and as "pure culture"—the idea of the life of the counsels in a secular situation does not appear as either paradoxical or eccentric. For we cannot see why this radicalism could not at one time more heavily emphasize the "eschatological" and at another time the "incarnational",[11] or why it should not be possible to live out in a worldly situation that Christian totality to which the "hundredfold" has been promised, since in any event every person remains ultimately in the world. In order to understand this more precisely, we must not forget that Jesus' first disciples paradigmatically united in their personal lives both the life of the counsels and that of the priesthood, even though these two states are by no means identical. The priestly state is primarily a function; the state of the counsels is a

---

[10] This formula excludes the possibility of defining the existence of the layman in the world negatively by first "bracketing" everything that *does not* pertain to the layman's existence, such as the "eschatological existence" of priests and religious.

[11] Cf. the formulations of *Primo Feliciter.* On the one hand, it says *relicto saeculo* ("having forsaken the world"), on the other *per contactum intrinsecum* ("through an intimate contact"). Cf. my essay in *Civitas* II (1956): 204.

life form. The function is rooted in the external structure of the Church (since interiorly *all* are essentially "priests") and exists for this structure. The sixty- and hundredfold fruit promised to those who "forsake all things" always exhibits in this connection the aspect of service and usefulness to the Church. Like Paul, but also like Timothy, that person can be engaged everywhere who sets himself free of all worldly bonds to a place, a career, and a family in order to be totally available for the needs of the Church. When the same Paul, however, says, "I wish that all would live as I do", meaning in celibacy, he understands celibacy not as a requirement for holding office and being active in the Church but as a state of virginity consecrated to Christ, a state that the first virgins in the Church showed to be possible even in the midst of the world. In this case, the "hundredfold" appears in association not with the eschatological but with the incarnational aspect. Both *Provida Mater* and *Primo Feliciter* have pointed to this association as being the particular ecclesial situation of the secular institutes. The experience of Catholic Action has shown that the "hundredfold" is here not to be taken as something purely interior and invisible, as a value of the sacrifice of one's life to God, but that in certain circumstances it has to manifest itself visibly in the Church. In certain circumstances, an "apostolate" rooted in the worldly milieu can be far more effective than much sermonizing from the outside on the part of priests and religious who do not belong to that milieu.

By "hundredfold" we understand the manifestation of the mystery of Christ's totality in the existence of the Christian who has this totality as his life form. This "hundredfold" is, of course, primarily a spiritual and invisible good. We have only to think of the fruitfulness of purely contemplative prayer, about which both the big Teresa and the little Thérèse knew so much. But the "hundredfold" implies also the possibility of realizing on a very earthly and sociological plane the life of him who has placed all things in Christ: "No one leaves house, brother, sister, mother, father, child, or farm for my sake and that of the gospel without gaining everything back a hundredfold — *already in this world* in the midst of persecutions: house, brother, sister, mother, child, and farm, and in the next world eternal life" (Mk 10:30). Again, this is not meant, or is not necessarily meant, in the sense of earthly compensation, as with Job in the Old Testament, but in a spiritual-ecclesial sense that is perhaps most beautifully demonstrated by the fruitfulness of the life of the counsels in the world. That the very foundations of the world are really affected by such a life, that we have not here to do with an "eschatological existence" that floats somewhere over the ground in Gnostic manner: this is a mystery of Faith, rooted in Christ's becoming a man, which we will later consider. But we can already say that, if the reshaping of what is worldly by what is Christian can be fundamentally affirmed in a worldly situation, then such giving of form must also be recognized to be possible and real in the life of the counsels. This holds also and especially if the life of the counsels experiences the mystery of remaining whole even as it must divide itself up practically. This is the particular mystery of the *asyngchytos* in the *adiairetos* (the "unmixed" in the "undivided") of Chalcedon, a mystery discernible only Christologically.

Just as it is impossible to determine univocally Christ's stance with regard to the world, so too is it impossible to pin down absolutely the stance of whoever follows him radically. This impossibility only reflects the common Christian suspension of being "in the world but not of the world". The person living in the state of the counsels *can* and *may* take an "eschatological" stance in an emphatic distance from "the world". But he can also (and this occurs in the secular institutes) choose his stance in the world, among Christians of the secular state and among men who are outside the Church. Christ himself did this, both as a workman and as a teacher and miracle worker. Paul did this implicitly when he renounced his own peculiar status as an apostle and the "poverty" proper to this status in order to earn his living as a tent weaver, and this not in make-believe fashion. From our accustomed perspective, such positioning may appear to be a kind of extrapolation outside the inherited scope of life forms, but then God's becoming a man is nothing but one great extrapolation out of the Divinity and its heaven: the unusual character of exterior appearances may for a while justify the shock. Instead of living with his brother in a community house, this Christian persists in the world in a kind of voluntary "banishment"—"as in a voluntary exile", says Carpentier.[12] But for such a Christian the world is not outside of Christ. It belongs to the risen Lord. Rather than Christ's having his place in the world, it has its place *in him*. In its becoming, its dying, and its rising, the world moves toward Christ. All earthly existence, even that of members of religious orders, remains an exile insofar as eschatological fulfillment still remains to be accomplished. However we might choose to look at it, over and over again we confront the realization that in this field of tension the particular feature of the life of the counsels consists in its being precisely a particular instance of *the one universal* Christian imperative.

Things really become more difficult when we bring the second field into our considerations. It is undeniable that in the gospel the Lord calls his disciples to an exclusive intimacy with his person, an exclusiveness that must replace for them everything that they must leave behind and renounce. House, brother, sister, mother, father, child, and farm are entrusted to the care of the Christian in the world through a communality of destiny that he at least shares with the men of the old eon. He has no right to renounce them, unless a strong call of the Lord loosens him from these bonds. On receiving this call he must remain indifferent to all else and must achieve a thorough renunciation in his heart: *fiat voluntas tua.* In this respect, the renunciation of the disciple is, again, but the particular instance of the general imperative, the actual living out of what every Christian must be prepared to do, even to the extreme of giving witness by the shedding of one's blood. For this reason we can see how, historically, the life of the counsels came to supersede and replace the condition of the martyr. Because every human being, however, the disciple included, is a personal, limited being existing in time and history, this "living out" must, as involving a human choice, be a *selection from a number of possibilities,* even when the life sought conforms to the *forma ecclesiae* and even when the person chooses the totality of Christ's reality. Whoever chooses Christ as his All by the same token renounces other possible objects of choice. He cuts through existing bonds and, indeed,

[12] Carpentier, *Nouvelle Revue théologique* (Apr. 1955), p. 409.

fundamentally through *all* bonds, in keeping with the Lord's univocal exigency. One must not even "bid farewell" or go "bury one's dead father". Now, this exclusiveness for Christ is, for both Master and disciple, no merely personal and private event, and this in a double sense. On the one hand, Christ calls those he especially chooses to live an "ecclesial existence" at the very heart of the Church. Whether exteriorly or interiorly, visibly or in a hidden manner, he calls them to become fruitful a hundredfold and to distribute themselves Eucharistically in the mysteries of the communion of saints. On the other hand, the call is an ecclesial happening also from the side of the one called, since he conceives of his Yes to discipleship as a corealization of Mary's and the Church's Yes, as an entering into the total Yes spoken by redeemed humanity to the redeeming God. Both these aspects, however, nowhere keep his discipleship from always remaining a personal, human act. For this reason, his vows can never be "pragmatized" one-sidedly. They retain a dimension of personal love for Christ and, through him, for the triune God, a dimension that the Church can only mediate but never simply claim and use for its own ends. The person who makes vows belongs to God first and only secondarily to the Church. He does not become an instrument of the visible Church in the same sense that a civil servant is an instrument of the state. When two Christians living in the world choose each other for marriage and thus bind themselves to one another in reciprocal trust, no authority can meddle in this relationship of trust under the pretext that the family is the building stone of the state. Even the Church holds the keys of the Kingdom of heaven only insofar as she uses them in accordance with the heavenly mysteries. These mysteries are, of course, to their very core personal as well as communitarian, as Mariology shows us, but in such a way that the aspect of community never threatens or cancels out the personal aspect.

The member of an order and the priest choose Christ in the way that a Christian living in the world chooses his wife and his wife chooses him. Here the varieties of existence become manifest. The person who marries subjects himself to a common destiny with his spouse. He surrenders the rights over his body and his entire person to

his wife and, through her, to his children. Love here takes on the form
of a flowing forth into other generations and families. It strives to
achieve a natural "hundredfold" and thereby accomplishes a kind of
dispersion and anonymity of the individual. This condition of being
"scattered forth" can never be undone and can never be controlled in
its totality, even though with the necessary care for one's family there
is enjoined as well the responsibility for the future, which in turn
requires some kind of planning in advance. With marriage there is
given the intrinsic necessity of possessing property and of free planning.
The bond and hard ascesis between persons in the old eon persists in
marriage and in everything that follows from it logically and naturally,
everything that constantly offers marriage an ethical corrective and
the married state so abundantly contains (the "care" of Heidegger and
of the Sermon on the Mount),[13] everything, in short, that is marriage's proper means to sanctification (I Tim 2:15). By intimately
associating the sacrament of matrimony with his own relationship to
the Church, Christ has blessed this happy-unhappy human destiny
(*heimarmenē, tychē*), which between birth and death offers space for
every sort of illusion and disillusion, hope and disappointment, striving and futility. Between the Christ-Church relationship and the
man-woman relationship in marriage, however, there is no identity,
only the analogy between carnal "image" (*Vor-Bild*) and the "original
likeness" (*Ur-Bild*), which attains to fulfillment at a higher stage. The
analogous character of the comparison is already evident in the fact
that the aspect of indissoluble fidelity between Christ and the Church
is, in marriage, confined to the earthly time span. After the death of a
spouse, the other spouse is totally free. Paul already said as much in
this connection (Rom 7:3), and in this light the question of the
Sadducees (Mt 22:23f.) appears as more than just a captious jest. The
whole structure of marriage belongs to temporality and bears the
stamp of the temporal at every level.

But Christ took human nature to himself in such a way that he also

---

[13] For this reason, it seems to us to be erroneous when people attempt to
combine the ethics of the family with the ethics of religious life by submitting
married couples to the regime of poverty and obedience proper to the orders. This
attempt exhibits an ignorance of the inner theological logic of both states.

assumed all of mankind's destiny in his Person, thus making human destiny into an expression of his relationship to the Father in the Holy Spirit. Christ does not take human destiny to himself as one who overcomes it stoically. Christ is the Man of Sorrows, come defenselessly to allow the sin of all to exhaust its rage upon himself. This is not a case of self-ruination, however, but rather the freedom to give one's life away and to take it back again. This is a case of being poured out over all heights and depths, even to the mystery of the Eucharist, and through it all there reigns a kingly sovereignty that accepts no commands except from the Father alone. While eros scatters, agape remains gathered and itself gathers. For this reason, the love of Christ for the Church (and, through her, for all mankind) opens out into the infinite and into a boundless fruitfulness and yet forever remains an exclusive and childless love between an "I" and a "Thou" (Cant. 6:9). A person enters into this mystery and partakes in its "inclusive exclusiveness" by virtue of the life of the counsels. This distinguishes also the mysterious and sublime solitude of the person who is a special disciple of the Lord. He is haunted by Christ's own solitude and aloneness, from which alone all community derives. His life is nourished by the *monē pros monon* ("alone with the Alone") between the Church and her Lord. It would, then, be erroneous to attempt considering and treating religious communities as if they were natural familial communities. Discipleship, too, involves a certain anonymity, but one that leads in a very different direction than the anonymity of an individual entangled in the web of destiny. In the case of discipleship, the anonymity involved is a transparency for the ever unique mystery of agape. The chosen disciple can serve only as a vessel and a tool for this mystery, but the mystery, in turn, imparts to him a radiance that makes him stand out and bestows on him a countenance very different from that of a personality that has been "steeled in life's battle".

From this perspective, the life form that previously appeared to be a *forma informans vitam christianam* (a "form in-forming the Christian life") now becomes a *forma subsistens in Christo* (a "form subsisting in Christ"). It thus becomes one life form among others at the level of human and earthly life forms, both established in its feasibility by Christ and guaranteed by him in its realizability. As such a *forma subsistens,* this life becomes the *forma informans* of the secular state, since marriage receives both its natural and its supernatural sacramental dignity only from the original sacrament between Christ and the Church (Eph 5:21–23). As total community, the Church remains "grounded on the foundation of the apostles and [Christian] prophets, and on Christ, the cornerstone", and only in this way do all become fellow citizens with the saints and members of God's household (Eph 2:19–20).

The important thing that must be realized is that the first ecclesiological tension can never be resolved without the second, that the universality of the spirit of discipleship cannot be infused into the Church without the living out of an exclusive concern for Christ, which finally may be seen to partake in his exclusive concern for the Father. This exclusiveness of Christ constitutes our theological (in the narrow sense) as well as our soteriological basis. It is the representation of God's eternal and blessed threefold nature, as well as the form of suffering for everyone, since in a world that emanates disintegration such exclusiveness may be seen as *the* fundamental scandal that actually provokes crucifixion. But it is the soteriological basis only because it is the *theological* basis as well. It is not the accumulation of all sins upon the Suffering One that effects redemption but the Son's forsakenness by the Father. All openness to the world in the Passion finally contains within itself as form this infinitely sublime closedness of the triune God. Only God redeems the world in his divine relations of Father and Son in the Spirit. Indeed, by its "contribution" to the event of redemption, the world only made itself more guilty than ever (Rom 5:16).

As God, Christ can never be "the Other" for man. In the words of Nicholas of Cusa, he is the *Non-Aliud,* the "not other", or as Ben Sirach says, "He is all" (Sir 43:29). Whoever would choose Christ exclusively as God would, by the same token, choose the universal. And, if this person is aware of the fact that God created the world and loves the world, he would also, for the sake of God, have to include the world in this "universal". One cannot choose God and exclude the world. For God has allowed his creation to partake in his eternal begetting of the Son: the Divine Word, the Son of the eternal Father, becomes man and "one of us". Only at this level does the universal become at the same time the exclusive, precisely in order to be truly universal. For no one comes to the Father except through the Son. Here we would have to examine anew the famous debate between Thomists and Scotists and ask whether the particularization of the universal God in the Incarnation is primarily founded on a theological and cosmological basis or on a soteriological one—in other words, whether the Incarnation is to be seen as the perfection of God's revelation or as the result of sin. According to our answer we would then come to consider the imitation of Christ as embodied in the "exclusiveness" of the life of the counsels either as the ultimate perfection of human life or as a sacrifice with Christ for the world, extending into the Resurrection.

Whatever may be the case, we can assert that the first field of tension leads into the second. The life of the counsels in the Church is not *only* a universal "spirit" that, precisely because it is spirit, can ultimately be lived beyond any distinction of states of life. This is what Protestants do and what many Catholics today are likewise attempting. The life of the counsels represents the spirit of the Church *as a state,* as a particular, visible, and sociological life form within the Church. This is so because Christ is "one among us", as well as the *Non-Aliud* and *to pan* ("the All"). Because this spirit is at the same time a state, therefore, as *forma vitae ecclesiasticae* (the "form of life in the Church"), it can also shape the life of Christians in the world into a "state". By so doing, it infuses into secular life the necessary strength and unity of state to convert the thousand varieties of human destiny into a following of Christ. The life of the counsels remains the original model of discipleship because it is not primarily founded on a "selective" choice (i.e., "I choose Christ as my partner instead of a wife") but on the action of a God who himself chooses and calls, a God who chooses man's whole existence, body and soul, interiority and history, and to whom man responds by giving him everything—the totality of what he is. He cannot give more, and this not only in a material sense but also formally: man cannot wholly account for himself, since he conceives of himself as an answer to God's call.

Just as with Christ the aspect of exclusiveness makes its appearance precisely when the Word becomes *flesh,* so too does the aspect of exclusiveness in discipleship (the challenge of the second paradox) make its appearance only in the sphere of the bodily. Considered abstractly, the "counsel of poverty" and the "counsel of obedience" could, in fact, be resolved almost wholly into a "spirit". In both instances what matters primarily in practice, both in the life of the counsels and in secular life, is precisely the spirit. There comes a point where it is nearly indifferent whether a Christian still calls certain goods nominally his own or whether he administers and uses them only as the goods of a community. The Christian in the secular state can be so detached from his goods interiorly that it would not bother him to give them away to the poor or to hand them over to someone else to be administered, while he retained only their use. The fact that there is found in the Church the example of those who have "left all things" has perhaps, for those who remain in the world, a primarily "pedagogical" significance and much less of an unconditional theological meaning. As we will soon see, something similar is the case with obedience. But the "states" become differentiated in the bodily sphere. Here we find the point of departure that then reaches over to the other spheres and shapes them differently according to the way chosen. This is why in 1 Corinthians 7 *virginity* remains for Paul the criterion for distinguishing the states, and for this reason as well virginity is also historically what first distinguishes the life of the counsels. Poverty and obedience as "counsels" are a consequence of a bridal relationship with Christ, and this relationship constitutes a life derived from the life of the bride-Church, whose original model is Mary. But precisely here it becomes clear that Mary, who like her Son had to make a real decision whether to marry or not to marry, remains a virgin in order to be a mother. This means that following Christ in the Church puts one, precisely *through* the choice of virginity, on the road to the total motherhood of the Church, which embraces both states or ways of life. For this reason we discover in genuine, Catholic virginity an experience of the body made in faith. The experience can be seen in the case of Mary to be an experience of Incarnation, in the case of the Church an experience of being a bride, in the case of Christ a Eucharistic experience. Such experience mediates a "supernatural" contact with the Christian state of matrimony, an event that can be confirmed even psychologically in the case of good priests and religious. Theologically, therefore, it is erroneous to describe the Christian who lives the counsels in the world as being incompetent in the affairs of marriage simply because he has no experience of them. The exclusiveness of a decision for God such as Christ and his Mother made, precisely at the service of all who were to be saved, can indeed be considered a sacrifice, but not in the sense of an atrophy or a mutilation of an essential aspect of man.

As far as *obedience* is concerned, we must remember that the states of perfection in the Church are analogous to each other and *only* analogous, but in such a way that the essence of the life of the counsels is preserved in all of them, including the secular institutes. One cannot, therefore, simply introduce the ideals of one form of life into another. In an unambiguously forceful manner, Bernanos has called our attention to the fact that precisely this can and has unjustly been the case, and that what is good for the religious state is perhaps not so good for the state of the layman in the world. But in order to understand Bernanos completely, we must see him as a novelist whose real subject is the most severe obedience to the counsels. In his half-fictionalized, half-historical figures of saints he has portrayed an obedience that, in deriving from an evangelical pattern, is a model *for all to follow.* Those theologians who polarize the two basic life forms in the Church as much as possible in order to preserve the freedom of the laity, thereby leaving no room for secular institutes, will have a difficult time maintaining the unity of ecclesial obedience as it is found in *all* states. They will also supposedly employ a concept of freedom derived from the model of the secular state, a concept that can conceive of freedom in the life of the counsels only negatively as "that which has been sacrificed to obedience" and that is, therefore, no longer present.

With a brevity perhaps open to misunderstanding, let us attempt to trace the relationship of freedom and obedience through the different states. We begin with the secular state, where "freedom" seems to be greatest and "obedience" most limited, since in this state a person takes most responsibility for family, career, and civil life. Even here we can see that the two spheres cannot merely exist alongside each other. A Catholic physician or lawyer, for instance, will be basically ready to exercise the freedom he enjoys in the spirit and in the sense of the Church's doctrine and recognizing a certain leadership on her part. In this case, the physician or lawyer does not mark off and delimit *from his own perspective* the area of the Church's competence but rather relies on the Church's awareness of the nature and limits of her own powers, corresponding to the *propriis principiis, propria methodo* ("following her own principles and methods", Dz. 1799) of Vatican I. The Church, in turn, is wary of interfering in the areas of the secular sciences and professions other than as called for by her mission of looking after the supernatural and eternal salvation of man and his world. Both the Church and the individual are aware of the mysterious character of ecclesial obedience, which, on the one hand, exists in order to teach the individual to be attentive and submit to God's word and voice, and which, on the other hand, itself represents the divine authority in the world. The layman who possesses the right ecclesial spirit will defend himself against possible encroachments of the Church's authority on the domain of his freedom as a layman, but in such a way that he does not thereby presume for himself an immediate, exclusive relation to God but rather keeps the *whole* field of his freedom fundamentally open to the maternal control of the Church—even the field of his free professional responsibility. Whoever would make this paradox out to be psychologically impossible or unbearable (as non-Catholics do with gusto) could do so only on anthropological or statistical considerations. These, however, prove as much theologically as would a poll on the monastic and clerical "states" trying to determine theologically the pros and cons of the religious life or of celibacy.

Let us move now to the opposite extreme, to that type of religious life that represents primarily the eschatological aspect of the Church. Because within the artificially circumscribed world of the monastery every kind of civil responsibility in the world is suspended, obedience becomes possible as a surrender of personal decision making into the hands of one's spiritual superior. This is discipleship to the very Cross, where the Lord could not touch even a single one of his own bodily members. Even this renouncement of secular freedom is, naturally, both an expression and a furthering of the Christian's eschatological freedom, which must accomplish this act of surrender both once and for all and yet anew every day. Naturally, too, there is presupposed a certain official charismatic character as being present in the person charged with spiritual leadership. To the one who makes the vows, the superior must mediate not his own will but the will of God in the place of that which has been given up. In order to be able to do this, the superior must live in a constant union with God through prayer.

In active orders things shift around in such a way that the one obeying, having basically sacrificed his freedom, receives it back again in obedience, and he can and should use his freedom out of obedience for free and responsible decision making. Tensions arise here between, on the one hand, an orientation toward the general spirit of the order, the particular personality of the superior and his intentions, and the objective context of the task at hand and, on the other hand, toward the specific nature of the situation, which demands a personal decision. These tensions must be borne out and are, again, to be resolved only in a supernatural fashion, which here means through the prayer life of both superior and subject. We must once again emphasize the fact that a vow of obedience is directed to God, even if through the hands of the superior who represents the order. The most precious of all gifts that a person can offer—that of his own freedom—may be made only to God and to him alone. The Church's representatives can, indeed, through God's special privilege, become costewards of such a gift in the name and in the spirit of God, but they can never use or misuse it for themselves, for their own advantage and purely personal plans and designs. Because the person obeying trusts in God insofar as he guides the Church and, therefore, also trusts in the superiors' solidarity with God in prayer, obedience remains one of those daring risks known only to Christian faith. The act of obedience is not achieved following from statistical probabilities but following from trust, in faith, in the Founder of the Church.[14]

[14] Cf. Joseph Loosen, S.J., "Gestaltwandel im religiösen Gehorsamsideal", *Geist und Leben* (1951): 196–209.

From this quarter, then, there is hardly any serious objection left that could be made against obedience in a secular institute. On the one hand, the same autonomous decisions are here involved as must be made by the layman in the secular state, decisions concerning above all one's profession and professional community and that leave a person mostly to his own resources, often making impossible an appeal to the opinion of one's spiritual superiors. As with the religious with vows, however, this responsibility, now largely or even totally "secularized", is accepted out of Christian and ecclesial obedience and remains permanently open to it.

In practice, this bond of obedience will, in the great majority of cases, do nothing other than lend support to the free responsibility that a person has ventured to assume. The bond of obedience will first of all educate one's sense of "responsibility". It will, in a fatherly and yet inexorable manner, strengthen responsibility and induce it to make the decisions exacted when the natural thing would be to draw back and become entrenched behind this or that "authority". Whoever has ever been in the position of exacting ecclesial obedience knows that such a measure usually has to be engaged only to make prevail, against (i.e., *for the sake of*) the obeying subject, that aspect of God's will that has already become evident to the obeyer in prayer. Such an imposition of obedience aims at not allowing the development of the Christian life of love to break off and atrophy prematurely, and thus to carry it through even against the opposition of a subject grown fatigued with trials. Obedience is, then, an aid for the individual never to lose his ideal from sight and ever to strive after it. Here also belongs the overall consideration of a comprehensive life calling, the opportunity of bringing together into a single, theologically unified act all elements of one's life: direct and indirect call from God, mediation of the Church through the suggestions of superiors, personal inclinations and aptitudes. In short, the kind of relationship existing between the secular competence of the one obeying and the salvific competence of the Church's representative who issues commands is here comparable in its content to that relationship as it exists for the layman living in the secular state. For with the layman, too, there lies at bottom the fundamental openness of indifference to the word of the Church. Only in its practical implementation does this relationship preserve the radicalism of the life of the counsels, a life form that here again shows itself to be not a special second ethics alongside the general Christian ethics but rather as the strictest and therefore most tension-fraught realization of the life of the counsels, established on the special authority of the Lord's calling. Whether this tension is bearable can be demonstrated only by the experience of the Church and of those Christians who live it out. All cries of warning that such a tension is psychologically impossible, dangerous, or inopportune and both offensive and incomprehensible for men will not hold back those Christians who themselves feel called to it.

The Christian in a secular institute is a Christian in the world, among other Christians and non-Christians in the world. He distinguishes himself from them only by the fact that he has given his whole existence—body and soul—to Christ and receives from him, through the mediation of the Church, the place indicated as his area of engagement for the Kingdom of God in the world. It is a consequence of the Incarnation that he occupies, preserves, and manages this "place" *in reality* and not merely in appearance. The eschatological aspect of the situation, in contrast, consists in overseeing this area of responsibility with one's whole existence, as a steward of God and as a messenger of his Kingdom. In either direction, he gives his fellow Christians by his life an example only of what Christian existence in the world is. He does this "undividedly", since he has identified his own existence with the Church's for Christ's sake, and for that very same reason he does it "Eucharistically". His going out into the world, to fellow humans and to whatever his calling might involve, is not the dissolution brought about by destiny but, through grace, is rather a form of the presence of Christ's saving mysteries.

3. Responses to the objections

1. The first objection arose out of a concern for the ideal of a lay Christian identity. Our answer to this objection must be free of slipshod pietistic rhetoric and must acknowledge the import of the

objection. A compelling and convincing answer can be given only by those persons themselves whose lives have been credibly shaped by a discipleship of Christ within the secular state. By means of the words on this paper we can show only that there exists no contradiction between personality and discipleship. In short, a call to (special) discipleship always addresses itself to the *individual,* in the most literal sense of the term. Kierkegaard knew this, and, in order to overcome his religious melancholy, he lacked only the Catholic manner of discipleship.[15] We have already said it: the followers of Christ are solitary, but out of sheer fullness, laden as they are with the mystery of totality. "Orders" and "institutes" are ecclesial and sociological frameworks in which these perpetually solitary individuals can live according to their calling: in a kind of community, a kind of "organization" of the specific and personal love relationship—an "organization" that, if it is not to become a self-contradiction, must always retain a certain trait of the fragmentary, of the fostering, but also of the "subsequent" rather than of the "precursory" (cf. the foreword to the *Constitutions of the Society of Jesus*). Rather than being "armored" for a holy war, the one chosen by the Lord is, indeed, left only more "exposed" by this framework in which he lives, "exposed" without protection to the pure flame of love, and by the same token exposed to a world that he confronts with an unprotected heart. It is ultimately the state of sainthood that shows the full blossoming of the truth contained in the rules and life form of the orders. It is above all to the saints that no one can deny a "personality", and yet it is precisely they who come from the state of the "chosen". This fact should not disgruntle lay Christians but rather make them rejoice, since that state is not a state "different" from their own but only its "particularity", emphatically demarcated as a pure, shaping form to *their,* the laity's, own benefit. It is the saints who, as God-formed personalities, are in a position to inform laymen. There is, to be sure, a structural distance between them, but this distance is precisely not to be found in the concept of personality. Only the more or less

---

[15] Cf. Erik Peterson, "Kierkegaard und der Protestantismus", in *Marginalien zur Theologie* (Munich, 1956), pp. 17f.

"misshapen" saints of orders and institutes could have inspired such a thought. But this is a matter no longer of theology but of statistics.

2. Are the counsels the easier way, today at any rate? Are they the socially secure way, while the person in the world is the prey of destiny in a very different sense? As we have seen, the gospel gives something like a supernatural assurance to the disciple, something like a guarantee that he who has chosen Christ, instead of everything else that gives security in the world, will not fall into the void. The "eschatological" step out of the world and into Christ is transformed, in the risen Lord, into a sheltering containment in him and in the world that heeds Christ's word and that has been incorporated into him. For this reason, an existence such as Paul's may, in the eyes of the world, seem precarious to the extreme; it is, nevertheless, secured in Christ, precisely that Paul may be able to suffer so much. Now it is just in secular institutes that something of this paradox comes to life again. In them a Christian receives that minimal support necessary for him to give himself unreservedly to his task. This support belongs to New Testament theology (even the prophets of the Old Testament had it) and is not to be relativized sociologically. And if the chosen disciple is not "flayed by destiny" in the same manner as the rest of men, he is not therefore any less a *dareis anthrōpos* — a "flayed man" — since he has been chosen for the Cross of Christ, and he has wedded himself interiorly to his suffering. What he suffers is enjoined more directly by the Lord than by "destiny". More suffering from the inside and less from the outside are here involved: participation in the form of the redemption. Precisely in the form of the secular institutes, such a participation can also be "suffered" in its essence as a result of the ruthless exposure of the disciple who loves in the midst of an uncomprehending, often inimical, hating, and loveless world. The disciple is very alone with his mission. The manner in which he experiences the supernatural protection proper to his mission is perhaps quite unconscious to him. Abandoned to the superior power of his environment, he scarcely has any hope for any success worthy of the name. He must hold his ground as one who has, by worldly standards, already been conquered. Often it is enough for him just to

be there. The usual means of publicity are largely denied him by his
secular vocation: he has to operate indirectly. He considers the comfortable interiors of family homes, and often of monasteries and
rectories too, and it seems to him he is an outsider, fallen between two
chairs, alone, really accepted by no one. By means of this very
palpable, very sensitive "outside" (how keenly Paul felt it!) he stands
exactly on the road that follows Christ, and in a very special way he
gains a share in the life form of the contemplative: the "wilderness of
God" experienced by the monk becomes palpable to him in the
"wilderness of the world".

3. We have spoken of the uneasiness caused in fellow human beings
and fellow Christians alike by one bound to obedience. Is it really *he*
who speaks and acts, or is he speaking and acting in the name of
another, of some group, of some kind of ecclesiastical freemasonry?
The question becomes all the more incisive as a community ranks
higher intellectually and educationally. The dogged fixation of many
congregations on some limited program or other initiated by their
founder or foundress, the *iurare in verba fundatoris* ("oath to the words
of the founder"), the often fanatical exposition and dissemination of a
doctrine that has been concocted and is then passed out as the distinctive feature of the congregation: all of these constrictions of Christian
freedom and intellectual latitude are profoundly detrimental to the
state of discipleship. "Spirit of the order" can mean only the Holy
Spirit, and full openness in the "spirit of the order" can mean only the
mediation of every individual member to a greater openness to the
Holy Spirit. And as these individuals hold secular posts in ever greater
personal responsibility, the superior must to that extent take refuge
more and more in the Spirit in order to strengthen that same Spirit in
the one obeying, strengthen him ever to act in the unity of the Spirit
that reigns between them. The same would basically hold here as for
spiritual direction in the sacramental situation of confession. Kings,
too, have had their father confessors, and neither the order that
provided them nor the kings' politics were necessarily harmed by this
contact. Reinhold Schneider has time and time again referred to the
confrontation between king and saint as being *the* fruitful terrain of

world history.[16] He rightly points to the fact that this confrontation has to be a meeting of two personalities, of which the one makes total claim for God, while the other must derive from this claim a decision for the secular situation: obedience and freedom at the same time. This relationship can work only when both parties acknowledge serving the same Master and the director does not attempt to over-power the one obeying; it works only when both understand the peculiar atmosphere of discipleship and have not secularized the mystery of ecclesial obedience in their hearts, turning it into a worldly thing.

But we should not let ourselves be enticed and yield to the general resentment against the life of the counsels, consciously seeking to cause offense under the pretext of truthfulness. This would have its countereffect on the Catholic in the secular state, since he too—forever obeying those mysterious orders from Rome—will always remain as offensive and sinister for the non-Christian as is the Christian religious for the secular Christian. Here, all Catholics stand *in eadem damnatione* ("equally damned"), and nothing can deliver them of that judgment but the truthfulness of obedience itself, which occasionally startles even outsiders, as in the cases of Thérèse of Lisieux and Francis Xavier.

4. We can ask what is understood by "little people". No one doubts that here it is not a matter of higher education and that an "education of the heart", nobility of soul, and magnanimity may be found in humble folk, and indeed in the proletariat, just as much as among the upper classes. In our day, the most ordinary men and women in secular institutes achieve such marvels under the impulse of the Holy Spirit that members of old-standing orders dedicated to education are stunned. The danger of the institutes lies in their emphatically charis-matic character. On this point they stand or fall, since *charisma* is their proper strength. Where the spirit dies out, the form cannot survive for long. Another danger lies in numbers and the possibility of splintering into tiny groups. But this, too, is the reverse of an advantage,

---

[16] Cf. my book *Reinhold Schneider* (Hegner, 1953), esp. pp. 175ff.

since big orders easily become formalized. An ideal situation would perhaps be achieved if the small groups succeeded in combining their interior mobility with the necessary openness to one another and to the possibility of collaboration among themselves. The smallness of a group is in itself no sign of subalternship. The greatest orders almost always accomplished their best work at the time when they were small groups—light cavalry and not heavily armed infantry.

5. The last objection brings up again the whole question of "states". The answer is to be found in the middle section of these reflections. There it became evident why a melting together of all the states is out of the question. The secular state (as the "general" form of the Church) needs the "particular" form in order to demonstrate to the world what is particular about Christianity. The crossing of the boundaries, attempted by many, will never be accomplished by the Church as a whole. We can bear our neighbors' burdens only in the form that Christ did it: in the suffering that the Father fashioned for the Son out of men's sins. Guilt always divides; innocence binds together. A common guilt can be an occasion of new and deeper love only in a common con-version away from itself. One thing is true, however: the states of life in the Church exist in order always to celebrate anew their "nuptials" with one another in the Church's bosom and very foundations. Already the fact that particular discipleship can become the shaping form of *all* discipleship in the Church sufficiently shows that the expression *two states* is only an approximate, defective one. Precisely in its act of giving shape, the form really reaches the matter it shapes. The very bases of the lay state are really affected by the state of the counsels and of discipleship, which mediates the life form of the apostles, the saints, and those who strive to imitate them. The love of one who follows Christ fundamentally transcends itself into its "other". Such love is both itself and this "other", just as Christ is both himself and the Church.

Throughout this essay we have addressed ourselves to the dialectical relationship of the "two lives" in the Church, not to the problem between hierarchical office and laity. In order to establish some order within this dialectical relationship, we could distinguish three levels that are cut through by the "two lives", levels at which these "lives" behave differently in each instance.

We have the level of love, of agape, which is a commandment for all in the Church. At the opposite end, we have the level of the exterior ecclesiastical organization of the life forms, which divides Christians into "states". In the middle, between these two, we have the level of the theological structure of the Church, which, on the one hand, is agape and, on the other, has a visible shape. Our question is: What *fundamentum in re* ("basis in reality") does ecclesiology offer for the separation of the states?

a.   The *level of agape* unites all in the Church by the common and unifying commandment of love of God and neighbor. An example: a layman in the world decides to dedicate his life in the world unreservedly to Christian love, there where he has always lived it. He further renounces marriage for that reason and even forms a group with other like-minded individuals. Now, this layman has in no way entered any new "state". To love the God of Christ with one's whole heart is nothing "eschatological". This is decisive for an understanding of secular institutes. *In order to evaluate their basic impulses, thus aiding them to attain their proper form, we must not have as our point of departure the question: To what extent can the religious life approximate secular life without ceasing to be religious life? but rather the opposite question: How far can lay, secular life go in living out Christian agape without becoming "eschatological" religious life?* Instead of the *relicto saeculo* ("leaving the world behind"), we would have the *in saeculo* ("in the world") of Pius XII in *Primo Feliciter.*

b.   The *level of ecclesiastical organization* has to draw certain boundaries as guidelines that, though possessing a certain "positivism" like all human legislation, nevertheless look to objective theological structures as their basis. Since what is here involved is the external face of the Church, the vows—as a total surrender to Christ in the Church—are primarily regarded as an engagement, in the Church, for the concrete Kingdom of God in the world, and therefore as service through the Church, which includes a connection with the function of the hierarchy.

Orders and congregations are, then, seen as "functions".[17] The radiance of their agape manifests itself as their "apostolate". The radicalness of death and Resurrection with Christ appears as the "going out of the world" required to work together fruitfully in the service of the Church. Now, it is not established a priori that secular institute–type communities belong unequivocally to the state of life in the Church we have been describing, called globally by many "the clergy". *Provida Mater* shows this when it speaks of the "new state" as being only analogically and not univocally comparable to the traditional "state of perfection". The decision has to be made at the third level.

c. The *level of ecclesiology.* As far as canonical law is concerned, the separation of the states is based on that ecclesiological *fundamentum in re* that we have discussed: the visible order of salvation. Totality and exclusiveness of existence for God take on the form of a decision to consecrate oneself, body and soul, to the Lord of the Church, in imitation of Mary and the Church herself. The point at which the states part their ways ontologically is the decision whether one wants to love men exclusively in God through Christ (this is the way of discipleship and of the counsels) or whether one loves God and the Church within the framework of a community of human love (this is the way of marriage).[18]

Such a fundamental decision cannot, for the Christian, be a private thing. In either case it ought to be an imitation *of* the Church *in* the Church. Of this decision we must ask the intentions with which it is made. It can be made out of a desire to make oneself available to the particular hierarchical and apostolic service of the Church. This is the case not only with most orders and congregations but also with most

[17] This is most clearly seen in the fourth vow of the Jesuits, which makes the whole order a special instrument of the Holy Father through a personal vow of obedience to him.

[18] We are here speaking, of course, of a *Christian* choice and not of celibacy for secular reasons, which is neutral in a Christian sense. Secular celibacy can derive from a personal decision based on a variety of advantages or duties or simply from the fact that marriage has not "happened". Theologically there is in the Church no "third state", even though, for the sake of practical organization, the people of the Church may be divided into many categories and groups.

secular institutes that serve a particular ecclesial need: spiritual direction; all kinds of aid to the clergy; teaching, fostering, and educational work; ministering to the sick and to families; work in news media and publishing houses; home and foreign missions. But the intention could also consist of wanting to be nothing other than a Christian among Christians in the world, whose only "specialization" would be the living of Christ's love. In this manner, the "Little Sisters and Brothers of Charles de Foucauld" reject every kind of "churchly activity".[19] They do not want to be "active as apostles"; they only want to *be there.* We could name other very illustrious institutes that persistently refuse being considered a part of any other but the lay secular state. It does not trouble them that canonically they have been classified as an "analogous state of the counsels", as had to be the case.[20] Precisely such a refusal to be included in the "eschatological contingent" not only poses the problem of ecclesial states in an unevadable manner. It also *connects* the "states" to one another in a fruitful way unsuspected until now. It allows the "form of sainthood" for the first time really to become the form of the layman in the world. In all this there is a mysterious manifestation of the freedom of the Holy Spirit. Just as no amount of barbed wire can hamper God's Spirit in its blowing, so too the form of saintliness in the Church can never be definitively classified into ecclesiastical categories of states. The form of holiness overflows these categories majestically and yet does not destroy them. It establishes these categories even as it transcends them.

[19] Whatever the ecclesiastical "state" they may include themselves in.

[20] At times these groups feel themselves *obstructed in their basic intentions* as a result of an all too impetuous classifying and publicizing activity from the side of the hierarchy and a well-meaning but not always felicitous help from the ranks of the older orders. In such a situation many groups prefer to remain in the anonymity of the pure secular state, an option possible today and approved by the Church. The work of classification is both good and indispensable, provided it does not detract from the original impulse of the spirit or break it off prematurely.

PART THREE

LITURGY AND AWE

1. The liturgy of the Church is an inexorable and, under the inspiration of the Spirit of God, indeed an infallible teacher educating man in reverence. That which is characteristic of every official liturgy of the higher cultures—the sense for religious good taste, for that which is appropriate and fitting in man's attitude to God, especially where he offers his worship in the context of a state, city, or confederacy—all these are transfigured to the highest degree in the cultic acts of the Church and fulfilled on a new level. The *lex orandi*—the law of prayer—of the Church is truly a *lex,* although this is of course *law* in a wholly interiorized sense: the law that her spirit of faith must impose upon itself, in order to be able to express and portray itself correctly: a law that this spirit of faith reads off its own self, a law that it itself is and yet is not, because the archetype of faith is the awesome love of Christ in the Holy Spirit for the Father, and the Church's Faith, while it bears the stamp of this archetype, can never identify itself with it for an instant. The Trinitarian distance of Christ from the Father, the immensely deep, not only divine-human but also divine reverence that breathes through all his statements about the Father, is the guiding image that stands in and above the reverence of the Church, which, as body and bride, will never equate herself with the Head and Bridegroom, despite all the unity that exists: indeed, the awareness of the ever greater uniting only deepens ever more and more the awareness of the insuperable distance between the Sanctifier and those who are sanctified, between the Lord and the handmaid of the Lord. The concealing of God on the Cross is still the exposure of the naked man, but under the Cross, herself deeply concealed, stands the *Mater-Ecclesia.*

In a spiritual sense, which is not to be pressed in a material direction, the law of praying is nevertheless the law of believing. This does not mean that theology in its individual details could be lifted out of the formulations of the liturgy. But the fact that the Church at prayer is inspired is the point from which all her other inspirations

Translated by Fr. Brian McNeil, C.R.V.

461

flow, especially of those inspirations that make a claim on her thinking and judging. For when she prays, the Church is entirely what she
ought to be and, through the infusion of the Holy Spirit from her
Head, also is at every moment: the body, the glory of the man, the
bride without spot, purified in the bath of water. How could it be
possible for her, therefore, to strike the wrong note when she prays?
And even if her innermost prayer has its foundation in the invisible
mystery, still her external daily and yearly prayer, to which she herself
has given the form, reproduces—according to the testimony of her
own consciousness—the decisive element of her inner attitude. This,
as has been said already, is an attitude of copying, of following and
imitating, of participating at a distance. This specific measure of
proportion, which is wholly unique (because it presupposes the mystery of the Trinity), this proportion between Father-Son and Son-
Church, which cannot be compared to anything else, can only be a
gift from above, if it is to succeed at all, and the fact that the Church's
liturgy does succeed in such purity, in such a transparent, still, and
irrefutably clear form, already bears in itself the attestation from
above. Nevertheless, liturgy is not simply revelation, the word of the
Bridegroom, but the work and the word of the bride who responds
in the Spirit; and for all her reliance on the word of God in order that
she may speak correctly, she remains aware that she is giving structure
to her own work. Precisely for this reason, it is, in an intensified sense,
a word of reverence: *uxor autem timeat virum suum,* "let the wife fear
her husband". This is a word that, more than all the other functions of
the Church's life, is the genuine, ecclesiastical pedagogical introduction into the correct disposition before God—not only a school of
prayer in the narrower sense but also a school and a practice of the
whole existence.

It is noticeable—and yet once again, something that is taken for
granted—with what reticence all the mysteries of the organic-nuptial
uniting of the redeemed man with the redeeming God are passed over
in silence in the liturgy rather than being brought into the light. The
disciplina arcani, which was employed by the first Christians as the
result of a very correct consideration, could not be adopted as an
external obligation to silence, nor did it need to be, since it was

inappropriate to the public character and to the catholicity of the Church; but on a deeper level, this was not necessary, because the Church already possessed in her innermost consciousness the required regulatory mechanism, perhaps more strongly in the Western Roman Church than in the Eastern Greek Church. She has the incorruptible ear for what is fitting, for what is appropriate for herself, and this does not follow in every respect the same nuances as the word of Scripture. The flame of judgment and the overpowering force of the prophets are not suitable here, nor is the subjective rambling of the wisdom literature; nor is the lordly character of the synoptic "logia", nor the superabundance—*perisseuein*—of the Pauline periods that bursts all the dams, nor the rapture of the Johannine Letters and the Apocalypse, which are caught up into mystical intangibility. All of this receives its place in the liturgy, but it is chosen with moderation and is given a framework characterized by moderation, which is an effective defense in principle against the identification of both words. The mysteries of the nuptial chamber are not ignored or forgotten for a moment, but they are more presupposed than described; they are revealed indirectly, by means of their fruitfulness, and even when one word or another alludes to them, this always takes place in the atmosphere of that reverent purity that is utterly purified by the penitence of the sinner and is also, thanks to the innocence of the bride without wrinkle and spot, irreproachable and free of all ambiguity.

The Church at prayer brings all personal piety back into this attitude in order to purify and clarify it—especially the subjective mysticism, which is always in danger of overflowing the limits of reverence and of laying claim for itself to the nuptial relationship of Christ and the Church. The liturgy does not lack boldness (*Da nobis per huius aquae et vini mysterium eius divinitatis esse consortes . . . offerimus tibi pro totius mundi salute,* "grant that we may be sharers in his divinity by means of this mystery of water and wine . . . we offer to you for the salvation of the whole world"; this is how we pray every day), but it is not the extreme formulae that appear to the Church to be the boldest but rather that unheard-of transparency of the entire attitude before God, in which the servant character of the handmaid of God expresses itself, and at the same time something is shown of the kingly mantle that the Bridegroom throws about her shoulders. The Roman liturgy is the wholly incalculable synthesis of an interior Marian-Petrine attitude of sheer service with an exterior form that bears the imprint of the Roman people and empire, something that possesses a lordly character but that has handed this over totally to the service of the interior attitude. This lordly character is not usurped (by a power-hungry hierarchy) but is made ready as it were unintentionally by Providence as an appropriate though not necessary instrument and field of expression of the Church's attitude.

2. Precisely at this point, however, it would be possible to introduce a relativization of the liturgy that would indicate its limitations, at first the general and fundamental limitations but then also those that obtain for our particular age of the world. Both aspects are important for our theme, and both support and reinforce each other, since the questions posed today derive their weight from the fundamental considerations, and it is perhaps precisely only by means of today's problematic that the general problematic becomes clear.

The central insight of today's theology (above all, of Biblical theology) is that nothing in revelation simply falls down from heaven. That which is new always grows at the same time out of a maturing process of that which is old. Even if the New Testament were not so open in the Old as some Church Fathers liked to think, still it was not so hidden as the New Testament scholars of past decades thought. Jesus makes use of the religious forms of the religion of his ancestors; taken in their "genuine" sense, they are very close to his own spirit, and indeed it is the same Spirit that inspires them. Therefore it is not surprising for us, who have come to know the Biblical history of time better, that the Christian liturgy should grow organically out of the Jewish liturgy. Just as Paul is aware that he possesses what Pharisaism "really" wanted to say, so the first Christian at prayer is aware that he possesses the true meaning of the Jewish psalms and hymns. The newness lies not so much in the form as in the fullness of the spirit that gives life to the old forms and then certainly develops individual parts of the old liturgy so that they become new, broadened forms. In the first phases, no emphasis is laid on the form: the vague poetical forms of the first hymnody, as this is glimpsed through the Letters of Paul, and indeed as it can still be seen in the Odes of Solomon and the Didache, is unpretentious, traditional, at times only a stylized kerygma, at times giving a light hint rather than creating a genuine form. The liturgy takes on a form in the full sense only gradually, in the struggle with the formed cultic forms of the public and of the secret pagan religions, in the Constantinian character and again in the Byzantine and Carolingian characters. Even if we do not enter upon the complicated history of the individual details, even the layman has the clear total impression that the Roman liturgy, as it is practiced today, is the only living piece that has survived of the imperial Church of the various social orders in the late Middle Ages. Here the spectator who takes part in the celebration experiences—with reverent astonishment, if he is not all too accustomed to these things—what a bishop was in this imperial Church, how it was attempted to copy on earth the heavenly liturgy of the angels and saints, indeed, how the entire world-view of that period experienced the two worlds of creation and redemption, of nature and the supernatural, of the cosmos and the Church, as an indissoluble unity, and knew how to represent this in a relationship of archetype and copy, portraying its meaning and its expression. This all-embracing relationship of meaning and expression is the fundamental mode of experience of those periods, a scheme that explains the "aesthetic" main characteristic both of the classical period and still of the Middle Ages (or rather, is identical with this main characteristic) and was the real presupposition for success on the part of Christian sacred art. It is not correct to define this schema out of hand as mythology and then to call its superseding "demythologization".

The decisive fact here is that we can no longer accomplish this unity as it was. Even when we feel at home today in a Romanesque or Gothic cathedral, and we believe that we understand it, it is—as experience has shown—absolutely impossible to set up such a cathedral in a creative manner today. These memorials of a past Christian age remain, in all their glory and even in their comprehensibility, something that is past. But what about the liturgy that is celebrated in them, which was developed in them (and, in a certain way, also for them)? Karl Barth once made the plea that the Münster in Basle should be given back to the Catholics, since a Protestant service was out of place in this architectonic setting. Our question is this: Is the appropriateness of Catholic liturgy to such a setting more than a historical, historicizing matter? In other words—and formulated more with a view to our theme here—is not that religious reverence in which our liturgy educates us somehow time conditioned, i.e., the expression of a religious-aesthetic sensibility of life in which the entire cosmos in its appearance was experienced as a *leitourgia,* as a great Platonic-Stoic-Neoplatonic play of gods, demigods, and heroes, of demons and souls, of hierarchies of angels that are at the same time powers of creation—a play that then lets itself be translated without any break of continuity in the Christian empire into a secular-spiritual court play in the presence of God and of his heavenly court? A play that is shot through and through with the profound concept of representation, something that can be applied both to the prince and to the priest. The "ceremony" certainly has its place still; i.e., it possesses its eloquent expression only within a ceremonial image of the world. And certainly our liturgy has grown slowly into a cohesion, and we have no difficulty in excising later, less essential strata in order to get back to the essential kernel: we can excise Baroque, Gothic, and Carolingian additions in order to penetrate through to an early Christian essential content: But is not this too a genuine construction partly of late antiquity and partly—in structures that can still be identified—of Judaism? Is this language ours; are these images and signs ours? Is it therefore as simple as the liturgical movement thinks—is it enough to let the people have a more active share in what happens in order for this to receive a relevant character for today? Does not perhaps this kind of liturgy demand something like a choir of "spectators" who stand in silent admiration and are somehow far away?

3. This brings us to the question of today's man. Indeed, there is no question that the old forms of the liturgy had a sense for form. They had, at least in the older strata, an unheard-of gift for impressive speech. The baroque had lost this ability. In the face of this example,

we wonder: Is there not also an element of flight in the liturgical enthusiasm of our days, a flight from the utter impossibility of creating speech of one's own that is full of reverence, out of the utter drying up of the power of making a religious impression, into a form that (as if by a miracle) has not found its place long ago in a museum but has remained in use down to our own times? A flight, at the same time, from the profanity of our times into a sacrality that is, so to speak, ready for use. A flight from the breakdown of every tradition in our existence into a piece of Western Tradition that bears witness to itself, the Tradition, enriched through the passage of the centuries, that still permits the living dimensions in the depths to become visible as they go back to the origins, to that mysterious confluence of the classical period and Christianity, indeed of Judaism and paganism?

Besides this, we are more than willing to admit that the Benedictines and other ancient orders, which live totally out of this Tradition and represent it in their education and indeed in their whole rhythm in a living manner in our present age, have a claim on these established forms of reverence. But what about us? And how will this majestic language of reverence look when the serious effort is undertaken to translate it into our everyday speech and into our modern, faded journalistic German? Does not this apparently insignificant experiment betray clearly the whole wretchedness of our situation? Does not the whole abyss that separates us from this glorious and beloved language open up? Who today can make a credible and uncontradicted translation of even one psalm? Luther indeed was able to find a language at the end of the Middle Ages, but has anyone been able to do this at the end of the modern period?

No one today is in the dark about the bottlenecks into which the practical execution of today's liturgical demands leads; Louis Bouyer has spoken very openly about this at the last congress of the Centre de Liturgie Pastorale (Strassbourg, 1958). This criticism was long overdue, but the speaker knew also that criticism is easy here—for example, in the case of the invasion of technical instruments and devices into services of worship—but that it is very difficult to do things better. Everything in this area that makes things "easier", e.g., that one can hear the preacher's voice better; that one can understand better what happens in the front of the church, at the altar, something that is hardly visible at all from behind; and also everything that intensifies by means of organization the congregation's sense of fellowship, such as the thorough rehearsal of the people's common responses to the address of the celebrant—it is difficult to see how this can be a genuine, an unambiguous demand made by reverence. Often it means that reverence is disturbed; or, if the people does not in fact allow itself to be disturbed, then one must say that it bears in itself the will to be reverent, that it has already brought this with itself from outside, and that it maintains itself within this will to reverence in spite of everything. But there are no doubt many who enjoy the climactic feeling of being a mature, active, and celebrating Church in a "modern" service more than they appreciate the genuflection of the handmaid of the Lord in profound humility of service before the incomprehensible presence of her Master and royal Bridegroom and the presence of the whole triune God.

We have perhaps dwelt for too long here on the questionable aspects, which should not be paid undue attention. If contemporary Church art has succeeded in shaking off the long Tradition of form, which had simply become a chain, replacing it here and there with a credible form—a form that is most credible where it is simplest—if, therefore, there exists a power of truth in the realm of our Faith that can reach back to the origin and bring it near, why should not this power be able to act effectively in the liturgical realm too, not now by tearing down and destroying all that has come into being in the past but by making it become transparent to the mystery that is made known therein? Why, for example, should not this power be able to experience the temporal strata of the Tradition in the liturgy as a manifestation of the fellowship of the saints? For the Baroque too, the Middle Ages, Charlemagne too and Constantine, as well as the earliest Church and even the Old Covenant join in the prayer of this liturgy: certainly they do not do so without us, but nor do we without them. A power with such an ability to relativize the temporal periods and their law and their weight and their mistaken attempts in the face of the one thing that is essential in the liturgical act—such a power would then be sufficiently virile, if it pleases the Holy Spirit to set his stamp upon new forms of reverence, to find a language in which a man of today, a congregation of today would be able to speak to God without necessarily taking foreign words from the past on their lips. For Sacred Scripture always remains the matrix for every historical language of Christianity. One will have to admit that the Protestants have some advantages over the Catholics when it comes to forming an ever new sacral language of reverence out of Scripture, in art. But for Catholics, it is surely the case that what is "modern" in this context will be found not so much in services with loudspeakers and in Masses broadcast on television and not at all in what can be "made" with technological means but at the place of encounter between the wilderness of a secularized culture that lacks words and reverence, stripped of its disguises, and the "wilderness" and the silence of the Trinitarian and Eucharistic God, for example, in the poor chapel of Charles de Foucauld and his wordless, liturgyless adoration, out of which, in a long period of incubation, something like a valid utterance, bearing in itself in a credible manner the testimony of reverence, can give birth to itself anew.

4. But, following directly from what has just been said, there is one further perspective that helps us on our way. Modern *life* in its public character and its rationalization lacks mystery, but this does not mean that modern *man* must necessarily lack reverence. The prepared spaces, times, and processes that are tuned to religious reverence and aim at this, and were ready for occupation by man, have been demolished for him, and this process will only intensify all the time. Thus, his reverence before God remains as it were homeless, like a bird that finds no place to rest. Not even the modernized service of worship offers him any longer a place for something of the silence and contemplation that he no longer finds in his apartments that are pervaded by the din of the radio.

The allusion to Charles de Foucauld reminds us that the real solution transcends the liturgy in the narrower sense and lies at the point where liturgy spans the gap between worship service and daily life and is the life-style that towers above both and is common to both.

It does not suffice for the liturgical style of the worship service to be transposed as such to daily life: the only result would be mannerism. The solution lies at the point where the Christian life is understood in a wholly primary sense as reverence's act of worship and is lived in this way. But this is the "style" of holiness. The language of Christian liturgy has also created a sensitivity to that which is holy as it is realized in life—not the other way round—just as this already bears the imprint of the language of the Bible. And "the holy" here is not simply a vague general sacrality of the universe (an idea that had already been torn to shreds by the utter scepticism of late antiquity) but is the Holy God himself, as the Church Fathers, who set their stamp on liturgical style, experienced him. The inner style of thinking about God, speaking about God, and living before God is constructed throughout in a uniform manner from the innermost proportionality to the most extreme formulation, by the totally dominant sensitivity for the measure that is demanded by the holy matter, that *metron, kanon,* "measurement" (*analogia*) that Paul too knows and that is practiced by the whole of Scripture. Why should the liturgical sense of life, which is portrayed in the highest degree by Dionysius the Areopagite and is transmitted by him to the Middle Ages, be foreign to modern man, who measures so much and works with numbers and proportions? Much in modern art reveals his sense of spiritual taste, of what is becoming in the presence of God, of religious decorum. And the illuminating grace will not refuse to him too the eye that measures distances and dares to set accents. But for all the ages of the world—and thus for our age too—the great and irrefutable accent remains the accent consecrated to God, the sacral life in the world. Today more than ever, this is the true place of refuge for the need for reverence. Men who consecrate their lives to God by making a holocaust of them in accordance with the counsel of the gospel and who give expression to this unique act in their daily life and in their disposition: such persons are, for those who are near them and often for a much wider circle, a sign that brings even the most cynical scepticism to silence for a moment. And if the old forms of religious life no longer seem sufficiently illuminating for the great multitudes, the Holy Spirit awakens in the Church new forms of life that set up the sign of scandal in the midst of the world in a way that cannot be overlooked. Reverence today cannot be invested safely in any mere word, not even in the liturgical word as such, but only where the word is backed up by life; and it is the duty of the Church's *martyrion* to see that this is the case in the liturgical word (where the Word becomes flesh and blood, and indeed slaughtered flesh and poured-out blood) in a manner that is credible for the world and for the age.

SEEING, HEARING, AND READING
WITHIN THE CHURCH

The human person has five different senses, five different access points to the reality of the world that surrounds him. The different nature of these access points is not without relevance for the reality itself that is grasped. We are no Platonists or rationalists, for whom the knowledge of the senses signifies nothing more than the arbitrary occasion, the external cause of an intellectual knowledge that is quite different in kind. With Aristotle and Thomas, we know that "nothing exists in the intellect that did not first exist in the sense". It is true that the things that stand "in the intellect" are precisely for this reason grasped differently and on a higher level than when they stood only in the realm of the senses, but these are the same things of the senses that are communicated through the senses. Thus, the individual character of the different senses enters the intellectual realm too: something heard is, even in the intellect, different from something that is seen, tasted, or touched, or at least it shows us the thing from a quite different perspective. Thus, a phenomenology of the various ways in which the senses perceive would have very great importance for an insight into our intellectual knowledge of reality; unfortunately, the average textbooks of philosophy, whether Christian or non-Christian, scarcely touch on this question.

My intention here is not even to sketch the rudiments of such a phenomenology; we cannot do this and do not wish to do this. We shall take only a few principles from the context of this scarcely existing science, which help us to find the direct access to our topic. For it is only when we grasp what seeing, hearing, and reading signify in the natural realm that we can grasp something of the meaning of these activities in the realm of the Church. We deal only with the two noblest activities of the senses, seeing and hearing (reading will show itself to be a subordinate function that can replace

Translated by Fr. Brian McNeil, C.R.V.

these two in a rough-and-ready fashion), since these two are the most significant in the sphere of the Church.[1]

From earliest times, seeing is held universally to be the noblest sense, that which discloses reality in the greatest depth. Seeing is the most materially relevant of the senses, because it alone unfolds before our person the world of objects, of the things that are spatially related and ordered. This material relevance has inseparably a double meaning: on the one side, it indicates an inner state of being enlightened (since the eye sees only in the light), a possibility of encompassing things in an overview, a comprehensibility. The eye is the organ with which the world is possessed and dominated, the immediate reflection in the sphere of the senses of the rational intellect that comprehends. Through the eye, the world is *our* world, in which we are not lost; rather, it is subordinate to us as an immeasurable dwelling space with which we are familiar. The other side of this material relevance denotes distance, separateness. All the other senses touch their object in some direct manner, and they have at least an instinct to come as closely as possible to this object. Only the eye needs separateness, in order to see. It is not through a close encounter that it comes to terms with things but through the look from a distance that tames them—like animals in the circus ring. This position of distance between that which sees and the object is such an essential dimension of the act of seeing that it always enters the very highest ecstasies of unity in seeing as an inherent, felt, and living proviso: when we enter a glorious landscape, we feel that it is glorious precisely in the unattainable solitude, in the intangible distance of its extension and its horizons, and that no matter how far we wander, our romantic yearning for its blue depths will never overcome this essential distance, will never be able to wander into the picture itself. Clarity and distance are the fundamental categories of our seeing. But this is wholly true only when we have "things", lifeless matters, before us. To the extent that the things become filled interiorly with life and become plants, animals, human beings, a new element is added to these categories (which remain valid even here): an inner reality shimmers through the exter-

---

[1] On tasting (eating), see the following chapter.

nal outlines of the things, creating for itself an immediate expression in these outlines and yet dwelling mysteriously closed within itself; and the more the life that appears is endowed with spirit, the more free will its self-revelation be in the areas of its sensual-material expression. Now there extends between the seeing eye and the living-intellectual objects, going beyond the distance of the separateness without however removing this, a relationship that consists of seeing into the foreign interiority, a relationship of comprehending, of insight, that goes as far as recognizing the same intellectual quality and the same act of seeing on the part of the object. The highest point, therefore, that an eye is able to attain is to look into another eye that sees. Two clarities, two separatenesses sink into one another and coincide without being blended together. This means that only those of equal rank can look into one another's eyes; even when the lord and the servant look into one another's eyes, they do so in a sphere in which they stand equally as intellectually endowed persons, in a sphere of confidence, of fidelity, of respect, and of love. Otherwise, one of them lowers his eyes or conceals himself and becomes rigid. Clarity and separateness, therefore, are not removed in this highest "moment" but have come to their most beautiful possibility. The Caesarean element of power that lies in all seeing is fulfilled when two inherent powers take the measure of one another and find it worthy of them to be the object of one another's seeing.

Hearing is a wholly different, almost opposite mode of the revelation of reality. It lacks the fundamental characteristic of material relevance. It is not objects that we hear—in the dark, when it is not possible to see—but their utterances and communications. Therefore it is not we ourselves who determine on our part what is heard and place it before us as object in order to turn our attention to it when it pleases us; that which is heard comes upon us, without our being informed in advance, and it lays hold of us without our being asked. We cannot look out in advance and take up our distance. It is in the highest degree symbolic that only our eyes—not our ears—have lids. Nor is it without significance that sound waves travel much more slowly than light waves, i.e., that we know instinctively, when a noise comes to our ear, that what we hear is basically already "over", and we have no more power over it. The basic relationship between the one who hears and that which is heard is thus the relationship of defenselessness on the one side and of communication on the other. We must develop this second point in closer detail. Even the sounds of dead nature "speak to us", and even their noiselessness can be a positive mode in which it penetrates to us as we listen; but in everything that lives, the voice becomes the great medium of self-communication. Only the voice discloses the inner mystery of that which lives, and the oscillating form of existence of the sound, full of presence and invisible, is itself the most appropriate bearer of this revelation, symbolically predestined to this task. Music is the art of interiority and of the spirit; its intensity is not the intensity of light but that of warmth. And yet the revelation of the sound and of the word communicates only the utterance, not the being itself. All speaking and singing conceal at the same time the speaker and the singer; an arrow speeds across and penetrates me more deeply than a look would have been able to do, but the bow from which the arrow comes does not itself come into my hand. No being is capable of giving total utterance to itself, even when it seeks help and aims to break out of its own interior. Thus hearing remains something intermediary and oscillating between the "Thou" and the "I", but something that streams from the one who speaks to the one who hears. The equality of stance between the two is fundamentally removed; even in a dialogue between equals in rank, the one who is at the moment hearing is in the subordinate position of humble receiving. The hearer belongs to the other and obeys him.

Reading is simultaneously a seeing and a hearing: in the seeing of the symbolically representative signs, the word of an absent speaker makes itself internally heard. But this also means that reading cannot be either genuine seeing or genuine hearing. For it is only the arbitrary sign that is directly seen, not the object or the person himself; and the voice of the speaker, whose sound accompanies me internally like a spirit and as if across great distances, is a voice that, as such, has never resounded forth. Reading is a seeing of recollection and of hope, a hearing out of the imaginative power of one's own soul. If these are alive, reading can almost take the place of the presence of the one who is distant: the letter, the book disappear; we look at the lines without seeing them; we fly above the pages as if on a magic carpet from the Thousand and One Nights. But if these are faded and dead, the paper becomes for us a lime twig on which we remain stuck or a wall (as in Japanese houses) that separates us from the reality. The distance that separates reading from seeing becomes greater because the object is not truly present to us; the element of domination gets the upper hand because the one who reads is alone by himself, and it is easy for him to dispose of the shadowy partner. And thus, to the same degree, the urgency of the word that presses upon him is reduced: he now sees only the "objective" element of truth contained in the written word and no longer sees the existential form of its existence, which alone makes it a word.

The distinguishing mode of the revelation of reality in the individual senses remains, we have established, in the understanding intellect too. As such, this asserts something essential about the intellectual meaning of existence in the world. And thus it is right, indeed necessary, that these sensual modes should play a role both in the analogous natural knowledge of God on man's part and in the supernatural revelation of God to man. As far as man's natural knowledge of God is concerned (a subject on which we shall not linger here), it can be said that this knowledge of God comes into being through the created beings, in their mirror and likeness, with certain natural abilities of the human spirit that one may conveniently call "intellectual senses". For the very fact that the various sensual modes stand in the sphere of the spirit means that they themselves are spiritualized, and that there exists in the human spirit a possibility of the experience of reality that corresponds to them. This does not mean that the human spirit would now suddenly possess its object in the same "intuitive" way as do the senses, seeing it, hearing it, touching it. But in the human spirit's own particular relationship to its object—here, the act whereby God displays himself in the created being—there is something that corresponds to the mode of the clear and objective act of seeing, something else that corresponds to the mode of hearing and being affected, and something else again that corresponds to the perception of smell and of taste or to the blind awareness of touch that nevertheless brings certainty and is blessed.

We shall not spend time here on these "intellectual senses", because they have received a priori a fulfillment in this supernaturally elevated world in which God has revealed himself, a fulfillment that goes beyond them into what the Fathers, following Origen, were accustomed to call the "spiritual senses", *sensus spiritales.* This sensual perception, which Origen described with the utmost care,[2] is at one and the same time the fulfillment of the natural-intellectual senses (*gratia perficit naturam*) and a wholly new sensitivity for the modes in which the divine appears in the world, a sensitivity that is only the result of the "infusion" of grace. The spiritual senses are the human range of senses adapted to the riches and the variety of the paths taken by God in his revelation, with the capacity simultaneously to "see his glory", "hear his word", "breathe his fragrance", "taste his sweetness", and "touch his presence". It is of course true that Origen himself gave this teaching a spiritualizing hue by bringing the bodily senses and the spiritual senses into a mutual relationship of total opposition: it is impossible, he says, for the external eyes or ears *and* the internal eyes or ears to be open at the same time. But a sensual character does not automatically imply sensuality in the negative sense of worldly or carnal lust; it is possible to intensify the modes of sensual perception without any rupture or inversion and bring them above themselves into the spiritual dimension. Only so is it possible to understand how a Bernard, a Francis, a Bonaventure, and an Ignatius, in their "application of the senses", bring the mode of the intellectual-spiritual sense into action directly in the mode in which the bodily sense acts.

Thus—to take simply what is important for us here—there exist a spiritual seeing, hearing, and reading. These functions can indeed be marked off less sharply from one another, because the unity of the Spirit and of the revelation no longer permits the same degree of differentiation as in the case of the material perception of the senses, but the positive content of this difference continues to exist undiminished. Spiritual seeing: already in nature, in which "the invisible dimension of God is seen visibly", and far more in the human appearing of Christ, through which the essence of the Father appears: "Philip, the

---

[2] See my selection of texts in *Geist und Feuer,* 2d ed. (1951), pp. 338–63.

one who sees me sees the Father also", in the form of a servant taken
by the Crucified, through which already the light of the glory of the
new age blazes: "And we have seen his glory, as the glory of the only
begotten of the Father", and, "Blessed are the eyes that see what you
see." And yet this clarity, which the "Light of the world" offers to our
eyes, remains concealed in the separateness of genuine human seeing:
"No one has seen God", says John's word so decisively that it does not
abolish but fulfills the word of the Old Testament: "No one can see
God and live." It is in this sense too that the greatest theologian of the
spiritual seeing, Origen, interprets Paul's word about seeing through
a mirror and an enigma: all seeing here below remains nonseeing and
separateness; and in Gregory of Nyssa's mysticism of the night, the
dialectic of seeing and nonseeing leads to an ultimate paradoxical
equation of the two. But this distant clarity of that which is all too
real (which the truth removes from us and sets behind the veil of
concepts, dogmas, and rites) aims always, through everything, at a
highest encounter face to face, when we "shall know just as we have
been known", and the gaze of the Creator and the gaze of the creature
shall coincide in the "glance of God's eyes".

In distinction from this aiming at the identity of the mutual gaze,
the hearing of God takes its starting point in the knowledge that the
Divine Being remains always far removed. In distinction to the clarity
of the God who is "light", it sets the darkness of the God who is
inscrutable Will and Life that pours forth. Only utterances *in actu* of
this will are revelations of God, but they pour forth upon us as such,
irresistibly and urgently. The Creator himself makes use of the
defenseless and needy openness of our finite spirit, which does not
bear its own object in itself but must await this passively from outside
itself, in order to make himself heard by the listening ear of our spirit.
"Let the one who has ears, hear!" Let him already hear God, with
Augustine, as a weak, enticing music that sounds through the confused noises of the world; let him hear him as the incarnate Word on
the hills of Galilee, recounting the knowledge of the Father before the
thousands who hang on his lips, speaking "like one who has authority"
and, even more, like one who is himself the subsisting Word. Let him
hear these human words as the revelation of the very life that flows

forth in the farewell discourses like an endless wave of the sea. Then he will understand also that the blood that flows on the Cross is only the continuing parable of this intellectual life that has already been poured out in the word, the parable of the substantial blood of God, so to speak, which the spear thrust of sin caused to well up from the heart of him who is eternal. The listening Church stands under the Word of God like the penitent woman who stands under the flowing blood of the Cross. The obedience of this act of hearing is the form of her service and of her readiness to serve. And when she herself speaks as one who teaches and proclaims, she herself listens while she speaks the word in the commission that she has received from the Word. She brings further the pouring forth and the sound of the voice: "As the Father has sent me, so do I send you." And therefore, the decisive attitude of the Church will be that of hearing: "Faith comes from hearing." And the Father himself prescribes this attitude: "This is my beloved Son: listen to him." If the act of seeing aims, through the separateness of the mirror and the likeness, at the encounter face to face of the highest, identical mutual gaze, the act of hearing aims upward into an ever more perfect obedience and thus into a creatureliness that distinguishes itself ever more humbly from the Creator. This humility will not be abolished in all eternity, because the truth of the relationship between God and man expresses itself ever more perfectly in it.

The reading of God certainly exists, just like the seeing and the hearing of God. For Sacred Scripture is the "word" of God, not of course the word that immediately flows forth but the word objectivized in signs, which continually finds occasion in these signs for a fresh streaming forth. In this sense, Scripture is in truth a kind of sacrament or sacramental, as Origen considered it; and even today, it is given the incensation in High Mass that is owed to the presence of God in it. And so the Lamb in the Apocalypse rests on the book with the seven seals, and the word itself reveals itself as Alpha and Omega, i.e., as the embodiment of all that can be expressed in the letters of the alphabet. And yet it is in this form of the word as book that we clearly see the secondary element that we noted in the case of every act of reading. It is, of course, true that the Alexandrine theology saw an immediate analogy between the materialization of the Logos in the flesh and the materialization in the book: in both, the word can be touched, seen, and grasped. But here we must not overlook a threefold corrective. First, the Alexandrines, as intellectual "Gnostics", stand in the Tradition of Hellenizing Judaism, which had already long carried out a magical-speculative cult with the Torah that had been elevated to the status of a semidivine being (perhaps the book symbols of the Apocalypse too are a certain echo of these speculations), a cult that is not in the least suggested by the Bible itself and that bears light traces of an intellectualism that deforms Scripture. Further, one must recall that the book, as a material book, had no significance whatsoever for the Christian Alexandrines, since they contemplated the written word only in its immediate connection with preaching, in which alone the word of God, which is "living force and life", receives a mystical presence. Finally, this Biblical theology is assessed correctly only when it is given its place in the entire movement of Alexandrinism, in its striving away from the symbol to the unconcealed truth, from the flesh of the Logos (in all its forms) to the Pneuma. Accordingly, Origen basically does not spend any time at all on the act of reading; unlike the acts of seeing and hearing, the act of reading does not emerge as a positive and significant mode of the experience of reality. Origen knows nothing of a "spiritual act of reading". Rather, the act of reading as such is always that which is a priori disappearing before the immediacy of the presence of the word. Thus, he would never have understood the parable of Augustine, who saw in Sacred Scripture a letter that the Father sent us from our homeland "in order to enkindle in us the yearning to return home". Here it is separateness that takes the place of immediacy; the book becomes a vicarious representation of the absent God and becomes prominent in its material character; the act of reading as such takes on a decisive significance that can be distinguished from the acts of hearing and seeing. This change can be illustrated best by means of the similar change in the understanding of the Eucharist. For Origen, the transfigured Body of Christ, since it is pneumatic, is absolutely supraspatial and therefore present everywhere; the Eucharist, since it is spatially limited, can be only a visible, cultic sign of this universal presence. For

Augustine, Christ's transfigured Body is "in heaven" — *surrexit, non est hic* — and the Eucharist is the sacramental "substitute" for this abiding distance between the old age and the new. It is clear that, if the danger exists in Origen of springing immediately away from the text and seeking "behind" the letter a second, hidden, esoteric-pneumatic meaning, there stands in the continuation of Augustine's understanding the no less pernicious literalism that clings to the material character of the "letter from God" and ultimately is no longer able, thanks to the sheer quantity of Biblical criticism, to perceive the message and the word. "Spiritual reading" will therefore have to maintain its position in the oscillating midpoint that is the proper position of all genuine reading: remaining with the text only in such a way that the meaning and the person who speaks shine through it without, however, flying over the text in such a manner that one fails to read, to hear, and to see the word that is given expression in the sign.

Fundamentally, however, both types that have now emerged in the case of the act of reading are nothing other than the two great ecclesial types of the East and of the West. The East is Johannine: it is the Church of seeing. The West is synoptic-Pauline: it is the Church of hearing. In the East, Logos means "meaning" and "idea"; in the West, it means *Verbum*, "word". A Christianity that gives seeing unambiguous preeminence above hearing must also have the modality of seeing as its fundamental structure; i.e., at the basis there are the objectivity and reality, the abiding encounter between the eye and the thing. This is why the world appears for the East fundamentally as a world of ideas and the Logos as the embodiment of all intellectual realities. The separateness that is also denoted by the act of seeing becomes clearly seen in the distinctively Eastern concept of the intermediary beings between God and the world, the heavenly and earthly hierarchies, the Byzantine-sacral court ceremonial (the liturgy does no more than transpose this into the ecclesiastical realm, just as theology transposes it into the cosmic realm), and the all-determining sense for representation. Thus the created universe becomes a great total sacrament and "mystery" in which the ecclesiastical-liturgical sacrament appears only as one particular function. If one wishes to be convinced that it is this partial significance that is attributed to the cultic mystery, one need do no more than open the pages of Maximus the Confessor's *Mystagogy*. The individual-mystical mystery and the universal-cosmic mystery stand beside the cultic mystery in a position of equal importance. The same is fundamentally true already of the Alexandrines, while in the Cappadocians and in the theology of the desert hermits (continued as the Athos theology of the Greek Middle Ages) the cultic mystery almost totally yields place to the cosmic-individual mystery. This can be understood only when we look upward from the basis of the objectivity of the act of seeing to the summit of the vision that is the aim of all seeing: to the unmediated encounter face to face of the creature with God, flying over all inequality of rank and qualitative difference. *Theôsis*, deification, is the ultimate cry, the ultimate goal of Eastern Christianity, because it is the ultimate meaning of the pure vision. This is why the East aims at (mystic-supernatural) identity, and why monophysitism is the genuinely Eastern heresy. The two or three "small" dogmatic differences between Rome and Byzantium were never more than the occasion, never the truly weighty reason, for the schism. The Eastern Church became heretical because she handed herself over to the absolutization of the inner dynamism of the act of seeing, which points ultimately, in its upward flight, to identity with God and to negation of the world. Thus the great Eastern systems, where they are Christian, tend to the form of a "thinking backward" from a radical systemic form, which as such inclines to gnosis and pantheism. It is only where this upward flight toward identity remains bound to the form of the abiding, objective separateness, so that the basic form of creatureliness and thus an intellectual position of hearing is maintained, that the Eastern form of Christian piety remains something that cannot be lost within the sphere of the Church.

Unlike this, the Christianity of hearing knows the abiding creatureliness, obedience, and worldly character of the one who hears and a relationship of immediacy, bypassing every representative intermediary form, to the word of revelation. The Western Church is the Church that is bowed down under the act of hearing and that inclines toward the world as an apostolic Church through the sending of the word. For this reason, she is also the Church that is visible in her abiding creatureliness as one earthly form among others, and it is no coincidence that the primacy of Peter came into view in her and not in the East. Thus she is also the Church in a hand-to-hand struggle with the age in which she lives, defenseless and vulnerable in the act of hearing (whereas the pneumatic Eastern Church is so to speak invulnerable, because she is already the new age, no longer "of this world"). Thus she too feels in an upward direction, not into the immediate vision, not in order to be deified but in order to have an ever closer contact with the will of God that leads her in the darkness. The comparative form that guides her is not the ever deeper sinking of the world in the presence of the light of God but the ever greater honor of God in the work of service of the world. But for this reason she, unlike the East, tends to both heresies of hearing: either one perceives in the word of God nothing more than the ray *in actu* that touches us and no longer perceives the objective-visible meaning (this aspect is initiated in Augustine's teaching on predestination and develops one-sidedly in Luther, Calvin, and Port-Royal), or else one becomes so absorbed in the service of the world that he forgets the very mission and the hearing and becomes a prisoner of this world to which he ought to have preached the word (the immanentism of the modern period). The erring paths of the West are the actualism of the pure word and the activism of pure activity. They will be avoided only when the abiding creatureliness does not close itself up in blindness but keeps the eye of its spirit open for the objective meaning of the word that is spoken—and likewise only when service of the world does not isolate itself in a Pelagian manner from the God who gives the mission but understands itself as a sacral, "sacramental" representation of this God in the world. Thus the entire form of the Catholic Church stands between the extreme East and the extreme West, between Athos and Wittenberg, pure vision and pure hearing. But it is decisive that, in this entire form, the rock of Peter rests visibly in the West, in Rome—not only because the pole of visibility belongs to the West in the equilibrium between the visible and the mystical Church but more decisively because the relationship between the world and God, both in the natural order and in the supernatural order, is given more decisive expression in the form of hearing itself. The basis of the gift of the relationship between friend and friend is the abiding relationship between Lord and servant, which is fulfilled by the gift.

Let us now cross over from this wholly general sphere of the Church into her visible-liturgical sphere, and let us deduce from the ideas that have been developed here a few consequences that arise directly.

A first significant consequence shows us at once that liturgy is possible neither in the radical East nor in the radical West. Where the Eastern piety of vision displays its character perfectly translated into life, on Athos, the liturgy can be only a preparatory stage. The perfect mystic separates himself from the community monastery to withdraw into the caves on the peaks, from which the mystical light of Athos was seen shining at night. The unambiguous tendency, from Clement of Alexandria *via* Origen, Evagrius, both Gregories and Maximus, is to transcend the visible liturgy and to find its "truth" in an individual-Gnostic immediate relationship to God. Even in Dionysius the Areopagite, the signs perceptible to the senses, to which he holds so fast, are only thin veils for a Gnostic-heavenly event: as signs they are indeed sacramental, but basically they are representative rather than themselves being efficacious. Thus, while it is true that the Eastern liturgy, where it genuinely unfolds itself, is a liturgy of seeing, in which the believer is permitted to see, through mirror and likeness, the supraheavenly mysteries of the new age in a great symbolic-representative sequence of scenes, it is nevertheless just as characteristic that this living sequence of scenes as it were solidifies into the "wall of images", the iconostasis—solidified like the ceremonial of the Byzantine court—and that this now divides the church interior into two, one space for the profane, uninitiated people who must be content with the "colorful reflection of the splendor" and one space for the mystic-initiated priest who always has the iconostasis at his back and already stands on the far side of all likenesses. This is, basically, the repetition of the Alexandrine division of the believers into the "simple" (*haplousteroi*) and "Gnostics" or "perfect" (*gnôstikoi, teleioi*).

But liturgy is no less impossible in the pure West, because the pure word makes all objectivization in image and sacrament impossible.

Thus the Protestant has nothing more than the pulpit and the seats for those who listen. And if we consider the other heresy of the West, that of activism in the world, then we shall not be wrong if we put the blame for this on the faded lifelessness and hurriedness that is so often found in Catholic worship. Where the world devours all our interest, even half an hour on Sunday is long; the sermon is reduced to a minimum, the ceremonies shrink, and thus ultimately even here the individual believer is left to his own resources, to his prayerbook, his missal, or his Rosary. The visible element of the liturgy is simplified until it is almost nothing more than a formal presence at the Holy Mass, while the mystical element of the liturgy is simplified to the point of becoming an interior recollection during this half-hour of lonely prayer.

It is neither the extreme idea of the East nor that of the West that will show us what liturgy truly is, but only the total form of the Church of East and West. This Church is fundamentally both creaturely and visible, formed of worldly beings who have no need of being ashamed that they belong to the world, since Jesus Christ took on a full, human, and worldly nature. Thus it is above all the iconostasis that falls away if a true liturgy is to be celebrated, since the iconostasis excludes what is worldly as profane ("pro-fane" means outside the sanctuary) from what is sacred. As Maximus the Confessor describes it, nave and altar, nave and pulpit form an inner unity with an analogy to the two natures, which are not reduced by their unity in Christ. On the basis of this weighty foundation, in which the Western Roman element predominates over the Eastern, the further equilibrium between East and West is now built up in harmonious balance. This is initially the equilibrium between seeing and hearing, "sacrament" and "word", objective and existential event of salvation. Against the all too Western tendencies, it will be necessary to emphasize the sacramental significance even of the sermon (as Origen understood this); the sermon is not only a moral-ethical exhortation and edification but also a true act of making present the Divine Word itself; and further, it will be necessary to emphasize that the coming transfigured world is made present in a real and representative manner through the sacramental total event of the liturgy. Against the overemphasized Eastern tendencies, it must be maintained that this presence of the new age is not the presence of a Platonic-pneumatic realm beyond this world that stands in no relationship to the present, lost world—in the manner, for example, in which a Russian icon floats as a transcendental "idea" above the real world of every day, to which it bears no relationship—but rather that it is precisely the real world of every day that is to be transfigured and transformed, i.e., that this real world must appropriate salvation to itself existentially in the sacramental event and transform the gift of grace into a moral-ethical life. Thus, just as both sacrament and word are "sacramental" in the Eastern sense, so both are also an "existential sermon" in the Western sense, the urgent word of God.

This implies a second equilibrium: against the Western type, it must be said that the liturgical event is not only a temporally and spatially limited act within the church building, out of which the Christian can take at most a couple of good resolutions for his apostolic activity in daily life; rather, the Church's liturgy is the form that concentrates the total liturgy of the world, which includes all daily life and in which the Christian has the liturgical function of effectively representing the divine in the world through his whole *being*. But against the Eastern type it must be objected that an act of representing God in the world that is limited to one's being is not enough, or indeed is quite impossible, unless the being is also an actively formed being that has been made one's own ethically and streams forth in the *act* of apostolic proclamation. The East is right to say that we must continue our act of worship in our daily life without any break of continuity, but the West sees more clearly that we must do this not as walking icons but as utterly everyday and genuinely secular human beings.

The final equilibrium is a direct consequence of this. Since the Church is not a mystical reality existing beyond this world, no heavenly pneumatic fellowship of the elect (as the extreme East is inclined to believe, e.g., among the Old Believers, and the extreme West in Protestantism) but a genuine, visible fellowship based on the genuine and visible Incarnation—therefore the Church's liturgy too is, to begin with, a genuinely worldly function among other functions, and the obligation to attend Mass on Sundays and to make one's Easter duties is indeed often an uncomfortable or even heroic profession of faith in the visible Roman Church. Therefore, genuine life of the senses and hearing has its abiding place in this liturgy. The sacramental event *ought* to unfold visibly in as beautiful and worthy a form as possible. If it is the case that, thanks to an increasing clericalization and a corresponding exclusion of the people, not only their ability to *see* truly in the Church but likewise the possibility to see anything objective and symbolic at all (since it is scarcely there to be seen) have strangely atrophied, then it is not possible to lament this state of affairs seriously enough. The same is true of the sermon, or even of the simple reading aloud of the word of God: both on the part of the preacher and on the part of the listening people, there is seldom the awareness that here the personal word is being made present, the direct continuation of the sending of the Son by the Father. This would, therefore, be first of all a matter of a new feeling on the part of the priest for the significance of sensual speaking and acting, and a new feeling on the part of the people for sensual hearing and seeing. But such a recovery must now take place explicitly in the sphere of the real and worldly Church, not in the sphere of an Eastern Church that is caught up out of the world, for otherwise one would cultivate only a falsely sacred awareness that engaged in an aesthetic flight from the world, feeling itself to be the holy community of the Lord thanks to a few well-drilled gestures or chants—but this would collapse in the face of the raw wind that blows outside the church door. The only way to attain an appropriate behavior on the part of the congregation in the liturgical celebration is not from the outside, through reforming and practicing new things in the limited liturgical sphere, but through education to a new sensual-intellectual total awareness of the Western-Eastern Church in her reality.

Since we are in the sphere of the Church, the new sensual seeing and hearing, which as such is predominantly Western, will have to change itself and interiorize itself directly into a spiritual perception and encounter with God. The Johannine Church is the secret heart of the Church of Peter. The rite exists for the sake of the inner mystery; the visible sacrifice of the Church exists for the sake of the invisible sacrifice on the Cross; when man remembers God, God remembers man and comes down to him. The spiritual seeing and hearing too must be learned anew, for God wishes to be met by the entire human person, body and soul. But our inner eyes are closed inertly; the inner ears are stopped shut. The word of Scripture, which has been heard too often, "says nothing to us any more", just like the celebration of the Mass. Here the Eastern Church can teach us secularized Westerners, if we attempt to accomplish in our own sphere what she possesses in hers.

One more word about the book and the act of reading. The German *"Volksschott-Bewegung"*, the movement that aimed to spread the use of a Latin-German missal among the laity, wanted to break down the invisible iconostasis between the people and the altar or pulpit and to create for the people a direct participation in the altar and the word. This movement took insufficient account of the fact that the people that stream into the church are not people who know how to read like Augustine or like Origen. For us moderns, a book is entertainment, distraction, instruction—in one or the other form, a substitute for real life. We vanish in the book; we forget ourselves while we read. The men of old read aloud, even when alone: they brought reality to the word in the sign. Something akin to shame or anxiety prevents us from reading aloud to ourselves: this would have existential consequences. We would be forced, while hearing ourselves, to perceive what we read sensually, intellectually, spiritually as "true". Our relationship to a book is quite different from that which still existed in the case of Goethe or Hölderlin, to say nothing of earlier generations. De facto, the "Schott" missal has become a kind of new iconostasis for us. We follow the real unfolding of the liturgy or the Scripture reading in it, as the general follows the military maneuvers on the map or the traveling snob follows the landscape in his Baedeker guide. We control the situation and thereby stand outside it. We have the word in black on white, but the word does not have us. We grasp; we are not ourselves grasped. We hold the libretto in our hand and could prompt "priest" and "people", but we ourselves are not "people" or "priest".

Something similar is true of the "Biblical movement". The intention was to bring the people into contact with the immediate word of God. The people received an inexpensive book that was also designed to speak to them in the most popular way possible. But when the people lost their timidity in the presence of the Bible, they also lost their reverence for it; the Bible is no longer the big, heavy book fitted with clasps, high up on a shelf out of reach of the children, out of which the father would read aloud a couple of sentences in the evening before one went to bed; now it lies in a corner, covered with dust, among a thousand other pamphlets, novels, and grammar books.

The act of reading is even more strongly atrophied among us than the acts of seeing and hearing. It will be very difficult to vitalize the great primary functions of the senses through reading, which always plays a secondary, vicarious role. And yet our eyes and ears must open themselves in order to perceive the presence of the Lord and his mission in the sphere of the Church and thereby to become capable of understanding the present day of the world too as a present day of God and a *kairos* of the Church.

If the mass of the people are no longer capable of this, then the individuals must achieve it. If even their senses lose their sharpness in the oncoming roar of civilization, then they must learn anew to look inward and to hear within, in order to begin from there to give form to their external sensual perception also, both their own and that of the Church. This is possible, because the God of the living, who allowed his Son to become a man, is a God for men. "What we have seen, heard, and touched of the Word of life, this we make known to you, so that you may have fellowship with us" (1 Jn 1:1–3). Every living Christian who has encountered God can speak these words in order to point others to the God who gave men senses in order that they might feel after him: "I planted the ear in man—am I not to hear? I formed the eye—am I not to see?" (Ps 93:9). "The hearing ear, the seeing gaze: God has made both of these" (Prov 20:12).

SEEING, BELIEVING, EATING

The Johannine farewell discourse of Christ is an utterance spoken after the Eucharist: the Word that has given itself as flesh and blood, the Word that has entered the believers and now speaks within the Church, which has her foundation in the Eucharist, as the word of the unity between Head and body, the word in the satisfied hunger of the soul, the word of common thanksgiving. Since it is virtually only Christ who speaks, this is already an eschatological word that sounds forth only from the Church in the state of fulfillment: the nuptial unity of the voice, in which the word of the bride is transubstantiated into the word of the Bridegroom and thus a word that no longer speaks in parables but openly (Jn 16:25) in the anticipation of the full understanding on the part of the bride herself. The morsel handed to Judas shows that this Eucharistic word is at the same time the Word that is given over into the Passion and the abyss of sin; Judas is the only one to be expressly named, while the Communion of the others, with the others, is meant to shine forth silently from the situation of the Last Supper, from the bequest of the washing of the feet, and from the final intimacy of the word that is poured forth and "preserved" (17:6) by the Church.

This is the highest level of the word: here it no longer speaks only as a word that gives itself and is received by man in faith but as a word that locates in itself faith (which is continually demanded anew) between the brackets of seeing (recognizing, understanding) and eating. This level remains the ideal that is the aim of all the Church's liturgy, for it is precisely *this* that is to be done in memory of him. The guarantee that the attainment of this ideal is made possible by Christ is the promise, taken up into the fulfilled word, of the Holy Spirit, who will be the full "remembrance" (Jn 14:26) of the entire word of Christ. All of Christ's exhortations to "remember" the word (15:20), indeed all the speaking so that they may "recall" this later (16:4) and "believe" because what was said has come to pass (13:19;

Translated by Fr. Brian McNeil, C.R.V.

491

14:29), indeed all that is unspoken, because they would not yet be able to bear it (16:12), is ultimately entrusted to the activity of the Spirit who leads them into all the truth of Christ (16:13f.). His work will be the anamnesis of the Church, which will therefore be more than a mere reminiscence and casting of the thought back: it will in fact be the positing of identity between the one who recalls and the one who is recalled: in the depth of the Eucharistic presence as sacrifice and meal.

This is so true for John that "believing" and "knowing" are virtually interchangeable terms in the farewell discourses: 16:30: "Now we *know*... this is why we *believe*"; 17:7: "Now they have *known* that all you have given me comes from you, for I have given them the words that you gave me, and they have received them and have in truth *known* that I came forth from you, and they have *believed* that you sent me"; 17:21, 23: "Thus they too shall be one, so that the world may *believe* that you have sent me ... perfectly one, so that the world may *know* that you have sent me." This is faith because it is the gift and the entrusting of oneself, and thus in fact love; it is knowledge, because the visible character of the love of the Father in the Son outshines and transfigures everything. It is an eschatological faith that even now almost dissolves into "the eternal life, namely, that they may know you, the only true God, and him whom you have sent, Jesus Christ" (17:3); even now it is almost the "vision of the glory ... before the creation of the world" (17:24).

This means that the disciples' "knowing" or "recognizing" or "understanding", at this eschatological point, which is attained with the final disclosure of the *Doxa* of Christ on earth, without removing the fact and the requirement of faith (cf. 14:10–11), penetrates and is dissolved in the sight that they have of the incarnate One in a manner that is inseparably the sight of the senses and the sight of the mind. This unity of seeing and knowing is archetypical in the Revealer himself (3:11), and since his vision is a living and perceiving vision, it can be separated out into "seeing and hearing" (3:32; cf. 15:15). In imitation, however, it is also something that concerns the believer. It is denied that the Jews have faith in God: "You have never heard his voice; you have never seen his form; you have never had his word abiding in you" (5:37–38). In the same way, it is denied that the world has the possibility of believing in the consoling Spirit, "because it neither sees him nor knows him" (14:17). Naturally, the text goes on to say of the disciples only that "you know him": the "seeing" will take place after the Resurrection. Indeed, what the world does see of Christ—that which is external—will soon be withdrawn from it too: "Yet a little while, and the world will see me no longer; but you see me, because I live, and you too will live" (14:19). They see him now, and they will see him later, because they bear in themselves Christ's life and word, and this fulfilled seeing is not endangered by the abyss of nonseeing in the Passion: "Yet a little while and you will see me no longer; and again a little while, and you will see me again" (16:16), because the mystery of the "hour" is a mystery of the Father; it is the mystery of the birth in pain, the birth that includes being alone and indeed "leaving alone" (16:31–32), "but I will see you again" (16:22). Thus even now, in the "last" hour of the world, the Lord spans the still-remaining gulf in the disciple between seeing with the sense and seeing with the mind: " 'Lord, show us the Father, and that is enough for us.' 'Have I been with you so long now, and you have not recognized me, Philip? The one who sees me, sees the Father' " (14:8–9, taking up again what was said at 12:45).

The eschatological integration of believing, knowing, and seeing that is anticipated in the farewell discourses on the basis of the presupposed gift of the Eucharistic food makes such a strong identification that it is scarcely possible for us to see here the process of the integration, which we would wish to follow and to reconstruct, both for the sake of the theological knowledge and for the sake of the practical accomplishment in life of the Eucharistic celebration. This process is visible in the so-called discourse of promise in John 6, which as such opens up the true path and genesis that lead to unity. We do not need to deal in this context with the question whether the explicitly Eucharistic passage 6:53–58 is originally Johannine or a later "ecclesiastical redaction" (if the latter, then one would also have to excise the *ex hudatos* at 3:5 and thus cut out the most important passage that links the sacraments), or whether the identification of Jesus with the "true bread" takes on its sharp point only through the Eucharistic passage, which brings the offense to its peak. Against the excision we have the symbolism of blood and water at the Cross (19:34) and the threefold testimony of Spirit, water, and blood (1 Jn 5:8) which, as it stands in its context, is woven inextricably into one with the (anti-Gnostic) theology of the Letter. Even although these passages do not speak explicitly of bread (while in contrast Jn 6 speaks explicitly of "hungering" and "thirsting" [v. 35] and goes on to mention the blood just as explicitly), the alternating sequence of water-Spirit (1:31–34), water-wine (2:9), water-Spirit (3:5, as well as the baptism of John and of Jesus, 3:22f.; 4:1–2), living water, unknown food, maturing corn (4:10, 13–14, 32, 35) with a reminiscence of the miracle at Cana (4:46), and, finally (if one joins chap. 6 directly to chap. 4) the miracle of bread (6:1–15) and the miracle of water (the walking on the lake, 6:16–21) is nevertheless a leitmotiv that cannot be overheard, finding its climax in the discourse of promise and later (chap. 5, chaps. 7–12) falling silent for a time, with the exception of slight hints (7:37–38; 9:7; 12:24) until it is fulfilled first in the Passover meal and in the Resurrection meal (bread and fish, 21:13).

The whole scene of John 6 — the miracle of food, the miracle on the lake, and the discourse of promise — is situated "shortly before the Passover feast of the Jews" (6:4), something that points ahead to the fulfillment at 13:1 ("It was on the day before the Passover feast").

A *first section* begins by playing variations on the concepts of "seeing", "sign", and "bread", understanding the last of these in a wholly material sense. The crowd "follow after" Jesus, "because they had seen the signs that he performed on those who were sick" (6:2). As so often in John, there occurs something like a breakthrough to Jesus on the basis of something one has "seen", "recognized", "known" (the Baptist, 1:34; the disciples at Cana, 2:11; Nicodemus, 3:2; the Samaritan woman, 4:19, 25; the Samaritans, 4:42; the official, 4:53). This can be a breakthrough to faith or an initial movement toward the Lord that is still wholly material, as in the case of Nicodemus and here. Jesus' "lifting his eyes" and his "seeing" the multitude at 6:5 correspond to this "having seen" on the part of the people. This "looking at" is a genuine action of the God-Man, not something like a mere "as if" that he could dispense with, since he knows in any case what it is he will see. This is an aspect of the mutuality of seeing, of looking at each other, that is found throughout the scenes of vocation at the Jordan (1:38–39: "He saw that they were following", "Come and see", "And they went with him and saw"; 1:42, "Jesus looked directly at him and said, 'You are Simon'"; 1:46–50, "Come and see", "When Jesus saw Nathanael coming, he said, 'See'", etc. . . . "I saw you under the fig tree", "You will see still greater things than these"), in which man's inchoative looking at the Lord is a priori held within and surpassed by the total, encompassing looking on the part of the Lord, a looking that however in turn promises a share in his own seeing.

The all-encompassing character of Jesus' seeing is expressed by the fact that "he knew what he wished to do" (6:6) and by the fact that his question to Philip and the following discussions about the price of the bread that would be needed and the shortage of supplies stands within the brackets of this seeing and knowing. After the miracle has been performed, the initial situation is repeated. "The people" see "the sign that Jesus had performed" and recognize in him the promised prophet. "But when Jesus recognized that they wanted to come and bear him off to make him King", he withdraws (6:14–15). Once again, a "sign" is seen and understood as a sign, but not as *the* sign that it was truly shown to be; the "following" of Jesus, which beforehand was material, now becomes demonic as man takes hold of the miracle worker and bears him off for his own purposes.

The miracle on the lake that follows confronts the believing disciples with the Lord, who is initially invisible but then appears on the lake in the night and the storm and draws near to the boat. This is what they "see"; this is what makes them "afraid" (6:19). Jesus' seeing is spoken of only in an implicit manner. However, the mutuality is clear at 6:21: the will that attempts to take up into the boat the Lord who is drawing close is superseded by the Lord, in that the boat "is immediately ashore, and at the point at which they had aimed" (6:21): *he* has taken *them* up.

Now the people once again "see" (6:22) the miracle in their own way: the only boat had left with the disciples and without Jesus, but Jesus is likewise absent. This is a wholly negative act of seeing the sign, but the evangelist attributes so much force to it that the crowd go off to look for Jesus with other boats. When they ask (in their craving for miracles) how he had come to the other shore, Jesus replies by taking away from them even the "seeing of a sign" and by leaving them only with the desire for earthly bread (6:26).

The transition to the *second section,* in which the theme of spiritual bread becomes dominant, plays with the concept of "works-work" (6:27–30). Jesus himself gives the slogan "to work" in the sense of giving oneself trouble, of being concerned about the bread that remains for eternal life, which the Son of Man gives (or "will give": this may already be Eucharistic redaction), for the Father has set his seal of attestation upon him. "To work", taken up by the people and understood in the sense of "doing" and "accomplishing" the "works of God", falls from the movement of faith down to the morality of recompense and must be turned round by Jesus, taking it beyond the starting point: the movement of faith is no longer the endeavor of man but a work carried out by God himself, as it were, only the echo of his chief work, the giving of the bread of life, something that is expressed in broad strokes of detail in what follows. But in order to be this echo too, the Jews demand a work of Jesus ("What work do you perform?"), something that they wish to "see" in order to be able to "believe".

Now there follows in detail (6:31–51a, most probably not in the original ordering of the material) the identification of Jesus with the bread of life that descends from the Father, since he is given over in such a way through his gift of self to the Father's will that he can be given out and distributed (vv. 32–33, 38, 50–51a). In the course of this discourse, over against the Jews who have seen without believing and who still want to see, the true interpenetration of Christ's seeing and the seeing of the believing man are explained—something that is possible only through the disclosure of the entire Trinitarian dimension. On the one hand, there exists the archetypical and unique seeing of the Father by the Son, for no one else has seen the Father (v. 46); on the other hand, there exists the fact that the Son is seen on earth, which is now mentioned together with "faith" (v. 40), and this faith is directed to the Son who sees the Father (v. 47) and mediates the eternal life. It is precisely this synthesis of seeing and believing that the Jews lack ("You have seen me, and yet you have not believed": v. 36), and this means that they fall out of the will of the Father that bears and accomplishes all things. The theme of the "will" is developed in three statements that follow each other: first, the Son comes, in order (or better: in order not!) to do not his own will but the will of the one who sends him; second, the will of the Father who sends him hands over "everything" to the Son, in other that he may bring it safely into eternal life; third, this same will of the Father allows the Son to encounter those who see and believe, whom he can save and raise up to life (vv. 38–40). When the Jews murmur (vv. 41–42), a more precise explanation is given of this mystery of the Father's will: the process whereby one comes to the Son (i.e., faith) is a "drawing" by the Father, or, as the prophet says, "letting oneself be led" by the Father, "hearing from the Father" (vv. 43–45). There is therefore a mysterious doubling of the word of God, which must already be present as gift in the one who hears, in order that he can run to meet the word that is given to him as bread. The word-bread that descends encounters itself in the faith that rises up to meet it; or, better, it encounters the will of the Father that is at work a priori in man, while on the other hand the believer, who bears the word in himself a priori as he goes to meet the word, has a share a priori in the word's vision of the Father in order to be able to see him. This is why he cannot be rejected by the Son (v. 37).

This Trinitarian miracle of the God who reveals himself in the Son leaves far behind itself all the shadow images of the Old Covenant, even that of the manna that descends from the physical heaven: for this stands ultimately on the side of those who "eat" and "have become filled" in order to hunger again and finally to die (v. 49). Here lies the decisive point: death stands against "life" (vv. 33, 35, 48, 50, 51), "eternal life" (vv. 40, 47, 51), and "resurrection on the Last Day" (in a fourfold refrain: vv. 39, 40, 44, 54). And the guarantee of this nondying, this life, this eternal life, is—in a unity that cannot be separated into its component parts but is wholly indissoluble—the "living bread" that bestows life and the "faith", which as such is the "possession of eternal life" (v. 47).

The encounter of these two, which both produce the same effect, is given the name "eating". The concept already lies unexpressed in the absolute identification of the Son-Word with the bread that is given by the Father (v. 32). It lies even more closely in the identification of "coming to me" and "hungering no more", of "believing in me" and "thirsting no more" (v. 35). Thus "faith", as the "possession of eternal life" (v. 47), is already implicitly described as eating, and the explicit designation (in vv. 50, 51a) adds nothing substantially new to this, other than the physical forcefulness and emphasis of the process: encounter as absorption and identification.

Here, before we go over to the third section, we should give space to a little reflection. The Christian who is quickly satisfied (precisely the one whom Origen liked to call the *haplousteros,* the "simpler one") is inclined at this point to think that all of this is meant "in a purely spiritual sense" and is therefore somehow "unreal". It is as if we had first the general process of revelation, the encounter between the contents of faith and the act of faith, and the divine grace, here attributed to the Father, which has a necessary accompanying role to play in this encounter. And it seems that one does not emerge essentially further than the Old Testament formulae of the wisdom literature, where the personified Wisdom also prepares allegorical feasts with bread and wine and invites men to her table (Prov 9:5f.; Is 55:1–3; Sir 24:19, 21). Nevertheless, quite apart from the fact that even the wisdom literature portrays more than a mere allegory, there remains the distinction that Jesus calls himself not the divine Logos but explicitly the "Son of Man" in the context of his being bread (v. 27). Although the ego that presents itself here again and again is certainly one that has descended from heaven, it is absolutely a human ego. It is therefore impossible to avoid seeing that here, in the encounter between bread and faith, the stage of the Eucharistic mystery has already been reached, if not in terms of the form, certainly in terms of the content. This is also the case because the abandonment of his own will and the identification of the Son with the will of the Father, i.e., the process that will lead inexorably to the Cross, to the slaughtered flesh, and the poured-out blood, is already named formally here as the precondition for the Word's becoming bread (v. 38). The revelation of the Son has from the very outset a Eucharistic structure, which implies also that the Faith that answers this revelation as its echo has the same structure.

We can express this by seeing the "spiritual communion" (which, for this reason, is no mere unreal communion, communion in a transferred sense only) as the foundation and at the same time as the content of the "sacramental" Communion: this brings us precisely into the center of Augustine's teaching on the Eucharist and likewise into the center of Mariology as formulated by Augustine: *prius concepit mente quam ventre,* "she conceived in the mind before conceiving in the womb". If one has understood that the establishment of this foundation does not in the least reduce or relativize the Eucharist, since this is only the introduction of the mystery into an ecclesial-liturgical form, then one will understand also the Eucharistic doctrine of Origen, who continually points back from the form to the content (as that which is truly real): from the flesh that is eaten to the Divine-human Word that is eaten. In John too, the communion with the Logos is always a communion with the incarnate Logos: the three Letters repeat this untiringly, although they do not describe it in liturgical-sacramental terms. At most, they presuppose the Sacrament, as the farewell discourses only presuppose and hint at the liturgical event ("a meal was held", 13:2). But presupposing it means *including* it as a reality, so that while it is indeed present, theologically speaking, in its distinctive particularity in the communion with the "living bread" described by John, it is not given individual emphasis. To such an extent does that last Apostle, at the close of the revelation, grasp the meaning of the sacraments in the eschatological character that is proper to them.

In what is clearly a new paragraph, the *third section* carries out the transition to the sacramental sphere. The word *flesh* is used (v. 51b), which is explained immediately, as a response to the renewed and stronger murmuring of the Jews, as the "flesh" of the "Son of Man", which must be eaten, and his "blood", which must be drunk (v. 53), and in the assurance that both are meant in the genuine sense of the words: as "true food", "true drink" (v. 55). There follows the effect that is attributed to the Eucharist in other passages too: the being in one another (v. 56), which unfolds its dimensions in the parallelism of the Mediator: "As the living Father has sent me and I live through the Father—so will the one who eats me live through me" (v. 57; cf. 17:21, 23). Otherwise, what is contained in this section is the repetition of the statements that have already been made.

In this position, the conclusion (vv. 60–71)—wherever it may have stood originally—makes good sense here. The offense that even the disciples now take is parried by Jesus through the question that challenges them by giving even sharper point to the paradox of eating the flesh, and yet offers the solution to this: "What if you were now to see the Son of Man ascending to where he was before?" (v. 62). For the believers, this seeing of the return to the Father (which will be the most extreme "sign" for those who see it and thus also, at least in an abstract sense, the most extreme occasion for scandal, for saying "no" in the face of the vision of the "opened heaven": 1:54) will be the response of faith, filled with grace, to the Son's seeing of the Father. Here, in the return, it is necessary to speak of the Spirit who gives life to the flesh of the dead Christ and who also raises up to faith the man who lies in the grave of sin. "The flesh is of no use": this is set in a provoking contradiction to the word spoken earlier about salvation to be found only in the flesh that is eaten. "The words that I have spoken to you are spirit and life": the word that, as bread, is life, was mentioned earlier, and now both concepts are mediated through the concept of the Spirit, i.e., of the divine power that brings about every miracle and raises all that has been said to the level of miracle.

Here there takes place the final disarming of the man who would achieve things on his own, the *krisis* between the one who in faith allows things to happen and the one who does not come to a decision. This is the reason for the reference to Jesus' knowing from the beginning who would believe and who would betray him (v. 64). Now it is "betrayal" that is said instead of "not believing", and the name of the traitor will be mentioned explicitly immediately after-ward (v. 71). The one who believes receives the one who has descended from heaven and keeps him in himself (v. 56). The one who does not believe "casts him out" (v. 37), abandons him to "perdition" (v. 39), and thus hands him over to death. He is a murderer (I Jn 3:15) and a devil (v. 70). The only thing that saves from this falling away into "no longer going about with Jesus", "going back on one's own steps" (v. 66) is the blind step that Peter takes forward; for it is necessary to "go to someone"; and since "we believe and know [v. 69] that you are the Holy One of God: to whom else should we go?" "You have words of eternal life." Precisely this is the reception of the word as the bread of eternal life; it is the communion of Peter and of the Twelve with him, and therein (as at Mt 16:18) the true foundation of the Church in the act of the Eucharist. In both passages, the most utterly personal following of Christ flows of itself into the Church and the sacramental fellowship.

This permits us to see the slow process of making concrete, i.e., the growing together of that eschatological unity of the perfect act that unites vision, faith, and meal in the identity of the love between Bridegroom and bride, as this is shown by the farewell discourses. And yet, in John that which is in the process of becoming is measured only by means of its orientation to that which is perfected: the sign (sēmeion) is measured against the entire revelation of the Father in the Son, the word of the Son against its total essence whereby it is "spirit and life", "living bread", "bread for the life of the world"; the seeing of the incarnate One is measured against faith's insight into his divinity (v. 69). John shows this inexorable dynamic in almost all of Jesus' encounters with whose who will come to faith, a dynamic that ends in the act of falling down in adoration: at one and the same time the abdication of all that is one's own in blind faith *and* the opening of one's eyes to the brightest light and to the evidential character that cannot be refuted: "You are . . . "

This insight teaches us once again the mystery, ever ancient and new, that all theology—i.e., all understanding of revelation—must always take place from above, viz., in descent from the fulfilled truth: from a point that, considered in human, philosophical terms, would be sheer utopia and an ideal that ought not to be taken into serious consideration but that is absolutely fulfilled reality in the realm of the grace of God, in the work and in the being of Christ, and also in the Church that has flowed forth from him, the bride without wrinkle and spot, purified in the water. Something of every striving, sinful, failing human being is kept safe at this point, even if "only" the living image that Christ has of him. But this image cannot be recognized in any other way than by entering the movement of faith, which for John is the movement of love itself: as vision, gift of self, and meal. And this love is the operation of the Father who draws to the Son and of the Son who mediates to the Father, the proof that his word is spirit and life.

EUCHARISTIC CONGRESS 1960

In the upper part of Raphael's *Disputation,* we see the heavenly Church gathered around the glorious humanity of Christ: next to him sit Mary and John the Baptist; above him thrones the Father; at his feet the dove of the Spirit flies down onto the monstrance, which rests on an exalted altar in the middle of the lower half of the painting, surrounded by the earthly Church, which surrounds the mystery in a high degree of movement: adoring, admiring, researching in books, teaching one another in dialogue and disputation. It is not the event of the Mass that is celebrated here, as in the fresco of the succeeding stanza; it is only the glory of the mystery, which dominates everything and radiates forth into the last corner of the picture, and the identity of the Redeemer in the form of his heavenly glory and in his earthly concealment in bread, mediated through the vertical descending of the *Creator Spiritus,* the Holy Spirit of creation. The greatest geniuses of Christian intellectual history are gathered in throngs around the mystery and are utterly absorbed in it; they are an emphatic representation of the people, who are absent but are intended to be seen there. In the background of this Eucharistic gathering in celebration there rises up—seen close at hand on the right and from the distance on the left—the unfinished building of St. Peter's, a parable of the Kingdom of God that cannot be built completely on earth.

The mystery at the heart of Christianity, which is here, before the general public, portrayed and handed over to the world to be looked at and made the object of discussion, essentially transcends the framework of what is merely earthly, merely human; in the sphere that is irradiated by it, man and his whole cosmos are taken beyond themselves and brought into relationship with a divine-human center that polarizes humanity and imposes a higher law on it. The feast of the new *Disputation,* which is to be celebrated in Munich at this time, is formed and justified out from this center, which unites in itself things

Translated by Fr. Brian McNeil, C.R.V.

that appear incompatible and perhaps also therefore unjustifiable to the man who thinks in a purely human fashion—and not to him alone but also to the Christian, to the extent that he remains a limited and mortal human being.

It is not to be wondered at that such a Congress appears questionable precisely to the religious man, with its massive deployment of people, its unavoidable external character, which at least borders on the profanation of what is holiest of all. In the face of this undertaking, which cannot take its stand upon an instruction of Christ that one would have to obey but derives from a merely spontaneous (not to say arbitrary) initiative of Christianity to glorify the mystery from which it lives, there is no Christian of our age who can exempt himself from the obligation to ask himself the anxious question: Is such an activity Christian? Is it not a terrible misunderstanding, the result of an enthusiasm that has been led astray, perhaps indeed already objective idolatry, worse even than the private Mass that Luther banished from the house of God, sheer profanity in the holy place? And even if it was perhaps permitted in a Catholic culture like that of the baroque to have that which is holy radiate out into the profane sphere, and the cosmos of creatures truly seemed bathed in this splendor that shone forth from the mystery, and even the ancient myths could be made transparent by the power of Calderon in his *Autos Sacramentales* to the central Eucharistic Mystery, and faith seemed strong enough to lend the church building the splendor of the profane feasting hall and thus to bathe the profane building in an indirect gleam of what was holy: If this perhaps did appear permitted and commanded for such centuries, does this suffice to justify it for our age, where the profane no longer appears capable of being sacralized, where what we still possess of wholesome holiness in our profanity must be protected in its purity if it is to have any effect at all? For it is not the cheap and external blendings that will reconcile Church and world anew but only the power and the clarity of the distinction, the recovery of the right gradient—a situation comparable to that of the earliest Christianity.

It is precisely those among us who are the best who make this very serious objection, and we should take it very seriously and borrow from it the slogan of Christian discernment. For in fact everything depends on what the intention of this undertaking is: A mere proclamation of religious enthusiasm using means invented by man? Then it would be a phenomenon of the history of religions, with existing analogies in all non-Christian religious fellowships. It would not be anything specifically Christian—at most, a forgivable accommodation made by the Church leadership to the wishes and needs of the soul of the people. If, however, the central intention is the objective and unique mystery of Faith itself, that divine-human mystery that utterly transcends and shatters the categories of what is purely human, even in the religious sphere, then does there exist at least a chance that this may provide not only an excuse for this feast but also a positive justification? It is our task to test this chance, and it is our goal to affirm it in Christian simplicity, without diplomatic and apologetic circumlocutions.

If we apply the criterion of faith in Christ, i.e., the criterion of Jesus Christ, to the forms in which the Church appears, then all of them are in principle questionable. Everything sacramental is questionable, because here human pious activity is introduced into a work that has already been performed by Christ, *opus a Christo operatum.* Infant baptism—no, every baptism—is questionable as soon as it is more than a mere sign; more questionable still is confession, if it is to be more than a reference to the redemption that has already taken place; priestly ordination is questionable, because it claims to impart powers that—considered from an earthly perspective—can only be misused by human beings. The whole hierarchy is questionable, since it is to mediate along the objective-ministerial path the unique One, the God-Man, and his grace, while he is essentially exalted high above all that is merely ministerial. Finally, an absolute and unconditional religion built upon contingent truths of history (which demand to be checked and ascertained ever anew) is questionable—a Faith that must demonstrate itself to be the highest reason and at the same time, by definition, cannot be established on the grounds of reason alone. Paul says that this religion must appear as folly to the wisdom of the reason, and one could translate just as well: as madness. And yet he calls it in the same breath the true wisdom, "God's mysterious, hidden wisdom", which "through proofs of Spirit and power" establishes itself as the correct wisdom in the world.

Therefore, since the Church is no human construct but something invented by God, she must unite things and cast a bridge that links contradictions that appear incompatible to our reason, which falls short. If one wishes to understand the Catholic Church in her life and in the claim she makes, this breadth is decisive: a breadth that is held together in an evident and demonstrable unity and is accordingly not syncretism, a rag bag of incompatible things. In order to cast light on the object of our reflections, we shall take three of these fields of tension.

1. First, the Church is the *unity of mystery and openness*. In order to be the Catholic, i.e., all-embracing, universal religion, she must be both. If she were *only* mystery—like, for example, the secret religions of the classical and later periods—then she would be a sect with select and initiated members. If she were only openness—like, for example, the Roman state religion or the religion of reason in the Enlightenment— then she would not be divine, positive revelation; she would not be the remaining, essential mystery of faith that, no matter how accessible it is to everyone, nevertheless lays claim to the whole person of the individual and reveals itself to him in the truth of the heart only to the extent that he makes the gift of himself. The word of God is proclaimed to all. But only some of these allow themselves to be affected by it. The field is the world, but only the seed that falls on good soil springs up and bears hundredfold fruit. "God spreads abroad everywhere the fragrance of the knowledge of Christ through us," says Paul, "for we are the good fragrance of Christ, to the glory of God, among those who are being saved and among those who are going to destruction; for the one part, a stink that brings about death, for the other part, a foretaste of living life" (2 Cor 2:14–16). Christ went about on the streets and preached the mysteries of God in the presence of all the people, on mountains, by lakes, in the cities, and on the village streets; the apostles did the same. Although there are things that he whispers into the ears of his disciples, he commands them at the same time to proclaim them later on from the rooftops (Mt 10:27).

Christianity is no secret religion, but God is powerful enough to preserve intact the depth of his mystery in his worldwide Church with her openness to the world. The kernel of the Catholic matter is expressed in Goethe's phrase about the "sacred public mystery", which means initially God's secret openness in the cosmos, and by Hölderlin's canonization of all that is seemingly profane in the world and in life. Ultimately, the Church has no walls about her but stands defenselessly open to the world: and this is because the act whereby the Father hands over the Son to the world of sinners is an original profanation of the holy—for what else did the Father do, when he gave us his Son, but throw pearls before the swine? "Pro-fane" means "outside, before the sanctuary": Christ lived there, outside, before heaven; he was born in the stable there, outside, before the city of David; he died between two criminals there, outside the gates of holy Jerusalem; and he set up his Church in Babylon-Rome there, outside the borders of the holy land. Again and again he has let his holy ones, who have borne witness with their blood, be thrown before the wild beasts; again and again he has let his sanctuaries be profaned by Vandals, Huns, Nazis, Communists, and bad Christians; again and again, through Judas (who never dies completely), he has let the *Domine, non sum dignus* be uttered in the full breadth of its meaning. Through the profanation of the holy God, the inaccessible light came into our region of darkness and the shadow of death, and through the ever renewed profanation of the holy Church the light that is present among us streams further out into the world.

But wait! Are we not playing an ambiguous game with words? Are we not explicitly instructed *not* to throw the pearls before the swine? Is not the mystery of the Eucharist celebrated by the Lord within the sacral liturgy of his ancestors, in the small circle of his disciples, in an intimacy that strengthens the Lord and his disciples and from which they go out into the profaning existence—but an intimacy that never anywhere belongs on the streets? Yes, indeed, boundary lines are set here: boundary lines of holy tact and of good Christian taste. The room that shelters and conceals is appropriate for the celebration that recalls the death of the Lord and for the adoration of his hidden love. Yet such church rooms are something completely different from the temple, the tabernacle of the Old Covenant, where God dwelt and throned between the cherubim. Our churches, on the other hand, are merely accidental tents set up here and there, capable of being taken down at a moment's notice, and the one who makes himself present in them is not essentially localized by the walls of the church: for us, the church is the place of our acts of worship, while for the risen Lord, his church is the world. He goes through doors that are closed; he does not even need to break them open, since they have no existence for him. Does not this too belong to our Faith? May and should we not bear witness once in a way—as an exception—to this too, by transferring our worship to the place where (as Christ sees it) it belongs—in the midst of the world? Dear brothers and sisters, have we not perhaps narrowed down the breadth of the Christian liturgy in the last decades in a way that flees from the world, out of sheer concern for the sacrality of our liturgical services? Have we not coddled and dressed up the liturgy in an aseptic, sterilized, germ-free environment, and did not Hitler take us at our word in a terrible way? Fine, if you yourselves transfer what you are concerned with to behind the walls of the churches, then remain there and get on with it as you like, but I will not allow you to enter the public sphere. That was the degradation of the Church to a sect, hemmed in more and more restrictively until there was no more air to support life in her innermost sanctuary. Or, put better—and this redounds to her honor— until the only presence she had in the public sphere was the true testimony, the testimony of blood. A clearer presence—you will object to me—than these ambiguities of a secularized liturgy. But must the one exclude the other? Is it inadmissible that—by way of an exception—the Church's worship should also appear once visibly in its cosmic dimension? So that both Christians and non-Christians may realize that this is the true intention: the Church is not a club; either she is the world, or she does not exist. In her, the world adores; the world gives thanks for its redemption; the world swears fidelity to the God of love. Even if this cannot take place every day, still it ought to happen on one occasion that the memorial of the certainty of redemption should be set up in the face of the whole sighing creation, which groans in travail, which is made subject to corruption because of sin, "for it is in hope that we have been saved".

The breadth that goes from mystery to openness has one last significance. Christ's commandment to eat his slaughtered flesh and to drink his poured-out blood, and to do this in commemoration of him, does not at all mean only a cultic-sacramental act. It does indeed mean this, but not only this. "Do this" means absolutely also: follow me in this in your life. If I have given my life for you, then you too should give your life for the brethren, for the world. After the Cross, there can exist no valid act of worship that does not inherently aim also at the existence, at imitation that goes as far as death. Already the Mass is in its kernel the offering up of the Church together with her Head: the act that unites to the Cross and enters the one valid, one redemptive act on the Cross (where the Head is, the body belongs too; the sacrifice, the consecration, and the Communion can have no other intention): thus an act that in itself already breaks open the doors of the church room and draws in all of the profane life of Christians. As for Christ, so also for the Christian there are ultimately no "inside" and "outside". If his whole life is not worship, liturgy, then he has not understood the first word about being a Christian. The coming celebration must also remind us of this: that sacred marriage feast between Christ and the redeemed world takes place everywhere, and we too are always the object of this.

2. We are the object of this: *as individuals and as a plurality,* or—let us use the ominous word—as a *mass.* Is it then the fault of us human beings that we are not only a person but also part of a mass? *Mass* means that which is concentrated in a mass, that which is kneaded, the dough. Who has made humanity into this dough if not the Creator, who took clay from the earth and blew his Spirit of personal being into this amorphous thing? What responsibility do we have for the fact that we are always both person and nature in a tragic and yet blessed blending of heaven and earth? Unmistakable individuals, and yet an anonymous mass with a million heads?

But one will object that Christianity is concerned only with the person; it lifts precisely those who are chosen and called out of the mass by making them become only then truly persons: Christianity and the mass are two entities that cannot be united with each other. Naturally, this obvious objection is right: that humanity in which the mass wins power over the person and the person abandons himself in intoxication or despair to the instincts of the mass is the deadly foe of Christ; this humanity forms the followers of the apocalyptic beasts. Seen from this point of view, one can say that the holy people is not a mass. And yet the objection does not think far enough. For even a holy people can be numbered in millions—why not? Even a holy people is as such a collective and anonymous. And this side of redeemed humanity too is assumed and portrayed by the Church. The Church is more than the sum of her members, of her individuals. She is an infinitely mysterious unity that has its origin from Christ as the fullness of his grace, a unity that we cannot describe with exactness either as personal or as impersonal: it is personal as the bride of Christ and impersonal as the body of Christ: a reality in which both sides of what it is to be human are redeemed, preserved, and justified.

What is this bread, then, that we hand over to God so that he may change it into his Son? Is it not dough; is it not a mass? Is it not—as already the liturgical prayers of the earliest Church say—individual grains trampled down, grains that must give up their individual being in order to become bread? And must not the grapes lose their skins that separate them from one another, so that the juice within them may mingle and become the intoxicating drink that the divine love deigns to assimilate to itself? Do not both things coexist in this process: the most utterly personal testimony in the shedding of one's blood, and the gift of self made over to what is anonymous, the gift that wills to attain salvation only together with all the brethren, with the great Adamic body of humanity? Is not this excessively cultivated personalism, which can see only the Individual (with a capital letter) in the Christian, an utterly bourgeois affair? Perhaps worse still: a preservation of self, an altar set up in secret to the idol "I"? When and where did a holy Christian ever display such an attitude? Did he not rather win his soul by being willing to lose it and by losing it de facto? Man-mass belongs just as much to the dough of the Eucharist as does man-person, and what a hope lies therein, what an anti-Jansenist hope that not only individual elect persons, plucked out of the *massa damnata,* are to reach salvation but rather both the individual and humanity, both prefigured in the Church, which is certain of salvation! How, then, should a feast of the Eucharist not be also a feast of the bread, of the dough? The more the better! There is no one whom we can afford to miss. And we, who go to adoration, take with us in the group that we form every group that does not go along with us. Group is group; group can represent group.

Let us reflect well on the fact that the power of this span can be only a supernatural power established by God. The state and the people can make demands of every citizen, but only of his earthly existence, not of his immortal soul. There exists the point at which the individual must assert himself as a person over against the state, even if—as in one of Schiller's tragedies—through his death. On the other hand, there can exist fellowships of free persons who unite and commit themselves to an idea, a world-view, a friendship, and perhaps attain thereby a strong moral or cultural, political power and yet will never become more than individuals. Only in the Church is it possible to bring both levels simultaneously into unity, into the unity of the redemption that has been established by God, in which the rights of the person are inalienably guaranteed, and yet there reigns a communism of the good things of salvation: in heaven, everything is personal, but nothing is private any longer.

3. The Church lives in an incomprehensible place between earth and heaven, between death and eternal life, between the old world that is passing away and the new and incorruptible world. The Christian has died with Christ in baptism but has also (as Paul assures him) risen up with Christ and ascended with him into heaven, and he lives in time on the basis of eternal life and oriented toward eternal life. As he follows Christ, he goes toward suffering and death, and yet he lives out of the real power of the risen Christ. Thus Christian existence embraces the *span between penitence and feast.* We are reminded of this by the Church year with its seasons of Advent and Lent and yet with its unbroken succession of feasts great and small. This sequence gives us a symbol of something that, on a deeper level, is a mutual

compenetration, a third paradox of our Christian existence. But just as heaven is victorious over earth, and resurrection over death, so for the Christian must even penitence, suffering, and death be lived out of a disposition of the celebration of a feast: the feast of the wedding of God with his redeemed world.

It is well known that the solemnities of the Old Testament all grew out of thanksgiving feasts for harvest. Where the earth bears fruit and holds feast, man holds a feast with it in thankfulness. Later, these feasts of nature were linked to historical reminiscences; but everywhere the joy at harvest shimmers through the Mazzoth feast of unleavened bread, the Pentecost feast of the firstfruits of the wheat harvest, and the feast of booths in the plucking of fruit and grapes, when people slept in booths in the open fields and beside the vineyard: and perhaps no one even today can celebrate a religious feast with such a natural joy and cheerfulness as the Jews. There are prayers, but there are also songs and dances as a means of giving thanks to God. Has this cheerfulness remained anywhere on the faces of the Christians who celebrate a feast? It is true that the mystery that they celebrate lies on a deeper level—but is it not also greater? Ought not the joy too be a much deeper joy? What are religious harvest thanksgiving festivals, even indeed when they are concerned with the rescuing of Israel, compared with the unforeseeable harvest of bread and wine in the New and eternal Covenant? The whole earth is now bread and wine. Must not the genuinely human joy be permitted to break through at this point? Would not a song by thousands of voices on the Theresienwiese be the expression of what the Apostle says: "Rejoice in the Lord always; again I say, rejoice. The Lord is near. Have no anxiety about anything but in everything bring your concerns to God with insistent prayer of petition and with Eucharist. And the peace of God, which surpasses all that one can imagine, will keep your hearts and thoughts in Christ Jesus" (Phil 4:4–7).

It is not a worldly enthusiasm that we are to draw forth from the feast but a strength that comes from the insight into the essence of God's love. And it is not herself that the Church celebrates; she is not enthusiastic about herself but only about her Head and Lord. It is not the emotional atmosphere that is important but the matter itself. And this is God, who becomes man among us in order to die for us. If we Catholics behave exactly and correctly, then it should not be possible for our Protestant brethren to find anything to object to in our feast. The object of our celebration is Jesus Christ in his love that goes until the end, in his power to lay down his life and to take it up again, in his creative might to make the gift of himself to us in the forms of bread and wine, in order to be inconceivably one with humanity. And if we Catholics include here the miracle of the Consecration too, which we are accustomed in our stammering way to call transubstantiation, still the object of our celebration is not at all this but rather the incarnate love of God itself, the mystery of the Last Supper that our Protestant brethren too know and celebrate; it is no Counter-Reformation festival that we are celebrating but a feast that goes back to the Middle Ages, when Christianity was not yet divided. And how else should we celebrate it than in the Spirit of the *Una Sancta?*